T0178125

Lecture Notes in Computer Science 12128

More information about this series at http://www.springer.com/series/7409

Maria Bielikova · Tommi Mikkonen ·
Cesare Pautasso (Eds.)

Web Engineering

20th International Conference, ICWE 2020
Helsinki, Finland, June 9–12, 2020
Proceedings

 Springer

Editors
Maria Bielikova (iD)
Slovak University of Technology
Bratislava, Slovakia

Tommi Mikkonen (iD)
University of Helsinki
Helsinki, Finland

Cesare Pautasso (iD)
University of Lugano (USI)
Lugano, Switzerland

ISSN 0302-9743   ISSN 1611-3349   (electronic)
Lecture Notes in Computer Science
ISBN 978-3-030-50577-6   ISBN 978-3-030-50578-3   (eBook)
https://doi.org/10.1007/978-3-030-50578-3

LNCS Sublibrary: SL3 – Information Systems and Applications, incl. Internet/Web, and HCI

This Springer imprint is published by the registered company Springer Nature Switzerland AG
The registered company address is: Gewerbestrasse 11, 6330 Cham, Switzerland

Preface

The International Conference on Web Engineering (ICWE) aims to promote research and scientific exchange related to Web Engineering, and to bring together researchers and practitioners from various disciplines in academia and industry in order to tackle emerging challenges in the engineering of Web applications and associated technologies, as well as to assess the impact of those technologies on society, media, and culture.

Supported by International Society of Web Engineering (ISWE), ICWE is the flagship conference for the Web Engineering community that focuses on different aspects of designing, building, maintaining, and using Web applications, interpreted in the widest sense.

Previous editions of ICWE took place in Daejeon, South Korea (2019), Cáceres, Spain (2018), Rome, Italy (2017), Lugano, Switzerland (2016), Rotterdam, The Netherlands (2015), Toulouse, France (2014), Aalborg, Denmark (2013), Berlin, Germany (2012), Paphos, Cyprus (2011), Vienna, Austria (2010), San Sebastian, Spain (2009), Yorktown Heights, NY, USA (2008), Como, Italy (2007), Palo Alto, CA, USA (2006), Sydney, Australia (2005), Munich, Germany (2004), Oviedo, Spain (2003), Santa Fe, Argentina (2002), and Cáceres, Spain (2001).

This volume collects the papers presented at the 20th International Conference on Web Engineering (ICWE 2020), virtually held during June 9–12, 2020, in Helsinki, Finland. It contains full research papers, short research papers, industry papers, posters, demonstrations, PhD symposium papers, tutorials, and extended abstracts of the keynotes presented at ICWE 2020. In addition, workshops will later publish their own post-proceedings, where workshop contributions will be disseminated to the wider audience.

The research track of the ICWE 2020 edition received 78 submissions, out of which the Program Committee selected 24 full research papers (30% acceptance rate), 6 short research papers (38% acceptance rate), 1 industry paper, and 3 education track papers. Additionally, the Program Committee accepted 7 demos/posters and 4 contributions to the PhD symposium. Also accepted was a tutorial lecture titled "From Linked Data to Knowledge Graphs: Storing, Querying, and Reasoning," as well as the following three workshops: the International Workshop on Web of Things for Humans (ICWE), the International Workshop on Semantics and the Web for Transport (Sem4Tra), and the International Workshop on Knowledge Discovery on the Web (KDWEB).

Reflecting the special global pandemic situation, the event was run online, with keynotes being live and individual sessions pre-recorded and discussed online to facilitate discussion in a best possible way. Being a conference on Web Engineering, ICWE 2020 moved to the Web with ease, and it seeked new ways and forms to convey the program using the website as a portal for the whole conference.

The excellent program would not have been possible without the support of the many people who helped with the successful organization of this event. We would like to thank all the organizers – in particular the local team, consisting of Niko Mäkitalo, Nyyti Saarimäki, and Kari Systä – for their excellent work in identifying cutting-edge and cross-disciplinary topics in the rapidly moving field of Web Engineering, organizing inspiring workshops and tutorials around them, as well as putting it all together to an inspiring event. A word of thanks also to the reviewers for their meticulous work in selecting the best papers to be presented. Last, but not least, we would like to thank the authors who submitted their work to the conference and all the participants who contributed to the success of the events. Finally, we want to thank you, authors and the ICWE community, for taking the time and effort to contribute to and participate in ICWE 2020.

June 2020

Maria Bielikova
Cesare Pautasso
Tommi Mikkonen

Organization

General Chair

Tommi Mikkonen   University of Helsinki, Finland

Program Committee Co-chairs

Maria Bielikova   Slovak University of Technology in Bratislava, Slovakia

Cesare Pautasso   University of Lugano, Switzerland

Local Co-chairs

Niko Mäkitalo   University of Helsinki, Finland

Kari Systä   Tampere University, Finland

Workshop Co-chairs

In-Young Ko   Korea Advanced Institute of Science and Technology, South Korea

Juan Manuel Murillo   University of Extremadura, Spain

Petri Vuorimaa   Aalto University, Finland

Tutorial Co-chairs

Marco Brambilla   Politecnico di Milano, Italy

Kari Salo   Metropolia University of Applied Sciences, Finland

Mahbubul Syeed   American International University in Bangladesh, Bangladesh

Demo and Poster Co-chairs

Maxim Bakaev   Novosibirsk State Technical University, Russia

Cinzia Cappiello   Politecnico Milano, Italy

Markku Laine   Aalto University, Finland

PhD Symposium Co-chairs

Alessandro Bozzon   Delft University of Technology, The Netherlands

Irene Garrigos   Universidad de Alicante, Spain

Petri Ihantola   University of Helsinki, Finland

Publicity Co-chairs

Flavius Frasincar	Erasmus University Rotterdam, The Netherlands
Niko Mäkitalo	University of Helsinki, Finland
Marco Winckler	Université Nice Sophia Antipolis, France

Industry Track Co-chairs

Christoph Bussler	Google, USA
Tomoya Noro	Fujitsu Laboratories, Japan
Antero Taivalsaari	Nokia Bell Laboratories, Finland

Web-Based Learning Track Co-chairs

Nick Falkner	The University of Adelaide, Australia
Terhi Kilamo	Tampere University, Finland
Ralf Klamma	RWTH Aachen University, Germany

Proceedings Chair

Nyyti Saarimäki	Tampere University, Finland

ICWE Steering Committee Liaisons

Florian Daniel	Politecnico di Milano, Italy

Program Committee

Ioannis Anagnostopoulos	University of Thessaly, Greece
Maurício Aniche	Delft University of Technology, The Netherlands
Myriam Arrue	University of the Basque Country, Spain
Sören Auer	Leibniz University of Hannover, Germany
Marcos Baez	University of Trento, Italy
Maxim Bakaev	Novosibirsk State Technical University, Russia
Hubert Baumeister	Technical University of Denmark, Denmark
Devis Bianchini	University of Brescia, Italy
Domenico Bianculli	University of Luxembourg, Luxembourg
Maria Bielikova	Slovak University of Technology in Bratislava, Slovakia
Matthias Book	University of Iceland, Iceland
Alessandro Bozzon	Delft University of Technology, The Netherlands
Marco Brambilla	Politecnico di Milano, Italy
Christoph Bussler	Google, USA
Carlos Canal	University of Málaga, Spain
Cinzia Cappiello	Politecnico di Milano, Italy
Richard Chbeir	University of Pau and Pays de l'Adour, France

Dickson K. W. Chiu	The University of Hong Kong, China
Pieter Colpaert	Ghent University, Belgium
Oscar Corcho	Universidad Politécnica de Madrid, Spain
Florian Daniel	Politecnico di Milano, Italy
Oscar Diaz	University of the Basque Country, Spain
Schahram Dustdar	Vienna University of Technology, Austria
Filomena Ferrucci	Università di Salerno, Italy
Sergio Firmenich	Universidad Nacional de La Plata, Argentina
Flavius Frasincar	Erasmus University Rotterdam, The Netherlands
Piero Fraternali	Politecnico di Milano, Italy
Martin Gaedke	Chemnitz University of Technology, Germany
Irene Garrigos	University of Alicante, Spain
Cristina Gena	University of Torino, Italy
Juan Manuel Murillo	University of Extremadura, Spain
Hao Han	The University of Tokyo, Japan
Jan Hidders	Delft University of Technology, The Netherlands
Radu Tudor Ionescu	University of Bucharest, Romania
Ashwin Ittoo	University of Liège, Belgium
Martin Johns	TU Braunschweig, Germany
Epaminondas Kapetanios	University of Westminster, UK
Ralf Klamma	RWTH Aachen University, Germany
Alexander Knapp	Universität Augsburg, Germany
Philipp Leitner	Chalmers - University of Gothenburg, Sweden
Oscar Pastor Lopez	Universitat Politècnica de València, Spain
Zakaria Maamar	Zayed University, UAE
Maristella Matera	Politecnico di Milano, Italy
Santiago Melia	Universidad de Alicante, Spain
Lourdes Moreno	Universidad Carlos III de Madrid, Spain
José Ignacio Panach	University of Valencia, Spain
Tomoya Noro	Fujitsu Laboratories Ltd., Japan
George Pallis	University of Cyprus, Cyprus
Jan Paralic	Technical University Kosice, Slovakia
Cesare Pautasso	University of Lugano, Switzerland
Vicente Pelechano	Universitat Politècnica de València, Spain
Euripides Petrakis	Technical University of Crete, Crete
V. Ramakrishnan	Stony Brook University, USA
Raphael M. Reischuk	ETH Zurich, Switzerland
Werner Retschitzegger	Johannes Kepler University, Austria
Filippo Ricca	DIBRIS Università di Genova, Italy
Thomas Richter	Rhein-Waal University of Applied Sciences, Germany
Gustavo Rossi	National University of La Plata, Argentina
Harald Sack	FIZ Karlsruhe Leibniz Institute for Information Infrastructure and KIT Karlsruhe, Germany
Abhishek Srivastava	Indian Institute of Technology Indore, India
Andrea Stocco	Università della Svizzera Italiana, Italy
Kari Systä	Tampere University, Finland

Stefan Tai	TU Berlin, Germany
Antero Taivalsaari	Nokia Bell Labs, Finland
Jeffrey Ullman	Stanford University, USA
Maria Esther Vidal	Universidad Simon Bolivar, Venezuela
Markel Vigo	The University of Manchester, UK
Michael Weiss	Carleton University, Canada
Erik Wilde	CA Technologies, Switzerland
Manuel Wimmer	Johannes Kepler University Linz, Austria
Marco Winckler	University of Paul Sabatier, France
Yeliz Yesilada	The University of Manchester, UK
Nicola Zannone	Eindhoven University of Technology, The Netherlands
Gefei Zhang	Hochschule für Technik und Wirtschaft Berlin, Germany
Jürgen Ziegler	University of Duisburg-Essen, Germany

External Reviewers

Anand Aiyer
Sabri Allani
Ali Aydin
Cristina Barros
Peter Bednar
Russa Biswas
Karam Bou Chaaya
David Chaves-Fraga
Dominik Ernst
Shirin Feiz Disfani
Andrea Gallidabino
Antonio Garmendia
Siggi Gauti
Genet Asefa Gesese
Cesar González Mora
Ibrahim Hammoud

Fabian Hoppe
Manuel Karl
David Klein
Kristína Machová
Elio Mansour
Frank Pallas
Demetris Paschalides
Jorge Ramírez
Ioannis Savvidis
Anis Tissaoui
Rima Türker
Michael Vierhauser
Bernhard Wally
Sebastian Werner
Sabine Wolny
Rita Zgheib

Sponsors

 Tampere University

 HELSINGIN YLIOPISTO
HELSINGFORS UNIVERSITET
UNIVERSITY OF HELSINKI

 HIIT | HELSINKI INSTITUTE FOR
INFORMATION TECHNOLOGY

 Metropolia

 A! Aalto University
School of Engineering

 ISWE
International Society for
Web Engineering e.V.

 Springer

 Helsinki

Contents

Testing of Web Applications

Emotion Detection

Location-Aware Applications

Sentiment Analysis

Open Data

Liquid Web Applications

Tutorial

User Interface Technologies

Detecting Responsive Web Design Bugs with Declarative Specifications

Oussama Beroual, Francis Guérin, and Sylvain Hallé[⊠]

Laboratoire d'informatique formelle, Université du Québec à Chicoutimi,
Saguenay, Canada
shalle@acm.org

Abstract. Responsive Web Design (RWD) is a concept that is born from the need to provide users with a positive and intuitive experience, no matter what device they use. Complex Cascading Style Sheets (CSS) are used in RWD to smoothly change the appearance of a website based on the window width of the device being used. The paper presents an automated approach for testing these dynamic web applications, where a combination of dynamic crawling and back-end testing is used to automatically detect RWD bugs.

1 Introduction

The only functionality of a web application with which the user interacts is via the web page. Today's users expect a lot from a web page: it has to load fast, provide the desired service, and be enjoyable to view on all devices: from a desktop to tablets and mobile phones. However, due to the somewhat complex relationship between HTML, CSS and JavaScript, the layout of web applications tends to be harder to properly specify in contrast with traditional desktop applications. The same document can be shown in a variety of sizes, resolutions, browsers and even devices.

Responsive Web Design (RWD) [15] attempts to provide a solution to this wide diversity, by providing a design methodology that easily adapts the layout to various screen sizes. In RWD, significant portions of a site's graphical user interface can be modified, or even added or removed depending on the specific type of device being used to view a page. However, this appealing feature comes with the drawback that a single web page can now have multiple possible layouts, making the presence of so-called layout "bugs" all the more prevalent. Such problems can range from relatively mundane quirks like overlapping or incorrectly aligned elements, to more serious issues compromising the functionality of the user interface. Detecting these bugs in a responsive application imposes the testing of the interface on all of its possible layouts, which multiplies the testing effort required, when compared to traditional web sites and desktop applications.

It has quickly become clear that detecting GUI bugs in RWD applications requires a new and more efficient testing approach, and especially the creation

© Springer Nature Switzerland AG 2020
M. Bielikova et al. (Eds.): ICWE 2020, LNCS 12128, pp. 3–18, 2020.
https://doi.org/10.1007/978-3-030-50578-3_1

of testing tools adapted to this specific use case. This is precisely the goal of this paper, which presents an automated technique that provides test oracles capable of verifying the consistency of a responsive layout over a wide range of window widths. Contrary to existing methods, which define hard-coded algorithms that can test a handful of predefined RWD bugs, our proposed approach defines such bugs as statements expressed in a declarative, domain-specific language designed especially for web interfaces. This language, implemented by the Cornipickle web testing tool [13], includes temporal operators that allow the correlation of elements of a page at multiple moments in time. The novelty of our approach is to leverage this feature by using an external web crawler (in this case, Crawljax [16]) to change a browser's window size multiple times, and instruct the UI oracle to take each of these window sizes as a distinct page. In such a way, we show that RWD bugs can be expressed as specifications over *sequences* of the same page at different sizes.

The important side effect of expressing RWD bugs as declarative specifications is that other types of RWD bugs, currently unforeseen, can easily be detected by simply writing the appropriate declarative specification that corresponds to their occurrence. To the best of our knowledge, this work is the first solution that tackles the issue of responsive web design testing from a purely declarative standpoint.

The rest of the paper is structured as follows. In Sect. 2, we describe the concept of responsive web design, and describe common examples of RWD bugs. Section 3 describes the current solutions and tools. In Sect. 4, the paper describes the proposed solution, which consists of combining a declarative language interpreter with a stateful crawler to efficiently detect behavioral bugs in Rich Internet Applications (RIAs). Section 5 shows that with a Cornipickle interpreter as the test oracle for an RIA crawler, one can automatically search and detect behavioral and RWD bugs in web applications.

2   Responsive Web Design Bugs

Before a few years ago, access to websites was conditioned by assumptions about the size of the device's screen. Desktop computers were the dominant device to access websites, and so designers created page layouts that assumed a minimum window size in order to be displayed properly. The situation has changed radically in the past decade, with the advent of smartphones and other devices with smaller screens. A 2019 report highlights that the percentage of internet users in the world via mobile devices and tablets is higher than the percentage of internet users that use desktop computers [11]. An alternative approach for proper site operation in a range of different viewport appliances and sizes was needed.

2.1   Adapting the Layout

A first solution to this problem was to use parameters extracted from HTTP headers: the request for a resource through a browser was followed by a so-called "user agent" string to identify the type of browser used. Reading the user agent string on the server side causes the release of two versions: a mobile version designed for small screen sizes, and a desktop version designed for large screens. This approach is not without shortcomings. Among its defects, the fact that it does not fit with new devices entering the market, such as tablets that are somewhere in the middle of mobiles and laptops in size, brings the need for another special version of the site. In addition, other versions of the site must be developed in order to satisfy all user devices. Even the assumption that desktop users have large monitors may not always hold: a browser window can share the screen with other applications, and hence not occupy the entire space available. Clearly, a better approach was needed.

Developers have been following the emergence of CSS *media queries* [18], that allow conditional style statements by media properties such as window size. Adapting a site for a specific window size at runtime has become possible, by writing different CSS rules depending on the dimensions of the viewport. Any valid CSS property can be enclosed within a media query, making it possible to enforce very distinct layouts depending on the result of these queries. If CSS rules alone are not sufficient, the standard also defines JavaScript events that are triggered when a media query fires, which makes it possible to write client-side code that reacts to specific changes in a window's dimensions, and to dynamically alter the layout by directly modifying element properties.

2.2   RWD Bugs

Due to the somewhat complex relationship between HTML, CSS and JavaScript and the multiplication of the devices in the market nowadays, the layout of web applications tends to be harder to properly specify in contrast with traditional desktop applications. The same document can be shown in a variety of sizes, resolutions, browsers and even devices, making the presence of so-called layout "bugs" all the more prevalent. Such problems can range from relatively mundane quirks from elements overlapping to viewport protrusions.

Walsh *et al.* describe five types of bugs in RWD websites [19]:

1. Element Collision: A bug in which elements overlap into one another. This bug can hamper the usability of websites if functional elements of the page are hidden because of this collision. This is shown in Fig. 1a.
2. Element Protrusion: Elements need to resize themselves when they are short on space, but they also need be large enough to contain all of their children. Element protrusion is a bug where an element protrudes outside of its parent due to a lack of space. The element can then be unreachable, hidden by another element, or on top of other elements. This is shown in Fig. 1b.
3. Viewport Protrusion: This bug happens when elements are pushed outside of the viewport and become inaccessible or hidden. This is shown in Fig. 1b, by taking the parent element as the whole viewport.
4. Wrapping Elements: This bug happens when a container is not wide enough to contain all the items and one or more items are pushed on a supplementary line. This is shown in Fig. 1c.

5. Small-Range Layouts: Depending on the implementation, some layouts can be correctly displayed in only a small amount of widths. For instance, a display could be only correct between 320 and 325 pixels of width.

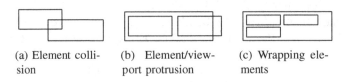

(a) Element colli-   (b) Element/view-   (c) Wrapping ele-
sion   port protrusion   ments

Fig. 1. Various categories of RWD bugs.

3   Existing Solutions

Related works on testing web applications for such kinds of bugs can be roughly divided in two families. The first concentrates on test oracles, i.e. mechanisms for expressing conditions that must be verified by the running application. The second family concentrates on means of finding errors in applications, by performing an exhaustive search of their state space.

There exist a number of tools and techniques for testing web applications. Most of them do not address the functional validation and are not able to test the asynchronous nature and extensive dynamic nature of modern web applications; they are not suitable to test the specific characteristics with respect to Ajax. These tools focus on HTML validation, and static analyses, load testing, broken link detection and protocol conformance.

We first mention web testing software such as Capybara [1], Selenium Web-Driver, or Sahi [2]. These tools provide various languages for describing the tests and writing assertions about the application. All these languages are imperative (i.e. procedural), and aimed at driving an application by performing actions. The testing part reduces to the insertion of assert-like statements throughout the script code. By definition, such assertions relate to the current state of the application; they are therefore ill-suited to express bugs that relate multiple states of the application. In fact, in order to express such bugs as assertions, a user must make use of variables to keep data about the state of the application at various moments, and then write assertions in terms of these variables.

Several tools have been developed to provide the service to display a page in a custom window of variable sizes using a web browser. With smart search and quick review features, Websiteresponsivetest [3] supports all major browsers to provide the exact preview of the website on any specific device. Similarly, Respondr [4] allows checking the responsiveness by simply entering the URL of a website. In addition, the device for which a website or web page is tested can also be chosen from the list given. The page can be previewed at an appropriate width. Screenfly [5] is a multi-device compatibility testing tool which allows previewing web pages as they appear on different devices. Moreover, it supports different screen sizes and resolutions.

The Responsive Web Design Bookmarklet [6] displays any web page in multiple screen sizes for previewing, simulating the viewport of different devices. It is a quick web design tool that can be viewed from a desktop to test any website's responsiveness. All these tools, however, are not automated, and the discovery of RWD bugs still must be done by manual visual inspection of each version of the page. Responsinator [7] helps site owners to get an idea of how their site will work on the most popular devices. Just by typing the website URL, the site will quickly show on screens of various sizes. ResponsivePX's [8] process involves entering the URL of the site and uses buttons to adjust the width and height of the viewport to find the exact breakpoint width in pixels.

Some work has also been done on the use of image analysis techniques to identify layout problems; in particular, WebSee [14] is a tool implemented in Java that leverages several third party libraries to implement some of the specialized algorithms. It applies techniques from the field of computer vision to analyze the visual representation of web pages to automatically detect and localize presentation failures. Applitools Eyes [9] is a commercial tool following a similar principle; it uses the pure image segmentation of the web pages and a pixel-by-pixel visual comparison. However, these approaches are geared towards the detection of static, overlapping or overflow-type bugs in a document, and currently do not support the checking of temporal patterns across multiple snapshots of the same page. We shall see in the following that comparing multiple versions of the same page is key to correctly identify RWD bugs.

The closest tool to our proposed approach is ReDeCheck [20], a responsive web design testing tool. At its core, ReDeCheck builds a *Responsive Layout Graph* (RLG), which accumulates information about the positioning, visibility and relative alignment of an element in multiple versions of the same page. It is inspired from the alignment graph used in X-PERT, a concept that was proposed and developed by Choudhary et al. [10]. ReDeCheck defines three kinds of constraints, respectively called Visibility, Width and Alignment, and reports a responsive layout bug when these constraints differ for an element in the RLG of two versions of the same page. As such, ReDeCheck can only verify a fixed set of predefined layout problems, and does not provide a general-purpose language for expressing assertions.

4   Proposed Solution

In this section, we propose a novel solution for the automated detection of RWD bugs. Instead of requiring the development of special algorithms and a dedicated setup, our approach leverages the combination of two *existing* web testing tools to perform this detection.

The main principle of our approach is shown in Fig. 2. First, a
tool for driving a browser window
is instructed to open the same web
page in a web browser multiple
times. Typically, the first such call
opens the page at a standard desktop window size (w_1), and subsequent calls progressively decrease
this width (w_2, w_3, etc.). As one
can see in the figure, each distinct
size results in a different page layout, with some jumps producing
more drastic changes than others
(such as the switch from w_2 to w_3).
For each of these pages, a summary

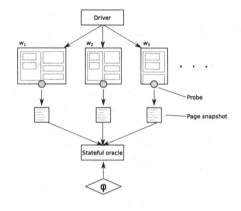

Fig. 2. The proposed framework for catching
RWD bugs.

of the layout is then produced; we call these summaries *page snapshots*. Such
snapshots can be created by the web crawler itself, or by some external mechanism (a "probe") fetching the state of some elements of the page and serializing
them into some format. The important point is that the succession of such snapshots be kept, in order to form a *sequence* of snapshots.

The second part of our approach involves a test oracle, which is fed the
sequence of page snapshots, and evaluates a condition, φ, on that sequence. Since
our approach involves comparing the state of elements in multiple snapshots
across the sequence, the test oracle should be *stateful*—that is, it must be able to
handle conditions that take into account the sequence of snapshots. The intuition
behind this setup is that a RWD bug will typically be detected as a particular
condition on the relative positioning of elements that holds for large window
sizes, and which suddenly stops to hold once reaching a smaller width.

This high-level setup constrains the tools that are available for actually implementing the solution. The driver must be able to call a page at different window
sizes, and must provide some mechanism for automatically fetching the page's
relevant content and produce a summary. On its side, the oracle cannot simply
evaluate an invariant condition on each page separately; on the contrary, it must
have some form of memory that makes it possible to correlate elements of a
page across multiple snapshots. Ideally, expressing these conditions should not
be done by writing low-level procedural code (such as pure Java, JavaScript or
Python), and allow the user to write RWD bug conditions at a higher level of
abstraction for increased modularity and reusability.

Based on these criteria, the solution we propose involves two well-known testing tools: Crawljax [16] as the web driver/crawler component, and Cornipickle
[13] as the stateful test oracle. This architecture was coded in an open source
plugin for Crawljax[1]. We briefly describe these two components in the following,
and explain how they have been made to interact with each other.

---

[1] http://github.com/liflab/crawljax-cornipickle-plugin.

4.1   A Stateful Oracle

The oracle within Cornipickle is on a server that receives requests in JSON format to evaluate a page. These requests are sent by a client browsing the website under test. The developer must inject a JavaScript probe generated by the application into his website to make the requests.

In a standard use case, a developer first writes a set of declarative statements, which are stored in Cornipickle's memory. These statements model the JavaScript code (called probe) that is to be inserted into the application under test so that the client can serialize every page. This probe is designed to report a snapshot of the relevant DOM and CSS data upon every user-triggered event. When such an event occurs, the probe collects whatever information is relevant on the contents of the page into JSON and relays that information to the Cornipickle server, which saves it into a log. Optionally, information on the current status of the assertions being evaluated (true/false) can be relayed back to the probe. An analytics dashboard can then retrieve the saved log and be consulted by the developer, to query the state of all properties input at the beginning of the process.

Cornipickle's language is constructed from first-order and linear temporal logic, such as quantifiers and temporal operators, allowing a user to specify complex relationships on various document elements at multiple moments in time, a feature that is absent from many scripting languages. As a matter of fact, Cornipickle provides operators borrowed from Linear Temporal Logic (LTL) [17] to express assertions about the evolution of a document's content over time. The *Always* x construct allows one to assert that whatever x expresses must be true in every snapshot of the document. Similarly, *Eventually* x says that x will be true in some future document snapshot, and *Next* x asserts it is true in the next snapshot.

One particular purpose of temporal operators is to compare the state of the same element across multiple snapshots. This can be done in Cornipickle with the construct *When* x *is now* y *then* z. If x refers to the state of an element captured in some previous snapshot, then y will contain the state of the same element in the current snapshot.

4.2   Browser Interaction with Crawljax

Crawljax is a tool for automatically exploring the dynamic state of modern web applications. Through programmatic interfaces, it has the capacity to interact with the client side code of the application. The detected changes in the dynamic DOM tree are committed as new states of the behavior. Many options are available with Crawljax to configure the crawling behavior: we can for example specify the links or the widgets to click on or not in the course of the crawling.

This crawler (Crawljax) interacts with Cornipickle through its plugin architecture. Every time a state is created or visited, Crawljax serializes the page and sends it to the interpreter for evaluation the same way the probe sends the page to the Cornipickle server in the traditional architecture. After the page has been evaluated by Cornipickle, the verdict is returned and our plugin outputs the result.

In order to find RWD bugs, we also created a Crawljax plugin that resizes the browser from a given width to another width. Because having a vertical scrollbar is not a problem in responsive design, only resizing horizontally is the correct approach in discovering RWD bugs. Since we explicitly want to find bugs related to RWD, the plugin slowly lowers the browser's width; these bugs show up on lower widths where the space available becomes increasingly scarce in reference to wider widths. It is possible to provide to the plugin the upper bound, the lower bound and the amount of pixels for the decrement. The plugin also highlights bugs it finds and takes a screenshot of the page. Thanks to Cornipickle's feedback mechanism, the user then gets screenshots where the elements responsible for the bug have red borders.

5   Experiments and Results

In this section, we illustrate how our combination of Cornipickle and Crawljax can be used to automatically detect RWD bugs in websites.

5.1   Defining a Common Language

Cornipickle only provides very low-level access to element properties. Since RWD bugs involve a recurring number of higher-level concepts (containment, overlapping, etc.), it is therefore useful to first define "macro-concepts" that will allow expressing bugs in a more natural way.

The first part of this core constructs defines basic concepts such as alignment and visibility. The definitions are shown in Fig. 3. The first statement defines a construct of the form "$x and $y are the same", using the "cornipickleid" property. This property is a unique value given to every element in the page during the serialization phase. Since it is unique, it can be used to identify if two elements are the same across two distinct snapshots of a page. The second statement simply defines a "not the same" construct as the negation of the previous one; it is only added for the sake of readability.

The definition of a visible element checks if its `display` property is set to `none`; invisible elements can be discarded from the analysis, as they do not cause any layout change. Also, this value is affected consciously by the developer so their position on the page is correct. Finally, the alignment of two elements is defined with the constructs "top-aligned" and "left-aligned". We say that two elements are top-aligned and left-aligned when their top and left values, respectively, are equal.

```
We say that $x and $y are the          Not ($x's display is "none")).
same when (
  $x's cornipickleid equals            We say that $x and $y are
  $y's cornipickleid).                 top-aligned when (
                                         $x's top equals $y's top).
We say that $x and $y are not
the same when (                        We say that $x and $y are
  Not ($x and $y are the same)).       left-aligned when (
                                         $x's left equals $y's left).
We say that $x is visible when (
```

Fig. 3. Constructs for visibility, sameness and alignment.

```
We say that $x x-intersects $y         We say that $x and $y
when ((($y's right - 1)                overlap when (
    is greater than $x's left) And       (($x is visible) And
  (($x's right - 1)                         ($y is visible)) And (
    is greater than $y's left)).         ($x x-intersects $y)
                                         And
We say that $x y-intersects $y           ($x y-intersects $y))).
when ((($y's bottom - 1)
    is greater than $x's top) And      We say that $x and $y do not
  (($x's bottom - 1)                   overlap when (
    is greater than $y's top)).          Not ($x and $y overlap)).
```

Fig. 4. Constructs for overlapping.

The second part of the core constructs deals with overlapping elements. The corresponding definitions are shown in Fig. 4. The first two constructs first define when two elements intersect horizontally and vertically, respectively. Overlapping elements are then defined as two elements that are both visible, and intersect both horizontally and vertically.

One can see that the first definition uses the expression "right - 1", which has for effect that in order to be declared as intersecting, elements should do so by at least two pixels. It overcomes a problem where Cornipickle relays dimensions and coordinates in integers (pixels), although the browser can work with floats in case of elements having dimensions in ratios. These floats are rounded and can cause 1 pixel differences between what is displayed and what is serialized.

Finally, RWD bugs routinely involve the concept of *containment*: the fact that the boundaries of an element are entirely enclosed within the boundaries of another. Containment constructs are shown in Fig. 5. These rules define two types of top-level containment: that of a child element within its parent, and also that of an arbitrary element within the browser's global viewport.

```
We say that $c is horizontally        We say that $c is fully
  inside $p when (                       inside $p when (
  ($c's left is greater than             If (($c is visible) And
    ($p's left - 2))                        ($p is visible)) Then (
  And                                       ($c is horizontally inside $p)
  ($c's right is less than                  And
    ($p's right + 2))).                      ($c is vertically inside $p))).

We say that $c is vertically          We say that $x is fully inside
  inside $p when (                      the viewport when (
  ($c's top is greater than              If ($x is visible) Then (
    ($p's top - 2))                         (($x's left + 2) is greater than 0)
  And                                       And
  ($c's bottom is less than                 ($x's right is less than
    ($p's bottom + 2))).                       (the page's width + 2)))).
```

Fig. 5. Constructs for containment.

5.2 RWD Declarative Properties

Now that we have defined useful concepts at an appropriate level of abstraction, it is possible to express responsive layout bugs as statements using the aforementioned constructs.

Scrollbar Bug. One of the first indications of a poorly responsive website is the presence of a horizontal scrollbar. To detect this bug, a simple Cornipickle property can be defined:

```
We say that there is an horizontal scrollbar
  when (
  the page's width is less than
    the page's scroll-width).

Always (Not (there is an horizontal scrollbar)).
```

This property is made of an auxiliary statement expressing the presence of a scrollbar, which is then used within an LTL temporal operator (Always) stipulating that the condition should not appear in any of the page snapshots.

Element Collision. The second kind of RWD bug is element collision, which occurs when two elements of the page overlap while they should not. Detecting such bugs is more delicate than it looks. Indeed, it does not suffice to report all overlapping elements inside a page, as many of them overlap for legitimate reasons: to start with, any element nested within its parent would trigger such a simple condition.

This is where the approach we propose, which is based on sequences of snapshots of the same page in various dimensions, can be put to good use. Rather than trying to guess which overlapping elements are suspect by looking at a single rendition of the page, we compare the overlapping state of these elements across successive snapshots. Elements are said to be colliding when they are non-overlapping in one snapshot, and overlapping in the next.

In order to express these properties, one must use the full expressive power of the Cornipickle language, as is shown below.

```
Always (
  For each $x in $(body *) (
    For each $y in $($x > *) (
      For each $z in $($x > *) (
        If ( ($y and $z are not the same) And
          ($y and $z do not overlap) ) Then (Next (
            When $y is now $a (When $z is now $b (
              $a and $b do not overlap)))))))).
```

The three *For each* constructs gather all the elements and their immediate children. It allows testing pairs of *siblings* (elements with the same parent) $x and $y for their overlap property. The Next operator then moves the focus to the next snapshot of the page; the two constructs *When x is now y* trace the same pair of elements and places them into variables $a and $b, respectively. This way, it becomes possible to compare the properties of a pair of elements over two successive snapshots of the page. Overall, the property says that if two siblings do not overlap at one point in time, these two siblings should not overlap either at the next point in time.

Note that, in the way the property is written, it does not check whether an element overlaps with a "cousin" (an element that shares the same grandparent): this is not necessary, because a colliding cousin necessarily violates the Element Protrusion property, which we shall describe later. The property could be done by testing every element with every other element but it is costly in performance.

Element Protrusion. This property tackles the problem of elements which overflows their container. As with the previous property, reporting all overflowing elements is not appropriate, as overflows can also occur for legitimate reasons. However, one can use the same device, and use LTL temporal operators to compare an element and its direct children across two snapshots of the page. It can be expressed in the Cornipickle language in this fashion:

```
Always (
  For each $x in $(*) (
    For each $y in $($x > *) (
      If ($y is fully inside $x) Then (Next (
        When $x is now $a (
          When $y is now $b (
            $b is fully inside $a))))))).
```

The property at the end has two *For each* constructs that return a pair composed of any element in the page and any of its direct children. Then, if the latter is fully inside the former in an initial screenshot, the same pair should be fully inside in the next one. This property was able to catch a bug on the website https://www.thelily.com/. It can be seen in Fig. 6 where the *div* with the menu buttons ends up outside of the menu bar and out of sight. In the first picture, all the buttons are correctly placed in the menu bar. In the second picture, the highlighted "About" button is protruding outside of the menu bar, its parent.

(a) Correct   (b) Buggy

Fig. 6. The Element Protrusion bug on the website thelily.com.

Viewport Protrusion. The Viewport Protrusion bug can be handled in a manner similar to the Element Protrusion bug, but using the whole viewport as the reference. It can be written in Cornipickle as follows:

```
Always (For each $x in $(*) (
    If ( $x is fully inside the viewport )
      Then (Next (
        When $x is now $y (
          $y is fully inside the viewport))))).
```

On the website https://www.slaveryfootprint.org, a Viewport Protrusion was found in a large width. Figure 7 shows how non-observable bugs can create problems at lower widths. In the first picture, the page's width is already small enough for the document's main *div* element to start protruding outside the viewport. Cornipickle reports it as a bug, although there is not (yet) any observable effect (all the graphical elements and the text inside that div are still completely visible). However, setting the window to an even smaller width makes the bug observable: in the second picture, the window is exactly 440 pixels wide, and we can now see the text overflowing outside the viewport.

Wrapping Elements. Wrapped elements are elements that are pushed on an additional line, although they were aligned with other elements on a single line at larger widths. We limited our implementation to elements that are inside a list.

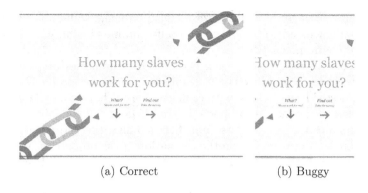

(a) Correct   (b) Buggy

Fig. 7. The Viewport Protrusion bug on the website slaveryfootprint.org.

```
We say that the list $x is          Always (
aligned when (                         For each $x in $(ul) (
  For each $y in $($x > li) (            If (the list $x is aligned)
    For each $z in $($x > li) (          Then (
      ($y and $z are top-aligned)          Next (
      Or                                     When $x is now $y (
      ($y and $z are left-aligned)))).        the list $y is aligned))))).
```

Finally, all the lists are taken in a first screenshot in order to compare their elements' alignment. They then need to still be aligned in the next screenshot.

An example of a wrapped element can be seen in Fig. 8. It could be argued that this is not a bug, however, at lower widths, the list is top-aligned again. This shows that having this list top-aligned is the desired layout.

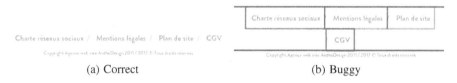

(a) Correct   (b) Buggy

Fig. 8. The Wrapping Element bug on the website anthedesign.fr. In the first picture, the list is top-aligned. At a lower width (second picture), the "CGV" element gets pushed on an additional line. The list was highlighted in red by the Cornipickle probe. (Color figure online)

5.3 Scalability Considerations

In order to assess the scalability of our approach on real-world web sites, we created a benchmark designed to measure the computation time of the Cornipickle interpreter on web pages of various sizes. All experiments and data are available as an external download[2], in the form of a self-contained instance of the LabPal experimental environment [12].

More precisely, we generated synthetic JSON summaries of pages, in the same format as the one produced by Cornipickle's JavaScript probe. Each page is made of two nested levels of lists, with each list element having a variable number of sub-list elements. Since all properties listed in Sect. 5.2 compare an element with either its direct children or its immediate siblings, this setup is sufficient to measure the impact of page size on the evaluation of the properties. While using "real-world" web pages seems like an appealing prospect at first sight, static pre-recorded files do not make it possible to run a controlled experiment where parameters can easily be varied. On the contrary, synthetic snapshots allow us to vary the size and structure of pages so that the interpreter's scalability can be measured.

We varied the number of child elements that each list item can have, and ran the Cornipickle interpreter on generated page summaries of the corresponding size. For each snapshot, we measured the total running time of the interpreter for evaluating each of the properties listed in Sect. 5.2. All experiments have been run on relatively modest hardware, consisting of an AMD Athlon II X4 640 1.8 GHz running Ubuntu 18.04, with a JVM of 3566 MB of memory.

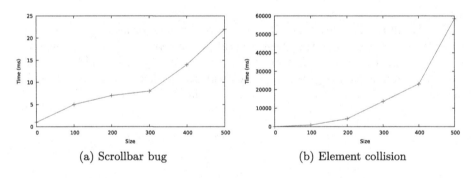

(a) Scrollbar bug   (b) Element collision

Fig. 9. Interpreter evaluation time for page summaries of increasing size.

Figure 9 shows the evolution of execution time for increasing page sizes. Due to lack of space, we only include running times for the fastest (Fig. 9a) and the slowest (Fig. 9b) of all properties. As one can see, checking for the presence of a scrollbar requires a negligible amount of time on the order of a few tens of milliseconds. The running time is roughly linear in the size of the page snapshot, as it appears that Cornipickle's design requires the ingestion and parsing of every page snapshot, regardless of the amount of data that is actually accessed inside this snapshot.

---

[2] https://github.com/liflab/cornipickle-benchmark.

The running time for evaluating the Element Collision property shows a much larger increase with respect to snapshot size. This is expected, considering the expression of the property as three nested quantifiers (cf. Sect. 5.2). The first ($x) loops over all elements of the page, while the second and third ($y and $z) each loop over all children of $x. Barring the overhead incurred by the remainder of the expression, a quick calculation shows that the interpreter runs in time $O(m^2)$, where m is the total number of elements in the page; this corresponds to the roughly quadratic execution time we observe experimentally.

To the best of our knowledge, our work is the first to rigorously measure the running time of the Cornipickle interpreter on page snapshots. Unfortunately, the running times we obtained cannot be compared with related works: the paper on ReDeCheck [20], the only other *automated* RWD testing tool, makes no mention of running time on the sample pages it was tested on. The other approaches mentioned in Sect. 3 all involve a manual inspection, and therefore it makes no sense to speak of running time for these tools. Nevertheless, figures gleaned from [20] can give us a few indications. All pages studied contained fewer than 400 lines of HTML code, and no more than 196 DOM nodes. The experimental results above indicate that pages of such a scale can be handled in under five seconds using our Cornipickle/Crawljax approach.

It shall be noted that our proposed approach is intended to be used in a development and testing context, where tests are run periodically, and a few seconds of waiting is considered reasonable. Performing the same analysis on production web sites in realtime is obviously not an option.

6 Conclusion

In this article we have presented an automated approach that allows the detection of RWD bugs. The effectiveness of the tool has enabled us to catch automatically some common problems encountered in real modern web applications. Cornipickle properties ensure that the pages of an application follow various kinds of constraints. A small application has been developed and integrated in order to test the visual rendering in the different possible viewports in order to catch the RWD faults.

One main advantage of the proposed approach is that it does not require the development of new tools or new algorithms; rather, it leverages the power of two existing systems, and allows RWD bugs to be expressed as declarative test oracle specifications. So far, our solution has concentrated solely on the five types of RWD bugs proposed by Walsh *et al.* [19]; however, the use of a general purpose declarative language opens the door to the elicitation of RWD bugs related not only to layout, but also functionality. We are currently exploring this line of research, which is left as future work.

Our solution also has some limitations. The use of Cornipickle limits us to constraints referring only to elements that are displayed. It makes bugs that are caused by the back end sometimes hard to catch; it is necessary to find displayed elements that can indirectly represent server states. In the same line, if Crawljax does not notify of a state change when the DOM changes, it is not possible to evaluate that page where a bug could have happened. Also, when a property evaluates to false, it is false for the rest of the crawl and no other bug can be caught with this property. This caused a problem with finding observable RWD bugs because most failures are non-observable and the properties had to find an observable bug as their first bug. Finally, our solution currently does not address cross-browser incompatibilities, multi-page analysis, or incorporate verdicts from other kinds of approaches, such as screenshot-level analysis. Overcoming these limitations could be the basis of future works. A comparison with bugs found by real human testers, as well as ReDeCheck, could be used as a baseline to calculate the precision and recall of our approach.

References

1. http://makandracards.com/makandra/1422-capybara-the-missing-api
2. http://sahi.co.in
3. http://www.websiteresponsivetest.com/
4. http://respondr.io/
5. http://quirktools.com/screenfly/
6. https://www.sitepoint.com/responsive-web-design-tool/
7. https://www.responsinator.com/
8. http://responsivepx.com/
9. http://www.applitools.com
10. Choudhary, S.R., Prasad, M.R., Orso, A.: X-PERT: accurate identification of cross-browser issues in web applications. In: Proceedings of the ICSE 2013, pp. 702–711, May 2013
11. Enge, E.: Mobile vs desktop traffic in 2019 (2019). https://www.stonetemple.com/mobile-vs-desktop-usage-study/. Accessed 3 July 2019
12. Hallé, S., Khoury, R., Awesso, M.: Streamlining the inclusion of computer experiments in a research paper. IEEE Comput. **51**(11), 78–89 (2018)
13. Hallé, S., Bergeron, N., Guérin, F., Beroual, O.: Declarative layout constraints for testing web applications. Log. Algebraic Methods Program. **85**(5), 737–758 (2016)
14. Mahajan, S., Halfond, W.G.J.: WebSee: a tool for debugging html presentation failures. In: Proceedings of the ICST 2015, pp. 1–8. IEEE, April 2015
15. Marcotte, E.: Responsive Web Design, 4th edn. Eyrolles, Paris (2013)
16. Mesbah, A., van Deursen, A., Lenselink, S.: Crawling Ajax-based web applications through dynamic analysis of user interface state changes. ACM Trans. Web **6**(1), 1–30 (2012)
17. Pnueli, A.: The temporal logic of programs. In: Proceedings of the FOCS 1977, pp. 46–57. IEEE Computer Society (1977)
18. Rivoal, F.: Media queries - W3C recommendation (2012). https://www.w3.org/TR/css3-mediaqueries
19. Walsh, T.A., Kapfhammer, G.M., McMinn, P.: Automated layout failure detection for responsive web pages without an explicit oracle. In: Proceedings of the ISSTA 2017. ACM (2017)
20. Walsh, T.A., McMinn, P., Kapfhammer, G.M.: Automatic detection of potential layout faults following changes to responsive web pages. In: Proceedings of the ASE 2015, pp. 709–714. ACM (2015)

Layout as a Service (LaaS): A Service Platform for Self-Optimizing Web Layouts

Markku Laine$^{(\boxtimes)}$, Ai Nakajima, Niraj Dayama, and Antti Oulasvirta

Aalto University, Helsinki, Finland
{markku.laine,ai.nakajima,niraj.dayama,antti.oulasvirta}@aalto.fi

Abstract. To personalize a web page, case-specific rules or templates must be specified that define the visuospatial layout of elements as well as device-specific adaptation rules for an individual. This approach scales poorly. We present *LaaS*, a service platform for self-optimizing web layouts to improve their usability at individual, group, and population levels. No hand-coded rules or templates are needed, as *LaaS* uses combinatorial optimization to generate web layouts for stated design objectives. This allows personalization to be controlled via intuitive objectives that affect the full web layout. We present an extensible architecture and solutions for (1) layout generation using integer programming, (2) data abstractions to mediate between browsers and layout generators, and (3) page restructuring. Moreover, we show how *LaaS* can be easily deployed as part of existing web pages. Results demonstrate that our approach can produce usable personalized web layouts in diverse scenarios.

Keywords: Self-adaptive web interfaces · Web-based interaction · Web personalization · Web layouts · Web service architectures

1 Introduction

Designing a *web layout* is laborious and challenging: Given elements can be laid out in many different ways, yet content and functionality need to appear interesting and presented in an appealing and accessible way. However, the "one design fits all" approach is inherently suboptimal from the usability point-of-view. For any individual user, a page designed for a larger population will always compromise the particular interests, expectations, and capabilities. Previous work suggests that layout personalization could bring significant per-user improvements in usability and experience and could relieve designers and developers from manual work. However, while there are computational methods and architectures for web personalization, no viable solution has been proposed how to adapt *full web layouts* to individuals without manually precoded rules or templates.

This paper contributes a novel service architecture design and computations for *objective-level web layout personalization*. That is, layouts are adapted by reference to desired effects on end-users: "I want this page to be improved for [design objective]". In objective-level control, the full layout of a page, including

© Springer Nature Switzerland AG 2020
M. Bielikova et al. (Eds.): ICWE 2020, LNCS 12128, pp. 19–26, 2020.
https://doi.org/10.1007/978-3-030-50578-3_2

elements and their positions and sizes will be *generated* given the user's data. No rules or templates are needed. This extends web personalization from content-level personalization to consider full layouts. In this paper, we explore selection time and visual saliency as two common objectives in layout optimization [5].

In the rest of this paper, we present *LaaS*, an architecture and computations for *self-optimization of web layouts*. Our cloud-based service architecture allows offloading computation effort to the cloud. The computational tasks of selecting and layouting elements on a page are NP-hard problems and not solvable in a browser for realistic problem instances. We make two further technical contributions. First, we extend combinatorial optimization based approaches [5] to permit adapting layouts to a wide variety of users, pages, and devices with no predefined rules or templates. Changes to existing codebase are minimal (1 line per page). This is practically out of reach of rule-based approaches, which scale up poorly. Second, we present a data abstraction for the visuospatial design of the page, which allows the optimizer to be agnostic of the underlying web technologies (here: HTML, CSS, and DOM). The architecture is easy to deploy and fully controllable by the service owners, who may want different outcomes on different pages and must trust that the outcomes produced are of high quality. The process is practically invisible to end-users. Moreover, thanks to the separation of a design task from the generator, proprietary machine learning methods can be incorporated to *LaaS*. We demonstrate the system with a clickstream-based generation of personalized web news portals, a realistic and challenging case with needs for variability in web layouts.

2   Related Work

LaaS focuses on the *grid layout*, a common design principle for organizing graphical UIs, available in many design tools, UI toolkits, and layout managers. Visual flow and motor selection are two important goals in their design [6,9]. After determining the visuospatial organization of a web layout, it must be implemented, typically using standard web technologies. Adaptation rules, such as for Responsive Web Design, must be added, which is often done by hand. Designers spend considerable time with repetitive tasks related to UI layouts. So far, no architecture has been proposed for web layout adaptation that is able to adapt the full layout for an individual without predefined rules or templates.

Web personalization has been a topic of interested since the 1990s. A number of machine learning and data mining methods have been proposed for modeling page contents and web usage patterns in order to drive the *recommendation* and *selection* of contents. Research on techniques for *presenting content* has focused on the *ordering*, *emphasis*, and *scaling* of contents [2], as well on message framing and use of colors. However, no method has been proposed that could handle any and all of these on the web.

Service architectures for adaptive web layouts have been either rule-based or template-based. For example, AERO is a template-based framework for web layout synthesis [10]. The approach is based on a suite of templates specified in HTML and CSS, of which one is selected in accordance with a customizable scoring function. An issue with both rule and template-based approaches is that they rely on decisions at design-time. In general, existing approaches are not well-suited for handling continuous and unanticipated changes.

Combinatorial optimization has been studied as a method for the GUI design [5]. Early research mostly used rules and design heuristics to generate layouts that adhere to known design guidelines and more recently data-driven approaches. *Model-based approaches*, on the other hand, use *white-box* (first principles) models that provide a theory-driven and transparent approach to layout generation. In the generative process, layout quality is measured against some model or design heuristic. When heuristics are used as objective functions, however, optimization systems scale up poorly due to the large number of rules. *Predictive models of user performance and experience* have been proposed to address this issue [5]. We found only one application of prediction-based methods for web layouts. In Familiariser [9], a visual search model was fit to a user's site visitation history and used in a browser-side optimizer to re-layout a page to make elements quicker to find. In *ability-based optimization*, UI designs are generated by taking into account motor or cognitive impairments of an individual, which are represented as parameters in predictive models [8]. For an overview of design objectives that can be modeled using predictive models, see [5].

The layout problem is recognized in operations research as an NP-hard problem, and our design problem is an instance of it. In combinatorial geometry, grid layout has been studied in the context of 2D bin packing, rectangular packing, and the guillotine cuts problem [5]. Generation of multiple, varied, near-optimal solutions has been discussed. An elementary version of the grid design problem has been previously proposed [4]. However, they merely attempted to find the most densely packed solution by squeezing elements closely together.

3   LaaS: Architecture and Computations

This section presents Layout as a Service (LaaS), a service platform architecture and computations that enable *objective-level web layout personalization*. The distributed system architecture consists of a set of loosely-coupled client-side and server-side components that communicate with each other over HTTPS using a REST API, as depicted in Fig. 1. The client-side components are dynamically loaded to the end-user's browser during the initial phase of a page load; Layout Parser and Layout Adapter are executed *before* the web page is displayed to the user, whereas Event Logger collects user behavior data *while* the user interacts with it. The server-side components are run *on demand* (e.g., daily, weekly) in the cloud; Design Task Generator generates a design task specification for the latest version of each layout, whereas Layout Generator optimizes them accordingly.

In the architecture, expensive computations, especially layout generation, are executed on the server side. The adaptation of layout elements, on the other hand, takes place in the browser to permit adaptation of both server-side and client-side rendered pages. The architecture is also designed in a modular way such that it is possible to plug in machine learning components that help in user modeling and/or design task generation.

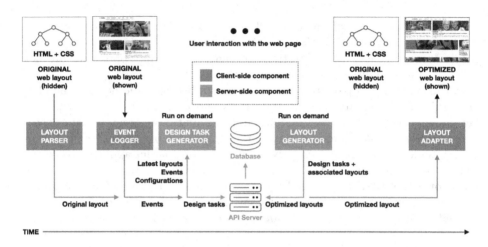

Fig. 1. *LaaS* architecture, including core components and interactions between them.

The following subsections describe the above-mentioned *LaaS* core components and their function in greater detail.

3.1   Layout Parser

In order to reproduce a web layout, Layout Parser *automatically* (1) assigns a unique identifier for each element, (2) parses the web page structure and styles, (3) detects and labels key elements, (4) precomputes permissible shapes for key elements, and finally (5) creates a user interface technology independent representation (JSON) of the *original layout*. This parsing process needs to be done *only once* per selected layout optimization level (individual, group, population).

3.2   Event Logger

Event Logger is responsible of capturing user interactions on a web page and sending the data to API Server. The collected data includes, among others: event type, layout identifier, client identifier, page URL, and other event-specific data (e.g., clicked element identifier, link target, and timestamp). Our current implementation records clicks and visits on web pages. Support for new event types and metrics (e.g., document scroll and time spent on the page) can be easily added by extending *LaaS* event logging capabilities.

3.3   Design Task Generator

To support adaptation on demand for any given target, as well as to support controllability, *LaaS* separates the design task from the generator. Design Task Generator (DTG) creates a specification of *design task*, which serves as a communication vehicle between the designer (here: DTG) and Layout Generator. It allows the designer to specify (1) various design objectives and constraints on a web layout to be generated and (2) compute per-element importance values based on collected user behavior data. We currently use click frequencies to obtain element importance values. However, the architecture is flexible enough to support other, more advanced computational methods, such as machine learning.

3.4 Layout Generator

We formulate a mixed integer linear programming model (MIP) in order to reorganize web pages as grid layouts. We chose MIP to achieve a balance between computational performance and solution quality. Our MIP formulation (1) ensures well-formed layouts that are rectangular and well-aligned and (2) optimizes them for stated design objectives, in our case selection time and visual saliency. Linearity of our model ensures better performance and enables use of suitable MIP callbacks [3]. Further, our MIP model has size depending solely on the number of elements involved, i.e., the size of our MIP model is independent of the canvas size. The MIP model works in three phases:

Phase 1: Layout Sanctity. We ensure a non-overlapping, non-overflowing grid where elements are placed within permissible size limits and in permissible locations. We use continuous decision variables to represent the location of all four edges of every individual element. Continuous decision variables avoid pixel-level discretization, which is important for the performance of the solver. To prevent overlapping elements, we use an approach introduced by Hart and Yi-Hsin [4]. Hence, the core MIP formulation developed in this phase provides non-overflowing, non-overlapping solutions with element sizes within limits.

Phase 2: Alignment. This phase computes and restricts the number of independent grid lines required to represent the selected candidate solution. It ensures that the resulting layouts are well-aligned and aesthetically acceptable. To represent overall alignment objectively, we define notional Cartesian grid lines on all pixels of the canvas. If any two (or more) elements have any of their edges aligned with each other, those elements share the single grid line for those edges. So, the *total number of grid lines actually utilised* in any feasible solution is a direct indicator of the overall alignment within that solution. The objective of minimizing the total number of grid lines achieves the design intent of well-aligned solutions.

Phase 3: Functional Layout. The functional placement formulation determines the placement and sizing of relevant elements to ensure that the layout has high usability. We have picked and implemented the following two design objectives, but any other objectives that can be efficiently represented in the MIP could be included (for previous work, see [5]).

- *Selection Time.* We use Fitts' law to compute the time required to reach a specific element on the screen. Fitts' law is widely used in model-based optimization as an objective function [1]. Selection time (ST) is a function of target distance (D) and size (W): $ST = a + b\log_2(D/W + 1)$. In our case, we assume that the user starts scanning the screen from the top-left corner. So, we use a linear function of the distance from the screen corner as a substitute approximation. If the design task instance prioritizes selection time, the optimizer attempts to minimize the predicted time required for important elements. The most obvious effect is that very important elements may become larger and placed closer to the top-left corner of the web page.

– *Visual Saliency.* Saliency refers to how attention-grabbing an element is given the rest of the page [7]. In our case, we compute saliency as the relative size of the element. While area would be a proxy for the saliency, this is further complicated by the requirement that the permissible areas of the element must be picked from within a fixed number of permissible shapes only. So, we pick the most salient size from the permissible shape set, if provided, and use that size for laying out elements. Similarly, color and other qualities could be implemented.

3.5   Layout Adapter

Restructuring hierarchical web pages is particularly challenging because even the smallest change to the DOM structure can break the web page's visual appearance, functionality, or both. Thus, Layout Adapter is designed so that it can reposition and resize web layout elements without changing the original tree structure. Once an *optimized layout* for the web page becomes available in the cloud, it can be fetched and applied *before* the web page is shown to the user.

3.6   Deployment

Enabling *LaaS* on a website can be done in just two steps. First, the service owner registers a website to obtain an embeddable `<script>` tag with a tracking identifier. Second, the obtained script is added on those web pages of the website, whose usability needs to be improved. Injecting the `<script>` tag into the web pages can be done either *manually* with minimal source code changes or *automatically* via our proxy server installation.

We also offer *LaaS* Control Panel for service owners to manage various *LaaS* related settings on their website, such as service status, design objectives, target elements, and data collection events.

4   Results

Figure 2 shows example outputs for WebNews, a custom news aggregator website hosted on our server. The original design shown in Fig. 2(a) has one template-based multi-column grid layout, to which in the initial design news articles from six different categories are allocated. Normally, adapting the *full layout* of a page like this would require predefined templates or a (very) large number of rules.

We divide the example results into two classes: demonstrator results done with simpler scenarios and two more realistic cases. Figure 2(b-d) shows adaptation results for different combinations of the two design objectives, using a single card as the illustrative example. The produced layouts are well-formed

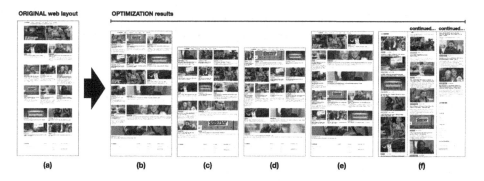

Fig. 2. Results for a web news page: (a) Original web layout with multiple content cards; (b) Optimized to improve selection time of a single card (Costco); (c) Optimized for visual saliency of the same card; (d) Optimized for both selection time and saliency of the same card; (e) Optimized for both and with more complex interest distribution (all sports and business cards); (f) Optimized for mobile device screen width.

and the element-of-interest (Costco) behaves as desired: it is moved to a closer position for selection in (b), more visually salient in (c), and both combined in (d). Figure 2(e) shows a more complex example, where a bimodal interest distribution (sports and business categories) is accounted for. Figure 2(f) shows the page adapted for a mobile screen. All layouts are properly formed: there are no holes and no overlapping elements. The layouts adhere to proper, well-aligned grids. This would be very laborious to achieve with a rule or template-based approach.

4.1 Discussion

There are two predominant methods for rendering layouts on the web: server-side rendering and client-side rendering. While client-side rendering has gained popularity over the past few years, a myriad of web applications (incl. WebNews), frameworks (e.g., WordPress), and libraries use or support server-side rendering, including React and Vue.js . The *LaaS* architecture is designed to work with both server-side and client-side rendered layouts; however, our research efforts have almost exclusively focused on the former up until this point.

Quality of Experience (QoE) [11] describes, from a holistic perspective, how well a service such as a website satisfies its users' expectations. While *LaaS* can produce usable personalized web layouts, we acknowledge that its use may unfavorably impact other QoE factors, such as page load times and aesthetics. However, according to our informal testing these effects are small and can be mitigated with the use of known techniques, such as caching and image re-cropping.

5 Conclusion

We presented first steps toward *objective-level* control of personalization, including an architecture and involved computations. We believe that at least within the scope of grid-based web layouts, this goal is within reach. The examples we showed would be very laborious to achieve with a rule-based approach. This result warrants more research on this approach. *LaaS* provides an extensible architecture concept for future work to build on. It supports, by design, easy deployment on many present-day pages and integration with widely used machine learning methods for user modeling and recommendations. The core MIP solutions, on the other hand, can be extended with other design objectives.

References

1. Bailly, G., Oulasvirta, A., Kötzing, T., Hoppe, S.: MenuOptimizer: interactive optimization of menu systems. In: Proceedings of the 26th Annual ACM Symposium on User Interface Software and Technology, UIST 2013, pp. 331–342, ACM (2013). https://doi.org/10.1145/2501988.2502024
2. Bunt, A., Carenini, G., Conati, C.: Adaptive content presentation for the web. In: Brusilovsky, P., Kobsa, A., Nejdl, W. (eds.) The Adaptive Web. LNCS, vol. 4321, pp. 409–432. Springer, Heidelberg (2007). https://doi.org/10.1007/978-3-540-72079-9_13
3. Castillo, I., Westerlund, J., Emet, S., Westerlund, T.: Optimization of block layout design problems with unequal areas: a comparison of MILP and MINLP optimization methods. Comput. Chem. Eng. **30**(1), 54–69 (2005). https://doi.org/10.1016/j.compchemeng.2005.07.012
4. Hart, S.M., Yi-Hsin, L.: The application of integer linear programming to the implementation of a graphical user interface: a new rectangular packing problem. Appl. Math. Model. **19**(4), 244–254 (1995). https://doi.org/10.1016/0307-904X(94)00033-3
5. Oulasvirta, A., Dayama, N.R., Shiripour, M., John, M., Karrenbauer, A.: Combinatorial optimization of graphical user interface designs. Proc. IEEE **108**(3), 434–464 (2020). https://doi.org/10.1109/JPROC.2020.2969687
6. Pang, X., Cao, Y., Lau, R.W.H., Chan, A.B.: Directing user attention via visual flow on web designs. ACM Trans. Graph. **35**(6), 1–11 (2016). https://doi.org/10.1145/2980179.2982422. Article No. 240
7. Rosenholtz, R., Li, Y., Mansfield, J., Jin, Z.: Feature congestion: a measure of display clutter. In: Proceedings of the SIGCHI Conference on Human Factors in Computing Systems, CHI 2005, pp. 761–770. ACM (2005). https://doi.org/10.1145/1054972.1055078
8. Sarcar, S., Jokinen, J.P.P., Oulasvirta, A., Wang, Z., Silpasuwanchai, C., Ren, X.: Ability-based optimization of touchscreen interactions. IEEE Perv. Comput. **17**(1), 15–26 (2018). https://doi.org/10.1109/MPRV.2018.011591058
9. Todi, K., Jokinen, J., Luyten, K., Oulasvirta, A.: Individualising graphical layouts with predictive visual search models. ACM Trans. Interact. Intell. Syst. **10**(1), 1–24 (2019). https://doi.org/10.1145/3241381. Article No. 9
10. Vernica, R., Venkata, N.D.: AERO: an extensible framework for adaptive web layout synthesis. In: Proceedings of the 2015 ACM Symposium on Document Engineering, DocEng 2015, pp. 187–190. ACM (2015). https://doi.org/10.1145/2682571.2797084
11. Wechsung, I., De Moor, K.: Quality of experience versus user experience. In: Möller, S., Raake, A. (eds.) Quality of Experience. TSTS, pp. 35–54. Springer, Cham (2014). https://doi.org/10.1007/978-3-319-02681-7_3

Structural Profiling of Web Sites in the Wild

Xavier Chamberland-Thibeault and Sylvain Hallé$^{(\boxtimes)}$

Laboratoire d'informatique formelle, Université du Québec à Chicoutimi,
Saguenay, Canada
shalle@acm.org

Abstract. The paper reports results of a large-scale survey of 708 web-sites, in order to measure various features related to their size and structure: DOM tree size, maximum degree, depth, diversity of element types and CSS classes, among others. The goal of this research is to serve as a reference point for studies that include an empirical evaluation on samples of web pages.

1 Introduction

Over the past years, several tools and techniques have been developed to analyze, debug, detect errors, or otherwise process the output produced by web applications. Many of these tools focus on an analysis of the Document Object Model (DOM) of a page, and accessorily to the Cascading Stylesheet (CSS) declarations associated to its elements. For example, X-PERT [2] and $\mathcal{X}$FIX [5] attempt to fix cross-browser issues; Cornipickle [3] is a general purpose interpreter for declarative specifications over DOM elements and their rendered attributes; ReDeCheck [6] performs an analysis of a page's rendered DOM to detect responsive web design (RWD) bugs.

A common point to these approaches, and to many others, is that their scalability –and ultimately, their success– is dependent on features of a page that are typically related to its *size*. Hence, the running time for ReDeCheck scales according to the number of DOM nodes in the target page; Cornipickle scrapes a page in time proportional to the number of DOM nodes, and evaluates a declarative property in time proportional to the number of elements matching any of the CSS selectors found in that property; some RWD constraints scale proportionally to the number of nodes and the maximum number of direct children they have; etc.

Most of the aforementioned works duly provide an empirical evaluation of the proposed tools on a sample of pages or websites. However, it is hard to assess where these samples lie across the whole spectrum of web pages that may exist "in the wild". For example, the experimental analysis in [6] is run against documents of up to 196 DOM nodes: is this typical of a large web page, or a small one? Without data making it possible to situate such values with

© Springer Nature Switzerland AG 2020
M. Bielikova et al. (Eds.): ICWE 2020, LNCS 12128, pp. 27–34, 2020.
https://doi.org/10.1007/978-3-030-50578-3_3

respect to a larger population, the authors, readers and reviewers alike are left speculating, with often conflicting viewpoints, to what extent the tested samples can be accepted as reasonably "real".

The present paper aims to address this issue. It reports on results of a large-scale analysis of 708 websites, with the goal of measuring various parameters related to the structure and size of their pages, such as the size of the DOM tree, degree distribution of its nodes, depth, distribution of various element types, diversity of CSS classes, etc. The goal of this research is to provide an objective (albeit partial) reference point allowing practitioners to quantitatively situate the samples used in research works that include an empirical evaluation. To summarize, the paper's contributions include a description of the methodology used to harvest and process data, a freely-available interactive package that can be used to explore the results, and a repository of all the raw data used in the analysis.

2   Methodology

To accomplish such an analysis, a few steps had to be followed. At first, we had to collect a large enough sample of websites for the analysis to be meaningful, then we had to find a way to collect the data from the previously found websites and, at last, process the recovered data. In this section, we shall present how each of those steps were fulfilled.

2.1   Website Collection

The first step of the process was to collect the list of websites to be included in our sample. We opted for a combination of two methods. First, we considered the first 500 most frequented websites in the world, by retrieving data from the latest list found on Moz [1]. However, this list contains many duplicates made of country-specific versions of the same platform. These duplicates have been removed, keeping only the first occurrence of each site. The remaining sites from this list (approximately 300) accounted for around 40% of our total sample.

This first sampling step provides us with a set of sites that are visited by the most users. However, this notion is orthogonal to the sample of sites most visited by an individual user. To illustrate this, consider a set of websites $\{s_0, \ldots, s_n\}$ and n users. Site s_0 is visited once by each user, and for each $i > 0$, site s_i is visited $n - 1$ times by user i. With $n = 10$, s_0 accounts for 53% of all traffic (compared to less than 5% for each of the remaining sites), but only accounts for 10% of all visits for any single user. That is, the fact that a site impacts the *most people* does not necessarily imply it impacts people *most significantly*.

In order to address this issue, we added a second part to our sampling step, by informally asking people around to provide us with the list of websites they use daily. Therefore, by combining these two data collection methods, we got the most commonly used ones in the world and various day-to-day websites. The complete dataset and scripts can be downloaded[1].

---

[1] DOI: https://doi.org/10.5281/zenodo.3718598.

2.2 DOM Harvesting

After the list of websites was established, the next step was to collect data on the DOM for each of these sites. This was done by creating a JavaScript program which is designed to run when the DOM of a page has finished loading.

The script starts at the **body** node of a page and performs a depth first preorder traversal of the integral DOM tree of that page. For every node, the script records and/or computes various features:

- *tag name*; this is used to record the usage proportion of elements
- *CSS classes* associated to the element; this is used to measure the diversity and distribution of CSS classes in a document
- *visibility status*; elements in the page can be made invisible in various ways: setting their position outside the viewport, setting their dimensions to 0, using the **display** or **visibility** CSS attributes; the script records if any of these techniques is applied on the rendered element
- structural information, such as degree and depth from the root.

For a given page, the output of the script is made of two files: the first is a JSON document containing a nested data structure that mirrors the structure of the page's DOM tree, where each node is a key-value map containing the features mentioned above. The file also contains global statistics computed on the DOM, such as the number of elements for each tag name, class and method of invisibility. The second document is a text file in the DOT format accepted by the Graphviz[2] library. It can be used to produce a graphical representation of the DOM, where each tag name is given a different color. An example of such a tree (for the Zippyshare.com website) is given in Fig. 1.

In order to actually harvest the data from a web page, we used the TamperMonkey[3] extension, which allows users to inject and run custom JavaScript code every time a new web page is loaded in the browser. This extension also presents the advantage that

Fig. 1. An example of a DOM tree represented graphically, as produced by our harvesting script. Each color represents a different HTML tag name. The root of the tree is the black square node. (Color figure online)

---

[2] https://graphviz.org.

[3] https://www.tampermonkey.net.

versions exist for multiple browsers, including Chrome, Firefox, Edge and Safari. For each website in our sample, the home page URL was loaded and our TamperMonkey script was run on this page.

It shall be emphasized that the harvesting step on each web page is performed in the browser, and hence operates on the DOM tree and on properties of the elements *as they are actually rendered* by the browser. That is, our script does not perform a simple scraping of the raw HTML code returned by the server. Doing so would miss all the elements that are dynamically inserted or modified by client-side scripts at load time. Overall, running the scripts over the 708 sites takes approximately 6.5 h and generates 62 MB of raw data.

2.3 Data Processing

As a second step, we aggregated these various measurements to compute statistics over the whole sample of pages, so as to get information such as distributions for various numerical parameters, using the LabPal experimental processing framework [4]. This library makes it possible to load, process, transform, and display empirical data in the form of tables, macros and plots. Our LabPal instance is designed such that every website is an experiment instance, whose task is to read the corresponding raw JSON files and compute various additional statistics on the structure of the DOM tree. These results are then collated in various ways into tables and plots.

It is to be noted that some of the recovered files were not used in the analysis. As was said earlier, the automated loading of web pages made us retrieve a lot of advertisement pop-ups –which arguably do not really count as "real" web pages, in the sense meant by most papers concerned with analyzing the DOM. Manually inspecting each file to judge whether it is an advertisement page or a normal web page is a tedious process. We therefore opted for a more general rule that would remove most of these pages: we took away from the analyzed data each page that contained fewer than 5 DOM nodes, or whose URL belonged to a list of domains that are known to be advertisement pages.

3   Results and Discussion

A full presentation of the results of the study cannot be done exhaustively in this paper due to a lack of space. In this section, we shall present a summary of the most important features, as well as a few interesting highlights and take-home points that should be taken from this study. The combined size of all websites visited amounts to a total of 623100 DOM nodes.

3.1 Website Profiles

DOM Tree Structure. A first statistic we computed is the number of elements in a web page across all sites. Figure 2a shows the cumulative distribution, where the line represents the fraction of all sites that have fewer than some number of elements. From this, we can observe that half of all websites have fewer than

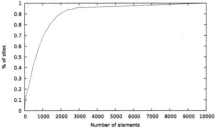

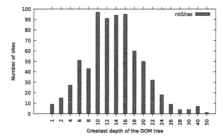

(a) Cumulative distribution of websites based on the size of DOM tree

(b) Distribution of websites based on DOM tree depth

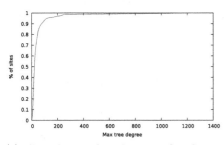

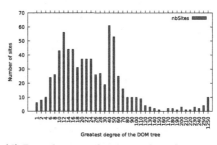

(c) Cumulative distribution of websites based on maximum node degree

(d) Distribution of websites based on maximum node degree

Fig. 2. Graphical summary of DOM profiling

700 nodes, and 90% have fewer than 2000. The distribution of the number of elements in a web page very closely matches an inverse exponential function. In our dataset, the fraction of the number of pages having x elements or less is given by the function $1 - \frac{0.83}{e^{0.0011x}}$; the coefficient of determination is $R^2 = 0.999$, which indicates a surprisingly strong fit with the regression.

We also computed the depth of the DOM tree for each website; this corresponds to the maximum level of nesting inside the top-level body element. The distribution across websites is shown in Fig. 2b. The distribution assumes a relatively smooth bell shape; 39% of all sites have a maximum depth between 10 and 16.

A complementary measurement to the depth of the DOM tree is the maximum degree (i.e. number of direct descendants) that a DOM node can have. This is represented in Fig. 2c. 50% of websites have a maximum degree of at most 22, while 90% of websites have a maximum degree of at most 80. This time, a good fit for the data is the function $1 - \frac{4.91}{x^{0.92}}$, with a high coefficient of determination of $R^2 = 0.894$.

A fourth statistic related to tag usage across websites. We measured the relative proportion of each HTML element name, excluding tags corresponding to inline SVG markup. Unsurprisingly, div is the most frequent tag, representing 26% of all elements in a page. It is followed by a (19%), li (11%) and span (10%).

Combined, these four elements account for two-thirds of all tags found in a page. No other tag has a frequency greater than 4%. Given that `div` and `span` have no special meaning, and are only used to enclose elements for display purposes, we can conclude that more than one third of all HTML markup is not semantic.

Visibility Status. Of all DOM nodes in the websites analyzed, 54% were invisible to the user by one of the available techniques. This is a rather surprising finding, which means that more than half of a page's markup corresponds to elements that are not immediately displayed to the user, such as scroll-down menus or pop-ups. Figure 4 shows the distribution of websites according to the fraction of nodes that are invisible. One can see that this distribution is fairly uniform, with a roughly equal number of websites for each 10% interval of invisible nodes (Fig. 4).

An interesting finding is that the techniques used to make elements invisible are not uniformly distributed. Of all invisible elements across the analyzed pages, 60% are made so by assigning them a negative position. Surprisingly, *none* of the websites analyzed used `display:none` or a dimension of zero to make nodes invisible.

nbElement	InvisibleType
0	Display
	widthOrHeight
131334	visibility
213840	outsidePosition
536700	negativePosition

Fig. 3. Total number of elements using each visibility.

CSS Classes. Another aspect of our study is concerned with the CSS classes associated with elements of the DOM, either directly with the `class` attribute, or programmatically using JavaScript.

We first checked whether there is a correlation between the size of the DOM tree and the number of distinct CSS class names occurring in the tree. This can be represented graphically with the plot of Fig. 5a. As one can see, there is a relatively loose dependency between the size of a website and the number of classes it contains. We also calculated, for each website, the average size of each CSS class (i.e. the average number of DOM nodes belonging to each distinct CSS class present in the document). The function $1 - \frac{1.72}{x^{1.93}}$, which represents the

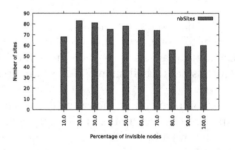

Fig. 4. Distribution of websites according to the fraction of all DOM nodes that are invisible.

fraction of all sites having an average CSS class size of x or less, fits the experimental data with a coefficient of determination of $R^2 = 0.931$.

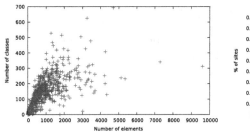
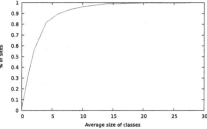

(a) Size of the DOM tree vs. number of (b) Cumulative distribution of websites
CSS classes   based on the average size of a CSS class

Fig. 5. Statistics about the use of CSS classes.

3.2   Threats to Validity

Website Sample. All the distributions and statistics computed in this study obviously depend on the sample of websites used for the analysis. Different results could be obtained by using different selection criteria. We tried to alleviate this issue by including in our sample a good fraction of sites selected using an objective and external criterion (the Moz top-500 list, which ranks sites according to their traffic). However, we also balanced this selection by including lesser known sites suggested by people based on their daily usage of the web. Finally, the relatively large size of our study (708) lessens the odds that our selection fortuitously picked only outliers in terms of size or structure.

Variance Due to Browser. A single browser was used in our study, namely Mozilla Firefox. Since there sometimes exists a discrepancy between the pages rendered by different browsers, the actual DOM trees obtained could differ when using a different browser. However, most compliance violations affect the way elements are *graphically* rendered on the page, but not the actual contents of the DOM tree from which the page is rendered; hence these discrepancies do not affect the statistics we measure in our study. It shall also be noted that our use of Firefox has been made out of commodity: nothing technically prevents the same scripts from running in other browsers, thanks to TamperMonkey's wide support.

Homepage Analysis. For all the sites considered, only the homepage has been analyzed. This is deliberate, so that the same methodology could be applied uniformly to all the sites in our study. Although many websites allow users to access to a different section after logging in, most of them have a relatively complete and usable homepage. There are, however, some exceptions; the most notable is Facebook, which shows nothing but a login form to non-authenticated visitors. This has repercussions on the reported page size and structure.

To minimize the impact of this phenomenon, it could be possible to choose a different page in each website, in order to pick one that is representative –for example, one of the pages shown to the user after logging in. This, however, would introduce considerable complexity: valid credentials would need to be provided for all these sites, and specific instructions on how to reach the desired page (automatically) would have to be defined. More importantly, the choice of the "representative" page would introduce an additional arbitrary element that could in itself be a threat to validity.

4   Conclusion

In this paper, we have presented various statistics about the structural content of web pages for a sample of 708 websites, which includes the 500 most visited sites according to Moz [1]. Our analysis has revealed a number of interesting properties of websites in the wild. For example: the distribution according to their size closely follows an inverse exponential; most pages have fewer than 2000 nodes and a tree depth less than 22; more than half of all elements are hidden, and the majority of them are concealed by setting them to a negative position; most websites have CSS classes containing on average 10 elements or less.

It is hoped that these findings, and many more included in our online experimental package, can be used as a reference point for future research works on website analysis. They can help situate a particular benchmark or sample used in an empirical study, with respect to a larger population of websites "in the wild". As future work, we plan to expand the amount of data collected on each page, and intend to periodically rerun this study in order to witness any long-term trends over the structure of websites.

References

1. The Moz top 500 websites. https://www.moz.com/top500. Accessed 20 October 2019
2. Choudhary, S.R., Prasad, M.R., Orso, A.: X-PERT: accurate identification of cross-browser issues in web applications. In: Notkin, D., Cheng, B.H.C., Pohl, K. (eds) Proceedings of the ICSE 2013, pp. 702–711. IEEE Computer Society (2013)
3. Hallé, S., Bergeron, N., Guerin, F., Breton, G.L., Beroual, O.: Declarative layout constraints for testing web applications. J. Log. Algebr. Methods Program. **85**(5), 737–758 (2016)
4. Hallé, S., Khoury, R., Awesso, M.: Streamlining the inclusion of computer experiments in a research paper. IEEE Comput. **51**(11), 78–89 (2018)
5. Mahajan, S., Alameer, A., McMinn, P., Halfond, W.G.J.: Automated repair of layout cross browser issues using search-based techniques. Proc. ISSTA **2017**, 249–260 (2017)
6. Walsh, T.A., McMinn, P., Kapfhammer, G.M.: Automatic detection of potential layout faults following changes to responsive web pages (N). In: Cohen, M.B., Grunske, L., Whalen, M. (eds) Proceedings of the ASE 2015, pp. 709–714. IEEE Computer Society (2015)

Performance of Web Technologies

Accelerating Web Start-up
with Resource Preloading

JiHwan Yeo$^{(\boxtimes)}$, Jae-Hyeon Rim, ChangHyun Shin, and Soo-Mook Moon$^{(\boxtimes)}$

Seoul National University, Seoul, Korea
{jhyeo,jhtop12,schyun9212}@altair.snu.ac.kr, smoon@snu.ac.kr

Abstract. Long start-up time of *web apps* or *web pages* at the client device may affect the user experience negatively. One bottleneck in reducing the start-up time is *resource loading* overhead. To reduce the overhead, resource *preloading* has been proposed, which load resources ahead of time, instead of loading them on time when they are used. For commercial client device such as smart TV, it is reasonable for the browser of the client to do resource preloading. Existing client-only technique remembers the resources accessed in the previous visit and then preloads them in the current visit. However, it preloads the resources in some arbitrary order, thus not dealing well when the preloading order is important, especially for user experience. One solution is employing a *resource dependence graph*, often used for preloading with proxy servers or web servers, but in client-only environment we need to compute the graph while preloading is in progress, and update the graph incrementally when the resources change. This paper proposes such a dependence graph-based, client-only resource preloading technique. For better user experience, we decide the preloading order based on those factors that affect user perception such as the size or the location of images in the screen. Our experimental results on Chromium browser with real web apps on an embedded board and on a commercial smart TV show that the proposed technique can improve the UX-related app start-up time (above-the-fold time or speed index) tangibly, allowing the user to really feel the difference.

Keywords: Web browser · Resource preloading · Smart device

1 Introduction

Web browsing is important for smart devices. For example, browsing is known to occupy 63% of the user time and 54% of the CPU time on the smartphone [22]. The *start-up time* of web pages or apps during browsing is an important factor affecting user experience and business revenue [3,4,18]. Amazon found that every 100 ms of latency costs them 1% in sales [9].

One big contributor to the start-up time is *resource loading*, which is the process of fetching the resources from the network [20]. An extensive research has been done to accelerate resource loading [2,11,13,15,19], and many of them

© Springer Nature Switzerland AG 2020
M. Bielikova et al. (Eds.): ICWE 2020, LNCS 12128, pp. 37–52, 2020.
https://doi.org/10.1007/978-3-030-50578-3_4

require infrastructural support of servers and proxies, which is hard to provide by the device manufacturers (e.g., smart TV makers) due to scalability or maintenance issues.

Client-only optimizations are more easily deployable and scalable. There are two popular client-only approaches: *caching* and *prefetching*. Caching stores resources locally and reuses them in the subsequent page accesses if they are still valid. Prefetching predicts the pages to visit and fetches the resources in advance. Although these methods are widely used, they have limited performance impact due to spoiled or un-cacheable resources or wrong predictions [10,12,17,21].

Another client-only method is resource *preloading*. Normally, a resource is loaded on demand when it is met during the HTML parsing of a web app (page). Preloading fetches resources in advance by reading all resource tags in the HTML file at the beginning of parsing and by requesting their loading using the browser threads. However, those resources accessed by the execution of JavaScript code during app start-up (e.g., web framework like jQuery) cannot be preloaded in this way. So, more aggressive preloading techniques have been proposed.

One technique is a profile-based solution which remembers resources accessed during the previous visit of a web page and uses it to fetch resources in advance when visiting the same page again [21]. This approach solves the limitations of caching and regular preloading, but it does not consider the preloading order of resources, so some critical resources might be delayed to be loaded (it should be noted that the preloading order does not affect correctness but only performance), or it is hard to implement elaborate preloading heuristic that requires precise ordering.

Another solution exploits proxy servers at the cloud [11] or the web servers [13]. Such remote servers proactively visit web pages in advance to decide the target resources for preloading. Since they work in an offline manner, they can build an elaborate data structure called a *dependence graph* to decide the preloading order. It estimates the dependence between resources using the loading start time and end time of each resource, where an overlap of loading time between two resources means independence. This information is used for preloading by the client so as to preload dependent resources earlier, thus more accurate preloading. Since proxy-cloud for commercial devices is unrealistic, we wonder if the client browser can exploit the dependence graph by itself.

We propose a *dependence graph-based preloading*, yet working on the client-only environment. There are two issues. First, every time we execute a web app (page), we need to update the dependence graph since new resources can be added or old ones can be obsolete (again, preloading of wrong resources does not affect correctness but only performance). So, we must update the graph concurrently while resource preloading is in progress at the client, and the existing method of building the graph from scratch by the proxy server at each proactive visit cannot work. In fact, preloading many resources at once at the client would make otherwise dependent resources appear independent, if only the start time and the end time were used. To handle this, we update the dependence graph incrementally, based not only on the loading time of a resource but also on the time the resource is actually used at the client.

Another issue is the preloading order that can best exploit the dependence graph, especially among non-dependent resources. Existing method uses their depth/height to decide the preloading order, but we propose a heuristic based on user experience factors so that the users can have better experience.

We modified chromium browser to implement proposed technique and experimented on an embedded board and on a commercial smart TV. The experimental results with real TV apps show a tangible performance improvement. Also, when there are updates of resources, we could recover the performance drop caused by the out-of-date dependence graph quickly, as it updates the graph incrementally.

The rest of the paper is as follows. Section 2 reviews related work on preloading or UX. Section 3 describes the proposed preloading technique. Section 4 has the UX-based heuristics. The implementation on Chromium is shown in Sect. 5. Section 6 shows the experimental results and Sect. 7 includes the summary and the future work.

2   Background on Resource Loading and Preloading

After downloading the HTML file of a web page, a web browser parses the HTML file to build a DOM tree. When a resource (e.g., image, JavaScript, CSS, JSON file) is met during the parsing, the resource is also downloaded, and then the parsing continues. This on-demand resource loading is slow since the browser needs to wait while the resource is being downloaded. To reduce the wait time, most browsers employ a *pre-loader* by default, which requests the download in advance for those resources explicitly specified in the HTML file. However, only those resources in the HTML tags can be preloaded, and many other resources to be requested as a result of JavaScript execution or those in the CSS or JSON files cannot be preloaded in this way.

HTML5 includes the preload directives [6], which allow the web developer to specify the resources that will be needed in a web page using an HTML tag. So for those dynamic resources to be requested by the JavaScript execution can also be preloaded if they are specified in a preload directive. However, this would be a burden for the developers who need to specify the resources manually in the web page. Also, there is a restriction on the resources allowed with preload directives. For example, if a web server can provide the resources specialized for each user, the client needs to send the user's identifier using *query string* in resource URL or *request header* along with the resource URL. Preload directive can only specify the resource URL, thus not allowing preloading for those resources with the request header.

To overcome the above limitations, two more aggressive preloading techniques have been proposed. One is a client-only approach, and the other is proxy-based approach.

One representative client-only preloading technique is *Tempo* [21]. It saves a list of resources loaded in the previous visits of a website using a *resource graph*, a hierarchically structured graph starting from the website root node, subdomain nodes, web page nodes, to subresource nodes. When accessing a website, Tempo preloads those subresources of a web page node if it was visited previously, or predicts then preloads if this is the first visit. The resource graph is updated at each visit for preciseness.

One problem of Tempo is that it does not specify the precise preloading order, which might make some critical resources be delayed to be loaded. For example, some smart TV apps download JSON files, which include resources (or another JSON files that include resources) to download, which will be added to the DOM tree to show the real time menus (e.g., today's movie lists) on the screen. If the JSON file were preloaded later than the menu resources, none of them are usable since the JSON file might have different resources than those of the previous visit. Actually, preloading of the menu resources might even delay the regular loading of the JSON file by monopolizing the network bandwidth. Another problem is that Tempo does not save the request headers, so it cannot preload user-specialized dynamic resources (e.g., user-specialized menus for smart TVs).

SWAROVsky is a representative proxy-based preloading technique [11]. Its remote proxy server proactively accesses the web servers that the client pre-notifies for possible future access, decides the target resources for preloading, and analyzes the order of resources. SWAROVsky performs this job repetitively (once in 30 min) and caches the resources as well, so when the client access the web page, it allows the client to perform preloading. It decides the preloading order by building a resource dependence graph during proactive access. The basic idea is that for each resource SWAROVsky observes the start time and the end time of resource loading, and if there is any overlap between two resources, they are classified as independent. On the other hand, a resource A is classified as dependent on a resource B, if there is no overlap between A and B, *and* B's end time is closest to A's start time. When the client requests the web page, the proxy server will send the resources in *topologically sorted order* of the graph. For the TV app example above, this will make the JSON file be preloaded earlier than the menu resources dependent on it. The dependence graph can save the request header, allowing preloading of user-specialized resources.

Although SWAROVsky allows more precise preloading, its remote proxy-based approach is unrealistic to employ by a smart device manufacturer, which cannot easily afford to provide and maintain a remote, scalable server for a huge amount of client devices. Also, if a web page is updated frequently (e.g., movie apps such as Neflix), there can be a difference between the resources of the proxy server and those of the current web server due to the 30-min delay.

Above discussions indicate that for smart devices, it is more realistic to take a dependence-based, yet client-only resource preloading approach. There is one challenge, though. The existing dependence graph of SWAROVsky is built *offline* at the remote proxy, while preloading is performed *online* at the client. The proposed approach requires performing both simultaneously at the client. Since every time when the web page is accessed, we need to make a new resource dependence graph since a new resource can be added or an old resource can be

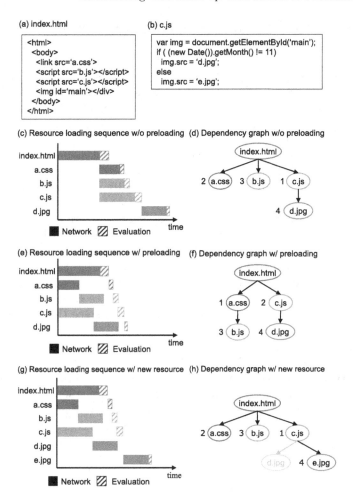

Fig. 1. Resource loading sequence and dependency graph without and with preloading

obsolete. The problem is that we need to make the graph while the resource preloading is in progress at the client. The existing graph cannot work properly; preloading of many resources at once would make otherwise dependent resources look independent if only the start time and the end time are used. Also, when a new resource is added, it will be likely to be loaded later than all other preloaded resources, thus making it dependent on them, which is not right.

Disabling preloading once in a while to build the precise graph from scratch would degrade the performance and affect user experience, thus not an option.

We propose a new technique of updating the dependence graph incrementally and concurrently with resource preloading. We also propose a preloading order heuristic that can best exploit the proposed precise dependence graph at the client.

3   Dependence-Based, Client-Only Preloading

This section describes the proposed technique, focusing on how to build and update the resource dependence graph at the client, concurrently while resource preloading is in progress. When the client runs a web app (page) for the first time, it will build a dependence graph (unlike SWAROVsky's, the graph can be built as the updates of the initial empty graph; see below). Figure 1 depicts how to build one for a simple web app.

Figure 1 (a) shows the HTML file (*index.html*), which accesses two JavaScript (*b.js* and *c.js*) resource and one CSS resource (*a.css*). The JavaScript code c.js accesses one image resource depending on a condition, as shown in Fig. 1 (b). Figure 1 (c) shows an example resource loading sequence for the first execution of the web app (with the default browser pre-loader), where *network* means the transmission time of a resource and *evaluation* means the time while the resource is used (e.g., execution time for JavaScript or CSS code or decoding time for an image). If we build the dependence graph using the start time and the end time of *network* (as depicted in Sect. 2), it will be Fig. 1 (d); *a.css*, *b.js*, and *c.js* are dependent on *index.html*, while they are independent to each other (thus being siblings in the graph), and *d.jpg* is dependent on *c.js* since the end time of *c.js* is closest to the start time of *d.jpg*.

When the app is run again in the next time, the client will preload resources based on the graph in Fig. 1 (d), where the preloading order heuristically decided by SWAROVsky is attached at each node. Among the three sibling resources who have the same *depth*, c.js is preferred since it has the longest *height*. Since a browser has multiple threads for resource preloading (e.g., maximum three in our example), it can request multiple resources simultaneously, while satisfying the preloading order. Let us assume that Fig. 1 (e) shows the resource loading sequences for the second run, where *c.js* and *a.css* are preloaded with *index.html*, followed by the preloading of *b.js* and *d.jpg*. The overall loading time is reduced, which also advances the use time of each resource, thus improving the app start-up time. Now, the question is how to rebuild a new dependence graph since we need to accommodate a new behavior; new resources can be added or old resources can be obsolete (for example, if *c.js* accesses *e.jpg* instead of *d.jpg* this time, we would need to add *e.jpg* while removing *d.jpg* in the new graph).

If we rebuild the dependence graph using Fig. 1 (e) as previously, the graph will be Fig. 1 (f), where a new dependence from *a.css* to *b.js* exists, which is not right. Actually, preloading of many resources at once would even make otherwise dependent resources look independent. If no resources are added or deleted, the previous graph in Fig. 1 (d) should still be valid, but if we build the graph using the start time and the end time of loading sequences of Fig. 1 (e), we will get a different, incorrect graph.

To handle this problem, we propose a different method. Basically, we will start from the same graph used in the previous run and update it as needed, based on the resource usage time as well as the start/end time, as follows.

First, if a preloaded resource is actually used in the current run, its dependence relationship in the old graph will be preserved. So if no resources are added or deleted as in Fig. 1 (e), we need no update for the old graph of (d).

Secondly, if a new resource is added in the current run, it will be loaded when it is needed, unlike other preloaded resources. If we consider only the start/end time, this new resource would be added to a leaf incorrectly. Instead, we try to find an existing resource, whose *use time* is earlier than and closest to the new resource's *start time*. Then, we add the new resource as a child of the node we found. Actually, there are many possible cases for the dependence, but we think that the most common case of adding a new resource is replacing an old resource by a new one (e.g., *c.js* in Fig. 1 (b) chooses a different resource depending on a condition, the menu resources of a JSON file is replaced by new ones, or a resource tag of the HTML file accesses a different resource). If so, the correct location in the graph would be the sibling of a deleted node. This heuristic tends to maintain the depth of the old graph unchanged, unlike when adding the new resource to a leaf. This would keep the depth of the original graph built with no preloading unchanged, thus more desirable. Actually, when we run the web app for the first time, we may build the first dependence graph as if we add new resources incrementally to the initial empty graph.

Finally, if a preloaded resource is not used in the current run, the corresponding node in the old graph should be deleted. If the deleted node is a leaf node, we simply remove it. If it has children nodes, we try to make them the children nodes of its sibling node. If there is no sibling, they will be the children of its parent node, which might reduce the depth of the graph. If deletion of an old node and insertion of a new node occur at the same time (i.e., replacement of a node), we perform the insertion first, then the deletion, which is likely to keep the whole depth of the graph unchanged.

Figure 1 (g) shows the resource loading sequence when execution of *c.js* accesses *e.jpg* instead of *d.jpg*, and Fig. 1 (h) shows the graph after the insertion and deletion.

Now, we mention the impact of proposed resource preloading when resource caching mentioned in Sect. 1 is also used. Generally, resource preloading will have a higher performance impact when the local cache is empty (*cold cache*) since it can significantly reduce the network latency of resource loading. Even if the resources are available in the local cache (*warm cache*), the resource preloading still has a performance impact by loading the resources from the disk cache to the memory of the browser, faster than when they are loaded on demand, especially when the browser is newly launched when the device (e.g., the TV) is turned on (if the browser accesses the same web page many times, the resources will eventually be saved to the memory cache, reducing the impact of preloading, though). Actually, not all resources can be cached; those resources whose contents are updated frequently cannot be cached as per the instructions of the web server. We performed preloading with both cold cache and warm cache in the experiment.

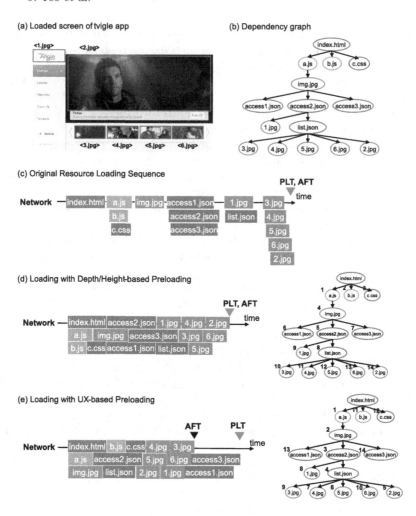

Fig. 2. UX-based Ordering vs. depth/height-based one for Resource Preloading

4   Preloading Order for Better User Experience

The only ordering requirement enforced by the original dependence graph is to preload the parent resources earlier than the child resources, thus in a topologically sorted order. Among the nodes with no paths in the graph, any ordering is possible, but the previous section followed the heuristics used by SWAROVsky, which prefers nodes closer to the root node (depth is smaller) and prefer those with the longest descending chain for the siblings whose depth is the same (height is longer). Figure 2 (a) shows an example of smart TV web app which includes 15 resources. Figure 2 (b) shows the corresponding dependence graph. Figure 2 (c) depicts an example of a regular resource loading sequence without preloading. Figure 2 (d) illustrates an example resource loading sequence with depth/height-based preloading when there are three preloading threads, with the preloading order attached to the dependence graph. Conceptually, they imply that the total page load time (PLT) as well as the above-the-fold time (AFT) [1] (which is what the user see) can improve with resource preloading.

One issue with the above preloading is that it tends to delay the preloading of the image resources located at the bottom of the graph, thus affecting the user experience. To improve it, we propose an ordering heuristic that favors images, especially those images that affect human perception. In fact, there have been many researches on prioritizing resource loading for quality-of-experience (QoE). They show that earlier loading of bigger images and those images closer to the center of the screen improves QoE [2,8]. Additionaly, the original finish time of loading an image is important [2,16].

Using these factors, we can define parameters such as the size of images, the distance from the center, and the original loading finish time. Then, we define a QoE score for each image resource with three terms, as follows:

$$QoE\ score = \frac{area}{window\ size} + \left(1 - \frac{distance}{max\ distance}\right) - \frac{finished\ time}{last\ image\ finished\ time}$$

The first, second, and the third terms considers the size factor, the distance-from-the-center factor, and the original loading time factor, respectively. We could give a different weight for each term, but our experiments showed that there was no notable difference for user perception. We sort the images in a descending order of the QoE score and decides the preloading order among them. Other resources in the dependence graph on which each image is dependent should be preloaded earlier than the image, and in this way we decide the final preloading order for all resources. Figure 2(e) shows the conceptual loading sequence based on the new preloading order attached in the dependence graph, obtained after sorting the QoE score of images. The image resources and the dependent resources are loaded earlier, which reduces the AFT, thus improving user experience (UX), while the PLT is similar. In fact, there is a video clip at https://youtu.be/EcQeWVd4gj4 that demonstrates the app start-up behavior for the three configurations (original, depth/height-based preloading, UX-based preloading) for the above TV app. It shows that preloading leads to much faster start-up than original start-up, and the UX-based preloading allows users to feel slightly faster start-up.

5   Implementation

We implemented the proposed preloading technique on the Chromium browser. For each run, we generated a resource table which records the start time, the end time, and the use time for each resource. During the process of each resource loading by the browser (e.g., initiating loading request, starting the fetch from the network, ending the fetch), some callback functions are called, so we modified those callback functions to record these times at the table. When the app start-up ends, we build or update the dependence graph using the resource table.

Table 1. Number of resources used for web apps

Apps	Browser pre-loaded resources	Warm cached resources	Total resources
Google Movies	4	22	23
Tvigle	3	40	56
POOQ	2	208	234
RU-tv	35	64	71
Plex	0	5	7

We implemented the preloading request logic by following the internal implementation of the preloading directives in the browser, but we send the request header as well as the URL. Chromium browser allows a maximum of 10 parallel preloading requests, yet 6 for a single host. The Chrome browser has its own priorities and scheduling rules for preloading requests, so we control the number of invocation of preloading requests appropriately, so as not to affect the original resource loading drastically.

For some resource, each run intentionally changes its URL by adding a random number at the end of the URL, even though it is actually the same resource (the server understands this, thus sending the same resource to the client). This is for preventing the resource from being cached. This causes a problem for our update of the dependence graph since such a resource might be classified as adding a new resource. This is a well-known problem. To handle this problem, we employ a URL matching heuristic in [14], to check if different URLs actually mean the same resource.

For implementation of UX-based ordering, we obtain the size and position of each image resource by accessing the layout event where the DOM tree and the CSSOM tree are merged to a render tree.

6   Evaluation

We performed two types of evaluation. One is to compare client-only resource pre-loading in Sect. 3 with regular resource loading. The other is to compare the ordering heuristics of depth/height in Sect. 3 and UX in Sect. 4.

6.1   Resource Preloading vs. Regular Loading

For the first evaluation, we evaluate the performance impact of the proposed dependence-based, client-only resource preloading, compared to regular resource loading. We experimented with five web apps used in a commercial smart TV listed in Table 1, which are URL-based apps, thus similar to browsing web pages. We performed the experiments on an embedded board (Odroid-C2) with 1.5GHz ARM CPU and 2GB memory (with Chromium version 66), and on a commercial

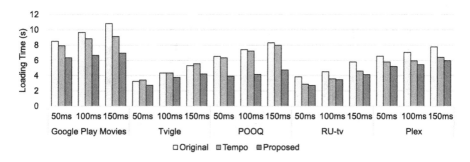

Fig. 3. Web app start-up time with cold cache

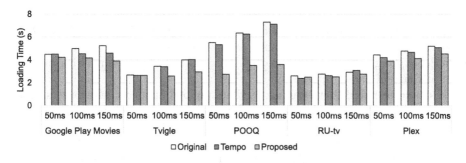

Fig. 4. Web app start-up time with warm cache

smart TV with an ARM-based SOC (with Chromium version 68). We measured the app start-up time until the first screen of a web is displayed on the screen. For the embedded board, we evaluate the performance impact based on diverse network conditions by saving all resources of a web app in a server and by emulating the network between the server and the client [7]. We experimented with the network bandwidth of 10, 25, 50, and 100 Mbps and the network latency of 50 ms, 100 ms, and 150 ms. There is no difference of app start-up time for the network bandwidth, so we report the result with the bandwidth of 100 Mbps only. To measure the app start-up time, we used above-the-fold time (AFT) [1], instead of page-load time (PLT). PLT measures the time when all resources included in the HTML are loaded, while AFT measures the time when all resources above the fold are displayed on the screen, thus better reflecting user experience. We experimented with both cold cache and warm cache.

For the smart TV experiment, we measured the wall clock time by connecting the TV to the internet by the Ethernet. Since the network latency would be even smaller than the 50 ms of the board experiment, it is worse environment to show the impact of preloading. Also, the TV is equipped with highly optimized warm cache specialized to the TV, so it is even disadvantageous. Finally, the CPU quality of the TV is worse than the board, which would make resource loading less critical to app start-up time. Nevertheless, we obtained tangible performance impact, as we will see shortly.

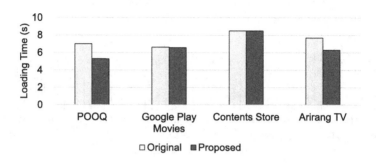

Fig. 5. Web app start-up time on a smart TV with warm cache

For the embedded board, we measure the start-up time for the original (*Original*), Tempo-based preloading exactly as implemented in [21] (*Tempo*), and ours with depth/height heuristic (*Proposed*). For the TV, we measured the start-up time of Original and Proposed.

It should be noted that Original also does preloading for some resources using the default pre-loader of the browser. Tempo or Proposed preloads on its own way.

Figure 3 shows the app start-up time on the embedded board with cold cache for three network latencies. The start-up time of our Proposed is shorted than Original and Temp for all five apps for all network latencies. For longer network latencies, preloading has a better impact, as we can expect. Our Proposed has an average improvement of 27% compared to Original. It is even better than Tempo by 11%, but we found that it is mostly due to the lack of specifying request headers, mentioned in Sect. 2. If we experiment with the same condition, the results were similar and we found that at the beginning of the start-up, Proposed preloads better resources than Tempo, but as the time goes on, the difference between two preloading methods become little (since resources are loaded even before invoking preloading requests). However, the second experiment with the ordering heuristics for UX in the next subsection will show the value of more precise ordering using the dependence graph.

Figure 4 shows the performance impact with warm cache. Proposed shows an average of 19% improvement over Original, which is better than 6% improvement of Tempo. The overall start-up time with warm cache is shorter than with cold cache, since cached resources are loaded from the local disks rather than from the network.

Table 1 shows the total number of resources used in each app. It also shows the number of resources preloaded by the browser pre-loader as well as the resources saved in the local cache when warm cache is used. For the cold cache experiment, the total resources minus the browser pre-loaded resources will be the target of preloading from the network for Proposed and Tempo. For the warm cache experiment, among these target resources, the cached resources will be preloaded from the local cache and the remaining resources will be preloaded from the network. Tvigle and POOQ have a relatively large number of un-cached

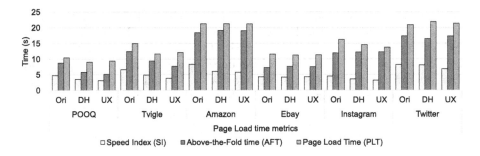

Fig. 6. UX-based vs. Depth/Height-based Ordering (lower is better)

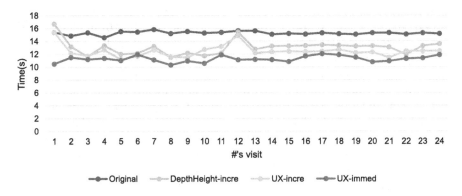

Fig. 7. Above-the-fold time for Tvigle app when resources change

resources, thus showing a higher performance impact of preloading, while others show less impact due to preloading from local cache.

Figure 5 shows the web app start-up time on the smart TV for four TV apps. Proposed shows an average of 13% improvement over Original, which is lower than the board experiment but still tangible. This is due to faster network latency, lower CPU performance, highly optimized caching policy of the TV, as explained previously. However, for Arirang TV and POOQ, the difference is 2 s and 1.5 s, respectively, so TV users can feel the difference with their eyes.

6.2 Preloading Order Based on UX vs. Depth/Height

We also experimented with preloading based on UX-based ordering compared with the depth/height-based ordering. We measure the AFT as well as the speed index (SI) [5] for this experiment (SI is another popular UX metric). The network delay is 150 ms and the cold cache is used. For this experiment, we used the two web apps for TV (Tvigle and POOQ) and four popular web pages (other TV apps did not show notable difference).

Figure 6 shows the AFT and SI for the original (*Ori*), the depth/height-based preloading (*DH*), and the UX-based preloading (*UX*). We also measured the

PLT for comparison. We can see that for two web apps, both AFT and SI of UX-based are better than Depth/Height by as much as 18% and 20%, respectively. For the web pages, AFTs are similar but SIs of UX-based ordering works better, exploiting the precise dependences of the dependence graph. One thing to note is that there is little difference of PLT for both UX and DepthHeight, so the total time to load all resources is similar, but user experience improves.

6.3 Update of Dependence Graph with Resource Change

If the resources of a web app (page) change as time goes on, our preloader based on the old dependence graph will preload the old resources and not preload the new correct resources, degrading the start-up time. So we proposed incremental update of the dependence graph to recover the start-up time from degradation.

To evaluate the performance impact of our incremental update of the dependence graph, we use the Mahimahi tool [14] to record web resources and replay the visits. Figure 7 shows the start-up time (AFT) for the Tvigle app when we ran the app 24 times with 12-h intervals. *Original* means the original start-up with no preloading, and *DepthHeight-incre* and *UX-incre* mean preloading with incremental update of the dependence graph. *UX-immed* means that we make two consecutive web app loads for each simulated visit. Browser re-compute the dependence graph and the UX-based order from scratch in the first web app load and measured the AFT in the second web app load. It would be a some-what ideal start-up time. We found that at the 12-th visit, around 10 resources were changed, so we can see a sharp increase of the start-up time for both depth/height and UX heuristics. However, we can recover it at the 13-th visit due to our incremental update of the dependence graph. This result indicates that our client-only preloading can cope with the change of resources by updating the graph on demand.

7 Summary and Future Work

In this paper, we proposed dependence-based, client-only solution for resource preloading. Unlike an existing client-only solution, we consider resource preload-ing order based on dependence graph. Unlike an existing dependence-based solu-tion working on an offline proxy server, our solution updates the dependence graph at the client online, even while preloading the resources. We also pro-posed ordering heuristics for better user experience. Our experimental results indicate that the proposed solution shows a tangible performance impact on real TV apps, on the commercial TV as well as on the embedded board.

As a future work, we can improve the heuristics to update the dependence graph. For a new resource added, if we can consider the network time as well as the use time for the candidate resources which the node is dependent on, we might be able to predict its right position in the graph. Also, when a resource is loaded and its event handler requests a new resource, they are dependent, which could be identified if we analyze the call stack of the JavaScript engine.

We can use machine learning to decide the preferable images for each web site, instead of the current fixed preference based on the size and the location of the images.

Acknowledgement. This work was supported by the National Research Foundation of Korea (NRF) grant funded by the Korea government (MSIT) (No. 2020R1A2B5B02001845) and LG Electronics.

References

1. Brutlag, J., Abrams, Z., Meenan, P.: Above the fold time: measuring web page performance visually. In: Velocity Web Performance and Operations Conference (2011)
2. Butkiewicz, M., Wang, D., Wu, Z., Madhyastha, H.V., Sekar, V.: Klotski: reprioritizing web content to improve user experience on mobile devices. In: 13th USENIX Symposium on Networked Systems Design and Implementation, pp. 439–453 (2015)
3. Everts, T.: New findings: for top ecommerce sites, mobile web performance is wildly inconsistent (2018). https://blog.radware.com/applicationdelivery/wpo/2014/10/2014-mobile-ecommerce-page-speed-web-performance/
4. Galletta, D.F., Henry, R.M., Mccoy, S., Polak, P.: Web site delays: how tolerant are users? Inf. Syst. Res. **17**(December 2002), 20–37 (2002)
5. Google: Speed index (2012). https://sites.google.com/a/webpagetest.org/docs/using-webpagetest/metrics/speed-index
6. Grigorik, I., Weiss, Y.: Preload (2018). https://www.w3.org/TR/preload/
7. Hubert, B.: tc(8) - Linux man page (2018). https://linux.die.net/man/8/tc
8. Kelton, C., Ryoo, J., Balasubramanian, A., Das, S.R.: Improving user perceived page load times using gaze. In: 14th USENIX Symposium on Networked Systems Design and Implementation, NSDI 2017, Boston, MA, USA, 27–29 March 2017, pp. 545–559 (2017)
9. Liddle, J.: Amazon found every 100ms of latency cost them 1% in sales (2008). https://blog.gigaspaces.com/amazon-found-every-100ms-of-latency-cost-them-1-in-sales/
10. Liu, X., Ma, Y., Liu, Y., Xie, T., Huang, G.: Demystifying the imperfect client-side cache performance of mobile web browsing. IEEE Trans. Mob. Comput. **15**(9), 2206–2220 (2016)
11. Liu, X., Ma, Y., Wang, X., Liu, Y., Xie, T., Huang, G.: SWAROVsky: optimizing resource loading for mobile web browsing. IEEE Trans. Mob. Comput. **16**(10), 2941–2954 (2017)
12. Ma, Y., Liu, X., Zhang, S., Xiang, R., Liu, Y., Xie, T.: Measurement and analysis of mobile web cache performance. In: Proceedings of the 24th International Conference on World Wide Web, WWW 2015, pp. 691–701. ACM Press, New York (2015)
13. Netravali, R., Goyal, A., Mickens, J., Balakrishnan, H.: Polaris: faster page loads using fine-grained dependency tracking. In: Proceeding NSDI 2016 Proceedings of the 13th USENIX Conference on Networked Systems Design and Implementation, pp. 123–136. USENIX Association (2016)
14. Netravali, R., et al.: Mahimahi: accurate record-and-replay for HTTP. In: Proceedings of the 2015 USENIX Annual Technical Conference (USENIC ATC 2015), pp. 417–429 (2015)

15. Ruamviboonsuk, V., Netravali, R., Uluyol, M., Madhyastha, H.V.: Vroom: accelerating the mobile web with server-aided dependency resolution. In: Proceedings of the Conference of the ACM Special Interest Group on Data Communication, SIGCOMM 2017, pp. 390–403. ACM Press, New York (2017)
16. Varvello, M., Blackburn, J., Naylor, D., Papagiannaki, K.: EYEORG: a platform for crowdsourcing web quality of experience measurements. In: Proceedings of the 12th International on Conference on emerging Networking EXperiments and Technologies, CoNEXT 2016, pp. 399–412. ACM Press, New York (2016)
17. Vesuna, J., Scott, C., Buettner, M., Shenker, S., Berkeley, U.C.: Caching doesn't improve mobile web performance (Much). In: USENIX ATC 2016 Proceedings of the 2016 USENIX Conference on USENIX Annual Technical Conference, pp. 159–165 (2016)
18. Vrountas, T.: How Slow Mobile Page Speeds Are Ruining Your Conversion Rates (2018). https://instapage.com/blog/optimizing-mobile-page-speed
19. Wang, X.S., Krishnamurthy, A., Wetherall, D.: Speeding up web page loads with Shandian. In: Proceedings of the 13th USENIX Conference on Networked Systems Design and Implementation, p. 15. USENIX Association (2016)
20. Wang, Z., Lin, F.X., Zhong, L., Chishtie, M.: Why are web browsers slow on smartphones? In: Proceedings of the 12th Workshop on Mobile Computing Systems and Applications, HotMobile 2011, p. 91. ACM Press, New York (2011)
21. Wang, Z., Lin, F.X., Zhong, L., Chishtie, M.: How far can client-only solutions go for mobile browser speed? In: Proceedings of the 21st International Conference on World Wide Web, WWW 2012, p. 31. ACM Press, New York (2012)
22. Zhu, Y., Reddi, V.J.: WebCore: architectural support for mobile Web browsing. In: 2014 ACM/IEEE 41st International Symposium on Computer Architecture (ISCA), vol. 10, no. 4, pp. 541–552, October 2014

An Analysis of Throughput and Latency Behaviours Under Microservice Decomposition

Malith Jayasinghe[✉], Jayathma Chathurangani, Gayal Kuruppu,
Pasindu Tennage, and Srinath Perera

WSO2, Colombo, Sri Lanka
{malithj,jayathma,gayal,pasindu,srinath}@wso2.com

Abstract. Microservice architecture is a widely used architectural style which allows you to design your application using a set of loosely coupled services which can be developed, deployed, and scaled independently. The service decomposition is the act of decomposing (breaking) a coarse-grained service into a set of fine-grained services that collectively perform the functionality of the original service. The service decomposition introduces additional overhead due to inter-service communication of services which impacts the performance. In this paper, we study the effect of service decomposition on the throughput and average latency. We perform an extensive performance analysis using a set of standard microservice benchmarks with different workload characteristics. Our results indicate that when we decompose a service into a set of micro-services the performance of the new application can improve or degrade. The factors which impact the performance behaviours are the number of service calls, the service demand, concurrency (i.e. number of concurrent users) and the decomposition strategy. In addition to the experimental performance evaluation, we analyze the performance impact of service decomposition using queueing theoretic models. We compare the analytical results with experimental results and notice that analytical results match well with the experimental results.

Keywords: Service decomposition · Orchestration · Choreography · Throughput · Latency · Closed system

1 Introduction

Micro-service architecture has become a popular architectural style because it allows organizations to develop robust and extensible applications. It separates a complex application into a set of loosely coupled services that communicate with each other using a set of lightweight protocols and these services can be deployed and scaled independently. Microservice applications have the ability to easily adapt to changing user requirements in contrast to monolithic applications.

Service decomposition is the act of decomposing (breaking) a coarse-grained service into a set of fine-grained services that collectively perform the

© Springer Nature Switzerland AG 2020
M. Bielikova et al. (Eds.): ICWE 2020, LNCS 12128, pp. 53–69, 2020.
https://doi.org/10.1007/978-3-030-50578-3_5

functionality of the original service. Service decomposition introduces additional overhead due to inter-service communication of services which impacts the performance. The objective of this paper is to investigate the effect of service decomposition on the performance of microservice applications. Although there is existing work [1,12,13,15–17] which investigates various performance behaviours of microservices, these do not specifically investigate performance behaviours of a microservice under service decomposition. In particular these work do not investigate the effect of the number of services, the number of concurrent users, service demand and the number of network calls on the performance. The main focus of existing work has been to compare the performance of monolithic and microservice applications [16,17], analyzing the tail latency behaviours of microservice applications [13,15], analyzing the performance of microservice applications running on containers [1,12], understanding the performance of microservices on server-less platforms [7] and how to develop the queueing theoretic and simulation models that can estimate the performance of microservice applications [8,14]. In this paper, we perform an extensive performance analysis using a set of standard microservice benchmarks and study the impact of service decomposition on the performance. The main contributions and key findings of this paper are as follows.

- Using 4 standard microservice benchmarks (I/O bound, CPU bound, etc), we investigate the impact of service decomposition on the performance of the services. We decompose each microservice into multiple microservices using two architectural styles (namely the orchestration and choreography) and then we investigate the performance by varying the number of concurrent users. We show that performance depends on a number of factors which include the number of concurrent users, the number of services, the number of I/O calls, and the decomposition method.
- When we decompose microservices we observed degradation in the performance under a lower number of concurrent users. This degradation in the performance (under lower number of concurrent users), however, is not highly significant and it increases (at a very low rate) with the increasing number of services.
- When we decompose microservice benchmarks under higher number of concurrent users the performance can degrade or improve depending on workload characteristics of the individual microservice. If the service is I/O bound then it is very likely to observe a degradation in the performance (as opposed to an improvement). In such cases, the overall throughput depends on the processing rate of the bottleneck service which is typically the one that has the highest number of incoming and out-going I/O calls. On the contrary, if the service is CPU bound then it is likely to observe an improvement in the performance. The main reason is that the additional resources (e.g. cores) available will help to boost the performance.
- We provide a Queueing-theoretic based analytical model which can be used to evaluate the performance in micro-service based architectures and we use this model to compare the experimental and analytical results. The results closely

match for majority of cases. In particular, we use mean value analysis which allows one to model the behaviour of a set of micro-services communicating with others. The mean value analysis (MVA) is a recursive algorithm used to find the expected waiting times, queue lengths in each service and throughput of a closed queueing network.

The rest of this paper is organised as follows. Section 2 presents the methodology we used in this paper. Section 3 presents the evaluation results. Related work is presented in Sect. 4. Section 5 concludes the paper.

2   Methodology

In this section we provide the methodology that we use in this paper to investigate the performance impact of service decomposition.

2.1   Microservice Benchmarks

The performance evaluation we carry out in this paper is based on a set of standard microservice micro-benchmarks. In total there are 4 microservice benchmarks, namely, the simple echo-service [15], the prime-check service[1], the news-portal microservice and news-portal service with cache [9]. The echo microservice represents an I/O bound microservice. It simply echos back the requested which is posted to it [15]. The prime-check is a part of the well-known system-bench benchmark (see footnote 1) which is used to evaluate the performance of CPU bound applications on multi-threaded systems. We implement the prime-check within the microservice and we carry out the analysis using different prime numbers (which represent different levels of CPU utilization). The prime-check microservice checks if a given number is a prime number or not. The higher the value of the prime number the more computationally intensive the service call becomes. We carry out the analysis using 3 levels of processing: CPU level 1 (small prime), CPU level 2 (moderate size prime) and CPU level 3 (large prime). The news-portal microservice is a famous use-case which relates to decomposition of microservices [9] with a database. The news-portal microservice serves users who request three different types of news, namely, the sports, politics and famous news (i.e. celebrity news). This news is stored in a database. We will provide the details of how we decompose each of these microservices sections into multiple microservices in the following sections.

2.2   Decomposition Strategy

This section provides the details on how we decompose the microservices we presented in the previous section. We decompose each microservice into a set of microservices following two main architectural styles, namely the choreography and orchestration.

---

[1] https://github.com/akopytov/sysbench.

1. Choreography: The service choreography can be thought of as a decentralized way to perform service composition in which there is a global perspective of the functionality of individual services and how they communicate with each other. Let us now provide the details of how we decompose the four microservices presented in the previous section (under Choreography)

   (a) Echo-Service: The echo microservice represents the simplest I/O bound service which echoes back the request that is posted to it. The echo microservice does not have any functionality which we can further break down into smaller units. As such when we decompose the echo service we simply forward the messages to the next service. Figure 1 illustrates the architecture when we decompose the service into 3 microservices.

Fig. 1. Decomposition of Echo and Prime Services

   (b) Prime-Service: The flow of messages in this use case is identical to the previous one. However, in this use case, we introduce processing into the service. The objective is to analyse the performance under different levels of processing. As pointed out we implement prime-check (a commonly used CPU benchmark) in the service where the service checks if a given number is a prime or not. Let n be the number which the user wants to perform the prime check. In the single service case, it simply performs the prime check and sends the response back to the client. In the case of two services the first service checks if the given number can be divided by a number in the range 2 to n/2. If yes it sends the response to the user. Otherwise, it sends a message to the second service which checks if the number can be divided by a number in the range n/2+1 to n−1. Once it receives the response it sends the response back to the client. Similarly, in the case of three services, the work is divided among the three services. In our experiments, we use different prime numbers to control the amount of processing.

   (c) News-Portal Service: The flow of the messages in this use case is similar to the previous 2 cases except that each micro-service has a database which contains news data. For the single service case we have all the news data (Famous, Political and Sports) in a single database. Then for the 2 services case, we have Famous and Political news in a single database and the Sports news in the other database. Lastly, we have Famous, Political and Sports news data in three separate databases for the 3 services case. The query we test is "get all types of news". Figure 2 illustrates this use case.

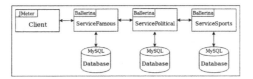

Fig. 2. Decomposition of news-service

(d) News-Portal Service with Cache: This use case is identical to the previous use case except that there is a cache which caches the recently accessed data in the database.

2. Orchestration: In service orchestration, there is a centralized way to perform service composition where there is a composite service (orchestrator) that coordinates the interaction among different services.

(a) Echo-Service: With single microservice, the client sends a message to an orchestrator service which will send a message to the echo-service which echos back the response to the orchestrator. The orchestrator will then send the response back to the client. When there is more than one echo-service the orchestrator sends a message to each echo-service and after receiving the response from each echo-service it sends the message back to the client. Figure 3 illustrates the orchestration with 3 echo services.

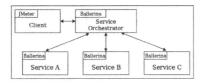

Fig. 3. Decomposition of Echo and Prime Service

(b) Prime-Service: Let n be the number to perform the prime check. In the case of a prime service, the client sends the request to orchestrator which sends a request to the prime-service which performs the prime-check and sends the response back to the orchestrator which sends the response back to the user. When there are 2 prime services the orchestrator receives a request from the client and it first sends a request to the first service which checks if the number can be divided by a number in the range 2 to $n/2$ and sends a response back to the orchestrator. If the number needs further checking it sends a request to the second service which then check if n can be divided by a number in the range $n/2 + 1$ to $n - 1$. Once the orchestrator receives the reply from the second service it sends the response to the client. Similarly, in the case of 3 services, the work is divided among the 3 participating services instead of 2.

(c) News-Service: Similar to the previous use case there is a composite service which sends the requests to a set of microservices. Each microservice fetches the data from its database and sends the reply back to the orchestrator. Once the orchestrator receives responses from all the microservices it sends the consolidated message to the user. Figure 4 illustrates this use case for the case of three microservices (i.e. famous news service, political news services, sports news service)

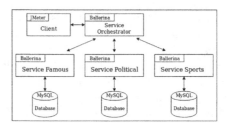

Fig. 4. Decomposition of news-service

(d) News-Portal Service with Cache: This use case is identical to the previous use case except that there is cache in each micro-service which caches the recently accessed data stored in the database.

The performance evaluation we carry out in this paper is a closed-system performance evaluation. Note that in a closed system there is a fixed number of users in the system. The most commonly used term for the number of users is concurrency (or the number of concurrent users). We conduct our performance evaluation under different levels of concurrencies. In total there are 4 microservice benchmarks and two architectural styles. This results in 8 use cases in total. For each of these use cases, we vary the number of microservices from 1 to 3 and perform tests by varying the concurrency.

2.3   Implementation Details

We implemented 8 use cases using Ballerina (Version 0.981.1), a programming language which is designed to network distributed applications. We used HTTP as an application layer protocol for our implementation. The source code for the implementation can be found in[2]. We use JMeter as the load testing client. We carry out our performance tests under different concurrent users (1, 2, 50, 100, 300, 500, 700, 1000) and message sizes (50 bytes, 400 bytes, 1024 bytes). The full set of results can be found in[3]. We run each service on machines with 4 cores and allocate 16 GB (15.5 GB usable) memory. The bandwidth of the network was 1 Gbps.

---

[2] https://github.com/gayalkuruppu/microservices-performance.

[3] https://github.com/gayalkuruppu/microservices-performance/tree/master/Results.

3   Performance Evaluation

3.1   Performance Behaviours for I/O Bound Service

Let us first take a look at the performance behaviour when we decompose an I/O bound service into a set of services. Figure 5 illustrates the performance behaviours for echo service under choreography (refer to Sect. 2.2). We observe the best throughput and the latency with just a single echo-service (compared to 2 and 3 echo services in a chain). Single echo-service performs significantly better compared to 2 and 3 (echo) services (in a chain) under high concurrency levels (note: Fig. 1 shows the architecture with 3 echo services). One may think that we should see an improvement in the performance (when we increase the number of services) because when we increase the number of services we provision more resources (i.e. core, memory, etc) to individual microservices. However, instead of performance improvements, we observe a performance degradation. Let us now explain why we observe this performance degradation. Recall that in this particular use-case each microservice receives the message from the previous microservice and forwards it to the next microservice and once it receives the response, it forwards it to the previous microservice. Since each microservice forwards the message back and forth there is no processing in the service level. However, there is processing associated with performing I/O and this processing becomes significant under high concurrency levels due to the significantly large number of network service calls. When we have one echo service it receives the request from the client and sends the response back to the client. When we have

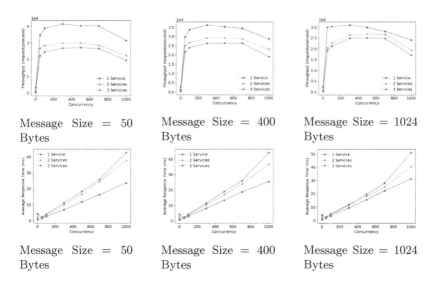

Message Size = 50 Bytes

Message Size = 400 Bytes

Message Size = 1024 Bytes

Message Size = 50 Bytes

Message Size = 400 Bytes

Message Size = 1024 Bytes

Fig. 5. Performance of (I/O bound) echo-service under service decomposition (with Choreography)

two echo services the first service forwards the message to the second service and once it receives the response from the second service it sends the response to the client. In this case, the first service has to perform two times more I/O compared to the single echo service case. Therefore, when we have two services communicating in this manner the first service becomes the bottleneck due to additional processing overhead of having to perform more I/O. This is the reason why we see a significant drop in performance when we increase the number of microservices from one to two. When we increase the number of services from two to three, we also see a degradation in the performance. However, this degradation is not as significant as the degradation we see when we increase the number of services from one to two. When we have three (echo) services the first and second service will need to perform more I/O compared to the last service (refer to Fig. 1). Therefore, the throughput of the use case will depend on the processing rate of the first and second services. In this case, we expect the processing rates of these two services to be similar (since they both do the same amount of I/O) and it to be similar to the processing rate of the first service when we have two services. Hence the throughput of 3 services should converge to the throughput of the two services. However, we do not exactly notice this behaviour rather we see that three services have lower performance compared to two services (under a higher number of concurrent users). We believe this is due to the effect of other factors (such as minor variations in hardware on which we run these tests).

3.2 The Performance Behaviours of Prime-Service with Different Processing Levels (Service Demands)

In the previous section, we discussed the performance behaviours under service decomposition for simple I/O bound service. We noticed that the performance degrades as the number of services increases in particular under high concurrency levels. In this section, we will investigate the performance behaviours under service decomposition for the prime-service with different levels of service demands. The way we control the service demand (i.e. the amount of processing) is by varying the value of the prime number. We carry out our analysis under 3 levels of processing, namely, CPU level 1 (minimal), CPU level 2 (moderate) and CPU level 3 (high). For each of these levels, we investigate the effect of the number of services on the throughput and the latency. Figures 6 and 7 show the performance behaviours under choreography and orchestration respectively. For CPU level 1, we notice similar performance behaviours as simple I/O bound echo service which we investigated in the previous section. This means that for CPU level 1, I/O overhead plays an important role. The service which has the highest number of incoming and out-going service calls becomes the bottleneck (service) and the processing rate of this service will determine the throughput of the application. For example, if we consider orchestration with the prime service under CPU level 1, the orchestrator service is the bottleneck service. As the number of primes-services increases, the number of prime-services the orchestrator has to communicate also increases. For example, when we have a single prime service, the orchestrator service communicates with two entities concurrently (i.e client and prime-service). When we decompose the prime service into two services, orchestrator communicates with 3 entities, namely, the client and the two prime services and so on. The increasing number of I/O calls increases the I/O overhead on the orchestrator. As a result, its processing rate decreases with an increasing number of prime-services. This results in the throughput and latency to degrade. Let us now consider the behaviour when we increase the processing i.e. by increasing the value of the prime number. When we increase the value of the prime number we can see a significant change in the performance behaviours (refer to Figs. 6 and 7). In particular, we notice that decomposing the service into multiple services under CPU level 3 has clear performance benefits. For example, if we consider service orchestration with prime-service when the prime number = 1000003, we notice that we get 2x improvement in the performance with 2 services (compared to single service) while we get 3x the performance with 3 services (compared to the single service). The reason for this behaviour is that the I/O overhead is no longer the main determinant of the performance it is rather the service level processing. For large prime numbers having more services means we have more resources to process the requests and therefore the performance improves with the increasing number of services.

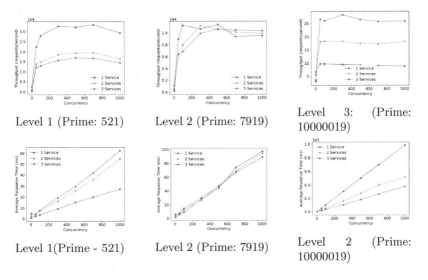

Level 1 (Prime: 521)   Level 2 (Prime: 7919)   Level 3: (Prime: 10000019)

Level 1(Prime - 521)   Level 2 (Prime: 7919)   Level 2 (Prime: 10000019)

Fig. 6. Performance of prime-service under service decomposition (with choreography)

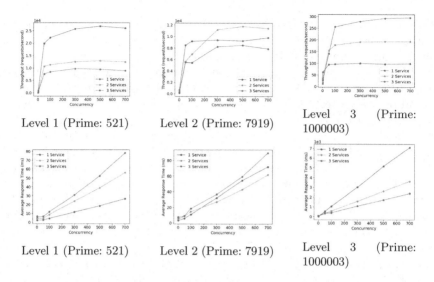

Level 1 (Prime: 521)   Level 2 (Prime: 7919)   Level 3 (Prime: 1000003)

Level 1 (Prime: 521)   Level 2 (Prime: 7919)   Level 3 (Prime: 1000003)

Fig. 7. Performance of Prime-service: decomposition (with orchestration)

3.3 Microservices with DB Back-Ends

Let us now investigate the performance impact of service decomposition for services with database back-ends using the news-portal service. Here, we decompose a news-portal service into multiple services. For more details, refer to Sect. 2. Figure 8 shows the performance behaviours for news-portal service with and without DB cache. Clearly, the use of cache has resulted in an improvement in the performance. We note the news-portal service by itself has the best performance. We see performance degradation when we decompose the service into multiple services. We noticed similar behaviour earlier with the prime-service with CPU level 1 and the simple echo service. In the database use cases there are three reasons why we do not get performance improvements with the increasing number of services (1) DB operations in news portal-service are not computationally heavy (simple select query) and in addition to this the size of the database is relatively small (less than 100 rows of the data in database tables). This means that processing times of the database queries are relatively small (we can expect this behaviour to change for other DB use cases) (2) when we increase the number of services the orchestrator has to do more I/O calls which will result in additional I/O overhead making its processing rate to reduce (we provided the same explanation in the previous sections when we explained the performance degradation we observed in prime service with CPU level 1 and simple echo service) (3) In addition to the I/O overhead the orchestrator has to prepare the consolidated message which it will send to the client. This processing further impacts the processing rate of the orchestrator. We observed similar behaviour for news-portal service under choreography as well.

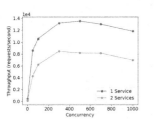

News-portal service

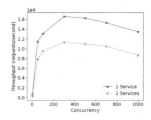

News-portal   service
with cache

Fig. 8. Behaviour of throughput under service Decomposition

Table 1. Variable declaration

M	Multi Programming Level (MPL)
μ_j	Service Rate of the jth Server
λ_j^M	Arrival Rate of the jth Server when the MPL is M
$E[T_j^{(M)}]$	Expected total time at the jth server when the MPL is M
$E[R]$	Expected Response Time
X	Throughput
Δs_i	Processing time overhead for I/O with i number of service calls

3.4 Analytical Performance Evaluation

In the previous sections, we investigated the performance impact of service decomposition using 4 microservices under two architectural styles. In this section, we will develop a qeueing theoretic-based analytical model and study the performance behaviours (throughput and response time. We use mean value analysis (MVA) which is a recursive algorithm to find the expected waiting times, queue lengths of a closed queueing network. MVA is established on arrival theorem which relates to the recursive relationship between a system with the total number of requests N, with the same system with the total number of requests $N-1$. Given the service rates μ_i and probability routines P_{ij}, i.e. the probability of a request travels from service i to j, we can find above expected response time and throughput under a given number of concurrent users. MVA analysis assumes exponentially distributed inter-arrival and exponentially distributed service times (markovian assumptions) which is also an assumption in the previous queueing theoretic-based performance models [2,3,6,10]. For example, Liu [6] uses markovian assumptions when developing performance models for SOA applications. We provide the notation we use in this analysis in Table 1.

$$E[T_j^{(M)}] = \frac{1}{\mu_j} + \frac{p_j \lambda^{(M-1)} E[T_j^{(M-1)}]}{\mu_j} \tag{1}$$

$$\lambda^{(M-1)} = \frac{M-1}{\sum_{i=1}^{k} p_i E[T_i^{(M-1)}]} \tag{2}$$

$$p_j = \frac{\lambda_j^{(M)}}{\sum_{i=1}^{k} \lambda_i^{(M)}} \tag{3}$$

$$\lambda^{(M)} = \sum_{i=1}^{k} \lambda_i^{(M)} \tag{4}$$

$$E[R] = \sum_{i=1}^{k} E[T_j^{(M)}] \tag{5}$$

$$X = \frac{M}{E[R]} \tag{6}$$

The asymptotic bounds for a closed system imply that the throughput of a closed system converges to its busiest server's service rate, which becomes the bottleneck. When we decompose a service into a set of microservices it results in each new service receiving requests and sending requests to other services. This introduces additional overhead on each microservice communicating with one another which impacts the throughput and the latency of microservices. As already pointed out, for those use cases where there is minimal processing in the service level, I/O overhead is the main determinant of the performance of the system. We introduce Δs_i, the service (processing) time overhead due to the ith additional I/O call (note: we will illustrate how we compute this using a concrete example later in this section).

Let us now provide a detailed analysis of one of the main use cases we discussed in the previous section. The analysis for the other use cases can be performed in a similar manner. We now provide the analytical performance evaluations for prime-service under service orchestration (and compare the analytical results with the experimental results).

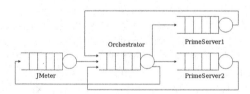

Fig. 9. Queueing model for orchestrator with 2 prime services

Figure 9 illustrates the queueing model for the case of two prime microservices. We can extend this model for the case of n services. We model each microservice as a server that process requests in a First-Come-First-Served (FCFS) manner until completion (note: in the case of database use cases each database server is modelled as a separate server). The processing rates for microservices are obtained by benchmarking each microservice on its own. Note that when using MVA we need to model the workload generator (in our case it is the JMeter). For JMeter, we use a large processing rate because it is capable of generating HTTP workloads at rates of over 50000 requests/second[4].

In order to obtain the throughput vs users and average latency vs users plots, we feed the processing rates of microservices, the routing probabilities and Δs_i. There is no direct way to analytically derive the Δs_i. As such we use experimental results to obtain Δs_i. Computing the Δs_i is rather straightforward from the experimental results. We need to obtain the maximum throughput for the orchestrator service and single service performance when the service is doing an I/O bound task and then decompose the single service into two services and obtain the maximum throughput. When we decompose the prime-service into two services the number of communication links for orchestrator increases by one resulting in a degradation in the maximum throughput. Using the differences in the maximum throughput for single service and two services cases we can compute Δs_1. Similarly, when we decompose the service into three services we can compute Δs_2. In our experiments, we compute Δs_1 (processing overhead on the orchestrator service due to having 2 services compared to a single service) and Δs_2 (processing overhead on the orchestrator service due to having 3 services compared to a single service) as $0.0769\,\mathrm{ms}$ and $0.125\,\mathrm{ms}$ respectively. In the case of CPU bound application in which the orchestrator does not become the bottleneck we still consider the Δs_i to adjust the throughput of the orchestrator service to cater for I/O overhead. However, in such cases the overall impact of Δs_i on the performance is minimal. Figures 10 and Figs. 11 illustrate the analytical and experimental results.

4   Related Work

There is existing work which investigates numerous performance behaviours of the microservice applications. One main category of such performance evalua-tions make efforts to compare the performance of monolithic applications with their microservice counterparts [16,17]. One of the key observations is the poor performance of microservices applications compared to monolithic implemen-tations. Existing work reports different levels of performance degradations in microservices applications compared to monolithics. The reason for such perfor-mance differences is the differences in the use cases and parameter values used in these evaluations. For example, Villamizar et al. [17] claim a 13% degradation in average latency in microservice applications compared to the monolithic using the Web server use case. Rudrabhatla [11] claims that there is a 72% degrada-tion in the throughput microservice applications compared to monolithic using acmeair benchmark[5]. There is existing work which specifically focuses on inves-tigating the tail latency behaviours of microservice applications [13,15]. Tennage et al. [15] in their recent paper extensively investigates the tail latency behaviours

---

[4] https://jmeter.apache.org/.
[5] https://github.com/acmeair/acmeair.

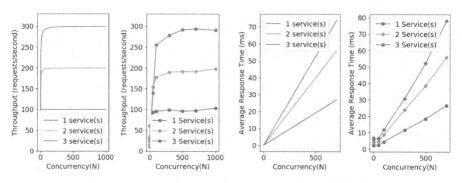

Analytical vs Experimental(CPU level 1)   Analytical vs Experimental(CPU level 1)

Fig. 10. Comparison of analytical and experimental results: CPU level 1

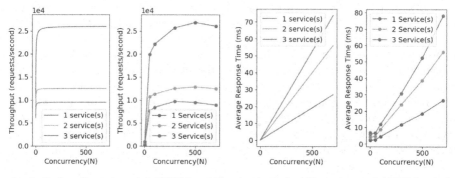

Analytical vs Experimental (CPU level 3)   Analytical vs Experimental (CPU level 3)

Fig. 11. Comparison of analytical and experimental results: CPU level 3

of microservices applications. They point out that the latency distribution of microservice applications have the power-low relationship however, they do not exhibit the heavy-tailed characteristics. They also show that the number of concurrent users and the service demand impact the tail latency behaviours of microservice applications. Sriraman et al. [13] investigate the ways in which the operating system (OS) and network overheads impact the microservice median and tail latency values. One of their main findings is that non-optimal OS scheduler decisions can result in tail latencies in microservice architectures.

Lloyd et al. [7] have done an extensive performance evaluation of the microservices application in server-less platforms. They have identified four main factors which impact the performance of microservices in server-less platforms and they show that performance variations in the microservice application on server-less can be up to 15x. Klock et al. [4] investigate the optimal deployment architectures for microservice-based applications based on a set of different functionalities under a different number of concurrent users. They point out that having multiple functionalities in one microservice is ideal for low concurrency levels and better to disperse the functionalities (features) among multiple services for optimum performance in high concurrency levels.

There are several existing researches [1,12] that investigate the performance characteristics of microservices application in containers Amaral et al. [1] have investigated the performance of microservices deployment on nested and master-slave containers. This study shows that nested-containers do not have an impact on the CPU utilization, however, there are some trade-offs in terms of network performance compared to bare-metal and regular containers. Nane Kratzk [5] investigates the performance impact of microservices running on containers, they show that although containers are stated to be lightweight, they have a significant impact on network performance. This can be in the range of 10% to 20%. Shadija et al. [12] investigate performance impact of running a set of microservices in a single container vs microservices partitioned across separate containers. They have observed a negligible increase in service latency for the multiple container deployment over a single container.

Efforts have been made to use queueing theoretic and simulations based models to estimate the performance of microservices-based applications [8,14]. Gribaudo et al. [8] present a parametric simulation-based method that allows one to model the behaviour of microservice architectures under different workload mixes and design alternatives. Sun et al. [14] present queueing theoretic model that models the relationship between workloads and performance metrics. They, then predict applications' response time by computing the parameters of the performance model using an adaptive fuzzy Kalman filter.

Our contribution in this paper differs from existing work where we specifically focus on investigating the way in which the service decomposition impacts the performance. We perform an extensive performance analysis by decomposing a service with different performance characteristics into a set of microservices. We carry out this analysis by varying the number of microservices, concurrent users and the method of decomposition.

5   Conclusion

In this paper, we extensively investigated the effect of service decomposition on the performance of microservices. For this analysis, we have used 4 standard microservice benchmarks. We showed that when you decompose a microservice the performance can improve or degrade. The factors which impacts the performance are the workload characteristics of the service being decomposed (I/O bound, CPU bound), the number of services, the number of incoming and outgoing service calls in each new service (after decomposing), the number of concurrent users. We extensively analyzed the behaviours by varying these parameters and provided the reasoning for the behaviours we observed.

References

1. Amaral, M., Polo, J., Carrera, D., Mohomed, I., Unuvar, M., Steinder, M.: Performance evaluation of microservices architectures using containers. In: 2015 IEEE 14th International Symposium on Network Computing and Applications, pp. 27–34. IEEE (2015)
2. Bondi, A.: Foundations of Software and System Performance Engineering: Process, Performance Modeling, Requirements, Testing, Scalability, and Practice, August 2014
3. Didona, D., Quaglia, F., Romano, P., Torre, E.: Enhancing performance prediction robustness by combining analytical modeling and machine learning. In: Proceedings of the 6th ACM/SPEC International Conference on Performance Engineering, ICPE 2015, pp. 145–156. ACM, New York (2015). https://doi.org/10.1145/2668930.2688047
4. Klock, S., Van Der Werf, J.M.E., Guelen, J.P., Jansen, S.: Workload-based clustering of coherent feature sets in microservice architectures. In: 2017 IEEE International Conference on Software Architecture (ICSA), pp. 11–20. IEEE (2017)
5. Kratzke, N.: About microservices, containers and their underestimated impact on network performance (2017)
6. Liu, H.H.: Software Performance and Scalability: A Quantitative Approach. Wiley, Hoboken (2009)
7. Lloyd, W., Ramesh, S., Chinthalapati, S., Ly, L., Pallickara, S.: Serverless computing: an investigation of factors influencing microservice performance. In: 2018 IEEE International Conference on Cloud Engineering (IC2E), pp. 159–169, April 2018. https://doi.org/10.1109/IC2E.2018.00039
8. Gribaudo, M., Iacono, M., Manini, D.: Performance evaluation of massively distributed microservices based applications. In: 31st European Conference on Modelling and Simulation, Proceedings of the ECMS, Hungary (2017)
9. Pacheco, V.: Microservice Patterns and Best Practices: Explore Patterns Like CQRS and Event Sourcing to Create Scalable, Maintainable, and Testable Microservices. Packt Publishing (2018). https://books.google.lk/books?id=gfi9tAEACAAJ
10. Romano, P., Leonetti, M.: Poster: selftuning batching in total order broadcast via analytical modelling and reinforcement learning. SIGMETRICS Perform. Eval. Rev. **39**, 77 (2011). https://doi.org/10.1145/2034832.2034861
11. Rudrabhatla, C.K.: Comparison of event choreography and orchestration techniques in microservice architecture. Int. J. Adv. Comput. Sci. Appl. **9**(8), 18–22 (2018)
12. Shadija, D., Rezai, M., Hill, R.: Microservices: granularity vs. performance. In: Companion Proceedings of the10th International Conference on Utility and Cloud Computing, pp. 215–220. ACM (2017)
13. Sriraman, A., Wenisch, T.F.: Micro-suite: a benchmark suite for microservices. In: 2018 IEEE International Symposium on Workload Characterization (IISWC), pp. 1–12, September 2018. https://doi.org/10.1109/IISWC.2018.8573515
14. Sun, Y., Meng, L., Liu, P., Zhang, Y., Chan, H.: Automatic performance simulation for microservice based applications. In: Li, L., Hasegawa, K., Tanaka, S. (eds.) AsiaSim 2018. CCIS, vol. 946, pp. 85–95. Springer, Singapore (2018). https://doi.org/10.1007/978-981-13-2853-4_7

15. Tennage, P., Perera, S., Jayasinghe, M., Jayasena, S.: An analysis of holistic tail latency behaviors of Java microservices. In: 2019 IEEE 21st International Conference on High Performance Computing and Communications, IEEE 17th International Conference on Smart City, IEEE 5th International Conference on Data Science and Systems (HPCC/SmartCity/DSS), pp. 697–705. IEEE (2019)
16. Ueda, T., Nakaike, T., Ohara, M.: Workload characterization for microservices. In: 2016 IEEE International Symposium on Workload Characterization (IISWC), pp. 1–10. IEEE (2016)
17. Villamizar, M., et al.: Evaluating the monolithic and the microservice architecture pattern to deploy web applications in the cloud. In: 2015 10th Computing Colombian Conference (10CCC), pp. 583–590. IEEE (2015)

W-ADE: Timing Performance Benchmarking in Web of Things

Verena Eileen Schlott[1]([⊠]) [iD], Ege Korkan[2][iD], Sebastian Kaebisch[3][iD],
and Sebastian Steinhorst[2][iD]

[1] Ludwig Maximilian University of Munich, Munich, Germany
`verena.schlott@campus.lmu.de`
[2] Technical University of Munich, Munich, Germany
`{ege.korkan,sebastian.steinhorst}@tum.de`
[3] Siemens AG, Munich, Germany
`sebastian.kaebisch@siemens.de`

Abstract. As the number of devices participating in the Internet of Things (IoT) rapidly grows, the challenge of interoperability across IoT platforms becomes more apparent. In order to limit fragmentation of IoT development and improve compatibility, web mechanisms and technologies can be applied, forming the Web of Things (WoT). The World Wide Web Consortium (W3C) supports the standardization of WoT by providing a platform-independent specification called Thing Description (TD). It is a machine-readable document that semantically describes metadata, interactions and interfaces of a device, indicating its functionality. However, it does not provide any information about timing performance, which is crucial for the design of optimal system compositions. In this paper, we present W-ADE, a development environment for WoT and TD that facilitates manual timing measurements and automated timing performance benchmarking of Thing interactions, merely with a TD available. Timing performance is guaranteed systematically, hence allowing optimization during the design phase of Thing mashups. Our evaluation shows that with 99.9% confidence W-ADE can predict average interaction timing performance within a range of ±5%, and is able to provide approximate network-independent static timing performance benchmarks for interaction affordances to 99.93%. To enable the design of heterogeneous IoT applications based upon these timing requirements, a proposal on how to annotate a TD based on the measured performance data is made.

Keywords: Web of Things · Thing Description · Timing performance · Performance benchmarking

1 Introduction

The *Internet of Things* (IoT) is a system of physical devices, such as sensors or actuators, which are able to communicate over various IP-level networking

© Springer Nature Switzerland AG 2020
M. Bielikova et al. (Eds.): ICWE 2020, LNCS 12128, pp. 70–86, 2020.
https://doi.org/10.1007/978-3-030-50578-3_6

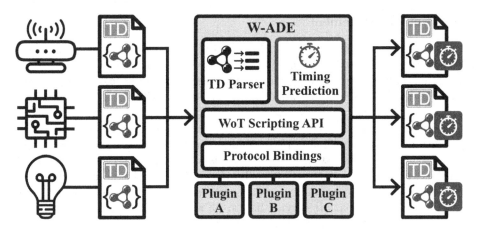

Fig. 1. The Web of Things (WoT) development environment W-ADE is a standalone application based upon the W3C WoT Architecture [6]. Its core includes a WoT runtime, protocol bindings, a Thing Description (TD) parser, and a timing performance benchmarking functionality. It can be extended with further plugins. W-ADE takes a TD as input and is able to return it, annotated with timing performance benchmarks.

interfaces and eventually can be connected to the Internet. These smart things, also referred to as *Things*, enable us to monitor and interact with the physical world in a fine-grained spatial and temporal resolution [1].

However, limitations become visible as soon as multiple Things from diverse vendors are integrated into one system. As universal application protocols and platform-independent standards are missing, companies come up with their own solutions, leading to fragmentation of IoT development. Thus, it requires complex integration work, technical expertise, and it is mostly mandatory to have real devices available to build heterogeneous system compositions [2].

The World Wide Web and its associated technologies are capable of providing solutions for the fragmented progression of IoT and offer the foundation for the next steps beyond basic network connectivity. Hence, web mechanisms are nowadays used to facilitate communication with IoT platforms - independent from their underlying technologies. This approach of integrating real-world devices into the Web is called the *Web of Things* (WoT) [3,4].

The World Wide Web Consortium (W3C) is seeking to standardize this web layer for IoT to enable effortless integration of heterogeneous devices. The core concept in this process is the *Thing Description* (TD) specification [5], further discussed in Sect. 2. A TD is an abstraction of a Thing's capabilities: It semantically describes its metadata, interfaces, and available protocols. It acts as exposed interface, facilitating the communication with the described IoT instance.

1.1 Problem Statement

IoT applications are often composed of not only a single but multiple devices, also referred to as *mashups*. The TD facilitates to design them without having the actual Things or other device documents (e.g. system specification) at disposal. To create reliable TD-based mashups, it is inevitable to have data on timing performance of the included Things. Timing is defined as the sum of the round trip delay time (RTD) plus the required processing time of the client application and Thing. Timing performance can therefore be understood as the required time to interact with a Thing. This is further discussed in Sect. 4. However, TDs currently do not provide such information. To obtain data on timing performance, a time-consuming manual process needs to be accomplished: for each protocol a compatible service has to be started and timing performance has to be measured manually. Although many qualitative and quantitative studies on performance of Things have been conducted, as outlined in Sect. 7, they are rather focusing on protocol or network than general application logic timing performance. Moreover, there is no tool available, which is capable of measuring timing performance, supports diverse IoT protocols (besides common web protocols) and is able to generate timing performance benchmarks at the same time. The question on how timing performance can be measured with only a client-side application available, as it usually is the case when including third party IoT devices, also remains unexplored.

1.2 Contribution

In this paper, we introduce *W-ADE*, the missing foundation block of a development and testing environment for WoT, TDs and mashups, illustrated in Fig. 1. It facilitates the automated generation of timing performance benchmarks as well as annotating a TD with the produced data - with only the associated TD available. In particular, the following contributions are made:

- In Sect. 3, we enable system designers to invoke single interactions of a Thing independent from its protocol, based only on its TD, and allow them to retrieve the associated timing performance.
- In Sects. 4 and 6, we introduce and evaluate a technique to automatically produce static and dynamic timing performance benchmarks for device interactions, giving estimations for worst-, best- and average-case execution with confidence interval limits.
- In Sect. 5, we propose a vocabulary set, aligned with the TD specification, to annotate existing TDs with observed timing performance.

Our approach is then compared to related work in Sect. 7. Finally, conclusions are drawn in Sect. 8.

2   W3C Web of Things

Our concept of providing information on timing performance evolves around the Thing Description standard. TD is one of the building blocks associated with the W3C WoT Architecture [6], which aims to prevent the further fragmentation of IoT development. The main idea is exposing device capabilities as resources in a description-oriented fashion through the WoT interface, that is, network interactions modeled as *Properties*, *Actions*, and *Events* [7]. This information can then be processed and interpreted by a *WoT Consumer*, also referred to as *Consumer*, an entity, for example another device, browser, or web application that is able to understand TDs and interact with Things [6].

Other important building blocks are the *WoT Scripting API* [7] and *WoT Binding Templates* [8]. The Scripting API is the description of a programming interface, representing the WoT Architecture. It allows scripts to discover, operate, and expose Things. The WoT Binding Templates provide guidelines on how to define Protocol Bindings for the description of network-facing interfaces [8].

2.1   Thing Description

In the WoT context, the TD acts as a defined representation of a Thing and can be considered the entry point for communication. As TDs are encoded in JSON-LD [9] format, they are machine-readable as well as human-understandable. The main goal is to preserve and complement existing IoT standards and solutions [6]. Thus, the TD is not a proposition for a new protocol to replace other standards but a way to represent them through syntactic and semantic information [10].

One of the TD's main parts is the interaction model, a formal definition of mapping application intent to concrete protocol operations [6]. A TD interaction can therefore be understood as the description of a specific capability of a Thing, representing the data structure, access protocol and access link [10]. Consequently, a TD instance comprises a list of a Thing's interactions and how to access them. The interaction affordance is based upon the before-mentioned WoT paradigms:

- **Properties**: Exposed values of a Thing that can be *read* (e.g. sensor data), *written* (e.g. to set configuration parameters) or *observed*.
- **Actions**: Invoking them triggers physical, possibly time consuming processes (e.g. moving a robot arm) or functions inside the Thing.
- **Events**: Used for signaling asynchronous notifications that are triggered by events (e.g. a pressed button alert).

An example TD including a Action, Event, and Property is shown in Listing 21.

2.2   Thing Description Based Mashups

As IoT systems usually consist of multiple devices, it is important to shift the focus towards mashups. Mashups in WoT are associated to digital mashups in

Web 2.0. These describe the technology of composing modularized web applications to create entirely new services [11]. Respectively, creating WoT mashups expresses the process of aggregating WoT-enabled Things[1] to form new applications. This is done by chaining together multiple interactions, whereby the TD provides required information. A smart-home mashup could for example compose a light sensor and window shutters that are opened as the sun rises.

2.3   Importance of Timing Performance Benchmarking for Mashups

In order to build reliable physical mashups, a way to analyze, describe, and generate timing performance benchmarks for included Thing interactions has to be found. Knowledge on timing performance is especially important if involved interactions trigger physical processes. As these executions can take a considerable amount of time. Furthermore, when the sum of different interactions influences the total mashup time, it is highly relevant to be able to extract data on their individual timing performance from their description. This becomes even more valuable when a mashup is more complex, due to including many interactions or having dependencies on each other's responses. Timing performance information is also required during the mashup's design phase. As then included Things might not be available and individual interaction request times cannot be measured.

Another example for the importance of the availability of timing performance benchmarks in a TD is, when a client application persistently requests data from a Thing (polling). It could send requests in a shorter time period than the device needs to process. This potentially leads to malfunctions or to a system overload. However, the TD does not yet include any performance related information such as timing behavior, measurement context or precision. As a remedy, this paper introduces a way to integrate timing aspects into TDs.

```
1 {
2      "@context": "https://www.w3.org/2019/wot/td/v1",
3      "title": "Coffee-Machine",
4      "securityDefinitions": { "basic_sc": {"scheme": "basic", "in":"header"},
5      "security": ["basic_sc"],
6      "base": "coaps://coffee-machine.example.com:5683",
7      "properties": {
8          "status" : { "forms": [{"href": "properties/state"}]}
9      },
10     "actions": {
11         "brew" : {"forms": [{"href": "actions/brew"}]}
12     },
13     "events":{
14         "error": {
15             "data": {"type": "string"}, "forms": [{"href": "events/error"}]
16 }    }    }
```

Listing 21. A Thing Description for a smart coffee machine that exposes the machine status, a brewing action and an error event functionality, together with their URIs.

---

[1] A Thing, that is accessible via its TD and can be consumed.

3   W-ADE: API Development Environment for WoT

To solely measure the time it takes to invoke an interaction, several operations need to be performed. Depending on a Thing's implementation and the choice of protocol, a compatible service which can communicate via this protocol eventually needs to be started on the Consumer. Then, the desired endpoint has to be extracted and a request to execute it has to be sent. Subsequently, the time until the response is received has to be manually measured. To obtain representative results, this process would have to be repeated numerous times. Depending on the number of interactions, the level of their diversity and the quantity of services that need to be utilized, this can become a time-consuming and error-prone process. To minimize the susceptibility to errors and overall lighten this series of actions, we developed *W-ADE*: *Web of Things API Development Environment*. It simplifies the TD-based interoperation with devices, can be expanded with required protocols and facilitates timing measurement of Thing executions.

3.1   Application Features and Implementation

W-ADE possesses WoT specific functionalities, typical features needed for API interaction, and the possibility to measure timing. Its core is based upon the W3C Scripting API reference implementation[2], making it compatible with WoT paradigms. It is able to parse and interpret TDs, enables users to edit them and execute chosen interactions in a specific order. W-ADE acts as Consumer to communicate with virtual or physical entities over various protocols[3]. As it supports diverse protocols existing in IoT ecosystems and web browsers are usually restricted, it is realized as a standalone Electron[4] application[5].

Since a TD is the interface for interactions and accessing API endpoints is a main use-case, functionalities, such as sending requests with optional input values and displaying responses, are implemented. Another substantial feature is entering, storing, and applying required security credentials. Beyond that, W-ADE measures the overall time it takes to send a request, process it on the target application, and finally receive a response. Utilizing the Node.js feature `process.hrtime()`, high-resolution real time measurements in nanoseconds are available. This and the size of the sent or received data, is then displayed. Further, W-ADE's architecture facilitates custom plugins, allowing it to be easily extended by numerous already existing WoT implementations. An overview of its system architecture is presented in Fig. 1.

---

[2] Node-wot (https://github.com/eclipse/thingweb.node-wot) is based upon the JavaScript runtime Node.js (www.nodejs.org/).

[3] Embedded Binding Templates [8] enable the incorporation of further protocols including custom ones and thus, facilitate interoperability for diverse vendors.

[4] A JavaScript based framework, which allows to build cross platform applications.

[5] W-ADE is available here: https://github.com/tum-esi/wade.

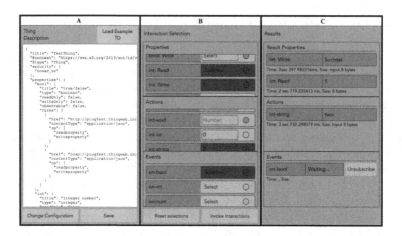

Fig. 2. W-ADE's GUI. Thing Descriptions can be uploaded and edited in the Editor (A). Interactions are parsed and visualized in (B), where input values can be entered and interactions can be selected. Results, including measured communication time and payload size of input or output are displayed in (C).

3.2 Workflow

To retrieve timing performance data of a Thing in W-ADE, first a TD has to be inserted: it can be pasted, uploaded, or fetched via a URI. This TD is then parsed and all available Properties, Actions, and Events with according input fields/ drop-downs are generated. Interactions can then be selected and invoked. If applicable, security credentials, e.g. user-password combinations or broker data, can be stored beforehand. Then, a request to the associated endpoint will be sent. Simultaneously, the internal measurement is started and stopped as soon as W-ADE receives the Thing's response. The elapsed time in milliseconds and if available, the size of the received data in bytes will be shown. The according user interface is illustrated in Fig. 2.

W-ADE provides the framework for timing performance testing, eases the work with TDs and due to its plugin architecture, is able to improve tooling around the WoT ecosystem. Nonetheless, to give reliable and reusable assertions on timing performance we introduce a more elaborate timing analysis technique for timing performance benchmarking in Sect. 4.

4   Automated Timing Performance Benchmarking

W-ADE aims to facilitate the automated generation of timing performance benchmarks of a Thing with merely its TD available; Premised that the specific device is WoT-enabled and consumable. We define the scope of timing performance in Sect. 4.1, elaborate our benchmarking technique in Sect. 4.2 and present its implementation in Sect. 4.3.

4.1   Timing Performance Possibilities in W-ADE

The time it takes to communicate with a Thing is dependent on factors like connection throughput, available bandwidth, network workload, loss rate, software characteristics, hardware architecture, latency of outgoing packets, packet size or used communication protocols [12,13]. To measure timing performance, common approaches are measuring the latency of outgoing packets or the throughput rate, while tweaking network conditions, manipulating bandwidth, or switching protocols [3,12,14]. In test scenarios, it is feasible to vary system configurations and retrieve data on the network environment or target devices. However, in real-world scenarios, mashup designers do not necessarily have access to manipulate devices or the opportunity to analyze internal application processes. Things could be connected via gateways and data on network conditions might be missing. As our objective is the facilitation of automated timing performance benchmarking on any capable machine, in any network environment, without knowledge about the target application, and while using any IoT-protocol, network-, protocol- and machine influences are not considered individually.

For this reason, W-ADE's timing performance technique is based on measurements of the overall round trip delay time (RTD), including the required processing time of the Consumer. The RTD is the sum of latency in each direction including the Thing's processing time. Latency indicates the total delay between endpoints [13]. In our case this relates to the total time elapsed, from the moment the data is sent until the response is received, expressed by Eq. 1.

$$T_{\text{dynamic}}(x) = T_{\text{consumer}}(x) + T_{\text{transfer}}(x) + T_{\text{process}}(x) \qquad (1)$$

- **T_{dynamic}**: Total *dynamic* time needed for transferring a message from the Consumer to a Thing and receiving a response for an interaction x.
- **T_{consumer}**: Consumer-side (in our case W-ADE's) processing time.
- **T_{transfer}**: Time needed for sending/ receiving messages over the network.
- **T_{process}**: Internal process time of a target Thing. It depends on the path of the internal execution and the time spent in the instructions on this path on this particular hardware [15]. Also covers physical interaction times.

Although the influences of $T_{consumer}$ and $T_{transfer}$ cannot be isolated reliably, it is possible under certain conditions to extract the static timing performance of an Action (a time-consuming physicial or virtual internal process). The IoT device must offer a Property-read as well as an Action interaction; Interactions must be implemented synchronously (not asynchronously or queued: responses are only send after a physical or internal process is finished)[6]; The application logic is comparable for all existing interactions; The time for reading a Property value is negligible (e.g. due to retrieving from memory); T_{dynamic} of the Action is bigger than T_{dynamic} of the Property-read. With these fullfilled prerequisities, we make the following assumption:

---

[6] It is assumed that interactions of a WoT-enabled Thing are mostly implemented to be synchronous, as conveyed in the WoT TD implementation report (https://w3c. github.io/wot-thing-description/testing/report.html). In future versions of the TD, information on interaction-implementation will be included.

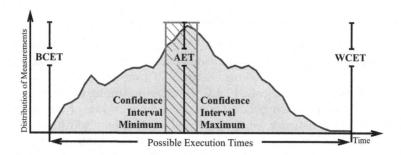

Fig. 3. Basic concept of our timing benchmarking technique. The curve depicts sample values of interaction timing performance. Its minimum indicates the estimated best-case execution time, its maximum the estimated worst-case execution time. The middle line represents the Average Execution Time, surrounded by its confidence interval.

$$T_{\text{static}}(x) = T_{\text{dynamic}}(x) - T_{\text{dynamic}}(y) \qquad (2)$$

$T_{\text{static}}(x)$ is the estimated *static* time of an Action x that does not change with network or client alternations. $T_{\text{dynamic}}(x)$ defines the *dynamic* time of the invoked Action x, $T_{\text{dynamic}}(y)$ the same for a Property-read y.

4.2 Benchmarking Technique

To provide meaningful timing performance benchmarks, timing constraints on measurements and reliable average timing values need to be determined. For this purpose, bounds on execution times have to be identified. This can be achieved by executing an interaction for several repetitions or a specific amount of time, while simultaneously measuring the elapsed time. Results are combined to estimate execution time bounds. These are specified by deriving the overall maximum and minimum observed execution time. This is commonly called worst-case execution time (WCET) and best-case execution time (BCET) [15]. Generally, the BCET is overestimated and the WCET underestimated, as the actual values are almost impossible to derive. Since we cannot guarantee that Things can be analyzed, they are treated as *black-box* components and estimated WCETs are utilized. Moreover, the average execution time (AET) for all measurements is computed (Fig. 3).

In order to offer reliable benchmarks, we use confidence intervals (CI)[7] to propose a range of plausible values for the AET. The CI is calculated as seen in Eq. 3, where $\bar{x}$ is the sample mean, σ the standard deviation, n the sample size and z^* represents the appropriate z^*-value from the standard normal distribution of the chosen Confidence Level (CL). The CL indicates the probability that the unknown parameter lies in the stated interval.

$$\bar{x} \pm z^* \frac{\sigma}{\sqrt{n}} \qquad (3)$$

---

[7] A CI, in statistics, refers to the probability that an unknown value will fall between a specific range of values, calculated from observed data [16].

To compute *static* timing, measurements of both a Property and Action are required. The *static* AET is computed from the difference of the *dynamic* AET values of the included Action and Property measurements (see Eq. 2). Its CI is calculated with Eq. 4: Elements have the same meaning as in Eq. 3, whereby subscript *a* represents Action and subscript *p* Property values.

$$\bar{x}_a - \bar{x}_p \pm z^* \sqrt{\frac{\sigma_a^2}{n_a} + \frac{\sigma_p^2}{n_p}} \tag{4}$$

Certain factors influence execution times and need to be considered when timing performance is measured and interpreted. One factor is the context dependence of execution times [15]. The execution time of individual instructions may vary by several orders of magnitude depending on the state of the processor. Thus, an execution time B can heavily depend on the state produced by execution A, e.g. for initial connection establishment, regarding memory or caching [15]. A task can also show variations depending on the payload or divergent environment behavior. To minimize this impact, the option of using measurements after a certain time has passed and an indefinite amount of interactions have been executed, is available and measurements can be repeated multiple times to reduce context errors. To remove the impact of initial connection establishment, the first measured values are removed. Further, timing anomalies, counter-intuitive influences on the local execution time of one instruction on the global execution time of the entire task [15], need to be considered and optionally be removed. We use the common approach of detecting outliers with the help of the interquartile range (IQR) that represents the width of the box in the box-and-whisker plot [17] and indicates how spread out middle values are, shown in Eq. 5.

$$IQR = Q_3 - Q_1 \tag{5}$$

$$min = Q_1 - 1.5 \times IQR \quad \text{and} \quad max = Q_3 + 1.5 \times IQR \tag{6}$$

The IQR is the difference of the third (Q_3) and the first quartile (Q_1). A Quartile divides the number of data points into four equal parts, or quarters. Q_1 marks where 25%, Q_3 where 75% of the data is below. Equation 6 defines how the minimum and maximum threshold can be computed to identify outliers. Outliers are defined as values that are more than one and a half times the length of the middle-value box, away. Identified outliers can then be removed.

4.3   Implementation

To put this technique into practice, a timing performance feature is implemented in W-ADE. Users need to select interactions, enter required inputs, and choose performance analysis settings, including the type of measurement - either *Iteration* or *Duration* - with the desired amount. Iteration indicates that measurements are executed a certain number of times, whereas Duration executes them for the entered time-period. Then, a delay before the beginning of overall measurements or before the beginning of each execution can be scheduled. To finally start the execution and computation process, the desired CL to calculate the

AET's CI has to be entered. Selectable options are 80%, 85%, 90%, 95%, 99%, 99.5% and 99.9%. To take into account potential environmental impacts, results are subdivided into *Possible* and *Realistic*. They respectively contain computed WCET, BCET, AET, CI limits for the AET, and the first measurement value. *Possible* results are computed considering all measurements except the first measured, whereas for *Realistic* results neither the first measured, nor detected outliers are included. Additionally, settings, general information, and all measured values in chronological order are displayed. To compute *static* timing, one Property, one Action, and the option `static timing` must be selected. As WCET and BCET are not applicable, they are not present in *static* results.

5   Timing Performance Annotation

To be able to apply timing performance benchmarks, results needs to be integrated into the TD, in reference to the appropriate interaction. For this purpose, we propose a vocabulary set, referred to as *InteractionTiming*, that describes timing performance benchmarks. It is compatible with present TD vocabularies, as it is based upon similar semantics and principles. Existing TD vocabularies are independent and extensible. They each define a collection of terms that can be interpreted as objects denoting Things and their Interaction Affordances [5].

As not all collected performance data discussed in Sect. 4 is significant for describing timing performance, only specific elements are included in our vocabulary. Figure 4 gives an overview of the main *InteractionTiming* vocabulary terms. The proposed term names are only suggestions and can be easily adjusted if they conflict with other TD terms. `staticTiming` characterizes *static* timing measurements and is added to the TD on the same level as `forms`. Other measurements are respectively summarized in `dynamicTiming` and are added to the particular `forms` element of the interaction. By default, both of them include `measurementContext` information, `confidence` data, and results categorized in `possible` and `realistic`. As `measurementContext` implies only contextual data, it is linked to by a JSON Pointer [18] and can be stored in another document. This default term set was elaborated with the aim of providing most information without including the entire set of results. An example of an annotated TD comprising *dynamic* and *static* performance data is depicted in Listing 51. For the sake of readability, only *Possible* measurement data is added and confidence information of the *dynamic* annotation is absent. We provide a complete annotated TD[8] externally[9]. As a TD can be presented as a JSON-LD file, its specification [5] also provides a JSON Schema [19] to syntactically validate TDs. To extend this Schema, we created an *InteractionTiming* JSON Schema, including detailed descriptions[10] and a TD JSON Schema extended with it[11].

---

[8] Available at www.ei.tum.de/fileadmin/tueifei/esi/WADE-files/td_annotated.json.

[9] The distribution of annotated TDs is not determined in this paper, since not even the W3C WoT working group has fully explored TD distribution possibilities so far.

[10] www.ei.tum.de/fileadmin/tueifei/esi/WADE-files/Interaction_Timing_schema.json.

[11] www.ei.tum.de/fileadmin/tueifei/esi/WADE-files/TD_Interaction_Timing_schema. json.

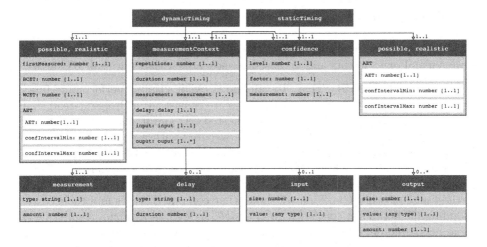

Fig. 4. Our proposed *InteractionTiming* vocabulary with term keys and values, including child elements and their data types. It is intended for annotating a Thing Description, in order to characterize timing performance of its associated Thing.

An annotated TD can be generated in W-ADE after results are computed. If desired, annotations can be further revised in the TD editor, before saving. An enhanced TD can be interpreted by a human and an automated system. It offers detailed semantics for describing how a Thing behaves regarding timing.

```
1  "brew": {
2    "staticTiming": {
3      "possible": {
4        "AET": {
5          "AET": 40078.83,
6          "confIntervalMin": 40072.32, "confIntervalMax": 40085.35
7    } } },
8    "forms": [{
9        "href": "actions/brew",
10       "dynamicTiming": {
11         "measurementContext": "#/measurementContext/
                   dynamicTimingContext_action/brew",
12         "possible": {
13           "firstMeasured": 40221.06,
14           "BCET": 40118.66, "WCET": 40962.02,
15           "AET": {
16             "AET": 40238.33,
17             "confIntervalMin": 40185.93, "confIntervalMax": 40290.74
18       } },
19         "confidence": {
20           "level": 99.9, "factor": 3.291, "numMeasurements": 100
21} } } ] }
```

Listing 51. A snippet of an annotated Thing Description, including *dynamic* and *static* timing data for the Action **brew**. *Dynamic* annotations are added to the particular **form** element, whereby *static* annotations are located on the same level as **forms**.

6   Evaluation

To prove the correctness and validate the quality of our technique, we conducted three virtual experiments and one use-case scenario with a physical IoT device.

Experiment 1, Validity Test: To validate W-ADE's timing performance functionality and to show that processed results are consistent, a Property-read that returns a 14 byte string of an externally hosted TD and its simulated Things[12] was selected. Then, a HTTP-request was executed with a chosen CL of 99.9% for 1000 iterations, 10 times. Different network conditions applied for the Consumer and simulated Thing. We then examined how results differed, to what percentage the CI fluctuates around the AET and verified whether AETs are in the range of other CIs. Figure 7 shows that computed AETs and their corresponding CI limits are consistent for *Possible*, as well as *Realistic* results. Only some negligible deviation, with a max. range of 10 ms in *Possible* and 4 ms in *Realistic* average AET values, were observed. Moreover, CI limits always lied within a range of ±5% of AETs and AETs values lied in their associated CI, including all other measured CIs (Fig. 5).

Experiment 2, Sanity Check: To evaluate W-ADE's credibility, we matched our measurements with measurements of an ADE[13] called *Postman*[14]. It acted as a control entity. In comparison to W-ADE, Postman is not able to parse or understand TDs. It can only communicate over HTTP and lacks functionalities to interpret and produce timing performance benchmarks. Using the same test Thing from Exp. 1, we executed an HTTP Property-write request with a 12 byte string-input, no output, and a CL of 99.9% for 1000 times, repeating it 10 times with W-ADE and Postman. To make result sets comparable, we applied W-ADE's technique onto Postman's results to processed the WCET, BCET, and AET with its CI. We used W-ADE's *Possible* results, as outliers were not removed from Postman, and rounded them to integers.

Results, presented in Fig. 6, show that Postman's and W-ADE's results are proportional to each other and consistent within. WADE's AET values showed a max. deviation of 5, 98% (min. 221 ms, max. 235 ms). Postman's values showed a similar max. deviation of 6, 42% (min. 103 ms, max. 109 ms). W-ADE added an average overhead (see $T_{client}(x)$ in Eq. 1) of about 121 ms and 111, 01% in comparison to Postman. This is expected, as Postman's default behavior keeps socket connections open[15]. W-ADE closes them after each request as keep-alive connections are only usable for polling, which should rather be implemented as event properties. This is the anticipated way of writing a Consumer application.

---

[12] This TD is provided by the W3C WoT working group for testing purposes.

[13] ADE stands for <u>A</u>PI <u>D</u>evelopment <u>E</u>nvironment and describes software that focuses on designing, building, and testing APIs.

[14] Postman (www.getpostman.com/) version v7.16.1. was utilized.

[15] This behavior cannot be changed in the current version of Postman.

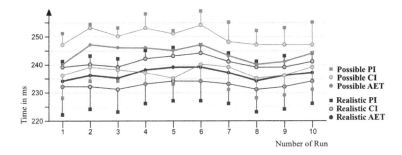

Fig. 5. W-ADE's measured, rounded *Realistic* (blue) and *Possible* (orange) average execution times (AET). Confidence intervals (CI) always lied within a 5% range (PI) around the average values. AETs always lied in their own and all other CIs. (Color figure online)

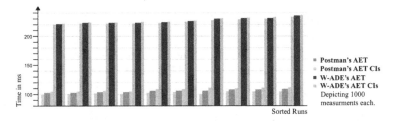

Fig. 6. Measured average execution times of W-ADE (blue) are compared to Postman's (yellow). Bars denote the average values for 1000 measurements each. Enclosing thinner bars respectively indicate confidence interval limits. Both systems produced consistent values, whereas W-ADE's expected overhead to Postman was also consistent. (Color figure online)

Experiment 3, Static Timing: To confirm the validity of our *static* timing approach, introduced in Sect. 4.1, we created a script that simulates a Thing, providing a Property-read that returns a 14 byte string and an Action, that returns the same variable after a predetermined delay of 1000 ms, simulating a physical process of a device. It was then exposed on the same machine running W-ADE, communicating over the same local network. 100 Action and Property HTTP requests were sent to the before-mentioned interaction with a chosen CL of 99,9% and measured with W-ADE, 10 times each. Due to network anomalies and other outliers adding a noticeable effect to timing, we used rounded *Realistic* values for our evaluation. As shown in Fig. 7, the computed average *static* AET of 999,30 ms matched the artificial delay of 1000 ms to 99,93%, whereby *Realistic* AET measurements resulted either 999 ms or 1000 ms. The min. lower limit of the CI was 998 ms and the max. 1001 ms. Giving a −0,2%/+0,1% range around the actual delay. This confirms that that computed results are able to anticipate actual interaction timing performance.

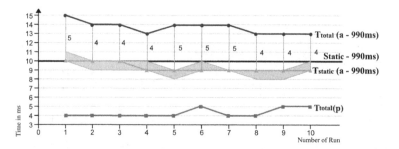

Fig. 7. Computed *static* timing performance of an Action. The upper curve indicates *dynamic* measurements (see Eq. 1) of Action a, the lower measurements of a Property p. The middle line shows the *static* timing with its confidence interval. For the sake of comprehension **990 ms are subtracted from both Action values.**

Use-Case with a Physical Device: To demonstrate the practicability of timing performance generation with a real Thing, we conducted *static* measurements analog to Exp. 3. Included components were W-ADE as client and a WoT-enabled[16] Pan-Tilt HAT module[17] (PTH) attached to a Raspberry Pi[18] (RP), both connected to the same network. The evaluated Action `scan` moves the robot arm from the outer-left to the outer-right position and the used Property `panPosition` returns the position of the pan module. Both HTTP interactions were executed 10 times with 1000 iterations each and a 99,9% CL, before the *static* timing of `scan` was calculated. Analog to Exp. 3, the evaluation was based on *Realistic* results. An average *static* AET of 40055 ms with a CI of 40053 ms - 40057 ms was measured for `scan`. Whereby the average *dynamic* AET of all measured Actions was 40063 ms, with a CI of 40049 ms - 40077 ms. Property measurements revealed an average AET of 8 ms and CI limits of 7,6 ms - 8,8 ms.

This proves that W-ADE enables the conduction of *static* timing performance on an actual physical IoT device. To once again validate that the *static* AET matches the actual time of a `scan` movement, manual, possibly error-sensitive chronometer based measurements, would be necessary.

7   Related Work

Numerous approaches on how the Web of Things can look, have been introduced to the world of IoT [20–22]. As the TD standard and associated WoT approaches not only present a well conceived concept, but also actively offer solutions to counteract the fragmentation of IoT, this work is based upon them. Many W3C WoT tools and services have already been contributed, nevertheless, there is little scientific work on them available. This might be due to the TD standard

---

[16] A WoT-enabled Pan-Tilt HAT: www.wotify.org/library/Pan-Tilt%20HAT/general.
[17] A set of horizontal and vertical motion servos, that can be moved individually.
[18] A small single-board computer, here a model **3B+** running **Raspbian 2019-09-26**.

being rather new and hardly distributed. Therefore, no service or approach to enhance a TD with timing information has been released.

While performance evaluation in IoT is the topic of many studies, they often focus on comparison of diverse protocol performance under specific circumstances, whereby the experiment environment is mostly controlled [3,14,23]. Other studies target network-performance regarding an IoT device [22,24], the general performance spectrum, or stress testing of Things [12]. In general, studies in the field of IoT performance do not deal with *dynamic* or *static* timing performance of Things and do not offer solutions on how to generate comparable benchmarks for this purpose. Choosing the best fitting communication protocol and determining network performance makes sense when setting up IoT platforms, but not when third-party Things need to be integrated into mashups or their general timing performance needs to be benchmarked. In contrary to existing studies, our proposed technique enables developers to actively use timing performance data for the design of real-world IoT systems and use cases.

8 Conclusion

Motivated by the problem of missing opportunities to easily measure and compare timing performance of IoT devices based on their TD, we introduced a technique which facilitates timing performance benchmarking, while considering environmental influences. Thereupon, we developed W-ADE, an API development environment and platform for the WoT ecosystem that implements our technique and additionally enables manual timing measurement of device interactions. To validate and demonstrate the applicability in practice, we tested our technique with a physical IoT device and conducted virtual simulations. We proved that W-ADE reliably predicts *static* timing performance of interactions and offers accurate timing performance benchmarks. Combined with our proposed *InteractionTiming* vocabulary to annotate TDs, mashup designers are now able to estimate and compare interaction timing performance; thus, optimize system compositions during design time.

References

1. Guinard, D., Trifa, V.: Building the Web of Things: With Examples in Node.js and Raspberry Pi. Manning Publications Co., Shelter Island (2016)
2. Guinard, D., Trifa, V., Pham, T., Liechti, O.: Towards physical mashups in the web of things. In: Proceedings of INSS, vol. 9, pp. 17–19 (2009)
3. Babovic, Z.B., Protic, J., Milutinovic, V.: Web performance evaluation for internet of things applications. IEEE Access **4**, 6974–6992 (2016)
4. Guinard, D., Trifa, V.: Towards the web of things: web mashups for embedded devices. In: Workshop on Mashups, Enterprise Mashups and Lightweight Composition on the Web (MEM 2009), Proceedings of WWW, vol. 15 (2009)
5. Kamiya, T., Käbisch, S., Kovatsch, M., McCool, M., Charpenay, V.: WoT thing description. Technical report, W3C (2019). www.w3.org/TR/2019/CR-wot-thing-description-20191106/

6. Matsukura, R., Lagally, M., Kovatsch, M., Toumura, K., Kawaguchi, T.: WoT architecture. Technical report, W3C (2019). www.w3.org/TR/2019/CR-wot-archit ecture-20191106/

7. Peintner, D., Nimura, K., Kis, Z., Hund, J., Nimura, K.: WoT scripting API. Technical report, W3C (2019). www.w3.org/TR/2019/WD-wot-scripting-api-20191028/

8. Koster, M.: WoT protocol binding templates. Technical report, W3C (2018). www.w3.org/TR/2018/NOTE-wot-binding-templates-20180405/

9. Champin, P., Kellogg, G., Longley, D.: JSON-LD 1.1. Technical report, W3C (2019). https://www.w3.org/TR/2019/CR-json-ld11-20191212/

10. Korkan, E., Kaebisch, S., Kovatsch, M., Steinhorst, S.: Safe interoperability for web of things devices and systems. In: Kazmierski, T.J., Steinhorst, S., Große, D. (eds.) Languages, Design Methods, and Tools for Electronic System Design. LNEE, vol. 611, pp. 47–69. Springer, Cham (2020). https://doi.org/10.1007/978-3-030-31585-6_3

11. Liu, X., Hui, Y., Sun, W., Liang, H.: Towards service composition based on mashup. In: 2007 IEEE Congress on Services, pp. 332–339. IEEE (2007)

12. Esquiagola, J., de Paula Costa, L.C., Calcina, P., Fedrecheski, G., Zuffo, M.: Performance testing of an internet of things platform. In: IoTBDS, pp. 309–314 (2017)

13. Huston, G.: Measuring IP network performance. Internet Protocol J. **6**(1), 2–19 (2003)

14. Chen, Y., Kunz, T.: Performance evaluation of IoT protocols under a constrained wireless access network. In: 2016 International Conference on Selected Topics in MoWNeT, pp. 1–7. IEEE (2016)

15. Wilhelm, R., et al.: The worst-case execution time problem – overview of methods and survey of tools. ACM Trans. Embed. Comput. Syst. (TECS) **7**(3), 36 (2008)

16. Neyman, J.: X—outline of a theory of statistical estimation based on the classical theory of probability. Philos. Trans. R. Soc. Lond. Ser. A Math. Phys. Sci. **236**(767), 333–380 (1937)

17. Tukey, J.W.: Exploratory Data Analysis, vol. 2. Reading, Massachusetts (1977)

18. Bryan, P., Zyp, K., Nottingham, M.: JavaScript Object Notation (JSON) Pointer. RFC 6901 (Proposed Standard) (2013)

19. Wright, A., Andrews, H., Luff, G.: JSON Schema Validation: A Vocabulary for Structural Validation of JSON. IETF Standard (2016)

20. Guinard, D., Trifa, V., Mattern, F., Wilde, E.: From the internet of things to the web of things: resource-oriented architecture and best practices. In: Uckelmann, D., Harrison, M., Michahelles, F. (eds.) Architecting the Internet of Things, pp. 97–129. Springer, Heidelberg (2011). https://doi.org/10.1007/978-3-642-19157-2_5

21. Käfer, T., Richard Bader, S., Heling, L., Manke, R., Harth, A.: Exposing internet of things devices via REST and linked data interfaces. In: Proceedings of the 2nd Workshop Semantic Web Technology Internet Things, pp. 1–14 (2017)

22. Duquennoy, S., Grimaud, G., Vandewalle, J.: The web of things: interconnecting devices with high usability and performance. In: 2009 International Conference on Embedded Software and Systems, pp. 323–330. IEEE (2009)

23. Yokotani, T., Sasaki, Y.: Comparison with HTTP and MQTT on required network resources for IoT. In: 2016 International Conference on Control, Electronics, Renewable Energy and Communications (ICCEREC), pp. 1–6. IEEE (2016)

24. Morabito, R., Farris, I., Iera, A., Taleb, T.: Evaluating performance of containerized IoT services for clustered devices at the network edge. IEEE Internet Things J. **4**(4), 1019–1030 (2017)

Comparing a Polling and Push-Based Approach for Live Open Data Interfaces

Brecht Van de Vyvere$^{(\boxtimes)}$ (iD), Pieter Colpaert$^{(\boxtimes)}$ (iD), and Ruben Verborgh$^{(\boxtimes)}$ (iD)

IDLab, Department of Electronics and Information Systems, Ghent University – imec,
Gent, Belgium
{brecht.vandevyvere,pieter.colpaert,ruben.verborgh}@ugent.be

Abstract. There are two mechanisms for publishing live changing resources on the Web: a client can pull the latest state of a resource or the server pushes updates to the client. In the state of the art, it is clear that pushing delivers a lower latency compared to pulling, however, this has not been tested for an Open Data usage scenario where 15 k clients are not an exception. Also, there are no general guidelines when to use a polling or push-based approach for publishing live changing resources on the Web. We performed (i) a field report of live Open datasets on the European and U.S. Open Data portal and (ii) a benchmark between HTTP polling and Server-Sent Events (SSE) under a load of 25 k clients. In this article, we compare the scalability and latency of updates on the client between polling and pushing. For the scenario where users want to receive an update as fast as possible, we found that SSE excels above polling in three aspects: lower CPU usage on the server, lower latency on the client and more than double the number of clients that can be served. However, considering that users can perceive a certain maximum latency on the client (MAL) of an update acceptable, we describe in this article at which MAL point a polling interface can be able to serve a higher number of clients than pushing. Open Data publishers can use these insights to determine which mechanism is the most cost-effective for the usage scenario they foresee of their live updating resources on the Web.

Keywords: Web API engineering · Performance and scalability · Open Data

1 Introduction

The Open Data deployment scheme [1] defines 5 steps that data publishers can undertake to raise the technical and semantical interoperability of their Open datasets on the Web. With the use of the Hypertext Transfer Protocol (HTTP) as a communication protocol, a dataset becomes technically interoperable with the Web of data [2, 3]. This allows Open Data consumers to retrieve a resource (e.g. a document that is part of the dataset) by sending an HTTP GET method to the Uniform Resource Identifier (URI) of the resource. For live changing resources, such as the measurements of a sensor, there are two communication mechanisms to share an update in a timely fashion to clients. First, there is pull where the client initiates the action to retrieve a resource. This category

© Springer Nature Switzerland AG 2020
M. Bielikova et al. (Eds.): ICWE 2020, LNCS 12128, pp. 87–101, 2020.
https://doi.org/10.1007/978-3-030-50578-3_7

has two representatives: HTTP polling and HTTP long polling. Next, you have push where the server pushes updates of a resource to the client. Server-Sent Events (SSE) and Websockets are implementations for this mechanism. Lubbers et al. [4] compared Websockets with HTTP polling for a dataset that updates every second and up to 100 k clients, but this was only a theoretical analysis of the bandwidth usage and latency. Depending on the size of the header information, a bandwidth reduction of 500:1 can be made with Websockets and a latency reduction of 3:1. Pimentel et al. [5] went a step further and investigated how the physical distance between publisher and consumer impacts the overall latency. They performed a comparison between polling, long polling and Websockets where a new sensor update of roughly 100 bytes is published per second. They defined formulas to check when polling or long polling is feasible for updates on time, dependent on the network latency. When the network latency exceeds half the update rate of the dataset, then Websockets is the better choice. However, there is no evaluation performed on the performance of the server under a high load of clients, which is an important factor that needs to be considered for Open Data publishing.

One of the key features of publishing data on the Web is HTTP caching, which has not been addressed in related work [4–6]. This allows a resource to become stateless and can be shared with proxy caches or Content Network Delivery (CDN) services to offload the server. With push-based interfaces like Websockets, caching of a resource is not possible as the server needs to actively push the content in a stateful manner to all subscribed clients. In previous work [7], a minimum set of technical requirements and a benchmark between pull (HTTP polling) and push (Websockets) have been introduced for publishing live changing resources on the Web. This benchmark tested with only 200 clients, which did not yield conclusive results on the latency or scalability issues that arise inside an Open Data ecosystem, where client numbers of 15 000 are not an exception [8]. In this article, we will run a similar benchmark between HTTP polling and SSE with up to 25 k clients. SSE is tested instead of Websockets, because it has a similar performance [6], communication is unidirectional which is suitable for Open Data and lastly, it only relies on HTTP instead of a Websockets protocol, which lowers the complexity of reusing a dataset.

The remainder of this article is structured as follows: we will provide in the related work section an overview of publication techniques and the current state of publishing RDF Streams on the Web. RDF Streams are applicable for describing live updating resources with the Resource Description Framework (RDF) and thus resolve the fourth step of the Open Data deployment scheme [1]. Thereafter, we conduct a field report to quantify how many live Open datasets are available on the Open Data portals of Europe and the U.S. to observe which update retrieval mechanism is used in different domains. In the problem statement section, we define our research questions and hypotheses, which we will then evaluate with a benchmark between HTTP polling and SSE. In the discussion and conclusion, based on the results of the benchmark, we will propose some guidelines for data publishers when to use pull or push interfaces.

2 Related Work

2.1 Web Publication Protocols

HTTP Polling. A client sends an HTTP GET request to the server, waits for a certain time interval after retrieving the response and starts again with requesting the resource. The benefit of this approach is that a resource becomes stateless and HTTP caching is possible. However, there is no strict guideline on how clients should time their request. For variantly updating resources, a client can not predict when the next update will be available. A higher polling frequency can minimize the latency on the client, but this comes at a higher bandwidth cost [4].

HTTP Long Polling. With long polling, the server only returns a response when a new update is available. This way, a client does not send redundant requests like HTTP polling. Also, the client does not wait before sending a request again. A resource becomes stateful as the server needs to maintain all the connections open. Pimental et al. [5] showed that long polling can have a similar performance as Websockets when the underlying network latency is lower than half the data measurement rate.

Server-Sent Events. With the growing demand for (near) realtime applications, HTTP is extended in 2014 with the support of Server-Sent Events (SSE). Similarly to long polling, the server holds the connection open for every client, but this remains open for pushing multiple updates instead of one. With the use of the EventSource API (supported by all browsers except IE and Edge), clients can receive updates of a resource in an event-driven fashion. Using SSE over HTTP/1.1 has the disadvantage that every requested resource requires a separate TCP connection, which can run into the limited number of connections a browser can open per domain. However, this is solved for servers that support HTTP/2, which multiplex all requests and responses over one connection.

Websockets. The Websocket protocol provides a bidirectional communication channel over one TCP connection for every client. HTTP is used to set up a handshake between client and server for transmitting data, but further communication happens over a raw TCP connection. The WHATWG Websocket standard describes how messages can be pushed between client and server, but there are also sub protocols (MQTT [9], CoAP, etc.) for more advanced features, for example a publish/subscribe broker to receive or send updates of a specific resource. Websockets has a similar performance as SSE [6], but a lower transmission latency when the server needs to send large messages above 7.5 kbytes. Also, for client to server communication provides Websockets a lower transmission latency [6] than using HTTP.

WebSub. The WebSub [10] specification extends the communication pattern between clients and servers from above protocols with a third actor hub. A resource can be retrieved from the publisher (server), but consumers can also subscribe for updates through a hub instead of polling the resource URL. A resource is coupled with one topic, which is exposed by one or more hubs for fault tolerance. Reusers of the data can receive updates by setting up a Web accessible server and subscribing to a topic. Hubs then send updates through HTTP POST requests (Webhook mechanism) to this server. While Open Data publishers can benefit from distributed hubs in an Open Data ecosystem, for example a hub can be reused by multiple data publishers, Open Data reusers are required to deploy a Web server to receive updates they are interested in. To enable the use case of autonomous intelligent agents [11] that wish to retrieve updates of a resource through a topic, then a service for subscribing to a topic must be made available. As this service will also need to decide on exposing polling or pushing to agents, we will not further elaborate on WebSub in this article.

2.2 RDF Streams

Arasu et al. [12] defines a stream S as a (possibly infinite) bag (multiset) of elements $\langle s, \tau \rangle$ where s is a tuple (the actual data without the timestamp of the element) belonging to the schema of S and $\tau \in T$ is the timestamp of the element. The Resource Description Framework (RDF) Stream Processing (RSP) Community Group, which focuses on processing RDF-modelled data, has applied this definition for RDF streams [13] where an RDF stream S is a (potentially) unbounded sequence of timestamped RDF statements in non-decreasing time order. TripleWave [14] is a tool that transforms Web streams, which only differs from an RDF stream by its data model [7], into RDF streams and republishes them with a polling and/or push-based (Websockets, MQTT) interface. These streams can be consumed by other RDF stream processors (RSP) for continuous query answering with SPARQL-based query models (C-SPARQL [15], CQLS [16], TPF Query Streamer [17]). Dell'Aglio et al. [18] describes for the publication of an RDF stream that both push-based and polling interfaces can be supported; the consumer may choose what it prefers. Also, several requirements [19] are defined for RSP query engines of which requirement 6 "timely fashion" acknowledges [18] that the timing of results depend on the application scenario and thus the requirements of the consumer of the data publication or query service. In the next section, we will look into how the timely fashion requirement is applied for live Open datasets.

3   Field Report on Live Open Datasets

This section gives an overview of how many live Open datasets are available in the European and U.S. Open Data portals, what the rate of publication is and which update mechanism is used. Datasets were retrieved by doing a full-text search on "real-time". Only working and up-to-date datasets are mentioned. Note that this is a non-exhaustive overview, because among other reasons not all Open datasets are harvested by these portals. We also briefly describe the update mechanisms that are used in the public transport and cryptocurrency trading domains.

On Table 1 we see that live Open datasets from only five countries are harvested by the European Open Data portal. While we can argue that there are more relevant datasets than on this overview, for example by browsing for Open Data portals of specific cities or using Google Dataset Search [21], we still get a broad view of the current state-of-the-art interfaces. Only 2 datasets have a push interface available, both using the Websocket protocol, of which only the Transport for London (TfL) API from the U.K. is free to use.

Interestingly, the True Time API from the U.S. offers the same functionality as the TfL API with arrival predictions for public transport, but uses polling instead of push-based update mechanism. On the one hand, we found live datasets related to the environment (water level, weather, etc.) that publish at a lower rate (from every minute to every hour) with a polling-based interface. On the other hand, we found mobility related datasets whose update interval fits between realtime (as fast as possible) and 5 min.

Table 1. Overview of live Open datasets according to their country, how fast it updates and whether a polling or push interface is used.

Country	Datasets	Update interval	Update mechanism
Belgium	Vehicles position (Public transport MIVB)	20 s	Polling
Belgium	Bicycle counter	Realtime	Polling
Belgium	Park+rides	Realtime	Polling
France	Parking and bicycle stations availability	60 s	Polling
Sweden	Notifications about Lightning Strikes	Realtime	Push-based
Ireland	Weather station information, the Irish National Tide Gauge Network	3600 s	Polling
UK	River level data	900 s	Polling
UK	Cycle hire availability & arrival predictions (Transport for London Unified API)	300 s	Polling
UK	Arrival predictions (Transport for London Unified API)	Realtime	Push-based
U.S.	Real-Time Traffic Incident Reports of Austin-Travis County	300 s	Polling
U.S.	True Time API (arrival information and location of public transport vehicles)	Realtime	Polling
U.S.	Current Bike Availability by Station (Nextbike)	300 s	Polling
U.S.	USGS Streamflow Stations	24 h	Polling
U.S.	NOAA water level (tidal) data of 205 Stations for the Coastal United States and Other Non-U.S. Sites	360 s	Polling
U.S.	National Renewable Energy Laboratory [20]	60 s	Polling
U.S.	RTC MetStation real time data	360 s	Polling
U.S.	Seattle Real Time Fire 911 Calls	300 s	Polling

We also examined the public transport domain where GTFS-RT, a data specification for publishing live transit updates, takes no position [22] on how updates should be published, except that HTTP should be used. OpenTripPlanner (OTP), a world-wide used multi-modal route planner which allows retrieving GTFS-RT updates and bicycle availabilities, also supports both approaches: setup a frequency in seconds for polling or subscribe to a push-based API.

When people want to trade money or digital coins, it is crucial that the latency of price tickings, books, etc. are as low as possible, otherwise it can literally cost them money. The rate of publication of these live datasets are also typically below 1 s. Therefore, publishers in the cryptocurrency trading domain heavily use push-based mechanisms for their clients. This however does not mean that a HTTP polling approach is not used. Websockets are de-facto used as a bidirectional communication channel is required for trading. We tested three publishers (Bitfinex, Bitmex and gdax) and saw over a span of one year that they were still available which makes us believe that Open push-based interfaces are a viable option for other domains as well.

4   Problem Statement

In the field report, we saw that there is no strict guideline whether to use polling or pushing for a certain dataset. Based on the insights from the field report and related work, we define the following research question:

Research question: Which kind of Web interface for server to client communication is best suited for publishing live Open Data in function of server-side cost, scalability and latency on the client?

Following hypotheses are defined which will be answered in the discussion:

H1: Using a Server-Sent Events interface will result in a lower latency on the client, compared to a polling interface.
H2: The server-side CPU cost of an HTTP polling interface is initially higher than a Server-Sent Events interface, but increases less steeply when the number of clients increases.
H3: From a certain number of clients onward, the server cost of a Server-Sent Events interface exceeds the server cost of a polling interface.

5   Benchmark HTTP Polling Versus Server-Sent Events

5.1   Evaluation Design

Update Interval of Live Dataset. The experiments focus on observing the latency on the client when a server needs to serve a high number of clients. As we want to observe the latency on the client per update and we expect a higher latency when the server works under a high load of clients, it is important to reserve enough time between updates. Table 1 shows that most datasets have an update interval in the range of seconds. By choosing a fixed update interval of 5 s for the live dataset in this experiment, there should be enough time to observe the latency on the client between two updates and still have a representative update interval according to Table 1. Also, an invariantly changing dataset allows to set HTTP caching headers according to the update interval, which is an opportune circumstance for HTTP polling.

Live Dataset. A JSON object with a size of 5.2 kB is generated every 5 s, which has a similar size as the park+rides dataset (5.6 kB) from Table 1. This object is annotated with a timestamp that indicates when this object was generated and is used by clients to calculate the latency on the client. Furthermore, it is published inside a HTTP document for clients that use HTTP polling or it is directly pushed to clients with SSE.

Latency on the Client. The goal of this benchmark is to observe the time between the generation of an update and when a client can further process it. We define this as the latency on the client of an update. For HTTP polling, this depends on timing its request as closely as possible after a new update is available. Based on the caching headers of a response (Cache-Control for HTTP/1.1 or Expires for HTTP/1.0), a client could calculate the optimal time for its next request. In this benchmark, we choose to continuously fetch the HTTP document with a pause of 500 ms between the previous response and the next request, because we expect a similar polling implementation by Open Data reusers like OpenTripPlanner.

Web API. The live data is published with a server written in the Node.js Web application framework Express and exposes 2 API routes: /polling to retrieve a JSON document containing the latest value with an HTTP GET request and /sse to receive updates through an open TCP connection with Server-Sent-Events. The latter is naively implemented server-side with a for loop that pushes updates to every client. Multiple optimizations are possible (multi-threading, load balancing, etc.), but to make a fair comparison between HTTP polling and SSE we focus on having a single-threaded implementation for both approaches. By only using a for loop, all work needs to be done by the default Node.js single-threaded event loop. For HTTP polling, we use nginx as reverse proxy and enable single threading by configuring the number of worker_processes to 1. In order that nginx can handle many simultaneous connections with clients, the number of worker_connections is set to 10 k.

HTTP Caching. Two HTTP caching components are available: one is implemented server-side using the HTTP cache of nginx, the other one at the client-side. When a client fetches the document containing the most recent update, it will first check if a non-expired copy is available in its cache (Fig. 1). Web browsers have this feature enabled by default, but the Node.js clients in this benchmark need to use the cacheable-request NPM package to support HTTP caching. An unexpected side effect of using nginx (version 1.17.7) is that it does not dynamically update the max-age value in the Cache-Control header when returning a copy from its cache. This means that a cached copy with a time-to-live of 1 s will still have a max-age of 5 s which leads into extra client-side caching for 5 s instead of 1 s. To circumvent this behaviour in our benchmark, we also added the Expires header, which indicates when the document is expired. This requires that the clocks of the server and clients are synchronized which is the case for the testbed we used. For future work, we suggest to use Varnish as reverse proxy, which dynamically updates the Cache-Control header. In Fig. 1, we see that the client makes a request to nginx when its cache is expired. When nginx's cache is also expired, then only the first request will be let through (proxy_cache_lock on) to retrieve the document from the back-end server over a persistent keep-alive connection that is configured. Other requests need to wait until nginx received the response and then pull from the updated cache. The max-age value is calculated by subtracting the time that is already passed (the current time - the time the last update is generated) from the frequency a new update is generated (5000 ms). The Expires header is calculated by adding the update frequency to the time of the last update. Finally, nginx removes the Cache-Control header, which obliges the client to use the Expires header for the correct timing of its cache.

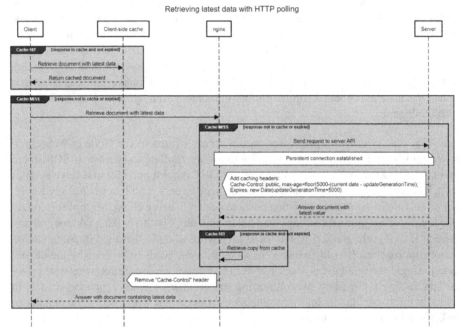

Fig. 1. Two cache components (client-side and server-side/nginx) are used for HTTP polling. As Nginx does not dynamically update the max-age value from the Cache-Control header, we fall back on the Expires header for client-side caching.

High Number of Clients. A benchmark environment is created using the Cloudlab testbed at the University of Utah, which had at the time of writing the biggest number (200+) among alternatives available to us of bare metal servers. This is necessary for our envisaged scenario where we need to deploy thousands of Web clients to simulate the impact on an Open Data interface. 200 HP ProLiant m400 [23] servers are used for our benchmark, each containing a CPU architecture with eight 64-bit ARMv8 (Atlas/A57) cores at 2.4 GHz, 64 GB of RAM, 120 TB of SATA flash storage. Notice that a m400 server uses ARM which is generally lower in performance than traditional x86 server architectures which could lead to faster detection of performance losses. Lastly, we use the Kubernetes framework to easily orchestrate the deployment and scaling of our server and clients that are containerized with Docker.

Logging Results. A time series database (InfluxDB) is deployed where clients log their latency on the client. Also, the visualisation tool Grafana is deployed to monitor whether all clients are initialized and polling or subscribed as expected and then to export the results as CSV. When an update is received on the client, only 10% is randomly logged to InfluxDB to prevent an excess of updates. We exported several minutes of recordings of the latency on the client per test, which we deem enough, for evaluation. To log the usage of the server and client (CPU and memory), we use the Kubernetes Metrics Server. Similarly to retrieving the resource usage of a Linux machine with the 'top' command, we can use 'kubectl top pods' to extract the resource usage of Kubernetes pods. For each test, we ran this multiple times and calculated the average for plotting. The Node.js back-end and nginx reverse proxy are deployed in one single pod. This means we can easily monitor the overall resource usage for HTTP polling from both components together.

5.2   Results

The results from our benchmark are split into two parts: first, we will show the latency on the client with density charts. Then we will look into the resource usage. We will first test HTTP polling without using nginx. This way, we demonstrate the performance boost nginx creates.

Polling Without Nginx. On Fig. 2, we can see a group of density charts for polling without using nginx. The y-axis represents the number of clients (100, 1000, etc.) that are deployed in polling mode, while the x-axis represents the time in ms it took to retrieve a new update. For every number of clients, there is a separate density chart showing the distribution of latencies on the client that are measured. A client still uses a client-side cache and polls every 500 ms, but it directly contacts the server Web API when its cache expires. For 100 clients, more than half of the updates is retrieved below 0.5 s. Up to 2000 clients, the majority of updates are retrieved beneath one second. Above 2000 clients, the server struggles to respond efficiently as the latency on the client is spread from 0 s up to 5 s. We were unable to deploy more than 5000 clients, because the server fails to handle the number of requests.

Polling. With nginx added to the server as a reverse proxy with HTTP caching enabled, we can see on Fig. 3.1 that the server is able to handle 8000 clients instead of 5000 clients and have a similar latency for 100 and 1000 clients as without nginx (Fig. 2). From 2000 clients on, a peak of the latency on the client appears between 1 s and 2 s. Also, a peak exists between 3 s and 4 s starting from 4000 clients. At 8000 clients, the distribution is evenly spread between 0 s and 2 s. Clients have a polling frequency of 500 ms and start polling at different times, which is one of the causes of this spread. In addition, all requests wait until the cache is updated and then nginx returns responses single-threaded. To see whether this is not caused by our client implementation, we performed a benchmark with the wrk HTTP benchmarking tool, which generates a significant amount of requests to test the HTTP response latency instead of the latency on the client to retrieve an update. A wrk benchmark was performed for 30 s, using 12 threads, keeping 400 HTTP connections open and timeout for response times above

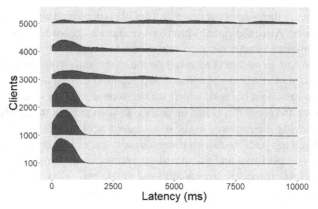

Fig. 2. Latency on the client with polling without using nginx. The server is able to answer effectively up to 2000 clients and becomes unstable above 5000 clients.

4 s. Wrk measured a maximum response latency of 3.89 s with 13 responses timed out above 4 s and could reach 2.52 k requests/s which acknowledges insights from the density charts on Fig. 3.1.

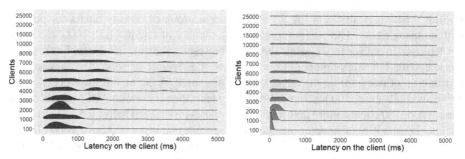

Fig. 3. Latency on the client with polling (Fig. 3.1) and Server-Sent Events (Fig. 3.2). Polling scales up to 8 k clients, while Server-Sent Events can serve 25 k clients.

Server-Sent Events. On Fig. 3.2 we can see that the maximal latency on the client with a SSE interface increases with the number of clients. For 5 k clients, the latency on the client is still below a second, but for 25 k clients this is evenly distributed between 0 s and 4 s. During implementation, we faced a kernel buffer issue where data transmission is queued until no data was written from Node.js to the HTTP response objects from clients. This caused an increasing minimal latency on the client and also a higher maximal latency on the client up to 1.5 s for 20 k clients. A continuous data transmission was achieved by running a sleep function of 1 ms per 1000 clients, because we saw on the density charts of Fig. 3.2 that SSE could respond efficiently up to 1000 clients.

Resource Usage. We measured the CPU and memory usage for the three above-mentioned approaches. The CPU metric of a Kubernetes pod, in which our server resides, is measured in mCPUs (milliCPUs). 1000 mCPUs are equivalent to 1 AWS vCPU or 1 Hyperthread on a bare-metal Intel processor with Hyperthreading. Memory usage is measured in mebibytes (MiB). On Fig. 4, we can see that polling without nginx has the steepest curve for CPU and that SSE still has a significant CPU advantage over polling with nginx. We believe this is caused by SSE having less overhead than polling, although nginx is able to minimize this with connections that are kept alive, gzip compression and caching. For 5000 clients, we see that nginx decreases CPU usage by half compared to polling without nginx. The memory usage stabilizes for polling (Fig. 5) with preference for polling with nginx. For SSE, this continuously increases with the number of clients as every client connection is held in memory.

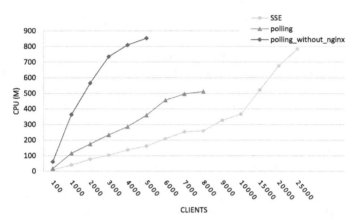

Fig. 4. CPU usage (in milliCPU) of polling and Server-Sent Events. SSE uses less milliCPU than polling.

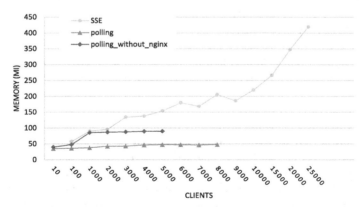

Fig. 5. Memory usage (in mebibytes) of polling and Server-Sent Events. Polling has a low memory footprint (<100 MiB), while SSE needs to keep every client connection continuously in memory.

6 Discussion

Based on the benchmarking results from previous section, we start our discussion by verifying our hypotheses. Thereafter, we will answer our research questions more in depth.

Our first hypothesis H1 states that a SSE interface will result in a lower latency on the client than with polling. When comparing the latency the client on Fig. 3, we see that SSE always has a lower maximal latency on the client than a polling interface with server-side cache enabled, so we accept H1. Surprisingly, to achieve this distribution for SSE from 0 s onwards, we had to add a sleep function of 1 ms between every 1000 clients. Otherwise, all responses are first stored in the kernel buffer before getting transmitted which causes a higher minimum latency on the client. This behavior is not described in implementation guidelines of SSE or Websockets so we hope that this article can help informing the Node.js community.

For our second hypothesis H2, we expected a faster growing server cost of SSE than polling. Previously [7], it was argued that the capabilities of HTTP caching would outperform the server cost of SSE for a high number of clients, although polling has an initial higher server cost. CPU usage results (Fig. 4) show that nginx indeed improves the CPU usage for polling, but it is still steeper than SSE, so we reject H2. Publishers should take note of the higher memory footprint of SSE, because all client connections are saved in memory. When data needs to be encrypted using TLS, then we expect that the server-side CPU cost for both polling and pushing will be only be slightly higher, because TCP connections are kept alive for both approaches and thus the time and resource expensive TLS handshake only needs to be done once for the first HTTP request [24].

Hypothesis H3 can also be falsified, because the CPU usage of polling grows apart higher than SSE for a large number of clients. In other words, answering requests with a cached copy still has a higher CPU cost than pushing updates directly. In terms of scalability, we saw in Fig. 3 that SSE is able to serve 25 k clients, while polling could only serve 8 k clients. From our hypotheses, we see that SSE is favored based on scalability, server cost and latency on the client.

The field report (Sect. 3) shows for the vehicle positions dataset that updates are generated every 20 s and polling is used. When an end user wants to reuse this information inside the OpenTripPlanner application, then a polling frequency (s) needs to be specified. This depends on the maximal latency on the client that an end user perceives as acceptable. Even if the update interval of the live dataset is known, e.g. every 5 s like in our benchmark, matching the polling frequency with this update interval would still create a latency on the client distribution between 0 s and the polling frequency. In the worst case, an HTTP response is returned just before a new update arrives, so the client will only fetch this update with the next request round. Given the results of our hypotheses, we question at which point the maximum acceptable latency on the client (MAL) of an end user must be in order that our polling interface can serve more clients than SSE. In the next paragraph, we will describe how we can theoretically calculate this MAL cut-off point between polling and SSE.

In our benchmark, we tested with the Wrk HTTP benchmarking tool that our polling interface could serve up to 2.52 k requests/s. When all users would have started polling at different starting times every 5 s, so they configured a MAL of 5 s, then our polling interface could have served theoretically up to 12.6 k clients (2.52 * 5) instead of 8 k from our benchmark. This can be generalized with the following formula, which states that the maximum supported number of requests/s of a polling interface (2.52 k in our case) must be higher than the expected number of users that make one request every MAL seconds:

$$Requests_{maxsupported}/s \geq Users * Request/MAL \tag{1}$$

Open Data publishers can calculate with formula (1) how many users with a certain MAL can be maximally served. In practice, users can configure a higher polling frequency than the expected MAL, so the number of users that can be served will probably be lower. To compare this with SSE, we see on Fig. 3.2 that SSE can maximally serve 25 k clients over a MAL of 4 s, which is still more than polling can serve (10 k clients) with this MAL. By increasing the MAL, we found that a MAL of 10 s allows our polling interface to serve the same number of clients (25 k) as SSE. This should not be interpreted as a universal number, because there are other factors that can influence this number: an AMD CPU architecture could be more performant than the ARM architecture we used or publishing in a global network could add extra network latency for polling [5]. Nonetheless, this number gives an indication that users must have a relatively high MAL (>10 s) in order that polling can serve a higher number of clients than pushing with the same amount of resources. This brings us to our research question where our single-threaded comparison shows that pushing is the best choice up to a maximum latency on the client of 10 s. For datasets where all users configure a MAL above 10 s, then a polling interface is capable to serve a higher number of clients, which can be calculated with formula (1).

Figure 4 showed that HTTP caching is crucial for a polling interface to lower the CPU usage, but for variantly updating datasets it is not possible to foresee when the next update will happen. For this use case, we advise to only cache the response for 1 s in the reverse proxy (micro caching), and thus still off-load the back-end Web API. At last, caching headers should always be set if possible, according to the arrival of the next update so the user can still configure its preferred MAL and bandwidth usage can be reduced.

7 Conclusion

In related work of the RDF Stream Processing Community Group [18] and the field report on live Open datasets (Sect. 3), we saw that publishing live changing resources on the Web leaves the options for polling and push-based mechanisms open. With this article, we shed some light into this topic by running a benchmark between a Server-Sent Event and polling interface. In contrast with traditional HTTP benchmarks, we focused on assessing the latency on the client of an update instead of the HTTP response latency. We extend existing work [5], because we saw that a push mechanism is also the best option when the server needs to handle a high number of clients. If the latency on the client must be as low as possible, then the server CPU cost of HTTP polling with caching enabled does not outperform pushing [7]. Data publishers can use our results, which reflect the performance of a pull and push mechanism over a single thread, to foresee when to scale their infrastructure in function of the number of clients and the expected maximum latency on the client. The application scenario that users have a maximal acceptable latency on the client (MAL) of at least 10 s makes polling more scalable than pushing, although this is a theoretical number. Configuring the MAL is a task that an Open Data reuser should be able to choose and this cannot be forced by the data publisher by setting a caching header. Because of this, caching headers should always be applied for invariant streams, but its timing should not be further than the next update. For variantly updating streams where the timing of the next update is unknown, we advise to use micro caching on the reverse proxy. At last, Open Data publishers should do user research (conduct a survey or investigate query logs [25]) to find out which MAL is most likely to be used for each dataset and verify if their current infrastructure is fit for this by applying formula (1). For example, the vehicle position dataset from the field report in Sect. 3 has a new update available every 20 s. If users also configure their polling frequency in function of this interval, so their MAL is above 10 s, then polling is the preferred interface based on the number of clients that can be served.

The "timely fashion" requirement is currently only applied for each component individually (from Web stream to RDF stream and RSP query engines). In future work, we would like to investigate how this requirement can be resolved from a true user perspective, such as Smart City Dashboards, and how this requirement goes top-down to all the underlying components.

Acknowledgements. We would like to express our gratitude to Raf Buyle and Pieter Bonte for their support during the writing process of this article.

References

1. Berners-Lee, T.: 5 Star Data (2009). https://5stardata.info/en/. Accessed 04 Mar 2020
2. Colpaert, P., et al.: Quantifying the Interoperability of Open Government Datasets. Computer **47**, 50–56 (2014)
3. Rezaei, R., Chiew, T.K., Lee, S.P.: A review on e-business interoperability frameworks. J. Syst. Softw. **93**, 199–216 (2014)
4. Lubbers, P., Greco, F.: HTML5 websocket: a quantum leap in scalability for the web (2010). http://www.websocket.org/quantum.html. Accessed 04 Mar 2020
5. Pimentel, V., Nickerson, B.G.: Communicating and displaying real-time data with websocket. IEEE Internet Comput. **16**, 45–53 (2012)
6. Słodziak, W., Nowak, Z.: Performance analysis of web systems based on XMLHttpRequest, server-sent events and websocket. In: Grzech, A., Borzemski, L., Świątek, J., Wilimowska, Z. (eds.) ISAT 2015, Part II. AISC, vol. 430, pp. 71–83. Springer, Cham (2016). https://doi.org/10.1007/978-3-319-28561-0_6
7. Rojas Meléndez, J.A., Van de Vyvere, B., Gevaert, A., Taelman, R., Colpaert, P., Verborgh, R.: A preliminary open data publishing strategy for live data in flanders. In: Companion Proceedings of the The Web Conference 2018, pp. 1847–1853. International World Wide Web Conferences Steering Committee (2018)
8. Colpaert, P., Verborgh, R., Mannens, E.: Public transit route planning through lightweight linked data interfaces. In: Cabot, J., De Virgilio, R., Torlone, R. (eds.) ICWE 2017. LNCS, vol. 10360, pp. 403–411. Springer, Cham (2017). https://doi.org/10.1007/978-3-319-60131-1_26

9. Naik, N.: Choice of effective messaging protocols for IoT systems: MQTT, CoAP, AMQP and HTTP. In: 2017 IEEE International Systems Engineering Symposium (ISSE), pp. 1–7 (2017)
10. Genestoux, J., Fitzpatrick, B., Slatkin, B., Atkins, M.: WebSub W3C Recommendation 23 January 2018. https://www.w3.org/TR/websub/. Accessed 04 Mar 2020
11. Taelman, R., Van Herwegen, J., Vander Sande, M., Verborgh, R.: Comunica: a modular SPARQL query engine for the web. In: Vrandečić, D., et al. (eds.) ISWC 2018, Part II. LNCS, vol. 11137, pp. 239–255. Springer, Cham (2018). https://doi.org/10.1007/978-3-030-00668-6_15
12. Arasu, A., Babu, S., Widom, J.: The CQL continuous query language: semantic foundations and query execution. VLDB J. **15**, 121–142 (2006)
13. Dell'Aglio, D., Della Valle, E., Calbimonte, J.-P., Corcho, O.: RSP-QL semantics: a unifying query model to explain heterogeneity of RDF stream processing systems. Int. J. Seman. Web Inf. Syst. (IJSWIS). **10**, 17–44 (2014)
14. Mauri, A., et al.: TripleWave: spreading RDF streams on the web. In: Groth, P., et al. (eds.) ISWC 2016, Part II. LNCS, vol. 9982, pp. 140–149. Springer, Cham (2016). https://doi.org/10.1007/978-3-319-46547-0_15
15. Barbieri, D.F., Braga, D., Ceri, S., Valle, E.D., Grossniklaus, M.: C-SPARQL: a continuous query language for RDF data streams. Int. J. Seman. Comput. **4**, 3–25 (2010)
16. Le-Phuoc, D., Dao-Tran, M., Xavier Parreira, J., Hauswirth, M.: A native and adaptive approach for unified processing of linked streams and linked data. In: Aroyo, L., et al. (eds.) ISWC 2011, Part I. LNCS, vol. 7031, pp. 370–388. Springer, Heidelberg (2011). https://doi.org/10.1007/978-3-642-25073-6_24
17. Taelman, R., Verborgh, R., Colpaert, P., Mannens, E.: Continuous client-side query evaluation over dynamic linked data. In: Sack, H., Rizzo, G., Steinmetz, N., Mladenić, D., Auer, S., Lange, C. (eds.) ESWC 2016. LNCS, vol. 9989, pp. 273–289. Springer, Cham (2016). https://doi.org/10.1007/978-3-319-47602-5_44
18. Dell'Aglio, D., Phuoc, D.L., Le-Tuan, A., Ali, M.I., Calbimonte, J.-P.: On a Web of Data Streams. DeSemWeb@ISWC (2017)
19. Dell'Aglio, D., Della Valle, E., van Harmelen, F., Bernstein, A.: Stream reasoning: a survey and outlook. Data Sci. **1**, 59–83 (2017)
20. Jager, A., D.; Andreas: NREL National Wind Technology Center (NWTC): M2 Tower (1996)
21. Brickley, D., Burgess, M., Noy, N.: Google dataset search: building a search engine for datasets in an open web ecosystem. In: The World Wide Web Conference, pp. 1365–1375. Association for Computing Machinery, New York (2019)
22. Google: GTFS Realtime Overview. https://developers.google.com/transit/gtfs-realtime. Accessed 04 Mar 2020
23. Hardware HP ProLiant m400 server at Cloudlab Utah. https://docs.cloudlab.us/hardware.html. Accessed 04 Mar 2020
24. Nginx SSL/TLS offloading. https://www.nginx.com/blog/nginx-ssl/. Accessed 04 Mar 2020
25. Vandewiele, G., et al.: Predicting train occupancies based on query logs and external data sources. In: Proceedings of the 7th International Workshop on Location and the Web (2017)

NuMessage: Providing Scalable and Reliable Messaging Service in Distributed Systems

Lubin Liu[1], Tong Liu[2(✉)] [iD], Xinglang Wang[1], Tao Xiao[1], Wei Fang[1], and HongYue Chen[1(✉)]

[1] eBay, Shanghai 200120, China
{lubliu,xingwang,taxiao,weifang,hochen}@ebay.com
[2] Shanghai University, Shanghai 200444, China
tong_liu@shu.edu.cn

Abstract. For e-commerce companies with complex businesses like eBay, messaging oriented middleware has become a critical component of a large-scale distributed system, to support real-time asynchronous communication. In this work, we introduce novel messaging oriented middleware named as NuMessage, which can provide universal messaging service, including supporting push and pull modes and different scenarios. We also propose a retry mechanism to guarantee each message can be delivered and processed at least once. Various interfaces are implemented in NuMessage, making it easy to deploy NuMessage in practice. Experiments are conducted in a real system, and the results show that NuMessage can achieve superior performance when there are message consuming failures happening. Moreover, we have adopted NuMessage in eBay for some time to process 12 billion of messages per day.

Keywords: Message oriented middleware · Retry mechanism design · Distributed messaging system

1 Introduction

As the businesses of large e-commerce companies, like eBay and Alibaba, become more and more complex, distributed system architecture is widely adopted, in which subsystems are built separately to support different businesses. Subsequently, *message oriented middleware* arises as an indispensable component in a large-scale distributed system (also called as *messaging system*), aiming to provide efficient and reliable communication among subsystems through a certain message delivering mechanism. Taking the advantage of message oriented middleware, application decoupling, asynchronous communication, traffic clipping and other functions could be achieved in a distributed e-commerce system.

This research is supported by NSFC (No. 61802245) and the Shanghai Sailing Program (No. 18YF1408200).

M. Bielikova et al. (Eds.): ICWE 2020, LNCS 12128, pp. 102–110, 2020.
https://doi.org/10.1007/978-3-030-50578-3_8

Some message oriented middleware [3–7,9] has been developed and widely-used by enterprises, such as RocketMQ [9] in Alibaba and Kafka [4] in LinkedIn. Traditional messaging systems based on the Java Message Service (JMS) specification [2] and the Advanced Message Queuing Protocol (AMQP) [8], always focus on providing diverse message delivery guarantees. For instance, each message is allowed to be acknowledged after consumption, according to the JMS specification. However, such messaging systems has poor performance in throughput, especially when there are many messages produced and accumulated. Developed as a log-processing messaging system, Kafka [4] has been widely used due to its high scalability and high throughput. Particularly, it applies to the applications, which can tolerate a few messages losing occasionally. However, due to the different requirements of various businesses (e.g., high throughput and fault intolerance), universal message oriented middleware, supporting different consuming modes and achieving high reliability and scalability, is in demand.

To meet the challenge, we develop novel messaging oriented middleware, called *NuMessage*, to support building a large-scale distributed messaging system with different business requirements. NuMessage can offer universal messaging service, which can be implemented based on any storage provider like file system, log system, and data base. NuMessage can be adopted to both point-to-point scenario and publish/subscribe scenario. Moreover, both push and pull message-consuming modes are supported in NuMessage. As our first attempt, a retry mechanism is proposed to process message consuming failures, which can guarantee each message can be delivered and processed at least once. Various interfaces including standard messaging APIs, RESTful APIs, and RPC APIs, are integrated, making NuMessage easy to be deployed in a distributed messaging system. In addition, another advantage is that the light-weight characteristic of NuMessage supports its clients can communicate with the HTTP protocol.

The rest of this paper is organized as follows. We introduce some basic concepts in Sect. 2 firstly. Then, we review some representative message oriented middleware which has been widely used in enterprises in Sect. 3. In Sect. 4, we describe the design of NuMessage and its key retry mechanism. In addition, we also implement NuMessage in Ebay and take two applications as examples. Experiments are conducted in a real system and the results are shown in Sect. 5. Finally, we conclude the paper in Sect. 6.

2   Basic Concepts

In this subsection, we introduce some basic concepts used in a messaging system, which is generally consisted of three components, i.e., message producers, message consumers, and specific message oriented middleware. The message oriented middleware is also called as a *broker* or a *message server*. A *message* is a structured object to hold data, transferred among message producers, the broker, and message consumers. A *message producer* is responsible to generate messages and send messages to the broker. Conversely, a *message consumer* is responsible to consume messages received from the broker. There are two models of messages applicable to different scenarios, i.e., *point-to-point* (P2P) model and *publish and subscribe* (Pub/Sub) model. In the P2P model, messages are sent to a specific *queue* until they are consumed or timed-out. The message in a queue can only be consumed by one consumer at the same time. The order of messages in a queue is guaranteed. In the Pub/Sub model, producers (also called *publishers*) send messages to a certain *topic* and then consumed by the consumers (also called *subscribers*) subscribed to the topic. A topic could be subscribed by multiple consumers and a message could be consumed by multiple consumers at the same time. The order of messages in a topic is not guaranteed. In some applications, multiple messages are produced or consumed together in a *batch*. In our paper, queues and topics used to hold messages, and message producers and consumers are collectively called *messaging resources*.

A messaging system can be divided into two modes, i.e., *push mode* and *pull mode*, according to how consumers receive messages. In the push mode, the broker actively pushes a message to the consumers who *subscribe* to the message, as soon as the broker receives the message. This mode is suitable for the applications with high real-time messaging capabilities. However, the disadvantage is that a large amount of messages will be accumulated at the consumer client when the processing rate of the consumer is slower than the sending rate of the producer. In the pull mode, consumers take the initiative to pull the required message from the broker, no matter how many messages are generated by producers. The unconsumed messages are stored at the message server. The disadvantage of this mode is that the timeliness of message processing is low.

3   Related Work

Until now, there are multiple message oriented middleware, such as IBM Web-Sphere MQ [5], RabbitMQ [7], ActiveMQ [6], ZeroMQ [3], RocketMQ [9], and Kafka [4], which have existed for long time and widely-used by enterprises. In this section, we review three representative message oriented middlewares.

ActiveMQ [6] is a popular and open source message queue framework produced by Apache, which fully supports the JMS specification [2]. ActiveMQ supports asynchronous message transfer, which reduces the coupling of producers and consumers. ActiveMQ also ensures messages reliably saved in the middleware and high-speed message persistence. Under the default setting of ActiveMQ, messages are pushed to consumers one by one.

RabbitMQ [7] is an open-source middleware based on AMQP [8], which is widely used in financial and payment systems due to its good performance in reliability, availability, and extensibility. However, RabbitMQ only supports P2P model, which limits its usage scenarios. Besides, RabbitMQ does not support message backtracking, which means a message is deleted once consumed.

Kafka [4] is a distributed Pub/Sub messaging system originally developed by LinkedIn, which is widely used due to its horizontal scalability and high throughput. Kafka is a well-designed and application-specific messaging system, which has several special characteristics as follows. Firstly, data are stored in a set of segment files and the broker simply appends messages to the last segment file.

Each message is addressed by its *offset* in the segment file, which avoids random access to the disk. Secondly, the information about how many messages have been consumed is saved by each consumer itself, and messages are actively required by consumers. Thus, the burden of the broker is significantly reduced. However, the broker does not know whether a message is consumed by all subscribers or not. The main disadvantages of Kafka are that messages may be re-consumed more than once by mistake, and Kafka lacks some useful functions like message-level acknowledgement mechanisms.

4   NuMessage Design

In this section, we first introduce the overview of our designed message oriented middleware *NuMessage*. Then, we explain the details of our proposed novel *retry mechanism* and the improved implementation of NuMessage. Finally, two examples are taken to show the usage of NuMessage in Ebay.

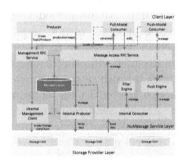
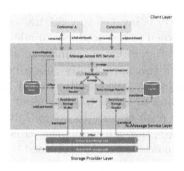

Fig. 1. Framework of NuMessage.   **Fig. 2.** Retry Mechanism.

4.1   Overview

Figure 1 shows the framework and data flow of our designed message oriented middleware NuMessage, which is mainly composed of four modules.

1. **Management Service:** A group of RPC APIs to manage (e.g., create, read, update, and delete) the messaging resources. Internal Management Client is contained in this service, which converts the requests (e.g., creating a producer or a topic) of clients to the instructions of storage providers.
2. **Message Access Service:** A group of RPC APIs for producers generating messages and consumers consuming messages. Both push and pull modes are supported in NuMessage.
3. **Internal Message Provider:** Internal Producer and Internal Consumer are included, which converts the request of producing/consuming messages to the instruction of writing/reading data into/from the storage provider.

4. **Ancillary Module:** Two ancillary engines are included in NuMessage as well, i.e., *filtering engine* and *push engine*, which make messages can be filtered according to user-defined rules and pushed to consumers in NuMessage.

In a messaging system implemented based on NuMessage, the storage provider could be implemented as a file system, a log system like Kafka, or a data base. Then, each storage unit holding messages is corresponding to a file, a topic, or a table, respectively. In any storage provider, we uniformly use *offset* to identify the location of a message recorded in a storage unit (e.g., rowID in Oracle DB).

Then, we describe the data flow in NuMessage in the following, as shown in Fig. 1, a new client (producer/consumer) firstly registers to NuMessage through the APIs provided by Management Service. To hold messages, a new topic or queue can be created by a provider, which is also supported by Management Service. Internal Management Client is invoked to create a storage unit or a client in the storage provider layer. All metadata (e.g., topic name, producer name, and their incidence relation) are saved in Metadata Store. To produce messages, a producer calls APIs provided by Message Access Service, and then Internal Producer is invoked to write messages into a storage unit. An acknowledgement is returned to the producer to inform it the message is persisted or not. In addition, two message consuming modes are supported in NuMessage. *In the push mode*, a consumer firstly subscribes to one or multiple specific topics/queues. Messages are periodically read by Internal Consumer from the storage provider according to the subscriptions of a consumer, and delivered to the consumer by the push engine. *In the pull mode*, consumers actively send requests to get messages, through calling the APIs provided by Message Access Service. Finally, an acknowledgement is returned to Message Access Service after the message is processed by the consumer.

4.2   Retry Mechanism

Some breakdowns may happen due to network instability or limited capacity of clients, such as (1) message loss during delivering from NuMessage to client, (2) processing failure at consumer client, and (3) acknowledgement loss during delivering from client to NuMessage. They lead to messages are lost during delivering or processing, which is unacceptable in some applications. To overcome the drawback, we adopt the acknowledge mechanism in NuMessage. In terms of consuming, if the acknowledgement of a message pushed to a consumer is not received, the message needs to be re-delivered to the consumer. To guarantee at least once delivery, we introduce a novel *retry mechanism*. The detailed design is plotted in Fig. 2.

Note that we build a specifical *BatchDetail Storage Unit* in storage prodiver, differing from source data storage units used to save normal messages. This special unit is used to store the status of each batch of messages consumed by a consumer client. Specially, each *batch detail record* stored in the unit contains the metadata of a consumed batch, such as batch ID, message IDs, batch status[1], expired time, and the count of retry times. When a consuming request arrives to Message Access Service, there are two consumption channels to get the corresponding messages, i.e., *normal consuming channel* and *retry consuming channel*, both of which are supported by Internal Consumer.

In the normal consumption channel, the request is sent to Normal Storage Reader by the distributor, which will read messages from source data storage units according to the offset recorded in Metadata Store. In the retry consumption channel, the request is sent to Retry Storage Reader, which will try the batch of messages failed before. Concretely, a cache storing the details of un-acked batches is maintained by Internal Consumer. A long-running thread BatchDetail Storage Reader periodically pulls batch details from BatchDetail Storage Unit and writes them into the cache. Retry Storage Reader reads messages from source data storage units according to the batch details recorded in the cache. In addition, the details of a batch with status := EMIT is created and written into BatchDetail Storage Unit by BatchDetail Storage Writer when the batch is read by Normal Storage Reader. The status of the batch is updated in BatchDetail Storage Unit, when its acknowledgement is returned by the consumer. If all messages in the batch are processed successfully by the consumer, BatchDetail Storage Reader will delete the record in the cache. If the batch is marked as failed in the acknowledgement, the details will be written into BatchDetail Storage Unit and then written into the cache. Failed messages will be retried sometime by the retry consumption channel. Otherwise, the expired time of the batch will be up, if there is no acknowledgement returned. Then, the batch will be retried by Retry Storage Reader based on the details recorded in the cache.

4.3   Improved Implementation

To enhance the efficiency of NuMessage in practice, we take three optimizing implementations as illustrated in the following.

---

[1] A batch has four statues:

1. SUCCESS means all messages in the batch have been processed successfully, and the batch will be deleted in storage.
2. EMIT indicates the batch is delivered to the client for the first time.
3. FAILED indicates that partial or all messages in the batch are marked as retry. A batch will be marked as failed as well if its acknowledgement is not returned before timeout. All failed batches will be redelivered.
4. ABANDONED means all messages in the batch are marked as abandoned, or the retry count has exceeded the upper bound.

Simplified Cache. A cache is used in NuMessage to record the details of failed batches. However, it is not necessary and memory-efficient to hold all batch details in the cache. Only a few key metadata are useful such as batch status, count of retrym and expired time. Then, each record in the cache has a fixed payload size of 26 bytes.

Instance Mapping. In NuMessage, the consuming service provided to each consumer client is supported by Internal Consumer. Thus, we need to map each novel consumer client to a proper internal consumer and keep the mapping balanced. Specially, if the number of consumer clients dose not exceed the upper bound asked by NuMessage, we will create a new internal consumer for the new client; otherwise, the client will be mapped to an existing internal consumer.

Channel Selection. When a consuming request arrives, a normal or retry consumption channel is selected by Internal Consumer to process the request. The default policy is simple random selection. We optimize the selection policy as follows. If the normal/retry channel returns an empty batch, Internal Consumer will change to the other channel.

4.4   Usage in Ebay

In this subsection, we introduce two practical usages of NuMessage in Ebay.

Search Data Federation (SDF) Service. SDF service is invoked by eBay business domain to save eBay item index update events to HBase [1]. The traffic volume of SDF service is quite heavy in eBay. For instance, the count of messages can reach to more than 4 billion per day. We implement a novel SDF service base on NuMessage, as shown in Fig. 3. Here, an index update event is written into NuMessage as a message by a SDF producer. Then, a SDF consumer reads the message out and invoke HBase write service (i.e., sdfwriter), to persistent the event in HBase. Thus, the invoke of SDF service by eBay business domain is decoupled with writing item index update into HBase.

Remote Procedure Call (RPC) Framework. RPC is a protocol of inter-process communication. We implement a RPC framework based on NuMessage in eBay, to deal with the applications containing a centralized control plane (regarded as RPC client) and multiple data planes (regarded as RPC servers). As shown in Fig. 4, the communication between the RPC clients and RPC servers is implemented by NuMessage, in which casts and calls generated by a RPC client are packed as messages, saved in multiple NuMessage queues and parallelly consumed by different RPC servers.

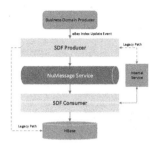 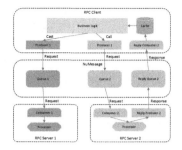

Fig. 3. SDF service based on NuMessage.

Fig. 4. RFC framework based on NuMessage.

5   Experimental Results

We conduct experiments based on a real system, comparing the performance achieved by NuMessage and Kafka [4], a popular open-source messaging middleware for log processing. We run our experiments on 5 machines deployed on the private cloud of eBay, each with 2 cores and 4 GB of memory. Two of them are used to run as client (producer/consumer) and server, respectively, while the other three machines are used as brokers. We carry out NuMessage in which the storage provider is implemented as log system Kafka. We test the performance of the consumer achieved by Kafka and NuMessage, which is measured by the average number of messages processed in a second. We run a single consumer client for Kafka and NuMessage respectively, and set the processing time of each message is 20 ms. In addition, we also consider two different scenarios, i.e., (1) no message retry happen, and (2) 20% messages are re-delivered.

The experimental results are presented in Fig. 5 and Fig. 6, respectively. We can find that the performance achieved by Kafka and NuMessage is lower than 50 messages/sec, since extra time is spent for the consumer pulling messages from the broker. As shown in Fig. 5, when there is no message retry, the performance achieved by NuMessage is slightly lower than Kafka. It is because NuMessage adds one more network hop to pull messages than Kafka. On the other hand, when there are 20% messages retried, NuMessage performs much better than Kafka, e.g., 18.4% higher throughput achieved. This is because Kafka has to block consuming for redelivering the failed messages, while NuMessage has the built-in non-blocking retry mechanism.

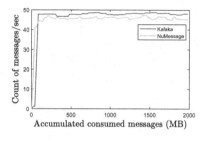

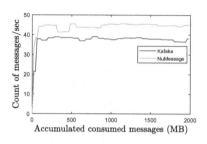

Fig. 5. Consumer performance when there is no message retry.

Fig. 6. Consumer performance when there are 20% messages re-delivered.

6 Conclusions

In this paper, we propose a novel messaging oriented middleware NuMessage, which can support push and pull modes and apply to different scenarios. Moreover, a retry mechanism is provided as our first attempt, which can guarantee at least once delivery in NuMessage. We also conduct experiments to show the superior performance of NuMessage. Until now, NuMessage has been adopted in practical systems of eBay, which process up to 12 billion of messages per day.

References

1. George, L.: HBase: The Definitive Guide: Random Access to Your Planet-Size Data. O'Reilly Media Inc., Sebastopol (2011)
2. Hapner, M., Burridge, R., Sharma, R., Fialli, J., Stout, K.: Java Message Service. Sun Microsystems Inc., Santa Clara (2002)
3. Hintjens, P.: ZeroMQ: Messaging for Many Applications. O'Reilly Media Inc., Sebastopol (2013)
4. Kreps, J., Narkhede, N., Rao, J., et al.: Kafka: a distributed messaging system for log processing. In: Proceedings of the NetDB, pp. 1–7 (2011)
5. Lampkin, V., et al.: Building Smarter Planet Solutions with MQTT and IBM WebSphere MQ telemetry. IBM Redbooks (2012)
6. Snyder, B., Bosanac, D., Davies, R.: Introduction to Apache ActiveMQ. Active MQ in Action, pp. 6–16 (2017)
7. Videla, A., Williams, J.J.: RabbitMQ in action: distributed messaging for everyone. Manning (2012)
8. Vinoski, S.: Advanced message queuing protocol. IEEE Internet Comput. **6**, 87–89 (2006)
9. Yue, M., Ruiyang, Y., Jianwei, S., Kaifeng, Y.: A MQTT protocol message push server based on RocketMQ. In: 2017 10th International Conference on Intelligent Computation Technology and Automation (ICICTA), pp. 295–298. IEEE (2017)

Machine Learning

A Credit Scoring Model for SMEs Based on Social Media Data

Septian Gilang Permana Putra[1], Bikash Joshi[1], Judith Redi[1],
and Alessandro Bozzon[2]($\boxtimes$)

[1] Exact Software, Delft, Netherlands
{septian.putra,bikash.joshi,judith.redi}@exact.com
[2] Delft University of Technology, Delft, Netherlands
a.bozzon@tudelft.nl

Abstract. Credit scoring is an important tool to assess the solidity of small and medium-sized enterprises (SMEs), and to unlock for them new options for credit and improvement of cash flow. Credit scoring is, in its most common form, used by (potential) creditors to predict the probability of SMEs to default in the future, as an inverse measure of creditworthiness. The majority of existing credit scoring methods for SMEs are solely based on the analysis of SMEs' financial data. While straightforward, these methods have major limitations: they may rely on very incomplete or outdated data, and fail to capture the very dynamic environment in which the business of SMEs evolves. In this paper, we propose an alternative approach to credit scoring for SMEs by enriching traditionally used financial data with social media data. We carried out our analysis on 25654 SMEs in the Netherlands, using 20 traditional financial indicators and 35 social media features. Experimental results suggest that the use of social media data in addition to traditional data significantly improves the quality of the credit scoring model for SMEs. Furthermore, we analyze the most important factors from social media data influencing the credit scoring.

1 Introduction

Small and medium-sized enterprises (SMEs) play an important role in the economy of every nation. In the Netherlands, for example, SMEs represent 99.8% of all enterprises, account for 64.2% of overall employment, and contributed to 61.8% value added of the non-financial business sector in 2017 [11]. In the Netherlands, as elsewhere in the world, supporting the financial needs of SMEs is crucial to the country's growth.

Credit analysis has emerged as an essential aspect of the modern economy, and especially for SMEs. Businesses need to evaluate the reliability of their customers before supplying services or goods. Likewise, financial institutes need to assess the probability of being paid back in full and on time before lending

M. Bielikova et al. (Eds.): ICWE 2020, LNCS 12128, pp. 113–129, 2020.
https://doi.org/10.1007/978-3-030-50578-3_9

money to SMEs. Credit scoring, defined as the process of assigning a quantitative measure to a potential borrower as an estimate of how likely they are to *default* (i.e. not repaying the debt in time), is a common credit analysis tool [15]. Creditors consider SMEs as high-risk clients, mainly because of their higher failure rate [3], and because of the difficulty to obtain reliable information about their financial situation as their financial reports are mainly for tax purposes and not publicly available. Because of these unique characteristics, creditors need to handle SME's credit risk separately from larger enterprises [3]. Hence, most of the commercial banks and other credit companies build specific credit scoring model for SMEs to enhance their credit decision process.

In the past two decades, plenty of credit scoring models have been proposed for SMEs. Recently proposed solutions rely on machine learning techniques and a fairly consistent set of predictors, namely financial ratios derived from accounting data (e.g. current ratio, return on asset (ROA), debt-to-equity ratio, etc.). Despite their proven predictive power [1,2,33], financial ratios have some limitations. As already mentioned, it is difficult for creditors to obtain financial data of SMEs. Moreover, there can be other factors beyond financial data which may influence the default behavior of SMEs such as their willingness and ability to repay the loan [16]. For this reason, a few studies have started including non-financial predictors [5,28], which incorporate knowledge about marketability, technology advantage, management quality, age, size, type of industry, and geographical area. While improving the accuracy of credit scoring, such data is difficult to obtain, as creditors should manage an on-site survey or have long enough historical relation with the borrowers to collect the data.

Social Media are popular among SMEs as tools to present themselves to the public and acquire new customers. Platforms such as LinkedIn and Facebook collect profiles of SMEs, reporting information on their business, their most recent initiatives, as well as their interactions with their customers. Creditors can access this alternative source of data using APIs provided by the platforms or using scraping technology. Arguably, SME lenders can also use this information to build a more comprehensive credit scoring model which is more transparent, faster and cheaper, and hence suitable for SMEs.

Despite its intrinsic richness [7], the use of Social Media information for credit scoring presents some non-trivial challenges. First, the data is not readily available unless provided directly from the company being assessed - which is not always the case; therefore, smart data collection techniques need to be devised for data acquisition. Second, scientific literature scarcely addresses the challenge of using social media data for credit scoring. Several companies provide commercial credit scoring service (partially) based on social media exist (e.g. Lenddo or Kabbage), but the nature and performance of their methods are concealed for obvious commercial reasons. In practice, best practices on how to use social media data in credit scoring are, to date, not yet set.

In this paper, we investigate how credit scoring for SMEs can make use of social media as part of a *default prediction* model. The main contributions of this work can be summarized as follows:

1. **Social media as an additional data source**. We investigate the use of social media data from Facebook as an additional source of data for building the credit scoring model. We show the techniques used to collect and process such data. We also present how features can be extracted from such unstructured data source which can be useful for the credit scoring model.
2. **A fuzzy matching method to retrieve social media ID**. We present a technique to improve the veracity of data collected from the social media. We can search the social media ID using some basic information but some irrelevant result may appear. We apply similarity-based instance matching to improve the quality of search result.
3. **Analysis of social media features influencing SME credit scoring**. We further analyze the impact of social media features on the performance of a credit *default prediction* model. There may be some distinct characteristics that make a SME more riskier than the others. In this research, we investigate which social media features relate to an SME's probability of default.

In the next section we summarise literature related to credit scoring and the use of social media metrics in business related topics. Then we present our data collection methods, where we describe how data is collected from different sources, including data acquisition from social media and public websites. The following section, introduces the credit scoring framework that we use to develop SME credit scoring. Finally, we present a detailed analysis of our results.

2   Related Work

2.1   Credit Scoring Models for SMEs

The term credit scoring originates from the banking industry, where it is used to denote methods to evaluate the creditworthiness of the potential borrowers. It has been popularly used in the context of large companies and consumer lending. However, it was only recently adopted to assess credit worthiness of SMEs. SMEs exhibit distinct characteristics as compared to consumer or large firms lending. Hence, creditors need to build models specifically designed for SMEs. Given its business relevance, it is no surprise that the development of models specifically for SMEs has attracted attention from scholars and practitioners. Those studies differ in the features associated with the credit default and the techniques used for building the scoring model. In this subsection, we will explore recent studies and highlight the features and techniques popularly used to develop credit scoring model for SMEs.

The majority of the credit scoring models designed for SMEs are variations of the techniques designed for consumer lending and large corporate lending. Discriminant analysis is one of the earlier works and popularly used for several years for credit scoring for SMEs.

Edmister [14] proposed one of the earliest works for predicting default of small businesses. He examined the predictive power of 19 financial ratios, and proposed a discriminant function which showed the effectiveness of financial ratios for predicting SME bankruptcy. On the other hand, the use of many financial ratios in the discriminant function affected the stability of the model. Edward Altman proposed a framework using Multivariate Discriminant Analysis (MDA) for predicting corporate bankruptcy. The discriminant function is showed to be very accurate in distinguishing between bankrupt and healthy companies. Even though the original work was designed specifically for medium and large company, several years later Altman [1] extended this work by building a specific model for SMEs, known as Z"-score This model uses only 4 financial ratios derived from accounting data. Because of its simplicity and stability, it is still popularly used for credit scoring of SMEs.

In [6], authors proposed credit scoring models for SMEs using three different machine learning algorithms and adding non-financial features. Their paper aimed to identify important features for small business. Their results suggest the effectiveness entrepreneur's personal and business characteristics in addition to the credit characteristic for SME credit scoring. Some of the non-financial features used in their work are: owner's age, occupation, amount, loan duration, interest rate, repayment method, location and sector.

Sohn et al. [28] built a logistic regression based model for technology based firms, where they assessed several attributes. Some of the useful non-financial features in their work are: knowledge management, technology experience, technology commercialization potential, product competitiveness etc. The outcome of their work is a robust classification model with high precision and recall. Altman et al. [4] combined non-financial features with financial features for SMEs which have insufficient financial information. The inclusion of non-financial features is reported to improve the prediction accuracy of the model by up to 13%. Pederzoli et al. [26] were the first to combine innovation-related features, i.e R&D productivity and value of the patent, with financial features to predict the default event on SME lending. Their research shows that combining innovation related features to the financial data can increase the accuracy of the model by 4.5%. Ciampi et al. [10] implemented SME credit scoring model by combining the geographical area, business sector and the size of SMEs with the financial features. They show that size, business sector, and geographical area are influential for credit scoring of SMEs. A credit risk assessment technique using both financial and non-financial features is also presented by [18]. Their results show that the use of non-financial features (e.g. size of company, ownership structure and corporate banking relationship duration) significantly improved the performance of their credit scoring model. Finally, Lee et al. [19] proposed an accounting ethics-based model which is said to reduce the default rate resulting from the moral hazard associated with unethical accounting behaviors.

Logistic regression has been conventionally used in many studies for credit scoring. It is preferred over other methods mainly because of its computational efficiency and interpretability. Altman et al. [3] used logistic regression to build SME default prediction model based on a set of financial ratios and proved its superiority to MDA.

Recently, more complex machine learning techniques such as support vector machines (SVM), decision trees, and artificial neural networks (ANN) have also been adopted for SME credit scoring. Ciampi et al. [10] implemented a model using various machine learning techniques, including Artificial Neural Networks. Bastos [30] evaluated a credit scoring models based on a variant of gradient boosting machine, extreme gradient boosting (XGBoost), across five credit datasets. The proposed XGBoost-based model achieves promising performances by producing high accuracy in all of the datasets used.

One of the main challenges in credit scoring modeling is class imbalance. Marques et al. [20] tackle this problem using re-sampling techniques to balance the number of samples before applying logistic regression algorithm to build the model. Their research proposed seven re-sampling algorithms, including various under-sampling and over-sampling techniques, such as One-Sided Selection (OSS), Neighborhood CLeaning rule (NCL), random under-sampling (RUS), under-Sampling Based on Clustering (SBC), random over-sampling (ROS), Synthetic Minority Over-sampling TEchnique (SMOTE), Safe-Level SMOTE, and combination of SMOTE and data cleaning, called SMOTE+WE. The experimental results demonstrate that in general, over-sampling techniques perform better than any under-sampling approach with the SMOTE+WE top the result. Brown et al. [9] showed that random forest and gradient boosting trees are better at dealing with class imbalance problems.

2.2   Use of Social Media Data in Credit Scoring

Oztamur et al. [25] analyzed the role of social media for SMEs from the perspective of firm marketing performance. In this study, the number of likes and followers, richness of content, interaction with customers and the use of language from Facebook and Twitter are chosen as criteria to asses the performance of SMEs. Similarly in [12] and [13], authors investigated the potential of Facebook data for microfinance credit scoring. In [22], McCann et al. compiled the measurement of social media in mainstream academic literature and other business-oriented publications.

Masyutin et al. [21] used the data collected from VKontakte, Russia's most popular social media platform, to discriminate between the solvent and delinquent borrowers in personal lending. The research showed that social media data can effectively enrich the classical application of credit scoring. Tan et al. [29] proposed a social media based credit scoring model for microloans. The research shows that incorporating social network metrics can improve the repayment prediction by 18%.

Zhang et al. [32] constructed a consumer credit scoring model by fusing social media information collected from social platform PPDai with the information that are used in the credit scoring traditional model. The model proved able to catch 86.02% default customer with overall accuracy 84.86%. In [31], authors used data collected from largest social media from China i.e. Weibo for conducting online credit scoring.

Even though social media data has been extensively used in credit scoring for personal or consumer lending, it has never been used in the context of SMEs. In this paper, we utilize this additional source of information for credit scoring for SMEs. Furthermore, we analyze the impact of various social media features on credit default prediction for SMEs.

3   Data Collection

Data for this research was provided by Exact[1], a large software company based in the Netherlands. It consists of general information about 218,778 SMEs, including sector, company size, website, and chamber of commerce number, along with their financial administration data for the past 5 years. Most of the financial features were derived from this data. On the other hand, the dataset did not include non-financial data (and specifically social media data) or bankrupcy information. Thus, we had to devise a method to acquire this extra information from publicly available data sources.

3.1   Public Data

We enriched the data from Exact with public data mainly for two additional information: bankruptcy label and non-financial data. The *Dutch Chamber of Commerce website*[2] offers information related to all of the legal entities that participate in economic transactions in the Netherlands, including SMEs. We used it to complete and validate the SMEs basic information, i.e. name, address, website and Chamber of Commerce (KvK in Dutch) number. Especially the latter, was then used to collect bankruptcy, the extra information we needed.

Information related to bankruptcy status of businesses is available in some public websites, such as faillissementen.com, faillissementsdossier.nl and drimble.nl, which can be searched based on KvK number or company name.

---

[1] The information made available by Exact for this research is provided for use for this research only and under strict confidentiality.

[2] www.kvk.nl.

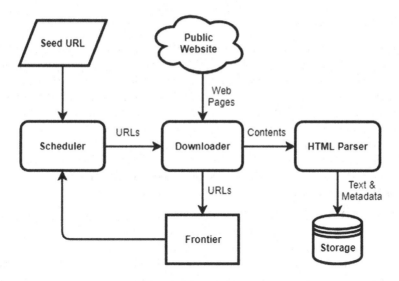

Fig. 1. Functional diagram of Web Scraper

To automatically collect bankruptcy information for over 200000 businesses in our initial dataset, we created a scraper that would use KvK number as an identifier to select the relevant SME. The architecture of our web scraper is illustrated in the Fig. 1 and explained below.

The scraping begins with a list of URLs called seed list. The URLs in seed list (**Seed URLs**) are constructed from the KvK number of the company of interest, and can be different for each public website. A **Scheduler** then handles the scraping strategy, choosing the URL from the queue to be sent to the **downloader** module.

The **downloader** module sends then the HTTP request to the website and retrieves the content of the HTML file, taking care of sessions, cookies and authentication, if needed. In this work, we use Selenium[3] as our HTML downloader. The HTML pages are then parsed via a python script based on the *Beautiful soup*[4] library, and the relevant information stored (in CSV format) in the designated **storage**.

Throughout the scraping, the **Frontier** module maintains the list of URLs discovered during the crawling process. Sometimes, the seed URL doesn't provide direct access to the desired information, and another hyperlink from the page needs to be accessed. Such URLs are stored by scrap frontier.

Using this method, we found that 217,280 out of 218,778 Dutch SMEs in our initial dataset have valid KvK numbers. From those with valid KvK numbers, 124,261 (57, 19%) have size information, 132,227 (60.85%) have sector information, 46,948 (21.61%) have website information, and 3264 (1.5%) have filed bankruptcy.

---

[3] https://www.seleniumhq.org/.
[4] https://pypi.org/project/beautifulsoup4/.

3.2 Social Media Data

Among the many social media platforms which contain information about SMEs, such as Facebook, LinkedIn, Twitter, Yelp etc, we decided to use Facebook for various reasons. Facebook is the most popular social media platform followed by LinkedIn and Twitter [23,27]. Moreover, it is the most popularly used platform for credit scoring and business performance evaluation in the literature. Facebook also allows companies to create their business page, which can be conveniently collected using Facebook's Graph API. However, for collecting data from Facebook's API, we need the username or user ID, information that is not present in our initial dataset. Hence, we obtained this information using the two methods described below.

Scraping SME's Website: Many SMEs report their social media account information in their website. Therefore, we scraped their websites to get their social media username or ID, specifically on Facebook: we could then easily parse the username or ID as the Facebook URL has specific pattern. In doing so, we considered the data trustworthy only if we got a one-to-one correspondence between the website information and the Facebook account, ultimately obtaining 17,866 Facebook accounts. One main limitation of this approach is that we could only obtain social media information for a subset of SME websites. However, for this subset we have high confidence on the correctness of SME Facebook account that we found.

Using Facebook Search API with Fuzzy Matching: To complement the previous approach and extend the dataset, we used Facebook's search API to search using the SME's name or brand name. Here the problem we had to tackle was that, often, the search result returned multiple accounts with similar names. Hence, we used a fuzzy matching technique to identify, among the many returned, the relevant social media account.

Our fuzzy matching technique is based on text similarity of name and address of the SMEs as per our initial dataset and those returned by the Facebook search API. To tune this fuzzy matching model, we used the knowledge of the unique SMEs-Facebook account pairs obtained from website scraping. We created two similarity features between the two texts (denoted as a and b in the following equations) comparing at token and phrase level, denoted as L_{phrase} and L_{token} respectively. They are computed as:

$$L_{phrase}(a, b) = 2 * M_{a,b}/(T_a + T_b) \tag{1}$$

$$L_{token}(a, b) = M_{a,b}/min(T_a, T_b) \tag{2}$$

Where M is the number of consecutive character matches and T is the total number of characters. We calculate both features for name and address. The probability of an item on search result to be relevant, denoted as $p(x, y)$, can be computed as the weighted combination of the similarity features as below:

$$p(x, y) = L_{phrase}(x_{name}, y_{name}) * w_{name,phrase}$$
$$+ L_{token}(x_{name}, y_{name}) * w_{name,token}$$
$$+ L_{phrase}(x_{address}, y_{address}) * w_{address,phrase} \quad (3)$$
$$+ L_{token}(x_{address}, y_{address}) * w_{name,address}$$

However, deciding the appropriate weights which can provide the best estimation for $p(x,y)$ is not trivial. Hence, we pose this as a classification problem. We try to predict whether a Facebook page from the list of multiple accounts is relevant or not. To train this prediction model, we use the SME-Facebook account pairs which we already collected from the first strategy. The prediction model can be used to identify the relevant Facebook pages. If there are multiple relevant pages returned from the classifier, we can use the class probabilities to chose the most relevant one.

Using this method, we are able to get additional 7,788 SMEs with Facebook accounts, which is 30.36% of our final dataset.

4 Credit Scoring Framework

This section presents the details of our credit scoring framework based on combination of traditional and social media data.

4.1 Feature Engineering

The first step of our framework is engineering features which are relevant for credit scoring of SMEs in terms of future bankruptcy.

Traditional Features: Traditional features include both financial and non-financial features. Here, we follow findings from literature: as financial features we also use financial ratios derived from accounting data, and we use business sector and size as non-financial features. All the traditional features used in our framework are listed in Table 1.

Social Media Features. Content generated by companies on their Facebook page is used to compute social media features. We use features proposed in earlier research, and we propose some new relevant ones. Features such as number of posts (photo and video) and days since last post are derived from [21]; so are number of story posts, number of days since last comment and number of days since the last visitor post.

Similarly, number of fans, number of mentions, rating volume and rating level, are derived from [24]. As suggested in [8], we use features such as average number and percentage of reactions, shares, and comments per post on the Facebook page. We adapt these features according to the new feature on Facebook with 6 possible reactions (like, love, haha, wow, sad and angry), dividing them into positive (like, love, haha and wow) and negative reactions (sad and angry). Along

Table 1. Traditional features for SME credit scoring

Name	Description
Equity	Book value of equity
Total assets (TA)	Total assets owned
Current assets	Assets that can be converted into cash within a year
Total liabilities (TL)	Total obligations and debts owned
Current liabilities (CL)	Obligations that are due within one year
Cost	Amount of money that has been used up to produce revenue
Tax	Amount of tax paid
Revenue	Amount of money received from the sold products
EBITDA	Earnings before interest, taxes, depreciation and amortization
EBIT	Earnings before interest and taxes
Net profit	Earnings after all of the expenses
Current ratio	Current assets/current liability
Quick ratio	Assets without inventory/current liability
Net margin	Net profit/revenue
EBIT margin	EBIT/revenue
Return on asset	Net profit/total assets
Debt ratio	Total liability/total assets
Debt-capital ratio	Total liability/(total liability+equity)
Sector	SMEs category based on SBI 2008
Size	Number of employees

those lines, we propose new features based on visitor posts such as number and percentage of positive and negative visitor posts. Additionally, we propose a set of features based on the trend of several activities. These features calculate the gradient of some features such as number of posts, shares and comments in the duration of six months. We calculate the trends of posts, shares, comments and reactions (both positive and negative). Table 2 lists all the social media features used in our experiments.

4.2   Model Development and Evaluation

Feature Selection. Feature selection is the process of selecting the subset of features most relevant for learning a model. In this project we perform feature selection in three steps. First, we screen out features with very low variance, weak predictive power, or seemingly illogical for the task at hand. Then we perform correlation based feature selection, where the correlation among the features is measured and one or more features are selected from the group of highly correlated features. Then we perform a recursive feature selection to finalize the set of most relevant features.

Table 2. Social media features for SME credit scoring

Feature name	Description
Fan Counts	Number of follower in Facebook
Talking About Count	Number of content which mention the page
Rating Count	Number of rating submitted
Overall star rating	Average rating submitted
Posts	Number of content created
Shares	Number of share in their posts
Comments	Average number of comments per posts
P reaction	Average number of positive reaction per post
N reaction	Average number of negative reaction per posts
Shared	Percentage of post which is shared
Commented	Percentage of post which has comments
P reacted	Percentage of post with positive reaction
N reacted	Percentage of post with negative reaction
Photo posts	Percentage of posts which contains photo
Video posts	Percentage of posts which contains type video
Story posts	Percentage of posts which contains text only
Visitor	Number of content created by others in the page
P vpost	Percentage of positive visitor posts
N vpost	Percentage of negative visitor posts
P comments	Percentage of positive comments in their posts
N comments	Percentage of negative comments in their posts
SL post	Number of day since their last post
SL visit	Number of day since last visitor post
SL comment	Number of day since last comments
t-posts	Trend of number of content created
t-shares	Trend of number of share in their posts
t-comments	Trend of average number of comments per posts
t-P reaction	Trend of average number of positive reaction
t-N reaction	Trend of average number of negative reaction
t-shared	Trend of percentage of post which is shared
t-commented	Trend of percentage of post which has comments
t-P reacted	Trend of percentage of post with positive reaction
t-N reacted	Trend of percentage of post with negative reaction
t-P comments	Trend of percentage of positive comments
t-N comments	Trend of percentage of negative comments

Handling Class Imbalance. To tackle the class imbalance problem, we use SMOTE+Tomek links algorithm, which is a variant of Synthetic Minority Over-sampling TEchnique (SMOTE) [17].

Classification Algorithms. In our experiments, we consider two most popularly used learning algorithms in the literature: Logistic Regression (LR) and xgboost. These two algorithms exhibit different characteristics; LR is a linear model whereas xgboost is gradient boosting based tree ensemble method. We don't consider Artificial Neural Networks (ANN) because of the structure nature of the data and the relatively limited size of the training set.

Evaluation Metrics. One of the main challenges in this work is to tackle the class imbalance inherent in the dataset. Hence, we choose evaluation metrics which work well in presence of class imbalance such as Area Under Curve (AUC) of ROC curve, F1-score, Matthews Correlation Coefficient (MCC), precision and recall. For the sake of completeness we also use accuracy, however, it is not very meaningful for imbalanced datasets.

5   Results and Discussion

5.1   Experimental Setup

Dataset. The final dataset used in our experiments consists of 25,654 SMEs, 194 of which filed for bankruptcy (0.756%). The significant drop in the number of SMEs is due the unavailability of social media data for many of the SMEs. Even though this dataset does not include all SMEs in the Netherlands, it is large enough to validate different approaches for this study.

Baselines. We compared the following models:

- Random Guess: randomly assign half of items to positive and the other half as negative.
- Weighted Guess: randomly assign x of items to positive, and the remaining $(1 - x)$ items to negative, where x is the ratio of positive samples.
- LR and XGBoost models using traditional features only denoted with a Traditional prefix in later parts of this paper.
- LR and XGBoost models using social media features only denoted with a SocMed prefix in the later parts of this paper.

We perform feature selection method as presented in the previous section to select the subset of most relevant features.

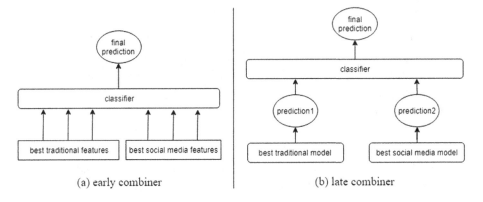

(a) early combiner   (b) late combiner

Fig. 2. The combined model

Combined Model. We experiment with different feature combination strategies for combining traditional and social media features. We use two methods to combine the features (Fig. 2):

- Early combining: we select the best features from the Traditional and SocMed models and train LR and XGB models. These models will be referred with a Early prefix in later parts of this paper.
- Late combining: we train a model on the output of the best performing models using traditional only and social media only features. The output used for training are bankruptcy prediction probabilities of the previous models. These models will be referred with a Late prefix in the later parts of this paper.

5.2 Experimental Results

Table 3 compares the performance of the 6 baseline and 4 proposed combined models. We can observe that performance of combined models are always superior to the baseline models for important metrics for imbalanced classification problem. Weighted Guess baseline has higher Accuracy as compared to others, but Accuracy is not a reliable metric for highly imbalanced datasets. Experiments show that using social media features alone doesn't perform well. However, when used in addition to the traditional features, they always provide additional information, hence resulting in an improved model.

We observe that early combined models always perform better than the late combined models. This is due to the fact that during early combining, we use both traditional and social media features together in the learning algorithm. Even though social media features are not sufficient themselves, when combined with traditional features, they enrich the learning process. However, for late combining model, we use class probabilities of models trained separately on traditional and social media features. Since the probability scores estimated by model based on social media features is very weak compared to the one based

Table 3. Performance of model developed using traditional features

Model	AUC	Accuracy	F1-score	MCC	Precision	Recall
Random Guess	0.50	0.50	0.01	0	0.01	0.50
Weighted Guess	0.50	**0.98**	0.01	0	0.01	0.01
Traditional, LR	0.70	**0.98**	0.09	0.08	0.07	0.11
Traditional, XGB	0.80	0.97	0.12	0.13	0.08	0.25
SocMed, LR	0.66	0.87	0.03	0.04	0.02	0.28
SocMed, XGB	0.68	**0.98**	0.04	0.03	0.04	0.04
Early, LR	0.75	0.96	0.10	0.12	0.06	**0.30**
Early, XGB	**0.83**	**0.98**	**0.15**	**0.15**	**0.12**	0.22
Late, LR	0.73	**0.98**	0.09	0.09	0.08	0.13
Late, XGB	0.81	0.97	0.14	0.15	0.10	0.26

on traditional features, combining them in late combiner results in an inferior model.

Moreover, among the early combined models, the model based on XGBoost performs better for most the metrics. Hence, in the following section we will analyze the most important features for the combined model based on early combining and using XGBoost algorithm.

5.3 Feature Analysis

Figure 3 shows the importance of various features in the combined model. As also stated in the literature, we also observed that Cost, EBIT, Total Assets, debt to capital ratio and liabilities (current and total) are important indicators for SME bankruptcy.

Whereas among the social media features, time since last post (SL_post) is the most influential factor for predicting bankruptcy followed by total number of followers (fan_count). This is very reasonable because time since last post indicates the activeness of the SMEs on social media. Usually, SMEs doing well in business and well engaged with their customers will be more active on social media and vice versa. Similar results were reported in [25] too. Similarly, the number of followers (fan_count) is established as another important feature. This is because the number of followers on Facebook indicates the popularity of the SME. Hence, this is a major indicator of how prone the business is for bankruptcy.

Number of content mentioning the page (talking about count) and number of days since last visitor (SL_visit) were also influential factors in the model. It was also self-evident as these features indicate the popularity and activeness of the SMEs which in-turn are directly correlated with possible bankruptcy.

Additionally, one of the trend features proposed in this work i.e. trend in number of shares in the post (t-shared), was particularly important for the model.

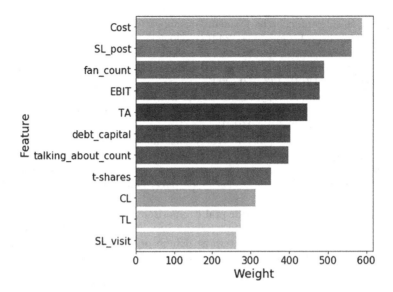

Fig. 3. Features used in early combining XGBoost model

Hence, the experiments confirmed the importance of the social media features used in literature for default prediction in the context of SMEs as well.

6   Conclusion

We presented a new method for SME credit scoring in terms of future bankruptcy prediction by combining social media features extracted from the data collected from Facebook with traditional financial and non-financial features. Moreover, we proposed a fuzzy matching based technique to improve the quality of data collected from Facebook. The experimental results suggest the superiority of this combined model as compared to the existing baselines which only take into account traditional features. Additionally, We present a detailed analysis of the results and especially focusing on the influence of social media features for default prediction.

References

1. Altman, E.I.: An emerging market credit scoring system for corporate bonds. Emerg. Markets Rev. **6**(4), 311–323 (2005)
2. Altman, E.I., Esentato, M., Sabato, G.: Assessing the credit worthiness of Italian SMEs and mini-bond issuers. Glob. Finance J. (2018)
3. Altman, E.I., Sabato, G.: Modelling credit risk for SMEs: evidence from the US market. Abacus **43**(3), 332–357 (2007)
4. Altman, E.I., Sabato, G., Wilson, N.: The value of non-financial information in small and medium-sized enterprise risk management. J. Credit Risk **6**(2), 1–33 (2010)

5. Angilella, S., Mazzù, S.: The financing of innovative SMEs: a multicriteria credit rating model. Eur. J. Oper. Res. **244**(2), 540–554 (2015)

6. Bensic, M., Sarlija, N., Zekic-Susac, M.: Modelling small-business credit scoring by using logistic regression, neural networks and decision trees. Intell. Syst. Acc. Finance Manag. **13**(3), 133–150 (2005)

7. Bocconi, S., Bozzon, A., Psyllidis, A., Titos Bolivar, C., Houben, G.J.: Social glass: a platform for urban analytics and decision-making through heterogeneous social data. In: Proceedings of the 24th International Conference on World Wide Web. WWW 2015 Companion, pp. 175–178. Association for Computing Machinery, New York, NY (2015). https://doi.org/10.1145/2740908.2742826

8. Bonsón, E., Ratkai, M.: A set of metrics to assess stakeholder engagement and social legitimacy on a corporate Facebook page. Online Inf. Rev. **37**(5), 787–803 (2013)

9. Brown, I., Mues, C.: An experimental comparison of classification algorithms for imbalanced credit scoring data sets. Expert Syst. Appl. **39**(3), 3446–3453 (2012)

10. Ciampi, F., Gordini, N.: Small enterprise default prediction modeling through artificial neural networks: an empirical analysis of Italian small enterprises. J. Small Bus. Manag. **51**(1), 23–45 (2013)

11. European Commission: 2018 SBA fact sheet Netherlands. European Commission (2018)

12. De Cnudde, S., Moeyersoms, J., Stankova, M., Tobback, E., Javaly, V., Martens, D.: Who cares about your Facebook friends? Credit scoring for microfinance (2015)

13. De Cnudde, S., Moeyersoms, J., Stankova, M., Tobback, E., Javaly, V., Martens, D.: What does your Facebook profile reveal about your creditworthiness? Using alternative data for microfinance. J. Oper. Res. Soc. **70**(3), 353–363 (2019)

14. Edmister, R.O.: An empirical test of financial ratio analysis for small business failure prediction. J. Finan. Quant. Anal. **7**(2), 1477–1493 (1972)

15. Feldman, R.J.: Small business loans, small banks and big change in technology called credit scoring. Reg. (Sep), 19–25 (1997)

16. Fridson, M.S., Alvarez, F.: Financial Statement Analysis: A Practitioner's Guide, vol. 597. Wiley, Hoboken (2011)

17. He, H., Garcia, E.A.: Learning from imbalanced data. IEEE Trans. Knowl. Data Eng. **9**, 1263–1284 (2008)

18. Khemakhem, S., Boujelbene, Y.: Predicting credit risk on the basis of financial and non-financial variables and data mining. Rev. Acc. Finance **17**(3), 316–340 (2018)

19. Lee, B.K., Sohn, S.Y.: A credit scoring model for SMEs based on accounting ethics. Sustainability **9**(9), 1588 (2017)

20. Marqués, A.I., García, V., Sánchez, J.S.: On the suitability of resampling techniques for the class imbalance problem in credit scoring. J. Oper. Res. Soc. **64**(7), 1060–1070 (2013)

21. Masyutin, A.: Credit scoring based on social network data. Bus. Inform. **3**(33), 15–23 (2015)

22. McCann, M., Barlow, A.: Use and measurement of social media for SMEs. J. Small Bus. Enterp. Dev. **22**(2), 273–287 (2015)

23. Michaelidou, N., Siamagka, N.T., Christodoulides, G.: Usage, barriers and measurement of social media marketing: an exploratory investigation of small and medium B2B brands. Ind. Mark. Manag. **40**(7), 1153–1159 (2011)

24. Neiger, B.L., et al.: Use of social media in health promotion: purposes, key performance indicators, and evaluation metrics. Health Promot. Pract. **13**(2), 159–164 (2012)

25. Öztamur, D., Karakadılar, İ.S.: Exploring the role of social media for SMEs: as a new marketing strategy tool for the firm performance perspective. Procedia-Soc. Behav. Sci. **150**, 511–520 (2014)

26. Pederzoli, C., Thoma, G., Torricelli, C.: Modelling credit risk for innovative smes: the role of innovation measures. J. Financ. Serv. Res. **44**(1), 111–129 (2013). https://doi.org/10.1007/s10693-012-0152-0

27. Silvestri, G., Yang, J., Bozzon, A., Tagarelli, A.: Linking accounts across social networks: the case of StackOverflow, Github and Twitter. In: Armano, G., Bozzon, A., Giuliani, A. (eds.) Proceedings of the 1st International Workshop on Knowledge Discovery on the WEB, KDWeb 2015, Cagliari, Italy, 3–5 September 2015, vol. 1489, pp. 41–52. CEUR-WS.org (2015). http://ceur-ws.org/Vol-1489/paper-05.pdf

28. Sohn, S.Y., Moon, T.H., Kim, S.: Improved technology scoring model for credit guarantee fund. Expert Syst. Appl. **28**(2), 327–331 (2005)

29. Tan, T., Phan, T.: Social media-driven credit scoring: the predictive value of social structures (2016)

30. Xia, Y., Liu, C., Li, Y., Liu, N.: A boosted decision tree approach using Bayesian hyper-parameter optimization for credit scoring. Expert Syst. Appl. **78**, 225–241 (2017)

31. Yuan, H., Lau, R.Y., Xu, W., Pan, Z., Wong, M.C.: Mining individuals' behavior patterns from social media for enhancing online credit scoring. In: PACIS, p. 163 (2018)

32. Zhang, Y., Jia, H., Diao, Y., Hai, M., Li, H.: Research on credit scoring by fusing social media information in online peer-to-peer lending. Procedia Comput. Sci. **91**, 168–174 (2016)

33. Zhu, Y., Zhou, L., Xie, C., Wang, G.J., Nguyen, T.V.: Forecasting SMEs' credit risk in supply chain finance with an enhanced hybrid ensemble machine learning approach. Int. J. Prod. Econ. **211**, 22–33 (2019)

Who's Behind That Website? Classifying Websites by the Degree of Commercial Intent

Michael Färber[1(✉)] [ID], Benjamin Scheer[2], and Frederic Bartscherer[1]

[1] Karlsruhe Institute of Technology (KIT), Karlsruhe, Germany
michael.faerber@kit.edu
[2] 1&1 IONOS SE, Karlsruhe, Germany
benjaminscheer.bs@googlemail.com

Abstract. Web hosting companies strive to provide customised customer services and want to know the commercial intent of a website. Whether a website is run by an individual person, a company, a nonprofit organisation, or a public institution constitutes a great challenge in website classification as website content might be sparse. In this paper, we present a novel approach for determining the commercial intent of websites by using both supervised and unsupervised machine learning algorithms. Based on a large real-world data set, we evaluate our model with respect to its effectiveness and efficiency and observe the best performance with a multilayer perceptron.

Keywords: Document classification · Web · Text mining · Machine learning

1 Introduction

Web hosting companies, such as 1&1 IONOS,[1] GoDaddy, and HostGator provide hosting services to millions of users ranging from individuals and non-profit organisations with no or little commercial intent to businesses with clear commercial intent. Apart from the size of the contract, web hosting companies are interested in cross-selling paid services with individual recommendations, such as SSL certificates or marketing services.

Websites can be clustered automatically given the readily available information on websites. Specifically, website classification can be considered as a document classification task, for which numerous methods have been proposed. However, no approach has been proposed to identify the commercial intent of websites on a large scale. In particular, applying document classification methods to websites is challenging as websites might have few words and coherent text structure compared to news articles, Wikipedia articles or research papers.

---

[1] This work was carried out in cooperation with the web hosting company 1&1 IONOS.

© Springer Nature Switzerland AG 2020
M. Bielikova et al. (Eds.): ICWE 2020, LNCS 12128, pp. 130–145, 2020.
https://doi.org/10.1007/978-3-030-50578-3_10

In this paper, we propose a novel approach to categorise websites based on its textual content into one of the following classes: *profit-oriented company, non-profit organisation, private website,* and *public institution.* To the best of our knowledge, our approach is the first one which can identify the commercial intent of websites on a large scale and, thus, is particularly useful for web hosting companies that want to improve their customer experience. Based on a large data set covering over 30,000 websites, we apply both supervised and unsupervised machine learning methods and evaluate them with respect to effectiveness and efficiency.

Overall, our main contributions are as follows:

- We propose a new classification schema for commercial intent that applies to any website.
- We present several machine-learning-based methods for content-based website classification.
- We evaluate our approaches with a large data set of 30,000 websites in the German language.
- We publish both implementation and data sets for subsequent research.[2]

The remainder of the paper is structured as follows: In Sect. 2, we give an overview of related works and argue for an approach based on the commercial intent. In Sect. 3, we introduce our classification schema, followed by describing the data preparation steps and evaluation data set in Sect. 4. Our applied approach and the evaluation results can be found in Sect. 5. Finally, we conclude the paper with an outlook in Sect. 6.

2   Related Works

Previous works differ either in the domain and used categories for website classification or in the used machine-learning-based approaches. In the following, we provide a detailed overview of *website classification schemas* and *website classification methods.*

Website Classification Schemas. Lindemann and Littig [1] identified a limited set of website categories by analysing textual data present on websites. They derived the following categories for websites by applying a task-specific algorithm: *academic, blog, community, corporate, information, nonprofit, personal,* and *shop.* This classification schema partly overlaps with the classes introduced in this paper. In contrast, we propose readily available, general-purpose approaches for website classification.

Thapa et al. [2] introduced the four non-topical categories *public, private, non-profit and commercial franchise* in the food domain. Although the four classes are similar to our classification schema, we follow a cross-domain approach that is applicable to the entirety of the web.

---

[2] See https://github.com/michaelfaerber/website-classification/.

Kanaris and Stamatatos [3] used seven categories for classifying websites: *blog, e-shop, FAQs, online newspaper, listings, personal home page*, and *search page*. However, these labels only describe some elements of a website and are not designated to indicate the commercial intent. For instance, blogs can be run in a *commercial* and *non-commercial context*. Furthermore, other important categories such as *corporate websites* are not included in this schema. The proposed categories might be sufficient for a benchmark data set, but cannot be used to categorise all websites on the web.

Meyer zu Eissen and Stein [4] used eight categories for website classification, such as *help, article, shop* and *non-private portrayal*. Note, that the categories are not driven by commercial intent. For instance, *non-private portrayal* contains websites of businesses and non-profit organisations.

Website Classification Methods. Bruni and Bianchi [5] applied machine-learning-based approaches to identify the commercial intent of websites. For each website, they aggregated multiple web pages into a single document for document classification and applied support-vector machines and random forests. Although similar to our approach, the scope is limited to a binary classifier for the e-commerce domain determining whether a website offers goods and services or not.

Studies using support-vector machines have been carried out by Sun et al. [6] in the academic domain and by Thapa et al. [2] in the food domain. The latter consider multi-label classification on a small balanced data set with about 100 websites. In contrast, we follow a single-label approach on a large data set and analyse the results of multiple machine-learning algorithms and imbalanced training data sets.

Sahid et al. [7] compared various algorithms for the task of website classification as well as different ways to weigh the given input texts. Specifically, they analysed the performance of Naive-Bayes, support-vector machines and multi-layer perceptrons for classifying the industry of e-commerce websites.

AbdulHussien [8] studied the suitability of random forests for website classification of health websites and provided an outlook of the potential benefits of neural networks. Note, that we do not use stemming in data preparation due to potential information loss. Xhemali et al. [9] explore the benefits of neural networks for website classification of training course websites and compare the results with other machine learning algorithms, such as Naive-Bayes and decision trees.

3   Website Categories

In this paper, we propose the following four categories for website classification having a distinct level of commercial intent. We argue that this classification is sufficient to categorise the entirety of the web.

Profit-Oriented Company. *(commercial intent: high)* A company or business is an economic, financial and legal entity acting according to economic principles. Their goal is to realise financial gain; as such, they are also referred to

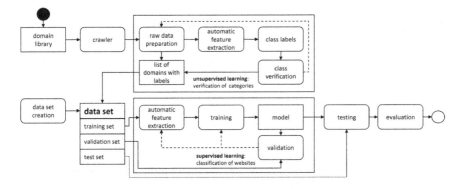

Fig. 1. Process of website classification

as for-profit organisations (FPO). Example websites are fahrschuleanik.de and dietz-fruchtsaefte.de.

Public Institutions. *(commercial intent: medium)* Public institutions are established on the basis of public law. Websites from public institutions include pages operated by federal and state governments as well as public institutions, municipalities, universities or state schools. Example websites are kit.edu and stuttgart.de.

Non-profit Organisation. *(commercial intent: low)* Following the notion of the *International Classification of Nonprofit Organisations* [10], a standard to classify non-profit organisations (NPO), an NPO fulfills the following criteria: (1) organised, (2) private, (3) self-governing, (4) non-profit-distributing, (5) voluntary. Example websites are tc-mudau.de and adac.de.

Private Websites. *(commercial intent: none)* A private website usually follows a private objective of an individual without commercial intent. Although the boundaries to other categories are sometimes ambiguous, we define a private website according to the following criteria: (1) No paid advertisement, such as Amazon affiliate links (2) No contact information or imprint, as this is required by law for German websites (3) The site is operated by an individual or a group of individuals. Example websites are fester.de and edithundsven.de.

4   Data Sets and Feature Extraction

In the following, we describe our data set, the required data preparation steps, and the feature extraction methods. Given an imbalanced distribution of classes, we consider three different training data sets and experiment with multiple feature extraction methods. An overview of the entire process, including training and testing, is provided in Fig. 1.

Data Sources. We start with a collection of websites, the *domain library*, consisting of two subsets: (1) The *directory-based subset* contains websites that are labelled automatically according to the type of directory and the information

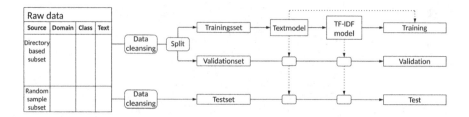

Fig. 2. Data preparation steps

provided by the directory. As the directory listings might not match exactly and contain websites of multiple classes, the labels were reviewed manually to a large extent. The websites of all four categories are retrieved from relevant pages dedicated to German websites such as *DMOZ*,[3] *project Curlie*,[4] *NPO Manager*,[5] and *Schulliste*.[6] (2) We use the *random sample subset* as a test data set that consists of a random sample of 1,500 domains with the German top-level domain *.de*, whereof only websites with useful content are considered.[7] All in all, we keep 1,109 websites and label them manually.

Data Cleansing. For each website, we crawl up to 30 pages and extract the textual information into a single document[8]. We remove non-visible textual information such as HTML markups, as well as special characters, non-German letters and numbers. Furthermore, we omit documents with less than 100 characters, as they are mostly error and domain parking pages.

Class Distribution. As the performances of some classification algorithms require knowledge of the a priori probabilities of the classes, we analyse the distribution of our four classes. Based on our *random sample subset*, we extrapolate the distribution of classes to be 73.2% commercial, 16% non-commercial, 9.1% private and 1.7% public institutions. Given the sample size and a total of approximately 16 million .de domains registered at DENIC, we derived a confidence level of 99% and a standard deviation of 4%.

Training & Validation Data Sets. Due to the imbalance in the class distribution, we experiment with three different data sets as depicted in Fig. 2. An overview of the subsets is given in Table 1. Note, that each data set is split into training and validation set with a ratio of 3 : 1.

1. **Balanced Data Set.** Each class is weighted similarly.
2. **Distribution Data Set.** Each class is weighted according to the distribution of the *random sample subset*.

---

[3] https://dmoz-odp.org/World/Deutsch/, accessed on 2019-10-24.

[4] https://curlie.org/de/Gesellschaft/Menschen/Pers%C3%B6nliche_Homepages.

[5] http://www.npo-manager.de/vereine/, accessed on 2019-10-24.

[6] http://www.schulliste.eu/, accessed on 2019-10-24.

[7] We remove unavailable domains or domain parking pages, i.e., websites with default content provided by the domain name registar.

[8] We consider only static visible textual information as input for classification, hence no HTML markups, meta tags or JavaScript.

Table 1. Absolute frequency of classes in the different data sets

Data set	Split	Comp.	NPO	Priv.	Publ.	Total
Full DS	Total	16,735	8,679	3,571	1,567	30,552
Balanced DS	Total	950	950	950	950	3,800
	Training	703	697	747	703	2,850
	Validation	247	253	203	247	950
Distribution DS	Total	10,450	1,306	2,283	239	14,278
	Training	7,827	966	1,740	175	10,708
	Validation	2,623	340	543	64	3,570
Quality DS	Total	2,100	1,500	1,500	930	6,030
	Training	1,600	1,000	1,000	600	4,200
	Validation	500	500	500	330	1,830
Test DS	Total	842	113	144	10	1,109

3. **Quality Data Set.** Similar to the distribution data set, but considering only documents whose class labels were reviewed manually.

Test Data Set. In all cases, the *random sample subset* is used as the test data set to establish a consistent basis for comparison.

Data Preparation Method. We analyse multiple feature extraction methods w.r.t. their suitability for website classification. The basis for all features are n-grams extracted from documents. We consider only n-grams that occur at least 1% and no more than 50% of the documents.

We consider the following *feature extraction methods*:

1. **Full Vocabulary without Weights.** We consider all words but stop words. Our list of stop words is based on the R package *stopwords* [11] for the German language that we extend by common words occurring in error messages, such as HTTP status codes.
2. **Full Vocabulary with Weights.** We consider all words and use weights based on tf-idf. We do not remove stopwords.
3. **Reduced Vocabulary with Weights.** We consider only the words of the 5,000 most frequent features and use weights based on tf-idf.
4. **1- & 2-grams with Weights.** We use n-grams with size 1 and 2 as features and use weights based on tf-idf.

Note, that *convolutional neural networks* follow a different approach. Instead of a bag-of-words representation, they are based on word embeddings. For our experiments, we choose a sequence length of 2,000 words and consider only the (i) 25,000 and (ii) 50,000 most common word embeddings of each data set.

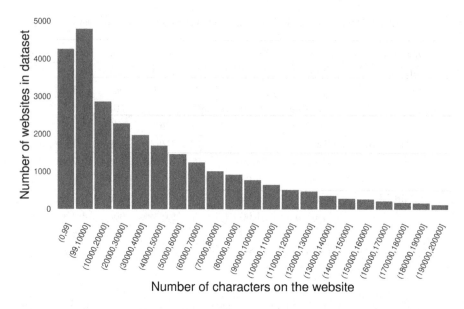

Fig. 3. Histogram of character count

Discussion. We publish the implementation and data sets online for subsequent research[9]. As shown in Table 1, the full data set contains 30,552 websites. The training and validation data sets are randomly chosen from the full data set and documents with less than 100 characters are omitted in the *data cleansing* step. The distribution of character counts is shown in Fig. 3.

5   Evaluation

5.1   Approach

As outlined in Table 2, 3, and 4, we use abbreviations to describe algorithms, data sets, and data preparation methods and introduce the following notation: $model_{training\ data\ set}^{preparation\ method}$. For instance, NB_B^T describes a Naive-Bayes classifier trained on the balanced data set with td-idf as feature weights.

5.2   Website Classification Using Unsupervised Algorithms

In Sect. 3, we argued that our four classes are sufficient to categorise the entirety of the web. Considering textual information, we show that unsupervised learning algorithms can distinguish these classes, too.

For a better visualisation, we analyse a subset of the *balanced data set* with *full vocabulary with weights* as the feature extraction method. For each class, we choose 300 documents and cluster them with the following methods:

---

[9] The data sets are freely available for research purposes at https://github.com/michaelfaerber/website-classification/.

Table 2. Abbreviations of algorithms

Abbrev.	Model
NB	Naive-Bayes
RF	random forest
GB	gradient boosting
SVO	support-vector machine one-versus-one
SVR	support-vector machine one-versus-rest
MP[i]	multilayer perceptron nr. i
CN[i]	convolutional neural network nr. i

Table 3. Abbreviations of data sets

Abbrev.	Training data
B	Balanced DS
D	Distribution DS
Q	Quality DS

Table 4. Abbreviations of preparation method

Abbreviation	Variant
U	Full vocabulary without weights
T	Full vocabulary with tf-idf weights
R	Reduced vocabulary (5,000 most popular words) with tf-idf weights
1G	Using 1-grams with tf-idf weights
2G	Using 2-grams with tf-idf weights
25k	Vocabulary with the 25,000 most popular word embeddings (CNN)
50k	Vocabulary with the 50,000 most popular word embeddings (CNN)

- **k-means** is often used for partitioning data. We set the number of clusters manually to $k = 4$ and achieved an accuracy of 0.65 and an $F1$-score of 0.64.
- **DIANA** is a hierarchical, divisive clustering algorithm. It achieved the best results with six clusters, consisting of four large clusters that represent our four classes. When we disregard the two small clusters, we achieve an accuracy of 0.71 and an $F1$-score of 0.71.

Both clustering methods confirmed that the introduced four classes can be found using unsupervised learning algorithms. We plot the data in Fig. 4 and conclude that, besides two negligible clusters (yellow and orange), the four classes are sufficient to classify the entirety of the web. Furthermore, we determine a strong overlap between company and private websites. The distinction between these classes turns out to be difficult using solely textual information. For instance, many of the red dots in the upper-right quadrant turn out to be private instead of company websites. As discussed in detail in Sec. 5.6 this is due to similar vocabulary in ambiguous cases, whereas a more distinctive vocabulary makes separation clearer for the other classes.

5.3   Evaluation Setup

In the following, we outline how we evaluated *seven machine learning methods* for website classification. We trained and evaluated all models using a server

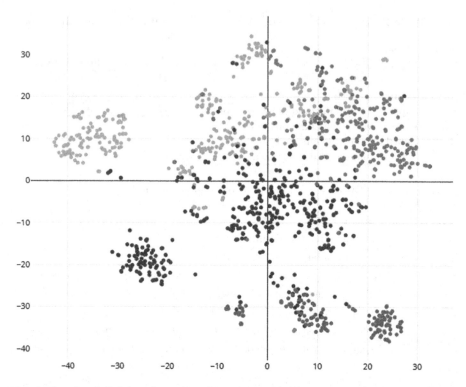

Fig. 4. Result of divisive clustering algorithm *DIANA*: company (red), NPO (blue), private websites (green), public institutions (purple) (Color figure online)

with 40 CPU cores, 565 GB RAM, Python 2.7 and R version 3.6. The training was conducted on a single GPU with 32 GB, model NVIDIA Tesla V100.

- **Guessing.** As a simple baseline, this method makes random guesses concerning the class assignment, using either the class distribution a priori or the most popular class as a fixed assignment.
- **Naive-Bayes.** We choose the Naive-Bayes classifier as one of our baselines.
- **Random Forest.** We use the R package *randomForest* with parameters $ntree = 500$ and $mtry = 150$, following the advice of Liaw & Wiener [12] for cases where only relevant features are to be found.
- **Gradient Boosting.** We use the R package *xgboost* with the booster *gblinear* and the parameters $n = 250$ and $k = 15$ for all models. All training was terminated before reaching *nrounds* rounds, when no improvements were observed. The standard value of $max.depth = 6$ was reduced in certain training variants and chosen between $[2 ; 6]$. The results show that model performance is affected by the composition of training data.
- **Support-vector Machine.** We run and evaluated both the SVM one-versus-one as well as SVM one-versus-rest variant using the R package *e1071*. A linear kernel and $cost = 200$ were used for all models.

- **Multilayer Perceptron.** We evaluated the following four MLP architectures:

  1. Two hidden layers with 10 neurons each.
  2. Two hidden layers with 30 and 15 neurons.
  3. Two hidden layers with 100 neurons each.
  4. Three hidden layers with 50, 10, and 50 neurons, i.e. the second layer acts as an artificial bottleneck.

  We chose *sigmoid function* for all hidden layers as it is suitable for text classification tasks and quick to calculate using backpropagation [13]. *Softmax* is used for all output layers. Due to the high dimensionality of our input, the highest amount of the neurons is located in the input layer. Therefore, most edge weights exist between input and the first hidden layer. During training, we used *Adam optimizer* [14] to achieve significantly faster run-times during training.

- **Convolutional Neural Network.** We evaluated the following two architectures, inspired by Chollet [15]: (i) Three convolutional layers with 128 filters each and kernel sizes of 3, 2 and 3. (ii) Two convolutional layers with a kernel size of 9. Both variants have an input layer of 2,000 neurons and a fully connected layer with 100 neurons feeding into an output layer with 4 neurons.

- Convolutional neural networks (CNN) do not use one-hot encoded inputs, but rather rely on vectorised contiguous text extracts of the same length (2,000 words in our case). The vectors are created using *fastText embeddings* [16]. A longer vector increases the number of trainable parameters drastically and may lead to *overfitting* and *longer training times*. Thus, we analyse whether a shallow CNN with a larger context window, i.e. kernel size, will lead to performance increases and reduced overfitting.

5.4   Evaluation Results

In the following, we present our evaluation results.[10]

Guessing. A simple classifier always guessing the most popular class achieves with 10.000 guesses an accuracy of 0.76 and a macro-F1 score of 0.215 on the test data set, representing the relative frequency of the company class. Another classifier that considers the class distributions for guessing achieves a lower accuracy of 0.60 and a macro-F1 score of 0.25. This shows, that the performance of guessing is highly dependent on the class distribution in the test data set.

Naive-Bayes. The results underline the dependence of performance on the training data. We achieve the best results using the balanced or (rather balanced) quality data sets with an accuracy of at least 0.72. The results using the (imbalanced) distribution data set were significantly lower.

The best performing model was NB_Q^R, with the highest micro-F1 score of 0.78 and the highest macro-F1 score of 0.57 as well as the second-highest accuracy

---

[10] We published the confusion matrices for each model at https://github.com/michaelfaerber/website-classification/.

Table 5. Overview of the best models for each MLP architecture

Model	Accuracy	Macro-F1	Micro-F1
$MP1_D^T$	0.866	0.689	0.870
$MP2_D^T$	0.861	0.679	0.867
$MP3_D^R$	0.849	0.676	0.855
$MP4_D^T$	0.861	0.710	0.869

of 0.75. Predictions for the classes companies and NPO were notably accurate with a score of 0.94 and 0.7, respectively.

Random Forest. In contrast to Naive-Bayes, we achieved the lowest scores with the balanced data set, whereas the model RF_Q^R achieved the highest score. The classes company and NPO are labelled with an accuracy of 0.94 and 0.86, respectively. The overall accuracy of 0.84 outperforms the Naive-Bayes classifier. Note, that the RF_D models could not label a single website of the class public institutions, possibly due to insufficient training data in the distributed data set.

A deeper look at the decision trees of each model shows that most private websites are classified following the exclusion principle, i.e. the trees split on words that are distinctive for a class. If none of the splits apply, the document is classified as a private website. This explains why even the best random forest models perform poorly classifying private websites.

Gradient Boosting. The best gradient boosting model (GB_Q^R) is trained using the quality set with the reduced weighted vocabulary (accuracy: 0.82, macro-F1: 0.66, micro-F1: 0.83). Similar to previous models, the distinction between private and company websites proves to be a difficult task. More than half of the websites classified as private are websites of companies or NPOs.

Support-vector Machine. The models SVO_D^T and SVR_D^T (accuracy: 0.86, macro-F1: 0.68, micro-F1: 0.86) achieve the best scores on the distribution data set and thus are chosen as best-performing variants. The difference between both models is marginal.

The output of an SVM using one-versus-rest can be interpreted as the confidence score of a class label. With this, we were able to analyse the effects of various thresholds for confidence values. Figure 5 shows the relationship between a given threshold, accuracy, and percentage of classified websites. About half of the websites can be classified with a threshold of 0.94, increasing the accuracy to 0.97. The idea behind this analysis reflects real-world settings, where particular difficult websites might be labelled manually.

Multilayer Perceptron. A summary of the best performing models for all four architectures is presented in Table 5, with the best overall model being $MP1_D^T$, achieving the highest accuracy and micro-F1 score.

Models trained on the quality and distribution data set achieve similar results, though no variant performs best in all metrics. As the largest data set

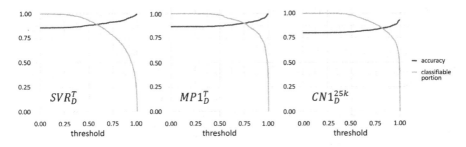

Fig. 5. Accuracy and ratio of classifiable websites depending on threshold value for SVR_D^T, $MP1_D^T$ and $CN1_D^{25k}$.

D has slightly better results, we conclude that the size of the training data has a strong influence on the performance.

Similar to SVMs, we can interpret the output of each classification as a confidence score for classification and analyse the effect of a manual threshold (as depicted in Fig. 5) for model $MP1_D^T$. A threshold of 0.92 allows for 75% of websites to be classified, increasing the accuracy to 0.94. Note, that raising the threshold does not lead to all classes being omitted equally. For instance, classifications of the classes private, NPO and public institutions are discarded earlier than the class company due to their relative frequency. Therefore, when choosing the ideal threshold value, the distribution of classes must be considered.

Convolutional Neural Network. $CN1_D^{25k}$ is the best performing CNN variant and achieves an accuracy of 0.80 and a micro-F1 score of 0.80. It achieves a macro-F1 score of 0.55, the second-highest of all CNNs. The larger context window of the shallow CNN does not provide any improvement. This implies that classes are defined rather by individual words than longer coherent sentences.

The analysis of output thresholds for the best performing variant $CN1_D^{25k}$ is depicted in Fig. 5. Considering a threshold of 0.92 the model can classify 75% of all websites and achieves an accuracy of 0.87. With a threshold of 0.99, about half of all websites can be classified with accuracy increasing to 0.92.

5.5   Comparisons

In the following, the best performing models of each algorithm are compared according to accuracy, micro-F1 and macro-F1 scores as well as the run-times of training and classification. Afterwards, we will discuss the shortcomings and difficulties faced.

Effectiveness. A summary of the results can be found in Table 6.

We achieve the best evaluation results for classification using a multilayer perceptron with a simple architecture. Experiments with dropout layers did not improve the performance of our models. The model $MP1_D^T$ achieves the highest scores in all three metrics. Similar performances are achieved by the SVM

Table 6. Overview of the best performing models for each algorithm

Model	Accuracy	Macro-F1	Micro-F1
$\mathbf{MP1}_D^T$	**0.866**	**0.689**	**0.870**
$\mathbf{SVR}_D^T$	**0.857**	**0.678**	**0.861**
SVO_D^T	0.854	0.676	0.858
RF_Q^R	0.844	0.552	0.840
GB_Q^R	0.821	0.664	0.834
$CN1_D^{25k}$	0.796	0.550	0.797
NB_B^R	0.736	0.571	0.762
Guessing	0.759	0.216	0.655

Table 7. Overview of training and classification run-time

Model	Training (sec.)	Testing (sec.)
$\mathbf{MP1}_D^T$	**46.0**	**0.5**
$\mathbf{SVR}_D^T$	6,223.0	36.7
SVO_D^T	917.0	20.1
RF_Q^R	815.1	0.3
$\mathbf{GB}_Q^R$	**2.0**	**0.1**
$CN1_D^{25k}$	94.2	0.2
NB_B^R	2.0	65.4

with one-versus-rest implementation, achieving only insignificantly lower scores compared to the MLP.

The Naive-Bayes classifier achieves the worst performance in comparison, though no parameters need to be optimised. Furthermore, it only requires very few training data and features. On top of that, the algorithm works well with balanced data, meaning no previous knowledge of class distribution is necessary. The classifier is therefore useful for a first analysis to determine the suitability of machine-based classification for a specific domain.

Despite successes in the latest researches on text classification, our results with CNN and pre-trained word embeddings did not yield good results. Other algorithms consistently achieve higher accuracy and F1-scores under similar training conditions. We conclude that for our use case models benefit rather from finding meaningful keywords within the text than interpreting coherent sentences.

We achieved similar results to the work done by Lindemann and Littig [1]. They also had difficulties to distinguish private websites from the categories "blog"[11] and "corporate."[12] They achieved an accuracy of 0.84 and a micro-F1 score of 0.84, which we surpassed with our MLP as well as SVM approaches.

Thapa et al. [2] achieve the best results (macro-F1: 0.74, micro-F1: 0.73) with an SVM classifier and multi-label approach on a balanced data set with about 100 websites. Although they consider additional features such as structural information and URIs, our model $MP1_D^T$ using a simple multilayer perceptron architecture (macro-F1: 0.69, micro-F1: 0.87) shows that basic textual information as a feature is sufficient for comparable performance on a large, imbalanced data set.

As depicted in Fig. 5, the outputs of the models $MP1_D^T$, SVR_D^T and $CN1_D^{25k}$ can be interpreted as confidence scores and thus allow experimentation with threshold values for classification. The performance of our MLP can be improved to 0.94, whilst still able to classify 75% of websites.

---

[11] "Blogs" fall under the categories of *private* or *company* according to our defined classes from Sect. 3.

[12] This is a subset of our *company* class.

Efficiency. If a model is implemented in a real-world setting and productive system, regular retraining on large data sets is required. Therefore, training time is an important metric. Considering the hardware configuration described Sect. 5.3, an overview of the run-times of our implementations with average training and testing time of the best models is given in Table 7.

The training times of the SVMs and the random forests are noticeably high. The longer training time for SVR_D^T over SVO_D^T was unexpected because fewer SVMs need to be trained [17], though they were implemented differently (SVR_D^T as a wrapper and SVO_D^T using the R package *e1071*).

The gradient boosting models exhibit the fastest training and testing, though many more pairs of hyperparameters need to be evaluated beforehand to determine the optimal setup, which is not accounted for in pure run-time analysis.

The Naive-Bayes classifier is the only algorithm with a higher run-time during testing compared to training. Because of its slow classification, it is better suited for cases where only a few classifications need to be made like local spam filters that must be retrained every time a new pattern emerges.

We conclude that a multilayer perceptron with a bag of words approach is the most promising solution to the task of website classification. Besides the best results, MLPs have a short classification run-time which can be easily improved through parallel processing with multiple GPUs.

Feature Extraction Method. A comparison between the four proposed training sets shows that a prior weighting of features through tf-idf is the most reasonable approach. No model achieved the best performance using non-weighted features. The average accuracy of all models using non-weighted full vocabulary reached 0.777, whereas the average accuracy of all models using weighted full vocabulary reached 0.798. This confirms results achieved by Sahid et al. in which weighting through tf-idf proved to be superior to non-weighted input [7].

Furthermore, a smaller vocabulary does not seem to necessarily lower performance scores. This effect is especially prominent for Naive-Bayes, random forest, and gradient boosting, where reduced vocabularies lead to the best results. A size of 5,000 words proves to be sufficient for our task at hand. All models trained using reduced vocabularies reached an accuracy of 0.794 on average. Finally, using 2-grams instead of 1-grams did not increase performance in our case. All models using 2-grams averaged an accuracy score of 0.789.

5.6   Classification of Private Websites

Our evaluation shows that both supervised and unsupervised algorithms cannot distinguish easily between private websites and company websites because private websites sometimes use commercial vocabulary in a non-commercial context. For instance, websites of musicians might be labelled as a private website in case of a school band whereas the portrayal of a singer might have a clear commercial intent. In some cases, this might be a challenge even during manual labelling. We conclude that the diversity of private websites creates a large feature space, leading to many cases where private websites are not classified correctly. A solution for this might be a multi-label classification approach as described by Thapa et al. [2]. However, in our case, a single-label approach was chosen to clearly define a distinct business strategy for the web hosting company.

5.7 Main Findings

1. We showed that there are many websites containing only few words and that distinguishing between private and company classes is a non-trivial task. Therefore, robust methods are required for website classification.
2. Our four proposed categories proved to be sufficient to cover the entirety of the web. As each class can be mapped to a target audience, we provide a real-world application for web hosting companies for determining their relationship and communication strategy with their customers.
3. Our work with unsupervised learning algorithms confirms the existence of our four proposed clusters. As for supervised learning, an MLP with a simple two hidden layer architecture proved to be the most suitable model for the task. Although SVMs achieved similar results, MLPs have a short classification run-time and, in general, run-times can be improved easily by parallel processing with multiple GPUs.
4. CNNs did not deliver superior results as performance is influenced rather by individual words than by longer coherent sentences.

6   Conclusion and Outlook

In this paper, we proposed four categories that can be used for website classification of the entirety of the web. We implemented various unsupervised as well as supervised machine learning algorithms for the purpose of automatic website classification. Furthermore, we discussed the efficiency and effectiveness of each method in a real-world setting. All in all, we achieved the best performance (accuracy: 0.866, macro-F1: 0.689, micro-F1: 0.870) using a multilayer perceptron that was trained on a data set with real-world distribution of classes using tf-idf as feature weights.

Experiences and insights gathered from this work could be applied to classifying other document types, categorization schemas, and languages. However, language-specific features might influence results, such as the required declaration of legal forms in Germany. Subsequent research can use our published implementations and data sets and, besides textual content, might consider additional features to improve our results, such as URIs and images.

References

1. Lindemann, C., Littig, L.: Classification of web sites at super-genre level. In: Mehler, A., Sharoff, S., Santini, M. (eds.) Genres on the Web. Text, Speech and Language Technology, vol. 42, pp. 211–236. Springer, Dordrecht (2011). https://doi.org/10.1007/978-90-481-9178-9_10

2. Thapa, C., Zaiane, O., Rafiei, D., Sharma, A.M.: Classifying websites into non-topical categories. In: Cuzzocrea, A., Dayal, U. (eds.) DaWaK 2012. LNCS, vol. 7448, pp. 364–377. Springer, Heidelberg (2012). https://doi.org/10.1007/978-3-642-32584-7_30

3. Kanaris, I., Stamatatos, E.: Learning to recognize webpage genres. Inf. Process. Manag. 45(5), 499–512 (2009)

4. Meyer zu Eissen, S., Stein, B.: Genre classification of web pages. In: Biundo, S., Frühwirth, T., Palm, G. (eds.) KI 2004. LNCS (LNAI), vol. 3238, pp. 256–269. Springer, Heidelberg (2004). https://doi.org/10.1007/978-3-540-30221-6_20

5. Bruni, R., Bianchi, G., et al.: Robustness analysis of a website categorization procedure based on machine learning. Technical report n. 04–2018 DIAG (2018)

6. Sun, A., Lim, E., Ng, W.K.: Web classification using support vector machine. In: Proceedings of the Fourth ACM CIKM International Workshop on Web Information and Data Management. WIDM 2002, pp. 96–99 (2002)

7. Sahid, G.T., Mahendra, R., Budi, I.: E-commerce merchant classification using website information. In: Proceedings of the 9th International Conference on Web Intelligence, Mining and Semantics. WIMS 2019, pp. 5:1–5:10 (2019)

8. AbdulHussien, A.A.: Comparison of machine learning algorithms to classify web pages. Int. J. Adv. Comput. Sci. Appl. (IJACSA) 8(11), 205–209 (2017)

9. Xhemali, D., Hinde, C.J., Stone, R.G.: Naïve bayes vs. decision trees vs. neural networks in the classification of training web pages. Int. J. Comput. Sci. Issues 4(1), 16–23 (2009)

10. Salamon, L.M., Anheier, H.K.: The International Classification of Nonprofit Organizations. Jossey Bass Publishers, San Francisco (1996)

11. Benoit, K., Muhr, D., Watanabe, K.: Stopwords: Multilingual Stopword Lists. R package version 1.0 (2019)

12. Liaw, A., Wiener, M., et al.: Classification and regression by RandomForest. R News 2(3), 18–22 (2002)

13. Amajd, M., Kaimuldenov, Z., Voronkov, I.: Text classification with deep neural networks. In: International Conference on Actual Problems of System and Software Engineering (APSSE), pp. 364–370 (2017)

14. Kingma, D.P., Ba, J.: Adam: a method for stochastic optimization. In: Proceedings of the 3rd International Conference on Learning Representations. ICLR 2015 (2015)

15. Chollet, F.: Deep Learning with Python, 1st edn. Manning Publications Co., Greenwich (2017)

16. Grave, E., Bojanowski, P., Gupta, P., Joulin, A., Mikolov, T.: Learning word vectors for 157 languages. In: Proceedings of the International Conference on Language Resources and Evaluation (LREC 2018) (2018)

17. Bishop, C.M.: Pattern Recognition and Machine Learning. Information Science and Statistics. Springer, New York (2007)

I Don't Have That Much Data! Reusing User Behavior Models for Websites from Different Domains

Maxim Bakaev[1]([⊠]) [iD], Maximilian Speicher[2] [iD], Sebastian Heil[3] [iD], and Martin Gaedke[3] [iD]

[1] Novosibirsk State Technical University, Novosibirsk, Russia
bakaev@corp.nstu.ru
[2] C&A Europe, Düsseldorf, Germany
maximilian.speicher@canda.com
[3] Technische Universität Chemnitz, Chemnitz, Germany
{sebastian.heil,martin.gaedke}@informatik.tu-chemnitz.de

Abstract. User behavior models see increased usage in automated evaluation and design of user interfaces (UIs). Obtaining training data for the models is costly, since it generally requires the involvement of human subjects. For interaction's subjective quality parameters, like aesthetic impressions, it is even inevitable. In our paper, we study applicability of trained user behavior models between different domains of websites. We collected subjective assessments of Aesthetics, Complexity and Orderliness from 137 human participants for more than 3000 homepages from 7 domains, and used them to train 21 artificial neural network (ANN) models. The input neurons were 32 quantitative metrics obtained via computer vision-based analysis of the homepages screenshots. Then, we tested how well each ANN model can predict subjective assessments for websites from other domains, and correlated the changes in prediction accuracies with the pairwise distances between the domains. We found that the Complexity scale was rather domain-independent, whereas "foreign-domain" models for Aesthetics and Orderliness had on average greater prediction errors for other domains, by 60% and 45%, respectively. The results of our study provide web designers and engineers with a first framework to assess the reusability and difference in prediction accuracy of the models, for more informed decisions.

Keywords: Web design · User experience · Machine learning · Training data

1 Introduction

Even though the thorough evaluation of user interfaces (UIs) became widely popular already in the early 90 s (e.g. [1]), it has not ceased to be a hot topic. User interfaces are becoming increasingly complex and sophisticated, which a visit to the Internet Archive's Wayback Machine easily proves. This, however, also raises the complexity of setting up and analyzing corresponding assessments. Besides, certain methods for evaluation are

© Springer Nature Switzerland AG 2020
M. Bielikova et al. (Eds.): ICWE 2020, LNCS 12128, pp. 146–162, 2020.
https://doi.org/10.1007/978-3-030-50578-3_11

often considered costly and inefficient in the industry. Especially the ability to carry out user tests is limited by the available resources ([2, 3, p. 180]). In many cases, this leads to the application of simpler and faster methods, like A/B testing, which is, however, not perfectly suited for determining qualitative aspects such as the usability or user experience of an interface [4]. One alternative to traditional user testing that has been repeatedly suggested in the literature is to employ models that predict subjective quality parameters – like usability – from (a) static [5] or (b) visual [6] properties of a user interface, or (c) from tracked interactions [7, 8].

Why is (efficient) evaluation of UIs important? With today's plethora of available websites and apps, it is crucial to properly test them in order to gain user acceptance. Users spend most of their time on other websites and disapprove of usability and user experience flaws [9]. Now, the more efficient an evaluation method is, the fewer resources are required, both, time- and money-wise, which leads to easier stakeholder buy-in, particularly in industry settings (yet, effectiveness must not be traded for efficiency). On top, the more user-friendly the interface and the more resource-efficient its creation process, the more sustainable it becomes, which is a consideration becoming increasingly important nowadays [3].

What are the advantages of user behavior models? Leveraging user behavior models to predict subjective interaction quality parameters is a promising approach to effective evaluation that uses fewer resources than traditional methods. First, libraries such as MOA and scikit-learn are widely available and make training machine-learning models relatively easy. Second, once such models have been trained, they can be applied as many times as wanted, without lengthy testing sessions and the involvement of real users.

So, what is the problem? Even though user behavior models need to be trained only once, obtaining high-quality training data is often a problem and huge amounts of data might be needed to obtain well-working models (e.g., ~23 GB of raw tracking data in the case of [10]). Therefore, it would be worthwhile to reuse existing models for as many UIs as possible, hence reducing the need for collecting hard-to-obtain training data. Yet, Speicher et al. [8] hypothesized that such models are only applicable within clusters of very similarly structured websites (since user interactions seem to be very sensitive to low-level details of an interface). This is the very question we intend to investigate in this paper.

Based on a set of features that are potentially more robust than user interactions with an interface, we build artificial neural network models (ANNs) for websites from a certain domain and investigate how accurately they can predict subjective assessments for different domains. Overall, this paper makes the following contributions:

1. We train ANN models for 7 different domains of websites, based on subjective quality assessments from 137 users.
2. We show that these ANN models can to a certain degree predict subjective interaction quality parameters of websites from other domains.
3. We show that there is a connection between prediction accuracy and distance between website domains, and we propose the corresponding distance measure.

In Sect. 2, we overview related work, while in Sect. 3 we describe our experimental study. In Sect. 4, we analyze the data and propose the regression model that relates the models' prediction accuracies and the distances between the domains.

2 Related Work

User behavior models are considered effective in representing research results in HCI and a solid basis for software tools that support UI designers [11], particularly in the evaluation of web UI prototypes and designs. Generally, they predict an interaction quality parameter, based on two sets of input: target user characteristics and UI representation. Interaction models are built for particular tasks (more rarely, task specification can be part of the input), whereas user experience models, which are a rather novel research topic, are more inclined towards reflecting cognitive processes and neural structures.

Despite the increasing recognition, their use in practical Web Engineering so far remains limited, for which we see two main reasons. First, building and training a new model for a project context imposes high skill requirements: a software development team rarely includes a computer scientist, a cognitive psychologist, etc. Second, even though more and more models are made available, it remains unclear how granular the input needs to be, i.e., how much re-training is needed for another group of users or a changed UI.

The endeavor undertaken in this paper relates to the topic of transfer learning, which in practical ML sometimes is also called pre-training. According to [12], transfer learning takes place when the knowledge contained in an existing model for a task T1 in a given domain D1 supports the learning of a not yet existing model for a task T2 from a domain D2, whereas $D1 \neq D2$. While also $T1 \neq T2$, the tasks should be related [13], which is the case for predicting quality parameters for websites from different domains. However, our approach is more radical in the sense that we intend to directly apply the model for D1 to D2, rather than to support the learning of a new model. This corresponds to skipping the second step (fine training) in the utilization of pre-trained user behavior models, which means a trade-off: saving on training data, but losing on the evaluation model's accuracy.

2.1 AI in UI Evaluation and Design

Classifiers for predicting quality parameters of UIs used in existing research include Random Forests, Naïve Bayes, ANNs, and non-ML-based models, among others. For instance, [10] collected a number of user interactions (mostly mouse and scrolling behavior) on search engine results pages and trained models that were able to predict the relevance of search results better than a generative state-of-the-art approach. They used Random Forests as the classifier of their choice. However, their solution is restricted to a very specific type of webpage and a single quality parameter. In [8], they employ a similar, but extended approach by tracking a similar (but larger) set of user interactions and learning several models in parallel to predict 7 different usability parameters (according to the INUTT instrument). Their classifier of choice is an incremental version of Naïve Bayes.

Such models in the context of UI evaluation and design have certain advantages and disadvantages. On the one hand, it is very cumbersome for a developer or researcher to manually identify patterns in website structure or user interactions that correlate with certain quality parameters (such as, "Users that change scrolling direction at least twice rate a website as more confusing"). In [8], the authors have tried this, but the correlations they found are mostly rather low ($r < .3$) and derived from the models they learned. Discovering these connections is much easier for machine learning classifiers. On the other hand, the models trained by classifiers are mostly not human-interpretable and the models themselves remain a black box.

The work of Grigera et al. [7] builds on a non-ML approach. They identified patterns of user behavior that hint at certain "usability smells", e.g., "user clicks a link and returns shortly after" → misleading link, and implemented a finder for each smell. This is a robust, easily understandable approach that is applicable to a large range of websites, but limited by existing knowledge about user behavior, not easily adjustable, and might prevent the detection of new patterns beyond the perception of the developers. None of the research described above aims at applying their learned models to user interfaces from a different domain. In [8], they tried but concluded that if it is possible, it is at best possible for interfaces that are structurally very similar. The approach in [7] is applicable to a range of websites from different domains, but not based on machine-learning approaches. Therefore, a comparison with our work is out of scope in this regard.

Indeed, [8] partly inspired the topic of this paper since we hypothesize that with different, more robust input attributes, applying models across domains of websites could be possible. For this, we orient at [6], since global, visual features of websites are potentially not as prone to differences in structure as user interactions. Their work builds on static visual properties of websites – metrics, as obtained through a screenshot-processing visual analyzer – and ANNs to predict subjective quality assessments (e.g., perceived complexity of a website).

2.2 The UI Visual Analysis Tools

The more traditional approach for extracting quantitative metrics of UIs is based on the analysis of UI code or model representation. It boasts high performance and accuracy and is particularly suitable for web UIs whose HTML/CSS code is easily available [14]. Code-based analysis is widely used to check compliance with accessibility guidelines and other standards and recommendations but is less suited for the assessment of such a subjective thing as user experience. On the other hand, the increasingly popular UI vision-based analysis, which is based on image recognition techniques, generally deals with the screenshot of a webpage as rendered in a browser. The main advantage of this UI "visual analysis" approach is that it assesses the UI as the target user witnesses it, so it is naturally good at considering layouts, spatial properties of UI elements, graphical content, etc. For instance, in [15], the authors perform automated data extraction from images and make use of Gestalt principles of human visual perception – this understandably would be highly problematic to do with code analysis. At the same time, the disadvantages of the vision-based approach include computational expensiveness and so far low accuracy for some of the metrics.

In view of the abundance and diversity of metrics proposed by various researchers in the rapidly developing metrics-based UI analysis field, we have previously developed the WUI Measurement Integration Platform[1] [14]. It is capable of collecting web UI metrics from different providers and storing them in the common structured representation for further analysis. The platform sends a web UI screenshot or website URI to a remote service using its supported protocol, waits for the output (WebSocket is mostly used) and saves it in the platform's database. Currently, the platform works with the two main UI visual analysis tools, which we also use for the purposes of the current research:

1. Visual Analyzer (VA), developed by Technical University of Chemnitz (Germany) and Novosibirsk State Technical University (Russia) [14];
2. Aalto Interface Metrics service (AIM), by Aalto University (Finland)[2] [16].

The potential number of UI metrics that can be obtained via the vision-based analysis is understandably boundless (the two analyzers that we exploit for this work are just a small portion of the available tools). It thus seems logical to assume that, just like for the general image recognition techniques, artificial neural networks should be an appropriate modeling method.

2.3 ANNs in User Behavior Modeling

Lately, artificial neural networks are back in fashion, with the advent of deep learning in AI. They have reasonable computational cost but are known to be "hungry" for diverse data, so their practical use in the fields where training data are scarce is limited. User behavior modeling is somehow divided with respect to this since the abundance of data varies due to the exact interaction quality parameter being predicted and the corresponding input. Still, the relatively novel recurrent neural networks are used for modeling sequences of user behaviors and are being introduced to predicting behavior on the web. Particularly, in [17], they consider domain switch – where two successive behaviors belong to different domains, which in that work are understood as "service categories in a large-scale web service".

We can speculate that for predicting user experience (as reported by users in their subjective assessments, making the training data quite costly) there is no guarantee that ANNs would be the most accurate method. Or, at least, quite special architectures and approaches would need to be developed for each of the subjective impressions, which has actually been done, e.g., for aesthetics [18]. However, in our current work, we are going to employ rather unsophisticated ANNs, since our goal is to obtain generalizable patterns of the models' applicability across website domains, not propose the most effective prediction model. So, our choice is further reinforced by the known "universal approximator" capability of ANNs, which theoretically makes them more general than, e.g., linear regression (which is, in a way an ANN with a single layer) or certain other methods.

---

[1] http://va.wuikb.info.

[2] https://interfacemetrics.aalto.fi/.

Since we are not going to perform neural architecture search and tinker with the ANNs' hyper-parameters, this somehow relaxes the requirements towards the amount of training data we would need. A popular "rule of thumb" for linear models is having 10 cases per predictor, so given the number of quantitative metrics the two chosen analyzers can produce (about 35), we would need to collect training data for about 350 websites per domain.

3 Research Hypotheses and Method

The goal of our experimental study was to check the applicability of models across domains of websites. Particularly, we formulated the following hypotheses:

- **Hypothesis 1:** There are significant differences in the quality of ANN user behavior models due to the website's domain.
- **Hypothesis 2:** The difference is smaller for domains that are more similar.

Material. In our experiment, we used screenshots of homepages of websites belonging to one of the 7 distinct domains described in Table 1. The requirements were:

1. The homepage is in English language (or the homepage of the website's international version).
2. Not representing a famous brand/company.
3. Maximum diversity of designs in the set.
4. The nominal number of websites per domain is 500.

Then we used our dedicated tool to automatically make screenshots of webpages located at the collected URIs. Since there is ongoing exploration of whether or not having above-the-fold screenshots is enough for predicting users' impressions, we settled on a compromise: for the universities (Univer) domain, the full webpage was captured, whereas for the other domains the capture was performed only for 1280×960 or 1280×900 pixels. Afterwards, the set of the automatically collected screenshots was manually inspected. The screenshots having some technical problems (most often, a pop-up covering a significant portion of the screen) or not obviously belonging to the specified domain were removed.

To investigate the influence of domain similarity on the applicability of models, we calculated pairwise domain distances for each combination of the 7 domains. For this calculation, each category was mapped onto the DMOZ hierarchy[3] of categories, as shown in Table 1. The domains of Food, Games, Health, News, and Univer have direct equivalents in DMOZ. For Culture and Gov, we identified sets of DMOZ categories that best match the websites of these domains contained in our dataset. As the resulting categories have the same depth in the hierarchy, all nodes to which a domain is mapped have the same distance to other domains.

Figure 1 shows the relevant section of the DMOZ category hierarchy used for domain distance calculation. To calculate the distance between two domains, we use the length

---

[3] using http://curlie.org/.

Table 1. Homepage domains and their mappings to DMOZ categories.

Domain name	Number of screenshots	Description	DMOZ Categories
Culture	807	Websites of museums, libraries, exhibition centers, other cultural institutions	Reference/Libraries, Reference/Museums
Food	388	Websites dedicated to food, cooking, healthy eating, etc.	Recreation/Food
Games	455	Websites dedicated to computer games	Games
Gov	370	E-government, non-governmental organizations' and foundations' websites	Society/Government, Society/Organizations, Society/Activism
Health	565	Websites dedicated to health, hospitals, pharmacies, medicaments	Health
News	347	Online and offline news editions' websites, news portals	News
Univer	497	Official websites of universities and colleges	Reference/Education/Colleges and Universities
	3429		

of the shortest path between the nodes corresponding to the two domains as per Table 1. This implies identifying the lowest common ancestor (LCA) and adding vertex distances $dist_v$ between both nodes and their LCA:

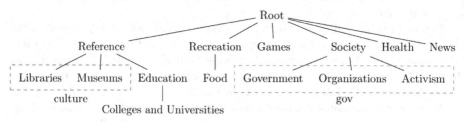

Fig. 1. DMOZ category hierarchy used for domain distance calculation (domains Culture and Gov comprising several DMOZ categories highlighted with boxes).

$$dist(D_1, D_2) = dist_v(dm(D_1), LCA(D_1, D_2)) + dist_v(LCA(D_1, D_2), dm(D_2)) \quad (1)$$

$$dm(D) = \underset{c \in DMOZ(D)}{\arg\min} \; dist_v(c, Root). \tag{2}$$

For distance calculation, domains D are represented by the corresponding DMOZ category that is the highest in the hierarchy, $dm(D)$. Table 2 presents the resulting domain distances for each domain pair.

Table 2. Domain distances based on the proposed measure.

Domain name	Culture	Food	Games	Gov	Health	News	Univer
Culture	0	4	3	4	3	3	3
Food	4	0	3	4	3	3	5
Games	3	3	0	3	2	2	4
Gov	4	4	3	0	3	3	5
Health	3	3	2	3	0	2	4
News	3	3	2	3	2	0	4
Univer	3	5	4	5	4	4	0

Design. The experiment used a within-subject design. The main independent variable was the screenshot domain (*Domain*). Derived independent variables were the pairwise distances between the domains (*Dist*), the 32 metrics for each screenshot (M_i – see the list in Table 3), and the subjects' assessments of each screenshots per the three subjective Likert scales (each ranging from 1, the lowest degree of the characteristic, to 7, the highest degree):

- How visually complex the WUI appears in the screenshot: *Complexity*;
- How aesthetically pleasant the WUI appears: *Aesthetics*;
- How orderly the WUI appears: *Orderliness*.

The dependent variable was the quality of the ANN models in predicting subjective assessments for each domain, as represented by absolute (*MSE*) and relative (MSE_{REL}) mean square errors. MSE_{REL} was calculated as the ratio between the model's *MSE* for the d-th domain and the *MSE* for the "native" domain of the model (i.e. the one whose data was used for training the model). Obviously, when d was the native domain, MSE_{REL} = 100%.

Participants and Procedure. In total, there were 137 participants (67 female, 70 male) in the survey, whose ages ranged from 17 to 46 (mean 21.18, SD = 2.68). They were mostly Bachelor's and Master's students of Novosibirsk State Technical University (NSTU), but also students and staff of some other universities, and specialists working in the IT industry. The majority of participants were Russians (89.1%), the rest

Table 3. Derived independent variables (M_i): the metrics for the screenshots.

Group	Metric	Mean	SD
Visual Analyzer (VA)	PNG filesize (in MB)	0.844	0.505
	JPEG 100 filesize (in MB)	0.848	0.453
	No. of UI elements	27.9	22.1
	No. of UI elements' types	4.430	1.279
	Visual complexity index	1248	1220
AIM – Colour Perception	Unique RGB colours	13742	10061
	HSV colours avg Hue	153	152
	HSV colours avg Saturation	0.225	0.140
	HSV colours std Saturation	0.271	0.083
	HSV colours avg Value	0.715	0.170
	HSV colours std Value	0.271	0.070
	HSV spectrum HSV	14157	8927
	HSV spectrum Hue	16396	7975
	HSV spectrum Saturation	16965	3865
	HSV spectrum Value	254.8	5.4
	Hassler Susstrunk dist A	18.0	14.1
	Hassler Susstrunk std A	28.3	14.5
	Hassler Susstrunk dist B	20.2	14.9
	Hassler Susstrunk std B	28.8	13.1
	Hassler Susstrunk dist RGYB	27.7	19.6
	Hassler Susstrunk std RGYB	41.3	17.4
	Hassler Susstrunk colorfulness	49.6	22.3
	Static clusters	3859	2030
	Dynamic CC clusters	693	449
	Dynamic CC avg cluster colors	12.4	1.4
AIM – Perceptual Fluency	Edge congestion	0.252	0.082
	Quadtree Dec balance	0.711	0.246
	Quadtree Dec symmetry	0.564	0.051
	Quadtree Dec equilibrium	1.000	0.002
	Quadtree Dec leaves	2876	2002
	Whitespace	0.340	0.265
	Grid quality (No. of alignment lines)	91.7	61.4

being from Bulgaria, Germany, South Africa, etc. The subjects took part in the experiment voluntary and no random selection was performed. All the participants had normal or corrected to normal vision and reasonable experience with websites.

The participants were provided a link to the online questionnaire that we specially developed for this study. In the survey, the screenshots were selected randomly from the pool of the available ones (with priority given to the ones that had a lower number of evaluations at the moment of selection) and presented to participants successively. The completeness of evaluation, i.e. ranking by all the 3 scales, was mandatory and controlled by the software. The default number of screenshots to be evaluated in each session was set at 100 for most of the participants. The assessment of the screenshots of the Univer domain was performed in a separate session (see in [19]), about 9 months before the other 6 domains, for which the screenshots were mixed into the single pool.

ANN Models. To construct and train ANN models, we used the Colab[4] service freely offered by Google (TensorFlow 1.15.0 environment with Keras, etc.). There was a separate model for each website domain and each subjective impression scale, so there were 21 models in total. In each model, the input values were the 32 metrics for the screenshots of the respective domain, and the single output was the respective subjective assessment.

The most widely used loss function for ANNs that perform a regression task is the mean squared error (MSE), which we will also use to represent the quality of the models. As for the architecture, the goal of our research was not to find the best one but to have comparable models for all domains and quality parameters. Therefore, we adopted the same generic architecture for all the datasets. The main hyper-parameters of the ANNs were set as specified in the following code:

```
def build_model(x):
  model = Sequential()
  model.add(Dense(units = 64, activation = 'relu',\
      input_shape = [len(x.keys())]))
  model.add(Dense(units = 64, activation = 'relu'))
  model.add(Dense(units = 1))
  model.compile(loss = 'mse', \
      optimizer = 'rmsprop', \
      metrics = ['mae', 'mse'])
  return model
```

The normalization of the input data was performed as follows:

```
def norm(x):
  return (x - x.describe().transpose()['mean']) / \
  x.describe().transpose()['std']
```

---

[4] Our full implementation is available at https://colab.research.google.com/drive/1PFFMkE9v SE7aWBlKdFSLEu0jnSQX7fHw.

For the models' training, the following configuration was specified:

```
TEST_SPLIT = 0.2
VAL_SPLIT = 0.2 # of the remaining 0.8
early_stop = ks.callbacks.EarlyStopping \
    (monitor = 'val_loss', patience = 10, \
    restore_best_weights = True)
```

Since `restore_best_weights` only works if the training was stopped by `EarlyStopping`, the nominal number of training epochs was set to 1000.

4 Results

4.1 Descriptive Statistics

For each of the 3429 screenshots, we attempted to calculate 32 metrics through our WUI Measurement Integration Platform performing in "batch" mode. However, for 345 (10.1%) of the screenshots the VA and AIM services would silently fail to produce some or all metrics (for some reason, *Whitespace* was especially problematic). The screenshots with incomplete metric values had to be excluded from further analysis, even though we do realize that this discard was not random. The metrics' means and standard deviations for the remaining 3084 screenshots are presented in Table 3.

For the 3084 valid screenshots there were 15134 full assessments, so on average 4.9 participants would provide their *Complexity*, *Aesthetics* and *Orderliness* ratings for a screenshot (see in Table 4). For the Univer domain, which was assessed in a separate session, this number was 8.6.

Table 4. Derived independent variables: the subjective impressions scales.

Domain name	Full assessments	Valid screenshots	Complexity		Aesthetics		Orderliness	
			Mean	SD	Mean	SD	Mean	SD
Culture	3280	746 (92.4%)	3.629	0.814	4.243	0.987	4.289	0.895
Food	1585	369 (95.1%)	3.658	0.811	4.699	0.945	4.657	0.865
Games	1570	362 (79.6%)	3.570	0.928	4.244	1.139	4.325	1.000
Gov	1494	346 (93.5%)	3.805	0.820	3.858	0.920	4.140	0.858
Health	2381	541 (95.8%)	3.728	0.789	4.154	0.900	4.399	0.822
News	1445	328 (94.5%)	4.157	0.857	3.795	0.833	4.164	0.817
Univer	3379	392 (78.9%)	3.570	0.636	4.047	0.825	4.417	0.632
	15134	**3084 (89.9%)**	**3.711**	**0.826**	**4.166**	**0.976**	**4.343**	**0.863**

We found significant Kendall's τ_b correlations between *Complexity* and *Aesthetics* ($\tau_{3084} = -0.046$, $p < 0.001$), as well as between *Aesthetics* and *Orderliness* (τ_{3084}

= 0.520, p < 0.001). *Complexity* and *Orderliness*, however, did not have a significant correlation (p = 0.359).

4.2 The ANN Models

Each of the 21 models that we constructed and trained was evaluated with its native testing dataset and 6 foreign ones (i.e., assessments for the screenshots of another domain), thus producing 147 *MSE* values. On average, predictions for the foreign datasets produced greater *MSEs*: +23% for *Complexity*, +60% for *Aesthetics* and +45% for *Orderliness*. T-tests suggested that for *Aesthetics* ($t_{47} = -6.11$, p < 0.001) and *Orderliness* ($t_{47} = -2.97$, p = 0.005) absolute *MSEs* were significantly different due to the model type (native or foreign). For *Complexity* ($t_{47} = -1.41$, p = 0.166), no significant effect was found. Detailed values for the absolute and relative *MSEs* per the subjective evaluation scales are presented in Tables 5, 6 and 7.

Table 5. The results of the *Complexity* models' evaluations (MSE and MSE_{REL}, %).

Testing dataset / training dataset	Culture	Food	Games	Gov	Health	News	Univer	Avg. MSE_{REL} for foreign models
Culture	0.820	1.145	1.116	1.308	1.320	1.491	0.937	
		140%	136%	159%	161%	182%	114%	**149%**
Food	1.126	1.231	1.689	1.100	1.260	1.343	1.120	
	91%		137%	89%	102%	109%	91%	**103%**
Games	1.229	1.062	1.346	1.375	1.405	1.549	1.047	
	91%	79%		102%	104%	115%	78%	**95%**
Gov	1.269	0.852	1.356	1.166	1.003	1.612	1.005	
	109%	73%	116%		86%	138%	86%	**102%**
Health	0.945	1.114	1.452	1.068	1.079	1.348	0.889	
	88%	103%	135%	99%		125%	82%	**105%**
News	1.456	1.497	2.778	1.745	1.616	1.497	1.506	
	97%	100%	186%	117%	108%		101%	**118%**
Univer	0.963	0.937	1.510	1.325	1.292	1.536	0.665	
	145%	141%	227%	199%	194%	231%		**190%**
								123%

The correlation between the models' MSEs averaged per domain and the respective domains' dataset sample sizes was not significant (p = 0.296). This finding suggests that the models had adequate amounts of training data, which caused no under- or over-fitting. Still, to compare the effects of Domain and of training data, we tried pooling all the domain-specific datasets into a single large one. We trained 3 ANN models (per the

Table 6. The results of the *Aesthetics* models' evaluations (MSE and MSE$_{REL}$, %).

Testing dataset training dataset	Culture	Food	Games	Gov	Health	News	Univer	Avg. MSE$_{REL}$ for foreign models
Culture	0.958	2.219	1.593	1.261	2.044	1.565	1.146	
		232%	166%	132%	213%	163%	120%	**171%**
Food	1.899	1.009	2.675	1.943	1.943	1.873	2.287	
	188%		265%	193%	193%	186%	227%	**208%**
Games	1.277	2.215	1.401	1.758	2.369	2.963	1.611	
	91%	158%		125%	169%	212%	115%	**145%**
Gov	1.264	2.168	1.605	1.196	0.934	1.099	1.126	
	106%	181%	134%		78%	92%	94%	**114%**
Health	1.680	1.918	1.912	1.525	1.174	1.047	1.395	
	143%	163%	163%	130%		89%	119%	**135%**
News	1.777	2.143	2.299	1.416	1.357	0.866	1.569	
	205%	248%	266%	164%	157%		181%	**203%**
Univer	1.316	2.495	1.493	1.166	1.301	1.084	1.024	
	128%	244%	146%	114%	127%	106%		**144%**
								160%

3 subjective scales) with the same hyper-parameters as we used before and evaluated them with testing sets, in which all the websites were mixed as well. The obtained *MSE* values were −33% for *Complexity*, −18% for *Aesthetics*, and −30% for *Orderliness*, compared to the averaged *MSEs* for the domain-specific models. So, for the two latter scales, the effect of a native training dataset was greater than of more training data.

4.3   Effects of the Domains' Distances

We found significant Pearson correlations between MSE_{REL} and *Dist* for *Aesthetics* (r_{49} = 0.313, p = 0.028) and *Orderliness* (r_{49} = 0.343, p = 0.016), but not for *Complexity* (r_{49} = 0.223, p = 0.123). However, if the native models (distance = 0) were excluded from the consideration, such correlations were no longer significant. But for this set of foreign models, we unexpectedly found significant **negative** correlations between the absolute *MSE* and *Dist*, for *Complexity* (r_{42} = −0.437, p = 0.004) and *Orderliness* (r_{42} = −0.347, p = 0.024), though not for *Aesthetics* (r_{42} = −0.149, p = 0.348). The averaged values for the absolute and relative *MSEs* per *Dist* are presented in Fig. 2 and Fig. 3 respectively.

Further, we performed regression analysis using the backwards selection method (entry 0.05, removal 0.1). We introduced 3 dummy variables with the values {0/1}: *Scale$_C$*, *Scale$_A$* and *Scale$_O$* to reflect to which of the subjective impression scales (*Complexity*, *Aesthetics* and *Orderliness*) belongs the model that produced the MSE$_{REL}$. The

Table 7. The results of the *Orderliness* models' evaluations (MSE and MSE$_{REL}$, %).

Testing dataset Training dataset	Culture	Food	Games	Gov	Health	News	Univer	Avg. MSE$_{REL}$ for foreign models
Culture	1.048	1.409	1.093	1.452	1.829	1.705	0.848	
		134%	104%	139%	175%	163%	81%	**133%**
Food	1.828	1.311	2.119	2.037	1.937	1.644	1.562	
	139%		162%	155%	148%	125%	119%	**142%**
Games	1.585	2.038	1.506	1.935	2.643	3.174	1.564	
	105%	135%		128%	176%	211%	104%	**143%**
Gov	1.287	1.676	1.210	1.061	1.116	1.385	1.263	
	121%	158%	114%		105%	131%	119%	**125%**
Health	1.557	1.511	1.414	1.465	0.992	1.211	1.312	
	157%	152%	142%	148%		122%	132%	**142%**
News	1.908	1.511	2.306	1.558	1.494	1.073	1.644	
	178%	141%	215%	145%	139%		153%	**162%**
Univer	1.275	1.495	1.456	1.066	1.366	1.862	0.839	
	152%	178%	174%	127%	163%	222%		**169%**
								145%

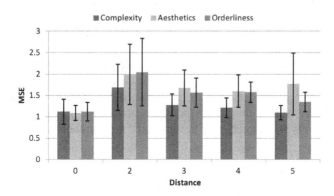

Fig. 2. Averaged absolute MSEs per distances between the domains.

resulting model included the factors of *Dist* (p < 0.001, Beta = 0.274), *Scale$_A$* (p < 0.001, Beta = 0.35) and *Scale$_O$* (p = 0.02, Beta = 0.208) and was highly significant ($F_{3,143}$ = 9.62, p < 0.001), although the R^2 = 0.168 was rather low:

$$MSE_{REL} = 0.958 + 0.084 Dist + 0.318 Scale_A + 0.189 Scale_O. \qquad (3)$$

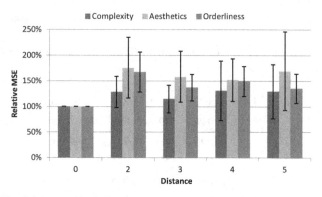

Fig. 3. Averaged relative MSEs per distances between the domains.

5 Discussion

Before we conclude this paper, we intend to have a look at the limitations of the described approach as well as questions that were left open.

First, while Complexity was the only scale without a significantly higher avg. MSE for foreign models, the peculiarity of this scale is further reinforced by its much lower correlation with the other two scales. Hence, we feel the need for more studies in various detailed dimensions of user experience.

Second, there also was an unexpected finding that absolute MSEs had significant negative correlations with the distance between the website domains. We thus believe that the measure of distance that we proposed deserves more exploration, possibly with more domains. Also, rather than relying on topical domains, it would be worthwhile to investigate a more structure-based approach to clustering and distance, e.g., as proposed by Hachenberg and Gottron [20].

Finally, the ANN models that were used for this research are only valid for the specific user groups that provided the subjective assessments. That is, they might not be representative target groups for all of the investigated domains. Hence, for better generalizability of our results, future work should investigate the influence of assessments from different user types on prediction accuracy and the correlations above.

6 Conclusions

In this paper, we sought to apply reuse, which has proven to be rather efficient in software engineering, to machine learning models and training data. For that, we built and trained 21 ANN models for websites from 7 different domains and evaluated how accurately they can predict subjective assessments of *Complexity*, *Aesthetics* and *Orderliness* for other ("foreign") domains. The assessments for the 3 subjective scales were provided by 137 participants of various nationalities, while the input data for the models were 32 metrics obtained through visual-based web UI analysis tools.

Concerning **Hypothesis 1** formulated prior to our experimental study, we found that although all the "foreign" models had on average higher mean square errors (+23%

for *Complexity*, +60% for *Aesthetics* and +45% for *Orderliness*), the difference for *Complexity* was not significant.

Exploring **Hypothesis 2**, we found that the measure of distance between the domains that we proposed in our study significantly affected *Aesthetics* and *Orderliness*. The regression model that we built for all the 3 scales was highly significant (but with a low $R^2 = 0.168$) and suggested that on average an extra point of distance adds 8.4% to the model's MSE, compared to the domain-specific ("native") model.

As for the validity of our study, we need to note the rather modest prediction accuracy of the ANN models, which should probably not be used for practical purposes. Yet, this is understandable since we did not seek to increase the models' MSEs by performing Neural Architecture Search, tweaking the hyper-parameters, etc. As our focus was on studying the effects of website domain similarity, we were reluctant to introduce these extra factors to the models. The amounts of training data per domains that we obtained for the study appear adequate, as we found no significant correlation between the models' MSEs and the sample sizes (p = 0.296). On the other hand, the control models that were trained on joined domain datasets had better MSE values, which is in line with the notorious "unreasonable effectiveness of data" in ML.

So, can we trust the predictions of ANN models for other domains than the original one? To answer this, we want to provide the reader with three key takeaways:

1. Our results suggest it is safe to assume user models for *Complexity* do not yield significantly less accurate results for foreign domains.
2. Domain distance indeed correlates with prediction accuracy for *Aesthetics* and *Orderliness*, so if you intend to reuse models, try to do so only for close domains. You can assume roughly 8.4% additional MSE per extra point of distance.
3. More research is required and it is always good, although often costly, to have more subjective assessments, but our study shows, with numbers, the trade-off for using available models and training data from different website domains.

When programmers' time became the prime cost in software, reuse came to be an integral part of SE. We believe that it can become similarly worthy in ML, at least for domains where training data is limited or expensive to get. So, in our work, we made a first step towards calculated trade-offs in the reuse of trained ML user behavior models.

Acknowledgment. The reported study was funded by RFBR and DST according to the research project No. 19-57-45006. We thank Vladimir Khvorostov from NSTU for his technical work on collecting the screenshots, the assessments, and the metrics. We are also grateful to all the colleagues who participated and organized assessments of websites.

References

1. Nielsen, J.: Enhancing the explanatory power of usability heuristics. In: Proceedings of the SIGCHI Conference on Human Factors in Computing Systems, pp. 152–158 (1994)
2. Nebeling, M. et al.: Crowdstudy: general toolkit for crowdsourced evaluation of web interfaces. In: Proceedings of the 5th ACM SIGCHI Symposium on Engineering Interactive Computing Systems, pp. 255–264 (2013)

3. Frick, T.: Designing for Sustainability: a Guide to Building Greener Digital Products and Services. O'Reilly Media, Inc., Sebastopol (2016)
4. Nielsen, J.: Putting A/B Testing in Its Place. Nielsen Norman Group, 14 August 2005. https://www.nngroup.com/articles/putting-ab-testing-in-its-place/. Accessed 13 Jan 2020
5. Beirekdar, A., Keita, M., Noirhomme, M., Randolet, F., Vanderdonckt, J., Mariage, C.: Flexible reporting for automated usability and accessibility evaluation of web sites. In: Costabile, M.F., Paternò, F. (eds.) INTERACT 2005. LNCS, vol. 3585, pp. 281–294. Springer, Heidelberg (2005). https://doi.org/10.1007/11555261_25
6. Bakaev, M.: Assessing similarity for case-based web user interface design. In: Alexandrov, D.A., Boukhanovsky, A.V., Chugunov, A.V., Kabanov, Y., Koltsova, O. (eds.) DTGS 2018, Part I. CCIS, vol. 858, pp. 353–365. Springer, Cham (2018). https://doi.org/10.1007/978-3-030-02843-5_28
7. Grigera, J., et al.: Automatic detection of usability smells in web applications. Int. J. Hum Comput Stud. **97**, 129–148 (2017)
8. Speicher, M., Both, A., Gaedke, M.: Ensuring web interface quality through usability-based split testing. In: Casteleyn, S., Rossi, G., Winckler, M. (eds.) ICWE 2014. LNCS, vol. 8541, pp. 93–110. Springer, Cham (2014). https://doi.org/10.1007/978-3-319-08245-5_6
9. Nielsen, J.: The Negativity Bias in User Experience. Nielsen Norman Group, 23 October 2016. https://www.nngroup.com/articles/negativity-bias-ux/. Accessed 14 Jan 2020
10. Speicher, M. et al.: TellMyRelevance! predicting the relevance of web search results from cursor interactions. In: Proceedings of the 22nd ACM International Conference on Information and Knowledge Management, pp. 1281–1290 (2013)
11. Chen, X., et al.: The emergence of interactive behaviour: a model of rational menu search. In: Proceedings of the 33rd ACM Conference on Human Factors in Computing Systems, pp. 4217–4226 (2015)
12. Lin, Y.-P., Jung, T.-P.: Improving EEG-based emotion classification using conditional transfer learning. Front. Hum. Neurosci. **11**, 334 (2017)
13. Torrey, L., Shavlik, J.: Transfer learning. In: Handbook of Research on Machine Learning Applications and Trends: Algorithms, Methods, and Techniques, pp. 242–264. IGI Global (2010)
14. Bakaev, M., et al.: Auto-extraction and integration of metrics for web user interfaces. J. Web Eng. **17**(6), 561–590 (2018)
15. Estuka, F., Miller, J.: A pure visual approach for automatically extracting and aligning structured web data. ACM Trans. Internet Technol. **19**(4), 1–26 (2019)
16. Oulasvirta, A. et al.: Aalto Interface Metrics (AIM): a service and codebase for computational GUI evaluation. In: 31st Annual ACM Symposium on User Interface Software and Technology Adjunct Proceedings, pp. 16–19. ACM (2018)
17. Kim, D. et al: Domain switch-aware holistic recurrent neural network for modeling multi-domain user behavior. In: 12th ACM International Conference on Web Search and Data Mining, pp. 663–671 (2019)
18. Dou, Q., et al.: Webthetics: quantifying webpage aesthetics with deep learning. Int. J. Hum Comput Stud. **124**, 56–66 (2019)
19. Boychuk, E., Bakaev, M.: Entropy and compression based analysis of web user interfaces. In: Bakaev, M., Frasincar, F., Ko, I.-Y. (eds.) ICWE 2019. LNCS, vol. 11496, pp. 253–261. Springer, Cham (2019). https://doi.org/10.1007/978-3-030-19274-7_19
20. Hachenberg, C., Gottron, T.: Locality sensitive hashing for scalable structural classification and clustering of web documents. In: Proceedings of the ACM CIKM (2013)

Improving Detection Accuracy for Malicious JavaScript Using GAN

Junxia Guo, Qiyun Cao, Rilian Zhao, and Zheng Li(✉)

College of Information Science and Technology,
Beijing University of Chemical Technology, Beijing, China
{gjxia,lizheng}@mail.buct.edu.cn

Abstract. Dynamic web pages are widely used in web applications to provide better user experience. Meanwhile, web applications have become a primary target in cybercriminals by injecting malware, especially JavaScript, to perform malicious activities through impersonation. Thus, in order to protect users from attacks, it is necessary to detect those malicious codes before they are executed. Since the types of malicious codes increase quickly, it is difficult for the traditional static and dynamic approaches to detect new style of malicious code. In recent years, machine learning has been used in malicious code identification approaches. However, a large number of labeled samples are required to achieve good performance, which is difficult to acquire. This paper proposes an efficient method for improving the classifiers' recognition rate in detecting malicious JavaScript based on Generative Adversarial Networks (GAN). The output from the GAN is used to train classifiers. Experimental results show that our method can achieve better accuracy with a limited set of labeled sample.

Keywords: Malicious code detection · JavaScript · GAN · Classifier

1 Introduction

Web applications are progressively more utilized for security-critical services, they have turned out to be a well-liked and precious target for the web-related vulnerabilities. As one of the key technologies to resist network attacks, JavaScript has become an open playground for the attackers to spread malware by injecting malicious JavaScripts. According to the Symantec 2019 Internet Security Threat Report [1], formjacking was one of the biggest cyber security trends of the year, with an average of 4,800 websites compromised with formjacking code every month in 2018, which mainly use malicious JavaScript code to steal important information.

Main techniques for detecting malicious code are static and dynamic methods. Static methods have high detection efficiency and do not need to execute

The work described in this paper is supported by the National Natural Science Foundation of China under Grant No. 61702029, No. 61872026 and No. 61672085.

M. Bielikova et al. (Eds.): ICWE 2020, LNCS 12128, pp. 163–170, 2020.
https://doi.org/10.1007/978-3-030-50578-3_12

JavaScript code, but are not good at detecting new malicious code. Dynamic methods usually require simulation of the environment to execute JavaScript code and analyze its runtime behavior, which lead to low efficiency. There are also methods that use both static and dynamic techniques, which usually perform static analysis first, and then simulate dynamic execution based on the results of the analysis. Researchers recently have enlisted machine learning approaches in the detection of malware, which extract features from programs and use classifiers to distinguish benign programs and malware. One advantage of using machine learning is that it can determine whether a code or a file is malicious or not without isolating it in a sandbox to perform the analysis. Another advantage is its predictive capability in detecting previously unknown malware. The advantage of using machine learning is even more apparent as malware becomes more polymorphic.

However, in order to use machine learning in classifying regular and malicious codes, usually we need to collect a large number of regular and malicious JavaScript samples, label them manually, and then perform model training. In fact it is difficult to collect sample data. In addition, manual labeling means high cost. This paper propose a method that uses Generative Adversarial Networks (GAN) to generate samples based on a small set of labeled sample and most unlabeled samples to improve the accuracy of the classifier. The contributions of this work are summarized below:

- It provides an efficient method to generate JavaScript samples, and follows on the improving of classifiers' accuracy when just has a small set of labeled samples.
- We design and implement a real-time detection tool for protecting web browsers from malicious JavaScript.

The rest of this paper is organized as follows. Section 2 presents the background of GAN and related work. Section 3 introduces the proposed model. The experiments and related analysis are shown in Sect. 4. Section 5 concludes the paper.

2 Related Work

JavaScript malicious code detection has been extensively studied in recent years. The studies are not limited to Web application architecture, also include the Android side JavaScript. Many machine learning based approaches are proposed. Research [11] shows how image tags, URL properties of style tags are used for malicious script injection resulting in URL redirection. Nunan et al. [15] proposed a machine learning based approach for the automatic classification of Cross Site Scripting attacks. This approach extracts features from the URLs and web documents, then uses them for analyzing classification performance. Andrew et al. [5] developed a supervised machine learning classifier based on four broad feature families: JavaScript properties accessed, HTTP cookies, HTTP referer information, and URL meta-features. Research [9] proposed a hybrid analysis method, in which, before performing classification-based detection to distinguish attacks, it analyzes for JavaScript code that works by conducting syntax analysis and dynamic instrumentation to extract internal features that are related to malicious code. Khan et al. [12] proposed an interceptor for the detection of malicious JavaScript attacks coming towards the client side. This approach based on the machine learning for detecting malware, especially previously unknown malware variants. The proposed approach is lightweight in nature with minimal runtime overheads. Detection is based on the static analysis of code for extracting features from given JavaScript to be fed into classifier for the classification process. Research [6] presented a malicious JavaScript detection model based on LSTM, in which features are extracted from the semantic level of bytecode and the method of word vector is optimized. Singh et al. [18] compared the aspects of attribute selection for detecting Malicious Websites using Machine Learning.

However, the attach techniques are also developed continuously. For exmple, Fass et al. [7] proposed an attack approach named HideNoSeek, which replaces benign sub-ASTs by their malicious equivalents (same syntactic structure) and adjusts the benign data dependencies without changing the AST so that the malicious semantics is kept. Thus, the continuous study on Malicious code detection is also necessary.

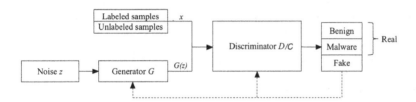

Fig. 1. The architecture of GAN this paper proposed.

3   Training Process

The learning model we propose in this paper is inspired by GAN [8]. GAN has shown good performance in generating realistic images [16,19], also can be used in image classification [10]. In this section, we describe the design of our method whose architecture is shown in Fig. 1. The discriminator network D in a normal GAN outputs an estimated probability that the input samples are generated from the G or not. Traditionally this is implemented with a feed-forward network ending in a single sigmoid unit, but it can also be implemented with a soft-max output layer with one unit for each of the classes [Real, Fake]. Once this modification is made, it is possible to find that D could have 2+1 output units corresponding to [Benign, Malware, Fake]. In this case, D can also act as a Classifier. We call this network D/C.

For learning the parameters of this GAN, we need to train the D/C to maximize the accuracy of discriminating the input data from the real data x or the generated data G(z). In addition, we need to train the G to minimize $\log(1-D(G(z)))$. Here we can use an alternative training method. Firstly, we fix G and optimize D/C to maximize the discrimination accuracy of D/C. Then, we fix D/C and optimize G to minimize the discrimination accuracy of D/C. This process alternates until the model achieves the global optimal solution, which is if and only if $p_{data} = p_g$. In the training process, we empirically update the parameters of D/C for k times and then update the parameters of G once.

Algorithm 1. The Training Process of GAN

Input: *epoch* :training times of GAN,
1: *labeled_data* :labeled samples,
2: *unlabeled_data* :unlabeled samples
3: **function** TRAIN(*generator, discriminator*)
4:    $i \leftarrow 0$
5:    **while** $i <$epoch **do**
6:        Sample a batch of samples ld from labeled_data
7:        Sample a batch of samples uld from unlabeled_data
8:        Label ld and uld using the D/C
9:        Update the D/C's weight θ_d by descending along the gradient $\nabla\theta_d\ Loss_D$
10:       Generate adversarial examples g from the generator for x
11:       Label g using the D/C
12:       Update the D/C's weight θ_d by descending along the gradient $\nabla\theta_d\ Loss_D$
13:       Update the G's weight θ_g by descending along the gradient $\nabla\theta_g\ Loss_G$
14:    **end while**
15: **end function**
16:
17: **function** SAMPLE(*generator*)
18:    Generate some samples data from the GAN's generator
19:    **return** data
20: **end function**
21:
22: **function** CLASSIFICATION
23:    $GAN \leftarrow TRAIN(generator, discriminator)$
24:    $generator \leftarrow GAN's\ generator$
25:    $data \leftarrow SAMPLE(generator)$
26:    Training classifier 100 times using data
27:    **return** average accuracy
28: **end function**

When training a GAN model, it is necessary to define a loss function to represent the loss between the model's prediction $\hat{y}$ and the real output y. The training process is the process of minimizing this loss. The loss function of the D/C is defined in Eq. 1,

$$Loss_D = L_{supervised} + L_{unsupervised} \qquad (1)$$

where:

$$L_{supervised} = -E_{x \sim p_{data}} log p_{model}(y|x, y \in \{0,1\})$$
$$L_{unsupervised} = -E_{x \sim p_{data}} log[1 - p_{model}(y|x, y = 2)]$$
$$+ E_{x \sim G(z), z \sim noise} log p_{model}(y|x, y = 2)$$
$$= -E_{x \sim p_{data}} log D(x)$$
$$+ E_{z \sim p_{uniform(0,1)}} log[1 - D(G(z))]$$

The loss function of the G is defined as Eq. 2.

$$Loss_G = E_{z \sim noise} log D(G(z)) \tag{2}$$

$p_{model}(y|x, y \in \{0,1\})$ is the set of samples that are recognized as real by the D/C, and $p_{model}(y|x, y = 2)$ is the set of samples that are recognized as fake by the D/C.

When the input is a labeled sample, it is in supervised learning mode. The D/C should distinguish that it is a benign or malware sample. So the $Loss_{supervised}$ should be minimized with respect to the weight of the discriminator. When the input is an unlabeled sample, it is in unsupervised learning mode. The D/C should distinguish the sample from generated samples, no matter it is benign or malware. So we can just minimize the $log(1 - D(G(z)))$. While the input is G(z) from generator, the D/C should distinguish it as fake.

Training this model is similar to training other GAN models. It takes labeled samples and unlabeled samples as input, and needs random variables z to generate G(z) by generator. First, fix G and optimize D/C to minimize the $Loss_D$. Next, fix D/C and optimize G to minimize the $Loss_G$. When D/C cannot classify the samples coming from real samples or coming from G, it means that the G has captured the distribution of real data. Finally, use G to generate samples as classifiers' input, and calculate the average accuracy of training classifiers. The whole process of training GAN is shown in Algorithm 1.

4   Empirical Study

To verify the effectiveness and usability of our method, which is applying the GAN in the identification of malicious JavaScript code, we designed the following research questions. **RQ1:** CAN the method we proposed in this paper improve the accuracy of classifiers? **RQ2:** Can the method we proposed in this paper be really used in the detection of malicious JavaScript?

4.1   Experimental Setup

The benign JavaScript dataset used in this paper is crawled from top 100 websites listed in Alexa [2]. We downloaded 5000 javascript code snippets from these websites. For collecting potentially malicious JavaScript, we visit common blacklists and services to track malicious URLs. As an example, we query the database service Harmur [14] for all malicious URLs that have been submitted. We crawl these URLs, collect JavaScripts and get about 2000 JavaScript code snippets. API features are used in this paper. We collect JavaScript API from W3school [3], and construct an 225-dimensional binary feature vector for each JavaScript code snippet based on 225 system level APIs.[1]

In order to validate the efficacy of samples generated by GAN, we use several different machine learning algorithms for comparison. The classifiers used in this paper include random forest (RF), logistic regression (LR), decision trees (DT), support vector machines (SVM), and k-nearest neighbor (KNN). Normally, the training of these classifiers depends on a large number of labeled samples, otherwise it will lead to lower accuracy. We use samples to train those classifiers 100 times, then calculate the average accuracy.

Adam [13] is used as the optimizer. We tuned the hyper-parameters on the validation set. 100 is chosen as the dimension of the noise vector z. The G's layer size is set to 100-500-256-225. The D/C's layer size is set to 225-256-500-1. The learning rate 0.001 is used for both the G and the D/C. The maximum number of epochs to train GAN is set to 1000. The epoch with the highest detection rate on the train set is finally chosen to test the performance of GAN.

4.2 Experimental Results

For malware detection, accuracy means the detection rate of malware. The accuracy results of original and generated samples with different training sets are shown in Table 1. Firstly, we analyze the case where the GAN is trained by 100, 200, 300, 400, 500 samples. In other words, we use those different numbers of samples to generate new samples and train the five classifiers.

Table 1. Accuracy of the classifiers use different original samples and generated samples. 'original' means the classifiers use the original samples to train, 'generate' means the classifiers use the generated samples to train.

		RF	LR	DT	SVM	KNN
100	original	65.24	67.98	64.78	74.08	81.40
	generate	70.86	73.14	70.25	75.26	81.81
200	original	69.42	72.91	65.89	75.86	85.88
	generate	73.02	74.14	71.50	77.63	87.32
300	original	76.36	80.33	73.19	80.87	88.91
	generate	79.17	83.93	76.83	84.82	89.64
400	original	77.56	81.64	75.86	85.73	90.94
	generate	79.57	84.06	76.12	86.94	91.08
500	original	78.05	84.35	76.25	86.41	91.54
	generate	81.96	86.62	78.13	88.09	93.79

---

[1] The API features used in this paper is listed at https://github.com/shi13san/proxy/ blob/master/Features-javascript%20apis.pdf.

In detail, for the RF, LR and DT, the accuracy of using generated set improves about 5% when using 100 samples as input to training GAN. When using other classifiers as the detector, GAN also can increase the accuracy when using generated samples, although 1%. That is to say, the proposed model has successfully learned to map the data distribution characteristics and can generate samples like the reality for these machine learning based malware detection algorithms.

In the five classifiers, KNN gives a comparatively better performance with respect to accuracy. From 100 samples to 500 samples, it always achieves higher accuracy than other classifiers.

Each of the 100, 200, 300, 400, 500 sample sets can be considered as a small set. Thus, we can say that our method has good performance with small set of labeled samples.

In the training process, the loss of our GAN model hovered around 0.05 near the 1000th training epoch, after which it shook a bit and was not very smooth. This reflects the fact that the training of GAN is usually unstable. How to stabilize the training of GAN have attracted the attention of many researchers [4,16,17].

4.3 Detecting Tool

Keeping in view the need for real-time detection of malicious JavaScript code, we design a tool fitting for the detection of real-time attacks based on the malicious code detection approach we propose above. This tool implements through putting a proxy, which we call MDproxy, between browser and server for the detection of malicious JavaScript code.[2]

The process of protecting a web browser by the MDproxy tool can be done in few steps. Firstly, when the web browser sends a request to the MDproxy using its URL, the MDproxy will forward the request to the web server and receive the response from the web server. Then, if the content type of response data is 'text/javascript' or 'application/javascript', it will be analyzed by the classifier which has been trained already. Finally, if the response data has malicious code, it will be replaced by a warning code. Otherwise the MDproxy forward the response data to the web browser.

5 Conclusion

In this paper, we proposed a method that uses GAN to generate samples and trained a model for detecting malicious JavaScript effectively. While comparing the overall performance of all the 5 classifiers on a different number of samples, we can find that when using samples generated by GAN the classifiers all have a comparatively better performance with respect to accuracy. Based on our testing, the MDProxy implemented in this paper can effectively intercept malicious JavaScript code in real-time.

---

[2] We share at https://github.com/shi13san/proxy.

References

1. Symantec 2019 Internet Security Threat Report. https://www.symantec.com/content/dam/symantec/docs/reports/istr-24-2019-en.pdf
2. Alexa Top Websites. https://www.alexa.com/topsites
3. W3School. http://www.w3school.com.cn/jsref/index.asp
4. Arjovsky, M., Bottou, L.: Towards principled methods for training generative adversarial networks (2017)
5. Denton, E., Chintala, S., Szlam, A., Fergus, R.: Deep generative image models using a Laplacian pyramid of adversarial networks, pp. 1486–1494 (2015)
6. Fang, Y., Huang, C., Liu, L., Xue, M.: Research on malicious JavaScript detection technology based on LSTM. IEEE Access 6, 59118–59125 (2018)
7. Fass, A., Backes, M., Stock, B.: HideNoSeek: camouflaging malicious JavaScript in benign ASTs. In: Proceedings of the 2019 ACM SIGSAC Conference on Computer and Communications Security, pp. 1899–1913 (2019)
8. Goodfellow, I., et al.: Generative adversarial nets. In: Advances in Neural Information Processing Systems, pp. 2672–2680 (2014)
9. He, X., Xu, L., Cha, C.: Malicious JavaScript code detection based on hybrid analysis. In: 2018 25th Asia-Pacific Software Engineering Conference (APSEC), pp. 365–374. IEEE (2018)
10. He, Z., Liu, H., Wang, Y., Hu, J.: Generative adversarial networks-based semi-supervised learning for hyperspectral image classification. Remote Sens. 9(10), 1042 (2017)
11. Jim, T., Swamy, N., Hicks, M.: Defeating script injection attacks with browser-enforced embedded policies. In: International Conference on World Wide Web. WWW 2007, Banff, Alberta, Canada, pp. 601–610, May 2007
12. Khan, N., Abdullah, J., Khan, A.S.: Defending malicious script attacks using machine learning classifiers Wirel. Commun. Mob. Comput. 2017(2017), 1–9 (2017). https://doi.org/10.1155/2017/5360472. Article ID 5360472
13. Kingma, D.P., Ba, J.: Adam: A method for stochastic optimization. arXiv preprint arXiv:1412.6980 (2014)
14. Leita, C., Cova, M.: HARMUR: storing and analyzing historic data on malicious domains. In: The Workshop on Building Analysis Datasets and Gathering Experience Returns for Security, pp. 46–53 (2011)
15. Nunan, A.E., Souto, E., Santos, E.M.D., Feitosa, E.: Automatic classification of cross-site scripting in web pages using document-based and URL-based features. In: IEEE Symposium on Computers and Communications, pp. 702–707 (2012)
16. Radford, A., Metz, L., Chintala, S.: Unsupervised representation learning with deep convolutional generative adversarial networks. arXiv preprint arXiv:1511.06434 (2015)
17. Salimans, T., Goodfellow, I., Zaremba, W., Cheung, V., Radford, A., Chen, X.: Improved techniques for training GANs. In: Advances in Neural Information Processing Systems, pp. 2234–2242 (2016)
18. Singh, A., Goyal, N.: A comparison of machine learning attributes for detecting malicious websites. In: 2019 11th International Conference on Communication Systems & Networks (COMSNETS), pp. 352–358. IEEE (2019)
19. Wang, S., Gao, H., Zhu, Y., Zhang, W., Chen, Y.: A food dish image generation framework based on progressive growing GANs. In: Wang, X., Gao, H., Iqbal, M., Min, G. (eds.) CollaborateCom 2019. LNICST, vol. 292, pp. 323–333. Springer, Cham (2019). https://doi.org/10.1007/978-3-030-30146-0_22

VISH: Does Your Smart Home Dialogue System Also Need Training Data?

Mahda Noura$^{(\boxtimes)}$, Sebastian Heil , and Martin Gaedke

Technische Universität Chemnitz, Chemnitz, Germany
{mahda.noura,sebastian.heil,martin.gaedke}@informatik.tu-chemnitz.de

Abstract. The main objective of smart homes is to improve the quality of life and comfort of their inhabitants through automation systems and ambient intelligence. Voice-based interaction like dialogue systems is the current emerging trend in these systems. Natural Language Understanding (NLU) model can identify the end-users' intentions in the utterances provided to spoken dialogue systems. The utility of dialogue systems is reliant on the quality of NLU models, which is in turn significantly dependent on the availability of a high-quality and sufficiently large corpus for training, containing diverse utterance structures. However, building such corpora is a complex task even for companies possessing significant human and infrastructure resources. On the other hand, the existing corpora for the smart home domain are either concerned with web services, focus on direct goals only, follow static command structure, or are not publicly available in English language which limits the development of goal-oriented dialogue systems for smart homes. In this paper, we propose a generic method to create training data for the NLU component using a generative grammar-based approach. Our method outputs, Voice Interaction in Smart Home (VISH) dataset consisting of five million unique utterances for the smart home. This dataset can greatly facilitate research in the area of voice-based dialogue systems for smart homes. We evaluate the approach by using VISH to train several state-of-the-art NLU models. Our experiment results demonstrate the capability of the corpus to support the development of goal-oriented voice-based dialogue systems in the context of smart homes.

Keywords: Smart home · Internet of Things · Web of Things · Goal-oriented interfaces · Training data generation · Dataset

1 Introduction

One of the main challenges of smart home is to enable end-users to control their smart devices to fulfill complex tasks, known as End-User Development (EUD) [2]. To reach this objective, it is vital that users can easily control how to use their smart objects (i.e., sense data from sensors and affect the physical environment) and how to combine the behavior of different objects to reach their

© Springer Nature Switzerland AG 2020
M. Bielikova et al. (Eds.): ICWE 2020, LNCS 12128, pp. 171–187, 2020.
https://doi.org/10.1007/978-3-030-50578-3_13

desired goal. One popular way of realizing such scenarios are graphical user interfaces which enable users to define relations between sensor events and actuator actions in a graphical way e.g., IFTTT[1] or Node-Red[2]. However, with the rise of modern voice-based user interfaces such as Amazon Echo and Google Home, new interaction mechanisms are becoming popular to make EUD approaches for smart environments more natural [11]. Moreover, goal-oriented interfaces for IoT provide an end-user-friendly mechanism by enabling the end-users to model their smart environments based on the desired goals (effects) rather than the concrete operations of the devices [5,10,12,15,17]: end-users specify a coarse-grained goal without providing a concrete way how to achieve it. For instance, end-users need to only state «it's too warm here», or «the noise is irritating me» instead of having to provide a solution like «turn on the air conditioner» or «reduce the volume».

Goal-based natural language (NL) spoken dialogue systems receive spoken language goal-related *utterances* from users as input, analyze their meaning to identify the user goal and extract named entities using Natural Language Understanding (NLU) components, and finally derive and execute a suitable solution, which may result in a set of actions on smart devices [15]. However, to ensure understanding of the meaning of the utterances and provide a good user experience, the NLU model requires a high-quality and sufficiently large *training corpus* with diverse utterance structures. The common process for developing such a dataset involves (1) recording sample utterances from users, (2) transcribing the utterances to text, (3) creating a training dataset by labelling the transcribed utterances and (4) training the NLU models on this dataset to extract and classify the required information. The recording, transcription and labelling causes a high level of human effort to achieve sufficient quality necessary for usable NL models, especially when the dataset grows in size due to the recording of many utterances by diverse speakers, data cleansing, transcribing each unique utterance, and labelling utterances with various entities, for each unique utterance. Moreover, manual/automatic transcription is error-prone due to the inclusion of foreign words, multiple users speaking at the same time, background noise or music. Labelling the utterances has the risk of subjective influences and different interpretations which could result in different sets of label for the same utterance.

The literature for gathering training data is based on live users in production (e.g., Amazon Alexa, Google Home), crowdsourcing [4,19], or performing controlled experiment with users in a smart home [7,18,22]. State of the art corpora for smart homes are either concerned mostly with invoking web services rather than physical devices, support only direct goals, follow fixed rules, or are not publicly available in English language which limits the research development of goal-oriented dialogue systems. In contrast, our work proposes an end-to-end approach, starting from sample utterance collection from users, mechanisms to enrich the dataset, generation of the final corpus called *VISH (Voice-Interaction for Smart Home)*, and is evaluated by training different state-of-the-art NLU models on the corpus. The results of this paper include the following contributions: (1) we present a systematic method for generating a corpus for dialogue systems using a generative-grammar based technique in a way that advocates reproducibility to create such a corpus, (2) public release of the VISH corpus in English language useful for several tasks such as automatic mapping of spoken utterances to configurations for Alexa's voice interface, Web of Things (WoT) composition using AI planning approaches, automated evaluation of spoken dialogue systems, pre-routing/pre-filtering step for specific processing units, and (3) demonstration of the usefulness of the corpus on different NLU models.

The rest of the paper is structured as follows. Section 2 discusses user goals in goal-oriented interfaces. After we present the proposed end-to-end method in Sect. 3 the procedure for creating the training corpus is presented in Sect. 4. Section 5 details the set of experiments performed and the results obtained from testing the corpus on different NLU models. In Sect. 6, the related work for existing smart home corpora is presented. Finally, Sect. 7 concludes the paper and provides future insights.

2   User Goals in Smart Homes

In this section, we first define the different user goals in a smart home setting and then present a conceptual model for goal-oriented interfaces for the Web of Things (WoT) domain which serves as the foundation of our work. Smart home user goals can be broadly divided into:

1. **Direct goals**, which is also referred to as *procedural goals* [8] specify a set of procedures that need to be performed for meeting the user's requirement, that is, how to satisfy the request. For example, remote device commands naming a specific device like «I'd like to adjust the thermostat to 22 degrees» are one type of direct goals. However, there are other direct goals which do not explicitly specify a target device like «clean the bedroom». Most direct goals are imperative, which means the actions, desired states and, related objects are present in user's utterances.
2. **Indirect goals**, which is also called *declarative goals* [8], an often-overlooked type of smart home interaction, best exemplified by «it's too hot here» specify the desired environment state that the user wants to achieve. In this kind of goals, users are interested in providing the overall effect rather than thinking in terms of individual devices/services. In this case, the dialogue system needs to infer the speaker's desired environmental change – a parameter and a change type– and decide which devices/services can satisfy the goal. For instance, the real intention of the above-mentioned goal is equivalent to the direct goal «turn on the air conditioner» or «open the window».

Goals are verbally expressed by users through utterances: natural language phrases that may form complete sentences or fragments of a sentence, that call for a state change in the physical environment. In the following, we provide a conceptual model for goal-oriented WoT interfaces.

Definition 1 (Goal-oriented WoT Interfaces): A Goal-oriented WoT domain is defined as 5-tuple GWoT $= \langle S, s^o, A, s^*, \gamma \rangle$, where:
$S = \{s_1, s_2, \ldots, s_n\}$ is a finite set of states including the initial state s^o and the goal state s^*. Each state is represented by a finite non-empty set of parameters $Par_s = \{p_1, p_2, \ldots, p_k\}$ expressing the facts known about this state. Each parameter $p_i \in Par_s$ has a finite domain of V^{p_i}. The parameters can be for instance brightness, noise, temperature.
A is the set of actions that link to the different operations of physical devices. An action $a \in A$ defines its functionality as 2-tuples: $a = (\text{effects}(a), \text{actuations}(a))$, where: effects$(a) = (p_i, t, v)$ of action a on parameter $p_i \in Par_s$ can be of the following types t:

- *increase* or *decrease*, for increasing or decreasing p_i (e.g., increase *brightness*)
- *toggle*, for switching between the possible values of p_i (e.g., from *on* to *off*)
- *assign*, for assigning a constant value v to p_i (e.g., set *temperature* to 22°C)

The actuations(a) are a set of HTTP or MQTT requests that can be sent to the physical devices that invokes the operations on the devices. $\gamma: S \times A \to S$ is the transition function between the states associated with actions from A performed on devices.

3   End-to-End Method

Our solution is designed for dialogue systems based on goal-oriented interfaces that call for a state change in the physical environment (e.g., «it's freaking cold in the bedroom» or «turn the heating on») rather than informational goals (e.g., «where is my vacuum cleaner?») or conditional commands (e.g., «when I'm away turn on the security system»). Accordingly, the dialogue system can be seen as an interface for end-users' actuating WoT devices.

Figure 1 depicts the engineering process that we propose for supporting EUD for WoT. The main steps are as follows:

1. Describe the WoT environments in an interoperable format using W3C Web of Things Description (TD) Model[3]. The semantic ontology should provide knowledge of the effects of each device action on the environment.
2. Automatically generate a running REST API of the modelled WoT devices using an API Generator [14, 16].
3. Search repositories for existing implementations for WoT devices or if they don't exist develop them.
4. Derive the user goal and extract custom named entities from the incoming request by the NLU component of the dialogue system Web service REST API, for which the presented training dataset is being generated. The API endpoint invokes an AI planner with the extracted named entities and classified intent (as JSON).

---

[3] https://www.w3.org/2019/wot/td.

5. Apply a planning technique to dynamically generate plans at runtime considering user goals, current state of the environment and the available WoT devices [13].
6. The corresponding plan will then result in invoking the set of WoT devices which consume RESTful and MQTT interfaces.

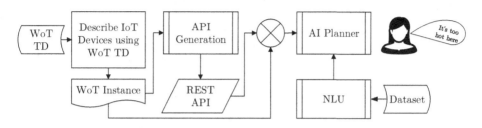

Fig. 1. The process for supporting EUD.

4   Voice Interaction Smart Home (VISH) Dataset

In this section we present the holistic approach that is employed for creating the training dataset for the development of voice-based goal-oriented dialogue systems in the smart home domain. Figure 2 illustrates an overview of the dataset creation workflow as BPMN diagram. There are two actors involved in this process:

– *Natural language engineer* is the actor who is in charge of collecting the utterance patterns and describing them through a formal language to support the dataset creation.
– *VISH Toolchain* is a system role representing our toolchain for supporting the NL engineer by automatically generating utterances based on the generative grammar.

The process consists of seven main steps which is described in the following in sequential order.

Step 1. Sample User Utterance Collection: As a first step, it is necessary to identify the different ways that end-users issue commands to their smart home dialogue systems. To realize this, we administered two different online questionnaires motivated from the study in [6] containing two scenario settings (1) unmediated and (2) mediated.

In the *unmediated scenario* setting the participants were not provided with any assistance and were told to imagine they have a smart home agent to which they can give arbitrary voice commands to control their houses. They were given the option to either write their commands as text or speak to the microphone by providing as many unique utterances they would trigger in their smart home.

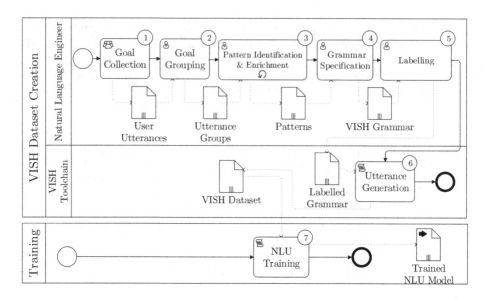

Fig. 2. The process for creating VISH corpus.

In the *mediated scenario*[4] setting, the participants were presented with a hypothetical smart home scenario describing some samples of instructions to an AI personal assistant. In addition, to simulate the capabilities of their imaginary smart home, a list of sample IoT sensors and actuators was provided as inspiration. The reason for this guidance was to allow the users to explore the devices themselves as they would do with a real deployed system over a long period of time. The participants were provided with additional time to look over the list of device capabilities before they could proceed. Next, we told participants that their AI personal assistant wants to assist them by automating their home on their behalf. We asked them to provide at least five different commands or goals starting with, «OK, Charlie ...» that they want their personal assistant to do without restricting them to the given devices.

These two questionnaires were administered three months apart and with different target groups. The unmediated scenario was conducted with international users while most respondents of the mediated scenario were students within Germany. Table 1 shows the number of responses that were received in each setting. A total of 823 goals were collected which includes 596 goals from 56 participants in the unmediated scenario setting and 227 goals from 45 participants in the mediated setting. One notable aspect we observed from the result of this experiment was that even our brief descriptions in the mediated setting resulted in receiving commands and goals that were more diverse in terms of semantic structure compared to the first questionnaire.

---

[4] https://bildungsportal.sachsen.de/umfragen/limesurvey/index.php/777955.

Table 1. Overview of questionnaire responses

Method	Number of users	Direct goals	Indirect goals
Mediated	45	453	243
Unmediated	56	110	117

Step 2. Utterance grouping. The initially collected utterances from end-users need to be analyzed to identify a set of patterns. The requests were grouped into different categories to form utterance groups. These groupings are derived based on similar grammatical structures, parameters and effect types.

Step 3. Pattern identification and enrichment. After the utterances have been grouped, for each group the words or phrases that represent constant or variable information were identified to form the patterns. These information serves as placeholders that are used to dynamically generate diverse utterances. For example, in the utterances «**open** the **shades** in the **bedroom**», the placeholders are highlighted in bold and refer to an action, awning device, and a location respectively.

Up to this step, a comparatively small corpus following low variability in syntactic structures and vocabulary can be created. However, the quality of interaction between the end-user and the dialogue system is highly dependent on a diversified dataset. Therefore, to further enrich the dataset with more diverse utterances this step consists of three main sub-tasks:

– **Utterance variation with placeholders**: Users can express the same intent to the dialogue system by providing a different number of placeholders and in different order. Therefore, a suitable approach for increasing the number of utterances in the training dataset is through consideration of all combinatorial variations of placeholders without repetition. For each original pattern with a given number of n placeholders, the maximum number of pattern variations resulting from this is:

$$\#\text{variations} \leq \sum_{i=0}^{n-1} \frac{n!}{i!} \tag{1}$$

– **Replication with different placeholders values and synonyms:** The extended patterns from the previous phase consists of different placeholders representing possible variables. A reasonable method for extending the number of possible utterances is to utilize these patterns to create a representative set of utterances covering different custom variable values and replacing variables with their synonyms. Specifically, for some placeholders in a pattern a *gazetteer* – a comprehensive list of representative values and synonyms that are expected as input from the user – is used. This allows to generate additional utterances by filling the placeholder with the values in the gazetteer. For example, a placeholder representing devices is instantiated with values such as "tv", "light bulb","window". For a placeholder like media-type the gazetteer lists synonyms like "track", "tune", "song", or "single". By adding n placeholders with X_i unique values of placeholder pl_i, this method allows to generate the following number of utterances:

$$\#utterances = \prod_{i=1}^{n} X_i \qquad (2)$$

- **Pattern paraphrasing:** The previous iterations already cover the different placeholders and corresponding values, the goal of this iteration is to increase the diversity of the utterance structures. In reality, users can use different expressions to refer to the same goal. For example, for the goal «open the shades», all the following utterance could be used to express the same semantic content:
  - Make the shades open
  - Could you wind up the blinds for me
  - The blinds are too low
  - I need some lights from the shades

Having this aspect in mind we create additional patterns by paraphrasing the existing patterns to create new training instances that are alternative functionality-relevant utterances. Unlike replacing the parameters with their equivalent synonyms, this step changes the syntactic structure of the utterance.

Step 4. Grammar Specification. Each identified pattern is represented using extended Backus Normal Form (eBNF) [1] rules that specify the grammatical structure of utterances according to the patterns. All rules together form a context-free grammar, called the VISH Grammar.

Definition 2 (VISH Grammar): The VISH Grammar G is a set of rules used to generate a set of NL utterances defined as a 4-tuple $G = \langle V_n, V_t, R, s \rangle$ where:

- V_n is a finite set of non-terminal symbols representing placeholders in the rules, (e.g., 'DeviceOnOff' or 'Turn' in Listing 1.1)
- V_t is a finite set of terminal symbols that appear in the utterance (e.g., 'on' or 'off' in Listing 1.1)
- $R : V_n \mapsto (V_n \cup V_t)*$ is a finite set of rules mapping each non-terminal symbol to a sequence of other non-terminal or terminal symbols. These production rules are used to generate the utterances.
- $s \in V_n$ is the starting symbol, a special non-terminal symbol that is the starting point of grammar generation.

The VISH grammar defines a language L representing smart home utterances. The following listing reports a sample of production rules in the VISH grammar.

Listing 1.1. VISH Grammar Extract

```
<DeviceOn> ::= <Intro>? (Activate|Turn On) <DeviceOnOff>
<DeviceOff> ::= <Intro>? (Deactivate|Turn Off) <DeviceOnOff>
<Intro> ::= 'I want to'|'could you'|'please'|'help me'
<Turn> ::= 'turn'|'switch'
<Activate> ::= 'activate'
<Deactivate> ::= 'deactivate'
<On> ::= 'on'
<Off> ::= 'off'
<DeviceOnOff> ::= 'lamp'|'tv'
```

With this grammar, we can build simple utterance like «could you activate the tv» or it's synonym form «turn on the tv». We believe this initial grammar for utterance generation is expressive enough to represent most goals in the smart home domain. The number of different goals in the smart home domain is rather constrained when compared to general question answering systems or general purpose dialogue systems. The current grammar consists of 259 rules and 218 terminal symbols.

Step 5. Labelling for Classification and Extraction. Some utterances contain smart-home-related information (entities) that needs to be extracted such as device, action, value etc. To support the extraction of this information the corresponding terminal symbols need to be labelled using Part Of Speech (POS)-like tags. In the smart-home-related utterances generated by the VISH grammar, the following concepts are supported for extraction:

- Device: Set the `DEVICE:thermostat` to 25 degrees
- Action: `ACTION:Mix` a smoothie for me
- Value: Change the colour of the hue to `VALUE:blue`
- Device state: Tell the robot to start `STATE:cleaning`
- Location: Turn the `LOCATION:bedroom` lights on
- Unit: Cook two `UNIT:ounces` of coffee
- Quantity: Brew `QUANTITY:three` tablespoons of tea

Some information that is not directly represented in the utterance as words (non-terminal symbols in VISH grammar) can be identified through classification requiring to further label the generated utterances with classes that correspond to:

- physical parameters p_i (temperature, humidity, brightness, air quality, noise, pressure, gas and colour)
- effect types t (increase, decrease, toggle, assign)
- direct/indirect nature of goals

For instance, the utterance: «The sound is disturbing me » is labelled as "`PARAMETER:Noise EFFECT:Decrease GOAL:Indirect`"

Step 6. Utterance Generation. In this step, the VISH toolchain is applied to the grammar to automatically generate all the possible utterances with the corresponding labels. The core of this step is a generator developed using the

NLTK[5] python library. The output of this step is the VISH dataset which consists of around 5 million labelled utterances. Table 2 shows the different NLP-related and smart-home-related characteristics of the VISH dataset.

Table 2. Characteristics of VISH dataset

Total Words:	33,618,437	Total Entities:	6,819,062
Total utterances:	4,743,745	Indirect Goals:	4,000,854
Unique words:	822	Direct Goals:	742,891
Entity Types:	7	Total Actions:	674,711
Effect Types:	4	Device Types:	305
Parameter Types:	8	Action Types:	130

Step 7. NLU Model. With the resulting VISH dataset, NLU models for smart home interfaces can be trained as demonstrated in the Evaluation Section.

5 Evaluation

The main objective of this evaluation is to show the applicability of the generated VISH dataset for training different general purpose NLU models to support identification of direct/indirect goals, parameters and intended effects as well as device, action, value extraction in the smart home context. This will enable the construction of dialogue systems exceeding the limited pattern-based interactions for smart home systems in subsequent work.

We first describe the evaluation procedure and the different NLU models that were trained on the VISH dataset and then we showcase the results.

5.1 Procedure

In order to evaluate the VISH dataset we use the open source NL toolkit Rasa[6] with different NLU models and configurations. The main motivation of using different NLU models is to reduce the bias from this variable. In the following we describe the steps of the evaluation process.

– **Dataset preparation:** Initially, the VISH training dataset was automatically transformed to Rasa's markdown syntax using the VISH toolchain. The markdown structures the dataset into lists of utterances grouped by intents. In natural language understanding, named entity recognition (NER) and intent classification are commmonly used to analyze utterances [23]. NLU models allow to identify the different required pieces of information in user utterances and to assign them an entity type. We employ *named entity recognition*

---

[5] https://www.nltk.org/.
[6] https://rasa.com/.

to perform the extraction of the seven types of smart-home-related entities from utterances as described in Sect. 4 Step 5. On the other hand, *intent classification* allows to derive the intent from user-provided NL input, which is required to identify corresponding actions [15]. For instance, the intent behind the utterance «it's too cold here» is to increase the temperature. Typically, an utterance is assigned to one intent. For that reason, we map combinations of the classification labels (cf. Sect. 4 step 5) on to intents for intent classification. This forms in total 29 number of unique intents.

- **Dataset division:** A standard evaluation method in machine learning is partitioning the training dataset into training and holdout sets. Accordingly we separated the VISH training dataset, 80% was used to train the different NLU models and 20% of the data is used for testing.

- **Training the dataset using NLU models:** We used different NLU models in Rasa which differ in the way intent classification and NER is performed. The NLU models that were used are namely *supervised embeddings pretrained embeddings convert* and *pretrained embeddings spacy*. The supervised embeddings model trains the word embedding model from the VISH dataset itself using a neural network. It utilizes *Conditional Random Field* (CRF) for NER, and a 2-layer softmax intent classifier on StarSpace embeddings of the utterances and intent labels. On the other hand, the ConveRT[7] model provides intent classification on a pre-trained sentence encoding embedding model, but does not support NER. As an alternative model for NER, we therefore employed the SpaCy[8] entity extractor, which utilizes CRF and a statistical Begin, Intermediate, Last, Other, Unigram (BILOU) transition model on pre-trained embeddings from GloVe and fastText. The training data from the previous step is used to train these three NLU models. We additionally, trained the NLU models using different number of epoch values to investigate the impact of training time on quality.

- **Tesing the NLU models:** After the training process, a test was performed using the holdout set on the trained NLU models to calculate the quality in terms of accuracy, precision and F1-score for intent classification and named entity extraction. The objective of this experiment is to show that the VISH dataset enables training of different state-of-the-art NLU models and configurations for use in smart home scenarios.

5.2 Evaluation Results

To provide a measure for the quality of the generated dataset, in this section we present the results obtained from testing the VISH dataset with the three different NLU models described in the previous step for intent classification and feature extraction.

Intent Classification. Table 3 provides an overview of the results of the NLU models for intent classifiers using supervised embeddings and pretrained embed-

---

[7] https://github.com/PolyAI-LDN/polyai-models#models.

[8] https://spacy.io/.

dings ConveRT. The F1-score of the supervised model is slightly higher compared to the pretrained ConveRt embeddings. With an increased number of epochs used to train the supervised embeddings model, classification quality slightly increases. However, it is feasible to use the VISH dataset even with smaller numbers of epochs to reduce training effort. Overall, the results for precision, recall and F1 of all models and configurations are very close to 1, demonstrating the feasibility of intent classification for smart home utterances leveraging the VISH dataset.

Table 3. Intent classification results

	Intent Classifiers				Mean
	Supervised 100	Supervised 300	Supervised 500	ConveRT	
P	.9834	.9849	.9886	.9756	.9831
R	.9834	.9849	.9886	.9756	.9831
F_1	.9834	.9849	.9886	.9756	.9831

Precision P, Recall R and F_1 score of intent classification using a 2-layer softmax NN trained with 100, 300 and 500 epochs on custom embeddings trained on VISH and on pretrained ConveRT embeddings (300 epochs) respectively

Entity Extraction. Table 4 gives an overview of the results of the NLU models using CRF and spaCy entity extraction techniques. The results show very comparable results for all models and entities, close to 1. Entity types with a greater variety of possible values, such as Value, Device and Action, show slightly worse results in the third and fourth digit only. The quality of entity extraction of both NLU models is not distinguishable.

Table 4. Named entity extraction results

		Entities							Mean
		State	Quantity	Value	Location	Device	Unit	Action	
Custom	P	1.0	1.0	.9980	1.0	.9999	1.0	.9998	.9997
	R	1.0	1.0	.9999	1.0	.9998	1.0	.9995	.9999
	F_1	1.0	1.0	.9989	1.0	.9998	1.0	.9997	.9998
spaCy	P	1.0	1.0	.9992	1.0	.9999	1.0	.9998	.9998
	R	1.0	1.0	.9983	1.0	.9998	1.0	.9995	.9997
	F_1	1.0	1.0	.9988	1.0	.9998	1.0	.9996	.9998

Precision P, Recall R and F_1 score of entity extraction using a CRF extractor on custom embeddings and on pretrained spaCy embeddings

Conclusion. The above results indicate that the VISH dataset can be successfully used to train state-of-the-art NLU models for both intent classification and entity extraction of smart-home-related utterances. The resulting quality is independent of the concrete NLU model or configuration used and the VISH dataset can be used for classifier/extractor training only as well as for training custom embedding models. The VISH dataset[9] is publicly available.

6   Related Work

The development of smart home dialogue systems based on machine learning algorithms requires a large corpus of labelled utterances to learn identifying the user goal. Building such a corpus is a complex task requiring significant human effort and infrastructure resources. Moreover, obtaining high quality user data to construct an accurate model is not possible before the model is deployed. This slows down research advances in the smart home domain. To tackle this problem, a set of datasets are available in the literature for smart homes each with their own benefits and limitations. Table 5 displays a qualitative comparison between the selected datasets for smart home domain where the columns indicate the features of the datasets. There are also some datasets collected in smart homes focusing on sensor measurements, however since they cannot be used to develop voice based dialogue systems we do not review them here.

The existing solutions use different approaches for the creation of datasets, namely data collection from smart home users in production, controlled experiments in the smart home, crowdsourcing and generative grammars.

Voice-based personal assistants like Google Home and Alexa collect training data from the users interaction with the system. Alexa assistant is based on Alexa Meaning Representation Language [9], that aims to understand the meaning of voice-based commands. For evaluating the performance of AMRL, a manually labelled dataset containing 20k samples were used. However, the data is not available publicly. IFTTT is an end-user programming paradigm designed for web services and IoT devices following a trigger-action model. The different recipes are developed by end-users and are also available on their website. However, IFTTT is not voice-based rather textual representation and the rules are constructed according to fixed Event-Condition-Action (ECA) patterns which limits diversity and flexibility. For this reason, only using IFTTT for training a dialogue system for smart home is not suitable.

In the speech community different controlled experiments are performed in the smart home using microphones to record datasets. For instance, the DIRHA corpus [7] was developed in an apartment with 40 microphones where the utterance of 24 native UK and US speakers were recorded. The recordings include phonetically-rich sentences, read and spontaneous home automation commands, keywords and conversational speech in four different languages. However, the utterances in DIRHA corpus are not smart home related since their intention is distant-speech recognition under background noise. The VocADom corpus and it's extension VocADom@A4H [18] corpus was recorded in Amiqual4Home smart home equipped with 500 sensors and actuators using eleven French participants.

---

[9] https://vsr.informatik.tu-chemnitz.de/projects/2019/growth/.

Table 5. Qualitative comparison between smart home datasets

Dataset	Size	L	DG	IG	A	Pr	E	De	Ac	Approach
Google Home	NA	en	✓	✗	✗	✗	✗	✓	✓	User
Alexa	20 K	en	✓	✗	✗	✗	✗	✓	✓	User
IFTTT	NA	en	◑	✗	✓	✗	✗	✓	✓	User, ECA rules
DIRHA	183	en	✗	✗	◑	✗	✗	✗	✗	Experiment
VocADom@4H	7 K	fr	✗	✗	✗	✗	✗	✗	✗	synthetic & Experiment
VoiceHome-2	1560	fr	✓	✗	✓	✗	✗	✗	✗	Experiment
Sweet-Home	1,5 K	fr	◑	✗	◑	✗	✗	✗	✗	Experiment
ATHENA	370	el	◑	✗	✗	✗	✗	✗	✗	Experiment
Genie	3 M	en	✓	✗	✓	✗	✗	✓	✓	Synthetic & crowdsourcing
Shilin et al	1 k	ru	✓	◑	✓	◑	✗	✗	✓	Crowdsourcing
VISH	**5 M**	**en**	✓	✓	✓	✓	✓	✓	✓	**User-derived generative grammar**

L indicates ISO 639-1 language codes, DG, IG, A, Pr, E, D, Ac respectively stand for direct goal, indirect goal, availability, parameter, effect, device and action, the symbols refer to: ✓ full-filled, ✗ not fulfilled, ◑ partially full-filled

The users were guided to interact with the smart home using voice commands for about an hour. However, this dataset is in French and the recordings/transcriptions cover conversations that are not directly related to controlling smart home. Similarly, the VoiceHome-2 [3] corpus was recorded for distant speech processing analysis in home. Sweet-Home [22] corpus is also a French dataset which was recorded with a single user with a simple set of commands following a strict grammar and it is not sufficient to cover a large set of intents with syntactic and lexical variation. On the other hand, ATHENA [21] is a Greek corpus collected using 20 participants that contains commands, keywords and conversations. However, this dataset is in Greek and not publicly available.

Crowdsourcing is used as a popular approach for corpus collection using anonymous contributors on platforms like Amazon Mechanical Turk. For example, Shilin et al. [19], used crowdworkers and domain experts to create a dataset. This work has some similarities to ours, in that in the first step sample commands are collected from users, and considering device parameters in entity extraction. In contrast, we consider extracting both device parameters (states) and physical parameters (e.g., brightness, temperature, colour). They only seek to collect a dataset with three levels of commands which is in a narrower focus than ours. Rather, we focus on indirect goals on a wider scope. Although their corpus is publicly accessible, it is in Russian language. The author of [20] also used the help of crowd workers to create a relatively small dataset related to smart home scenarios which is restricted to only static trigger-action patterns in IFTTT. Campagna et al. [4] elaborate on Genie toolkit which is capable of understanding compound commands provided to virtual assistants using a semantic parser. To train their neural model, they collect a dataset using synthesized data generated from NL-templates provided by developers which is then paraphrased by crowdsourced workers to make them natural. Our approach is similar to theirs in using synthesized data for training. However, the utterances in our case are created based on a generative-grammar based approach. Chatito[10] and Chatette[11] are tools which support generating NL datasets using a generic Domain Specific Language (DSL). Our solution for generating the VISH dataset is similar to Chatito in that we also generate all the possible utterances using defined grammar. However, to generate a corpus for smart home the developer needs to provide the grammar from scratch. In contrast, we provide the grammar used to generate VISH dataset, which can be further extended to support new goal structures.

7   Conclusion and Future Work

Goal-oriented natural language dialogue systems for smart homes can considerably simplify and enhance end-users lives. However, creating such a system is challenging due to the lack of labelled training data representing diverse utterance structures. In this paper, we introduced a systematic method for generating training data for smart home goal-oriented dialogue systems using a generative-grammar-based technique. The method can also be used by engineers to get training data for spoken dialogue systems in their own domains (e.g., smart city, smart health, etc.). The resulting VISH dataset consists of about 5 million labelled utterances and is publicly available (See footnote 9) for usage and further research. The dataset was evaluated by training three different NLU models. All models used performed with high quality on the VISH dataset for NLP tasks like intent classification and named entity recognition. In addition, we trained the NLU models in different configurations and reported on quality impact. The results suggest that the VISH dataset can be used to support goal-oriented dialogue system for smart homes. In the future, we plan to test the dataset in interactive sessions with goals received from end-users in a live setting. In addition we plan to integrate our custom NLU pipeline trained on the VISH dataset with our existing goal-based planning for smart home composition solution, GrOWTH.

References

1. International Organization for Standardization/International Electrotechnical Commission 14977:1996 information technology-syntactic meta-language-extended BNF. In: Standard. International Organization for Standardization, Geneva, CH (1996). http://standards.iso.org/ittf/PubliclyAvailableStandards/
2. Barricelli, B.R., Valtolina, S.: Designing for end-user development in the Internet of Things. In: Díaz, P., Pipek, V., Ardito, C., Jensen, C., Aedo, I., Boden, A. (eds.) IS-EUD 2015. LNCS, vol. 9083, pp. 9–24. Springer, Cham (2015). https://doi.org/10.1007/978-3-319-18425-8_2
3. Bertin, N., et al.: Voicehome-2, an extended corpus for multichannel speech processing in real homes. Speech Commun. **106**, 68–78 (2019)

---

[10] https://github.com/rodrigopivi/Chatito.
[11] https://github.com/SimGus/Chatette.

4. Campagna, G., Xu, S., Moradshahi, M., Socher, R., Lam, M.S.: Genie: a generator of natural language semantic parsers for virtual assistant commands. In: Proceedings of the 40th ACM SIGPLAN Conference on Programming Language Design and Implementation, pp. 394–410. ACM (2019)
5. Catania, V., Delfa, G.C.L., Monteleone, S., Patti, D., Ventura, D., Torre, G.L.: Goose: goal oriented orchestration for smart environments. Int. J. Ad Hoc Ubiquit. Comput. **32**(3), 159–170 (2019)
6. Clark, M., Newman, M.W., Dutta, P.: Devices and data and agents, oh my: how smart home abstractions prime end-user mental models. Proc. ACM Interact. Mob. Wearable Ubiquit. Technol. **1**(3), 44 (2017)
7. Cristoforetti, L., et al.: The DIRHA simulated corpus. In: LREC, pp. 2629–2634 (2014)
8. Georgievski, I., Aiello, M.: Automated planning for ubiquitous computing. ACM Comput. Surv. (CSUR) **49**(4), 1–46 (2016)
9. Kollar, T., et al.: The alexa meaning representation language. In: Proceedings of the 2018 Conference of the North American Chapter of the Association for Computational Linguistics: Human Language Technologies, Vol. 3 (Industry Papers), pp. 177–184 (2018)
10. Li, T.J.-J., Labutov, I., Myers, B.A., Azaria, A., Rudnicky, A.I., Mitchell, T.M.: Teaching agents when they fail: end user development in goal-oriented conversational agents. In: Moore, R.J., Szymanski, M.H., Arar, R., Ren, G.-J. (eds.) Studies in Conversational UX Design. HIS, pp. 119–137. Springer, Cham (2018). https://doi.org/10.1007/978-3-319-95579-7_6
11. Luger, E., Sellen, A.: "Like Having a Really Bad PA" the gulf between user expectation and experience of conversational agents. In: Proceedings of the 2016 CHI Conference on Human Factors in Computing Systems, pp. 5286–5297 (2016)
12. Mayer, S., Verborgh, R., Kovatsch, M., Mattern, F.: Smart configuration of smart environments. IEEE Trans. Autom. Sci. Eng. **13**(3), 1247–1255 (2016)
13. Noura, M., Gaedke, M.: An automated cyclic planning framework based on plan-do-check-act for web of things composition. In: Proceedings of the 10th ACM Conference on Web Science, pp. 205–214 (2019)
14. Noura, M., Gaedke, M.: WoTDL: Web of things description language for automatic composition. In: 2019 IEEE/WIC/ACM International Conference on Web Intelligence (WI), pp. 413–417. IEEE (2019)
15. Noura, M., Heil, S., Gaedke, M.: GrOWTH: goal-oriented end user development for web of things devices. In: Mikkonen, T., Klamma, R., Hernández, J. (eds.) ICWE 2018. LNCS, vol. 10845, pp. 358–365. Springer, Cham (2018). https://doi.org/10.1007/978-3-319-91662-0_29
16. Noura, M., Heil, S., Gaedke, M.: Webifying heterogenous Internet of Things devices. In: Bakaev, M., Frasincar, F., Ko, I.-Y. (eds.) ICWE 2019. LNCS, vol. 11496, pp. 509–513. Springer, Cham (2019). https://doi.org/10.1007/978-3-030-19274-7_36
17. Palanca, J., Val, E., Garcia-Fornes, A., Billhardt, H., Corchado, J.M., Julián, V.: Designing a goal-oriented smart-home environment. Inf. Syst. Front. **20**(1), 125–142 (2016). https://doi.org/10.1007/s10796-016-9670-x

18. Portet, F., et al.: Context-aware voice-based interaction in smart home-vocadom@ a4h corpus collection and empirical assessment of its usefulness. In: 2019 IEEE Intl Conference on Dependable, Autonomic and Secure Computing, International Conference on Pervasive Intelligence and Computing, International Conference on Cloud and Big Data Computing, International Conference on Cyber Science and Technology Congress (DASC/PiCom/CBDCom/CyberSciTech), pp. 811–818. IEEE (2019)

19. Shilin, I., Kovriguina, L., Mouromtsev, D., Wohlgenannt, G., Ivanitskiy, R.: A method for dataset creation for dialogue state classification in voice control systems for the Internet of Things. In: R. Piotrowski's Readings in Language Engineering and Applied Linguistics, pp. 96–106 (2018)

20. Tahir, A.: Smart home scenarios (2019). https://doi.org/10.6084/m9.figshare.8327096.v1

21. Tsiami, A., Rodomagoulakis, I., Giannoulis, P., Katsamanis, A., Potamianos, G., Maragos, P.: Athena: a Greek multi-sensory database for home automation control uthor: isidoros rodomagoulakis (ntua, greece). In: INTERSPEECH (2014)

22. Vacher, M., Lecouteux, B., Chahuara, P., Portet, F., Meillon, B., Bonnefond, N.: The sweet-home speech and multimodal corpus for home automation interaction (2014)

23. Wang, X., Yuan, C.: Recent advances on human-computer dialogue. CAAI Trans. Intell. Technol. 1(4), 303–312 (2016)

Neighborhood Aggregation Embedding Model for Link Prediction in Knowledge Graphs

Changjian Wang[1,2] and Ying Sha[3,4(✉)]

[1] Institute of Information Engineering, Chinese Academy of Sciences, Beijing, China
wangchangjian@iie.ac.cn
[2] School of Cyber Security, University of Chinese Academy of Sciences,
Beijing, China
[3] College of Informatics, Huazhong Agricultural University, Wuhan, China
shaying@mail.hzau.edu.cn
[4] Hubei Engineering Technology Research Center of Agricultural Big Data,
Wuhan, China

Abstract. Link prediction has become a hot topic of knowledge graphs (KGs) in recent years. It aims at predicting missing links between entities to complement KGs. The most successful methods for this problem are embedding-based. Most previous works only consider the triples to learn the embeddings of entities and relations, so the information they can utilize is limited. However, KGs are graph-structured data, we can use the neighborhood information to improve the quality of embeddings, thus improving the performance of link prediction task. In this paper, we propose NAE (neighborhood aggregation embedding model), a novel approach for link prediction. NAE consists of an aggregator and a predictor. The aggregator aggregates the embeddings of multi-order neighbors with different weights to generate a new embedding for each entity. Further analysis shows that the performance of some existing methods such as TransE and DistMult can be improved by integrating our aggregators. The predictor predicts the probability distributions of target entities. It uses convolutional neural network (CNN) to capture more interactions between the new entity embeddings and the relation embeddings. We also propose a highly parameter efficient model NAE-S by simplifying the predictor, which can obtain competitive performance with fewer parameters. Compared with DistMult, NAE-S achieves the same performance with 16x fewer parameters. Experimental results show that our method outperforms several state-of-the-art methods on benchmark datasets.

Keywords: Knowledge graph embedding · Link prediction · Semantic web · Graph neural networks

1 Introduction

Knowledge graphs (KGs) such as YAGO [26], Freebase [1], NELL [4], and DBpedia [15] are collections of real-world facts. Each fact that represents a relation r

© Springer Nature Switzerland AG 2020
M. Bielikova et al. (Eds.): ICWE 2020, LNCS 12128, pp. 188–203, 2020.
https://doi.org/10.1007/978-3-030-50578-3_14

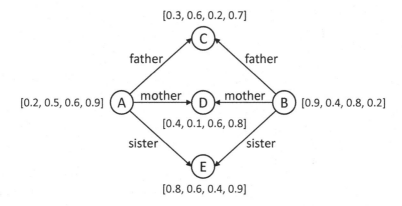

Fig. 1. A example of KG in the form of a graph. We randomly assign an embedding vector to each entity and generate new embedding vectors for A and B by simply aggregating their first-order neighbors (i.e., A = (A + C + D + E)/4, B = (B + C + D + E)/4). The cosine similarity between A and B is improved (from 0.67 to 0.97).

between a head entity h and a tail entity t is usually denoted as a triple $\langle h, r, t \rangle$. KGs are useful resources in various applications such as question answering [9], information extraction [5], recommendation [30], etc. However, these applications are vulnerable to the incompleteness of KGs, i.e., missing links between entities. Therefore, many works are devoted to solving this problem called *link prediction* or *knowledge base completion*.

In recent years, many embedding-based models have been proposed to solve link prediction and obtained state-of-the-art performance. In these models, entities and relations are represented as vectors or matrices. By simple operations like addition [2,16,31] or multiplication [21,28,33], the representations of entity and relation in a triple constitute a scoring function. The object of these models is to optimize this scoring function so that it scores valid triples higher than invalid triples. For example, the scoring function of TransE [2] is $-\|\mathbf{h} + \mathbf{r} - \mathbf{t}\|_{1/2}$, where $\mathbf{h}$, $\mathbf{r}$, $\mathbf{t}$ are the vector representations of head entities, relations and tail entities respectively. For link prediction, we can get the most plausible triples by sorting the scores of all candidate triples. Instead of using simple operations, ConvE [7] and ConvKB [19] use convolutional neural networks (CNNs) to construct the scoring functions, which makes their models more expressive. However, most of these methods only consider the triples individually, so the information they use to learn the embeddings is limited.

In fact, if we treat the entities as nodes and the triples as edges, KG is naturally graph-structured. We can utilize the graph structure information of KGs, not just triples, to improve the quality of entity embeddings. One of the most important information in graph-structured data is the neighborhood information. Nodes with same neighbors usually have some similarities (e.g., A and B in Fig. 1). If we make similar nodes get similar embedding representations, it will be helpful for link prediction task (e.g., if we know that A's embedding is similar to

B's and $\langle A, bornIn, F \rangle$ is a fact, there is a high possibility that embedding-based models predict $\langle B, bornIn, F \rangle$ is also a fact).

As a powerful method for processing graph-structured data, graph neural networks (GNNs) [3,6,10,14,29] have received extensive attention in recent years. GNN is a kind of model which generates the representation of a node by iteratively aggregating the representations of its neighbors. Inspired by GNNs, we find we can make the embeddings of similar entities more similar by simply aggregating the embeddings of their neighbors. As is shown in Fig. 1, the cosine similarity of A and B is improved after neighborhood aggregation even without training. Based on this observation, we construct our *aggregator*. The aggregator can only coarsely improve the quality of entity embeddings, and we also need a *predictor* to optimize this entity embeddings along with the relation embeddings. Similar to [19], in the predictor, we use 1D CNN instead of simple operations to capture more interactions between entity embeddings and relation embeddings for link prediction task.

More specifically, in this paper, we propose a novel model NAE (*neighborhood aggregation embedding model*) for link prediction in KGs. Figure 2 shows the architecture of NAE. NAE consists of two parts, an aggregator and a predictor. In order to utilize the information of neighbor entities, we first convert KG into a graph. The aggregator aggregates the embeddings of multi-order neighbors for each entity. We use random walks to distinguish the importance of one entity's neighbors, which is determined by the transition probability from this entity to its neighbor in a Markov chain. After the aggregator, each entity will have a new embedding. For each triple, the predictor using the new embedding of entity and the embedding of relation to predict the probability distribution of the target entity. We use CNN to construct the predictor, which consists of a convolution layer, a projection layer, and a softmax layer. We also propose a simplified version of NAE called NAE-S. NAE-S simplifies the predictor of NAE by restricting the number of filters to 1 and replacing the projection matrix with the entity embedding matrix. We evaluate our method on four benchmark datasets: WN18 [2], FB15k [2], WN18RR [7], and FB15k-237 [27]. Experimental results show that our NAE model outperforms several state-of-the-art models and our NAE-S model achieves competitive performance with fewer parameters.

In summary, our contributions are as follows:

- We propose a novel model for link prediction called NAE. The aggregator of NAE imporves the quality of entity embeddings by aggregating the neighborhood information in KGs. The predictor of NAE captures more interactions between entity embeddings and relation embeddings by CNN.
- The aggregator part of our method can easily extend to other existing methods and improve their performance without introducing additional parameters. This makes it possible for our aggregator to be a component of other link prediction methods.
- We also propose a parameter efficient model NAE-S, which simplifies the predictor part of NAE. Compared with ConvE and DistMult [33], NAE-S is 2x parameter efficient than ConvE and 16x than DistMult.

2   Related Work

In recent years, the most successful methods for link prediction are embedding-based. There are mainly three categories of these models, including translational models, bilinear models, and neural network-based models.

As a representative of translational models, TransE [2] represents entities and relations as vectors in the same space and the relations are interpreted as translations operating between entities. TransH [31] is an extension of TransE, which projects entity vectors into relation-specific hyperplanes by projection vectors. Similar to TransH, TransR [16] projects entity vectors into relation-specific spaces by projection matrices. TransD [11] simplifies TransR by using the product of two vectors to construct the projection matrix. Using the same principle as TransE, TorusE [8] embeds entities and relations on a torus to solve the regularization problem.

Different from translational models, bilinear models represent relations as matrices and combine two entity vectors by multiplication. RESCAL [21] is the most generalized bilinear model where each relation matrix is a full matrix. DistMult [33] simplifies RESCAL by restricting the relation matrices to diagonal matrices to decrease the number of parameters. Since DistMult can only deal with symmetric relations, ComplEx [28] extends DistMult by using complex numbers instead of real numbers to better model asymmetric relations. SimplE [12] is a simple interpretable fully expressive bilinear model that addresses the independence among the two embedding vectors of the entities.

Translational models and bilinear models have fewer parameters, less computational cost and are easy to extend to large knowledge graphs. However, they are less expressive than neural network-based models. NTN [25] has a standard linear neural network architecture, which combines two entity embeddings by a relation-specific tensor and gets the score by a nonlinear hidden layer and a linear output layer. One problem of NTN is that it requires a large number of parameters, and a convolutional neural network-based model may be a better choice since its parameter efficiency. ConvE [7] and ConvKB [19] are two models which utilize the convolutional neural network for link prediction. ConvE applies 2D convolution over a matrix which is constructed by reshaping the embeddings of head entity and relation. The feature maps generated by convolution are vectorized and then matched with all candidate tail embeddings through a projection layer and an inner product layer. ConvKB applies 1D convolution over a matrix constructed by the triple. The vectorized feature maps are computed with a weight vector via a dot product to give a score for the triple.

In addition to previous works which only consider the triples, there are some works which are similar to ours to capture more information using the graph structure of KGs. TransE-NMM [20] constructs neighbor-based vector representations for entities and applies it on TransE. However, they only consider the first-order neighbors and their TransE-based model is less expressive than our CNN-based model. R-GCN [23] and SACN [24] are two end-to-end models where the encoders are extensions of GCN and the decoders are based on existing models. They require multiple iterations and multiple layer-specific weight matrices that need training to aggregate high-order neighborhood information, while we only need a transition matrix without training. Another difference is that they learn the scoring function of the triples, while we directly learn the probability distributions of target entities.

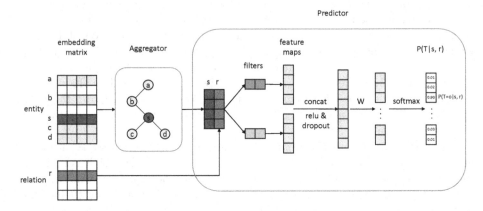

Fig. 2. NAE architecture. Take the triple $\langle s, r, o \rangle$ as an example. The aggregator generates a new embedding for s by aggregating the embeddings of its multi-order neighbors. The predictor constructed by CNN utilizes the new embedding of s and the embedding of r to predict the probability distribution of the target entity.

3   Background

3.1   Problem Definition

A knowledge graph $\mathcal{K} = \{\langle h, r, t \rangle\} \subseteq \mathcal{E} \times \mathcal{R} \times \mathcal{E}$ is a collection of valid triples, where $\mathcal{E}$ and $\mathcal{R}$ are the sets of entities and relations respectively. Each triple $\langle h, r, t \rangle$ is a fact in the real-world, indicating that there is a relation r between a head entity h and a tail entity t.

Link prediction typically refers to the task that predicts the head or the tail entity given a relation and another entity, i.e., predicting t given h and r ($\langle h, r, ? \rangle$) or predicting h given r and t ($\langle ?, r, t \rangle$). For example, $\langle Washington, capitalOf, ? \rangle$ means to predict which country's capital is Washington, and $\langle ?, capitalOf, USA \rangle$ means to predict which city is the capital of the USA. Note that by adding the inverse relation set $\mathcal{R}^{-1}$ to $\mathcal{R}$, $\langle h, r, t \rangle$ can also be represented as $\langle t, r^{-1}, h \rangle$, so these two tasks can be transformed into one task, i.e., $\langle S, R, ? \rangle$ where S and R denote h and r or t and r^{-1}. Instead of learning the scoring function which consists of the representations of head entities, tail entities, and relations, we directly learn the conditional probability distribution of the target entity $P(T|S, R)$ given S and R. An entity with a higher probability is more likely to be the target entity which we want to predict.

3.2   Graph Neural Networks

The main idea of GNNs is to use node features to learn the representations of nodes from the graph structure. Most GNNs can be described as neighborhood aggregation models which iteratively update the representation of a node by aggregating representations of its neighbors [32]. Formally, the general form of GNNs is:

$$h_{\mathcal{N}(v)}^k = \text{AGGREGATE}_k \left(\{ h_u^{k-1}, \forall u \in \mathcal{N}(v) \} \right)$$
$$h_v^k = \sigma \left(\mathbf{W}^k \cdot \text{COMBINE}_k \left(h_v^{k-1}, h_{\mathcal{N}(v)}^k \right) \right),$$

(1)

where $\mathcal{N}(v)$ is the set of first-order neighbors of node v, h_v^k is the feature vector of node v at the k-th layer, $\mathbf{W}^k$ is a layer-specific trainable weight matrix. $\sigma\,(\cdot)$ is an activation function, AGGREGATE is an aggregator function such as mean and pooling, and COMBINE combines the representations of the node itself and its neighbors. AGGREGATE and COMBINE are defined by specific models.

The representations of nodes at last layer will be used for specific tasks. For node classification, one of the most widely used applications of GNNs, the probability distribution of node's class is:

$$P = \text{softmax} \left(\mathbf{W}^l h_v^l \right).$$

(2)

Our approach generally follows this form, except for several differences: we do not need the initial features of entities; we learn an entity embedding matrix rather than multiple layer-specific weight matrices; our aggregator function is not iterative; our predictor is based on CNN, which combines relation information to predict the probability distribution of the target entity.

4   Methodology

In this section, we will describe the two parts of our method, including an aggregator and a predictor. The purpose of the aggregator is to obtain the new embedding of each entity. These new embeddings will be used in our predictor for link prediction task.

We first convert the triples into a graph $G = (V, E)$ where V is the set of nodes and E is the set of edges. We treat entities as nodes. If there is any relation between two entities, there is an edge between the two nodes.

4.1   Aggregator

The role of the aggregator is to generate a new embedding for each entity based on the embeddings of its neighbors. The general form of our aggregator is:

$$\mathbf{n}_i = \sigma \left(\sum_{j \in \mathcal{N}_1^k(n_i)} a_j \mathbf{n}_j \right),$$

(3)

where $\mathbf{n}_i$ is the embedding of entity i, $\mathcal{N}_1^k(n_i)$ is the set of 1th to k^{th}-order neighbors of entity i, a_j is the embedding weight of neighbor entity j, and $\sigma(\cdot)$ is an activation function.

According to this general form, we mainly need to determine how to choose the weights of embeddings. An easy way is to assign a same weight to all neighbors in $\mathcal{N}_1^k(n_i)$, i.e., $a_j = 1/|\mathcal{N}_1^k(n_i)|$. Although the computational complexity of this method is small, it cannot distinguish the importance of neighbors. As a compromise, we use random walks to distinguish the importance of different neighbors, i.e., the neighbor entities which are easier to reach in random walks on G will have higher weights. Random walk on a graph is a special category of Markov chains where each node is a state. The weight of node i's 1th-order neighbor j is the one-step transition probability from state i to state j:

$$a_j = p_{ij} = \frac{1}{deg(n_i)}, \quad j \in \mathcal{N}_1(n_i), \tag{4}$$

where $deg(n_i)$ is the degree of the node i. For k^{th}-order neighbors, the weights are determined by k-step transition probability:

$$a_j = p_{ij}^{(k)} = \sum_{r \in V} p_{ir}^{(m)} p_{rj}^{(k-m)}, \quad j \in \mathcal{N}_k(n_i). \tag{5}$$

In order to combine the embedding information of the node itself, we add a self-connection edge to each node in G, so the adjacency matrix of this new G is $A = A' + I_{|V|}$, where A' is the adjacency matrix of the original graph, and $I_{|V|}$ is the identity matrix. For all entities, the weight matrix of their first-order neighbors, i.e., the one-step transition probability matrix is:

$$\mathbf{P} = D^{-1}A, \tag{6}$$

where D is the degree matrix, $D_{ii} = \sum_j A_{ij}$. According to the properties of Markov chains, the embedding weight matrix of kth-order neighbors is $\mathbf{P}^k$.

We represent the entity embedding matrix as $\mathbf{M} \in \mathbb{R}^{|\mathcal{E}| \times d}$, where d is the embedding dimension of entities and the i-th line of $\mathbf{M}$ represents the embedding representation of the i-th entity. By aggregating the embeddings of neighbors from 1th to k^{th}-order with different weights, we get a new entity embedding matrix:

$$\widetilde{M} = \sigma\left(\sum_{j=1}^{k} \mathbf{P}^j \mathbf{M}\right). \tag{7}$$

4.2   Predictor

Our predictor is a model which uses entity information and relation information to perform link prediction task. The entity information is entity embeddings obtained by the aggregator and the relation information is relation embeddings.

As an efficient feature extractor, CNN has been widely used in many fields, such as images, natural language, audio, etc. In recent years, some works begin to apply CNN for link prediction [7,19]. In our model, we utilize 1D CNN to captures more interactions between entity embeddings and relation embeddings. For each triple $\langle s, r, o \rangle$, our model predicts the probability distribution of the target entity o:

$$P = \text{softmax}\left(\mathbf{W}\sigma\left(\text{concat}\left([\mathbf{s}; \mathbf{r}] * \mathbf{\Omega}\right)\right)\right), \tag{8}$$

where $\mathbf{s} \in \mathbb{R}^d$ and $\mathbf{r} \in \mathbb{R}^d$ are entity and relation embedding vectors from $\widetilde{M}$ and relation embedding matrix $M_r \in \mathbb{R}^{|\mathcal{R}| \times d}$ respectively, $*$ denotes a convolution operator, $\mathbf{\Omega}$ denotes the set of filters, concat denotes a concatenation operator, and $\mathbf{W} \in \mathbb{R}^{|\mathcal{E}| \times d|\mathbf{\Omega}|}$ is a projection matrix.

The architecture of our predictor is shown in Fig. 2. After the aggregator, we get a new embedding for each entity. For each training triple, we first combine $\mathbf{s}$ and $\mathbf{r}$ into an matrix $\in \mathbb{R}^{d \times 2}$. Then we perform the convolution operation on this matrix using multiple filters $\in \mathbb{R}^{1 \times 2}$. Next, we concatenate the multiple feature maps generated by the filters to a vector. We also apply dropout and activation function to this vector. Finally, we project this vector to $\mathcal{E}$-dimensional space using $\mathbf{W}$ and get the probability distribution of the target entity using the softmax function.

Like many neural network-based models, our NAE model is expressive, but there are too many parameters need to learn. To reduce the parameters, we propose a simplified model called NAE-S. NAE-S simplifies the predictor by restricting the number of filters to 1, i.e., $|\mathbf{\Omega}| = 1$, and replacing the projection matrix $\mathbf{W}$ to the entity embedding matrix $\mathbf{M}$ (i.e., output embedding [22]). Under this model, the probability distribution of the target entity is:

$$P = \text{softmax}\left(\mathbf{M}\sigma\left(\alpha\mathbf{s} + \beta\mathbf{r}\right)\right), \tag{9}$$

where α and β are two parameters of the filter. Noted that NAE-S has only two more parameters than some parameter efficient models such as the translational model TransE and the bilinear model DistMult, which makes it possible for our method to scale to large KGs.

We train our models by minimizing the following cross entropy loss function:

$$\mathcal{L} = -\sum_{o' \in \mathcal{E}} \mathbf{1}_{\mathcal{K}}\left(\langle s, r, o' \rangle\right) \log P(T = o'|s, r), \tag{10}$$

where $\mathcal{K}$ is the set of valid triples and $\mathbf{1}_{\mathcal{K}}(x)$ is an indicator function, i.e., if $x \in \mathcal{K}$ then $\mathbf{1}_{\mathcal{K}}(x) = 1$, else $\mathbf{1}_{\mathcal{K}}(x) = 0$.

5   Experiments

5.1   Datasets

For evaluating our proposed method, we select four benchmark datasets, including WN18 [2], FB15k [2], WN18RR [7], and FB15k-237 [27].

WN18. WN18 is a subset of WordNet [18]. WordNet is a lexical database of English which groups English words into sets of synonyms (termed synsets).

These synsets correspond to entities in KGs, and they are linked by conceptual-semantic and lexical relations. A total of 151,442 triples that contain 40,943 entities and 18 relations are extracted to construct WN18.

FB15k. FB15k is a subset of Freebase [1]. Freebase is a large knowledge base composed of multi-source structured data. There are a large number of general facts stored in Freebase that cover more than 39 million topics such as people, places, and things. FB15k is a collection of 59,2213 triples extracted from Freebase. These triples consist of 14,951 entities and 1,345 relations.

WN18RR and FB15k-237. It has been noted by [27] that there are many inverse triples of training triples in the validation and testing set of FB15k, e.g., $\langle a, hyponym, b \rangle$ in the training set and $\langle b, hypernym, a \rangle$ in the testing set. This makes it easy to predict such kind of triples once we know that the two relations are reversible. To address this problem, FB15k-237, a subset of FB15k, and WN18RR, a subset of WN18, are created by removing reversible relations to form more challenging and realistic datasets.

All these datasets consist of three parts: training set, validation set, and testing set. Table 1 presents the statistics of these four datasets.

Table 1. Statistics of the experimental datasets. #train, #valid, and #test represent the number of triples in training set, validation set, and testing set, respectively.

Dataset	$|\mathcal{E}|$	$|\mathcal{R}|$	#train	#valid	#test
WN18	40,943	18	141,442	5,000	5,000
FB15k	14,951	1,345	483,142	50,000	59,071
WN18RR	40,943	11	86,835	3,034	3,134
FB15k-237	14,541	237	272,115	17,535	20,466

5.2 Evaluation Protocol

As mentioned in Sect. 3.1, we convert the two tasks ($\langle h, r, ? \rangle$ and $\langle ?, r, t \rangle$) of link prediction into one task $\langle S, R, ? \rangle$ where S and R denote h and r or t and r^{-1} respectively. After training, we use the trained model to test each triple $\langle S, R, ? \rangle$ in the validation set and the testing set, and we can get the probability distribution of the target entity $P(T|S, R)$. We rank the candidate entities of each testing triple by descending order according to the probability values. Our evaluation is performed on these rankings.

To compare the performance of our method and others on benchmark datasets, we choose three common evaluation metrics, including Hits@N, MR, and MRR. Hits@N denotes the proportion of the hit triples in the testing set. A hit triple is a testing triple whose target entity ranks in top N in the ranking. MR is the mean ranking of the target entities. MRR is the mean reciprocal ranking of the target entities. Higher Hits@N, lower MR, and higher MRR indicate better performance.

Consider a situation that $\langle e_1, r_1, e_2 \rangle$ exists in the training set and $\langle e_1, r_1, e_3 \rangle$ exists in the testing set. When we predict $\langle e_1, r_1, ? \rangle$, there is a high probability that e_2 ranks higher than e_3 since $\langle e_1, r_1, e_2 \rangle$ has been learned by the model. However, this will degrade the performance of the model, although both are correct. In order to avoid this misleading behavior, we use the filtered setting proposed by [2], i.e., removing such type entities (e.g. e_2) that exist in the training, validation, or testing set before ranking.

5.3 Experimental Setup

We train our models using Adam optimizer [13]. We use grid search to select the hyperparameters of our models. Hyperparameter ranges are as follows: learning rate lr in {0.01, 0.001}, embedding dimension d in {50, 100, 200}, maximum order of neighborhood k in {1, 2, 3} , the number of filters f in {1, 3, 5}, dropout dp in {0, 0.1, 0.2, 0.5}. We use ReLU as the activation function σ. For NAE model, we find the following hyperparameters work well on the four datasets: $lr = 0.001$, $d = 100$, $k = 1$, $f = 1$, $dp = 0.2$ on WN18; $lr = 0.001$, $d = 100$, $k = 1$, $f = 5$, $dp = 0.1$ on FB15k; $lr = 0.01$, $d = 100$, $k = 1$, $f = 1$, $dp = 0.5$ on WN18RR; $lr = 0.001$, $d = 100$, $k = 2$, $f = 5$, $dp = 0.5$ on FB15k-237. For NAE-S model, the following hyperparameters work well on WN18RR and FB15k-237: $lr = 0.001$, $d = 100$, $k = 1$, $dp = 0$ on WN18RR; $lr = 0.001$, $d = 100$, $k = 3$, $dp = 0.5$ on FB15k-237. Best models are selected by using early stopping according to MRR on the validation sets.

Table 2. Link prediction results on WN18 and FB15k. The best score is in bold and the second best score is in underline.

Method	WN18					FB15k				
			Hits@N					Hits@N		
	MR	MRR	1	3	10	MR	MRR	1	3	10
TransE [2]	**251**	—	—	—	0.892	125	—	—	—	0.471
ComplEx [28]	—	0.941	0.936	0.945	0.947	—	0.692	0.599	0.759	0.840
ANALOGY [17]	—	**0.942**	**0.939**	0.944	0.947	—	0.725	0.646	0.785	0.854
R-GCN [23]	—	0.814	0.686	0.928	**0.955**	—	0.651	0.541	0.736	0.825
SimplE [12]	—	**0.942**	**0.939**	0.944	0.947	—	0.727	0.660	0.773	0.838
ConvE [7]	504	**0.942**	0.935	**0.947**	**0.955**	64	0.745	0.670	0.801	**0.873**
NAE	261	0.938	0.927	0.945	**0.955**	**53**	**0.765**	**0.705**	**0.805**	0.867

5.4 Results

We first evaluate our NAE model on WN18 and FB15k. Table 2 shows the results. Our NAE model obtains the best MR, MRR, Hits@1, and Hits@3 on FB15k. For WN18, most methods perform very well and the results are similar. Our model obtains the best Hits@10, the second best Hits@3 and MR. Compared with the second best result, the two metrics with the highest relative improvement are MR (absolute/relative improvement is 11/17%) and Hits@1(absolute/relative improvement is 0.035/5%) on FB15k.

As mentioned in Sect. 5.1, WN18RR and FB15k-237 are two more challenging and realistic datasets since they remove reversible relations which are easy to learn. We evaluate our NAE and NAE-S on these two datasets. Table 3 shows the results. On WN18RR, our NAE model obtains the best MR, Hits@1, Hits@3, Hits@10 and the second best MRR. The two metrics with the highest relative improvement are MR (absolute/relative improvement is 2437/48%) and Hits@10 (absolute/relative improvement is 0.05/10%). Our NAE model achieves the best results in all metrics on FB15k-237, and MR (absolute/relative improvement is 70/28%) and MRR (absolute/relative improvement is 0.02/7%) have the highest relative improvement. We note that our parameter efficient model NAE-S performs well on these two datasets. NAE-S obtains the second best results in all metrics on FB15k-237 and the second best MR, Hits@3, Hits@10 on WN18RR.

Table 3. Link prediction results on WN18RR and FB15k-237. Results marked * are taken from [7].

Method	WN18RR					FB15k-237				
			Hits@N					Hits@N		
	MR	MRR	1	3	10	MR	MRR	1	3	10
DistMult [33]*	5110	0.43	0.39	0.44	0.49	254	0.241	0.155	0.263	0.419
Node+LinkFeat [27]	—	—	—	—	—	—	0.226	—	—	0.347
R-GCN [23]	—	—	—	—	—	—	0.248	0.153	0.258	0.414
ConvE [7]	5277	**0.46**	0.39	0.43	0.48	246	0.316	0.239	0.350	0.491
CrossE [34]	—	—	—	—	—	—	0.299	0.211	0.331	0.474
NAE	**2673**	0.45	**0.41**	**0.46**	**0.54**	**176**	**0.337**	**0.246**	**0.372**	**0.522**
NAE-S	2822	0.42	0.36	0.44	0.52	179	0.334	0.245	0.366	0.511

6   Analysis

6.1   Extendibility

In this part, we study the effect of our aggregator on the performance of other existing methods. The aggregator of our method is easy to extend to other existing methods without introducing additional parameters that need to be learned. Specifically, we replace our predictor by TransE and DistMult to construct two new models. We evaluate these two new models on FB15k-237 and compare them with the original models.

Table 4. Experimental results on FB15k-237 of extending our aggregator to TransE and DistMult.

Model	TransE					DistMult				
			Hits@N					Hits@N		
	MR	MRR	1	3	10	MR	MRR	1	3	10
Original	255	0.271	0.179	0.304	0.452	254	0.241	0.155	0.263	0.419
With aggregator	236	0.284	0.193	0.319	0.467	273	0.265	0.177	0.294	0.445
Absolute improvement	19	0.013	0.014	0.015	0.015	−19	0.024	0.022	0.030	0.026
Relative improvement	7%	5%	8%	5%	3%	−7%	10%	14%	12%	6%

Table 4 reports the results. For TransE with the aggregator, all metrics are improved, and the highest relative improvement metric is Hits@1 (8%). For DistMult with the aggregator, most metrics are improved except MR. Compared with TransE, the overall improvement of DistMult is higher. The highest relative improvement metric on DistMult is Hits@1 (14%). The experimental results show that our aggregator can effectively improve the performance of existing methods, which makes it possible for our aggregator to be a component of other link prediction methods.

6.2 Ablation Study

We perform an ablation study on our NAE model. Section 6.1 has shown that the aggregator improves the performance of existing methods, and in this part we investigate the effect of removing the aggregator part of NAE on performance.

We carry out the experiment on FB15k-237 and the results are shown in Table 5. Compared to the full model, the results of the model without the aggregator decline in all metrics, up to 15% relative decrease in MR. The results demonstrate that the aggregator is a critical part of our method.

Table 5. Ablation study on FB15k-237

Model	MR	MRR	Hits@1	His@3	Hits@10
NAE	176	0.337	0.246	0.372	0.522
Without aggregator	203	0.310	0.223	0.338	0.485
Absolute decrease	27	0.027	0.023	0.034	0.037
Relative decrease	15%	8%	9%	9%	7%

6.3 Parameter Efficiency

We compare our NAE-S model with a bilinear model DistMult and a neural network-based model ConvE on parameter efficiency.

Table 6 shows the results on FB15k-237. NAE-S performs better than Dist-Mult and ConvE with the same number of parameters. The performance of NAE-S with 0.95M parameters is on par with ConvE with 1.89M parameters. Similar results are also reported on NAE-S with 0.46M (0.23M) parameters and ConvE with 0.95M (0.46M) parameters. NAE-S with 0.12M parameters still performs better than DistMult with 1.89M parameters in most metrics. Overall, NAE-S is 2x parameter efficient than ConvE, 16x than DistMult.

Table 6. Parameter comparison on FB15k-237. Results of DistMult and ConvE are taken from [7]. P.C. and E.S. represent the parameter count and the embedding size respectively.

Model	P.C.	E.S.	MRR	Hits@1	Hits@3	Hits@10
DistMult	1.89M	128	0.23	0.15	0.25	0.41
	0.95M	64	0.22	0.14	0.25	0.39
ConvE	1.89M	96	0.32	0.23	0.35	0.49
	0.95M	54	0.30	0.22	0.33	0.46
	0.46M	28	0.28	0.20	0.30	0.43
NAE-S	1.89M	128	0.33	0.24	0.37	0.51
	0.95M	64	0.32	0.24	0.35	0.49
	0.46M	32	0.31	0.22	0.34	0.47
	0.23M	16	0.28	0.21	0.31	0.44
	0.12M	8	0.26	0.18	0.27	0.41

7   Conclusion and Future Work

This paper proposes a neighborhood aggregation embedding model NAE and its simplified version NAE-S for link prediction in KGs. We consider the graph structure information of KGs, not just triples, to improve the quality of entity embeddings. NAE consists of an aggregator and a predictor. The aggregator generates a new embedding for each entity by aggregating the embeddings of its neighbors. The weights of neighbor entities are determined by the transition probabilities in a Markov chain. Our aggregator can easily extend to existing methods such as TransE and DistMult without introducing additional parameters, and improve their performance. This makes it possible for our aggregator to be a component of other link prediction methods. The predictor utilizes CNN to capture more interactions between entity embeddings and relation embeddings to predict the probability distributions of target entities. NAE-S simplifies the predictor part of NAE by restricting the number of filters to 1 and replacing the projection matrix with the entity embedding matrix to reduce the number of parameters. Further analysis shows that NAE-S is highly parameter efficient, achieving the same performance as ConvE and DistMult with 2x and 16x fewer parameters. Experimental results on benchmark datasets show that our NAE outperforms several state-of-the-art models and our NAE-S obtains competitive performance with fewer parameters.

In the future, we plan to explore the following directions: 1) we have implemented our aggregator by sparse matrix multiplication to reduce the memory usage, and we plan to reduce the computational cost by sampling neighbors. 2) We also plan to add relation information to our aggregator to further improve the quality of embeddings.

Acknowledgments. This work was supported in part by the National Key Research and Development Program of China under Grant No.2016YFB0801003.

References

1. Bollacker, K., Evans, C., Paritosh, P., Sturge, T., Taylor, J.: Freebase: a collaboratively created graph database for structuring human knowledge. In: Proceedings of the 2008 ACM SIGMOD International Conference on Management of Data, pp. 1247–1250. ACM (2008)
2. Bordes, A., Usunier, N., Garcia-Duran, A., Weston, J., Yakhnenko, O.: Translating embeddings for modeling multi-relational data. In: Advances in Neural Information Processing Systems, pp. 2787–2795 (2013)
3. Bruna, J., Zaremba, W., Szlam, A., LeCun, Y.: Spectral networks and locally connected networks on graphs. In: 2nd International Conference on Learning Representations, ICLR 2014, Banff, AB, Canada, 14–16 April 2014, Conference Track Proceedings (2014). http://arxiv.org/abs/1312.6203
4. Carlson, A., Betteridge, J., Kisiel, B., Settles, B., Hruschka, E.R., Mitchell, T.M.: Toward an architecture for never-ending language learning. In: Twenty-Fourth AAAI Conference on Artificial Intelligence (2010)
5. Daiber, J., Jakob, M., Hokamp, C., Mendes, P.N.: Improving efficiency and accuracy in multilingual entity extraction. In: Proceedings of the 9th International Conference on Semantic Systems, pp. 121–124 (2013)
6. Defferrard, M., Bresson, X., Vandergheynst, P.: Convolutional neural networks on graphs with fast localized spectral filtering. In: Advances in Neural Information Processing Systems, pp. 3844–3852 (2016)
7. Dettmers, T., Minervini, P., Stenetorp, P., Riedel, S.: Convolutional 2D knowledge graph embeddings. In: Thirty-Second AAAI Conference on Artificial Intelligence (2018)
8. Ebisu, T., Ichise, R.: Toruse: Knowledge graph embedding on a lie group. In: Thirty-Second AAAI Conference on Artificial Intelligence, pp. 1819–1826 (2018)
9. Fader, A., Zettlemoyer, L., Etzioni, O.: Open question answering over curated and extracted knowledge bases. In: Proceedings of the 20th ACM SIGKDD International Conference on Knowledge Discovery and Data Mining, pp. 1156–1165 (2014)
10. Hamilton, W., Ying, Z., Leskovec, J.: Inductive representation learning on large graphs. In: Advances in Neural Information Processing Systems, pp. 1024–1034 (2017)
11. Ji, G., He, S., Xu, L., Liu, K., Zhao, J.: Knowledge graph embedding via dynamic mapping matrix. In: Proceedings of the 53rd Annual Meeting of the Association for Computational Linguistics and the 7th International Joint Conference on Natural Language Processing (Volume 1: Long Papers), pp. 687–696 (2015)

12. Kazemi, S.M., Poole, D.: Simple embedding for link prediction in knowledge graphs. In: Advances in Neural Information Processing Systems, pp. 4284–4295 (2018)
13. Kingma, D.P., Ba, J.: Adam: A method for stochastic optimization. arXiv preprint arXiv:1412.6980 (2014)
14. Kipf, T.N., Welling, M.: Semi-supervised classification with graph convolutional networks. arXiv preprint arXiv:1609.02907 (2016)
15. Lehmann, J., et al.: Dbpedia-a large-scale, multilingual knowledge base extracted from wikipedia. Seman. Web **6**(2), 167–195 (2015)
16. Lin, Y., Liu, Z., Sun, M., Liu, Y., Zhu, X.: Learning entity and relation embeddings for knowledge graph completion. In: Twenty-ninth AAAI Conference on Artificial Intelligence (2015)
17. Liu, H., Wu, Y., Yang, Y.: Analogical inference for multi-relational embeddings. In: Proceedings of the 34th International Conference on Machine Learning-Volume 70, pp. 2168–2178. JMLR. org (2017)
18. Miller, G.A.: Wordnet: a lexical database for English. Commun. ACM **38**(11), 39–41 (1995)
19. Nguyen, D.Q., Nguyen, T.D., Nguyen, D.Q., Phung, D.: A novel embedding model for knowledge base completion based on convolutional neural network. In: Proceedings of the 16th Annual Conference of the North American Chapter of the Association for Computational Linguistics: Human Language Technologies (NAACL-HLT), pp. 327–333 (2018)
20. Nguyen, D.Q., Sirts, K., Qu, L., Johnson, M.: Neighborhood mixture model for knowledge base completion. arXiv preprint arXiv:1606.06461 (2016)
21. Nickel, M., Tresp, V., Kriegel, H.P.: A three-way model for collective learning on multi-relational data. In: Proceedings of the 28th International Conference on Machine Learning, vol. 11, pp. 809–816 (2011)
22. Press, O., Wolf, L.: Using the output embedding to improve language models. arXiv preprint arXiv:1608.05859 (2016)
23. Schlichtkrull, M., Kipf, T.N., Bloem, P., van den Berg, R., Titov, I., Welling, M.: Modeling relational data with graph convolutional networks. In: Gangemi, A., et al. (eds.) ESWC 2018. LNCS, vol. 10843, pp. 593–607. Springer, Cham (2018). https://doi.org/10.1007/978-3-319-93417-4_38
24. Shang, C., Tang, Y., Huang, J., Bi, J., He, X., Zhou, B.: End-to-end structure-aware convolutional networks for knowledge base completion. In: Proceedings of the AAAI Conference on Artificial Intelligence, vol. 33, pp. 3060–3067 (2019)
25. Socher, R., Chen, D., Manning, C.D., Ng, A.: Reasoning with neural tensor networks for knowledge base completion. In: Advances in Neural Information Processing Systems, pp. 926–934 (2013)
26. Suchanek, F.M., Kasneci, G., Weikum, G.: Yago: a core of semantic knowledge. In: Proceedings of the 16th International Conference on World Wide Web, pp. 697–706. ACM (2007)
27. Toutanova, K., Chen, D.: Observed versus latent features for knowledge base and text inference. In: Proceedings of the 3rd Workshop on Continuous Vector Space Models and their Compositionality, pp. 57–66 (2015)
28. Trouillon, T., Welbl, J., Riedel, S., Gaussier, É., Bouchard, G.: Complex embeddings for simple link prediction. In: International Conference on Machine Learning, pp. 2071–2080 (2016)
29. Veličković, P., Cucurull, G., Casanova, A., Romero, A., Lio, P., Bengio, Y.: Graph attention networks. arXiv preprint arXiv:1710.10903 (2017)

30. Wang, H., Zhang, F., Zhao, M., Li, W., Xie, X., Guo, M.: Multi-task feature learning for knowledge graph enhanced recommendation. In: The World Wide Web Conference, pp. 2000–2010 (2019)
31. Wang, Z., Zhang, J., Feng, J., Chen, Z.: Knowledge graph embedding by translating on hyperplanes. In: Twenty-Eighth AAAI Conference on Artificial Intelligence (2014)
32. Xu, K., Hu, W., Leskovec, J., Jegelka, S.: How powerful are graph neural networks? In: International Conference on Learning Representations (2019). https://openreview.net/forum?id=ryGs6iA5Km
33. Yang, B., Yih, W.t., He, X., Gao, J., Deng, L.: Embedding entities and relations for learning and inference in knowledge bases. arXiv preprint arXiv:1412.6575 (2014)
34. Zhang, W., Paudel, B., Zhang, W., Bernstein, A., Chen, H.: Interaction embeddings for prediction and explanation in knowledge graphs. In: Proceedings of the Twelfth ACM International Conference on Web Search and Data Mining, pp. 96–104. ACM (2019)

Testing of Web Applications

Automatic Model Completion
for Web Applications

Ruilian Zhao⬛, Chen Chen⬛, Weiwei Wang$^{(\boxtimes)}$⬛, and Junxia Guo⬛

Beijing University of Chemical Technology, Beijing 100029, China
{rlzhao,gjxia}@mail.buct.edu.cn, chenchen_buct@outlook.com,
vivioe_wang@163.com

Abstract. Model-based testing is one of the most effective methods for testing web applications, where the integrity of models determines the effectiveness and efficiency of testing. Static/dynamic analysis techniques are widely used to construct models for web applications. However, it is almost impossible to build a complete model for web applications by static analysis techniques since web applications are driven by events, and web pages are generated dynamically. Dynamic analysis techniques construct models through monitoring the execution of web applications and capturing the pivotal behavior information. But it is challenging to explore all possible behaviors, resulting in incomplete models. So, the combination of dynamic and static analysis techniques is a viable way to construct a more complete model for web applications. Extended Finite State Machine (EFSM) is considered more suitable to represent modern web applications. So this paper defines an integrity criterion for EFSM models of web applications and proposes a model completion method by combining dynamic analysis and static analysis techniques. Static analysis is used to collect all behaviors from the source code of web application, identify the uncovered ones from the EFSM model built according to the integrity criterion, and find feasible transition sequences for the uncovered behaviors on the EFSM model. Furthermore, we design multiple priority rules for transition sequence generation to improve its efficiency. The dynamic analysis is employed to simulate the execution of feasible transition sequences on the EFSM model such that the uncovered behaviors can be added into the model to improve its integrity. We implement our method in a prototype tool called *AutoMC* and conduct a series of experiments on five open-source web applications. The experiment results show that our method can complete the model of web applications, and the priority rules provide effective guidance in transition sequence generation. The model's integrity improved by 22.68% on average.

Keywords: Model completion · Web applications · EFSM model · Lookahead search

Supported by the National Natural Science Foundation of China under Grant No. 61672085, No. 61702029 and No. 61872026.

M. Bielikova et al. (Eds.): ICWE 2020, LNCS 12128, pp. 207–227, 2020.
https://doi.org/10.1007/978-3-030-50578-3_15

1   Introduction

With the popularity of web applications, ensuring the quality and security of web applications has become a common concern both in industry and academia. Model-based testing (MBT), as one of the most effective methods, is widely used in web application testing. In the method, the model is the foundation, and the integrity of the model has a significant impact on the test effectiveness.

Generally, the model is an abstract representation of software under test, and it can be constructed with the help of dynamic/static analysis techniques. For web applications, which are driven by events and whose web pages are generated dynamically, it is almost impossible to build a complete model by static analysis techniques. For example, research [4,16] builds the model of the web application through static analysis. But the dynamic features of web pages changed by Ajax events are less likely to be captured by static analysis techniques, causing the model incomplete. Dynamic analysis techniques are widely used in model construction, which captures the pivotal behavior information as *traces* by monitoring the execution process of web application and then map traces to models. For example, some studies [13,14,19] use dynamic analysis to capture user behavior to build the corresponding models of web applications. But it is hard to explore all possible user behaviors, especially if events and related DOMs are hidden in deep layers or require complex interactions. So, the models built by dynamic analysis techniques are also mostly incomplete. Beyond the question, the combination of dynamic and static analysis techniques is a viable way of constructing a more complete model for web applications. However, few studies focus on the construction of complete models by using static and dynamic analysis techniques.

In modern web applications, an event may result in different web pages due to different execution conditions and cause various changes in the parameter(s) or DOM elements. Thus, the dynamic behaviors involve not only web pages and events, but also the trigger conditions and follow-up operations on the parameter(s) or DOM elements. In the previous work [19], EFSM (Extended Finite State Machines) model is considered more suitable to abstract modern web applications, which is constructed based on user behavior traces. The EFSM model consists of state nodes and transition edges, where the states represent web pages and the transitions represent the trigger-events, trigger-conditions and follow-up operations. Furthermore, the integrity of the EFSM model of web applications can be evaluated from different perspectives, such as event coverage, web pages coverage, and so on. But in modern web applications, the event and corresponding execution conditions together determine the reached web page and follow-up operations. So, we think that the event and its execution conditions can represent the behavior of web applications.

Combining the above analysis, we define an integrity criterion based on the events and execution conditions coverage for EFSM models of web applications and propose a model completion method combines dynamic and static analysis techniques. We use static analysis to collect all behaviors, containing events and trigger-conditions, from the source code of web application, identify the uncovered ones from the model built according to the integrity criterion, and search feasible transition sequences on the model for the uncovered behaviors. The dynamic analysis is employed to execute feasible transition sequences on the model such that the uncovered events and conditions can be added into the model to improve its integrity.

For the model completion, finding a feasible transition sequence from the model and then supplementing the model based on the sequence are two crucial problems. As we know, there are many approaches to generate a feasible sequence to cover the uncovered objective, such as meta-heuristic search algorithms [10, 15,20]. Lookahead search is considered as an effective method to generate a feasible sequence for covering the objective [7]. In general, there are more than one candidate to be chosen in the current search location. So, some priority rules need to be set up to rank candidates. Arlt used event dependence information to narrow the search space when generating event sequences from the conventional UI model [2,11]. Inspired by their work, we take the dependency, such as data dependency between transitions of EFSM, to design the priority rules. That is, the uncovered objective is treated as the initial transition for transition sequence generation. Then, the transition with the highest priority is inserted at the front of the transition sequence one by one until reaching the entrance of the model. Once the new expanding transition makes the transition sequence infeasible, the current transition sequence is backtracked to the previous one, and the transition with the next highest priority is chosen. If all alternative transitions do not expand the current transition sequence, then the transition sequence backtracks to the previous one again. Besides, control dependency is taken into account in sequence generation. After that, test inputs making the sequence executable are generated by using a search-based algorithm, such as the Genetic algorithm (GA). So far, a feasible transition sequence that can go through the uncovered objective from the entrance of the EFSM model has been generated. Then, the feasible transition sequence is dynamically executed through simulating users' interaction with the web application. Finally, the uncovered objective (event and conditions) is traversed, the follow-up web page and operations can be identified. Afterward, the newly reached web page is abstracted into the state. The event, conditions, and follow-up operations correspond to the transition. And the EFSM model is supplemented with the state and transition. Consequently, the integrity of the EFSM model of the web application is improved.

The contributions of our work are summarized below:

1. We define an integrity criterion to evaluate completeness of EFSM model of web applications.
2. We propose an automatic model completion method based on static analysis and dynamic execution for EFSM models of web applications.
3. We design priority rules to guide the selection of candidates, improving the efficiency of the lookahead search.
4. We conduct a series of experiments on five open source web applications to validate the effectiveness of our method, and further analyze the impact of different priority rules on feasible sequences generation and model completion.

2   EFSM Model of Web Applications

In the modern web application, web pages and events are two primary components that reflect the dynamic behavior of web applications. An event execution may transfer to different web pages due to different execution conditions, and cause changes in parameter(s) or DOM elements. Thus, besides web pages and events, the trigger conditions and follow-up operations are also essential to depict dynamic behaviors of web applications. EFSM is a widely used model that consists of states and transitions, where the states represent web pages and the transitions represent the trigger-events, trigger-conditions and follow-up operations. It is an enhanced model of FSM (Finite State Machines), which adds preconditions of transitions and actions. In the previous work [19], EFSM is adopted to describe dynamic behaviors of web applications, and its definition is as below.

Definition 1 ***EFSMs of web applications.*** *The EFSM model of web applications is defined as a 5-tuple* (S_0, S, I, O, T), *where* S *is a finite set of states,* $S_0 \in S$ *is the initial state of the model,* I *is a finite set of input declarations,* O *is a finite set of output declarations,* T *is a finite set of transitions. Each member of* S *is represented as a URL, and corresponding DOM. Each member of* I *expresses an input parameter. Each member of* O *represents an output parameter. Each member of* T *signifies a transition from one state to another, remarking changes in the structure of the web page, such as URL or DOM. Furthermore, a transition* t *is denoted by a 5-tuple* $<$***src, event, cond, act, tgt***$>$, *where* ***src(t)*** *and* ***tgt(t)*** *represent the source and target state of transition* t, *respectively;* ***event(t)*** *signifies the event triggered on current source state by users;* ***cond(t)*** *describes the triggered conditions in associated event handler functions; and* ***act(t)*** *indicates the follow-up operations on the parameters or DOM elements caused by user event callbacks or server responses. Specifically, an* ***event(t)*** *can be further expressed as* ***event(t,inputList)***, *meaning event occurs with a list of input parameters, and an* ***act(t)*** *can be further described as* ***act(t,paraList)***, *implying action implements with a list of input or output parameters.*

For transition t, if its $event(t)$ is triggered and $cond(t)$ is met, then $act(t)$ is performed, and the state transfers from $src(t)$ to $tgt(t)$. The $event$, $cond$ and act parts of a transition t are optional. For a web application, the EFSM is constructed based on user behavior traces. It is difficult for the dynamic analysis technique to capture all possible behaviors, which makes traces insufficient. Thus, the corresponding EFSM of web applications is also incomplete. Our automatic model completion method aims to solve this problem.

3   Case Study of Model Completion for Web Application

In this section, we conduct a case study on a simple web application to illustrate our model completion method. The article management module of the web application *phpaaCMS*, which is an open-source article management system, is taken as an example. The corresponding EFSM model built based on user behavior traces is shown in Fig. 1.

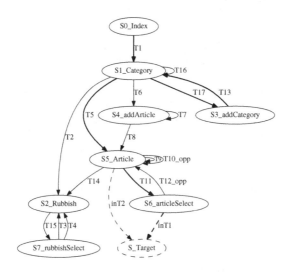

Fig. 1. The EFSM model of article management module

As Definition 1, the transition T_1 can be expressed as $<src:S_0;$ *event: click,link=Admin; cond:null; act:null; tgt:S_1* $>$, representing that on the *index page* (S_0), a user clicks *Admin* link (event), and enters into the *article category* page (S_1). Similarly, the transition T_{10} can be expressed as $<src:S_5;$ *event:click,Xpath:(//img[@alt='delete'])[2]; cond:a=='delete'&&id; act:null; tgt:S_5* $>$, representing that on the *article page* (S_5), users click the *delete* button to delete an article, the *delete* condition is triggered and the request is sent to web server. Then web server returns the response *delete* and enters the *article page* (S_5). The details of other transitions of the EFSM model are as below. T_5 is $<src:S_1;$ *event:click,Xpath://input[@value='Add article']; cond:null; act: null; tgt:S_5* $>$, T_{11} is $<src:S_5;$ *event:click,name=checkbox (id); cond:null; act: id=getCheckedIds('checkbox'); tgt:S_6* $>$, T_{12} is $<src:S_6;$ *event:click,id=Xpath: (//img[@alt='deleteAll'])[2]; cond:a=='deleteAll'&&id; act:null; tgt:S_5* $>$, T_{13} is $<src:S_3;$ *event:click,name=button (pid,name,seq); cond:null; act:null; tgt: S_1* $>$, and T_{17} is $<src:S_1;$ *event:click,Xpath://input[@value='Add category']; cond:null; act:null; tgt:S_3* $>$.

The EFSM model is constructed by user behavior traces. Obviously, the less frequently used behaviors are hard to be explored. Such as the *batch transfer* event, which is an event that users select multiple articles and transfer them to another group in batches. In general, the EFSM models constructed based on traces are incomplete. More specifically, the *batch transfer* event is rarely triggered because, usually, an article has been correctly classified when it is

```
1   <script type="text/javascript">
2   function doAction(a,id){
3   if(a=='deleteAll'&&id){//opposite condition
4           if(confirm('Delete all?')){ $.ajax({
5           data:'act=deleteAll&id='+getCheckedIds('checkbox'),
6                   success:function(data) {......}//T10     });}}
7   if(a=='delete'&&id){//opposite condition
8           if(confirm('Delete?')){ $.ajax({
9                   data:'act=delete&id='+id,
10          success:function(data) {......}//T12 });}}
11  if(a=='moveAll'&&id){//uncovered condition
12          if(confirm('All transferred?')){$.ajax({
13              data:'act=moveAll&id='+getCheckedIds('checkbox'),
14          success:function(data) {......}//T14 });}}}
15  </script>
```

Listing 1.1. JavaScript code of the event handler *doAction*

created. Thus, the *batch transfer* event and its execution condition, which is at line 11–14 of its corresponding event handler *doAction* shown in Listing 1.1, are difficult to appear in user behavior traces. Without loss of generality, we assume that the *batch transfer* event and its execution condition is not included in the EFSM model built, which is called as the uncovered behavior. How to identify uncovered behaviors and their priority rule is discussed in detail in Sect. 4.

Aiming at uncovered behaviors, we try to supplement them into the incomplete model. In general, different execution conditions in an event handler mean that the same event or the same type of event is handled in different ways. Hence, the uncovered conditions and its opposite conditions are likely to be activated from the same web page. Correspondingly, in the incomplete EFSM model, transitions covering opposite conditions are likely to be derived from the same state. For example, for the uncovered condition at line 11, its opposition conditions are in lines 3 and 7 in the listing1.1, which are involved in the transitions T_{10} and T_{12} with source states S_5 and S_6, respectively. The uncovered condition may also be derived from $S5$ or $S6$, but with a transition different from T_{10} and T_{12}, such as inT_1 and inT_2 in Fig. 1. To complete the EFSM model in Fig. 1, transitions inT_1 and inT_2 as well as their follow-up states should be supplemented into the model.

To generate a feasible transition sequence that can go through the inT_1 or inT_2 from S_0, lookahead search is employed. But which transitions (inT_1 or inT_2) should be considered first as the start for the sequence generation? The dependency between these two transitions and their preceding transitions can be analyzed. In *phpaaCMS*, to trigger *batch transfer* event, one or more articles should be selected, which is reflected in transition T_{11} of the EFSM model. Thus, we think it is more reasonable that T_{11} is treated as the preceding transition to cover the *batch transfer* event and its condition. So, we give higher priority to inT_1 as the initial transition of transition sequence generation. The priority rule for initial transitions is defined in Sect. 4.

During expanding transition sequences, we consider the dependency between transitions. The priority rules for preceding transition are defined in Sect. 4. Concretely, the less irrelevant variables are introduced by the preceding transitions, the less negative impact on sequence feasibility. The more relevant variables defined by the preceding transitions, the more significant the positive impact on sequence feasibility. Therefore, the preceding transitions can be prioritized when expanding the transition sequence. For example, for the EFSM model shown in Fig. 1, inT_1 is chosen as the start of the transition sequence generation, and its source state is S_6. The preceding transition of S_6 only has T_{11}. Thus, the partial sequence, $[T_{11}, inT_1]$ and the associated state S_5 can be obtained. Moreover, the state S_5 has four preceding transitions, which are T_5, T_8, T_9, and T_{10}, respectively. Since transition T_5 introduces the least irrelevant variables, compared to the other three transitions, T_5 is chosen to expand the sequence. As a result, the partial transition sequence $[T_5, T_{11}, inT_1]$ is generated, and state S_1 is gotten. Then, the preceding transitions of S_1 include T_1, T_{13}, and T_{16}. T_{13} defines the most data-relevant variables. So T_{13} is selected to expand the sequence, forming the sequence $[T_{13}, T_5, T_{11}, inT_1]$ and obtaining the state S_1. Subsequently, T_1 is added into the transition sequence, forming the final transition sequence $[T_1, T_{17}, T_{13}, T_5, T_{11}, inT_1]$. Then, the test inputs making this sequence executable are generated by using a search-based algorithm. Moreover, the sequence is further dynamically executed to determine the state that inT_1 can reach, namely the state S_Target in Fig. 1. And then, the transition inT_1 and state S_Target are supplemented into the EFSM model to improve its integrity.

4   Approach of Model Automatic Completion for Web Application

The integrity of the web applications' model seriously affects test effectiveness. But it is difficult to construct a complete EFSM model automatically based on user behavior traces for web applications. In this section, we define an integrity criterion for the model of web applications, and describe how to supplement the incomplete model built according to the integrity criterion by combining static lookahead analysis and dynamic simulation execution.

4.1   The Integrity Criterion for EFSM Model of Web Application

Web applications are one of the event-driven software, and their behaviors are activated by events. An event execution with different conditions may transfer to different web pages and cause changes in parameter(s) or DOM elements. That is, the event and its execution conditions triggered together determine the reached web page and follow-up operations. Thus, the behavior of web applications can be represented by the event and execution conditions in corresponding event handlers. To differentiate from the conditions on the transition of EFSM, the execution conditions triggered by events in the event handler are called JS branches. Therefore, the integrity criterion for the EFSM model of web applications is designed based on the events and JS branches coverage.

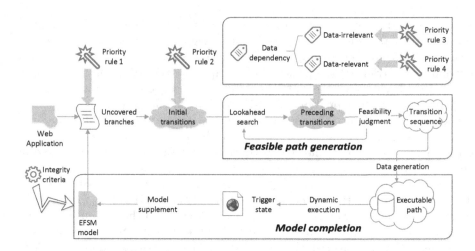

Fig. 2. The framework of automatic completion model for web applications

Definition 2 *All events & JS branches coverage criterion. If all the events and JS branches in the event handlers of a web application appear in its corresponding model, we call the model satisfying All events & JS branches coverage criterion.*

Based on this integrity criterion, the uncovered events and JS branches can be identified from the model built with the help of static analysis. Considering that all events coverage is easily achieved, this paper focuses on how to complete the model according to the uncovered JS branches.

4.2   Overview of Model Completion Method

To supplement the EFSM model built, we propose a model completion method which combines static and dynamic analysis techniques. Static analysis is used to collect all events and JS branches of a web application, identify the uncovered ones from its model, and find feasible transition sequences to traverse the uncovered one by lookahead search. Dynamic analysis is used to execute the transition sequence such that the corresponding transition and follow-up state can be added into the model to improve its integrity. Furthermore, to improve the efficiency of the transition sequence generation by lookahead search, a series of priority rules are designed to guide the selection of preceding transitions. The framework of our model completion method is shown in Fig. 2.

In more detail, for an uncovered JS branch, we first determine the initial transition for sequence generation. If there is more than one transition can be selected, such as inT_1 or inT_2 in Fig. 1, the transition with the highest priority is picked out as the initial transition. Then, the candidate transition with the highest priority is inserted at the front of the transition sequence one by one until reaching the entrance of the model. Besides, the feasibility of the generated partial transition sequence is judged, once a new preceding transition is added. After getting the feasible transition sequence, we generate data for the input variables of the transition sequence to make it executable. Then this sequence is dynamically executed, and a follow-up reached state is obtained. Finally, the initial transition and reached state are further used to supplement the EFSM model.

4.3   The Design of Priority Rules for Transition Sequence Generation

In transition sequence generation by lookahead search, there are usually more than one candidate transition to be chosen on the current search location. So, we design a series of priority rules to improve its efficiency. In this section, we will introduce these priority rules in detail.

The Priority Rule for the Selection of Uncovered Branches

In general, multiple uncovered branches are corresponding to the EFSM model built for a web application. Assume that the uncovered JS branch set is $UB = \{ub_1, ub_2, ..., ub_n\}$ $(n > 0)$, and the selected branch from UB for supplementing the EFSM model is called as target branch, denoted by tb, where $tb \in UB$.

Different tb will result in different transition sequences, which may have different completion effects on the EFSM model. If there are more than one uncovered branch, the dependencies between JS branches may exist. So, it is critical to determine which branch should be prioritized as the *target branch* to supplement the EFSM model. The more opposite branches of an uncovered branch appear in the EFSM model built, the more transitions can be chosen as the initial transition, the more likely it is to generate transition sequence to cover the uncovered branch. Therefore, the following priority rule is set for the uncovered branches.

Rule 1 *The priority rule for uncovered branches.* *The more opposite branches that an uncovered branch has in the EFSM model, the higher the priority of the uncovered branch is.*

The Priority Rule for the Selection of Initial Transitions

For a target branch $tb \in UB$, the corresponding transition is called as *target transition*, denoted by tt. tt is an initial transition for transition sequence generation. There may be more than one transition covering the opposite branches of tb. Thus, for tb, more than one initial transition exists. Without loss of generality, assume that there are m initial transitions for the target branch tb, and the initial transition set is $INT=\{ inT_1, inT_2, \cdots, inT_m \}$ $(m > 0)$, where $tt \in INT$.

As described in Sect. 3, the initial transition is selected as the starting point for sequence generation. However, the feasibility of initial transitions is affected by its preceding transition. Considering the data dependency between the initial transition and its preceding direct transition, the stronger the dependency between them, the greater the impact on the sequence feasibility, the higher priority should be given. The data dependency between transitions of the EFSM model are defined as below:

Definition 3 *Data dependency between transition.* *For two transitions T_i and T_j in the EFSM model, suppose that T_j is the preceding transition of T_i, the variables defined in T_j are $DV_{Tj} = \{dv_{j1}, dv_{j2}, \cdots, dv_{jk}\}$, and the variables used in T_i is $UV_{Ti} = \{uv_{i1}, uv_{i2}, \cdots, uv_{il}\}$. The def-use variables of T_j and T_i are $DU(T_j, T_i) = DV_{Tj} \cap UV_{Ti}$. If $DU \neq \phi$, we think there is a data dependency between transitions T_i and T_j. The more variables in DU, the stronger the data dependency.*

Based on this definition of data dependency between transitions, we give the following priority rule to set the appropriate priority for the initial transitions.

Rule 2 *The priority rule for initial transitions.* *Suppose the initial transition set is $INT = \{inT_1, inT_2, ..., inT_m\}$ ($m > 0$) for the target branch tb. The preceding transition sets of inT_i and inT_j are $preT_{inTi}$ and $preT_{inTj}$, where $preT_{inTi} = \{t_{i1}, \cdots, t_{ip}\}$ and $preT_{inTj} = \{t_{j1}, \cdots, t_{jq}\}$, respectively. The defined variable set, with respect to the preceding transition t_{ir} in $preT_{inTi}$, is DV_{tir}. The used variable set, with respect to the initial transition inT_i in INT, is UV_{inTr}. Then, the degree of data dependency between $preT_{inTi}$ and inT_i is defined as the maximum of the def-use variables between $preT_{inTi}$ and inT_i, that is, $\max_{r=1}^{p} |DU(t_{ir}, inT_i)|$. If the degree of data dependency between $preT_{inTi}$ and inT_i is stronger than that of $preT_{inTj}$ and inT_j, the initial transition inT_i is given a higher priority than inT_j.*

The Priority Rules for the Selection of Preceding Transitions

For a target transition tt, we try to search a feasible transition sequence through adding the preceding transition one by one until reaching the entrance of the EFSM model built, such that the tt can be supplemented into the model.

There may be more than one preceding transitions concerning the current transition sequence, which is named as partial sequence and denoted by $pSeq$. Among these preceding transitions, the transition that is conducive to generating a feasible transition sequence should be prioritized to expand the partial sequence. As mentioned above, the data dependency between the preceding transition and partial sequence has an influence on the feasibility of the sequence. If a preceding transition T_j has a data dependency with any transition T_i in $pSeq$, we call that T_j and $pSeq$ have a data dependency. The preceding transitions can be grouped into data-relevant transition and data-irrelevant transition for the current sequence, which are defined as below:

Definition 4 *Data-irrelevant transition*. *The preceding transitions that have no data dependency with the transition sequence pSeq are called data-irrelevant transitions of pSeq.*

Definition 5 *Data-relevant transition*. *The preceding transitions that have a data dependency with the transition sequence pSeq are called data-relevant transitions of pSeq.*

For data-irrelevant transitions, they do not affect the feasibility of the current sequence directly. However, if a data-irrelevant transition is added into the current sequence, the variables used in the conditions of data-irrelevant transition can be expanded into the used variables set of the partial sequence. It is observed that the more variables are used in the sequence, the more significant negative impact on the feasibility of the sequence. Thus, the following priority rule is given for the data-irrelevant transitions.

Rule 3 *The priority rule for the data-irrelevant transitions*. *Suppose that the partial sequence pSeq involves in n data-irrelevant preceding transitions set, denoted by $DIT=\{diT_1, diT_2, ..., diT_n\}$ ($n > 0$). The used variable sets of preceding transitions diT_i and diT_j ($0 < i, j < n$) are $UV_{diT_i}=\{v_{i1}, \cdots, v_{il}\}$ and $UV_{diT_j}=\{v_{j1}, \cdots, v_{jk}\}$, respectively. If the number of variables in UV_{diT_i} is less than that of UV_{diT_j}, then diT_i is given a higher priority than diT_j.*

For data-relevant transitions, they directly affect the feasibility of the partial sequence. It is observed that the more variables defined in the preceding transition are used in the current sequence, the easier to find inputs to make the sequence feasible. So, we give a higher priority to the preceding transition that defines more variables used in the partial sequence. Specifically, for data-relevant preceding transitions, the involving variables can be defined in *events* or *actions*, expressed by $evtDV=\{v_1, \cdots, v_m\}$ and $actDV=\{v_1, \cdots, v_n\}$. Among them, the variables in $evtDV$ can be assigned by the external input, while variables in $actDV$ cannot. Thus, variables in $evtDV$ are more likely to make the partial sequence meet its conditions than that of $actDV$. Therefore, we believe that variables in $evtDV$ are more important than that of $actDV$.

In general, there may be more than one data-relevant preceding transitions concerning a partial sequence. To evaluate the priority of data-relevant transitions quantitatively, we set different weights for variables in $evtDV$ and $actDV$ of a preceding transition. The priority of data-relevant transitions drT for the partial sequence $pSeq$ is computed as Eq. 1.

$$prio(drT) = \frac{|evtDV(drT) \cap UV(pSeq)| \times \alpha + |actDV(drT) \cap UV(pSeq)| \times \beta + 1}{|UV(pSeq)| + 1}$$

(1)

Where $evtDV(drT)$ represents the set of variables defined in events of a data-relevant preceding transition drT, $actDV(drT)$ represents the set of variables defined in action of drT, and $UV(pSeq)$ represents the set of variables used in the partial sequence $pSeq$. The values of different weights, i.e., α and β, are determined in the experiment.

Rule 4 *The priority rule for the data-relevant transitions. Assume that the partial sequence pSeq has n data-relevant transition set, which is $DRT\{drT_1, drT_2, ..., drT_n\}$ $(n > 0)$. If the $prio(drT_i) > prio(drT_j)$ $(0 < i, j < n)$, the transition drT_i is set to a higher priority than drT_j.*

4.4   Feasible Transition Sequence Generation for Target Transition

For a target transition tt, we try to find a feasible transition sequence to traverse it such that its follow-up state as well as operations can be identified, and tt can be supplement into the EFSM model. To further improve the efficiency of transition sequence generation by lookahead search, the preceding transitions are selected one by one based on the above priority rules until reaching the entrance of the EFSM model.

Concretely, for uncovered branches UB, a target branch tb is selected from UB based on the priority rule for uncovered branches selection first. As mentioned in Sect. 3, for a target branch tb, more than one initial transitions may exist. According to the priority rule for the initial transition, the initial transition with the highest priority is selected as the target transition $tt \in VT$. Then, tt is taken as the starting point of transition sequence generation, and the lookahead search is employed to pick out the preceding transitions based on the priority rules for the preceding transitions. In more detail, firstly, the candidate transition is selected from the data-relevant preceding transition set associated with the current transition sequence, based on the priority rule for the data-relevant transitions. If multiple data-relevant transitions have the same highest priority, we consider the control distance between the data-relevant transitions and the transition using the defined variables of the partial sequence. The smaller the distance is, the more significant the impact of data-relevant transitions on the feasibility of the partial sequence. So we select the transition with smaller control distance. If there is no transition in data-relevant preceding transitions set, the candidate transition is selected from the corresponding data-irrelevant preceding transition set based on the priority rule for the data-irrelevant transitions. If there are still multiple candidate transitions with the same priority, they are selected randomly. Then, the chosen transition is inserted at the front of the current transition sequence to extend the sequence. At the same time, the feasibility of the extended sequence is verified based on study [6]. If the chosen preceding transition makes the extended transition sequence infeasible, the next candidate transition, that is, the transition with the next highest priority is selected from the corresponding preceding transition set. If all alternative transitions do not expand the current transition sequence, then the transition sequence backtracked to the previous one. Otherwise, the extended sequence is treated as the current sequence, and the sequence is expanded continuously until reaching the entrance of the EFSM model. Therefore, for a target branch, the algorithm of feasible transition sequence generation is shown in Algorithm 1.

Algorithm 1. Feasible transition sequence generation based on priority rules

Require: webapp, EFSM, targetJS
1: $M = GetOppositeBranch(targetJS)$ // M is the opposite branch set of the target branch.
2: $S = GetSourceState(M)$ // S is the source state set of the transitions mapped by the opposite branches.
3: $INT = AddInitialTrans(targetJS, S)$ // INT is the initial transition set.
4: $RankInitialTrans(INT)$ // Prioritize the initial transitions.
5: **while** INT *is not empty* **do**
6:      $P = InitSequence(Top(INT))$ // Top() is a function that selects the highest priority transition.
7:      $INT.remove(Top(INT))$
8:      $FailedTrans = []$ // Records the transitions that fail to expand forward.
9:      **do**
10:         $F = GetPrecedingTrans(P) - FailedTrans$ // Removes failed preceding transitions.
11:         $D = GetDataRelevantTrans(F)$ // D is the data-relevant transition set.
12:         **if** D *is not empty* **then** $F = RankDataRelevantTrans(D)$
13:         **else** $F = RankDataIrrelevantTrans(F)$ // Prioritize the preceding transitions.
14:         **end if**
15:         **while** F *is not empty* **do**
16:            **if** $IsFeasible(Top(F), P)$ **then** $P = ExpendSequence(Top(F))$
17:               **break** // Judge the feasibility to extend the partial sequence.
18:            **else** $F.remove(Top(F))$
19:               $FailedTrans.add(Top(F))$
20:            **end if**
21:         **end while**
22:         **if** $ExpandSequence$ *is false* **then** $P = Bracktrack(1)$
23:            **if** P *is empty* **then break** // Try the next candidate initial transition.
24:            **end if**
25:         **end if**
26:      **while** *entrance is not reached*
27:      **return** P
28: **end while**
29: **return** $false$ // Generation fails.

4.5 Model Completion Based on Feasible Transition Sequence

In order to supplement the target branch into the EFSM model built, its follow-up state and operations need to be identified. Then, the feasible transition sequence should be executed dynamically to traverse the target transition. For each potential feasible transition sequence, we find the input parameter values that trigger the sequence by applying the GA-based test data generation system we developed earlier for EFSM models [22], making the sequence executable. The transition sequence is dynamically executed through simulating users' interaction with web applications.

Finally, the state triggered and follow-up actions by target transition can be identified from the execution results. If the triggered state is the same as one of the existing states in the EFSM model built, which is decided by the comparison of their DOM structures , then the existing state is taken as the target state of the target transition. Otherwise, the triggered state is new, then we add this state to the state set S of the model, and the target state of this transition is set to the new state. If the transition sequence generation for a target branch fails, this branch will be placed last, and another uncovered branch is taken into account. If all uncovered branches own its corresponding executable transition sequence, or the time budget is reached, the model completion is terminated.

5   Experiment

To verify the effectiveness of the proposed method, we have implemented our automatic model completion method in a prototype tool called *AutoMC*, and conduct a series of experiments on five different types of web applications as well as their associated EFSM models built. The results are analyzed in detail below. Moreover, the following research questions motivate our experiments:

RQ1: Can the transition sequence generation method generate feasible transition sequences to traverse the uncovered behavior?
RQ2: Is our model completion method based on the feasible transition sequence effective in improving the model integrity?
RQ3: How effective are the priority rules in transition sequence generation method?

To answer these research questions, the metrics used to measure the effectiveness of our method are introduced firstly. Above all, we count the number of JS branches that are not covered by the EFSM models built based on user behavior traces ($NUJB$), the number of traversed branches by feasible transition sequences generated ($NTJB$), and the number of branches that are successfully supplemented to the model ($NSJB$). Then, for the model before and after completion, we observe the number of states (NS) and transitions (NT). Further, we measure the *JS branch coverage* of the model according to the integrity criterion. For the priority rules, we compare the total number of transition sequences generated (NTS), the average generation time of each feasible transition sequence (AGT(ms)), the average length of the feasible transition sequences (ALS), and the average time of model completion computed by four methods for five web applications to measure their role in our method. The details of the four methods are described below.

5.1   Experimental Subjects

We selected five open source web applications from https://sourceforge.net as our experimental subjects, which are commonly used in theoretical research and practical application. Table 1 shows the details of the web application, such as the number of lines of code (LOC), the number of all *JS branches* (NJB), and functional description. The source code of web applications is analyzed by the Esprima tool [1] to get all the JS branches. The EFSM models are constructed based on the user behavior traces, which are discussed in our early work [19]. The uncovered JS branch is identified by comparing it with its corresponding EFSM model, whose number, i.e., NUJB, is listed in column 4 of Table 1, as our target branches.

Table 1. Web applications used in the study

App Name	LOC	NJB	$NUJB$	Functional description
SchoolMate	8181	89	18	Student management system with admin role
Addressbook	47481	25	5	Addressbook management system
Webchess	4722	25	8	Online chess game
FAQForge	1712	8	3	FAQ management tool
phpaaCMS	15949	61	7	Article management system

5.2   Experimental Implementation and Results Analysis

Experimental Implementation

For uncovered branches, *AutoMC* is employed to generate the corresponding feasible transition sequences based on a series of priority rules, dynamically execute the generated feasible transition sequence with the help of *selenium* tool to verify its triggered states and follow-up operations, and insert the target transitions into the EFSM models to improve their integrity. When analyzing the DOM structure of the triggered state, the *BeautifulSoup* library is used to parse the HTML file and the elements, as well as attribute nodes of the DOM tree, are compared to determine whether the triggered state is the new state. Besides, the different weights for α and β in Eq. 1 are set as 10 and 1 through experiments, which make the path generation most efficient.

Experimental Results Analysis

For RQ1. To validate whether our transition sequence generation method can find feasible transition sequences to traverse the uncovered behavior, we analyze the results of sequence generation for five web applications, and show the results in Table 2. As can be seen from this table, our method can generate feasible transition sequences for almost all uncovered branches except one in *Webchess* to support model completion.

Table 2. The results of transition sequence generation

	SchoolMate	Addressbook	Webchess	FAQForge	phpaaCMS
$NUJB$	18	5	8	3	7
$NTJB$	18	5	7	3	7

In *Webchess* web application, one uncovered branch is not traversed by the transition sequence generated. Through manual inspection and analysis, the reason was found to be due to the selection strategy of candidate preceding transitions. When there are data-relevant transitions and data-irrelevant transitions in preceding transitions at the same time, to improve the efficiency, we only consider the data-relevant transitions and select the candidate transition from them based on the priority rule for data-relevant transitions. Experiments show that this method can generate feasible transition sequences faster, but it may miss the potential feasible transition sequences that are related to data-irrelevant transitions.

For RQ2. To answer the effectiveness of our method in improving the model integrity, we analyze the results of model completion according to feasible transition sequences generated, and details the results in Table 3. Further, Fig. 3 shows the *JS branch coverage* of the model before and after model completion.

Table 3. The models before and after model completion

		SchoolMate	Addressbook	Webchess	FAQForge	phpaaCMS
$NTJB$		18	5	7	3	7
$NSJB$		16	5	7	3	6
Model before completion	NS	41	19	13	10	50
	NT	118	33	30	17	83
Model after completion	NS	45	20	14	11	54
	NT	140	38	39	22	91

It can be seen from Table 3 that the NS and NT in the EFSM model supplemented increase, and the JS branch coverage in Fig. 3 shows an upward trend after model completion. Thus, it can be drawn that our model completion method can improve the integrity of the original EFSM model.

However, two branches in *SchoolMate* and one in *phpaaCMS* are not added to the EFSM model. Through manual analysis, we found this is because the test data generation method is unable to generate complex data for the transition sequence generated, causing the sequence inexecutable. As a result, the corresponding transition can not be supplemented into the EFSM model built.

For RQ3. To analyze the effectiveness of the priority rules in transition sequence generation, we implement different transition sequence generation methods by using different priority rules. In more detail, the priority rules for uncovered branches and initial transitions directly determine whether the lookahead search can be activated. So, in the process of generating the transition sequence, we mainly distinguish different priority rules for preceding transitions, thus forming four different methods as below: (1) lookahead search without priority rules for preceding transitions called *LS*; (2) lookahead search with all priority rules except for that for data-relevant transitions, called *AutoMC-DR*; (3) lookahead search with all priority rules except for data-irrelevant transitions, called *AutoMC-DI*; (4) lookahead search with all priority rules, namely our method, called *AutoMC*. To eliminate the randomicity interference of the experiment, these four methods of transition sequence generation are run 100 times for each

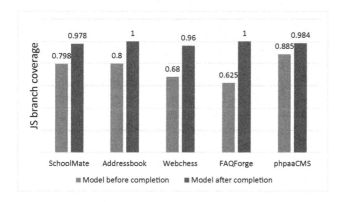

Fig. 3. The JS branch coverage of the model before and after completion

Table 4. The results of transition sequence generation by different methods

Method		SchoolMate	Addressbook	Webchess	FAQForge	phpaaCMS
LS	$NTJB$	18	5	8	3	7
	NTS	267	451	680	256	496
	AGT	36.93	15.24	187.14	12.10	4.29
	ALS	21.80	24.39	145.07	16.23	8.99
AutoMC-DR	$NTJB$	18	5	8	3	7
	NTS	275	455	689	258	518
	AGT	18.89	13.90	183.30	11.17	4.39
	ALS	16.78	23.02	135.78	14.89	8.98
AutoMC-DI	$NTJB$	18	5	7	3	7
	NTS	1744	478	606	294	521
	AGT	7.88	7.51	28.12	2.59	2.72
	ALS	12.09	19.82	30.47	12.87	8.99
AutoMC	$NTJB$	18	5	7	3	7
	NTS	1743	483	618	293	520
	AGT	8.02	6.70	25.09	2.37	3.03
	ALS	12.08	18.95	29.56	11.50	8.95

uncovered branch. The results of the transition sequences generated by different are shown in Table 4.

From the $NTJB$, we can see that these four-generation methods can generate feasible transition sequences to traverse almost all uncovered branches. But in terms of generation efficiency, these generation methods vary a lot. In more detail, within the same number of iterations, the NTS of LS is less than that of the other three lookahead search with priority rules (AutoMC-DR, AutoMC-DI, and AutoMC). That is, lookahead search with priority rules can generate more feasible transition sequences in the same iteration. Besides, the AGT of LS is higher than that of AutoMC-DR, AutoMC-DI, and AutoMC. This shows that lookahead search with priority rules uses less time to generate each feasible sequence. Thus, it can be seen that the priority rules make the lookahead search more efficient in feasible transition sequences generation. Furthermore, compared AutoMC-DR with AutoMC-DI in NTS and AGT, it can be inferred that the priority rule for data-relevant transitions has a more positive impact on transition sequence generation. From the ALS, we can see that the use of priority rules can significantly shorten the length of the generated transition sequence, especially on *Webchess*. Through manual analysis, we found that the reason is that there are more data-relevant transitions in the model of *Webchess*. If the appropriate transition is not selected in time, there will be many unnecessary loops traversed, resulting in long transition sequences.

Therefore, lookahead search with priority rules produces better results and efficiency then a simple lookahead search in the transition sequences generation. The priority rule for data-relevant transitions have a more significant impact than that of data-irrelevant transitions. So, it can be concluded that our method with all priority rules performs best in transition sequence generation.

Based on the transition sequences generated by $AutoMC$, the model is completed by simulating users' interaction of the transition sequence. The average time of model completion for five Web applications is 8.13 min, 0.84 min, 7.51 min, 0.88 min, and 1.45 min, respectively, which is acceptable.

6   Related Work

In recent years, model-based testing (MBT) methods are widely used in web applications. Modeling for web applications is one of the most essential tasks in MBT, which is usually time-consuming. Most of the modeling methods use static/dynamic analysis to build the model. Because of the event-driven and dynamic characteristics of the web application, it is difficult for static analysis techniques to construct a complete model. Research [4,12] extracts models through static analysis but lacks consideration of the dynamic characteristics, resulting in the incomplete models. Ricca and Tonella construct a UML class diagram [16] to model the static and dynamic feature of web application. During the stage of processing the forms and the pages linked to them, the tester manually selects test inputs, including the data used to fill out the forms, which is usually time-consuming and error-prone. Dynamic analysis techniques can capture user behavior information as traces to build models. Mesbah et al. [13,14] use dynamic analysis to build the behavior models of web applications. But because it is difficult to explore all possible user behaviors, the models are usually incomplete. Ricca and Tonella present a diversity-based web test generation algorithm [5]. A navigational model of the dynamic web pages is extracted and each web page is modelled in form of page objects, which creates methods based on the actions statically extracted from each test state. In most cases, the resulting methods may miss complex interactions that are possible on the web GUI, causing the incomplete models. In Wang's work [19], a minimum user behavior trace set generation method based on dynamic analysis is proposed to build the EFSM model. Due to the same reason, the integrity of the EFSM model also cannot be guaranteed. To alleviate this problem, in Su's work [18], the FSM model is constructed by combining the dynamic and static analysis techniques. Dynamic analysis infers events from the UI level of the page, but it may miss some complex events. The static analysis can scan all the event listeners and connect the missed events with the widget through the resource ID during the execution. However, inaccurate positioning and failing to find the target UI element will result in the infeasible event sequences. Thus, the model is still incomplete.

To supplement the incomplete model, this paper proposes a model completion method combining dynamic analysis and static analysis. In our method, the transition sequence generation is the core of the model completion. Some of the approaches in automated test sequence generation can inspire, such as symbol execution, random testing, and meta-heuristic search algorithms. For example, research [8] proposes a model-based testing method for Android applications. And symbol execution is used to explore the program paths of each event handler. On this basis, targeted event sequences are generated by lookahead search in the UI model. Inspired by this, we consider lookahead search is an effective way to generate sequences for covering the objective. *Kudzu* [17] and *crawljax* [13] explore the state space of web applications by randomly selecting events, which uses heuristic search strategies to create event sequences. Crawljax relies on the heuristics algorithm to detect event handlers, but it may not be able to detect all event handlers. Research [3] developed a tool, named *Artemis*, based on feedback oriented testing for JavaScript applications. Artemis instantiated event sequences by using different priority ranking functions and generated inputs with a simple feedback mechanism, thereby creating effective event sequences. In research [9], the feasibility of the transition sequence on the EFSM model is estimated by analyzing the data flow correlation between actions and conditions. In research [21], an automatic unit test generation method combining static and dynamic is proposed. First, dynamic analysis is used to infer the call sequence model from the sample execution. Then, static analysis is used to identify the dependencies between methods based on the fields they may read and write. Finally, the inference model (tends to be accurate but incomplete) and the static deterministic dependency information (tends to be conservative) are used to create legitimate and diversified tests. Inspired by their work, the dependency information between transitions is helpful to guide sequence generation.

7 Conclusion

In this paper, an automatic model completion method is proposed for the EFSM model of the web application, including target-oriented transition sequence generation and model completion based on the transition sequences generated. The core idea is to generate feasible transition sequences for uncovered branches, collect the information of model completion by dynamically executing the transition sequences, and insert the corresponding transition into the EFSM model. In the transition sequence generation, we propose a series of priority rules as a guide to reduce the search space in the lookahead search. The completed model is evaluated by the proposed integrity criteria. We believed that the way the integrity criterion is defined and used can be also viewed as a potential adequacy criteria for generated test cases. Experimental results show that the proposed method can generate feasible transition sequences for uncovered branches and complete the EFSM model built based on user behavior traces. The integrity of the model has been significantly improved. The average JS branch coverage of the model increased from 75.76% to 98.44%.

References

1. http://esprima.org/
2. Arlt, S., Podelski, A., Bertolini, C., Schäf, M., Banerjee, I., Memon, A.M.: Lightweight static analysis for GUI testing. In: 2012 IEEE 23rd International Symposium on Software Reliability Engineering, pp. 301–310. IEEE (2012)
3. Artzi, S., Dolby, J., Jensen, S.H., Møller, A., Tip, F.: A framework for automated testing of javascript web applications. In: Proceedings of the 33rd International Conference on Software Engineering, pp. 571–580. ACM (2011)
4. Athaiya, S., Komondoor, R.: Testing and analysis of web applications using page models. In: Proceedings of the 26th ACM SIGSOFT International Symposium on Software Testing and Analysis, pp. 181–191. ACM (2017)
5. Biagiola, M., Stocco, A., Ricca, F., Tonella, P.: Diversity-based web test generation. In: Proceedings of the 2019 27th ACM Joint Meeting on European Software Engineering Conference and Symposium on the Foundations of Software Engineering, pp. 142–153 (2019)
6. Cheng, J., Zheng, L., Zhao, R.: Infeasible path detection for EFSM models. J. Inner Mongolia Univ. (Nat. Sci. Ed.) **42**(5), 498–504 (2011)
7. Dutt, S., Shi, O.: A fast and effective lookahead and fractional search based scheduling algorithm for high-level synthesis. In: 2018 Design, Automation & Test in Europe Conference & Exhibition (DATE) (2018)
8. Jensen, C.S., Prasad, M.R., Møller, A.: Automated testing with targeted event sequence generation. In: Proceedings of the 2013 International Symposium on Software Testing and Analysis, pp. 67–77. ACM (2013)
9. Kalaji, A.S., Hierons, R.M., Swift, S.: Generating feasible transition paths for testing from an extended finite state machine (EFSM). In: 2009 International Conference on Software Testing Verification and Validation, pp. 230–239. IEEE (2009)
10. Kalaji, A.S., Hierons, R.M., Swift, S.: Generating feasible transition paths for testing from an extended finite state machine (EFSM). In: International Conference on Software Testing, Verification, and Validation Workshops, pp. 230–239 (2010)
11. Lam, W., Kask, K., Larrosa, J., Dechter, R.: Residual-guided look-ahead in and/or search for graphical models. J. Artif. Intell. Res. **60**, 287–346 (2017)
12. Marchetto, A., Tonella, P., Ricca, F.: State-based testing of Ajax web applications. In: 2008 1st International Conference on Software Testing, Verification, and Validation, pp. 121–130. IEEE (2008)
13. Mesbah, A., Bozdag, E., Van Deursen, A.: Crawling Ajax by inferring user interface state changes. In: 2008 Eighth International Conference on Web Engineering, pp. 122–134. IEEE (2008)

14. Mesbah, A., Van Deursen, A., Lenselink, S.: Crawling Ajax-based web applications through dynamic analysis of user interface state changes. ACM Trans. Web (TWEB) **6**(1), 3 (2012)

15. Rao, S., Jahan, H., Liu, D.: A search-based approach for test suite generation from extended finite state machines. In: International Conference on Progress in Informatics and Computing, pp. 82–87 (2017)

16. Ricca, F., Tonella, P.: Analysis and testing of web applications. In: Proceedings of the 23rd International Conference on Software Engineering, pp. 25–34. IEEE Computer Society (2001)

17. Saxena, P., Akhawe, D., Hanna, S., Mao, F., McCamant, S., Song, D.: A symbolic execution framework for javascript. In: 2010 IEEE Symposium on Security and Privacy, pp. 513–528. IEEE (2010)

18. Su, T., et al.: Guided, stochastic model-based GUI testing of android apps. In: Proceedings of the 2017 11th Joint Meeting on Foundations of Software Engineering, pp. 245–256. ACM (2017)

19. Wang, W., Guo, J., Li, Z., Zhao, R.: EFSM-oriented minimal traces set generation approach for web applications. In: 2018 IEEE 42nd Annual Computer Software and Applications Conference (COMPSAC), vol. 1, pp. 12–21. IEEE (2018)

20. Wu, T., Yan, J., Zhang, J.: A path-oriented approach to generating executable test sequences for extended finite state machines. In: 2012 Sixth International Symposium on Theoretical Aspects of Software Engineering (TASE), pp. 267–270. IEEE (2012)

21. Zhang, S., Saff, D., Bu, Y., Ernst, M.D.: Combined static and dynamic automated test generation. In: Proceedings of the 2011 International Symposium on Software Testing and Analysis, pp. 353–363. ACM (2011)

22. Zhao, R., Harman, M., Li, Z.: Empirical study on the efficiency of search based test generation for EFSM models. In: 2010 Third International Conference on Software Testing, Verification, and Validation Workshops (ICSTW), pp. 222–231. IEEE (2010)

Almost Rerere: An Approach for Automating Conflict Resolution from Similar Resolved Conflicts

Piero Fraternali, Sergio Luis Herrera Gonzalez[(✉)],
and Mohammad Manan Tariq

Dipartimento di Elettronica, Informazione e Bioingegneria, Politecnico di Milano,
Piazza Leonardo da Vinci 32, 20133 Milan, Italy
{piero.fraternali,sergioluis.herrera}@polimi.it,
mohammad.tariq@mail.polimi.it

Abstract. Concurrent development requires the ability of reconciling conflicting updates to the code made independently. A specific case occurs when long living feature branches are integrated to a rapid changing code base. In this scenario, every integration test will require to manually resolve the same conflicts at every iteration. In this paper we propose a framework for automating the detection and resolution of conflicts in the code updated by distinct developers, one of which may be a code generator. The tool learns how to solve conflicts from past experience and applies resolutions, encoded as replacement regular expressions, to conflicts not seen before. Experiments show that the number of automatically resolved conflicts and the quality of the solution increase as the system acquires experience.

Keywords: Automatic conflict resolution · GIT · Code integration

1 Introduction

The development of large and complex software applications requires distributing programming tasks among multiple developers. In Model Driven Development, this scenario may also include code generators that produce implementation code from high level models. When the same code base is updated concurrently by different actors, whether human or automatic, the possibility arises that the same portion of the code is affected, generating inconsistencies between the changes made by the actors and/or the code base. This occurrence is called *conflict* [8].

Conflict management is particularly relevant in the engineering of Web and multi-channel applications, because the implementation of the functional and of the presentation requirements is often assigned to distinct developers working on the same code base. Albeit the presentation aspects of Web-based interfaces can be factored out in CSS rules, the separation of concern is in reality partial, because it is a common practice to add presentation-oriented elements to the page structure to support the selective application of presentation styles.

© Springer Nature Switzerland AG 2020
M. Bielikova et al. (Eds.): ICWE 2020, LNCS 12128, pp. 228–243, 2020.
https://doi.org/10.1007/978-3-030-50578-3_16

Therefore, the concurrent update of structure and of the presentation aspects produces conflicts, which require the continuous alignment of the two facets of development to preserve the change of either aspect.

To support distributed development, Version Control Systems (VCS) [29] offer functions to share code, track changes, and identify conflicts. When conflicts are signalled by the VCS, the resolution is delegated to the developer, which makes code integration a time-consuming task [17]. Conflict resolution is also repetitive because similar or identical conflicts appear at every iteration. A significant case occurs in Model Driven Development when the source model and/or the model-to-text transformation templates are modified. In this case, the code generator applies the same transformation rules to many spots in the code overwriting the manually integrated code and producing multiple changes with the same pattern. In our previous work [6], we have addressed the management of the conflicts between handwritten and generated code, albeit the Virtual Developer approach helps reducing the conflicts between handwritten and generated code, still the need persists of manually resolving many similar conflicts.

In this paper we develop a method to let a VCS learn how to resolve similar conflicts. A conflict and its resolution can be modelled as a pair (*before-state*, *after-state*), where the before state contains the line(s) of the code affected by concurrent inconsistent updates and the after state comprises the code provided by the developer to resolve the inconsistency. The key idea is to exploit the conflict resolutions implemented by human developers in the past to create rules applicable to future (similar) conflicts. Intuitively, this requires the following process. When the first conflict is resolved manually, its resolution pair is processed to derive a *Conflict Resolution Rule (CRR)*. Then the first *Conflict Cluster (CC)* is created and the rule is associated with it. When a new resolved conflict arrives, its before state is compared with the existing CCs. If it is similar to some existing CC, it is added to it and the CRR associated with the CC is applied to resolve it; otherwise, the user is prompted to provide a resolution and a new (CC, CRR) pair is created. A quality metrics on the resolution provided by the CRR is monitored; as the system observes more and more manual conflict resolutions, the quality of the resolution computed by the CRR increase and the user may accept that the rule is applied without supervision.

The contribution of the paper can be summarized as follows: 1) We introduce the problem of automating the resolution of similar conflicts in concurrent application development and define the version control framework and workflow needed to handle it. 2) We apply the Hierarchical Agglomerative Clustering (HAC) algorithm with the Jaro-Winkler string similarity measure [30] to group similar conflicts in Conflict Clusters. A CC includes conflicts that may be resolved by the same rule. 3) We adapt the approach of [2] and [3] to automatically synthesize Conflict Resolution Rules for the conflicts of a CC. A CRR is a search and replace regular expression extracted from a set of conflict resolutions specified as pairs (*before-state*, *after-state*). Specifically, the CRR is the best fitted search and replace expression that maps the before states of all the conflicts in the CC into the respective after state. 4) We illustrate a reference implementation, called *Almost Rerere*, which extends the functionality of the popular Git VCS[1]. Almost Rerere builds on top of the *Git Rerere* plug-in, which resolves automatically conflicts *identical* to already seen instances and helps developers pre-check partial revisions before integrating a complete revision into the master branch. Almost Rerere can resolve conflicts *similar* to those observed in past iterations and can be used throughout the development process to support the semi-automatic resolution of previously unseen conflicts. It learns more and more precise CRRs as the application development progresses. 5) We evaluate the approach in the development of a web application using a Model-Driven Development tool that generates conflicts with the handwritten code and by extracting conflicts and resolutions from the history of submissions of large Git open source project repositories.

2   Related Work

The relevant related work refers to the identification of code similarities and to the generation of string rewriting rules from input/output examples.

Code similarity has been studied for software analysis, evaluation of refactoring issues, clone and plagiarism detection, etc. Textual approaches use direct string matching and comparison techniques for the detection of similarities, a wide set of this type of algorithms is available e.g. Jaccard Coefficient [19], Levenshtein Distance [18], Longest Common Subsequence (LCS) [26], Jaro [11] and Jaro-Winkler [30] similarity, Needleman Wunsch algorithm [27], Smith Waterman algorithm [28], etc. Ducasse et al. [9] used string-based Dynamic Pattern Matching (DPM) to detect code clones. Marcus and Maletic [21] applied latent semantic indexing (LSI) for finding similar code segments. Token-based approaches use lexical analysis for transforming the code into sequences of lexical tokens and the resulting sequences are then compared searching for duplicated sub-sequences of tokens. Tools implementing this approach are CCFinder [14], DUP [1] and CP-Miner [20]. Syntactic approaches use parsing to convert the source code into an Abstract Syntax Tree (AST). ASTs can then be analysed using tree-matching [4,12,15] and metrics-based methods [22]. The above-described approaches are combined with advanced clustering techniques, e.g., to provide intelligent recommendations or to identify bugs automatically. Kreutzer et al. created C3 (Clustering of Code Changes) a tool that scans code repositories to automatically detect code fixes by clustering code changes using diff-based and AST-based metrics.

The problem of synthesizing string-to-string transformations from a set of input/output examples is NP-Complete [10]. Nevertheless, some approaches have been developed to solve specific instances of the problem, many of them related to code editing. LAPIS [25] uses an assisted approach in which the user provides an initial search & replace expression that the system can improve or a set of positive and negative examples that are used to infer similar sections of the text.

---

[1] https://git-scm.com/.

LASE [24] uses a syntactic approach to create a context-aware edit script from examples and uses the script to automatically identify edit locations and apply the transformation to the code. The approach was later extended with RASE [23], an automatic refactoring tool for clone removal. A different approach was proposed by Bartoli et al. in [2] and [3], in which they used Genetic Programming (GP) and cooperative co-evolution to synthesize search & replacement patterns based on examples of the desired behaviour. The search pattern is a regular expression (regex) that defines the portions of the string to be replaced and the portions to be reused by the replacement pattern.

In this work, we aim at developing a language-independent tool able to handle conflicts in modern web and mobile projects mixing several languages. We base our tool on textual approaches for the similarity computation and conflict clustering tasks and adapt the algorithm of Bartoli et al. for conflict resolution. A text-based method presents advantages over syntactic techniques that require the creation of AST and are language-dependent. It can be applied to any semi-structured string, is independent of the text format, and can perform context-dependent rule extraction.

3   Background

3.1   Conflict Resolution

The concurrent development of software applications requires the management of possibly conflicting updates to the same code base by different developers. A typical workflow, in which the same code base is updated inconsistently by two developers (D1 and D2) producing a conflict, proceeds as follows.

Developers D1 and D2 initialize their local code base C1 and C2 from the current content of the central code-base C, which comprises the status of the project resulting from n preceding revisions. D1 and D2 start working independently on their local revisions, R_{D1}^1 and R_{D2}^1, initially equal. D1 introduces a new feature by applying changes to R_{D1}^1, creating a new local revision R_{D1}^2. Next, D2 independently updates R_{D2}^1 to introduce another feature, creating a new local revision R_{D2}^2. D1 submits his local revision to the central code-base generating a new shared revision R_C^2. No conflicts arise because D1 applied his update to the shared consolidated revision ($R_C^1 = R_{D1}^1$). Now D2 submits his revision to the central code-base. The operation creates a conflict because the submitted revision does not derive from the *current* shared revision ($R_C^2 \neq R_{D2}^1$). D2 performs conflict resolution and generates a new local revision R_{D2}^3, which integrates the feature locally developed by D2 and the current state of the central code-base (which comprises the feature developed and submitted by D1). He submits R_{D2}^3 to the central code-base and produces a new shared revision R_C^3.

The following example illustrates the content of a conflict. The markers <<<<<<< and >>>>>>> delimit the conflict area, and inside the conflict area the marker ======= separates the two colliding updates.

```
1   <h3>List</h3>
2   <table class="table table-hover table-condensed">
3   <!-- Conflict area Start -->
4   <<<<<<<
5       <thead class = "header">
6   =======
7       <thead class= "table_header">
8   >>>>>>>
9   <!-- Conflict area End -->
10          <tr>
11              <th>#</th>
12              <th>First Name</th>
13              <th>Last Name</th>
14          </tr>
15      </thead>
16      ...
17  </table>
```

The conflict illustrated above can be resolved by the following CRR:

```
{
    "regex": "(?:([^2])[^_]eader(\"))++",
    "replacement": "$1table_header$2"
}
```

The above CRR searches for the character sequence "eader" preceded by a case insensitive character and between quotes, and replaces the characters between the quotes with the string "table_header", leaving the rest unmodified.

3.2 Git Rerere

Git Rerere (**RE**use **RE**corded **RE**solution)[2] is a component of Git conceived to resolve conflicts that have already been handled in previous code integration steps. When a new conflict occurs the tool automatically records it in a pre-image file and once the conflict has been resolved manually by the developer it stores the conflict resolution in a post-image file. When the same conflict occurs again, Git Rerere reuses the recorded solution to manage the conflict automatically. Git Rerere is typically used in the development a long-lived feature branch where developers execute several testing cycles before the release of the feature. The pre- and post-images of a conflict are stored in a sub-directory named by *hashing* the content of the conflict area of the file. When a conflict occurs, Rerere extracts the conflict area, generates the hash, searches for the directory with that name, extracts the post-image and uses it to perform a merge with the current state of the file, thus resolving the conflict and preserving the rest of the non-conflicting

---

[2] https://git-scm.com/docs/git-rerere.

changes. Git Rerere is designed to automate the resolution of multiple identical
conflicts and cannot handle similar pre-images to apply a recorded solution to
a non-identical conflict. This aspect shows up also in the internal organization
of the tool. Due to the use of conflict hashes as access keys to the directory
organization, any change in the hash of a conflict prevents finding the recorded
solution. Moreover, when multiple conflicts in a source file occur, Rerere generates a single hash per source file using all conflict areas. If a new conflict occurs
in a file where a previously resolved conflict existed, a new hash is created and
the previously resolved conflict is no longer retrieved.

Almost Rerere aims at resolving automatically not only the conflicts that are
identical to previously seen instances, but also those that are *similar* to instances
solved in the past. It identifies conflicts with the same pattern, clusters them
based on a similarity criterion, and associates each cluster with a rule synthesized
from the conflict resolutions of the cluster. It does not depend on the stability
of the *hash* of the conflicts but rather exploits the changes in the conflict text
to learn a pattern that characterizes a family of related conflicts and to build a
replacement rule that can be applied to resolve future similar occurrences.

4   Proposed Approach

The proposed approach consists of three main steps: the identification of similar
conflicts using the Jaro-Winkler string similarity metrics; 2) the grouping of
similar conflicts using an agglomerative hierarchical clustering algorithm; 3) the
synthesis of conflict resolution rules by giving clusters in input to a genetic
algorithm that computes a search and replacement expression.

4.1   Almost Rerere Architecture

Figure 1 shows the architecture of Almost Rerere, which comprises four main
components: the Submission Manager, the Cluster Manager, the CRR Generator, and the Conflict Resolver.

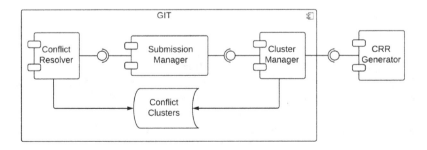

Fig. 1. *Almost Rerere* architecture

The Submission Manager extends *Git Rerere* and orchestrates the processing of a merge or commit command issued by the developer. The Cluster Manager implements the online hierarchical clustering algorithm that assigns an input conflict to an existing or new cluster. The CRR Generator exploits the method proposed in [3] and is triggered every time a conflict is added to a cluster. It synthesizes a CRR in the form of a regex & replacement expression that can be applied to the resolution of the conflicts of that cluster. Finally, the Conflict Resolver is called when a new conflict occurs. It searches for the cluster with the highest similarity index to the conflict, extracts the CRR, applies it, and returns the result as the possible solution to the conflict.

4.2 Conflict Cluster Generator

The core contribution of Almost Rerere is the recognition that a new conflict is similar to an occurrence already addressed in the past, so that a generalization of the previously applied resolution can be reused to cope with the new conflict. Generalizing a CRR requires identifying a pattern common to multiple conflicts, which consists of a constant and of a variable part. The constant part is used to match the conflicts that can be addressed by the CRR. The variable part enables addressing the differences in the conflicts with the same pattern. This approach requires two elements: a metrics for quantifying the distance between conflicts and an algorithm to group conflicts based on such a distance.

Almost Rerere computes the distance between conflicts based on a string similarity measure. Several string similarity algorithm were evaluated on a test data set of about 200 code line pairs. The *Jaro-Winkler* similarity algorithm showed the highest similarity scores of code lines in the same pair in 80% of cases and was selected for the implementation of the clustering algorithm. A similarity threshold was determine by calculating the precision, recall and F_1 for several thresholds, it was determine that 0.80 was the value maximizing F_1. The intuition behind the Jaro-Winkler algorithm performing better on the conflict data set is that it gives more importance to differences near the start of the string than to those near the end. It is common in many programming languages that the beginning of a line of code comprises reserved words, e.g. type declarations (*int, double, String*), access declarations (*public, private, protected*), flow control specifications (*if, while, switch*), etc. that are likely to remain unchanged. The end of a code line, on the other hand, is occupied by variables and operations declared by the developer, which are more likely to be updated.

The conflicts are grouped using hierarchical agglomerative clustering (HAC) [13]. When a conflict with its respective resolution is received from the Submission Manager, the cluster with the highest similarity score is searched. If the similarity score of the retrieved cluster is below a threshold (0.80), a new cluster is generated and the conflict is assigned to it; otherwise the conflict is added to the cluster. In both cases, the CRR generator is called to create a new rule or an improved version of an existing rule for the cluster. Each cluster has a unique id and contains an array of objects composed by the conflict and its resolution. Figure 2 shows an example.

```
 1  {
 2      "1": [
 3          {
 4          "conflict":"if (g instanceof UndirectedGraph){",
 5          "resolution":"if (g instanceof UndirectedGraph<?,?>){"
 6          },
 7          {
 8          "conflict":"if (!(graph instanceof DirectedGraph)){",
 9          "resolution":"if (!(graph instanceof DirectedGraph<?, ?>)){"
10          },
11          {
12          "conflict":"if (this.graph instanceof UndirectedGraph){",
13          "resolution":"if (this.graph instanceof UndirectedGraph<?,?>){"
14          }
15      ]
16  }
```

Fig. 2. Example of Conflict Cluster

4.3   CRR Generator

The CRR Generator exploits the general-purpose string search & replacement algorithm of [3], which takes as input a series of examples, consisting of pairs describing the original string and the desired modified string and outputs a search pattern and a replacement expression. The former is a regular expression that describes both the portions of the string to be replaced and those to be reused; the latter describes how to build the output string.

The method of [3] employs a Genetic Programming algorithm inspired by concepts of biological evolution such as reproduction, mutation, recombination, and selection. The best regular expression is chosen based on a fitness function. The set of examples is divided in three subsets: training, validation and testing. The training examples are used to generate an initial population of 16 candidate expressions for each training sample. The validation set is used to measure the fitness of the candidates in the initial population. The candidate expressions are applied to the test samples and the precision and recall with respect to the ground truth are computed, as well as the expression complexity. Next, the best candidates are selected and recombined in the next iteration of the process. Finally, the test set is used to evaluate the best candidate expression.

The method of [3] has been adapted to take as input a conflict cluster, to dynamically partition the input samples into the training, validation and testing sets, and to output a CRR for each cluster. As an example of the generated CRR, Fig. 3 shows the rule generated from the cluster of Fig. 2.

```
1  {
2      "1": [
3          {
4              "regex": "(h)(?=\))",
5              "replacement": "$1<\?,\?>"
6          }
7      ]
8  }
```

Fig. 3. The CRR generated from the CC of Fig. 2

The CRR searches for a character **h** followed by a closed parenthesis and the replacement expression then inserts the expression **<?,?>** after the character **h** to implement the desired transformation.

When the number of available samples is small, the algorithm is sensitive to the way in which the samples are assigned to the training, testing, and validation sets. To mitigate this problem, the samples are randomly divided into the training, testing and validation sets and the algorithm is executed multiple times. If the generated CRR is the same across the executions, which indicates that the algorithm has converged, it is saved. Otherwise, all solutions are kept, and the CRR is composed as the disjunction of the computed expressions. In the experiments, two rounds of execution proved to afford the best trade-off between performance and accuracy of the synthesised CRRs.

4.4 Conflict Resolver

This component has the responsibility to resolve the new conflicts when the developer executes a *git merge* command. The component searches for the cluster with the highest similarity measure with respect to the incoming conflict. The CRR of the selected cluster is applied and the result is returned to the developer.

5 Evaluation

Almost Rerere was evaluated in two case studies: the development from scratch of a web-based crowd sourcing platform using an Agile Model-Driven Development tool and approach, and the resolution of conflicts extracted from the reproduction of commits in the Git repositories of long-run open-source projects.

5.1 Integration of Handwritten and Generated Code

The goal of the test was to make an evaluation of how Almost Rerere could help in resolving conflicts during the life-cycle of a Model-Driven Development project. The application was developed using IFMLEdit.org[3] [5], an online tool

---

[3] https://ifmledit.org/.

for the rapid prototyping of web and mobile applications based on the Interaction Flow Modeling Language (IFML) [7]. The developed application was a
web-based crowd-sourcing platform for the selection and annotation of images.
The development process of the application was divided into seven sprints. At
each sprint, the developers applied changes to the IFML model, to the code generation templates, which combine HTML, JavaScript and CSS, and manually
modified the automatically generated code to add non-modelled features. Two
developers worked in parallel, the main repository of the code was the master
branch, each developer worked on his own branch and integrated the changes to
the master branch once completed. During the sprints, both developers updated
the code generation templates. When the code was generated from the modified
templates, the changes would propagate to all the relevant pages. In other cases,
the changes were made directly on the generated code. Both developers committed changes to their local branch. When the local branches were merged into the
main repository, conflicts arose because independent changes were applied to the
same lines of code. Whenever a conflict was detected, Almost Rerere intervened
to resolve the conflict or to record the manual resolution provided by the developer. During the seven sprints about 200 conflicts were resolved. Figure 4 shows
the total number of conflicts and the number of those resolved by Almost Rerere
at each sprint. In the first sprint, it can be observed that no conflict is resolved,
because no recorded conflicts existed at that point. In the second sprint, only 4
conflicts were resolved, because the number of samples available was small. As
the number of occurring conflicts increased, also the number of resolutions by
Almost Rerere grew.

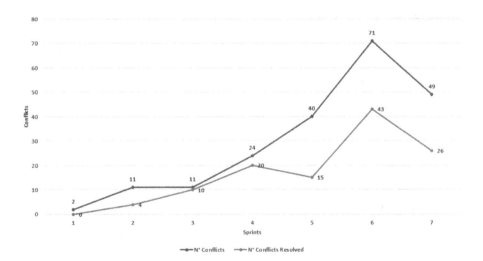

Fig. 4. Total conflicts vs. conflicts resolved by Almost Rerere

Overall Almost Rerere proposed a resolution for 57% of conflicts occurred
during development. The quality of the resolution depends on the intra-cluster

similarity. Almost Rerere created 21 clusters for 121 different conflicts. 7 of those clusters have an intra-cluster similarity above 90%. By manual inspection, it was observed that for those clusters the CRR provided a good result directly applicable to solve the conflicts. In other 7 cases, clusters have intra-cluster similarity below 90% and the proposed resolutions required manual inspection to verify that they were syntactically and semantically correct. In the remaining cases, the cluster contained only 1 or 2 samples and Almost Rerere could not generate a CRR for such isolated cases. It was observed that when a cluster had few samples, the generated CRR was very sensitive to small variations, such as spaces. As the number of conflicts in a cluster increased, the tool was able to generalize the CRR by taking into account the possible variations.

5.2   Large Project Repositories

To evaluate the quality of the automatic resolution provided by Almost Rerere, it was necessary to know the actual resolutions committed by developers and use them as ground-truth. In [16], nine data sets based on Git repositories from active Java open-source projects were created by extracting all the differences between the sequential commits to the master branch. From six such repositories, we extracted all the single-line changes and used them as conflicts resolved by developers. For each single-line change, the original state was considered as the conflict and the after state as the resolution. Almost Rerere was fed with the content of each conflict file, to execute the cycle of resolving the conflict, adding it to the corresponding cluster and updating the generated CRR. The provided resolution for each conflict was compared to the ground-truth and the similarity index between them was saved.

Almost Rerere provided resolutions for a high number of conflicts in each repository: Ant 54%, Cobertura 70%, Eclipse SWT 59%, FitLibrary 54%, JGrapT 68%, JUnit 49%. Table 1 shows the statistics of the evaluated repositories. Overall Almost Rerere resolved 55,7% of conflicts.

Table 1. Total conflicts, clusters and resolved conflicts

Repository	N° conflicts	N° cluster	N. conflicts resolved	% resolved
Ant	10500	1294	5667	53,97
Cobertura	1260	179	885	70,24
Eclipse SWT	1355	382	799	58,97
FitLibrary	4399	337	2371	53,90
JGraphT	3200	238	2135	66,72
JUnit	4424	388	2166	48,96
Total	**25138**	**2818**	**14023**	

Table 2. N° conflicts by resolution similarity intervals

Repository	100–90%		89–80%		<79%	
Ant	3717	65,59%	791	13,95%	1159	20,45%
Cobertura	577	65,19%	100	11,29%	208	23,50%
Eclipse SWT	567	70,96%	128	16,02%	104	13,01%
FitLibrary	1690	71,27%	434	18,30%	247	10,41%
JGraphT	1748	81,87%	221	10,35%	166	7,77%
JUnit	1470	67,86%	370	17,08%	326	15,05%
Total	**9229**		**2044**		**2210**	

Table 3. N° of cluster by intra-cluster similarity intervals

Repository	100–90%	89–80%	79–0%
Ant	127	485	682
Cobertura	27	33	119
Eclipse SWT	62	116	204
FitLibrary	48	132	157
JGraphT	26	86	126
JUnit	43	162	183
Total	**333**	**1014**	**1471**

To verify the quality of the generated resolutions, they were classified according to the Jaro-Winker similarity with the original resolution. Three intervals were considered: 100–90% for which synthesized resolution was equal or almost identical to the original one; 89–80% for which the synthesized resolution was close to the original one with only small variations; $\leq$79%, for which the synthesized resolution was rather different from the original one and required the developer's intervention (see Table 2). Out of the 14.023 conflicts resolved, 65,8% of the resolutions had a similarity score with the original resolution exceeding 90%. This shows that Almost Rerere was able to synthesize an accurate resolution in most cases based on previously resolved similar conflicts. Table 3 classifies the clusters by their intra-cluster similarity. It can be observed that the clusters with less than 79% intra-cluster similarity account for almost 50% of the total clusters. They represent conflicts that are not common (occurred only once) or not similar to other conflicts. It was also observed that in trivial cases Almost Rerere could provide accurate resolutions even with very few examples, whereas in more complex cases it required more samples to generalize. For example, in the JGraphT repository, Almost Rerere created a cluster with 40 conflicts with intra-cluster similarity of 84%. Some examples of conflicts are:

```
1  [
2    {
3      "conflict":  "public  BreadthFirstIterator(  Graph  g  )  {",
4      "resolution":  "public  BreadthFirstIterator(  Graph<V,  E>  g  )  {"
5    },
6    {
7      "conflict":  "public  UnmodifiableGraph(  Graph  g  )  {",
8      "resolution":  "public  UnmodifiableGraph(  Graph<V,  E>  g  )  {"
9    },
10   {
11     "conflict":  "public  CycleDetector(  DirectedGraph  graph  )  {",
12     "resolution":  "public  CycleDetector(  DirectedGraph<V,  E>  graph  )  {"
13   }
14 ]
```

The common pattern is the addition of the generic expression $<V, E>$. In this case the learning process was simple and with only four samples Almost-Rerere converged to a CRR that provides a correct resolution:

```
1  [
2    {
3      "regex":  "(h)(  )",
4      "replacement":  "$1<V,$2E>  "
5    }
6  ]
```

A different case is exemplified in the Cobertura repository, where a cluster contained the following conflicts:

```
1  [
2    {
3      "conflict":  "return  numberOfCoveredBranches;",
4      "resolution":  "return  getRawCoverageData().getNumberOfCoveredBranches();"
5    },
6    {
7      "conflict":  "return  numberOfCoveredLines;",
8      "resolution":  "return  getRawCoverageData().getNumberOfCoveredLines();"
9    },
10   {
11     "conflict":  "return  numberOfLines;",
12     "resolution":  "return  getRawCoverageData().getNumberOfValidLines();"
13   },
14   {
15     "conflict":  "return  numberOfBranches;",
16     "resolution":  "return  getRawCoverageData().getNumberOfValidBranches();"
17   }
18 ]
```

In this case Almost Rerere, based on the first conflict, generated a CRR that transforms the name of the variable into a getter method respecting the Java notation. When the second conflict occurred, the CRR continued to work well. For the third conflict, the expression did not generated the expected result because the resolution added the word Valid to the name of the method. Almost Rerere integrated the ground truth of the third example into the cluster and generated a composite CRR, with different patterns for the two cases:

```
1  [
2    {
3      "regex":  "(m*+)\w(umberOfCovered)(\w++)(;)",
4      "replacement":  "$1getRawCoverageData\(\)\.getN$2$3\(\)$4"
5    },
6    {
7      "regex":  "\w(\w\w\w\w\w\w\w)(\w+)",
8      "replacement":  "getRawCoverageData\(\)\.getN$1Valid$2\(\)"
9    }
10 ]
```

The composite CRR also worked when the fourth conflict occurred and provided an accurate resolution. This examples shows that Almost Rerere can adapt quickly when different unseen examples become available. Still it is sensitive to small changes when the number of samples available is small.

6   Conclusions

The paper describes an approach for the automatic resolution of conflicts during code integration on Git repositories. The approach is based on the synthesis of a search regular expression and a replacement expressions from previously resolved similar conflicts. A reference implementation, *Almost Rerere*, which extends the functionality of *Git Rerere*, was introduced, and the components in charge of executing the different steps of the approach, such as conflict clustering, regular expression generation and conflict resolution, were described. The proposed approach was evaluated in two use cases showing that it was able to resolve more than 55% of the observed conflicts. It was also shown, in the second use case, that more than 65% of the generated resolutions had a similarity score above 90% with the ground truth. Future work will focus on improving the Cluster Manager by adding a dynamic re-clustering capability to keep cluster intra-similarity high, this would prevent the CRR and CC become outdated over time. It would also extend the approach for the detection and resolution of multi-line conflicts.

References

1. Baker, B.S.: On finding duplication and near-duplication in large software systems. In: Proceedings of 2nd Working Conference on Reverse Engineering, pp. 86–95. IEEE (1995)
2. Bartoli, A., Lorenzo, A.D., Medvet, E., Tarlao, F.: Inference of regular expressions for text extraction from examples. IEEE Trans. Knowl. Data Eng. **28**(5), 1217–1230 (2016)
3. Bartoli, A., De Lorenzo, A., Medvet, E., Tarlao, F.: Automatic search-and-replace from examples with coevolutionary genetic programming. IEEE Trans. Cybern. (2019). https://doi.org/10.1109/TCYB.2019.2918337
4. Baxter, I.D., Yahin, A., Moura, L., Sant'Anna, M., Bier, L.: Clone detection using abstract syntax trees. In: Proceedings of International Conference on Software Maintenance (Cat. No. 98CB36272), pp. 368–377. IEEE (1998)
5. Bernaschina, C., Comai, S., Fraternali, P.: Ifmledit.org: model driven rapid prototyping of mobile apps. In: Proceedings of the 4th International Conference on Mobile Software Engineering and Systems, pp. 207–208. IEEE Press (2017)
6. Bernaschina, C., Falzone, E., Fraternali, P., Herrera, S.: The virtual developer: integrating code generation and manual development with conflict resolution. ACM Trans. Softw. Eng. Methodol. (TOSEM) **28**(4), 20 (2019)
7. Brambilla, M., Fraternali, P.: Interaction Flow Modeling Language: Model-Driven UI Engineering of Web and Mobile Apps with IFML. Morgan Kaufmann (2014)
8. De Souza, C.R., Redmiles, D., Dourish, P.: Breaking the code, moving between private and public work in collaborative software development. In: Proceedings of the 2003 International ACM SIGGROUP Conference on Supporting Group Work, pp. 105–114. ACM (2003)

9. Ducasse, S., Rieger, M., Demeyer, S.: A language independent approach for detecting duplicated code. In: Proceedings IEEE International Conference on Software Maintenance-1999 (ICSM 1999). Software Maintenance for Business Change (Cat. No. 99CB36360), pp. 109–118. IEEE (1999)
10. Hamza, J., Kunčak, V.: Minimal synthesis of string to string functions from examples. In: Enea, C., Piskac, R. (eds.) VMCAI 2019. LNCS, vol. 11388, pp. 48–69. Springer, Cham (2019). https://doi.org/10.1007/978-3-030-11245-5_3
11. Jaro, M.A.: Advances in record-linkage methodology as applied to matching the 1985 census of Tampa, Florida. J. Am. Stat. Assoc. **84**(406), 414–420 (1989)
12. Jiang, L., Misherghi, G., Su, Z., Glondu, S.: Deckard: scalable and accurate tree-based detection of code clones. In: Proceedings of the 29th International Conference on Software Engineering, pp. 96–105. IEEE Computer Society (2007)
13. Johnson, S.C.: Hierarchical clustering schemes. Psychometrika **32**(3), 241–254 (1967)
14. Kamiya, T., Kusumoto, S., Inoue, K.: CCFinder: a multilinguistic token-based code clone detection system for large scale source code. IEEE Trans. Softw. Eng. **28**(7), 654–670 (2002)
15. Koschke, R., Falke, R., Frenzel, P.: Clone detection using abstract syntax suffix trees. In: 2006 13th Working Conference on Reverse Engineering, pp. 253–262. IEEE (2006)
16. Kreutzer, P., Dotzler, G., Ring, M., Eskofier, B.M., Philippsen, M.: Automatic clustering of code changes. In: Proceedings of the 13th International Conference on Mining Software Repositories, MSR 2016, pp. 61–72. ACM, New York (2016)
17. Le Nguyen, H., Ignat, C.L.: An analysis of merge conflicts and resolutions in git-based open source projects. Comput. Support. Coop. Work (CSCW) **27**(3–6), 741–765 (2018)
18. Levenshtein, V.I.: Binary codes capable of correcting deletions, insertions, and reversals. Sov. Phys. Doklady **10**, 707–710 (1966)
19. Li, C., Lu, J., Lu, Y.: Efficient merging and filtering algorithms for approximate string searches. In: 2008 IEEE 24th International Conference on Data Engineering, pp. 257–266. IEEE (2008)
20. Li, Z., Lu, S., Myagmar, S., Zhou, Y.: CP-Miner: Finding copy-paste and related bugs in large-scale software code. IEEE Trans. Softw. Eng. **32**(3), 176–192 (2006)
21. Marcus, A., Maletic, J.I.: Identification of high-level concept clones in source code. In: Proceedings 16th Annual International Conference on Automated Software Engineering (ASE 2001), pp. 107–114. IEEE (2001)
22. Mayrand, J., Leblanc, C., Merlo, E.: Experiment on the automatic detection of function clones in a software system using metrics. In: ICSM, vol. 96, p. 244 (1996)
23. Meng, N., Hua, L., Kim, M., McKinley, K.S.: Does automated refactoring obviate systematic editing? In: Proceedings of the 37th International Conference on Software Engineering, vol. 1, pp. 392–402. IEEE Press (2015)
24. Meng, N., Kim, M., McKinley, K.S.: Lase: locating and applying systematic edits by learning from examples. In: Proceedings of the 2013 International Conference on Software Engineering, pp. 502–511. IEEE Press (2013)
25. Miller, R.C., Myers, B.A.: Lapis: smart editing with text structure. In: CHI Extended Abstracts, pp. 496–497 (2002)
26. Nakatsu, N., Kambayashi, Y., Yajima, S.: A longest common subsequence algorithm suitable for similar text strings. Acta Inform. **18**(2), 171–179 (1982)
27. Needleman, S.B., Wunsch, C.D.: A general method applicable to the search for similarities in the amino acid sequence of two proteins. J. Mol. Biol. **48**(3), 443–453 (1970)

28. Smith, T.F., Waterman, M.S., et al.: Identification of common molecular subsequences. J. Mol. Biol. **147**(1), 195–197 (1981)
29. Tichy, W.F.: RCS–a system for version control. Softw.: Pract. Exp. **15**(7), 637–654 (1985)
30. Winkler, W.E.: String comparator metrics and enhanced decision rules in the Fellegi-Sunter model of record linkage (1990)

Generation of Realistic Navigation Paths for Web Site Testing Using Recurrent Neural Networks and Generative Adversarial Neural Networks

Silvio Pavanetto$^{(\boxtimes)}$ (iD) and Marco Brambilla$^{(\boxtimes)}$ (iD)

Dipartimento di Elettronica, Informazione e Bioingegneria,
Politecnico di Milano, P.za L. da Vinci 32, Milano, Italy
{silvio.pavanetto,marco.brambilla}@polimi.it

Abstract. A robust technique for generating web navigation logs could be fundamental for applications not yet released, since developers could evaluate their applications as if they were used by real clients. This could allow to test and improve the applications faster and with lower costs, especially with respect to the usability and interaction aspects. In this paper we propose the application of deep learning techniques, like recurrent neural networks (RNN) and generative adversarial neural networks (GAN), aimed at generating high-quality weblogs, which can be used for automated testing and improvement of Web sites even before their release.

Keywords: Web engineering · Data mining · Deep learning ·
Recurrent neural networks · Generative adversarial networks · Testing

1 Introduction

Weblogs represent the navigation activity generated by a specific amount of users on a given website. This type of data is fundamental, e.g. for a company, because it contains information on the behaviour of users and how they interface with the company's product itself (website or application). The first useful information that can be extracted from weblog is the quality of the website, as described in the work of Berendt and Spiliopoulou [2], where they try to understand navigation patterns that are present in the data. This is explained also in the work of Singh et al. [15] in 2013, that shows an overview of the web usage mining techniques by applying pattern recognition. In addition, one could analyze these patterns and the statistics about users activities with visualization tools as explained in the work of Bernaschina et al. [3].

If a company could have a realistic weblog before the release of its product, it would have a significant advantage because it can use the techniques explained above to see the less navigated web pages or those to put in the foreground, but users and time are needed to produce them, making it an expensive task.

M. Bielikova et al. (Eds.): ICWE 2020, LNCS 12128, pp. 244–258, 2020.
https://doi.org/10.1007/978-3-030-50578-3_17

Because of this limit, our focus is on the generation part, since this particular task is little explored, but it is often a recurring theme also in the research world due to the lack of publicly available data.

In fact, open source libraries like Flog Generator [9] and Fake Apache Generator [1], or the work by Lin et al. [10], generate logs in a random manner and cannot be used as datasets that represent the users behaviour. Therefore, being able to create an algorithm that generates high-quality weblogs would be relevant from a scientific and commercial point of view.

What we did was apply deep learning methods for generating more realistic navigation activities, starting from a RNN (Hochreiter Sepp and Jürgen Schmidhuber [8]), which has been seen that it can be used for generating complex sequences with long-range structure (Alex Graves et al. [7]). Then trying a GAN (Goodfellow et al. 2014 [5]): neural networks aimed at generating new data, such as images or text, very similar to the original ones and sometimes indistinguishable from them, that have become increasingly popular in recent years.

The challenge is to evaluate which algorithm for the generation of log data could be the best and to verify if the GAN is applicable to this problem. Our work starts with the implementation of a generative algorithm based only on the theories already presented in the literature concerning the analysis and generation of weblogs. Then we introduce the algorithms that falls into the category of deep learning: an RNN and a GAN, verifying the effective generative capacity of these neural networks.

This paper is structured as follows: first, we talk about the state of the art for web mining and discrete data sequences generation topics. Then, there is a section about the methods used in this work, followed by an implementation and experiments part. Lastly, we close with the conclusions and future works.

2   Related Work

Berendt and Spiliopoulou [2] in 2000 have demonstrated the appropriateness of the "Web Usage Miner" (WUM): a set of tools which discovers navigation patterns subject to advanced statistical and structural constraints. This work was intended to understand the quality, defined as the conformance of the web site's structure to the intuition of each group of visitors accessing the site, of a specific website as a whole and not considering every page as a single. For doing this, they used data mining techniques such as sequence pattern mining and apriori algorithm.

The work of Singh et al. [15] in 2013 shows an overview of the web usage mining technique by applying pattern recognition on weblog data, defined as the act of taking in raw data and making an action based on the 'category' of the pattern. They divide their work into three parts: Preprocessing, Pattern discovery and Pattern analysis.

Generally speaking, these works that analyse web log data for pattern discovery, use almost the same approach based on data pre-processing and data mining techniques previously explained, in addition to a clusterization in some cases (Vedaprakash et al. [16] and Mahoto et al. [11] are examples).

Regarding weblog data generation, the open source malicious log detection library [10] tries to generate new access log data, by inserting in some malicious activities with the purpose of identifying them. The problem with [10] and other open source libraries such as Flog Generator [9] or Fake Apache Generator [1], is that they create these logs in a random manner. Instead, in this work we produce them in a completely different and more structured way. With respect to deep learning techniques used to produce discrete data, we can start with LSTM in recurrent neural networks (RNNs), presented for the first time by Hochreiter Sepp and Jürgen Schmidhuber [8]. This type of RNNs was widely used in the subsequent works, like the work by Alex Graves [7] that shows how Long Short-term Memory recurrent neural networks can be used to generate complex sequences with long-range structure, simply by predicting one data point at a time. Their approach is demonstrated for text (where the data are discrete) and online handwriting (where the data are real-valued). Due to the success of this type of neural network applied to data sequences (real-valued and discrete ones), this work proposes a Long Short-term Memory recurrent neural networks approach as the first deep learning method.

In the past few years, new techniques have been presented for generating high-quality data; the most famous and promising is the GAN (Goodfellow et al. 2014 [5]) that uses a discriminative model to guide the training of the generative one. However, it has limitations when the goal is for generating sequences of discrete tokens. A major reason lies in that the discrete outputs from the generator make it difficult to pass the gradient update from the discriminative model to the generative model. In addition, the discriminative model can only assess a complete sequence, while for a partially generated sequence, it is non-trivial to balance its current score and the future one, once the entire sequence has been generated. Yu et al. [17] try to solve this problem, proposing a sequence generation framework, called SeqGAN. Modeling the data generator as a stochastic policy in reinforcement learning (RL), SeqGAN bypasses the generator differentiation problem by directly performing gradient policy update. The RL reward signal comes from the GAN discriminator judged on a complete sequence and is passed back to the intermediate state-action steps using a Monte Carlo search. However, in their work they use a 'oracle' model, that is a randomly initialized LSTM as the right model, to generate the real data distribution $p(x_t|x_1, ..., x_{t-1})$ for their experiments and evaluations. In this way, they have a significant benefit: it provides the training dataset and then evaluates the exact performance of the generative models. In our approach we use real data as training data instead, and at the end of the GAN training we evaluated the results with different metrics.

3 Deep Learning Based Log Generation

In this section we present our statistical and deep learning approaches for generating weblogs. The core idea is to develop a recurrent neural network and a generative adversarial network (GAN) for generating new weblog data, and compare the generation performance of these methods with the statistical algorithm.

3.1 Statistical Approach

To this day the only public libraries simply create logs in a completely random manner. This approach is very coarse and therefore we decided not to consider it even as a baseline. We propose instead a method composed by two main parts: the first analyses a website and extracts statistical information, the second uses those data for generating new weblogs. The input must contain some important elements, such as the *Entry Points*[1], the *Confidences*[2], the *Mean Times*[3] and the *Web Site Graph*[4].

The implementation uses the state of the art methods for the extraction of knowledge from logs and applies this information on the creation process. Regarding the actual implementation of this algorithm, first we need to set different variables to produce new logs, like the *Maximum number of IPs at the same time*, a *List of users IPs*, the *Number of navigation sessions* and so on. Once all the configuration parameters are set, the algorithm can start the generation part where, if S is the total number of navigation sessions previously established, it repeats S times the computation of the *Navigation Path*, that consists of:

- *Selection of Entry Point:* The first thing that the algorithm needs to compute for every navigation session, is the entry point of the sequence. This page is selected among all the home pages that has been received as input by the algorithm, using the associated probability of being selected. It is not possible to start the navigation with a page that is not present on the home pages list.
- *Computation of Next URL:* After the selection of the entry point, the algorithm chooses the next URL until the sequence length is reached: this is the exit condition of every loop iteration. This URL is selected by retrieving all the possible subsequent pages for the previous computed URL and then by picking one of them using the probability of moving from one page to another.
- *Computation of Residence Time:* After each couple of URLs is chosen, it is necessary to calculate the number of seconds that the user will spend on page A before moving to page B or terminating the navigation. This is done by looking at the *Mean Times* that come as input to the algorithm and picking the mean time that corresponds to that couple of pages.

---

[1] A list of pages that represent the possible entry points for every navigation session. A probability to start the navigation with that page is associated with each one.

[2] The confidences are the probabilities for moving from a specific page to another, or, the probabilities for moving to a new page at a particular moment T, knowing the complete navigation path done from the beginning of the session (In this case, session means a portion of continuous time in which the user is browsing without leaving or interrupt the navigation.), until T.

[3] A list of mean times expressed in seconds that correspond to the quantity of time that users spend on that page on average.

[4] The graph representing the entire web site, where each page is associated with a list of possible subsequent pages.

Once the loop cycle is completed and all the sequences have been generated, the algorithm produces a log file that contains all the navigation activity of the users, created previously. The requests are sorted by time, and then the file is created. As we illustrated, this first statistical algorithm is guided with constraints such as the probabilities of moving from one page to another during the navigation of every user and the residence time on each page, that are already computed when the algorithm starts its execution. Instead, Deep Learning techniques do not need any hand-designed feature extraction phase, because they empower the model with the capability of learning features optimized for the task at hand.

3.2 RNN-Based Approach

Among the deep learning algorithms, we chose the Recurrent Neural Networks [14] (Rumelhart et al. 1986), that are neural networks dedicated to the processing of sequential data. Simple RNNs are useful when the temporal dependencies to be learned are not too long. When this happens, the gradients propagated over many stages tend to vanish (most of the time) or explode (more rarely). Even if we consider stable structures with a reasonable number of parameters, long-term dependencies lead to exponentially smaller weight updates for long-range interactions compared to the short-term ones. The best solution to this problem found as of today are gated RNNs, which are based on creating paths through time that have derivatives that neither vanish nor explode. One of the most effective models employing gated units is Long Short-Term Memory (LSTM) [8].

Due to these features regarding Recurrent Neural Network and their memory capacity, we implemented an RNN that receives a list of navigation sessions as input and trains itself with them. After the training phase, the network is ready to predict and produce new sequences.

Unlike the statistical algorithm, we do not need to specify the probability of moving among pages. For this reason, the input for the recurrent neural network consists of a list of sequences of URLs, together with the seconds of permanence on that page (*secInPage*) and the index that represents the number of pages already visited in the same session (*indexSession*). Every sequence corresponds to a navigation session made by a specific user.

The main characteristic that we want our RNN to learn is the sequence of pages that a specific user will visit and in which order he will make his navigation. For this reason, we started by feed the network with only the *url* feature, then we added the *secInPage* and *indexSession* features. We come up with the architecture shown in Fig. 1, where we can see that there are two principal layers, composed by the *CuDNNLSTM* previously discussed. Each of these layers consists of 50 neurons and is followed by a dropout operation that avoids overfitting. The output of the second layer, after the dropout, is flattened to obtain a single 2D vector containing the inputs for the last layer: the Dense layer, which produces the final output of the network.

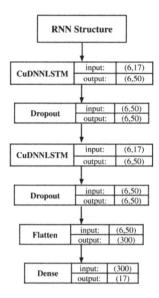

Fig. 1. The structure of the RNN. Parameters are set as follows: length of every sequence is 6, number of classes is 17, number of neurons is 50 and number of data point after the flatten operation is 300.

3.3 GAN-Based Approach

As discussed in the previous section, in the task of generating sequential synthetic data that mimics the real one, recurrent neural networks with long short-term memory (LSTM) cells have shown excellent performance. The most common approach to training an RNN is to maximize the log predictive likelihood of each valid token in the sequence given the previously observed tokens. However, the maximum likelihood approaches suffer from exposure bias in the inference stage: the model generates a sequence iteratively and predicts next token conditioned on its previously predicted ones that may never be observed in the training data. Such a discrepancy between training and inference can incur accumulatively along with the sequence and will become prominent as the length of sequence increases.

Generative Adversarial Network (GAN) proposed by Goodfellow and others [6] is a promising framework for alleviating the above problem. Specifically, in GAN a discriminative net D learns to distinguish whether a given data instance is real or not, and a generative net G learns to confuse D by generating high-quality data. This approach has been successful but has been applied almost only in computer vision tasks of generating samples of natural images (Denton et al. 2015 [4] is an example).

For these reasons and because of his capability of learning the probability distribution of training data and his hidden features, we thought that trying to build a GAN that generates synthetic discrete data would be an interesting challenge and a useful work for understanding if these type of Neural Networks are adaptable also to this task. Unfortunately, applying GAN to generating sequences has two problems. Firstly, GAN is designed for generating real-valued, continuous data but has difficulties in directly generating sequences of discrete tokens, such as texts or URLs in our case.

As such, the gradient of the loss from D w.r.t. the outputs by G is used to guide the generative model G (parameters) to slightly change the generated value to make it more realistic. If the generated data is based on discrete tokens, the "slight change" guidance from the discriminative net makes little sense because there is probably no corresponding token for such slight change in the limited dictionary space.

Secondly, GAN can only give the score/loss for an entire sequence when it has been generated; for a partially generated sequence, it is non-trivial to balance how well as it is now and the future score as the entire sequence.

GAN Parametrization. For the development of this net, the input data is a list of sequences of URLs, encoded as integers. Every sequence in this dataset corresponds to a navigation session like the RNN input case, and has a pre-fixed length.

Looking deeper at the implementation of the GAN, the sequence generation problem is denoted as follows: Given a dataset of real-world structured sequences, train a $\theta-$ parameterized generative model G_θ to produce a sequence $Y_{1:T} = (y_1, ..., y_t, ..., y_T), y_t \in Y$, where Y is the vocabulary of candidate URLs. This is interpreted as a reinforcement learning problem. In time-step t, the state s is the current produced URLs $(y_1, ..., y_{t-1})$ and the action a is the next URL y_t to select. Thus the policy model $G_\theta(y_t|Y_{1:t-1})$ is stochastic, whereas the state transition is deterministic after an action has been chosen, i.e. $\delta^a_{s,s'} = 1$ for the next state $s' = Y_{1:t}$ if the current state $s = Y_{1:t-1}$ and the action $a = y_t$; for other next states s'', $\delta^a_{s,s''} = 0$.

Additionally, we also train a ϕ-parameterized discriminative model D_ϕ to provide a guidance for improving generator G_δ. $D_\phi(Y_{1:T})$ is a probability indicating how likely a sequence $Y_{1:T}$ is from real sequence data or not. The discriminative model D_ϕ is trained by providing positive examples from the real sequence data and negative examples from the synthetic sequences produced by the generative model G_θ. At the same time, the generative model G_θ is updated by employing a policy gradient and MC search based on the expected end reward received from the discriminative model D_ϕ. The reward is estimated by the likelihood that it would fool the discriminative model D_ϕ.

Also, while the generator improves, we need to re-train periodically the discriminator to keep a good pace with the generator. Also, to reduce the variability of the estimation, we use different sets of negative samples combined with positive ones.

GAN Structure. Lastly, we want to add some information about the two neural networks structure that compose the GAN:

– *Generator:* We used a recurrent neural network as the generative model.
– *Discriminator:* In this case, we choose the CNN as our discriminator because these types of networks has been shown off great effectiveness in text classification, and our task is very similar to that one. A kernel applies a convolutional operation to a window of words to produce a feature map. At the end of this phase, a max-over-time pooling operation is applied over the feature maps. To enhance the performance, we used a fully connected layer with sigmoid activation that outputs the probability that the input sequence is real.

4   Evaluation

4.1   Context and Dataset

The evaluation methods and the algorithms employed in this work use the public 1995 NASA Apache web logs [12]. This public dataset is a standard Apache web log file. A typical configuration for the access log, that also applies in this case, is the Apache standard syntax for the HTTP requests. This standard format can be produced by many different web servers and read by many log analysis programs. The log file entries produced will look like the following (that is the standard apache format[5]): *127.0.0.1 - frank [10/Oct/2000:13:55:36 -0700]" GET /apache_pb.gif HTTP/1.0" 200 2326*
This dataset was selected for its size, number of entries and because is one of the few publicly available web log files: the lack of open web log data is in fact one of the issues that this work tries to solve. In particular, the size is 205.2 MB that corresponds to data recorded from Jul 01 to Jul 31(1995) and the total number of rows is 1891697.

URL Depth Problem. One of the main critical aspects to manage concerns the depth of every URL to be kept, present in each request. That is, if we have, for example, a request with a URL like this:

/home/shuttles/1969/apollo_11.html

we can notice that there are 4 steps in the request link: *home - shuttles - 1969* and *apollo_11.* Every step in this navigation path that leads to the *apollo_11.html* page represents a folder or eventually a category of the website that goes from the home page, that is the page with less specificity, to the page of the shuttle "apollo11", that is specific for that type of shuttle. This is a common conceptual representation of pages in every website, but for the task of this work, represents a problem whose complexity increases exponentially in certain situations.

For clearing this concept, is helpful looking at the Table 1, where we can see how fast the number of different pages in the website grows with the URL depth variable. In fact, we have only 19 unique pages when only a single part of the URL is kept, while we have almost ten times this number with only one more depth level.

---

[5] http://httpd.apache.org/docs/1.3/logs.html.

Table 1. The numbers of different pages with respect to the URL depth variable

URL depth	Number of pages
1	19
2	115
3	275
4	402

The problem with the algorithms that we tried to develop is that every URL is seen as a category and the neural networks are asked to predict the next page in a sequence among all. This means that if in the first case (depth = 1) the networks have to learn 19 different categories, in the last one (depth = 4) the network will have to learn 402 categories, and this is feasible only with a huge amount of training data, that is not available for our work.

Metrics. For evaluating the quality and realism of log produced by the different methods, we used a metric called the BLEU score [13]. BLEU, or the Bilingual Evaluation Understudy, is a score for comparing a candidate translation of text to one or more reference translations, or also, is an algorithm for evaluating the quality of text which has been machine-translated from one natural language to another. Quality is the correspondence between a machine's output and that of a human.

Every URL is treated as a unique "word" in the vocabulary, composed of all the pages of a particular website. Using this metric, scores are calculated for individual translated segments—generally sentences—by comparing them with a set of good quality reference translations. Those scores are then averaged over the whole corpus to reach an estimate of the translation's overall quality. Transferring this to our case, the translated segments are the generated navigation sequences, while the good quality reference translations correspond to our original dataset: the NASA weblog.

4.2 Experiments with RNN

The framework used for the implementation of the network is Keras, a high-level neural networks API, written in Python and capable of running on top of TensorFlow, CNTK, or Theano, while the type of LSTM cell is CuDNNLSTM: This type of LSTM cell must be run on GPU and is based on cuDNN, developed by Nvidia. cuDNN provides highly tuned implementations for standard routines such as forward and backward convolution, pooling, normalization, and activation layers.

For evaluating the performance of the network, we trained it on a training set, and then we checked the prediction accuracy on a test set. The problem with this type of evaluation, in this case, is that in the test data we could encounter some URLs that were not seen in the training phase, and the results would not

Table 2. RNN experiments: hyper-parameters tuning, URL Depth = 1

#test	1	2	3	4	5
Length sequence	6	6	6	6	6
Neurons	50	50	20	50	40
Layers	2	3	2	4	3
Dropout	0.2	0.25	0.25	0.25	0.2
Shuffle	True	True	True	True	True
Batch size	30	30	30	20	40
Activation	Softmax	Softmax	Softmax	Softmax	Softmax
Optimizer	Adam	Adam	Adam	Adam	Adam
Loss	cat. cross-ent.	cat. cross-ent.	cat. cross-ent.	cat. cross-ent.	cat. cross-ent.
Metrics	Accuracy	Accuracy	Accuracy	Accuracy	Accuracy
Epochs	50	50	65	70	100 (early stop)
Average accuracy	74,13%	74,17%	74,69%	**74,76%**	**74,76%**

Table 3. RNN experiments: BLEU performance and best accuracy with respect to the URL Depth

URL Depth	#classes	BLEU	Best accuracy
1	19	0.6482	74,76%
2	115	0.4739	58,23%
3	275	0.3655	31,05%

have been accurate because the network could not learn something that it has never seen. For this reason, we split the data in training and test by checking that all the URLs in the test set would be present also in the training set. In addition to this, we adopted some techniques to avoid overfitting, such as *dropout, early stop training,* and *data shuffle.*

In the Table 2 the results of the hyper-parameters tuning are visible for the URL depth equal to one, while in Table 3 we can see the evaluation results in terms of BLEU and best accuracy, with respect to the URL depth.

As mentioned before, the URL Depth problem is crucial because it increases the complexity of learning the correct features and the network performs worse.

4.3 Experiments with GAN

In this algorithm, the training set for the discriminator is comprised by the generated examples with the label 0 and the instances from the training set with the label 1. Dropout and L2 regularization are used to avoid over-fitting. Also in this case, we tried to generate new sequences using three different URL depth level to understand how the GAN performs respect to this parameter.

In this algorithm, the most important parameters to tune are the number of training epochs for the generator and the discriminator. In fact, we noticed that if the RNN (generator) is not sufficiently pre-trained before starting the adversarial training, the generator improves quite slowly and unstably. The reason is that in this GAN, the discriminative model provides reward guidance when training the generator and if the generator acts almost randomly, the discriminator will identify the generated sequence to be unreal with high confidence and almost every action the generator takes receives a low (unified) reward, which does not guide the generator towards a good improvement direction, resulting in an ineffective training procedure.

This indicates that in order to apply adversarial training strategies to sequence generative models, a sufficient pre-training is necessary. For the evaluation of this algorithm, we started with the analysis of the generator loss, relating it to the URL depth and to the number of pre-training epochs of the generator before the adversarial training. We run the training with three different values of pre-train generator epochs and three different values of URL Depth. The results that emerge from these analyses are the following:

- Adding a discriminator to the RNN allows the GAN to lower the loss of the generator and to improve its limits.
- Increasing the value of URL Depth variable, the loss value also increases regardless of the generator pre-train epochs value. This is observable in the Figs. 2 and is a further confirmation that increasing the number of URLs is critical for the complexity of the computations that the network must do.
- The variance of the loss in all the cases decreases when the number of pre-train epochs increases. In the Table 4, is notable that the minimum variance value occurs when the generator is pre-trained with 100 epochs and this is valid for the 3 different URL Depth values. This correspond to a better stability of the generator with respect to the cases with lower pre-train epochs.
- The minimum value of the loss is reached with 15 pre-train epochs, when the depth is equal to 1 and 2, while with a depth equal to 3, the minimum value is obtained with 100 pre-train epochs. This means the generator can get the lowest loss value with few epochs, but a good stability of the network is reached only with a high number of pre-train epochs.

We generated 3 different sets of sequences with respect to the URL depth and to the number of pre-train epochs for the generator and we computed the BLEU score against the original set of sequences. The results are shown in Table 6. We can see that adding a discriminator to the RNN (the generator) improves the scores in each of the 3 cases only if the number of pre-train epochs for the generator is enough to make the generator robust. If we train the generator only for 40 epochs and then we start the adversarial training, the data generated by the RNN will receive always a low score as a reward by the discriminator.

This is in contrast with the assessments previously made, where we showed that the lowest loss values are reached with 15 or 40 pre-train epochs, but agrees on what concerns the stability of the network that is improved with 100 pre-train epochs. This demonstrates that in the case of generative models the analyses of pure loss are not enough to understand if these models produce high-quality data (Table 5).

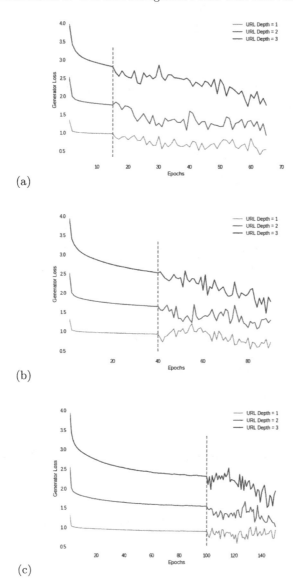

(a)

(b)

(c)

Fig. 2. Generator loss with 15, 14, and 100 pre-training epochs respectively, in relation to different URL Depth.

Table 4. GAN experiments: variance of the generator loss, related to the URL Depth and the pre-train epochs

	URL Depth = 1	URL Depth = 2	URL Depth = 3
15 Epochs	0.0151	0.0324	0.0673
40 Epochs	0.0255	0.0239	0.0614
100 Epochs	**0.00832**	**0.0179**	**0.0550**

Table 5. GAN experiments: minimum value of the generator loss, related to the URL Depth and the pre-train epochs

	URL Depth = 1	URL Depth = 2	URL Depth = 3
15 Epochs	**0.3916**	**0.9308**	1.7240
40 Epochs	0.5451	1.0667	**1.4720**
100 Epochs	0.5922	1.0215	1.5121

Table 6. GAN experiments: BLEU performance with respect to the URL Depth

URL Depth	BLEU, 40 pre-train epochs	BLEU, 100 pre-train epochs
1	0.6071	**0.7243**
2	0.4328	**0.5471**
3	0.3321	**0.4839**

5 Comparison: Statistical Approach vs RNN vs GAN

For the final comparison between all the techniques explored in this work, we opted to use another metric in addition to **BLEU**, that is a human judgment, since a weblog is a composition of navigation sequence and every sequence is something that is decided and created by a human. For this reason, we chose 5 of our colleagues with the same skills and knowledge: we showed him all the pages of the website and the possible navigation paths. Specifically, we mix 50 real sequences and 50 generated from GAN and RNN.

Then the judges are invited to pronounce whether each of the 100 sequences is created by human or machines. Once regarded to be real, it gets +1 score, otherwise 0. Finally, the average score for each algorithm is calculated. The experiment results are shown in Table 7, from which we can see the significant advantage of GAN over the RNN and Statistical method in weblog generation.

Table 7. Weblog generation performance comparison

Algorithm	Statistical	RNN	GAN
Human score	0.4335	0.5400	**0.6450**
BLEU	0.5811	0.6482	**0.7243**

6   Conclusions

In this paper, we proposed a step forward towards automatic production of high-quality weblog using deep learning techniques, such as recurrent neural network and generative adversarial neural networks. We provided an analysis of state of the art, aimed to identify the techniques to be used in order to reproduce and improve the best performances reached today with generative approaches for discrete sequences of data. We first implemented the state of the art algorithm, that improves the performances reached with random techniques, using data mining and generating navigation sequences based on association rules. Then we implemented a recurrent neural network that tries to learn the probability distribution of the input data and is capable of predicting the right URLs to complete a given incomplete sequence with good performances when the number of features is not very large, while it is not robust in the other case. Finally, we developed the GAN by adding a convolutional neural network as the discriminator, to allow the RNN to improve itself, applying the so-called min-max game between the two networks. Our experiments support the hypothesis that generative adversarial neural networks are the best families of models to handle weblog generation and that they can outperform the recurrent models especially when the number of feature variables increases substantially. We showed that using both the BLEU and the Human metric, the GAN overcomes the RNN and the statistical approach when the generator is well trained. Instead, when the pre-train epochs for the generator are not enough or too much, the quality of the generated sequences is lower than that of RNN, but is still higher than the statistical one.

Future Work. In addition to the possibility of including more variables in the training of the network that could improve the quality of the generated weblog, we mentioned the work proposed by [3] for visualizing the statistics taken from weblogs on a graphical representation of a particular website or app, using a model-driven approach. With the GAN used, a future work could be to generate new weblogs and fed the model of the website with them. Then, one could compare two models where one of them is fed with human generated logs and the other with the GAN logs.

References

1. Basu, K.: Fake apache log generator (2015–2018). https://github.com/kiritbasu/Fake-Apache-Log-Generator
2. Berendt, B., Spiliopoulou, M.: Analysis of navigation behaviour in web sites integrating multiple information systems. VLDB J. Int. J. Very Large Data Bases **9**(1), 56–75 (2000)
3. Bernaschina, C., Brambilla, M., Koka, T., Mauri, A., Umuhoza, E.: Integrating modeling languages and web logs for enhanced user behavior analytics. In: Proceedings of the 26th International Conference on World Wide Web Companion, pp. 171–175. International World Wide Web Conferences Steering Committee (2017)
4. Denton, E.L., Chintala, S., Fergus, R., et al.: Deep generative image models using a Laplacian pyramid of adversarial networks. In: Advances in Neural Information Processing Systems, pp. 1486–1494 (2015)
5. Goodfellow, I., et al.: Generative adversarial nets. In: Ghahramani, Z., Welling, M., Cortes, C., Lawrence, N.D., Weinberger, K.Q. (eds.) Advances in Neural Information Processing Systems, vol. 27, pp. 2672–2680. Curran Associates, Inc. (2014). http://papers.nips.cc/paper/5423-generative-adversarial-nets.pdf
6. Goodfellow, I., et al.: Generative adversarial nets. In: Advances in Neural Information Processing Systems, pp. 2672–2680 (2014)
7. Graves, A.: Generating sequences with recurrent neural networks. arXiv preprint arXiv:1308.0850 (2013)
8. Hochreiter, S., Schmidhuber, J.: Long short-term memory. Neural Comput. **9**, 1735–80 (1997). https://doi.org/10.1162/neco.1997.9.8.1735
9. Kwon, M.: Flog, an apache log generator (2017–2018). https://github.com/mingrammer/flog
10. Lin, C.H., Liu, J.C., Chen, C.R.: Access log generator for analyzing malicious website browsing behaviors. In: 2009 Fifth International Conference on Information Assurance and Security, pp. 126–129. IEEE (2009)
11. Mahoto, N., Memon, A., TEEVNO, M.: Extraction of web navigation patterns by means of sequential pattern mining. Sindh Univ. Res. J.-SURJ (Sci. Ser.) **48**(1), 201–208 (2016)
12. NASA: Nasa apache web log (1995). ftp://ita.ee.lbl.gov/html/contrib/NASA-HTTP.html
13. Papineni, K., Roukos, S., Ward, T., Zhu, W.J.: Bleu: A method for automatic evaluation of machine translation. In: Proceedings of the 40th Annual Meeting on Association for Computational Linguistics, ACL 2002, Stroudsburg, PA, USA, pp. 311–318. Association for Computational Linguistics (2002). https://doi.org/10.3115/1073083.1073135
14. Rumelhart, D.E., Hinton, G.E., Williams, R.J.: Learning representations by back-propagating errors. Nature **323**(6088), 533 (1986)
15. Singh, N., Jain, A., Raw, R.S.: Comparison analysis of web usage mining using pattern recognition techniques. Int. J. Data Min. Knowl. Manag. Process (IJDKP) **3**, 137–147 (2013)
16. Vedaprakash, M.P., Prakash, M.P.O., Navaneethakrishnan, M.M.: Analyzing the user navigation pattern from weblogs using data pre-processing technique. Int. J. Comput. Sci. Mob. Comput. **5**, 90–99 (2016)
17. Yu, L., Zhang, W., Wang, J., Yu, Y.: SeqGAN: sequence generative adversarial nets with policy gradient. In: Thirty-First AAAI Conference on Artificial Intelligence (2017)

Emotion Detection

Scalable Real-Time Confusion Detection for Personalized Onboarding Guides

Michal Hucko[ID], Robert Moro[(✉)][ID], and Maria Bielikova[ID]

Faculty of Informatics and Information Technologies, Slovak University
of Technology in Bratislava, Ilkovicova 2, 842 16 Bratislava, Slovakia
{michal.hucko,robert.moro,maria.bielikova}@stuba.sk

Abstract. Onboarding of new employees is a common process in all
companies. Many hours of qualified employees' time need to be invested
to teach new employees how to use the company's internal systems. This
process can be significantly eased by onboarding solutions leveraging
application guides. However, if not personalized, the guides can quickly
become annoying to users. This can be overcome by employing emotion
detection in real-time, but the solutions face several major challenges,
such as scalability, detection time, or model retraining. In this paper, we
describe how we tackled these challenges and implemented an emotion
detection-based personalization module in the onboarding solution *Yes-
Elf*. The module leverages the mouse interaction data of users to detect
their confusion. We show the scalability of our solution in the production
environment which has been deployed to three customers with more than
200 concurrent users.

Keywords: Affective computing · Confusion detection ·
Personalization · Scalability · Real-time detection · YesElf

1 Introduction

Affective computing as a research field emerged in 1995 with the publication of
Rosalind Picard [18] where she presented the idea of emotion-aware machines,
which could dramatically change the way we interact with the computers. Emotions are an essential part of our everyday lives and we apply them in our communication and decision-making. Our decisions or preferences are based not only on
rational thinking and exact mathematical equations, but many times the mood,
the emotions or the feelings are the main decision makers. Therefore, to make
the machines understand the human behavior and thinking, is to make them
understand our emotions.

Affective computing deals with two main problems. The first one is how to
detect human emotions during human-computer interaction. The subfield aiming to solve this problem researches various computer input sources (mouse,
keyboard, eye tracker and many others) as potential indicators of human emotion. The second subfield of the affective computing deals with incorporating the

© Springer Nature Switzerland AG 2020
M. Bielikova et al. (Eds.): ICWE 2020, LNCS 12128, pp. 261–276, 2020.
https://doi.org/10.1007/978-3-030-50578-3_18

emotions into the computers. The pioneer researcher in this respect is Marwin Minsky with his book *The Emotion Machine* [12]. In this paper, we address this second problem. More specifically, we try to involve emotion thinking into the *Yeself* to personalize guides during the onboarding of the users.

Project *YesElf* is an onboarding platform for web-based applications. The onboarding of new users to a web application (or even more experienced users to a new functionality within the application) is achieved by the means of personalized guides, which consist of a series of hints (guide steps) displayed as pop-up bubbles near relevant user interface elements [9]. *YesElf* provides tools for designing custom web guides and it can be integrated with any existing web-based application by inserting a JavaScript snippet into its source code. In the paper, we focus on the design and implementation of a production-ready emotion detection module, which is responsible for personalization of *YesElf*'s guides for the confused users. The use of the emotion detection in this case is to ensure that the guides are shown only to the users who might need them (because they are confused) and not to interrupt or annoy others.

We understand confusion as *"a situation in which people are uncertain about what to do or are unable to understand something clearly"*.[1] Based on this definition, a confusion in a web application is a moment when a user has no idea how to continue to finish his or her task. We detect the moments of user confusion based on the user mouse interaction data, with the accuracy comparable to the state-of-the-art solutions as presented in our initial study in the confusion detection on the web [9].

During the design and development of the production-ready confusion detection module we faced the following challenges, which are addressed in the paper:

1. As the detection is based on the mouse activity, we needed to develop a *real-time scalable mouse logger* that would not put too much strain on the client or the server.
2. Confusion detection is very context-dependent, which (at least for now) hampers the use of one general model for multiple web applications. We needed to develop a system able to detect confusion leveraging *domain specific classifiers*.
3. The feedback loop of a confusion detection system has to be fast, i.e., the delay between the occurrence of a user's confusion and the action taken by the system has to be low. In other words, we needed the detection module to be able to work in *real-time*.
4. Lastly, the model has to be able to learn and improve its accuracy over time. Therefore, we needed to address the *model retraining* and create an environment for gathering the users' feedback to the actions taken by the system based on its assumption that a user is confused.

The rest of the paper is structured as follows. In Sect. 2 we discuss the state-of-the-art in the onboarding and the emotion-aware systems. Next, Sect. 3

---

[1] https://www.merriam-webster.com/dictionary/confusion.

describes the architecture and the implementation decisions applied in the development of the emotion detection module. The method designed for improving the detection model accuracy directly in the production environment is presented in Sect. 4. In Sect. 5 we describe the production integration of the module and evaluate its scalability on the production data from three customers with more than 200 concurrent users. We conclude the paper with Sect. 6, in which we summarize the contributions and discuss our future work.

2   Related Work

The problem with the user onboarding is attracting attention of big companies dealing with the new employees on a daily basis. A lot of senior employees' time needs to be invested to the onboarding process of new employees without any immediate profit. The problem can be stated as follows: *How can be the process of onboarding automatised?* There are various existing approaches to onboarding applying techniques such as microlearning and gamification [7], blended and flipped learning [8,13,22], or the use of virtual or augmented reality [6]. However, currently there are no solutions incorporating emotions into the user onboarding. For this reason, we cannot refer to any work done in this specific area. This opens up the opportunity for the *YesElf.*

To find the systems applying emotions in the human-computer interaction, we need to look at the domain of technology-enhanced learning (or e-learning). This domain is similar to the user onboarding in its goal to provide users with some new information or knowledge. According to the literature, e-learning systems are the most popular applications of emotion detection (however, it has been successfully used also in other domains, e.g. in usability testing [21]). A survey [20] reviewed 26 different works of emotion and personality detection in the educational domain. Many approaches employ facial expression recognition [3,14], other also utilize data from other sensors, e.g., EEG [11].

The work of Ashwin, Jose et al. [1] presented an e-learning system supported by facial emotion detection system. They addressed the problem of processing time of machine learning approaches applied in the production environment. The facial detection methods need to process lots of image data. For this reason, it is hard to provide fast results of predictions to the system. The authors noticed a trade-off between the processing time and the accuracy of the method applied in the system. They presented the implementation of their emotion detection method on the graphical processing units (GPUs). This approach helped them to increase the processing capability of the system up to two times.

Another application of emotion detection in e-learning is the paper of Kung-Keat and Ng [10]. The proposed method detects the emotions of confusion, boredom, and excitement based on the user inputs of keyboard and facial expressions video. The learning materials of the system change based on the detected emotion of the user. As the authors mention, it is very challenging to design a system capable of processing the input data in multiple stages in the real time. In general, the real-time processing problem is closely connected the long processing time mentioned earlier.

The emotion detection-based systems are growing in popularity also in the field of recommender systems. In a recent paper of Qian et al. [19], the authors present the *EARS* emotion-aware recommender system based on a hybrid information fusion. *EARS* leverages the user data from clicking activity and social networks in order to incorporate the human emotion into the product recommendations.

We can see application of mouse interaction data in various emotion-aware approaches. For example, in [16,17] Pentel predicts the moments of user confusion in a computer game based solely on the mouse movements with satisfying accuracy. The approaches such as Pentel's usually employ mouse features known from the domain of biometric authentication [5].

As to the real-time mouse logging, it is (in case of web-based interfaces) typically implemented by injecting a *Java-Script* snippet into the source code of a web application. The injection can be done by the owner (developer) of the web application or by the means of a web proxy [2] or a browser extension [23]. In addition, we can distinguish between two major mouse logging approaches:

- In case of *time-based mouse logging*, the mouse device needs to be constantly checked for changes every n-milliseconds (*refresh time*). This approach can reach very high precision in case of a very low refresh time. However, the trade-off lies in the high processing time on the side of client. Sending constant messages to the mouse results into process overload in the browser. Therefore, it is not very suitable for us, since our goal is to provide as light-weighted solution to the end user as possible.
- On the other hand, *event-based mouse logging* is more processing time friendly. In this case, the mouse coordinates are logged only after an event. When the mouse remains still, no event is logged. Although this approach saves the processing time, it has its own limitations connected to the *JavaScript* implementation of the mouse listeners. The listener only tracks the event of a mouse move when the cursor travels distance greater than x pixels (x varies across different browser implementations). For this reason, we have to keep in mind the threat of a potential data loss.

To sum up, even though there are some works considering some of the aspects of a production deployment of emotion detection systems (such as input data processing time in [1] discussed above), most aspects (scalability, model retraining, deployment and adaptation to different contexts) rest unaddressed.

3   Infrastructure for Scalable Guide Personalization

The core functionality of *YesElf* is to create custom guides for any customer[2] web application. It is a client-server application consisting of these main modules (see Fig. 1):

---

[2] Throughout the rest of the paper we use the word *customer* to denote the owner of the web application who decided to integrate the *YesElf*. Under the term *user* we understand the user of the *customer's* application.

1. *YesElf client.* The part of the *YesElf* loaded to the user's browser through the *JavaScript* snippet. It is responsible for displaying the created guides.
2. *YesElf guide server.* The module which communicates with all running *YesElf clients.* It is responsible for guide data delivery.
3. *YesElf WebSocket server.* It ensures the asynchronous communication from *YesElf guide server* to *YesElf client.*

However, from the user perspective, the main interface for customers is the *YesElf editor*, where the guides can be setup. Each guide consists of a series of hints (pop-up like guide steps) attached to the *HTML* elements in the web application. By default, each guide is displayed to every user, based only on some trivial heuristics (display only first time, display after n seconds without activity, etc.). However, this sort of guide behavior may annoy the users, as their ability to control the user interface may vary. It is very hard to set up the rules for guide appearance in advance and not to annoy the users over time.

To overcome this problem, we developed an emotion detection method able to detect moments of user confusion in the real-time leveraging mouse interaction data [9] and integrated it into *YesElf*. The method processes the mouse interaction data into mouse movements (sequences of consecutive mouse events) and extracts a set of features, such as total distance of a mouse movement, its duration, acceleration, etc. The features are used to train a classifier (confusion detector) employing logistic regression.

The trained model is then used to personalize the guides. More specifically, each time the method detects that the user is confused, the YesElf client is notified and may take an action (e.g., prompts a user to display a list of available guides). To integrate the method into the *YesElf* and make it work in the real-time (i.e., to be able to detect user's confusion within milliseconds from its occurrence), we implemented an emotion detection module consisting of several components (mouse logger and confusion server being the main ones) and extended the basic *YesElf* modules as follows (see Fig. 1):

1. *YesElf client.* It prompts the user to display the list of guides if `confused` event is received. We also extended this module by mouse tracking and logging functionality.
2. *YesElf logger server.* REST API responsible for storing the tracked data and confusion detection initialization.
3. *YesElf confusion server.* Asynchronous process responsible for confusion detection.
4. *YesElf guide server.* It receives the `confused` event and sends it to the client using a *WebSocket server*.

3.1   YesElf Client

To run *YesElf* in a customer's web application, a *JavaScript* snippet must be inserted into the source code. After that each time a browser loads the web

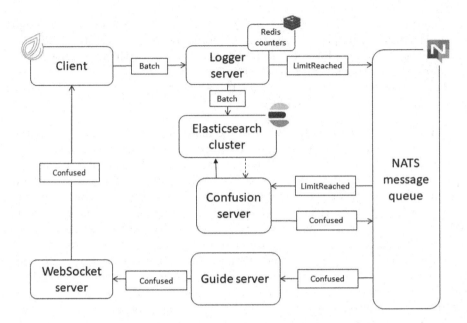

Fig. 1. Architectural diagram of *YesElf* with the integrated guides personalisation module.

application, the *YesElf client* is being loaded with it. The client itself its only 500 kilobytes big. This compact implementation helps us to overcome the long processing time problem mentioned in the related works. The client has two major responsibilities. The first one is to display the guides. The client monitors which guides have been opened before, and which guide step needs to be displayed based on the implemented rules. The state information is persisted into the local store of the browser thanks to the *React* implementation.

The most important part of the *YesElf client* from the emotion detection perspective, is the *user tracking*. The *YesElf client* monitors the mouse movements in the target web application. For this purpose, it leverages the *JavaScript* mouse listeners. The whole solution closely resembles the *Observer* design pattern. After mouse event is emitted, the mouse position is recorded into the mouse log. The sample code used for getting the current position of the mouse within the document is displayed in Fig. 2. The tracking frequency of the mouse logging can be configured in the *YesElf editor* ranging from 0 up to 60 samples per second (which follows from the modern browsers' limitations). Each of the mouse log fields is described in Table 1.

Besides the mouse position, we also track the element beneath the mouse cursor. This kind of logging gives us the ability to leverage the sequence of elements in the confusion detection. Moreover, this logging feature enriches the analytical ability of *YesElf*, since we are able to create more in depth analysis of user confusion based on the element activity.

Table 1. Fields and descriptions of mouse log used for recording.

Field	Description
ApplicationId	Field responsible for identification of target application
OrganisationId	Field responsible for identification of client (organisation) the log belongs to. Each client (organisation) can have multiple applications which integrate *YesElf*
ConversationId	Field responsible for session distinction
Event	Type of the mouse event. One of `mousemove`, `mouseup`, `mousedown`, `scroll`
Xpos	The X coordinate of the mouse cursor within the rendered document object model (DOM)
Ypos	The Y coordinate of the mouse cursor within the rendered DOM
Timestamp	The client timestamp when the log was recorded
Url	The uniform resource locator where the log was recorded
UserId	Identifier of the logged user in case of authenticated access
VisitorId	Unique identifier of the current visitor. The field is being used in case of anonymous application usage. Also one `UserId` may have many `VisitorId`s. The id is being stored in the local storage of the user's browser
Relative	The relative CSS selector for the HTML element beneath the mouse cursor. The selector is logged for every mouse event
TagOnly	The tag only CSS selector for the HTML element beneath the mouse cursor. Logged in case of `mouseup` and `mousedown` events
Xpath	The Xpath of the HTML element beneath the mouse cursor. Logged in case of `mouseup` and `mousedown` events
ClassOnly	The class only CSS selector for the HTML element beneath the mouse cursor. Logged in case of `mouseup` and `mousedown` events

```
export const getMousePos = e => {
    let cx;
    let cy;
    if (e.pageX || e.pageY) {
        cx = e.pageX;
        cy = e.pageY;
    } else if (e.clientX || e.clientY) {
        cx = e.clientX + document.body.scrollLeft + document.documentElement.scrollLeft;
        cy = e.clientY + document.body.scrollTop + document.documentElement.scrollTop;
    }
    // Sometimes the mouse coordinates are negative (e.g., in Opera)
    if (cx < 0) cx = 0;
    if (cy < 0) cy = 0;

    return { xpos: cx, ypos: cy };
};
```

Fig. 2. Sample *JavaScript* code used for estimating cursor position (taking into account also user's scroll) in any of the modern web browsers.

One of the biggest tracking challenges we faced, was the transition of the mouse logs to the *Yeself logger server*. Dispatching the log to the logger server, each time it is captured, leads to the already mentioned processing overload on the side of the *YesElf client* (in the worst case, there would be 60 post events per each second). To minimize this processing time, we developed a batching mechanism which samples mouse logs on the client side into the batches of logs and dispatches them to the server once in n seconds. Also in this case, the variable n can be configured per application in the *YesElf editor*. Although this solution solves the issue with the processing time, it brings up the issue of vanishing logs after hard navigation (i.e., changing the URL in the browser), or closing the browser window. In these logging cases, the mouse records within the batch in the browser memory are discarded. To overcome this problem, we developed a mechanism sending the incomplete batch before the navigation or window close leveraging the *JavaScript*'s window `beforeunload` event[3]. This approach sends the incomplete batch each time the browser is closed, or in case of a hard navigation event.

Another issue connected with the user tracking of the mouse is the maximal data bandwidth. As showed before, the mouse log incorporates the information about the *HTML* element (`TagOnly`, `ClassOnly`, `Relative`, `Xpath`) and all the other user data (`VisitorId`, `ApplicationId`, `SessionId`) and the application information (`ApplicationId`, `OrganisationId`). As we send the logs in batches, the same information repeats within logs many times. To keep the data bandwidth as small as possible, we encode the fields within the batch. We leverage the dictionary encoding method, where the target values are encoded as integers with the dictionary. To decode the batch on the server side, we incorporate the dictionary within every batch. By employing this method, we reduced the average batch size by 25% and minimized the impact of batch bandwidth.

3.2 YesElf Logger Server

The *YesElf logger server* component is responsible for mouse data storing. It communicates with the *YesElf client*, by receiving the batches through the *HTTP POST* request. It is a simple *Django REST API*[4]. Before storing the data into the *ElasticSearch* database cluster, the batches need to be decoded as mentioned above. For each application, a separate month-based *ElasticSearch* index is being held. We chose a non-relational highly scalable *ElasticSearch* database[5], because of the amount of data we need to store. For example, a customer's application with up to 200 active users per day can produce mouse activity of 2GB. Having multiple customers in the same time leads up to hundreds gigabytes of data being stored. Scalability of the *ElasticSearch* helps us to overcome this challenge.

Besides the data storage, the *YesElf logger server* is responsible for confusion detection initiation. The whole confusion detection is based on user activity.

---

[3] https://developer.mozilla.org/en-US/docs/Web/API/Window/beforeunload_event.

[4] https://www.django-rest-framework.org.

[5] www.elastic.com.

Every n user mouse events the logger server fires a confusion initiation message to the *YesElf* confusion server. To count the active user mouse activity, *YesElf logger server* counts user mouse logs in the *Redis* database[6]. After each n logs the *YesElf logger server* fires a message (labeled as `limitReached`) to the confusion server through the *NATS* message queue[7]. *NATS* provides asynchronous messaging, which is the key means of communication between the components during the detection because of the non-deterministic processing time.

3.3   YesElf Confusion Server

The confusion server is the heart of confusion detection in *YesElf*. It is an asynchronous subscriber for the *NATS* message queue. Every time the `limitReached` message is received, the *YesElf confusion server* tries to detect confusion based on the `ApplicationId`, `OrganisationId`, `VisitorId`, `UserId` and `Timestamp` extracted from the message. The online detection works as follows:

1. *Data extraction.* YesElf confusion server gets the user's past activity (last n seconds) from the *ElasticSearch* cluster, based on the user data from the *NATS* message.
2. *Model extraction.* For each application, *YesElf* stores a unique model in the *ElasticSearch* database, which is selected during the model extraction based on the *NATS* message content. The models are being pre-trained and stored in the database manually outside of the confusion server. We train the models leveraging the Python's `scikit-learn` library [15]. The trained models are persisted to the byte files, which are stored in the *ElasticSearch*, using the Python's `pickle` library.
3. *Feature calculation.* We calculate mouse features from the last n seconds of the user activity needed for the confusion model to be applied on.
4. *Detection.* We classify the computed feature vector from the previous step as an occurrence of user confusion or no confusion.

Each result of confusion classification is stored in a dedicated *ElasticSearch* index. This enables us to evaluate the performance of the model, and reevaluate the predictions. We discuss the retraining part in a later section. In case of a positive confusion prediction (i.e., a moment of user confusion is detected), the confusion server sends a *NATS* message (labeled as `confused`) to the guide server component. Each type of a *NATS* message has its own dedicated queue.

3.4   YesElf Guide Server

The *Yeself guide server* is a *JavaScript* API written in the *express* framework[8]. Besides its other functionality, it is implemented as an asynchronous subscriber for the `confused` *NATS* message sent from the *YesElf* confusion server. After it

---

[6] www.redis.io.

[7] www.nats.io.

[8] www.expressjs.com.

receives the message, the guide server finds the right *YesElf client* the prediction is addressed to, leveraging the message data.

It communicates with all running *YesElf clients* through the *WebSocket* communication protocol. We run a separate *YesElf web socket server* instance dedicated for this kind of communication. Moreover, the *YesElf guide server* is responsible for supplying the right guides with the guide steps to the client. The guide server is a highly scalable component. Because there are thousands of concurrently running clients, we run multiple instances of the guide server.

4   Model Retraining

The main challenge in our confusion detection approach is the *context dependency*. Having one confusion detection model for all kinds of applications is inefficient as we reach much lower accuracy in prediction. To overcome this problem, we must train separate confusion classifiers for each context (customer's application). To implement this solution in the production environment, we decided to store the trained models in the *ElasticSearch*. Using the `pickle` library, we can easily load the demanded model on the side of *YesElf confusion server*. Moreover, we can store the historical models to compare the results.

To get more accurate results of user confusion detection, *YesElf* is capable of retraining the existing confusion models. However, to retrain the models, we need to gather labeled data from the users which will serve as new training data. For this purpose, we proposed and implemented a feedback mechanism described in this section.

4.1   YesElf Context Help

Before discussing the model retraining mechanism, we must present the way the *YeslElf* guides are displayed to the confused users. When *YelElf* is integrated into a target application, the application is enhanced with a small HTML element called a *YesElf context help*. The design of the element is fully configurable and it can be placed anywhere in the target web application (in most cases in one of the corners). After clicking on the element, a small list with *YesElf* guides (internally referred as *tours*) pops up. An opened context help with the guides list for a given context[9] is shown in Fig. 3.

The default state of the context help is *closed*, meaning that the whole guide list stays hidden until the user clicks on the context help. As the *YesElf client* is responsible for the guide visualization, each time it receives a message from the guide server through the websocket server about a user being confused, it fires up one of the following reactions:

1. *Context help shake.* In case a user is detected to be confused, the context help shakes up n times (one shake per second). The number of shakes can be configured in the *YesElf editor*.

---

[9] Under the term *context* we understand the *URL* for which the context help is displayed, as each guide is situated at a specific *URL*.

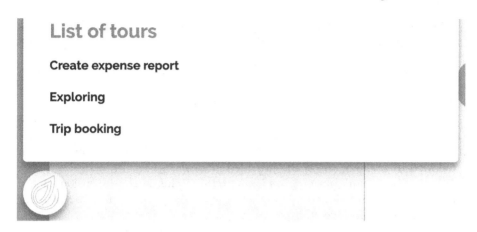

Fig. 3. Demonstration of an opened *YesElf* context help with a list of guides (*tours*) for a given context (URL).

2. *Pop up question.* In case a user is detected to be confused, a pop up question emerges next to the context help with the text *Do you need help?* and two buttons *Yes* and *No*. If the user clicks on *No*, nothing happens and the question disappears. If the user clicks on *Yes*, the context help displays the guide list.

To prevent too much user distraction the confusion reaction timestamp is cashed in the browser local storage and the application owner can specify a minimal time distance between two consecutive positive confusion reactions. For the moment, we did not analyse the impact of the proposed confusion reactions on the end users and their behavior. However, the experiences from the web applications where the *YesElf* is deployed suggest that the users tend to click on the context help even without any system prompt when they are not sure how to continue with their task. The proposed confusion reactions should notify also the users that would not otherwise click on the help (even when confused) and prompt the others to click on the context help sooner and thus help them to finish their task in less time.

4.2 Gathering User Feedback

Each time the *YesElf logger server* initiates the confusion prediction event, it generates a so called `predictionId`. This identifier is sent through all the components and refers to exactly one prediction on the side of *YesElf confusion server*. If the detection ends up with a result that the target user is not being confused, the `predictionId` is recorded to the confusion index with the rest of the confusion log. However, if the user ends up being detected as confused, the `predictionId` is propagated to the *YesElf client* and all the following user activity is labeled with it. In this case, the `predictionId` has a specified expiration time, configurable in the *YesElf editor*.

The goal of the `predictionId` propagation is to monitor what the user does after the confusion reaction is fired. One of the following reactions are possible:

1. *Nothing.* The user ignores any confusion reaction, or he or she closes the pop up question.
2. *Reaction accepted.* The user reacts to the action, by either clicking on *Yes* in the pop up question, clicking on the shaking context help, or clicking on the context help n seconds after the shake.
3. *Reaction with guide opening.* This is the extension of the previous reaction followed by opening one of the provided guides.
4. *Reaction with guide opening and interaction.* This is the extension of the previous reaction followed by interacting with the opened guide (by entering the n-th of its m guide steps).
5. *Reaction with guide finishing.* This is the extension of the previous reaction followed by finishing the opened guide.

These reactions help us label the cases when the model detects users to be confused either as *true positive* or *false positive*. If the user does *Nothing*, it is clearly a false positive case. However, the *Reaction accepted* reaction from a user can be easily mistaken with just the curiosity of a user after shaking is noticed (or the question pops up). Also the opening of a guide can just be the result of a curiosity. This can be partially filtered out based on the user history; if a user opens an already seen guide, it is probably not just from the curiosity. The most reliable are the last two reactions.

The *false negative* cases can be labeled based on the users' clicks on the context help when no prompt is presented to them. Alternately, a question can pop up at random and ask them if they feel confused. However, this is not always possible to do in a production scenario as it can lower the user experience.

After gathering enough data from the confusion model, the owner of the application is able to run retraining of the model. The retraining part can be initiated from the *YesElf editor* by starting a dedicated Python job on a confusion server. The job trains the model and stores it into the *ElasticSearch* cluster. After the retraining, the owner is able to choose the model in the *YesElf editor*.

It is important to point out that the retraining part of the *YesElf* is still under the development and has not yet been evaluated.

5   Production Integration

As previously mentioned, the guide personalization module is a part of the *YesElf project* developed by the *Brainware* company[10]. It is being developed with three environments: *development, acceptance,* and *production.* The whole development part takes place in the *development* environment. Each time a new feature is implemented, the code is checked by someone else than its author (a researcher and also a developer) during the *code review.* After the features are accepted, the

---

[10] www.yeself.com.

development code base is deployed to *acceptation* environment. Here the integration, unit and acceptance tests are run. After the successful run of all the tests, the code base is deployed to the *production*, ready for the clients. Each component described in the previous sections is a separate dedicated Docker container. For the container orchestration we use the *Docker Swarm*[11]. All the services are easily scalable by running on multiple hosts. For monitoring the health of the application, containers log the activity directly into the *ElasticSearch* cluster.

Currently, three customers use the guide personalization module of the *YesElf* with more than 200 concurrent users. In Fig. 4, we can see the aggregated count of mouse logs being stored to the *ElasticSearch* cluster every 30 s from a chosen day (the figure shows a time window of approximately 15 min between 16:03 and 16:19). The graph was taken from the *Kibana* application[12], an analytical tool monitoring the state of the *ElasticSearch* cluster. In the figure, we can see up to 2500 concurrent logs being stored to the database every 30 s. This capability supports the scaling potential of the logging solution.

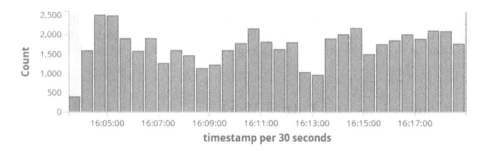

Fig. 4. The aggregated count of mouse logs being stored to the *ElasticSearch* cluster every 30 s (during a time window of approximately 15 min between 16:03 and 16:19). The graph was taken from *Kibana*, an analytical tool for *ElasticSearch*.

Figure 5 demonstrates the confusion detection capability of the system. It shows a daily count of predictions for one of the customers. We can see up to 10 000 predictions per day (more than 1000 predictions per working hour). The distribution reflects the common behavioral pattern of the company as employees work from Monday to Friday.

So far, the accuracy of the confusion detection has been evaluated in the controlled conditions of a user study [9] employing also eye tracking [4] for comparison. The achieved results are comparable to the state-of-the-art in this domain; however, to maintain the accuracy in different web applications, the model needs to be retrained for each specific context.

---

[11] https://docs.docker.com/engine/swarm/.
[12] www.elastic.co/products/kibana.

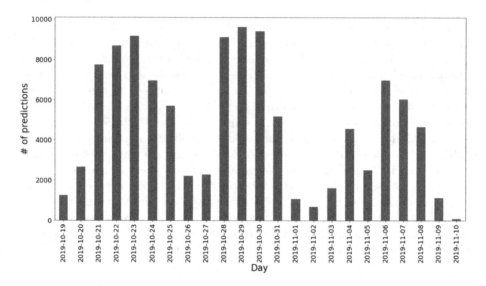

Fig. 5. Histogram of daily predictions for a specific *YesElf* customer. A standard working week is from Monday (e.g., 2019-10-21) to Friday (e.g., 2019-10-25). There was a holiday on Friday, November 1, which explains the low number of predictions that were made that day.

6   Conclusions and Future Work

In this paper, we introduced a guide personalization module based on emotion detection, which we integrated and deployed into an existing system—the onboarding platform *YesElf*. Our module leverages the mouse interaction data to detect the moments of users' confusion in the real time. The confused users are provided with the *YesElf* guides to help them overcome their confusion.

The production deployment of emotion detection systems is accompanied by many challenges, such as scalable user input logging, real-time prediction, model retraining and adaptation to new contexts, which are poorly addressed by the existing works. Our main contributions lie in tackling these problems. In the paper, we described the architecture for scalable guides personalization – the whole solution is scalable, orchestrated and containerised Docker implementation. The detection takes place on a dedicated server. To ensure prompt confusion detection and consequent system reaction (in order of tens to hundreds of milliseconds) the confusion detection module leverages asynchronous message passing queues. We demonstrated the capability of our solution to scale and provided analytical insights to the logging component of the module.

Currently, the biggest limitation of the system is the performance of the confusion method itself. Even though our method achieves results comparable to the state-of-the-art solutions [9], it is obvious that the method is very context (application) dependent. It means that it reaches lower accuracy in applications for which it was not specifically trained. As a consequence, to make the predictions as accurate as possible, we need to gather labeled data for each application, in which we wish to use the confusion detection method. Addressing this problem, we developed a model retraining mechanism based on the implicit feedback of the users (followed after a positive confusion prediction). Currently, we are working on evaluation of this approach.

Besides the evaluation of the model retraining, we plan to more closely examine the ways of prompting the confused users. At the moment, we are evaluating the shake and the popup question options as described in Sect. 4.1.

Acknowledgements. This work was partially supported by the Slovak Research and Development Agency under the contracts No. APVV-15-0508, APVV-17-0267 and by the Scientific Grant Agency of the Slovak Republic, grants No. VG 1/0667/18 and VG 1/0725/19. The authors would also like to thank the company Brainware for supporting their research.

References

1. Ashwin, T., Jose, J., Raghu, G., Reddy, G.R.M.: An e-learning system with multifacial emotion recognition using supervised machine learning. In: 2015 IEEE 7th International Conference on Technology for Education (T4E), pp. 23–26. IEEE (2015)
2. Atterer, R., Wnuk, M., Schmidt, A.: Knowing the user's every move: user activity tracking for website usability evaluation and implicit interaction. In: Proceedings of the 15th International Conference on World Wide Web, WWW 2006, New York, NY, USA, pp. 203–212. Association for Computing Machinery (2006). https://doi.org/10.1145/1135777.1135811
3. Bahreini, K., Nadolski, R., Westera, W.: Towards multimodal emotion recognition in e-learning environments. Interact. Learn. Environ. **24**(3), 590–605 (2016). https://doi.org/10.1080/10494820.2014.908927
4. Bielikova, M., et al.: Eye-tracking en masse: Group user studies, lab infrastructure, and practices. J. Eye Mov. Res. **11**(3) (2018). https://doi.org/10.16910/jemr.11.3.6
5. Chudá, D., Krátky, P., Burda, K.: Biometric properties of mouse interaction features on the Web. Interact. Comput. **30**(5), 359–377 (2018). https://doi.org/10.1093/iwc/iwy015
6. Funk, M., Bächler, A., Bächler, L., Kosch, T., Heidenreich, T., Schmidt, A.: Working with augmented reality?: A long-term analysis of in-situ instructions at the assembly workplace. In: Proceedings of the 10th International Conference on PErvasive Technologies Related to Assistive Environments, pp. 222–229, PETRA 2017. ACM, New York (2017). https://doi.org/10.1145/3056540.3056548
7. Göschlberger, B., Bruck, P.A.: Gamification in mobile and workplace integrated microlearning. In: Proceedings of the 19th International Conference on Information Integration and Web-based Applications & Services, iiWAS 2017, pp. 545–552. ACM, New York (2017). https://doi.org/10.1145/3151759.3151795
8. Hewett, S., Becker, K., Bish, A.: Blended workplace learning: the value of human interaction. Educ.+ Train. **61**(1), 2–16 (2019)
9. Hucko, M., et al.: YesELF: personalized onboarding for web applications. In: Adjunct Publication of the 27th Conference on User Modeling, Adaptation and Personalization, pp. 39–44. ACM (2019)

10. Kung-Keat, T., Ng, J.: Confused, bored, excited? An emotion based approach to the design of online learning systems. In: Fook, C.Y., Sidhu, G.K., Narasuman, S., Fong, L.L., Abdul Rahman, S.B. (eds.) 7th International Conference on University Learning and Teaching (InCULT 2014) Proceedings, pp. 221–233. Springer, Singapore (2016). https://doi.org/10.1007/978-981-287-664-5_19
11. Lin, F.R., Kao, C.M.: Mental effort detection using EEG data in e-learning contexts. Comput. Educ. **122**, 63–79 (2018). https://doi.org/10.1016/j.compedu.2018.03.020
12. Minsky, M.: The Emotion Machine: Commonsense Thinking, Artificial Intelligence, and the Future of the Human Mind. Simon and Schuster (2007)
13. Nederveld, A., Berge, Z.L.: Flipped learning in the workplace. J. Workplace Learn. **27**(2), 162–172 (2015)
14. Paxiuba, C.M., Calado, J., Lima, C.P., Sarraipa, J.: CADAP: a student's emotion monitoring solution for e-learning performance analysis. In: 2018 International Conference on Intelligent Systems (IS), pp. 776–783, September 2018. https://doi.org/10.1109/IS.2018.8710542
15. Pedregosa, F., et al.: Scikit-learn: machine learning in Python. J. Mach. Learn. Res. **12**(Oct), 2825–2830 (2011)
16. Pentel, A.: Employing think-aloud protocol to connect user emotions and mouse movements. In: 2015 6th International Conference on Information, Intelligence, Systems and Applications (IISA), pp. 1–5. IEEE (2015)
17. Pentel, A.: Patterns of confusion: using mouse logs to predict user's emotional state. In: UMAP Workshops (2015)
18. Picard, R.W.: Affective Computing. MIT Press (2000)
19. Qian, Y., Zhang, Y., Ma, X., Yu, H., Peng, L.: Ears: emotion-aware recommender system based on hybrid information fusion. Inf. Fusion **46**, 141–146 (2019)
20. Santos, O.C.: Emotions and personality in adaptive e-Learning systems: an affective computing perspective. In: Tkalčič, M., De De Carolis, B., de de Gemmis, M., Odić, A., Košir, A. (eds.) Emotions and Personality in Personalized Services. HIS, pp. 263–285. Springer, Cham (2016). https://doi.org/10.1007/978-3-319-31413-6_13
21. Stefancova, E., Moro, R., Bielikova, M.: Towards detection of usability issues by measuring emotions. In: Benczúr, A., et al. (eds.) New Trends in Databases and Information Systems, pp. 63–70. Springer, Cham (2018). https://doi.org/10.1007/978-3-030-00063-9_8
22. Thai, N.T.T., De Wever, B., Valcke, M.: The impact of a flipped classroom design on learning performance in higher education: looking for the best "blend" of lectures and guiding questions with feedback. Comput. Educ. **107**, 113–126 (2017)
23. Vigo, M., Harper, S.: Real-time detection of navigation problems on the world 'wild' web. Int. J. Hum.-Comput. Stud. **101**, 1–9 (2017). https://doi.org/10.1016/j.ijhcs.2016.12.002

Creating and Capturing Artificial Emotions in Autonomous Robots and Software Agents

Claus Hoffmann[1]([✉])[iD] and Maria-Esther Vidal[2][iD]

[1] Research Group Robots and Software Agents with Emotions,
Sankt Augustin, Germany
hoffmann.claus@web.de

[2] TIB Leibniz Information Centre for Science and Technology,
Hannover, Germany
Maria.Vidal@tib.eu

Abstract. This paper presents ARTEMIS, a control system for autonomous robots or software agents. ARTEMIS is able to create and capture artificial emotions during interactions with its environment, and we describe the underlying mechanisms for this. The control system also realizes the capturing of knowledge about its past artificial emotions. A specific interpretation of a knowledge graph, called an Agent Knowledge Graph, represents these artificial emotions. For this, we devise a formalism which enriches the traditional factual knowledge in knowledge graphs with the representation of artificial emotions. As proof of concept, we realize a concrete software agent based on the ARTEMIS control system. This software agent acts as a user assistant and executes the user's orders. The environment of this user assistant consists of autonomous service agents. The execution of user's orders requires interaction with these autonomous service agents. These interactions lead to artificial emotions within the assistant. The first experiments show that it is possible to realize an autonomous agent with plausible artificial emotions with ARTEMIS and to record these artificial emotions in its Agent Knowledge Graph. In this way, autonomous agents based on ARTEMIS can capture essential knowledge that supports successful planning and decision making in complex dynamic environments and surpass emotionless agents.

Keywords: Autonomous agents · Artificial emotions · Agent Knowledge Graphs

1 Introduction

Data-driven technologies in conjunction with smart infrastructures for management and analytics, increasingly offer huge opportunities for improving quality of life and industrial competitiveness. Semantic data models like RDF and OWL, have been proposed to represent knowledge in data-driven systems. Albeit

© Springer Nature Switzerland AG 2020
M. Bielikova et al. (Eds.): ICWE 2020, LNCS 12128, pp. 277–292, 2020.
https://doi.org/10.1007/978-3-030-50578-3_19

expressive, the aim of these models is to represent entities, and the meaning of their features and relations. **The Problem and Proposed Solution.** Our research is guided by the following questions: i) how to create artificial emotions and ii) how to capture these emotions in a knowledge graph of an agent. For the creation of artificial emotions, we developed the ARTEMIS robot or software agent control system. The Component Process Model (CPM) of the emotion psychologist Scherer [22] and the Psi theory of the cognitive psychologist Dörner [7] provide the theoretical basis for ARTEMIS. Thus, ARTEMIS relies on a solid theoretical background, which we briefly introduce in Sect. 3. Knowledge bases are essential components of autonomous robots or software agents. They are the cornerstone for their planning and decision-making. There are several ways to realize such knowledge bases. We suggest for this purpose a particular version and interpretation of knowledge graphs or Agent Knowledge Graph. This particular version and interpretation of knowledge graphs are designed to capture relevant knowledge for autonomous agents. It allows autonomous robots or software agents to mimic human "problem solving" in complex environments to a certain extent.

Knowledge graphs [9] are in general, becoming more and more important: Large companies such as Google, Facebook, or Microsoft now all operate their interpretations of knowledge graphs. The interpretation of Google's knowledge graph is optimized to enrich search results with semantic information. The interpretation of Facebook is designed to map social relationships. Our interpretation of knowledge graphs, we call Agent Knowledge Graph, is intended to support autonomous robots and software agents in planning and decision making in complex environments.

Our Contributions. We present the design of our robot or software agent control system ARTEMIS. The control system is capable of creating and capturing artificial emotions. In this paper, the basis for the creation of artificial emotions is the appraisal of interactions of the agent with other autonomous agents. Both cognitive processes and need processes are involved in realizing these appraisals. We demonstrate how ARTEMIS implements both types of processes. It is also vital that the ARTEMIS control system contains an Agent Knowledge Graph which stores the emotions and makes them available for later planning and decision-making processes. We further discuss the semantic and the episodic part of the Agent Knowledge Graph and provide a formalism to store artificial emotions. We have conducted a user study, and the observed results suggest that human test subjects consider the artificial emotions generated by ARTEMIS plausible. Further experiments evidence that knowledge about past artificial emotions contained in the Agent Knowledge Graph helps autonomous agents to successfully plan and make decisions in complex dynamic environments, outperforming, thus, emotion-free agents.

We have organized the paper as follows. In Sect. 2, we will give an overview of possible application areas of ARTEMIS, using a motivating example. In Sect. 3, we look at the foundations of how emotions are created and stored in an Agent Knowledge Graph. In Sect. 4, we devise an Agent Knowledge Graph able to model the problem presented in the motivating example. In Sect. 5, we discuss

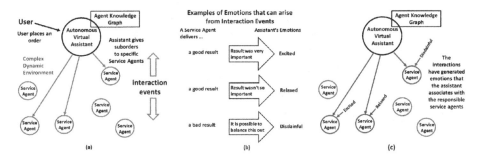

Fig. 1. Motivating example. (a) An autonomous virtual assistant executes a user's order in a complex environment. For this purpose, the virtual assistant selects the most suitable service agents, which in turn are also autonomous. Several interactions take place between the user assistant and the service agents. (b) The autonomous virtual assistant appraises these interactions. These appraisals create artificial emotions. For reasons of comprehensibility, we present the created emotions in this figure as text. In truth, they are encoded as points in a space that correspond to these text representations. We will discuss this later in this paper. (c) The resulting artificial emotions are associated in the Agent Knowledge Graph with the corresponding interaction events and with the causative service providers. The Assistant thus gains an attitude towards the Service Agents over time, which provides useful information for its future selections of cooperation partners.

related approaches and their relevance to the ARTEMIS control system. In Sect. 6, we present our experimental prototype and describe our experimental results. In Sect. 7, we discuss our conclusions and our future work.

2   Motivating Example

We motivate our approach using a typical situation that may be present in a wide variety of data-driven scenarios. Examples of application scenarios include the selection of a) machines in future 'Smart Factories', b) means of transport in 'Supply Chains 4.0', and c) information sources by an autonomous information broker in a 'decentral dataspace' like an 'Industrial Data Space'. The exemplary application scenario moves within the context of the so-called Service Web (see [8]). With this exemplary scenario, we can study principal problems of service selection without getting lost in the details of concrete application areas. The process of the exemplary application scenario is as follows (see Fig. 1a). An autonomous agent takes on the role of an autonomous virtual assistant for its user. The autonomous virtual assistant accepts the orders of its human user. To execute an order, the autonomous virtual assistant searches its knowledge base for a suitable plan. A plan defines a list of steps. For each plan step, the autonomous virtual assistant has to find a suitable service agent that performs the step. Autonomous service agents offer their services at different prices and are differently trustworthy. The autonomous virtual assistant has to decide which service agent fits best with the current situation. The following conditions form the basis for the exemplary application scenario:

1. In complex dynamic environments (e.g., 'Industry 4.0' applications) conditions for cooperation with autonomous service agents, can change from time to time. Present cooperation partners may leave the environment of the autonomous virtual assistant, and others may arrive. As a result, the search for suitable cooperation partners becomes a permanent task.
2. The cooperation partners of the autonomous virtual assistant are autonomous themselves and try to maximize their outcomes. Therefore, the results of cooperation are often uncertain. The autonomous virtual assistant always has to expect that cooperation partners do not meet the agreements and provide results that do not fulfill expectations. This violation of expectations can have numerous reasons. One reason could be that cooperation partners are not capable of delivering their promised services. Another reason could be that they did not understand their mandate correctly. It is also possible that they deliberately do not execute the job correctly in order to gain an advantage for themselves.

These conditions provide the basis for a complex interaction between the assistant and the service agents. Appraisals of these interactions create corresponding emotions in the virtual assistant. For example, 'Excited' when something goes well in contrast to expectations (and the result was very important) and 'Disdainful' when a cooperation partner performs poorly (and it is possible to balance this out) (see Fig. 1b). Through numerous interactions with the service agent, the assistant gains experience on the reliability of cooperation partners. Emotions are created and stored in the Agent Knowledge Graph of the assistant (see Fig. 1c). Over time, the assistant gains essential knowledge that helps for future effective planning and decision-making. Conventional approaches without artificial emotions would only determine whether an interaction was successful or not. The emotion-based approach, on the other hand, is much more differentiated. Emotions summarize the agent's assessment of the entire underlying situation. An essential function of emotions is to adapt the planning and decision-making of an autonomous actor to a particular situation. Scherer [22] describes this as follows: "Emotions are mechanisms that enable the individual to adapt to constantly and complexly changing environmental conditions" (from [22]). This applies to both current and remembered emotions.

3   Creating and Capturing Artificial Emotions

We first discuss how artificial emotions are created and their meaning. Then, we define the problem of capturing artificial emotions in Agent Knowledge Graphs.

3.1   Preliminaries

We present the ARTEMIS control system for creating artificial emotions. An Agent Knowledge Graph stores these created emotions. ARTEMIS resorts to the theoretical basis of the Scherer's [22] Component Process Model (CPM)

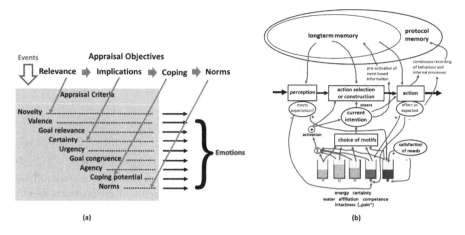

Fig. 2. Fundamentals for the creation of emotions. (a) Scherer's appraisal pattern [22] defines steps that have to be taken in order for emotions to form. For this purpose, the appraisal pattern defines appraisal objectives and appraisal criteria. The appraisal criteria subdivide the appraisal objectives. Emotions are created by applying the appraisal criteria to analyze events. However, Scherer's model does not describe any concrete mechanism on how appraisals should take place. (Eva Hudlicka inspired this picture, see [14]). (b) In ARTEMIS Dörner's Psi theory is the basis to realize Scherer's appraisal pattern. The Figure shows an overview of the structure of Psi (cut-out and own translation from [4]). The Psi theory defines an architecture of autonomous agents. This Figure primarily describes the interaction of need processes and cognitive processes. As this Figure shows, Dörner uses the concepts of motive and intention. We cannot discuss here in detail what exactly is meant by this. For the sake of simplicity, these terms could be replaced for the moment by the term goal.

and the Dörner's [7] Psi theory. In the Component Process Model, Scherer [22] defines an appraisal pattern for events. The Scheer's and Dörner's approaches are presented next.

Scherer's Appraisal Pattern for Events. Scherer (e.g., [20–22]) describes the objectives of the appraisal process of events: "There are four major appraisal objectives that an organism needs to adaptively react to a salient event: (1) How relevant is this event? Does it directly affect me or my social reference group? (relevance); (2) What are the implications or consequences of this event and how do they affect my well-being and my immediate or long-term goals? (implications); (3) How well can I cope with or adjust to these consequences? (coping potential); (4) What is the significance of this event for my self-concept and for social norms and values? (normative significance)." (Scherer [22, p. 50]) Scherer subdivides the four appraisal objectives into more detailed appraisal criteria (see Fig. 2a). The appraisal criteria include novelty, valence, goal relevance, urgency, goal congruence, responsible agent, coping potential, and norms (see Scherer [22, p. 51]). With his proposal, Scherer presents a theoretically sound appraisal pattern. However, he does not give any precise information on how to realize it. Scherer, however, gives hints on the boundary conditions for implementation; he also emphasizes the existence of needs and goals as essential prerequisites for the appraisals of events. Further, Scherer's criteria point out that computational agents who have no needs or goals cannot have real emotions (Scherer [22, p. 52]).

3.2   An Outline of Dörner's Psi theory

The Psi theory defines an architecture of autonomous systems (see, e.g., [5–7]). For experimental purposes, Dörner and his research team have realized the Psi theory as a computer simulation. The following scenario is the basis of this computer simulation: a virtual robot must protect its life on an island and at the same time, fulfill a task. The robot can alternatively be controlled by human test subjects or by Dörner's system. Dörner demonstrates that in a simulated environment, the realization of the Psi theory exhibits a similar behavior as the human test subjects.

Dörner's Psi theory shows that it is advantageous whenever needs are the basis of a control system of autonomous agents. For the realization of needs, Dörner proposes a simple model. Dörner models the 'need processes' using tanks that can have varying filling levels. If 'needs' are satisfied, the corresponding tanks are full. Each tank possesses an inlet and an outlet. Successes, reported by efficiency signals, raise the fill level of the tanks. Failures, reported by inefficiency signals, lower the level. Figure 2b shows needs represented by tanks. The actual fill level of these tanks (and thereby the actual strength of the needs) influences, for example, the arousal level as well as different behavior tendencies of the agent.

In the Psi theory, needs such as energy, integrity, or belonging activate goals that an agent must achieve in order to meet the needs. Sometimes some of these goals compete with each other and cannot be achieved at the same time. In this case, the control system must select a goal. The basis for a selection is how strongly the goals are activated and how difficult it is to achieve them. Further, there is a selection threshold that regulates the change of goals; it prevents an agent from switching between targets too quickly.

3.3   Creation of Artificial Emotions in ARTEMIS

We expand the knowledge of events that have taken place to include knowledge about the artificial emotions associated with them. To create emotions, we devise the ARTEMIS control system for autonomous agents (see Fig. 3). Artificial emotions are the result of the agent's appraisals of events (see Fig. 4a). First, we discuss the components of the ARTEMIS control system. As a starting point, we present the need system which is the basis of the ARTEMIS approach. This need system generates values for the parameters 'Pleasure', 'Arousal', and 'Dominance'. The parameter values generated by the need system are then mapped

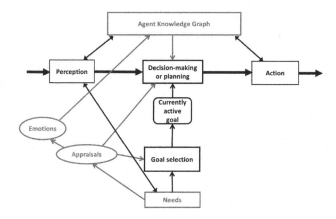

Fig. 3. The ARTEMIS architecture. An overview of the structure of the ARTEMIS control system. The Dörner's Psi theory represents the basis for many essential components of this architecture (shown in the black parts of the Figure). In ARTEMIS, an Agent Knowledge Graph realizes parts of the long term and protocol memory of the Dörner's Psi theory (see Fig. 2b). In contrast to the Dörner's approach, ARTEMIS has a specific appraisal component which appraises events based on both cognitive processes and need processes. Based on these appraisals, ARTEMIS creates artificial emotions. The results of these appraisals influence the 'decision-making/planning', or 'goal selection' components of the control system and modulate their effects (red arrows). An Agent Knowledge Graph captures these artificial emotions. (the red parts of the Figure are ARTEMIS specific realizations) (Color figure online)

to the PAD cube of emotions and define emotions there (Fig. 4b). Then, we discuss how the Dörner's Psi theory can realize the appraisal pattern defined in the Scherer's theory.

The Need System of ARTEMIS. Here, we present seven needs captured in the ARTEMIS control system. Why does our control system work with these seven needs as opposed to the Psi architecture? The answer is: Dörner uses the needs to be found in Fig. 2b in the context of psychological research questions. We do not conduct psychological research but build autonomous agents within the scope of artificial intelligence applications. So, we have adapted the needs of the Dörner's Psi theory to ARTEMIS. The chosen needs are better suited to our research questions; they are as follows:

1. Preserve existence (e.g., execute orders, make sure that services can be paid),
2. Avoid pain (for robots it could mean to avoid structural damages, for software agents it could mean not spending too much money),
3. Be agile (change methods and maybe partners from time to time, get neither bored nor boring),
4. Affiliation (the need for robust social integration and a good relationship with others),

5. Certainty (being knowledgeable about the environment. Certainty results from the ability to explain and predict events based on knowledge about the environment),
6. Competence (effectiveness and the ability to deal with real-world problems),
7. Avoid damages (for robots, it means maintaining machines or buildings and not overloading machines; for software agents, it represents the ability of not making decisions that endanger the environment).

The ARTEMIS emotion model uses a dimensional theory of emotions [18]. Different emotions are characterized in terms of the three dimensions of a PAD cube (see Fig. 4b). The three dimensions are described by the parameters: "Pleasure", "Arousal", and "Dominance". The values for these parameters are provided by the need system in the following way.

- Pleasure - Rising and falling of the strength of needs determine the level of pleasure.
- Arousal - A combination of the strengths of all needs determines the level of arousal.
- Dominance - The levels in the tank of the need for certainty and the need for competence determine the dominance of the agent.

Let *Eff*, *Ineff*, *Cert*, *Comp* be efficiency, inefficiency, certainty, and competence, respectively. Then, the former parameter values are defined as follows:

```
for ( i= 1 to NumberNeeds )
  L(Need[i]):= W(Eff)*Signal(Eff) − W(Ineff)*Signal(Ineff)
  L(Need[i]):= Max(0,Min(1,L(Need[i])))
  Need[i]:= ln(1+L(Need[i]))
  Arousal := ln(1+(Need[i]) * W[i])
  Pleasure := W(Eff)*Signal(Eff) − W(Ineff)*Signal(Ineff)
  Dominance := Need[Cert] * (1 − Need[Comp])
```

The strength of the needs depends on the corresponding levels (represented with the variable L) of the associated need tanks. The levels of the need tanks are calculated continuously. The level can only take values between 0 and 1. The efficiency and inefficiency signals have a weight W, which models the strength of their impacts (see [5]).

Artificial Emotions Based on PAD Parameters. The combination of PAD parameters forms a cube, as shown in Fig. 4b. The values of the parameters correspond to points in this cube. In the literature there are different proposals for mappings the points of the PAD cube to emotions. For our approach, we lean on the emotion mapping from Mehrabian [17,18]. Mehrabian considers only octants (subcubes) of the PAD cube. However, it makes perfect sense to name the extreme points of the PAD cube after these octants. So-called dimensional approaches make it possible to define vague boundaries of emotion categories. In our approach, the intensity of emotions increases from the center to the edges

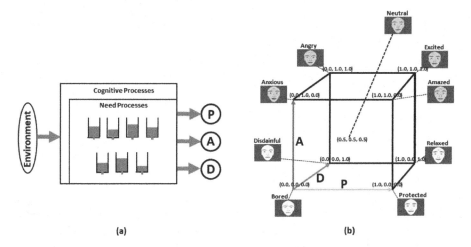

Fig. 4. Creation of artificial emotions in ARTEMIS. (a) Dörner's Psi theory is the basis for cognitive and need-based evaluations of events. In this way, ARTEMIS realizes the Scherer's appraisal pattern. The appraisal processes generate values for the parameters (P)leasure, (A)rousal, and (D)ominance. (b) The values of these parameters determine points on or in a cube. ARTEMIS maps these points to artificial emotions. Mehrabian's dimensional emotion theory [17,18] inspires this mapping.

of the cube. According to Peter Gaerdenfors [10, p. 48], the PAD cube equips emotions with meaning. The PAD parameters receive their values through need processes; as a consequence, the artificial emotions defined by ARTEMIS, finally, receive their meaning through need processes. An essential aspect of our approach is that the representations of the artificial emotions of ARTEMIS are not meaningless strings, but are grounded in the corresponding need processes.

Scherer's Appraisal Pattern in ARTEMIS. Some appraisal steps that Scherer defined (see Fig. 2a) can be realized directly or indirectly by the needs of ARTEMIS. Cognitive processes are the basis for these appraisal steps.

- 'Certainty' can be realized directly based on the 'need for certainty'. The filling level of the 'certainty tank' provides the necessary information for this purpose.
- The feature 'Coping potential' follows from the filling levels of the tanks 'certainty' and 'competence'.
- The filling level of the 'Preserve Existence' tank can be used to deduce the parameter 'Urgency'.
- Novelty is a comparison of the current event with the agent's expectations. Dörner's Psi achieves this by pre-activating need-based information in long-term memory.
- A determination of valence, goal congruence, goal relevance, agency, and norms require cognitive evaluations. Due to a lack of space, this is not explained in this paper.

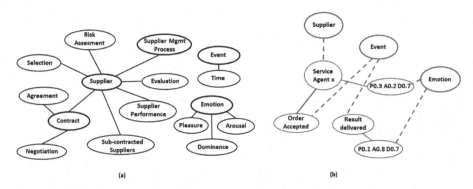

Fig. 5. Realizing the Agent Knowledge Graph. The Agent Knowledge Graph contains both semantic and episodic information. The semantic part of a Knowledge Graph contains general knowledge about the environment. The episodic part of the Agent Knowledge Graph contains information about specific entities and events that have occurred and the artificial emotions associated with it. (a) The semantic knowledge of the virtual assistant for the example presented in the motivating example (Sect. 2) looks like this. The template for this knowledge comes from Graupner [11]. It shows an Agent Knowledge Graph for the process scenario of supplier management. We added the concepts 'Event' and 'Emotion'. (b) Information about instances, actual events that occurred, and associated artificial emotions are represented in this part of the Agent Knowledge Graph.

4   The Agent Knowledge Graph

Previously, the process followed by ARTEMIS to create artificial emotions was described. In this section, we describe how ARTEMIS captures artificial emotions in an Agent Knowledge Graph. The Agent Knowledge Graph has a semantic and an episodic part. The semantic part of the Agent Knowledge Graph serves to classify information. A protocol of the events that take place represents the basis for the episodic part, such as interactions between the virtual assistant and the service agents are established (see the motivating example in Sect. 2). An Agent Knowledge Graph is an essential part of the ARTEMIS architecture (see Fig. 3). In Dörner's theory, a self-defined type of neural network is defined to realize the memory of Psi. However, for practical reasons, we have decided that ARTEMIS uses established methods of knowledge graphs for this purpose.

4.1   Realizing Semantics in an Agent Knowledge Graph

Knowledge specified by Graupner [11] forms the basis for the assistant's semantic part of an Agent Knowledge Graph. This knowledge provides the necessary conceptual information for the assistant about the problem area. We show an example of the organization of the semantic part of the Knowledge Graph in Fig. 5a. Since the Graupner's example is a supplier management system, the focus is on the supplier concept. Suppliers are related to many other concepts such as 'Risk Assessment', 'Evaluation', 'Supplier Management Process', 'Selection', 'Supplier Performance', 'Sub-Contracted Suppliers', and 'Contract'. The 'Contract' concept in turn is related to the 'Negotiation' and 'Agreement' concepts (see Fig. 5a). In ARTEMIS, we extend this model with the concepts 'Event' and 'Emotion'.

4.2 Episodic Knowledge in an Agent Knowledge Graph

While semantic knowledge specifies what the environment of an autonomous agent consists of, episodic knowledge describes what is going on in its world. In addition to the abstract semantic knowledge, a virtual assistant possesses episodic knowledge, such as knowledge about specific service providers, events, or artificial emotions (see Fig. 5b). The interactions of the assistant with the service providers create episodic knowledge; this episodic knowledge is enriched with emotional information. Over time this emotional information leads the assistant to develop a subjective attitude towards the service providers in its environment. This subjective attitude supports the assistant in future problem situations and enables the selection of appropriate cooperation partners in this dynamically complex environment. In our running example, the information stored in the episodic part refers to the abstract concepts supplier, event, and emotion. Information about a specific service provider (here, Service Agent x) is recorded. Events assigned to the specific service agents are 'Order accepted', and 'Result delivered'. Mainly the Events 'Service delivered' are predestined to generate artificial emotions, which are then also stored in the episodic part of an Agent Knowledge Graph.

5 Related Work

Research in the field of computers and emotions currently focuses on the recognition of user emotions. For example, one tries to recognize emotions in texts (emotional analysis), human faces, or the language (see [12]). This research direction has already achieved significant results. Emotion analysis will be essential for machines to be able to react appropriately to the emotions of their human users. Such analyses are, therefore, crucial for the next step in human-computer interaction (HCI). Here, however, the approach presented in this paper is not the recognition of human emotions. Instead, the focus is on creating and memorizing artificial emotions in autonomous agents. These artificial emotions help to adapt the behavior of autonomous robots and software agents to the respective environment. It is also crucial that the communication of these artificial emotions (e.g., by face, voice or gestures) can help users to understand the decisions and actions of the system. The basis of this understanding is the fact that human users can often well imagine that they probably would have had similar emotions in similar situations and that they would have acted or decided similarly on this foundation. The approach presented in this paper, therefore, has two results. On the one hand, it serves to improve the performance of autonomous agents. On the other hand, it is also a contribution to the research area of HCI.

There are diverse approaches to create artificial emotions. Marsella et al. [16] give an overview of this. So far, most approaches for agents with artificial emotions use the model from Ortony, Clore, and Collins (OCC) [19]. However, the OCC approach relies on a purely cognitive assessment of events. We, on the other hand, rely on the approach of the emotion psychologist Scherer and the cognitive psychologist Dörner. Scherer's research has shown that realistic judgments must both consider cognitive processes and need processes. According to Scherer, this is more promising for creating realistic artificial emotions for autonomous actors. Dörner's theory can be used to realize the appraisal pattern required by Scherer. With ARTEMIS, we now present a model that realizes these vital requirements from these two researchers.

The problem of capturing emotions has been tackled in the literature as a data analytics problem, and different formalisms have been proposed for knowledge representation to effectively solve this problem (e.g., [1,13]). Additionally, Chekol and Stuckenschmidt [2] present a formalism to represent temporally in probabilistic knowledge graphs. Albeit expressive for event representation or for performing data analytics, the semantics encoded in the emotions cannot be naturally represented in any of these approaches. In our approach, the artificial emotions of an autonomous agent have a meaning.

6   Experimental Study

We implemented a prototype of the virtual assistant to assess the performance of ARTEMIS. We aim to answer the following research questions (RQ): **RQ1)** Can a virtual assistant generate artificial emotions that are plausible for human test subjects? **RQ2)** Can captured artificial emotions make the virtual assistant more efficient? The experimental configuration is as follows:

A Synthetic Virtual Assistant: We implemented a synthetic scenario to evaluate the feasibility and behavior of ARTEMIS. A virtual assistant is created, which can call 100 service agents. In this scenario, 50 of these service agents are somewhat reliable, and 50 are rather unreliable without the virtual agent having any information about them. The virtual assistant selects its cooperative partners from this pool. It initially selects its cooperation partners at random following a uniform distribution. With a large number of interactions, it can use the artificial emotions generated during individual interactions and captured in its Knowledge Graph. The assistant executed 300 test runs.

Implementation: We realize the virtual assistant by a dynamic system based on difference equations; the system is implemented in Python 3.5.3. An Agent Knowledge Graph is modeled as an RDF graph using RDFLib [3]; in order to realize the episodic part of the Agent Knowledge Graph, events are described based on the ontology LODE [15].

Evaluation Metrics: We measure the performance of ARTEMIS in terms of time; it represents to the elapsed time between the submission of an order to the virtual assistant and the completion of the order; it corresponds to the absolute wall-clock system time reported by the Python `time.time()` function.

User Evaluation: We conducted an evaluation where 30 human test subjects evaluated the virtual assistant in the above described synthetic scenario. We asked the participants to asses the plausibility of the artificial emotions that the virtual assistant created when fulfilling an order of the user. We presented nine scenarios to each test subjects. The basis for the scenarios is the motivational example (compare Sect. 2). The test subjects were asked to assess the plausibility of the created artificial emotions within the scenarios. The artificial emotions were presented to the test subjects in both pictorial and textual form.

6.1   Results of the User Study

All the users answered the questionnaires independently and evaluated the presented artificial emotions; 270 evaluations were thus available. The test subjects stated in seven evaluations that they could not understand the artificial emotions presented "very well" or "well". In a later optional interview, five of them stated that in one of the scenarios, they would tend to the emotion "indifferent" rather than to the emotion "disdainful". In nine evaluations, the test persons indicated that they could not decide. In 254 assessments, subjects indicated that they could understand the artificial emotions presented well or very well and that they could imagine having similar emotions in similar situations (Table 1). Additionally, the performance of the virtual assistant was evaluated in terms of time; the behavior of the virtual assistant was observed without and with remembered emotions. The virtual assistant was executed for 300 runs. As a result, we observed that the effectiveness– in terms of average time– was enhanced by up to 40% whenever the virtual assistant was able to fall back on remembered emotions from earlier test runs for its decision-making process.

Table 1. Results of the user evaluation. Artificial emotions are evaluated in a user study; they are represented both as text and as images. In 53.33 % of the cases, the users understand very well the emotions while 40.74 % just understand them well.

User question	Positive answers	Percentage positive answers %
I fail to understand at all	3	1.11 %
I fail to understand	4	1.48 %
I cannot decide	9	3.33 %
I can understand well	110	**40.74 %**
I can understand very well	144	**53.33 %**

Discussion: As far as we have been able to investigate this, the proposed approach opens up productive and promising research and application fields. These initial results suggest that the approach implemented in ARTEMIS works and enables autonomous agents to reach their goals faster. It turns out that remembered artificial emotions are helpful for successful agent planning and decision making in complex environments. Furthermore, the results of the experiments show that the approach can help to make decisions of a computer system more plausible for users. The system can thus make clear its internal situation on which it grounds its decision making. However, further experiments considering different scenarios and types of goals are required to thoroughly asses the pros and cons of a model able to create and capture artificial emotions.

7   Conclusion and Future Work

We have tackled the problem of creating and capturing knowledge about artificial emotions. To generate artificial emotions, a suitable model, as well as a system that implements this is required. For this purpose, we have developed the ARTEMIS control system for autonomous agents with artificial emotions. The Psi theory of the cognitive psychologist Dietrich Dörner is the basis of essential components of the ARTEMIS control system. We added a specific appraisal and an emotional component. In ARTEMIS, event appraisals create artificial emotions. The appraisal pattern described by the emotion psychologist Klaus Scherer is the basis for this. However, Scherer does not provide any information on how to realize this appraisal pattern. In ARTEMIS, we use Dörner's Psi theory to implement Scherer's appraisal pattern.

For capturing knowledge about artificial emotions, we developed the concept of an Agent Knowledge Graph as a formalism for empowering autonomous robots and software agents with this knowledge. In addition to knowledge about facts, Agent Knowledge Graphs also represent subjective knowledge of individual autonomous agents. Captured artificial emotions form this subjective knowledge. Artificial emotions are collected together with other information (e.g., point in time) about events in Agent Knowledge Graphs. As time goes by, the captured artificial emotions form a subjective world view of the agents. This subjective world view helps agents to plan and decide successfully in complex dynamic environments. Artificial emotions of autonomous robots or software agents based on ARTEMIS have a meaning. This meaning can be derived as follows. According to Peter Gaerdenfors [9, p. 48], the PAD cube equips emotions with meaning. The PAD parameters receive their values through need processes; as a consequence, the artificial emotions defined by ARTEMIS finally get their meaning from the underlying need processes.

We empirically investigated the behavior of ARTEMIS in a synthetic scenario in which a virtual assistant had to select suitable cooperation partners from a pool of 100 service agents. In three hundred interactions, the virtual assistant developed an emotional attitude to many of these service providers. We have evaluated the feasibility of the artificial emotions the assistant created by a group of thirty human test subjects. The test subjects confirmed that most of the artificial emotions generated by the virtual assistant were comprehensible to them. Furthermore, we measured the execution time of the virtual assistant in a setting with and without remembered artificial emotions. The results of the evaluation reveal that the virtual assistant could reach their objective on average in 40% less time than the configuration without remembered artificial emotions. The observed results reveal the potential of the proposed approach. Nevertheless, we recognize that this formalism is still in an initial phase and that further studies are required to provide a general approach that can represent artificial emotions in any scenario. The development of general approaches able to capture artificial emotions while manage conflicts that may arise in different agent interactions are part of our future work.

Acknowledgments. We thank Christoph Lange from Fraunhofer Institute FIT for his valuable comments regarding our work. This work has received funding from the European Union's Horizon 2020 research and innovation programme under grant agreement No 822404 (QualiChain).

References

1. Candrlic, S., Katic, M.A., Pavlic, M.: A system for transformation of sentences from the enriched formalized Node of Knowledge record into relational database. Expert Syst. Appl. **115**, 442–464 (2019)
2. Chekol, M.W., Stuckenschmidt, H.: Towards probabilistic bitemporal knowledge graphs. In: Companion of the The Web Conference 2018 (WWW 2018), Lyon, France, 23–27 April 2018, pp. 1757–1762 (2018)
3. RDFLib Homepage. https://rdflib.readthedocs.io/en/stable/. Accessed 14 Jan 2020
4. Dörner, D., Schaub, H., Detje, F.: Das Leben von PSI. Über das Zusammenspiel von Kognition, Emotion und Motivation - oder: Eine einfache Theorie komplexer Verhaltensweisen. In: von Lüde, R., Moldt, D., Valk, R. (eds.) Sozionik aktuell, vol. 2. Informatik Universität Hamburg, Hamburg (2001)
5. Dörner, D.: The mathematics of emotion. In the logic of cognitive systems. In: Fifth International Conference on Cognitive Modelling, 10–12 April 2003. Universitätsverlag Bamberg, Bamberg (2003)
6. Dörner, D., Gerdes, J.: Motivation, emotion, intelligence. In: ICSAI, Yantai, China (2012)
7. Dörner, D., Güss, C.D.: PSI: a computational architecture of cognition, motivation, and emotion. Rev. Gen. Psychol. **17**(3), 297–317 (2013)
8. Dominique, J., Fensel, D., Davies, J., González-Cabero, R., Pedrinaci, C.: The service web: a web of billions of services. In: Tselentis, G., et al. (eds.) Towards a Future Internet: A European Research Perspective, pp. 203–216. IOS Press, Amsterdam (2009)
9. Ehrlinger, L., Woess, W.: Towards a definition of knowledge graphs. In: SEMANTiCS 2016 (Posters and Demos Track), Proceedings, Leipzig, Vol. 1695 (2016)
10. Gaerdenfors, P.: The Geometry of Meaning: Semantics Based on Conceptual Spaces. The MIT Press, Cambridge (2014)
11. Graupner, S., Netzad, H.R.M., Singhal, S.: Making processes from best practice frameworks actionable. In: 2009 13th Enterprise Distributed Object Computing Conference Workshops (2009)

12. Hakak, N.M., Mohd, M., Kirmani, M., Mohd, M.: Emotion analysis: a survey. In: 2017 International Conference on Computer, Communications and Electronics (Comptelix). Manipal University Jaipur, Malaviya (2017)
13. He, S., Liu, K., Ji, G., Zhao, J.: Learning to represent knowledge graphs with gaussian embedding. In: Proceedings of the 24th ACM International Conference on Information and Knowledge Management (CIKM 2015), Melbourne, VIC, Australia, 19–23 October 2015, pp. 623–632 (2015)
14. Hudlicka. Alternative Theoretical Perspectives on Emotion Representation and Modeling. https://www.slideshare.net/hudlicka. Accessed 14 Jan 2020
15. LODE: An ontology for Linking Open Descriptions of Events. http://linkedevents.org/ontology/2010-10-07/. Accessed 14 Jan 2020
16. Marsella, S., Gratch, J., Petta, P.: Computational models of emotion. In: Scherer, K.R., Bänziger, T., Roesch, E. (eds.) A Blueprint for Affective Computing: A Sourcebook and Manual. Oxford Univ Press, Oxford (2010)
17. Mehrabian, A.: Framework for a comprehensive description and measurement of emotional states. Genet. Soc. Gen. Psychol. Monogr. **121**, 339–361 (1995)
18. Mehrabian, A.: Pleasure-arousal-dominance: a general framework for describing and measuring individual differences in temperament. Curr. Psychol. Dev. Learn. Pers. Soc. Winter **14**(4), 261–292 (1996). https://doi.org/10.1007/BF02686918
19. Ortony, A., Clore, G.L., Collins, A.: The Cognitive Structure of Emotions. Cambridge University Press, Cambridge (1988)
20. Sander, D., Grandjean, D., Scherer, K.R.: A systems approach to appraisal mechanisms in emotion. Neural Netw. **18**(4), 317–352 (2005)
21. Scherer, K. R.: Appraisal considered as a process of multilevel sequential checking. In: Appraisal Processes in Emotion: Theory, Methods, Research, vol. 92(120), p. 57, New York (2001)
22. Scherer, K.R.: The component process model: architecture for a comprehensive computational model of emergent emotion. In: Scherer, K.R., Bänziger, T., Roesch, E.B. (eds.) Blueprint for Affective Computing: A Sourcebook, pp. 47–70. Oxford University Press, Oxford (2010)

On Emotions in Conflict Wikipedia Talk Pages Discussions

Maksymilian Marcinowski[1] and Agnieszka Ławrynowicz[1,2]

[1] Faculty of Computing and Telecommunications, Poznan University of Technology, Poznań, Poland
{mmarcinowski,alawrynowicz}@cs.put.poznan.pl
[2] Center for Artificial Intelligence and Machine Learning (CAMIL), Poznan University of Technology, Poznań, Poland

Abstract. Unjustified anti-social behaviour in Internet discussions, such as vulgarisms and insults, is tantamount to the outbreak of an online conflict that destroys the merits of the discussion. Recognising the characteristics of conflict discussions and modelling their dynamics can help to predict and prevent derailing. We propose to use emotion labels as characteristics and propose a new dataset, extending the non-conflict and such conflict conversations from Wikipedia talk pages that derailed due to a personal attack with an emotional context based on the Plutchik's model. We also present the results of the analysis of this dataset aimed at identifying specific, emotion-based features of conflict (derailed) discussions, which are potentially useful in predicting the outbreak of conflict in online conversations. Furthermore, we introduce the phenomenon of escalation of emotions using both the Plutchik's model and EmoWordNet lexicon and show its dynamics in these approaches. With this new dataset and analysis, we hope to open up new possibilities for research in detecting the outbreak of an online conflict.

Keywords: Online discussion · Emotions · Conflictual interactions

1 Introduction

Recognising the characteristics of online conflict discussions can help to predict and prevent their derailing. Recent works researched such various characteristics, including: politeness [9], hostile comments [6], sentiment features such as sentiment transition [8], mood and contextual features [2], or hate speech [3].

We hypothesize that emotions can be a good discriminating descriptor between conflict and non-conflict discussions. Importantly, models that capture the characteristics of the discussions need to take their *sequential* nature and *dynamics* into account, rather than individual posts. To facilitate research in this direction, we provide a new resource and its analysis according to two interpretable characteristics: *sequential patterns of emotions* in sequences of posts and *emotion intensity in the course of a discussion*. Our analysis aims to answer

© Springer Nature Switzerland AG 2020
M. Bielikova et al. (Eds.): ICWE 2020, LNCS 12128, pp. 293–301, 2020.
https://doi.org/10.1007/978-3-030-50578-3_20

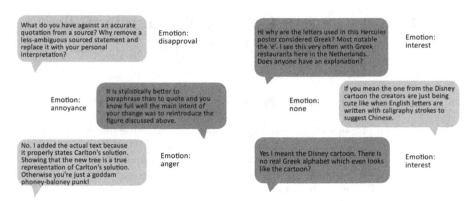

Fig. 1. Excerpts from a conflict (left) and a non-conflict (right) conversation.

the following research questions: **RQ1**: Are there any recurring sequential patterns of emotions occurring in conflict discussions? **RQ2**: Is it possible to notice conflict escalation in the discussions by recognizing emotions?

Our contributions are as follows: i) a new dataset, an extension of a subset of Wikipedia Talk Pages dataset [9] with emotion labels of posts (see Fig. 1 for a sample of annotated posts), we coined **EmoWikipediaTalkPages**, ii) an analysis of how emotion labels are related to a trajectory of a conversation, including detecting sequential patterns of emotions (i.e., of emotion labels) and investigating emotion intensity over time to capture the conflict escalation.

2   Models of Emotions

We have selected two models for annotating discussion posts: Plutchik's model [7], since it allows to express emotion intensity and it provides various ways the emotions relate to one another, which helps bring clarity and guidelines to human annotators, and the model of the EmoWordNet lexicon [1], which helps us to link the emotion labels with the natural language.

Plutchik's Model is a theory of emotions [7] distinguishing eight basic emotions: anger, anticipation, disgust, fear, joy, sadness, surprise and trust, which can be presented on the diagram (called "wheel of emotions"). We will denote an individual emotion by e. The degree of adjacency of emotions represents their degree of similarity, and the additional dimension represents levels of *intensity*. Three levels of emotion together form a *petal*, which we will denote by p, labelled with the name of the basic emotion. Emotions in empty spaces (between petals) are called the *dyads* (denoted further by d), i.e. feelings composed of two basic emotions. A *primary dyad* links common emotions that are one petal apart.

EmoWordNet [1] is a lexicon, containing 67 000 words and terms from English WordNet, expanded with 8 scores for each one, which represent 8 emotions: afraid, amused, angry, annoyed, don't care, happy, inspired and sad. The scores take values from 0 to 1 that estimate expressiveness and intensity of the emotion and they add up to 1 for each element of the lexicon.

3 Dataset

3.1 Original Dataset

The original dataset was a corpus provided by Zhang et al. [9] containing 1270 dialogues that consist of a total of 5839 comments/posts. Out of 1270 conversations, exactly half were annotated as conflict (derailed) discussions, i.e. that end with a personal attack.

3.2 Extending Dataset

We extended the dataset with the help of 63 respondents-volunteers, students aged 20–25 years. Their task was to annotate each of the comments/posts presented to them by clicking on a Plutchik's wheel of emotion in a place that represents the emotion that they think dominates the post. In order to make the task more affordable and enjoyable for the respondents, they were given a sample made of 10 dialogues of 3 posts each (30 posts divided into ten triplets - ten fragments of conversations), so that they could also judge the posts in certain context. For this reason we had selected conversations in which the number of comments is divided by 3 from the entire original dataset. The selection limited the number of conversations to 586 of which 237 were the conflict ones. Each post was annotated by 3 respondents, to check the reliability of annotation.

We further extended the dataset with values calculated on the basis of EmoWordNet lexicon (described in more detail in Sect. 5.2).

The EmoWikipediaTalkPages dataset is publicly available at https://doi.org/10.5281/zenodo.3631670.

4 Analysis

4.1 Basic Statistics

The respondents annotated a total of 624 posts in 151 whole conversations, each of which was annotated by three different annotators. Of the annotated conversations, 50 were conflict (containing a total of 249 posts) and 101 were non-conflict (containing 375 posts).

Each post was annotated by 3 respondents to check the compliance of annotators. The results point to a considerable variety of the annotations. Only approximately 6% of the posts were annotated by 3 respondents unanimously (36 times) and 54% posts were annotated with three different emotions (340 times). Out of the emotions chosen unanimously, it was most often the *none* annotation - 15 of

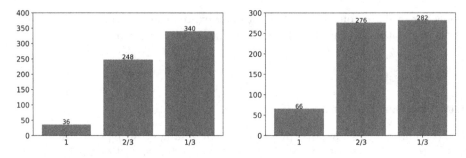

Fig. 2. Compliance of respondents in annotating posts considering particular emotions (left) and petals of emotions (right): "1" denotes 3 identical annotations of the post, "2/3" denotes 2 identical annotations and one other, "1/3" denotes 3 different annotations

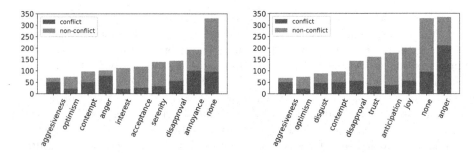

Fig. 3. Number of annotations containing the 10 most frequently chosen emotions (left) and petals of emotions (right) - in conflict and non-conflict conversations

36 times. Considering each level of the emotions' petal as an equal annotation, the compliance of annotators is slightly greater. A situation, in which one of the emotions dominates the respondents' choices, refers to 55% of the posts in such case (342 times), so 45% were annotated with emotions belonging to three different petals (282 times) (Fig. 2). Among the 66 unanimous decisions, most annotations (25 times) had been made with emotions from the *anger* petal.

Considering each emotion separately, the most frequent individual annotation was *none* (330 occurrences), which occurred far more often in non-conflict discussions. In conflict discussions the most frequent annotation was *annoyance*, the second most frequent generally (193 occurrences). Given the petals of emotions, the petal representing *anger* was the most commonly chosen (335 times) (Fig. 3).

4.2 Closed Sequential Patterns of Emotions

Let us denote by $<s_1, s_2, ..., s_i>$ a sequence of items, i.e. an ordered list of elements, such as posts in an online conversation or their labels, e.g. `<surprise, love, surprise>`, where `love` is a primary dyad and `surprise` an individual emotion. Sequential pattern mining consists of finding the complete set of frequently occurring subsequences, given a set of sequences and frequency (support) threshold. To answer research question RQ1, we performed mining of closed sequential patterns, i.e. patterns not included in any other patterns with the same support, with the ClaSP algorithm [5], using the implementation from SPMF library. [4]. Thanks to the expressiveness of the Plutchik's model, we could mine patterns within the following experimental settings (the results are in Table 1):

1. for all of the annotations for single emotions, i.e., where each item s_i was an individual emotion e_i (subtables a, b)
2. for all of the annotations to the level of detail of a petal with a primary dyad treated as a separate petal, i.e. where each item s_i was a petal p_i or a dyad d_i (subtables c, d)
3. for all of the annotations to the level of detail of a petal with a primary dyad treated as one of the adjacent petals, i.e. for a sequence `<surprise, love, surprise>`, the input to the pattern mining algorithm was `<surprise, {joy, trust}, surprise>` and this sequence supports both patterns: `<surprise, joy, surprise>` and `<surprise, trust, surprise>` (subtables e, f)
4. for triplets of annotations and the use of wildcard - three annotations of each post are aggregated and the output is the most common emotion among them or a wildcard (*) when each of the annotations is different (subtables g, h).

Considering the settings which include all of the annotations made in the conflict discussions, only one closed pattern consisting of more than one element has a support greater than 50% - it is `<anger, anger>` (59% support, 88 occurrences), discovered in the configuration with a primary dyad treated as one of the adjacent petals. Also for this pattern, the difference between support in conflict and non-conflict conversations is the most significant - in the non-conflict ones the pattern appeared 36 times (it means only 12% support).

Taking all settings into account there are 21 multi-elemental closed patterns with a support greater than 20%, all of which were discovered in conflict discussions. The most common pattern for non-conflict dialogues in any configuration is the same - `<none, none>`.

Table 1. The most common multi-elemental closed sequential patterns discovered during the analysis of EmoWikipediaTalkPages in particular configurations

(a) conflict

pattern	support (occ.)
<none, annoyance>	18% (27)
<annoyance, anger>	17% (26)
<none, anger>	16% (24)

(b) non-conflict

pattern	support (occ.)
<none, none>	18% (56)
<disapproval, none>	9% (27)
<interest, none>	8% (25)

(c) conflict

pattern	support (occ.)
<anger, anger>	40% (60)
<none, anger>	30% (45)
<disapproval, anger>	19% (28)

(d) non-conflict

pattern	support (occ.)
<none, none>	18% (56)
<anticipation, none>	13% (39)
<joy, joy>	11% (33)

(e) conflict

pattern	support (occ.)
<anger, anger>	59% (88)
<none, anger>	38% (57)
<anticipation, anger>	35% (52)

(f) non-conflict

pattern	support (occ.)
<none, none>	18% (56)
<joy, joy>	17% (53)
<anticipation, none>	16% (49)

(g) conflict

pattern	support (occ.)
<none, anger>	10% (5)
<none, rage>	8% (4)
<none,aggressiveness>	8% (4)

(h) non-conflict

pattern	support (occ.)
<none, none>	10% (10)
<interest, none>	9% (9)
<acceptance, none>	5% (5)

5 Do the Emotions Escalate?

To answer research question RQ2, we analyse the emotion intensity level and whether it grows in conflict discussions. Escalation of emotions is understood as an increase in intensity of emotions over the course of conversation that leads to conflict. We have verified the occurrence of this phenomenon in EmoWikipediaTalkPages dataset by using two methods of evaluating the intensity of emotions: the level of intensity of emotions occurring in posts according to the annotations based on Plutchik's model of emotions and the aggregated value of scores of particular words or terms occurring in posts according to the EmoWordNet lexicon based on the model provided by Rappler Mood Meter.

5.1 Analysis of the Annotations

The Plutchik's model has three levels of intensity, therefore the measurement of the intensity of emotions in the course of conversations was done using the levels from the model: emotions in the first level of the model were assigned a value of 1, emotions in the second level of the model and primary dyads were assigned a value of 2 and the most intense emotions were assigned a value of 3. The *none* annotation was assigned a value of 0. Conversations were divided into groups according to their length and then, for each group separately, the average intensity of emotions in consecutive posts was calculated.

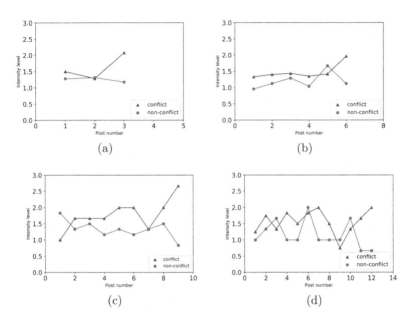

Fig. 4. Mean levels of emotions in consecutive posts in conversations consisting of: 3 (a), 6 (b), 9 (c) and 12 (d) posts, according the experiment's results.

The graphs in Fig. 4 illustrate a significant issue – the mean level of intensity of emotions at the end of conflict discussions is clearly higher than at their beginning, regardless of their length. It does not occur in non-conflict discussions. Moreover, all conflict conversations end at an mean higher emotional intensity level than non-conflict dialogues. Also noticeable can be an effect that may be called "calm before the storm", i.e. a temporary decrease in the mean level of emotion intensity in about 2/3 of the length of conflict discussions.

5.2 EmoWordNet

In order to juxtapose EmoWordNet lexicon with the dataset of conversations, each post from the dataset had been lemmatised and cleared of "stop words", then the scores of particular emotions in each term were summed up for each post and divided by the number of terms in the post to provide 8 mean emotion scores of each post. For the statistics, the maximum of these values for each post was selected, so the statistics presented in the graphs in Fig. 5 include average maximal mean emotion score of posts.

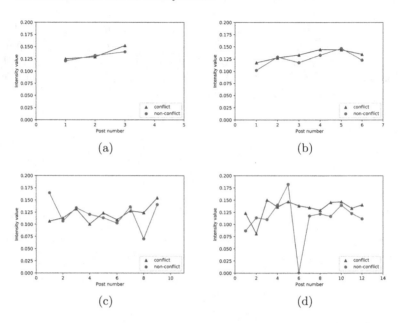

Fig. 5. Mean levels of emotions in consecutive posts in conversations consisting of: 3 (a), 6 (b), 9 (c) and 12 (d) posts, according to the EmoWordNet lexicon.

As in the case of annotations based on the Plutchik's model, the average score according to EmoWordNet lexicon is higher at the ends of conflict conversations than at the beginnings, which at the same time does not occur in non-conflict conversations. The average ending score of conflict conversations is also higher than that of non-conflict ones for all lengths.

6   Conclusions

We proposed a dataset of online conversations extended with emotion labels and presented the results of analysis of the dataset in the context of finding distinctive emotion-based features of conflict discussions which contain a personal attack.

The statistics show the difference in the nature of conflict and non-conflict discussions. Main emotions considered to be negative, such as aggression or especially anger, dominated conflict conversations, while emotions such as joy or serenity appeared more often in non-conflict dialogues. Furthermore, there are some specific features of the trajectory of conflict discussions, supported by both the annotations analysis and EmoWordNet-based scores, as an upward trend in the intensity of emotions throughout the entire length of the discussion, that distinguish them from non-conflict ones. The analysis provides some premises that the identification of emotions occurring in online discussions may contribute to the detection and prediction of conflicts in them. In the future work, we plan to use the results of this paper, and the dataset within, to train a machine learning model to detect emotions and conflict in text automatically.

Acknowledgements. This research has been partially supported by the statutory funds of Poznan University of Technology.

References

1. Badaro, G., Jundi, H., Hajj, H., El-Hajj, W.: EmoWordNet: automatic expansion of emotion lexicon using English WordNet. In: Proceedings of the Seventh Joint Conference on Lexical and Computational Semantics, pp. 86–93. Association for Computational Linguistics, June 2018. https://doi.org/10.18653/v1/S18-2009
2. Cheng, J., Bernstein, M.S., Danescu-Niculescu-Mizil, C., Leskovec, J.: Anyone can become a troll: causes of trolling behavior in online discussions. In: Proceedings of the 2017 ACM Conference on Computer Supported Cooperative Work and Social Computing (CSCW 2017), pp. 1217–1230 (2017)
3. Davidson, T., Warmsley, D., Macy, M.W., Weber, I.: Automated hate speech detection and the problem of offensive language. In: Proceedings of the Eleventh International Conference on Web and Social Media (ICWSM 2017), pp. 512–515 (2017)
4. Fournier-Viger, P., Gomariz, A., Gueniche, T., Soltani, A., Wu., C., Tseng, V.S.: SPMF: a Java open-source pattern mining library. J. Mach. Learn. Res. (JMLR) **15**, 3389–3393 (2014). http://www.philippe-fournier-viger.com/spmf/
5. Gomariz, A., Campos, M., Marin, R., Goethals, B.: ClaSP: an efficient algorithm for mining frequent closed sequences. In: Pei, J., Tseng, V.S., Cao, L., Motoda, H., Xu, G. (eds.) PAKDD 2013. LNCS (LNAI), vol. 7818, pp. 50–61. Springer, Heidelberg (2013). https://doi.org/10.1007/978-3-642-37453-1_5
6. Liu, P., Guberman, J., Hemphill, L., Culotta, A.: Forecasting the presence and intensity of hostility on instagram using linguistic and social features. In: Proceedings of the Twelfth International Conference on Web and Social Media (ICWSM 2018), Stanford, California, USA, 25–28 June 2018, pp. 181–190 (2018)
7. Plutchik, R.: A psychoevolutionary theory of emotions. Soc. Sci. Inf. **21**(4–5), 529–553 (1982). https://doi.org/10.1177/053901882021004003
8. Wang, L., Cardie, C.: A piece of my mind: a sentiment analysis approach for online dispute detection. In: Proceedings of the 52nd Annual Meeting of the Association for Computational Linguistics (ACL 2014) Volume 2: Short Papers, pp. 693–699 (2014). https://doi.org/10.3115/v1/p14-2113
9. Zhang, J., et al.: Conversations gone awry: detecting warning signs of conversational failure. In: Proceedings of ACL (2018)

Location-Aware Applications

Geospatial Partitioning of Open Transit Data

Harm Delva[✉], Julián Andrés Rojas, Pieter-Jan Vandenberghe,
Pieter Colpaert[✉], and Ruben Verborgh

IDLab, Department of Electronics and Information Systems,
Ghent University – imec, Ghent, Belgium
{harm.delva,pieter.colpaert}@ugent.be
https://idlab.technology/

Abstract. Public transit operators often publish their open data as a
single data dump, but developers with limited computational resources
may not be able to process all this data. Existing work has already
focused on fragmenting the data by departure time, so that data consumers can be more selective in the data they process. However, each
fragment still contains data from the entire operator's service area. We
build upon this idea by fragmenting geospatially as well as by departure
time. Our method is robust to changes in the original data, such as the
deletion or the addition of stops, which is crucial in scenarios where data
publishers do not control the data itself. In this paper we explore popular
clustering methods such as k-means and METIS, alongside two simple
domain-specific methods of our own. We compare the effectiveness of
each for the use case of client-side route planning, focusing on the ease
of use of the data and the cacheability of the data fragments. Our results
show that simply clustering stops by their proximity to 8 transport hubs
yields the most promising results: queries are 2.4 times faster and download 4 times less data. More than anything though, our results show that
the difference between clustering methods is small, and that engineers
can safely choose practical and simple solutions. We expect that this
insight also holds true for publishing other geospatial data such as road
networks, sensor data, or points of interest.

Keywords: Linked open data · Mobility · Maintainability · Web API
engineering

1 Introduction

People who rely on wheelchair-accessible public transportation have very specific
information needs when they are looking to buy a house. Real estate websites
can include this information in their item listings, but only if they can find and
access relevant datasets. Fortunately, many public transit operators publish their
offering as open data, often using de facto standards such as the General Transit

© Springer Nature Switzerland AG 2020
M. Bielikova et al. (Eds.): ICWE 2020, LNCS 12128, pp. 305–320, 2020.
https://doi.org/10.1007/978-3-030-50578-3_21

Feed Specification[1] (GTFS) or official standards such as Network Timetable Exchange[2] (NeTEx). However, these standards result in large data dumps: the combined GTFS feed of the public transit companies that operate in the Brussels area (SNCB, STIB, De Lijn, and Tec) is already over 1 GB of raw data. Searching for *"GTFS memory issues"* on the Web shows that many people have learned the hard way that this is more data than their personal laptops, Raspberry Pis, or entry-level VPSs can handle.

A popular use case for open transit data is route planning. The ideal route depends on many factors such as ticket prices, transfer times, walking distances, reliability, and arrival times. The value ascribed to each of these factors is ultimately subjective, and will likely change over time due to external factors such as the weather. However, contemporary route planning services offer little in terms of personalization because they sacrifice flexibility to provide better query time performance [3,12,14]. For example, an algorithm that relies on precomputed shortest paths is ill-suited to generate scenic routes. Alternatively, the route planning can be done directly on the client, and this has the benefit that more flexible algorithms become viable because users can only saturate their own CPUs. Client-side applications come with their challenges though, and ingesting the data is particularly difficult in this case. The European Commission reported that in 2019 the average price for 2 GB of mobile data within the EU28 was still €10 [9], which means that client-side route planners have to be conservative in which data they download.

These examples show that the way data is published can restrict how the data can be used. What may be feasible for a corporation may not be feasible for a regular person, even though the Open Definition[3] defines open data as data that can be *"freely used, modified, and shared by anyone for any purpose"*. Our goal is thus clear: we want to improve the way open transit data is published, so that more applications become more viable for more people.

2   Related Work

We identify three domains of related work which we discuss in the following subsections: (i) research in the field of Linked Data and the Semantic Web has focused on making data reusable and interoperable, (ii) existing mobility data specifications and what sets them apart, and (iii) how are public transit networks currently being partitioned and for what purpose. To close off this section we also briefly discuss Voronoi Diagrams, as our proposed method makes extensive use of them.

Note that throughout this paper we use three similar, but different, terms: *cluster*, *partition*, and *fragment*. In essence, clusters are partitions; *clustering* merges similar items while *partitioning* starts from the set of all items – so that clustering individual public transit stops partitions the network itself. A planar

---

[1] https://developers.google.com/transit/gtfs.

[2] http://netex-cen.eu/.

[3] https://opendefinition.org/.

space, such as the world, can also be partitioned, in which case each partition can be called a *region* instead. Fragments on the other hand come from the field of Linked Data and refer to Linked Data Fragments, i.e. resources on the Web.

2.1   Linked Data Fragments

To facilitate interoperability with other datasets, Open Data is often *Linked Data* as well. Tim Berners-Lee outlined the four principles of Linked Data [7]: 1) use URIs as names for things, 2) use HTTP URIs so that people can look up those names, 3) when someone looks up a URI, provide useful information using standards such as RDF, and 4) include links to other URIs so that they can discover more things. In the conceptual framework of *Linked Data Fragments* [17], this is just one interface to access Linked Data. You could also publish the data as one large data dump, or provide a querying API on top of the data. What all these interfaces have in common is that they expose a *fragment* of the entire dataset, so they can all be considered Linked Data Fragments. Data dumps and query APIs are the two extremes on the Linked Data Fragments axis [17]. This axis illustrates the trade-offs between different methods of publishing Linked Data on the Web. Data dumps put the data processing burden on the client's side, but allow the most flexibility for clients. Query APIs on the other hand put the processing burden on the server side but always restrict, in some way, the way the data can be used.

2.2   Mobility Data

The *General Transit Feed Specification (GTFS)* is, at the time of writing, the de facto standard for publishing public transit schedules. A single feed is a combination of 6 to 13 CSV files, compressed into a single ZIP archive. Its core data elements are stops, routes, trips, and stop times. Stops are places where vehicles pick up or drop off riders, routes are two or more stops that form a public transit line, trips correspond to a physical vehicle that follows a route during a specific time period, and stop times indicate when a trip passes by a stop. This data is not only useful for route planning applications, other applications include embedding timetables in mobile applications, data visualization; accessibility analysis, and planning analysis [1].

The Linked Connections specification [8] defines a way to publish transit data that falls somewhere in the middle of the Linked Data Fragments axis. Connections are defined as vehicles going from one stop to another without an intermediate halt. These connections are then ordered by departure time, fragmented into documents, and are then published over HTTP. Clients can use the semantics embedded in each fragment to solve their own queries. This, combined with the fact that each fragment is easily cacheable, make Linked Connections servers more scalable than full-fledged route planning services.

2.3   Partitioning Public Transit Networks

Researchers in the field of route planning have noted that methods based on partitioning have been successful for accelerating queries on road networks, but that adapting those methods to public transit networks is harder than expected [5,6]. One of the main differences is that road networks are, for the most part, topological networks. Public transit networks on the other hand are also inherently time-dependent. On top of that, it is not even clear *what* exactly needs to be partitioned as different algorithms can require wildly different data models [10].

The Scalable Transfer Patterns [4] algorithm aims to greatly reduce preprocessing times of the original Transfer Patterns [3] algorithm. The authors compared 4 different techniques to partition stops into clusters of roughly equal size: 1) *k-means* using the stops' geographical locations, 2) a merge-based clustering with a utility function that punishes big partitions and rewards pairs of partitions with high edge weights between them, 3) a general-purpose graph clustering algorithm called *METIS* [16], and 4) a road partitioning method called *PUNCH* [11]. They found that k-means, despite being completely oblivious to the network structure outperformed both METIS and PUNCH while their own merge-based approach performed the best of all. HypRAPTOR [10] is another route planning algorithm that uses METIS to partition the network graph, but which uses clusters of trips instead of stops.

2.4   Voronoi Diagrams

Voronoi diagrams are one of the fundamental data structures in computational geometry [2]. Although they can be applied to any metric space, we only consider Euclidean spaces in this paper for the sake of simplicity. Given a set of seed points in a Euclidean space, a Voronoi diagram partitions that space into regions so that each region contains exactly one seed point, and every point in a region is closer to that region's seed point than to any other region's. Formally this means that for a given Euclidean space X with distance function d, and a set of seed points $P \subset X$, each point $p_i \in P$ yields a corresponding Voronoi region $R_i \subseteq X$ where

$$R_i = \{x \in X \mid d(x, p_i) \leq d(x, p_j) \text{ for all } i \neq j\}$$

3   Method

The Linked Connections publishing scheme enables applications to access data for a specific point in time, but each data fragment still contains data from the entire transit operator's service area. Figure 1 shows that some regions served by the Flemish public transit operator, De Lijn, are more popular than others, implying that it makes sense to partition by location as well. Existing work has shown that partitioning public transit networks can improve query times of route planning services, so we investigate if similar improvements can be obtained for the publishing of raw data.

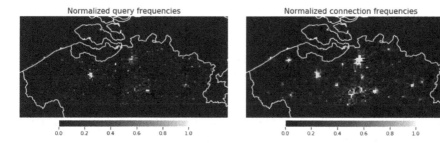

Fig. 1. Visualized on the left are the departure and destination locations, based on one week of query logs from the Flemish public transit operator De Lijn. Visualized on the right are the locations of all connections in their network during the same time period. Note that there are many places with a considerable amount of connections that are in low demand.

However, first we should consider what is necessary to make publishing fragmented data viable in the real world. We make a distinction between data owners and data publishers, with a clear distinction between their responsibilities. A *data owner* focuses on maintaining the data quality, while a *data publisher* focuses on making the data accessible. Both roles come with their own challenges, and as such it is not uncommon for data owners to outsource the data publishing to third parties. This means that data publishers may not have control over the actual data – they have to adapt when the data changes. For example, public transit operators routinely add and remove temporary stops due to maintenance works, and these changes have to be reflected in the published data with as little friction as possible.

3.1 Rationale

Existing work has focused on clustering stops, or trips, into discrete sets of objects. If a data publisher were to follow this approach, they would have to explicitly assign a label to every new stop the data owner adds. Failing to do so would cause them to publish incomplete data, as unlabeled stops will not be in any published cluster. This labeling of new stops is relatively easy for clustering algorithms such as k-means, but for algorithms such as METIS [16] this involves recomputing the entire clustering.

Rather than searching for an algorithm that supports updates, we propose to publish the clusters in a robust way by partitioning the physical world instead of creating discrete sets of stops. The resulting partitions are published as separate resources, allowing any agent to infer to which cluster every stop belongs. In other words, data publishers do not have to explicitly label every stop themselves – the data speaks for itself. This benefits both the data publishers and consumers: the maintenance effort required by the publisher is lower, and data consumers have access to complete and factual data.

3.2 Data

Guided by the insights provided by Fig. 1, we will focus on the Flemish public transit network for the remainder of this paper. To provide some context: Flanders is a small region within Europe, but with 487 inhabitants/km^2 in 2019, it is also one of the most densely populated [13]. The public transit network is also dense; at the time of writing there are 35,791 stops spread out over 13,522 km^2 for a density of 2.6 stops/km^2. There are roughly 1 million connections on a regular weekday, and the corresponding Linked Connections data results in over 10 million RDF triples per day. We use data from the first whole week of December 2019 as the input data for the methods discussed in this section.

3.3 Clustering

We start by adapting two clustering methods that are often used to partition transit networks: k-means and METIS. However, both methods disregard one important feature of transit networks; k-means does not consider network connectivity and METIS does not consider physical locations. This leads us to propose an additional method, called *Hub*, which clusters stops by their proximity to important transportation hubs. As others have shown good results from hierarchical methods, we also consider a merge-based adaption of Hub, appropriately named *Merged*. The remainder of this subsection discusses how each method is used to generate a geospatial partitioning.

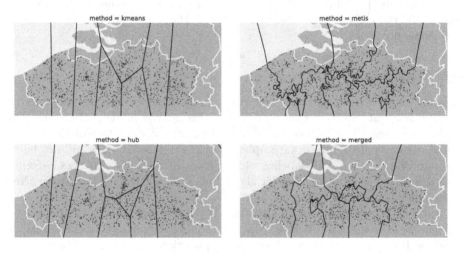

Fig. 2. The 8 partitions each evaluated method creates. Note that the two methods on the top row create regions of roughly equal sizes, while the approaches at the bottom create regions of varying sizes. The approaches in the left column create regions with simple shapes, while the ones on the right create irregular shapes.

K-Means. Despite its simplicity, existing work has found k-means to be competitive with more complex methods [4], so we consider it among the state of the art for this particular use-case. As the name implies, this algorithm distributes a given set of points in exactly k clusters, where every point belongs to cluster with the nearest cluster mean. Iterative heuristics exist to compute this clustering, and we used the implementation from scikit.learn[4] with default parameters and using the stops' WGS84 coordinates as input.

To obtain a spatial partitioning from this, we create a Voronoi diagram using the cluster means as seed points. Because the Voronoi cells of two adjacent points on the convex hull share an infinitely long edge, we add some extra padding points that represent the bounding box of the operator's service area – and then discard all infinite edges.

METIS. METIS is another algorithm that is used to partition public transit networks [4,10], so we consider it to be among the state of the art as well. Since it is a graph clustering algorithm, we must represent the public transit network as a graph. We follow the conventional approach of creating a vertex for every stop, and connecting them with an edge if they are connected through a single connection. Every edge is assigned a weight that corresponds to how many connections connect those stops. We used a Python wrapper[5] of the reference implementation to compute the clustering, using the `contig` option to force contiguous partitions.

The METIS algorithm only sees the network as a connectivity graph though – it does not know anything about the physical location of the stops. This means that even though it creates contiguous partitions, those partitions are not contiguous in the physical world. We obtain a clean spatial partitioning using an additional post-processing step that 1) creates the Voronoi diagram of all stops, 2) merges all Voronoi cells that belong to the same cluster, and 3) merge isolated areas into the surrounding cluster.

Hub. Hub is the first of our own methods that aims to incorporate both the geospatial and the graph-like nature of public transit networks. It iteratively selects the stops based on which trips pass through it. In the first iteration it selects the stop with the most unique trips, in the subsequent iterations it selects the stop with the most unique trips that the previous stop(s) do not have. After k iterations it contains the k most important hubs, which lead us to name this method *Hub*. These selected stops are then used as seed points to create a Voronoi diagram. To illustrate the simplicity of this approach, Listing 1 contains all the necessary code to implement this, up until the creation of the Voronoi diagram.

---

[4] https://scikit-learn.org/0.20/modules/clustering.html#k-means.
[5] https://metis.readthedocs.io/en/latest/.

```
1  def hub(k):
2      done_trips = set()
3      selected_stops = []
4      for _ in range(k):
5          best_stop = None
6          best_stop_score = 0
7          for stop, trips in stop_to_trips.items():
8              stop_score = len(set(trips) - set(done_trips))
9              if stop_score > best_stop_score:
10                 best_stop = stop
11                 best_stop_score = stop_score
12         selected_stops.append(best_stop)
13         done_trips.update(stop_to_trips[best_stop])
14     return selected_stops
```

Listing 1. The *Hub* method can be implemented in just 14 lines of Python code.

Merged. Instead of stopping the Hub algorithm after k iterations we can also let it terminate, and then use the Jaccard similarity coefficient to merge the two most similar adjacent Voronoi regions until only k remain. As there is a finite amount of trips, this algorithm has a clear termination condition: it stops when all trips are covered by one of the selected stops. This makes the process more complex, but existing work has shown good results using hierarchical clustering techniques [4]. We have named this approach *Merged*, for obvious reasons.

3.4 Hypermedia Controls

As discussed at the beginning of Subsect. 3.1, we want our published data to be easy to maintain. Our idea is to publish the partitioning itself, so that clients have all the information they need to decide to which cluster every stop belongs. We have already discussed how to obtain the partitionings, now we discuss how to publish them.

The partitions are published on the Web as stand-alone resources using the TREE[6] and GeoSPARQL[7] vocabularies. The TREE vocabulary is used to describe a partitioning as a collection of regions, and the wktLiteral datatype from the GeoSPARQL vocabulary is used to describe individual regions. GeoJSON is another common way to define geometries, but since GeoJSON polygons are incompatible with JSON-LD we chose to use the simpler string representation: WKT. Listing 2 contains a JSON-LD snippet of a single partition resource.

These partition resources are then used to fragment Linked Connections data. This two-step approach allows for reusing existing partitions, such as administrative regions. A modified Linked Connections server can ingest a given partitioning, and fragment the data accordingly. The server creates one view per

[6] https://github.com/TREEcg/specification.
[7] http://www.opengis.net/doc/IS/geosparql/1.0.

```
1 {
2   "@id": "https://example.org/clusters/hub_4",
3   "tree:member": [
4     {
5       "@id": "https://example.org/clusters/hub_4/1",
6       "geo:asWKT": "POLYGON ((4.170761972221639 50.7079439...
7     }, ...
8   ], ...
9 }
```

Listing 2. JSON-LD representation of a partitioning. Note that both the partitioning and the individual regions are separate resources, allowing other datasets to refer to them.

region, and then creates an index of all generated views using the TREE vocabulary, which links every view to the geospatial area it covers. Listing 3 contains a JSON-LD snippet of such an index.

```
1  {
2    "@id": "https://example.org/connections",
3    "@type": "tree:Node",
4    "tree:relation": [
5      {
6        "@type": "tree:GeospatiallyContainsRelation",
7        "tree:node": "https://example.org/connections?cluster=
   ↪ https%3A//example.org/clusters/hub_4/1",
8        "tree:path": [
9          "lc:departureStop",
10         "geo:asWKT"
11       ],
12       "tree:qualifiedValue": {
13         "tree:value": {
14           "@id": "https://example.org/clusters/hub_4/1"
15         },
16         "tree:path": "geo:asWKT"
17       }
18     }, ...
19   ], ...
20 }
```

Listing 3. JSON-LD representation of a view index. The `tree:node` property points to a data page from the original Linked Connections specification. The `tree:qualifiedProperty` property defines which geospatial area that page covers by referring to an existing published geospatial partition.

4   Evaluation

In the introduction we declared our intent to make more applications viable by improving the way we publish data. We gave client-side route planning as an example of a use case that needs to be conservative in the amounts of data they download, so we focus on this application to evaluate our data.

We have adapted an existing library for client-side route planning that uses Linked Connection data, so that it can interpret our hypermedia controls. This library uses the *earliest arrival time* variant of the Connection Scan Algorithm. This algorithm, similar to Dijkstra's algorithm, builds a list of which stops are reachable and how long it takes to reach them. A client that knows the location of each stop can also infer which clusters are reachable, so our adapted route planner simply fetches data for all reachable clusters – slowly growing its list of data sources. We focus on the use-case of client-side route planning because this a relatively demanding application.

As mentioned in Sect. 3, we use 1 week of Linked Connection as input for the clustering algorithms. We then use each method to create 4, 8, 16, and 32 clusters. A redis-backed server creates an ordered list of all connections within every generated region, and exposes these using the hypermedia controls defined in the Subsect. 3.4. The same server also hosts a version of the data with one cluster that contains all the data, i.e. without any geospatial partitioning. Altogether we test 17 (4 partitionings for each of the 4 methods, and the baseline) different partitionings, and each data fragment contains 20 min of data.

We make extensive use of letter-value plots [15] because our results have a long tail, which causes visualizations such as box plots to label many results as outliers. These plots show the median value as a black line, and then show the 75%, 87.5%, ... quantiles as separate boxes, making it easy to compare these statistics.

4.1   Efficiency

As a proxy for how easy the geospatially fragmented data is to use, we measure how much work a client needs to do to solve a query. Specifically, the time it takes for the same client to solve the query with a given partitioning, as well as how much data was downloaded. We compare those values to those of the baseline; the unpartitioned data.

5,000 queries were randomly selected from a query log that was given to us by the transit operator itself. All these queries were received on the same day, but throughout the day. We eliminate as many variables as possible to isolate the impact of the partitioning; the client and server run on two separate machines on the same local network, a constant 20 ms of latency is added per response, and the client only processes one query at a time.

Figure 3 shows that having just a few clusters already significantly improves the query performance, but that adding more clusters has diminishing returns, because even without the overhead of ingesting unnecessary data the client still has to compute the actual route. The METIS results are somewhat surprising;

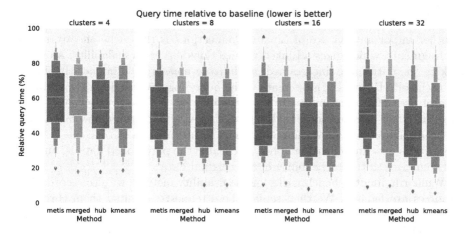

Fig. 3. The median query time with just 4 clusters is already 58% that of the original query times, and using 8 clusters further improves this to 45%. Note the diminishing returns as more clusters are added, using 16 or 32 clusters reduces the relative query times to 41% and 42%, respectively. The Hub and k-means methods yield very similar results, while METIS performs significantly worse.

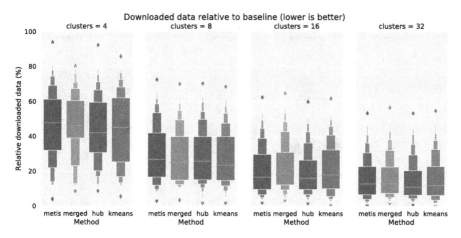

Fig. 4. Using just 4 clusters is enough to reduce the amount of downloaded data to 45% of the original amount of downloaded data, and adding more clusters consistently improves this metric. Although all methods seem competitive in this metric, the Hub method has a consistently low median and 75% percentile.

they are slightly worse across the board, and even become worse when going from 16 to 32 clusters. As Fig. 2 shows, the clusters from METIS are more complex than those from other methods, which makes them harder to interpret for a client. Figure 4 shows that the amount of downloaded data does keep decreasing by adding more clusters – theoretically we can avoid all unnecessary data by creating a cluster per stop.

4.2 Cacheability

Another important feature of Linked Connections is the cache effectiveness of the fragments, which gives a Linked Connections server its scalability. As we are making the data more fine-grained, we have to measure the impact this has on the cache effectiveness. Unfortunately, the query logs we use do not contain any form of user ID, which makes it hard to simulate a real-world scenario where there are client-side and server-side caches. Instead, we measure how fast a cache warms up in every configuration, and what the hit rate of a warm cache is. These two metrics give an indication of how cacheable the partitioned data is, and how this compares to the cacheability of the original data.

While running the benchmarks for the usability metrics, we also record which resources are fetched. We then replay these requests, running them through a simulated LRU cache to measure the hit rates. To measure the hit rates on a warm cache we first run all requests through a cache, and then create 1,000 samples of 500 requests to measure the overall hit rate of each sample. The hit rates on a cold cache are obtained by doing the same starting from a cold cache, and by varying the amount of requests per sample. We set the cache size to 20 MB, and each partitioning results in roughly 70 MB of gzipped data, so we expect to see many cache evictions.

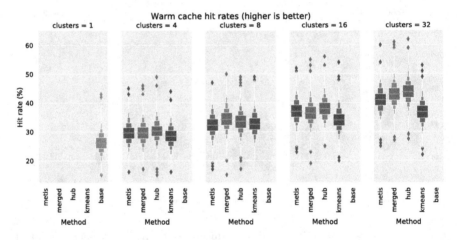

Fig. 5. Less valuable cache space is wasted on irrelevant data by using a fine-grained partitioning. The median hit rate on a warm cache using the unpartitioned data is 26%, the highest hit rate, 44%, is obtained using the Hub method with 32 clusters. The k-means method scores noticeable worse than the other methods.

Figure 5 and Fig. 6 show that partitioned data can improve the cache hit rate, but that caches take longer to warm up. The cache effectiveness when using 8 clusters surpasses that of the baseline at around 350 requests, regardless of the clustering method. The average query downloads 9 resources at this granularity, so that the cache effectiveness is better than the baseline's if the data is used to answer more than 39 queries per day.

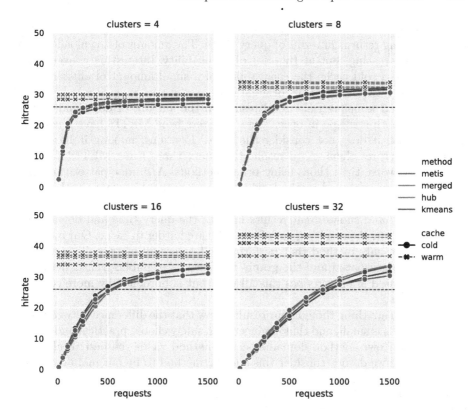

Fig. 6. Line plots of the median cache hit rates per configuration, showing that caches take longer to warm up with a fine-grained partitioning. However, any method with 4 or 8 clusters matches the hit rate of the original data on a warm cache (26%) after 350 requests.

5 Discussion

In the introduction we stated that our goal is to improve the way public transit data is published to make more applications viable. We found related work in the field of route planning, where the data is fragmented to improve query-time performance. However, our findings show that results from this field do not easily translate to publishing data on the Web, because, as stated in Sect. 3, we want the processed data to stay in sync with the raw data. We resolve this by moving some of the clustering logic to the client, which in return can then avoid downloading and parsing a lot of irrelevant data. Knowing which clusters to publish is just as important as knowing how to publish them though, so we also compare different clustering algorithms – and how they affect the performance of a client-side route planner.

The number of clusters has a noticeable impact on all evaluated metrics. Even a small amount of clusters can make a client-side route planner twice as

fast. More clusters do not necessarily lead to better results though, as we quickly
see diminishing returns in terms of query times. The amount of downloaded data
does keep decreasing, but at the cost of cacheability. Interestingly, even when
starting from a cold cache the cacheability of a small amount of clusters is on
par with the cacheability of the original data.

METIS and k-means yield good results in the amount of downloaded data
metric, but both struggle in other tests. Clusters from METIS have a complex
shape because it does not consider the stops' locations, making it harder for
clients to interpret them. As a result, the query times using METIS data are
consistently worse than those using other methods. A similar pattern presents
itself for the merge-based method, which is also noticeably worse in the query
time metric – more so than in the downloaded data metric. The k-means method
on the other hand shows great results in both the query time and downloaded
data metrics, but the resulting data fragments are harder to cache. Our own Hub
method is the only method that performs well across all metrics. This method
combines the geospatial and the graph-like features of public transit networks.
The merge-based approach does this all well, but is burdened by more complex
cluster shapes.

More than anything though, our results show that the difference between clustering methods is small, and that engineers can safely choose practical and simple
solutions. Our own method domain-specific method yields the best results, but
it is so simple we do not consider this specific method to be our main contribution; it is the realization that simple methods can, and do, outperform complex
methods. And it is this insight that is useful for web engineers – one does not
have to be a domain expert to publish quality data.

6   Conclusion

In this paper we investigated what data publishers can do to make their open
transit data easier to use. Based on research from the field of route planning,
we explored the idea of geospatially partitioning public transit networks. We
evaluated 4 different clustering methods for the use-case of client-side route
planning: k-means, METIS, and two domain-specific methods of our own. The
partitions were obtained using Voronoi diagrams, and were then published with
the appropriate hypermedia controls that clients can use to discover clusters of
public transit stops.

Our goal was to make open transit data more useful, so that more people
can use it in more applications. We focused on the use case of client-side route
planning, which have to be conservative in which data they download as mobile
data is still expensive. And in that regard, we succeeded. A simple clustering
algorithm and 8 clusters is all it takes to download 4 times less data, and to
answer queries 2.4 times faster. Preliminary results show that the cacheability,
and thus the scalability, of this approach is on par with the existing Linked
Connections publishing scheme.

More than anything though, we have found that the difference between clustering methods is small, and that engineers can safely go for simple solutions

– any geospatial fragmentation is better than no fragmentation at all. Future work can investigate if this translates to the publishing of other geospatial data such as road networks, sensor data, or points of interest. We postulate that it does, simply because the world is not uniformly populated – data from densely populated regions will be in higher demand. Additionally, our approach should be tested in the real world, comparing it to both route planning services and existing Linked Connections servers.

References

1. Antrim, A., Barbeau, S.J., et al.: The many uses of GTFS data–opening the door to transit and multimodal applications 4 (2013). Location-Aware Information Systems Laboratory at the University of South Florida
2. Aurenhammer, F.: Voronoi diagrams–a survey of a fundamental geometric data structure. ACM Comput. Surv. (CSUR) **23**(3), 345–405 (1991)
3. Bast, H., et al.: Fast routing in very large public transportation networks using transfer patterns. In: de Berg, M., Meyer, U. (eds.) ESA 2010. LNCS, vol. 6346, pp. 290–301. Springer, Heidelberg (2010). https://doi.org/10.1007/978-3-642-15775-2_25
4. Bast, H., Hertel, M., Storandt, S.: Scalable transfer patterns. In: 2016 Proceedings of the Eighteenth Workshop on Algorithm Engineering and Experiments (ALENEX), pp. 15–29. SIAM (2016)
5. Bauer, R., Delling, D., Wagner, D.: Experimental study of speed up techniques for timetable information systems. Networks **57**(1), 38–52 (2011)
6. Berger, A., Delling, D., Gebhardt, A., Müller-Hannemann, M.: Accelerating time-dependent multi-criteria timetable information is harder than expected. In: 9th Workshop on Algorithmic Approaches for Transportation Modeling, Optimization, and Systems (ATMOS 2009). Schloss Dagstuhl-Leibniz-Zentrum für Informatik (2009)
7. Berners-Lee, T.: Linked data-design issues (2006). http://www.w3.org/DesignIssues/LinkedData.html
8. Colpaert, P., Llaves, A., Verborgh, R., Corcho, O., Mannens, E., Van de Walle, R.: Intermodal public transit routing using liked connections. In: International Semantic Web Conference: Posters and Demos, pp. 1–5 (2015)
9. European Commission: mobile broadband prices in Europe 2019 (2019). http://www.w3.org/DesignIssues/LinkedData.html
10. Delling, D., Dibbelt, J., Pajor, T., Zündorf, T.: Faster transit routing by hyper partitioning. In: 17th Workshop on Algorithmic Approaches for Transportation Modelling, Optimization, and Systems (ATMOS 2017). Schloss Dagstuhl-Leibniz-Zentrum fuer Informatik (2017)
11. Delling, D., Goldberg, A.V., Razenshteyn, I., Werneck, R.F.: Graph partitioning with natural cuts. In: 2011 IEEE International Parallel & Distributed Processing Symposium, pp. 1135–1146. IEEE (2011)
12. Dibbelt, J., Pajor, T., Strasser, B., Wagner, D.: Connection scan algorithm (2017)
13. Flanders: population: size and growth (2019). https://www.statistiekvlaanderen.be/en/population-size-and-growth-0
14. Geisberger, R., Sanders, P., Schultes, D., Delling, D.: Contraction hierarchies: faster and simpler hierarchical routing in road networks. In: McGeoch, C.C. (ed.) WEA 2008. LNCS, vol. 5038, pp. 319–333. Springer, Heidelberg (2008). https://doi.org/10.1007/978-3-540-68552-4_24

320 H. Delva et al.

15. Hofmann, H., Kafadar, K., Wickham, H.: Letter-value plots: boxplots for large data. Technical report, had.co.nz (2011)
16. Karypis, G., Kumar, V.: A fast and high quality multilevel scheme for partitioning irregular graphs. SIAM J. Sci. Comput. **20**(1), 359–392 (1998)
17. Verborgh, R., et al.: Querying datasets on the web with high availability. In: MikaMika, P., et al. (eds.) ISWC 2014. LNCS, vol. 8796, pp. 180–196. Springer, Cham (2014). https://doi.org/10.1007/978-3-319-11964-9_12

Efficient Live Public Transport Data Sharing for Route Planning on the Web

Julián Andrés Rojas(✉)⬤, Dylan Van Assche⬤, Harm Delva⬤,
Pieter Colpaert⬤, and Ruben Verborgh⬤

IDLab, Department of Electronics and Information Systems,
Ghent University – imec, Ghent, Belgium
julianandres.rojasmelendez@ugent.be

Abstract. Web-based information services transformed how we interact with public transport. Discovering alternatives to reach destinations and obtaining live updates about them is necessary to optimize journeys and improve the quality of travellers' experience. However, keeping travellers updated with opportune information is demanding. Traditional Web APIs for live public transport data follow a polling approach and allocate all data processing on either data providers, lowering data accessibility, or data consumers, increasing the costs of innovative solutions. Moreover, data processing load increases further because previously obtained route plans are fully recalculated when live updates occur. In between solutions sharing processing load between clients and servers, and alternative Web API architectures were not thoroughly investigated yet. We study performance trade-offs of polling and push-based Web architectures to efficiently publish and consume live public transport data. We implement (i) alternative architectures that allow sharing data processing load between clients and servers, and evaluate their performance following polling- and push-based approaches; (ii) a rollback mechanism that extends the Connection Scan Algorithm to avoid unnecessary full route plan recalculations upon live updates. Evaluations show polling as a more efficient alternative on CPU and RAM but hint towards push-based alternatives when bandwidth is a concern. Clients update route plan results 8–10 times faster with our rollback approach. Smarter API design combining polling and push-based Web interfaces for live public transport data reduces the intrinsic costs of data sharing by equitably distributing the processing load between clients and servers. Future work can investigate more complex multimodal transport scenarios.

Keywords: Public transport · Web interfaces · Live updates · Route planning

Available online at https://julianrojas.org/papers/icwe2020-main-track/.

M. Bielikova et al. (Eds.): ICWE 2020, LNCS 12128, pp. 321–336, 2020.
https://doi.org/10.1007/978-3-030-50578-3_22

1   Introduction

Thanks to route planning applications, understanding printed time tables at a bus or train station has turned to instantly retrieving route planning advice on our smartphones. Access to such information may increase the usage of public transport services [5] and has a positive impact on its quality of experience [21]: travellers with access to live updates can reduce their waiting times, adjust their travelling choices for more efficient journeys and achieve higher satisfaction levels [14]. Today, many cities around the world recognize the value of providing reliable access to live information and devote considerable effort on maintaining and evolving their Web APIs, e.g., London, Helsinki, and San Francisco [1].

However, sharing live public transport data is a resource-demanding process that may (i) limit data accessibility; (ii) increase the costs of new solutions; and (iii) impose additional processing load for route plan recalculations upon live updates. Traditional Web API architectures for live public transport data usually follow a polling-based approach that allocates all data processing load on either *data providers* (e.g., public transport operators) or *data consumers* (e.g., route planning applications) computational infrastructure. In terms of required computational resources, two main strategies prevailed: (i) publishing a fully-fledged *live route planning API*; or (ii) providing a *data dump or feed* containing live schedule updates.

With live route planning APIs, most *data providers* limit data accessibility due to high maintenance and scalability costs [1]. Despite offering reliable information, live route planning APIs entail high costs because all processing resides on data provider infrastructure. These costs increase proportionally with the number of clients and motivates API request limitations, thus limiting data accessibility. For *data consumers*, this approach requires minimal effort in terms of processing resources, as clients only need one request per route planning query. Dealing with live updates also means that consumers check for query updates more frequently, further increasing the load on providers infrastructure and potentially conflicting with API request limits.

In contrast, a data dump or feed increases the computational costs for *data consumers* because they need to handle data integration. This approach represents a low cost solution for *data providers*, as they only require to maintain online a resource with the latest updates. However, static and live data need to be separated for client consumption. This separation increases infrastructure costs for consumers that need to store and integrate static schedules and their live updates for one or more public transport services.

In both cases, handling live data requires additional processing for route plan recalculations on data updates. Changing transport schedules may quickly render previously calculated route plans invalid. For example, a vehicle route could have been cancelled or a suggested transfer is no longer possible due to delays. Applications need to refresh query results as soon as new updates are available to avoid providing incorrect information. This generally involves full algorithm recalculations, which increase processing load. Thus, cost-efficient data sharing solutions that allow full accessibility, to accurate and opportune information for travellers are needed for both *data providers* and *data consumers*.

An *in-between* approach, namely the *Linked Connections* (LC) specification [7], defines a data sharing approach that equitably distributes processing load between data providers and consumers for route planning query processing over public transport networks. To measure the impact of polling- and push-based data sharing approaches on CPU, RAM, bandwidth and query response time, we implemented LC-based server and client-side applications. We (i) measure processing costs and query execution performance using the Connection Scan Algorithm (CSA) [12] for route planning calculation; (ii) simulate a Web-scale environment with up to 1,500 concurrent clients, using real data from the Belgian Railway operator; and (iii) extend CSA with a rollback mechanism that allows efficient route plan refreshing upon live updates, while avoiding full query recalculations.

The results show polling as a more efficient alternative on CPU and RAM for *data providers* but hint towards push-based alternatives when bandwidth is a concern. For *data consumers* there is no significant difference in CPU and RAM usage for route planning query processing. However, there is a significant improvement of 8–10 times with respect to query processing performance, using our proposed CSA rollback mechanism. Smarter API design that combines polling and push-based data sharing approaches can reduce the intrinsic costs of data sharing on the Web, by equitably distributing processing loads between providers and consumers. Moreover, by moving algorithm execution to the client-side, clients have more granular control on application state (e.g., previous query executions), which for this case increases efficiency on handling live data updates.

The remainder of this paper is organized as follows. We first present an overview of related work regarding live public transport data sharing on the Web and route planning over public transport networks. In Sect. 3 we describe the reference architecture, data models and implementation details of the evaluated approaches. Section 4 presents the experimental setup including data characterization, queries and Web interfaces used to achieve comprehensive results. In Sect. 5 we present the obtained results. Finally, on Sect. 6 we discuss the results, present our conclusions and our vision for future work.

2   Related Work

The Web became the preferred platform for sharing public transport data. Different technologies, approaches and standards were proposed to publish and consume both static and live data. In this section we present an overview of such related work.

2.1   Public Transport Standards

TriMet (Portland, Oregon) became the first public transport operator to integrate its schedules into Google Maps in 2005. This collaboration fostered the creation of GTFS[1], which at the time of writing, is regarded as the *de-facto* standard for sharing public transport data. The European Committee for Standardization (CEN) standards: Transmodel[2] and the more recent NeTEx[3], describe a conceptual model to facilitate the exchanging of network topology and timetable data. GTFS-realtime[4] and SIRI[5], are among the main reference standards for live schedule updates and vehicle positions. Both define protocols to exchange live updates for predefined timetables, modeled using GTFS and Transmodel standards respectively.

2.2 Public Transport Data on the Web

Implementations of live route plannings APIs limit accessibility by imposing request limitations to deal with the computational costs on their server infrastructure. CEN proposes the *Open API for distributed Journey Planning* (OJP)[6] as a standard for interoperable route planning APIs, but to the best of our knowledge there are no available implementations.

Public transport data dumps require expensive data integration tasks. Static data dumps contain extensive planned schedules, which scale proportionally to the size and complexity of the transport network [15]. Additionally, periodic live updates depend on static schedule data and need to be integrated each time before they can be used to answer route planning queries [6]. Most currently available dumps[7] on the Web follow GTFS and GTFS-RT standards [1].

An *in between* approach, namely the Linked Connections (LC) specification[8], was introduced by Colpaert et al. [7]. LC builds on the *Linked Data Fragments* conceptual framework [29] to model and publish public transport data on the Web. Data are organized in vehicle departure-arrival pairs called *Connections*, and sorted by departure time in cache-able and hypermedia enabled documents. Client applications can process route planning queries by downloading and performing a route planning algorithm over relevant documents. Live data are handled by the server, updating and re-sorting the *Connections* when updates occur [24]. LC allow clients and servers to share processing load of route planning query processing, in contrast to traditional approaches where processing tasks are assumed by one side or the other.

2.3 Route Planning Algorithms

Route planning has been extensively studied throughout the years. Bast et al. [3] and Pajor [22] present a comparative analysis of multiple route planning algorithms. Most algorithms are defined as extensions of Dijkstra's algorithm [13]

---

[1] https://developers.google.com/transit/gtfs.
[2] http://www.transmodel-cen.eu/.
[3] http://netex-cen.eu/.
[4] https://developers.google.com/transit/gtfs-realtime.
[5] http://www.transmodel-cen.eu/standards/siri/.
[6] http://www.transmodel-cen.eu/standards/ojp/.
[7] https://transitfeeds.com/.
[8] https://linkedconnections.org/.

using graph-based data models to represent transportation networks. Alternative approaches such as RAPTOR [10], CSA [12], Transfer Patterns [4] and Trip-based routing [30] exploit the basic elements of public transport networks to calculate routes directly on the timetables.

Regardless of the algorithm, in the presence of live schedule updates, subjacent data structures need to be updated to properly reflect the new available information. This means that previously obtained results for a certain query may become invalid and also need to be updated. Related work address this issue for road network route planning with live traffic updates [19]. However, there are no solutions for route planning on public transport networks.

2.4 Live Streaming Data on the Web

Two different approaches exist to publish/consume data streams on the Web: (i) polling-based approaches (e.g., REST APIs); (ii) pushing-based approaches (e.g., Server-Sent Events, WebSockets or MQTT). In the public transport domain, most *data publishers* follow a polling approach to publish live updates [1]. Other works advocate for pushing-based approaches, arguing faster communication between clients and servers [9,23,26] and more bandwidth efficiency [20]. Deolasee et al. explore an adaptive solution that allows clients and servers to use one approach or the other, given data coherence requirements [11]. Shortcomings of both approaches are highlighted on [2,18]. There are no studies that conclude which approach is optimal for sharing live public transport data. On previous preliminary work we evaluated HTTP and WebSockets APIs for publishing live open datasets. Results showed that WebSockets perform better on response time, but more exhaustive evaluations are still required [25].

Other related works study different aspects of general live data streams. The SOSA ontology [16] defines a semantic model to describe interactions between entities involved in acts of observation, actuation, and sampling, including for example, current vehicle positions and estimated departure/arrival times. VoCaLS [28] introduces a metadata description model of data streams on the Web. Stream querying is also studied by Dell'Aglio et al. [8], Taelman et al. [27] and Le-Phuoc et al. [17].

3 Reference Architecture

We designed and implemented a system architecture (Fig. 1) to evaluate the performance of different strategies for live public transport data sharing on the Web. In this section we present the design choices and implementation details of its different modules.

3.1 Publishing Live Public Transport Updates

We follow the LC specification for public transport data publishing. LC achieves higher *cost efficiency*, compared to equivalent full server-side route planning

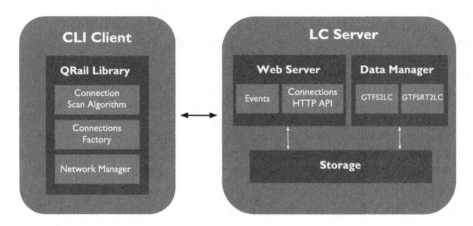

Fig. 1. Reference architecture used to evaluate polling (HTTP) and push-based (SSE) approaches for publishing and consuming live public transport data for route planning.

APIs [7]. The data publishing module in the reference architecture is called *LC Server*. For its implementation we extended the Linked Connections Server[9] (LCS), given its capabilities of integrating live updates out of the box [24]. The server is implemented as a Node.js application and consists of the following submodules:

- **Data Manager.** Transforms both static and live public transport data to the LC data format. It takes as input GTFS and GTFS-RT data sources and uses the gtfs2lc[10] and gtfsrt2lc[11] libraries to perform data transformations.
- **Web Server.** Exposes polling and push-based Web interfaces that clients use to access static and live data. The polling interface is a HTTP API that provides access to *Connection* documents and to the latest live updates using a reference date as input. The pushing interface is based on SSE and provides clients with updates in vehicle schedules.
- **Storage.** Represents data storage on disk. Documents containing sets of ordered *Connections* and spanning a predefined time window, are created by the *Data Manager* and persisted on disk as files. Data are serialized using the JSON-LD[12] format.

We study the cost and performance of polling and pushing Web interfaces. The polling interface of the LCS defines this access URL:

{operator}/connections?departureTime={iso-date}

Where operator is the name of the public transit operator and iso-date is the date and time for which a client requires information of vehicle depar-

---

[9] https://github.com/linkedconnections/linked-connections-server.
[10] https://github.com/linkedconnections/gtfs2lc.
[11] https://github.com/linkedconnections/gtfsrt2lc.
[12] https://www.w3.org/TR/json-ld11/.

tures. Upon request the LCS retrieves the document that contains *Connections* departing closest to the given departure time. It also checks if there are any available live updates that involve the requested document and merges them. An example of a *Connection* is shown in Listing 1.

```
{
    "@context": {
        "lc": "http://semweb.mmlab.be/ns/linkedconnections#",
        "gtfs": "http://vocab.gtfs.org/gtfs.ttl#"
    },
    "@id": "http://irail.be/connections/8885001/20200131/IC3231",
    "@type": "lc:Connection",
    "lc:departureStop": "http://irail.be/stations/NMBS/008885001",
    "lc:arrivalStop": "http://irail.be/stations/NMBS/008885068",
    "lc:departureTime": "2020-01-31T09:54:00.000Z",
    "lc:arrivalTime": "2020-01-31T09:58:00.000Z",
    "lc:departureDelay": 60,
    "lc:arrivalDelay": 60,
    "lc:direction": "Courtrai",
    "gtfs:trip": "http://irail.be/vehicle/IC3231/20200131",
    "gtfs:route": "http://irail.be/vehicle/IC3231",
    "gtfs:pickupType": "gtfs:Regular",
    "gtfs:dropOffType": "gtfs:Regular"
}
```

Listing 1: LC formatted as JSON-LD. The properties *departureDelay* and *arrivalDelay* indicate that live data is available for this *Connection*.

Schedule documents can be cached by clients, which can reuse them to answer more than one query. This reduces the amount of requests that need to be handled by the server. However, live updates quickly invalidate caches and clients need to request again updated LC documents for new queries. In the worst case, all *Connections* of a document change due to a live update, but the majority of the time only a handful of *Connections* are updated, causing that significant parts of LC documents are sent over and over again. For this reason, we extended the LCS implementation and added a new resource to its HTTP API that allows to retrieve only *Connections* that have changed since a given time: {operator}/events?lastSyncDate={iso-date}. This resource allows clients to synchronize their local caches with the latest available data.

We also implemented a pushing Web interface using SSE. Clients can subscribe to it on {operator}/events/sse and receive the latest schedule updates as they occur. We use the W3C standardized SOSA ontology to identify and semantically describe schedule updates for particular *Connections*. Our implementation is available online[13].

---

[13] https://github.com/DylanVanAssche/linked-connections-server.

3.2 Consuming Live Public Transport Updates

A command line interface (CLI) client application[14] was implemented for processing route planning queries on top of LC-based data. It implements the CSA algorithm on its *Profile* variant [12]. This allows calculating not only the *Earliest Arrival Time* but also later route alternatives, providing a maximum amount of desired vehicle transfers along the way. The selection of this algorithm is based on the data model defined by the LC specification. LC defines a sorted by departure time array of *Connections*, which is the data structure that CSA requires to process queries.

This client consist of a library called *QRail Library*[15] that was built using the Qt framework[16]. We selected this framework due to its cross-platform portability including Android or iOS. The client's modules are the following:

- **Network Manager.** Handles the communication capabilities of the client. It was built by extending the Qt *QNetworkAccessManager* library to handle SSE-based interactions. It keeps an in-memory local cache to store the latest available schedule information.
- **Connections Factory.** Retrieves data (either from cache or from the server) and builds *Connection* Qt objects to calculate route plans.
- **Connection Scan Algorithm.** Contains the implementation of the CSA *Profile* variant.

3.3 Dynamic Rollbacks for CSA

We extended CSA to address the problem of needing to perform complete route plan re-calculations, every time a new update is available on the client. Full route plan re-calculations increase the amount of requests and processing that both clients and servers need to handle, thus increasing computational costs.

Given a route plan query (e.g., from Bruges to Brussels departing today at 17:00), CSA starts its execution by scanning *Connections* departing no earlier than 17:00 until it finds the earliest arrival route. From this point, the algorithm performs predefined scan cycles, going back in time over the *Connections* array and adding every time for example, 30 min to the earliest arrival time. This allows finding later alternative route plans for the given query.

In our implementation, every time a new *Connections* document is requested during algorithm execution, we create a snapshot CSA's internal state containing the *Connections* currently involved in the, so far discovered routes. Thanks to these snapshots we can determine the exact index in the *Connections* array, from which CSA needs to recalculate when there are updates in the route plans. Given that CSA *Profile* goes back in time over the *Connections* array, the closer an updated *Connection* is to the departure stop, the faster the recalculation process will be. The set of snapshots is kept in memory and updated every time a new query is processed.

---

[14] https://github.com/DylanVanAssche/QRail/tree/develop/cli/qrail-cli.

[15] https://github.com/DylanVanAssche/QRail.

[16] https://www.qt.io/.

4   Evaluation

We study different approaches to efficiently publish and consume live public transport data, in terms of computational resources (CPU, RAM and bandwidth) and route planning query processing performance. For this we define the following research questions:

- **RQ1.** What is the most *cost-efficient* approach, in terms of computational resources, to publish live public transport data, considering polling and push-based technologies in a LC-based architecture?
- **RQ2.** What is the impact of polling and push-based approaches on LC-based clients, in terms of computational resources and route planning query processing?
- **RQ3.** What is the impact of the CSA rollback mechanism on the performance of a LC-based client for route planning query processing in terms of execution time?

To address these research questions, we defined a hypothesis for each of them:

- **H1.** A pushing approach will lower resource consumption on average, due to avoiding processing new client requests to obtain new schedule updates.
- **H2.** A pushing approach has lower computational cost on clients, since is not necessary to send every time a new request to the server to get the latest updates, thus reducing bandwidth and communication establishment processes.
- **H3.** On average, a rollback mechanism results in lower processing times for processing route planning queries.

We designed two different experiments to test our hypotheses. Next, we describe the testing data and the setups for each of the experiments.

4.1   Real-World Test Data

We used real data from the Belgian railway operator NMBS[17]. NMBS publishes both GTFS and GTFS-RT data dumps as open data[18]. We collected the timetable and all emitted live updates for November 2019 (we make the data available online[19]). We analyzed these data to understand how live updates happen, i.e., what the low and peak hours normally are, to run our experiments considering representative data. Figure 2(a) shows the amount of *Connections* updated during the entire month, having the 28th of November as the day with the highest amount (over 13.63 million). Figure 2(b) zooms in into this day, clearly showing peak hours around 07:00 and 17:00, and registering 17:00 as the peak hour of the day with more than 900,000 updated *Connections*.

---

[17] https://www.belgiantrain.be/.

[18] https://www.belgiantrain.be/en/3rd-party-services/mobility-service-providers/public-data.

[19] https://github.com/julianrojas87/ICWE2020-results.

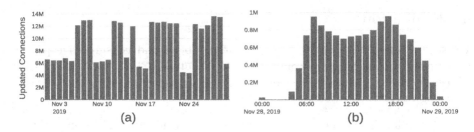

Fig. 2. The amount and distribution of *Connection* updates allow to visualize the behavior of the transport network regarding its low and peak times. Week days and especially their mornings and afternoons, consistently show higher number of updates.

We used the iRail query log dataset[20] as a reference. This dataset contains a registry of over one million real route planning queries per day, received by the iRail API[21]. We analyzed the queries that were executed on the week days during November 2019 and classified them by the amount of *Connections* used by their *Earliest Arrival Time* route, since routes with higher amount of *Connections* require a higher processing effort to be computed.

4.2   Experiment 1: Publishing Live Public Transport Updates

The first experiment was designed to test the computational resource (CPU, RAM and bandwidth) consumption of LC-based live public transport data publishing, following polling (HTTP API) and push-based (SSE) approaches. We setup a server with a Quad core Intel E5520 (2.2 GHz) CPU and 12 GB of RAM. We progressively instantiate up to 1500 clients requesting/receiving live data updates. Each client starts its operation 0.5 s after the previous to avoid overload peaks on the measurements and simulate a more realistic environment, where clients issue requests at any point in time and not necessarily synchronized with the live updates frequency.

For the polling scenario every client requests a new data update every 30 s, which corresponds to the update frequency of NMBS GTFS-RT feed. We also disabled serve-side caching, to obtain a clearer image of the actual operational costs of the server. In the pushing scenario, the clients subscribe once to the SSE interface and the server pushes new data to them every 30 s. The experiment was executed during 20 min for each scenario.

4.3   Experiment 2: Consuming Live Public Transport Updates

The second experiment was designed to measure the CPU, RAM and bandwidth usage of a LC-based client, consuming live public transport updates following

---

[20] https://gtfs.irail.be/logs/.
[21] https://api.irail.be/.

polling (HTTP API) and push-based (SSE) approaches. The client application was deployed on a machine with a Quad core Intel E5520 (2.2 GHz) CPU and 12 GB of RAM. We handpicked routes with different amount of updated *Connections*. This was intended to avoid evaluating routes without updates and thus, with no significant impact on client resources.

We ran the experiment for each selected query using our client on a polling and a pushing scenario, and a reference test client without the rollback mechanism described in Sect. 3.3. The evaluation run for 15 min on each scenario, where clients requested/received live updates every 30 s. Table 1 shows an overview of the selected routes.

Table 1. Set of route planning queries extracted from the iRail API logs. This table shows the number of *Connections* and the total travel time of the *Earliest Arrival Time* route.

From	To	*Connections*	Travel time (min)
Hasselt	Sint-Truiden	2	15
Leuven	Diest	2	32
Landen	Diest	5	43
Eppegem	Brussels-Shuman	6	23
Mechelen	Brussels-Congress	6	30
Leuven	Schaarbeek	11	29
Asse	Antwerp-Berchem	18	87
Antwerp-Central	Alken	23	94

5   Results

Here we present the results obtained for the experiments described in Sect. 4.

Figure 3 presents the measurements made for Experiment 1. Figure 3(a) shows a mean CPU usage of 10.8% for the pushing approach. For the polling approach we obtained a mean usage of 1.7%.

In terms of RAM, Fig. 3(b) shows a mean consumption of 563.8 MB for the pushing approach. For the polling approach we measured a mean consumption of 423 MB. Bandwidth measurements for pushing showed a total data exchange of 6.5 GB serving up to 1,500 clients during the measured time (20 min). For pulling, the server exchanged a total of 15.8 GB under the same conditions (figure not included for the sake of space).

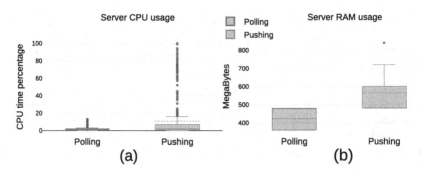

Fig. 3. Polling shows a lower resource consumption for both CPU and RAM.

Figure 4(a) shows the bandwidth usage for the three test scenarios, defined in Experiment 2. After 800 s the reference client exchange a total of 45.7 MB. The rollback clients exchanged 5.4 MB and 3.6 MB for polling and pushing respectively. In terms of RAM (Fig. 4(b)), no significant difference was measured for polling and pushing with a mean consumption of 70.6 MB and 71.1 MB respectively. The reference client shows an increased average RAM usage of 102.1 MB. CPU usage (figure not shown for the sake of space) maintained the same tendency with average consumption of 12.15% (polling), 12.22% (pushing) and 19.2% (reference).

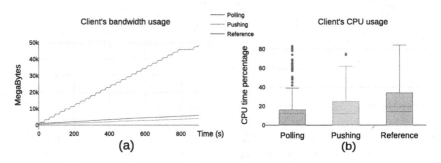

Fig. 4. The rollback clients give a significant reduction of bandwidth. There are no major differences in terms of RAM consumption.

Figure 5 presents the results obtained for testing our rollback mechanism and its impact on route planning query processing. The rollback mechanism is between 8–10 times faster in every set of route planning queries.

Average route planning query execution time

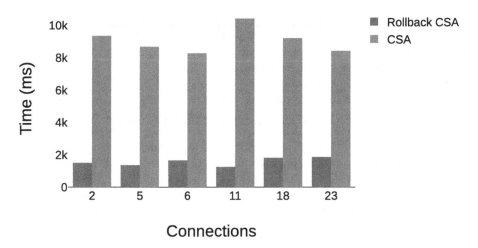

Fig. 5. The rollback mechanism significantly improves the performance of query recalculation.

6 Conclusion and Future Work

Experiment 1 was designed to test H1, related to RQ1. In terms of CPU usage, the polling approach uses on average 10 times less resources than the pushing approach. RAM memory measurements are closer between the two approaches, with pushing using around 140 MB more than polling. This can be explained by the operational characteristics of pushing and also by the setup of the experiment. In the pushing approach the server sends new data to all subscribed clients, when a new live update is received. This explains the various CPU peaks and the higher average usage. RAM memory consumption is also higher for pushing, because the server needs to keep an in-memory registry of all subscribed clients.

The lower resource usage of polling can also be explained by the distribution of client requests. A new client was added every 0.5 s from the start of the experiment and every client did a new request every 30 s, giving a maximum request load was of 50 requests/second with 1500 clients. This load was easily handled by the server given its hardware capabilities. Further tests with synchronized clients and different live update frequencies can provide a more complete picture for polling. Nevertheless, the results provide an indication of the required resources when using one approach or the other, giving polling as a less demanding approach for CPU and RAM.

Pushing requires lower bandwidth because clients do not send requests for new data updates. In conclusion, we reject H1 and consider polling as more *cost-efficient*, especially considering that with server-side caching in place, resource consumption could be improved.

Results of Experiment 2 relate to RQ2 and H2, and show no significant difference in CPU or RAM for pulling or pushing on the client. This is explained by the usage of our rollback mechanism, and confirmed by the higher consumption of resources measured for the reference client. Therefore, we reject H2. However, pushing uses the least amount of bandwidth. This is of utmost importance if we consider that route planning applications may be executed on mobile devices using data connections subject to charges.

The second part of Experiment 2 relates to RQ3 and H3. Results show significant improvements in route planning query recalculations using our rollback mechanism. By keeping snapshots of CSA's internal state, full recalculations are avoided and faster times are achieved. Therefore we can *accept* H3. This is an important result from the perspective of end-users, which need to be informed of journey changes as soon as possible.

In general, results show us that there is no *silver bullet* approach. Different aspects need to be considered to fulfill data provider, data consumer, and end-user requirements. Further evaluations may be performed to complement these results. However, this study already provides an informative base ground for public transport data publishers and route planning application developers. It also highlights the benefits of moving algorithm execution to the client-side, as is having more granular control of application internal state, which make possible to design smarter and more efficient clients.

Future work could study the impact of client-side route planning integrating multiple modes of transportation, as well as explore alternative algorithms and evaluate their performance, including end-user testing.

References

1. Ably: The maturity of public transport APIs 2019. Technical report (2019). https://files.ably.io/research/whitepapers/the-maturity-of-public-transport-apis-2019-ably-realtime.pdf
2. Agarwal, S.: Toward a push-scalable global internet. In: 2011 IEEE Conference on Computer Communications Workshops (INFOCOM WKSHPS), pp. 786–791, April 2011. https://doi.org/10.1109/INFCOMW.2011.5928918
3. Bast, H., et al.: Route planning in transportation networks. CoRR abs/1504.05140 (2015). http://arxiv.org/abs/1504.05140
4. Bast, H., Hertel, M., Storandt, S.: Scalable transfer patterns. In: 2016 Proceedings of the Eighteenth Workshop on Algorithm Engineering and Experiments (ALENEX) (2016)
5. Brakewood, C., Macfarlane, G.S., Watkins, K.: The impact of real-time information on bus ridership in new york city. Trans. Res. Part C: Emerg. Technol. **53**, 59–75 (2015). https://doi.org/10.1016/j.trc.2015.01.021. http://www.sciencedirect.com/science/article/pii/S0968090X15000297
6. Cirillo, F., et al.: Atomic services: sustainable ecosystem of smart city services through pan-European collaboration. In: 2019 Global IoT Summit (3GIoTS), pp. 1–7, June 2019. https://doi.org/10.1109/GIOTS.2019.8766431

7. Colpaert, P., Verborgh, R., Mannens, E.: Public transit route planning through lightweight linked data interfaces. In: Cabot, J., De Virgilio, R., Torlone, R. (eds.) ICWE 2017. LNCS, vol. 10360, pp. 403–411. Springer, Cham (2017). https://doi.org/10.1007/978-3-319-60131-1_26

8. Dell'Aglio, D., Della Valle, E., Calbimonte, J.P., Corcho, O.: RSP-QL semantics: a unifying query model to explain heterogeneity of RDF stream processing systems. Int. J. Seman. Web Inf. Syst. (IJSWIS) **10**(4), 17–44 (2014)

9. Dell'Aglio, D., Le Phuoc, D., Le-Tuan, A., Ali, M.I., Calbimonte, J.P.: On a Web of data streams. In: ISWC 2017 - DeSemWeb (2017)

10. Delling, D., Dibbelt, J., Pajor, T.: Fast and exact public transit routing with restricted pareto sets. In: Proceedings of the Twenty-First Workshop on Algorithm Engineering and Experiments, ALENEX 2019, San Diego, CA, USA, January 7–8, 2019, pp. 54–65 (2019). https://doi.org/10.1137/1.9781611975499.5

11. Deolasee, P., Katkar, A., Panchbudhe, A., Ramamritham, K., Shenoy, P.: Adaptive push-pull: disseminating dynamic web data. In: Proceedings of the 10th International Conference on World Wide Web, WWW 2001, pp. 265–274. Association for Computing Machinery, Hong Kong, Hong Kong (2001). https://doi.org/10.1145/371920.372066

12. Dibbelt, J., Pajor, T., Strasser, B., Wagner, D.: Connection scan algorithm. J. Exp. Algorithmics **23**, 1.7:1–1.7:56 (2018). https://doi.org/10.1145/3274661, http://doi.acm.org/10.1145/3274661

13. Dijkstra, E.W.: A note on two problems in connexion with graphs. Numerische Mathematik **1**, 269–271 (1959). https://doi.org/10.1007/BF01386390, https://link.springer.com/10.1007/BF01386390

14. Dziekan, K., Kottenhoff, K.: Dynamic at-stop real-time information displays for public transport: effects on customers. Transp. Res. Part A: Policy Pract. **41**(6), 489–501 (2007). https://doi.org/10.1016/j.tra.2006.11.006. http://www.sciencedirect.com/science/article/pii/S0965856406001431

15. Fayyaz, S.K., Liu, X.C., Zhang, G.: An efficient general transit feed specification (GTFS) enabled algorithm for dynamic transit accessibility analysis. PLoS ONE **12**(10), 1–22 (2017). https://doi.org/10.1371/journal.pone.0185333d

16. Janowicz, K., Haller, A., Cox, S.J., Phuoc, D.L., Lefrançois, M.: SOSA: a lightweight ontology for sensors, observations, samples, and actuators. J. Web Semant. **56**, 1–10 (2019). https://doi.org/10.1016/j.websem.2018.06.003. http://www.sciencedirect.com/science/article/pii/S1570826818300295

17. Le-Phuoc, D., Dao-Tran, M., Parreira, J.X., Hauswirth, M.: A native and adaptive approach for unified processing of linked streams and Linked Data. In: International Semantic Web Conference, pp. 370–388 (2011)

18. Loreto, S., Saint-Andre, P., Salsano, S., Wilkins, G.: Known issues and best practices for the use of long polling and streaming in bidirectional HTTP. RFC 6202, April 2011. https://tools.ietf.org/html/rfc6202

19. Malviya, N., Madden, S., Bhattacharya, A.: A continuous query system for dynamic route planning. In: 2011 IEEE 27th International Conference on Data Engineering, pp. 792–803, April 2011. https://doi.org/10.1109/ICDE.2011.5767844

20. Martin-Flatin, J.P.: Push vs. pull in Web-based network management. In: Integrated Network Management VI. Distributed Management for the Networked Millennium. Proceedings of the Sixth IFIP/IEEE International Symposium on Integrated Network Management. (Cat. No.99EX302), pp. 3–18, May 1999. https://doi.org/10.1109/INM.1999.770671

21. Monzon, A., Hernandez, S., Cascajo, R.: Quality of bus services performance: benefits of real time passenger information systems. Transp. Telecommun. J. **14**(2), 155–166 (2013)
22. Pajor, T.: Algorithm Engineering for Realistic Journey Planning in Transportation Networks. Ph.D. thesis (2013). https://d-nb.info/1058165240/34
23. Pimentel, V., Nickerson, B.G.: Communicating and displaying real-time data with websocket. IEEE Internet Comput. **16**(4), 45–53 (2012). https://doi.org/10.1109/MIC.2012.64
24. Rojas, J.A., Chaves-Fraga, D., Colpaert, P., Verborgh, R., Mannens, E.: Providing reliable access to real-time and historic public transport data using linked connections. In: Proceedings of the ISWC 2017 Posters & Demonstrations and Industry Tracks (2017). http://ceur-ws.org/Vol-1963/paper637.pdf
25. Rojas, J.A., Van de Vyvere, B., Gevaert, A., Taelman, R., Colpaert, P., Verborgh, R.: A preliminary open data publishing strategy for live data in flanders. In: Companion Proceedings of the The Web Conference 2018. WWW '18 (2018)
26. Stonebraker, M., Çetintemel, U., Zdonik, S.B.: The 8 requirements of real-time stream processing. SIGMOD Record **34**, 42–47 (2005)
27. Taelman, R., Verborgh, R., Colpaert, P., Mannens, E.: Continuous client-side query evaluation over dynamic linked Data. In: Sack, H., Rizzo, G., Steinmetz, N., Mladenić, D., Auer, S., Lange, C. (eds.) ESWC 2016. LNCS, vol. 9989, pp. 273–289. Springer, Cham (2016). https://doi.org/10.1007/978-3-319-47602-5_44
28. Tommasini, R., et al.: VoCaLS: vocabulary and catalog of linked streams. In: Vrandečić, D., et al. (eds.) ISWC 2018. LNCS, vol. 11137, pp. 256–272. Springer, Cham (2018). https://doi.org/10.1007/978-3-030-00668-6_16
29. Verborgh, R., Vander Sande, M., Colpaert, P., Coppens, S., Mannens, E., Van de Walle, R.: Web-scale querying through Linked Data Fragments. In: Bizer, C., Heath, T., Auer, S., Berners-Lee, T. (eds.) Proceedings of the 7th Workshop on Linked Data on the Web. CEUR Workshop Proceedings, vol. 1184, April 2014
30. Witt, S.: Trip-based public transit routing using condensed search trees. In: ATMOS (2016). https://arxiv.org/pdf/1607.01299.pdf

Web-Based Development and Visualization Dashboards for Smart City Applications

Douglas Rolim, Jorge Silva, Thais Batista⬤, and Everton Cavalcante(✉)⬤

DIMAp, Federal University of Rio Grande do Norte, Natal, Brazil
douglasrolim@gmail.com, jorgepereirasb@gmail.com, thaisbatista@gmail.com,
everton@dimap.ufrn.br

Abstract. Smart city applications are inherently characterized by the integration of data from heterogeneous sources and the need of considering geographical information that represents the real-world urban space. To address these concerns, some platforms have been proposed in recent years offering common services and facilities to ease the development of smart city applications. Nonetheless, the existing platforms do not offer high-level interfaces to provide developers with proper tools that could reduce the complexity of developing applications, neither an interface to organize data visualization to end-users. Aiming at tackling such limitations, this work presents Web-based dashboards to support development and data visualization in smart city applications: the former is tailored to application developers, whereas the latter is suited to visualize data. This paper presents the use of these dashboards in association with a platform that integrates heterogeneous urban data with geographical information while supporting the development of smart city applications on top of this data.

Keywords: Smart city applications · Application development · Development dashboard · Visualization dashboard

1 Introduction

Several challenges surround the smart cities ecosystem both at the stage of developing applications, and the consumption of the huge amount of heterogeneous data that is often available in this scenario. Application development is a time-consuming and error-prone task where developers have to deal with the complexities of the geospatial nature of city development, the underlying middleware platform, as well as the programming environment. From the end-users perspective, to have a coherent vision of the city, it is necessary to deal with the massive number of geospatial data generated on daily basis, understand them and how they are related.

In fact, although smart cities middleware platforms potentially support the development and integration of smart city applications [2], several significant

M. Bielikova et al. (Eds.): ICWE 2020, LNCS 12128, pp. 337–344, 2020.
https://doi.org/10.1007/978-3-030-50578-3_23

challenges remain open, mainly related to the need of having a broad knowledge of the specificities of the platform to create an application and organize data visualization to end-users. The needs of smart cities application development go further mashup facilities, requiring user-friendly support for managing geospatial data, integrating heterogeneous city information with geographic location, and querying, composing, and displaying smart cities data.

Aiming to tackle these issues, this paper presents a conceptual architecture for two Web-based dashboards: (i) the *development dashboard* supports the application development through a user-friendly interface that reduce the need of writing complex and specific code of the underlying smart cities platform; (ii) the *visualization dashboard* which provides an interface with geospatial dashboard, including the city map and data plotted over it, and services for linking, querying, and analyzing city information with geographic location. While the development dashboard lowers developers technical barriers, the visualization dashboard enables decision support and real-time monitoring of several city data.

This paper also presents the implementation of the proposed architecture over a smart city platform, *Smart Geo Layers* (SGeoL) [3], a middleware platform which integrates various types of government data sources and collaborative data, provided by individuals and companies, bringing together a series of georeferenced layers related to several domains. For example, the schools layer groups information about the different schools of a city, such as: its geographical location, number of students, number of teachers, students grade, etc. In SGeoL, each layer offers a different view of the city and they can be overlapped, based on its geographical properties. The implementation of the dashboards relies on well-consolidated technologies used in Web environments.

This paper is structured as follows. Section 2 presents the conceptual architecture of both dashboards. Section 3 presents details about the implementation of both dashboards. Section 4 discusses about related work. Section 5 contains the final remarks.

2   Architecture

The conceptual architecture of both the development and visualization dashboards is composed of four main elements: *security manager, authenticators, resource providers*, and *resource consumers*. This organization makes it possible to flexibly create an infrastructure for middleware platforms that consider geographic data, which can also be adapted to possible singularities, such as the specific data model used. Figure 1 defines the proposed architecture for the development dashboard and for the visualization dashboard, including their interactions with the underlying middleware platform.

The *Resource provider* represents the resources provided by the middleware platform. In the case of the SGeoL middleware, examples of resources are *layers* and *smart city entities*, e.g., schools, green areas, squares, hospitals, etc. The *Resource consumers* are components that use resources provided by the *Resource provider* component. For example, in the case of the visualization and development dashboard, consumers are: data integration and synchronizer component, map manager component, query generator component, etc.

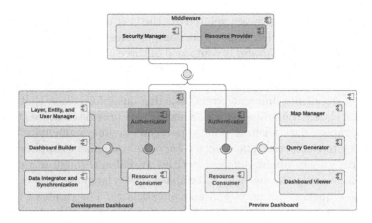

Fig. 1. Development dashboard and Visualization dashboard conceptual architecture.

The *Security Manager* is a middleware element that can authenticate users to verify if they are authorized to access an application or consume resources from the *Resource Provider* component. Once a user is authorized by the *Security Manager component*, the *Authenticator* component of both dashboards stores the session information of the authenticated user. This session information is used by all other components of the development dashboard to consume the resources provided by the *Resource Provider* component, as well the components of the visualization dashboard as to display visual UI elements that the user is allowed to access. For example, a user of the visualization dashboard that has read-only permission for a given layer can view the layer data using their credentials, but the edit layer button is not enabled since he/she does not have update permission.

The *Development Dashboard* is composed of three components: (i) *Layer, Entity, and User Manager*, (ii) *Dashboard Builder*, and (iii) *Data Integrator*. The *Layer, Entity, and User Manager* component uses the features provided by the APIs responsible for listing, authoring, displaying, editing, and deleting layers, entities, and users. In addition to managing elements, this component also manages the access policy of applications, users, and layers.

The *Dashboard Builder* component offers the ability of creating dashboards to each layer, individually. For example, in order to build a dashboard for the school layer that displays students performance statistics over the course of a successful term, a developer can select a board that shows a line chart for student's performance data (number of students approved, failed and evaded, etc.) with respect to different school periods. The union of these and other tables constitutes a dashboard of the school layer.

The *Data Integrator and Synchonization* component consumes the capabilities provided by the *Data Integration and Synchronization* API. This component facilitates the integration of data from companies, governments, organizations or even devices, reducing issues related to the use of legacy systems, use of proprietary software or other issues that hamper integration services.

The *Visualization Dashboard* is composed of three components: (i) *Map Manager*, (ii) *Query Generator*, and (iii) *Dashboard Viewer*. The *Map Manager* component allows an integrated, multidimensional data analysis, considering the correlation of data from different layers, bringing out information that would be obscured in a classic (one-dimensional) view. It also provides features that allow editing geographic data such as points, polygons or line segments of the entities belonging to the layers. The *Query Generator* component simplifies the way users perform queries about different entities available through a user-friendly interface, eliminating the need of a database query language knowledge. The result of these queries can be stored and reused later. The result of this query can be named, saved, and used later, eliminating the need of having to rewrite the query. The *Dashboard Viewer* component displays dashboards predefined by developers of layers at the time of their creation or editing, allowing users to view, monitor or correlate different data layers, intuitively and directly. In addition, it allows the user to compose a personal dashboard as a favorite dashboard which are displayed on their personal dashboard.

3   Implementation

The Vue.Js JavaScript framework[1] was used for implementing both development and visualization dashboards. Vue.Js powers sophisticated single-page applications when used in combination with modern tools and libraries. A modular structural architecture (see Fig. 1) was defined with the following modules: *Core*, *Maps*, *Dashboard*, and *Security*. The *Core* module contains all files common to the other modules, e.g., language selection, navigation bars and menus, login/logout buttons, etc. The *Maps* module is responsible for presenting geographic data and for providing basic operations that can act on the map elements, such as creating, reading, updating, and deleting layers and entities. The *Dashboard* module includes components of *boards* (such as graphics, pictures, light indicator, and historical data) for presenting data and composing dashboards. The *Security* module is in charge of the communication between interfaces and the middleware security component. This module has components, routes, and interfaces for user input, password recovery, registration of new users, definition of roles, etc. It also stores the state of the user's token data and allows other modules to make use of these for the consumption of the middleware APIs.

Each module is structured as follows: (i) *components*: includes all components belonging to the specific module, which can be reused using the name of the component or through events. For example, the dashboard module has components (boards) used for composing the dashboard. (ii) *services*: includes all configuration files, addresses and methods for consuming the APIs of the services used by the module; (iii) *stores*: stores the unique state data, that is, a single object that contains the state at the application level and shares it with the other

---

[1] https://vuejs.org.

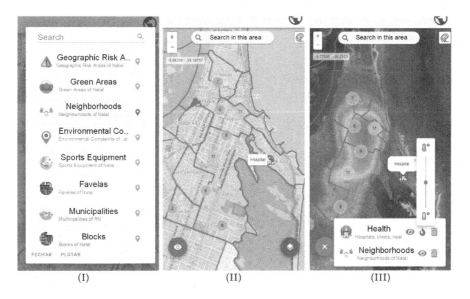

Fig. 2. Layers selection, layer overlay, and layer view control.

modules; and (iv) *routes*: responsible for configuring the internal routes of each module. For example, the *dashboard module* has a main route that presents a set of board and another route for presenting one board with a specific identifier.

3.1 Visualization Dashboard

The *Visualization dashboard* provides the simplest level of control. In order to provide a feeling of familiarity to the user, the interface was developed inspired by map applications, such as Google Maps and OpenStreetMaps. A user can select the available layers (Fig. 2-I), such as, *Green Areas, Neighbourhood, Cities, Health,* among others. By selecting the layers of *hospitals* and *neighborhoods* (Fig. 2-II), for example, the location of the *hospitals* overlapping the polygons of *neighborhoods* is displayed. An user can select to display in satellite mode or use the layer control component (Fig. 2-III), where an user can hide/exhibit layers, activate/deactivate heat maps with intensity control, or remove a layer from the display. Furthermore, when clicking on an entity represented by a polygon or marker on the map (Fig. 2-II), a navigation drawer opens (Fig. 3-I). On this view, the names and values of the properties of the selected entity are presented. It is also possible to edit a value by clicking on it (Fig. 3-II) or even to edit the polygon geometry or marker location. To edit a polygon or a marker (Fig. 3-III), an user can paste a GeoJSON code or load a DXF file for CAD models.

In addition to the layer selection features, it is possible to use the friendly interface query tool to select specific layer entities, eliminating the need for knowing the query language. The query tool allows: (i) to name the query, (ii) to select the color of the returned entities (Fig. 4-I), (iii) to compare values using

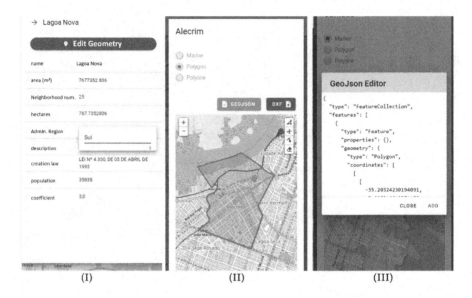

Fig. 3. Entity editing, geographic data editing, and import from GeoJson.

the buttons of the logical operators or even use captions (Fig. 4-II). For example, in the neighborhood layer, to query entities with a population greater than 40,000 inhabitants (Fig. 4-III). The results can be saved and reused, without the need of repeating the query.

3.2   Development Dashboard

The development dashboard provides features for the developer to manage applications, users, layers and entities, as well as tools for importing and synchronizing data. The developer has access to all the main features of the development dashboard, such as user management, layers, data import and synchronization. Furthermore, the developer can add new layers or edit or remove an existing one (if allowed). Once a developer owns a layer or have permission to edit it, he/she can add (Fig. 5-I), edit or remove entities.

If the developer wants to import data from other applications or systems, it is possible to use the *import interface*. This interface handles data importation in different contexts and or common approaches (Fig. 5-II). The first one uses the resources provided by NGSI-LD, which supports Linked Data. The second is a simpler import to be used when data do not need standardization through a context source. Then, it is possible to select whether the importation will use either CSV, JSON or XLS files or through APIs (Fig. 5-III). Once the data source type has been selected, the developer will have a wizard to instruct him/her with the necessary configurations, either to submit files or select the desired APIs in order to import data.

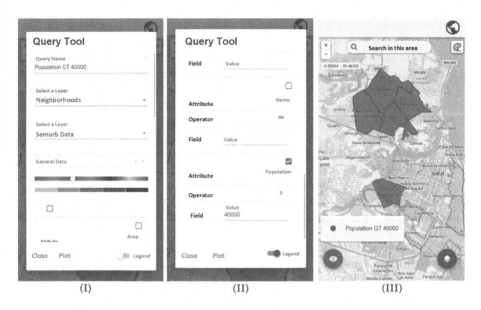

Fig. 4. Query tool and visualization of query results.

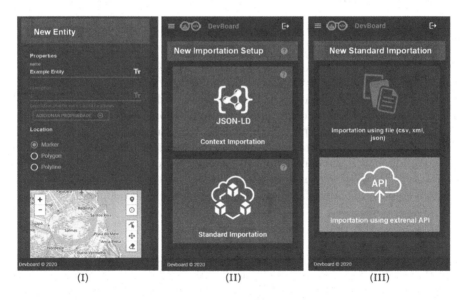

Fig. 5. Add new entity, import configuration, and selection of data source type.

4   Related Work

Dashboards have proven to be very useful for viewing, analyzing and monitoring information in smart city environments. Freeboard[2] is a tool that allows setting

---

[2] https://freeboard.io/.

up customized dashboards for monitoring device and smart cities data. Although Freeboard allows easy creation of customized dashboards, it does not support managing users and their access levels, neither tools for importing data, a useful feature in smart city environments in which data often need to be combined.

ThingsBoard[3] is an open-source platform for device data collection, data processing, data visualization, and data management. Similarly to Freeboard, ThingsBoard uses the concept of widgets, which can be connected to data sources and used to compose dashboards according to users' preferences. This platform also facilitates the use and integration of different data sources, users, and access permissions configurations.

Glue.things [1] allows managing access control to the data produced by the devices in addition to offering a dashboard on which developers can develop applications through mashups. Even though Glue.things supports application development, it does not support data integration and importation of heterogeneous data sources. On the other hand, the dashboards presented in this paper allow integrating data from several sources and types (e.g., APIs provided by third-party systems, CSV files, XML files, etc.), an essential concern in a smart city environment. Moreover, it lack support for geospatial information whereas our proposal includes the integration of maps, data analytics, and geographic visualization and querying.

5 Final Remarks

In this paper, we presented the architecture of Web-based development and visualization dashboards for smart city applications that aim to provide friendly interfaces for developers and users. The purpose of the proposal is twofold: (i) to reduce the complexity of developing smart cities applications and (ii) to allow better understanding the typical plethora of heterogeneous data in this scenario. While visualization dashboards can gather, exhibit, and advise on smart cities data, development dashboards support sustainable development of smart cities applications. We have shown how the proposed architecture was grounded on a smart city platform, providing a set of facilities to both developers and users.

References

1. Kleinfeld, R., Steglich, S., Radziwonowicz, L., Doukas, C.: glue.things: a mashup platform for wiring the Internet of Things with the Internet of Services. In: Proceedings of the 5th International Workshop on Web of Things, pp. 16–21. ACM (2014)
2. Santana, E.F.Z., Chaves, A.P., Gerosa, M.A., Kon, F., Milojicic, D.: Software platforms for smart cities: concepts, requirements, challenges, and a unified reference architecture. ACM Comput. Surv. **50**(6), 1–37 (2017)
3. Souza, A., et al.: A geographic-layered data middleware for smart cities. In: Proceedings of the 24th Brazilian Symposium on Multimedia and the Web, pp. 411–414. ACM (2018)

---

[3] https://thingsboard.io/.

Sentiment Analysis

Detecting Rumor on Microblogging Platforms via a Hybrid Stance Attention Mechanism

Zeng Lingyu, Wu Bin$^{(\boxtimes)}$, and Wang Bai

Beijing University of Posts and Telecommunications, Beijing, China
wubin@bupt.edu.cn

Abstract. Microblogging platforms are important social media in the Internet age. Considering the amount of users on microblogging platforms, the rumor spreading on microblogging platform could have a negative effect on individuals, groups and the whole society. Hence, automatic rumor detection is an important research issue. Stance information contains crucial features for rumor detection, because users discussing rumors tend to express more querying and denying stances. Moreover, different user stances have different importance. Motivated by this inspiration, in this paper, we propose a Rumor Detection Model with a Hybrid Stance Attention Mechanism (RDM-HSAM). The RDM-HSAM consists of four modules. The first module is a stance module, in which the tweet-level stance representation is constructed. The second module is the attention module in which a hybrid attention mechanism is used to construct the event-level stance representation of a microblogging event. The hybrid attention mechanism is consisted of two attention mechanisms, i.e. content attention mechanism and user attention mechanism which are applied at the stance information and user profile respectively. The third module is a rumor module which captures the content features and temporal features of a microblogging event. The fourth module is an integrate module in which event-level stance representations and rumor representations are concatenated together to detect rumors. Experiments on a real-world dataset from Weibo platform demonstrate that our proposed model RDM-HSAM improves the performance of rumor detection in terms of both efficiency and accuracy compared to other methods, and the accuracy of our model achieves 94.9%.

Keywords: Rumor detection · Stance mining · Attention · Neural networks

This work is supported by the National Key Research and Development Program of China (2018YFC0831500), the National Natural Science Foundation of China (NSFC) under Grant No. 61972047 and the NSFC-General Technology Basic Research Joint Funds under Grant U1936220.

M. Bielikova et al. (Eds.): ICWE 2020, LNCS 12128, pp. 347–364, 2020.
https://doi.org/10.1007/978-3-030-50578-3_24

1   Introduction

Microblogging platforms are crucial social media as well as research foci in the Internet age [23,24]. A rumor is defined as a statement or a story whose truth-value is unverifiable or deliberately false by social psychology literature [1]. Once rumors on microblogging platforms were out of control, massive panic and social unrest would be scattered in our community and the sphere of influence could be extraordinarily large.

To address this problem, many automatic rumor detection methods are proposed. Jing Ma et al. [3] propose a model based on recurrent neural network to learn the hidden representations that capture the variation of contextual information of relevant posts over time. Natali Ruchansky et al. [4] propose a model that combined text, response and source characteristics. Feng Yu et al. [5] propose a model based on convolutional neural network which can extract key features scattered among the input sequence and shape high-level interactions among significant features.

Stance is defined as a user's attitude of a piece of information. Stances are usually divided into three categories: supporting stance, querying stance and denying stance. Sometimes, a neutral stance is added to these three categories. Mendoza et al. [2] found that in hot events, most of the user stances related to real information are supportive, while more than half of the user stances related to rumor information are opposed and questioned. Similar to that, on microblogging platforms, users discussing rumors tend to express more querying and denying stances. Hence stance information is a crucial feature for rumor detection. The profile of the whole microblogging event stance is also a profile of group wisdom. There are some existing approaches that take stance information into account. Zhe Zhao et al. [6] work on early rumor detection using cue terms such as "not true", "unconfirmed" or "debunk" to find querying and denying tweets. Jing Ma et al. [7] detect rumor and stance jointly by neural multi-task learning. The main drawback of these methods is that they treat all the stance information equally but it is not proper on microblogging platforms.

The intuition underlying our model is that not all the stance information is equally valuable for the group wisdom profile, consequently, it is unequally important for rumor detection.

First, information of tweets with different stances is unequally valuable. In a microblogging event, the number of supporting tweets is much larger than that of querying and denying tweets in most cases. If we treat all the stance information equally, the information of querying and denying tweets is easily concealed. Moreover, even conveying the same stance, information with more persuasive clues should be paid more attention to.

Figure 1 is an example of a microblogging event, in which R_0 is the root tweet and R_1 to R_n are retweets. The text contents of the tweet and retweets are the comment made by users. As shown in Fig. 1, R_1 is a sequence of characters generated by default on the circumstance of a lack of comment when users publish posts. This kind of meaningless text has no value for gathering group wisdom, yet it accounts for a large proportion of all texts. To avoid a concealment of valuable information, the neglect of the valueless information is required. Furthermore, R_2 is a supporting tweets which is a repetition of root tweet and R_3, R_{n-1} and R_n convey querying and denying stance respectively. All of them are valuable for rumor detection, but among them, R_{n-1} and R_n are more valuable because they contain more persuasive clues.

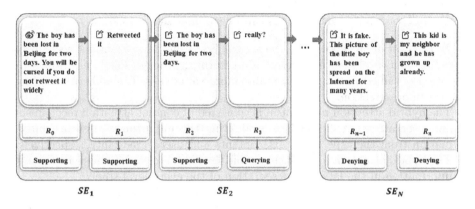

Fig. 1. An example of microblogging event. A microblogging event is defined as a collection of a root tweet and all its related retweets. R_0 in Fig. 1 is the root tweet. R_1 to R_n are retweets. An event can be divided into several subevents, which are notated as SE_1 to SE_N.

Second, not all the users are equally reliable. Hence, the information released by different users has different importance for rumor detection. There are three types of account on the microblogging platform. The first type is the official account which has the highest credibility mostly. The second type is the ordinary personal account. Some of ordinary personal accounts are more susceptible to rumors and others are more resistant. The stances of resistant users are more reliable. The third type is the robot account. Some of robot accounts are manipulated by somebody and the stances of them are fabricated to mislead public opinion.

Motivated by this inspiration, we have a hypothesis that making full use of the valuable and reliable stance information by paying different attention to different tweet-level stances can gather group wisdom more effectively and consequently, enhance the rumor detection model performance. To test the hypothesis, we propose the Rumor Detection Model with a Hybrid Stance Attention Mechanism (RDM-HSAM) in this paper.

RDM-HSAM consists of four modules: stance module, attention module, rumor module and integrate module. The first module is a stance module, in which the tweet-level stance representation containing stance information is constructed. The second module is the attention module in which a hybrid attention mechanism is used to construct the event-level stance representation of a microblogging event. The hybrid attention mechanism is consisted of two attention mechanisms, i.e. content attention mechanism and user attention mechanism which are applied at the stance information and user profile respectively. The third module is a rumor module which captures the content features and temporal features of a microblogging event. The fourth module is an integrate module in which event-level stance representations and rumor representations are concatenated together to detect rumors.

Overall, our main contributions can be summarized as follows:

- To the best of our knowledge, we are the first to use the attention mechanism in an event-level stance representation learning process. The latent representation obtained in this way contains more valuable and reliable information for rumor detection.
- The hybrid attention mechanism is consisted of content attention mechanism and user attention mechanism, evaluating the importance of stance information from the aspects of text contents and users' credibility respectively. The hybrid attention mechanism enable the model to contain more important information in the latent representation of the event-level stance.
- Experiments on a real world data set from Weibo platform demonstrate that our proposed model RDM-HSAM improves the performance of rumor detection in terms of both efficiency and accuracy compared with other methods, and the accuracy of our model achieves 94.6%.

2   Related Work

2.1   Rumor Detection

Initially, the automatic rumor detection of social media is based on hand-craft feature set. These methods construct the feature set manually at the beginning. Then they extract the features of the data according to the feature set, and finally all the extracted features are put into a machine learning classifier for rumor detection. Sejeong Kwon et al. [8] construct a feature set including content features and propagation features. Jing Ma et al. [9] extend the feature set with user features. Although these methods have good performance in rumor detection, their disadvantages are also obvious. First, hand-made feature sets require daunting manual labor. Second, the construction of feature sets depends on researchers' logical thinking and fail to extract more high-dimensional abstract features.

To overcome the shortcomings of these hand-crafted feature based methods, rumor detection methods based on deep learning are proposed. Jing Ma et al. [3] propose a model based on recurrent neural network to learn the hidden representation of microblogging events. The model converts the microblog event into a sequence of subevents and capture the variation of contextual information over time. Natali Ruchansky et al. [4] propose a model that can integrate text information, response information and source information. Feng Yu et al. [5] propose a model based on convolutional neural network to extract the key features scattered in the input sequence and form the high-level interaction between the important features. Jing Ma et al. [10] use tree structure recurrent neural network to leverage non sequential propagation structure for rumor detection. The disadvantage of these methods is that none of them use the information from the stance perspective.

There are also some existing approaches that take the stance information into account. Zhe Zhao et al. [6] use cue terms such as "not true", "unconfirmed" or "debunk" to find querying and denying tweets and then they use this clue to detect rumor. Jing Ma et al. [7] detect rumor and stance jointly by multi-task learning method. The main disadvantage of these methods is that they treat all the stance information equally, ignoring the fact that the information has different importance for rumor detection.

2.2 Stance Mining

Stance mining based on viewpoint mining can be divided into three different granularities: document level, sentence level and aspect level [11–15]. Stances are mined by identifying viewpoint sentences and extracting viewpoint in the form of five or six tuples. Liu Bing et al. [11] propose a model to abstract viewpoints into five tuples: Opinion = entity, aspect, opinion orientation, holder, time. Among them, entity is the object of viewpoint, aspect is the element of entity, opinion orientation is the tendency of viewpoint, holder is the holder of viewpoint, and time is the publish time. These stance mining methods are not suitable for the stance mining on microblogging platforms because the text on the microblogging platform is too colloquial to extract tuples.

Deep learning based methods are more suitable for the stance mining on microblogging platforms. IKM team [16] proposes a conventional-neural-network-based voting scheme in SemEval stance mining contest. Jing Ma et al. [3] detect rumor and stance jointly by neural multi-task learning. Xu Chang et al. [17] use a self-attention mechanism for Cross-Target Stance Classification.

2.3 Attention Mechanism

Attention mechanism has been widely used in natural language processing [18–21]. In the general definition of attention mechanism, key vectors and query vectors are need for attention values calculation. Besides, value vectors $v = [v_1, v_2, \ldots, v_n]$ are also needed for attention mechanism. There is a one-to-one correspondence between the n tokens of the value vector sequence v and the key vector sequence k. In an attention mechanism execution process, given a sequence of key values $k = [k_1, k_2, \ldots, k_n]$ and the vector of a query q, attention mechanism computes the alignment score between k_i and q by a compatibility function $f(k_i, q)$, which is a measure of the dependency between k_i and q. Then a softmax function is used to transform the scores $[f(ki, q)]_{i=1}$ to a probability distribution $p = (z|k, q)$ where z represents the importance of v_i to q on a specific task. That is, the larger $p = (z = i|k, q)$ is, the more important information v_i contributes to q. The above process can be summarized by the following equations.

$$\alpha = [f(k_i, q)]_{i=1}^n \tag{1}$$

$$p(z|k, q) = softmax(\alpha) \tag{2}$$

Specifically,

$$p(z = i|k, q) = \frac{\exp(f(k_i, q))}{\sum_{i=1}^n \exp(f(k_i, q))} \tag{3}$$

The output of the attention mechanism is a weighted sum calculated form all the tokens of value vector sequence v. The weight of v_i used in calculation is given by $p = (z = i|k, q)$ which measures the importance of v_i to q. The above process can be summarized by the following equation.

$$h = \sum_{i=1}^n (p(z = i|k, q)v_i \tag{4}$$

$f(k_i, q)$ is differently computed in different methods. Additive attention and multiplicative attention are the two mostly commonly used attention mechanism. In additive attention mechanism, $f(k_i, q)$ is calculated as following:

$$f(k_i, q) = \omega^T \sigma(W_k k_i + W_q q) \tag{5}$$

where $\sigma(*)$ is an activate function and ω is a weight vector. Multiplicative attention uses inner product or cosine similarity for $f(x_i, q)$, i.e.,

$$f(k_i, q) = \langle W_k k_i, W_q q \rangle \tag{6}$$

In practice, additive attention often outperforms multiplicative one in prediction quality, but the latter is faster and more memory-efficient due to optimized matrix multiplication.

3   Problem Definition

3.1   Preliminaries

A microblogging post is formulated as R $= \{$ u, text, t$\}$ in which u is user information, text is the comment that user creates when he/she publishes tweet and t is the publish time. Given a microblogging event, we align all the tweets to a sequence according to the publish time and consequently a microblogging event is formulated as E $= \{R_0, R_1, R_2, \ldots, R_i, \ldots, R_n\}$, where R_0 is the root tweet and R_1 to R_n are retweets.

On microblogging platforms, stance is the attitude of users towards the authenticity of the root tweet. Stances are classified into three types in our research, i.e. supporting stance, querying stance and denying stance. All the tweets that do not explicitly raise questions and objections are regarded as potential supporting tweets.

3.2 Goal

The main purpose of our research is identifying whether a root tweet is a rumor. The input of the rumor detection task is $E = \{R_0, R_1, R_2, \ldots, R_i, \ldots, R_n\}$. To construct a latent representation of event-level stance profile, we also raise a stance mining task in our paper.

4 Model

In this section, we introduce the proposed model. We first present the overall structure of the stance attention rumor detection model, then we detail the stance module, rumor module, attention module and integrate module respectively.

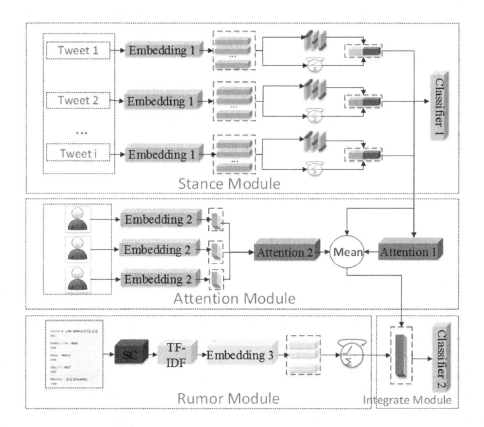

Fig. 2. The overall structure of the hybrid stance attention rumor detection model.

As illustrated in Fig. 2, there are four mini modules as follows: stance module, attention module, rumor module and integrate module. First, stance module is a module where tweet-level stance representations are learned. Second, hybrid attention mechanism is leveraged to construct event-level stance representation. Third, the rumor module captures the content features and temporal features of a microblogging event and constructs a latent representation containing the information directly related to rumor detection. Finally, the integrate module combines the rumor representation with the event-level stance representation as the input of the ultimate rumor detection.

4.1 Stance Module

Given a microblogging event $E = \{R_0, R_1, R_2, \ldots, R_i, \ldots, R_n\}$, the input of the stance module, notated as Text = $\{text_0, text_1, text_2, \ldots, text_i\}$, is the text of the post in the microblogging event E except the meaningless text. The meaningless text, as the R_1 shown in Fig. 1, is the text generated by default on the circumstance of a lack of comment when users publish posts.

To convert the text into a data format that the model can process, all the texts are put into an embedding layer firstly. Then a recurrent neural network and a convolutional neural network are used to extract event-related features and grammatical features respectively. The reason that we use two different network structures to extract features is that there are two different ways of users to expression stances in microblogging platforms, and the information of these two different expressions is suitable for two types of deep learning networks to extract.

Grammatical Feature. Microblogging platform is a social media full of colloquial content. When users express querying stances, a colloquialism they commonly use is "really?", and when it comes to denying stance, the colloquialism could be "It is not true" or "That's a totally crap". In this case, grammatical features are adequate for stance classification. As shown in Fig. 1, R_3 is a typically expression of querying and without root tweet content, we can also tell the stance of R_{n-1} because he/she said "it is fake" at the beginning. To capture these common expressions effectively, we construct a convolutional neural network. The network structure is shown in Fig. 3(a). The input of the grammatical feature extraction module is a matrix in which each row represents one character in the sentence. After convolutional process, the vectors obtained by convolution kernels with different window size are concatenated together to form the overall grammatical feature vector, which is represented as ts_i^g.

Event-Related Feature. Unlike R_3 and R_{n-1}, R_n says that the boy in the picture is his/her neighbor and he has grown up, indicating the boy could not be lost for two days. Although it is a post with denying stance, it is impossible for the model to classify the stance unless taking the information of root tweet into consideration. To deal with the problem above-mentioned, we construct

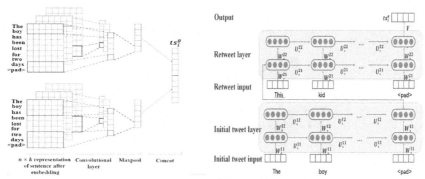

(a) The convolutional neural network used for grammatical feature extraction

(b) The recurrent neural network used for event-related feature extraction

Fig. 3. The neural networks used in stance module

a recurrent neural network to capture the event-related feature. The network structure is shown in Fig. 3(b). First, a recurrent neural network used GRU cell is constructed to encode root tweet, and then the output of the root tweet layer is used as the initial state of the retweet layer. In this way, the information of root tweet is taken into consideration during the retweets' feature extracting process. The output of the event-related feature extraction module is annotated as ts_i^e.

4.2   Attention

Given a microblogging event $E = \{R_0, R_1, R_2, \ldots, R_i, \ldots, R_n\}$ and the corresponding stance module input Text $= \{text_0, text_1, text_2, \ldots, text_i\}$, the inputs of the attention module is the user set notated as $U = \{u_0, u_1, u_2, \ldots, u_i\}$ and the output of the stance module. Two different attention mechanisms are used in attention module. Content attention mechanism use the output of the stance module to evaluate that how much important information a text contains and user attention mechanism use the user set U to evaluate that how reliable the user's stance is. For each attention mechanism, we calculate element-wise multiplication of the attention scores and x_1 to x_n. Then, we sum up all the vectors along the column and get two vectors from the two attention mechanism. Finally, we calculate the mean value of the two vectors and the representation of the event-level stance is obtained.

Content Attention. In a microblogging event, the number of supporting tweets is much larger than that of querying and denying tweets in most cases. Moreover, even with the same stance, we should pay more attention to that the stance information that contains more persuasive clues. Therefore, an attention mechanism is leveraged in our model to identify the important information during

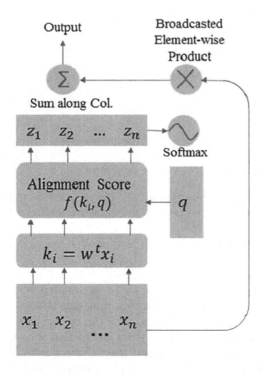

Fig. 4. The attention mechanism used for content attention.

the event-level stance representation learning process. The attention mechanism used in the model is shown in Fig. 4.

As shown in Fig. 4, x_i is a concatenation of ts_i^e and ts_i^g, i.e. the stance vector of the i-th tweet. k_i is the key vector of x_i. At the beginning, the stance vectors of tweets are put into a full connection layer to get the key vectors of them. Vector q is the querying vector which can be seen as a latent representation of a query. In this task, the querying is "whose stance information is more important for rumor detection?" The value of the querying vector is randomly generated and optimized as a parameter during the training process. Additive attention is used in our model, which means the alignment score is calculated as following:

$$f(k_i, q) = \omega^T \sigma (W_k k_i + W_q q) \tag{7}$$

The alignment scores are annotated as z_1 to z_n. To normalize the alignment scores, z_1 to z_n are put into a softmax layer in which all the alignment scores are mapped to the interval from 0 to 1.

User Attention. The credibility of different users is unequal. In general, official accounts have the highest credibility while robot accounts with fabricated stances have the lowest one. Meanwhile, in personal accounts, some of them are more susceptible to rumors and others are more resistant. The more resistance an account has, the more reliable its stance is. Therefore, we construct a user attention mechanism to evaluate the credibility of a user. The user attention mechanism used in the model has the same structure with the content attention mechanism. The difference between them is that the inputs of user attention mechanism are user profile vectors. In this paper, we construct the initial user profile vector according to the user feature set shown in Table 1. The initial user profile vector is put into an embedding layer for higher dimensional representation.

Table 1. Features used in initial user profile vectors

Future name	Description
Followers	Number of followers
Friends	Number of mutual follower
Gender	Man, woman
Registration time	Registration time of the account
Historical microblogs	Number of status
Verification type	Ordinary user, celebrity, government, enterprise, medium, school, website, organization, pending enterprise, application, junior expert, senior expert, deceased expert

4.3   Rumor Module

To extract content features and temporal features related to rumor detection directly, we construct a recurrent neural network for rumor feature extraction. Given a microblogging event $E = \{R_0, R_1, R_2, \ldots, R_i, \ldots, R_n\}$, the input of the rumor module is text of all the post in the microblogging event. Putting a post into the recurrent neural network once a time is inappropriate because it requires a recurrent neural network with thousands of layers. Hence, in rumor module, we firstly split a microblogging event into N subevents. Given the subevent number N and a microblogging event with n posts, first, we calculate the average number of posts per interval as n/N. n/N is a non-integer in most cases. Since N is a large number, if we put ceil(n/N) posts in each interval, the last few intervals may be empty while if we put floor(n/N) posts in each interval, there may be a lot of extra posts in the last interval. So we alternately set the number of posts in each interval to ceil(n/N) and floor(n/N). ceil(n/N) is the nearest integer greater than n/N and floor(n/N) is the nearest integer less than n/N. If the total number of posts involved in the event is less than N, we put a post in each interval, and the last intervals are empty.

After subevent construction process, we treat a subevent as a document and use the TF*IDF value of the vocabulary terms as input. We prune the vocabulary by keeping the top-K terms according to the word frequency, so the input dimension is N*K. The matrix of event is sparse, so we implement a embedding layer to convert the sparse input into dense representations.

GRU cell is suitable for long-distance dependency problem. The gate units not only keep the text content of subevents but also inject the inter-dependent evidence from its precious steps which lead to a good extraction of both content information and temporal information. Hence we construct a two-layer recurrent neural network using GRU cell in the rumor module.

4.4   Integrate Module

In the integrate module, the vector learning form stance module and rumor module are concatenated together and put into two fully connection layers and a softmax layer. The output of the softmax layer is annotated as p_c. Let g_c, where c denotes the class label, be the ground-truth 2-dimensional multinomial distribution on an event. Here, the distribution is of the form [1, 0] for rumors and [0, 1] for non-rumors. For each training instance, our goal is to minimize the sum of L2-regularization penalty and the cross entropy loss that between the probability distributions of the prediction and ground truth.

5   Metrics and Datasets

5.1   Metrics

For an N-categorization task, accuracy, recall, precision, and F1 score are used as metrics to measure the quality of the model.

5.2   Dataset

There are two datasets used in experiment, the first one is Weibo stance dataset and the second one is Weibo rumor dataset. Both datasets are public datasets. The Weibo rumor dataset is published by Jing Ma in 2016 [3] and the Weibo stance dataset is published by Lingyu Zeng in 2019 [22]. The basic information of datasets is shown in Table 2.

Table 2. Statics of datasets.

Rumor dataset	Statics	Stance dataset	Statics
User	2,746,818	User	110,012
Posts	3,805,656	Posts	156,577
Events	4,664	Events	541
Rumors	2,313	Rumors	330
Non-rumors	2,351	Non-rumors	211
Avg. time length/event	2,460.7 h	Supporting stance	189,390
Avg of posts/event	816	Denying stance	7,701
Max of posts/event	59,318	Querying stance	8,364

6   Experiment

6.1   Model Training

We train all the CNN and RNN models by employing the derivation of the loss through back-propagation with respect to all the parameters. We use the Ada-Grad algorithm for parameter update. After fine tune, we set the vocabulary size K as 10,000, the embedding size of rumor module, stance module and attention module as 300, 128 and 128 respectively. Filter windows of CNN is 2, 3, 5 and the feature maps of them is 100. The size of hidden units is 128 and the learning rate is 0.0001. Subevent number N is empirically set as 50. We firstly trained the stance module separately by putting the vector concatenating grammatical vector and event-related vector into a classifier. In the stance module training process, all the data of the Weibo stance dataset is used for training. The parameters of the stance module are fixed in the later rumor detection model training process. For rumor detection experiments, we randomly choose 10% of the Weibo rumor data for test and the rest for training.

6.2   Rumor Detection

To empirically evaluate the performance of our method on rumor classification, we perform experiments on Weibo dataset. We compared our stance mining assisting model with several baselines including:

- SVM-TS: a linear SVM classification model proposed by Jing Ma et al. in 2015 by using time-series structures to model the variation of social context features [9].
- DT-Rank: a decision-tree-based ranking model proposed by Zhe Zhao et al. in 2015 [11]. We implements their features and enquiry phrases.
- RFC: a random forest classifier proposed by Sejeong Kwon et al. in 2013 [8]. They utilize temporal volume curve to detect rumors.
- GRU-2: a deep learning model proposed by Jing Ma et al. in 2016 [3]. It is configured with a two-layer conventional neural network.
- CMAI: a deep learning model proposed by Feng Yu et al. in 2017 [5]. It is configured with two-layer of GRU hidden units.
- Multi-task: A multi-task method proposed by Jing Ma in 2018 [7]. It trains stance mining task and rumor detection task jointly.
- SMAM: A stance mining assisting model proposed by Lingyu Zeng in 2019 [22]. It learns the stance representation without attention mechanism.
- Our models: (1) Simple-RNN is a model that only contains the rumor module. The output of the rumor module is put into a full connection layer and a softmax layer to detect rumor. (2) RDM-SN is a model with stance module, rumor module and integrate module. The event-level stance representation is an element-wise average value of all the tweet-level stance representations. (3) RDM-HSAM is an overall model with stance module, attention module, rumor module and integrate module.

We implement SVM with LibSVM, decision tree model with scikit-learn and RNN model with TensorFlow. Table 3 shows the performance of different methods.

Table 3. Performance of different methods in rumor detection

Method	Class	Accuracy	Precision	Recall	F1
SVM-TS	R	0.849	0.839	0.885	0.861
	N		0.878	0.830	0.857
DT-Rank	R	0.731	0.738	0.712	0.726
	N		0.726	0.747	0.737
GRU-2	R	0.910	0.876	0.956	0.913
	N		0.952	0.864	0.903
RFC	R	0.849	0.786	0.959	0.864
	N		0.947	0.739	0.830
SVN-CSD	R	0.875	0.849	0.909	0.878
	N		0.904	0.841	0.872
CAMI	R	0.933	0.921	0.945	0.933
	N		0.945	0.921	0.932
Multi-task	R	0.917	0.920	0.921	0.915
	N		0.932	0.920	0.919
SMAM	R	0.939	0.929	0.950	0.940
	N		0.951	0.928	0.939
Simple-RNN	**R**	**0.891**	**0.882**	**0.901**	**0.891**
	N		**0.901**	**0.881**	**0.891**
RDM-SN	**R**	**0.917**	**0.906**	**0.929**	**0.917**
	N		**0.928**	**0.905**	**0.916**
RDM-HSAM	**R**	**0.949**	**0.937**	**0.961**	**0.949**
	N		**0.961**	**0.936**	**0.948**

Table 3 shows the performance of different methods and our model outperforms all the baselines.

Specifically, SVM-TS, DT-Rank and RFC are models based on machine learning and the rest of models are based on deep learning. The greater performances that deep learning models obtained indicate that using deep learning method to detect rumor is the prospect of rumor detection task.

DT-Rank is a decision-tree-based ranking model implementing enquiry phrases. In their model, they use a keyword matching method to find enquiry phrases features. DT-Rank achieves 0.731 accuracy, indicating that the key words matching method is insufficient for stance mining and rumor detection. Multi-task is a multi-task method training stance mining task and rumor detection task jointly. Joint training is not conducive to the optimal convergence of rumor detection model. Hence we trained stance module and the other modules separately and achieve a better performance in the rumor detection experiments. Besides, the Multi-task model uses a recurrent neural network to learn tweet-level stance latent representations but we propose a more efficient stance feature extraction structure. SMAM is a model mining stance information on subevent level. Compared with SMAM, RDM-HSAM mine stance in tweet-level at the beginning, avoiding a distortion of data. Mining stance on subevent level requires a processing of data which could distort data. Compared with these stance-aware methods, our model has a better performance.

The simple-RNN model achieves 0.891 accuracy on the dataset, indicating that the basic RNN can learn discriminative features effectively. RDM-SN with a better performance than the simple-RNN model validates the enhancement effect of the event-level stance information. Compared with RDM-SN which do not use attention mechanism in event-level stance representation learning process, the model with attention mechanism, i.e. RDM-HSAM achieves better performance, indicating the effectiveness of attention mechanism. The experiments demonstrate that more important stance information is contained in the event-level stance latent representation owing to the attention mechanism.

6.3 Early Detection

In order to effectively control rumors, rumors need to be identified as early as possible. Hence, early detection is extraordinarily valuable in rumor detection task. Given a detection deadline, early detection is a detection only using the tweets published before the time point.

Figure 5 shows the accuracy of the baselines and our models. Compared with the manual feature set method, the deep learning methods have better performances. It proves that the deep neural network can extract more explicit features in rumor detection task. Our model has a better performance after 24 h. This is explainable because it will take a while for users to browse rumors and express their stances. Compared with the time lag caused by the authority's rumor verification, 24 h is an acceptable time lag considering the high accuracy and large quantity of data that can be processed once.

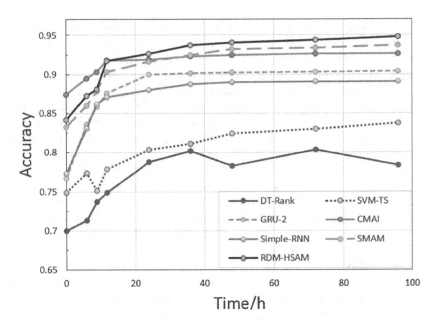

Fig. 5. Results of rumor early detection.

7   Conclusion

In this paper, we propose a rumor detection model with a hybrid stance attention mechanism. In the model, stance module extracts the stance feature and
construct tweet-level stance representation. Attention module leverages a hybrid
attention mechanism to construct the event-level stance representation. Rumor
module extracts content features and temporal features directly related to rumor
detection, and integrated module concatenates event-level stance representations
and rumor representations together to detect rumor. Experimental results show
that our method has a better performance compared with baselines, improving
rumor detection efficiency on microblogging platforms. In the future, we will
further develop unsupervised models due to the massive unlabeled stance data.

References

1. O'Reilly, T., Xuan, W.: What is Web2.0. Internet Wkly. (40), 38–40 (2005)
2. Mendoza, M., Poblete, B., Castillo, C.: Twitter under crisis: can we trust what we
   RT. In: Proceedings of the First Workshop on Social Media Analytics, pp. 71–79
   (2010)
3. Ma, J., Gao, W., Mitra, P., et al.: Detecting rumors from microblogs with recurrent
   neural networks. In: The International Joint Conference on Artificial Intelligence,
   pp. 3818–3824 (2016)
4. Ruchansky, N., Seo, S., Liu, Y.: CSI: a hybrid deep model for fake news detection.
   In: Proceedings of the 2017 ACM on Conference on Information and Knowledge
   Management, pp. 797–806 (2017)

5. Yu, F., Liu, Q., Wu, S., et al.: A convolutional approach for misinformation identification. In: Twenty-Sixth International Joint Conference on Artificial Intelligence, pp. 3901–3907 (2017)
6. Zhao, Z., Resnick, P., Mei, Q.: Enquiring minds: early detection of rumors in social media from enquiry posts. In: The 24th International Conference on World Wide Web, pp. 1395–1405 (2015)
7. Ma, J., Gao, W., Wong, K.F.: Detect rumor and stance jointly by neural multi-task learning. In: Companion Proceedings of the The Web Conference 2018. International World Wide Web Conferences Steering Committee, pp. 585–593 (2018)
8. Kwon, S., Cha, M., Jung, K., et al.: Prominent features of rumor propagation in online social media. In: International Conference on Data Mining, pp. 1103–1108. IEEE (2013)
9. Ma, J., Gao, W., Wei, Z., et al.: Detect rumors using time series of social context information on microblogging websites. In: ACM International on Conference on Information and Knowledge Management, pp. 1751–1754 (2015)
10. Ma, J., Gao, W., Wong, K.F., et al.: Rumor detection on Twitter with tree-structured recursive neural networks. In: Proceedings of the 56th Annual Meeting of the Association for Computational Linguistics, pp. 1980–1989 (2018)
11. Zhang, L., Liu, B.: Aspect and entity extraction for opinion mining. In: Chu, W.W. (ed.) Data Mining and Knowledge Discovery for Big Data. SBD, vol. 1, pp. 1–40. Springer, Heidelberg (2014). https://doi.org/10.1007/978-3-642-40837-3_1
12. Liu, B., Zhang, L.: A survey of opinion mining and sentiment analysis. In: Aggarwal, C., Zhai, C. (eds.) Mining Text Data, pp. 415–463. Springer, Boston (2012). https://doi.org/10.1007/978-1-4614-3223-4_13
13. Blei, D.M., Ng, A.Y., Jordan, M.I.: Latent Dirichlet allocation. J. Mach. Learn. Res. **3**, 993–1022 (2003)
14. Lv, P., Luo, Z., Cai, D., et al.: Effective mining product features from Chinese review based on CRF. Comput. Eng. Sci. **2**, 359–366 (2014)
15. Jin, W., Ho, H.H., Srihari, R.K.: OpinionMiner: a novel machine learning system for web opinion mining and extraction. In: Proceedings of the 15th ACM SIGKDD International Conference on Knowledge Discovery and Data Mining, pp. 1195–1204 (2009)
16. Chen, Y.C., Liu, Z.Y., Kao, H.Y.: IKM at SemEval-2017 task 8: convolutional neural networks for stance detection and rumor verification. In: Proceedings of the 11th International Workshop on Semantic Evaluation, pp. 465–469 (2017)
17. Xu, C., Paris, C., Nepal, S., et al.: Cross-target stance classification with self-attention networks. arXiv preprint (2018)
18. Veyseh, A.P.B., Ebrahimi, J., Dou, D., et al.: A temporal attentional model for rumor stance classification. In: Proceedings of the 2017 ACM on Conference on Information and Knowledge Management, pp. 2335–2338 (2017)
19. Zhou, Y., Cristea, A.I., Shi, L.: Connecting targets to tweets: semantic attention-based model for target-specific stance detection. In: Bouguettaya, A., et al. (eds.) WISE 2017. LNCS, vol. 10569, pp. 18–32. Springer, Cham (2017). https://doi.org/10.1007/978-3-319-68783-4_2
20. Zhang, H., Goodfellow, I., Metaxas, D., et al.: Self-attention generative adversarial networks. arXiv preprint (2018)
21. Rush, A.M., Chopra, S., Weston, J.: A neural attention model for abstractive sentence summarization. arXiv preprint (2015)
22. Lingyu, Z., Chenguang, S., Bin, W., et al.: SMAM: detecting rumors from microblogs with stance mining assisting task. In: Proceedings of Fourth International Conference on Data Science in Cyberspace, pp. 242–249 (2019)

23. Dabiri, S., Heaslip, K.: Developing a Twitter-based traffic event detection model using deep learning architectures. Expert Syst. Appl. **118**, 425–439 (2018)
24. Hogenboom, F., Frasincar, F., Kaymak, U., et al.: An overview of event extraction from text. In: DeRiVE@ISWC, pp. 48–57 (2011)

A Hybrid Approach for Aspect-Based Sentiment Analysis Using Deep Contextual Word Embeddings and Hierarchical Attention

Maria Mihaela Truşcă[1]([✉]), Daan Wassenberg[2], Flavius Frasincar[2][iD],
and Rommert Dekker[2][iD]

[1] Bucharest University of Economic Studies, 010374 Bucharest, Romania
maria.trusca@csie.ase.ro
[2] Erasmus University Rotterdam, Burgemeester Oudlaan 50,
3062 PA Rotterdam, The Netherlands
daan.wassenberg@hotmail.com, {frasincar,rdekker}@ese.eur.nl

Abstract. The Web has become the main platform where people express their opinions about entities of interest and their associated aspects. Aspect-Based Sentiment Analysis (ABSA) aims to automatically compute the sentiment towards these aspects from opinionated text. In this paper we extend the state-of-the-art Hybrid Approach for Aspect-Based Sentiment Analysis (HAABSA) method in two directions. First we replace the non-contextual word embeddings with deep contextual word embeddings in order to better cope with the word semantics in a given text. Second, we use hierarchical attention by adding an extra attention layer to the HAABSA high-level representations in order to increase the method flexibility in modeling the input data. Using two standard datasets (SemEval 2015 and SemEval 2016) we show that the proposed extensions improve the accuracy of the built model for ABSA.

Keywords: Multi-hop LCR-ROT · Hierarchical attention · Contextual word embeddings

1 Introduction

Since the evolution of the Social Web, people have benefited from the opportunity to actively interact with others sharing content from both sides. As a result, the amount of opinionated texts has risen and people had to face the problem of filtering the extra data in order to get the desired information [21]. In this context, sentiment analysis turns out to be an important tool that can find sentiments or opinions at the level of a document, sentence, or aspect [11]. Among all levels of analysis, the most fine-grained analysis is the one orientated to aspects [18]. The main tasks of ABSA are target extraction (TE), aspect detection (AD), and target sentiment classification (SC). Whereas, the TE task is concerned with

© Springer Nature Switzerland AG 2020
M. Bielikova et al. (Eds.): ICWE 2020, LNCS 12128, pp. 365–380, 2020.
https://doi.org/10.1007/978-3-030-50578-3_25

identification of targets, i.e., attributes of the entity of interest, the aim of the AD task is to learn aspects that have a broader meaning and refer to the targets' categories. However, in this paper, we focus only on the identification of targets' sentiments (SC task) computed at the sentence level.

Deep Neural Networks (DNNs) have recently shown a great potential for sentiment classification tasks and gradually replaced rule-based approaches. While the main advantage of DNNs architectures is flexibility, rule-based classifiers imply more manual labour that confers a higher level of domain-control. The two approaches can be easily combined in a two-step method that utilises a backup classifier for all inconclusive predictions of the main classifier. One of the first two-step sentiment classification methods utilises a dictionary-based method and a Support Vector Machine (SVM) algorithm [5]. Given that this method is a bit naive, we try to tackle the sentiment classification of targets using the more refined Hybrid Approach for Aspect-Based Sentiment Analysis (HAABSA) that obtains state-of-the-art results for the SC task [24]. The first step of this hybrid method employs a domain ontology [19] to determine the sentiments of the given targets. All the sentences for which the ontology is inconclusive input a Left-Center-Right separated neural network with Rotatory attention (LCR-Rot) [28], as the backup model.

In [24] two extensions of the neural network are proposed, namely Inversed LCR-Rot and Multi-hop LCR-Rot, but since the second one was shown to be the most effective, we choose it as the backup model. In this paper, we propose two extensions for HAABSA to improve the quality of the sentiment predictions. First, we replace the non-contextual GloVe word embeddings with deep contextual word embeddings, i.e., ELMo [15] and BERT [6] in order to better consider the semantics of words context. Second, we introduce a hierarchical attention, by supplementing the current attention mechanism with a new attention layer that is able to distinguish the importance of the high-level input sentence representations. We call the new model HAABSA++. The Python source code of our extensions can be found at https://github.com/mtrusca/HAABSA_PLUS_PLUS.

The rest of the paper is organized as follows. Section 2 briefly introduces the related works. Section 3 presents the details of the utilised datasets. Section 4 discusses the hybrid approach together with the extensions we propose and Sect. 5 presents the experimental settings and the evaluation of our methods. Section 6 gives our conclusions and suggestions for future work.

2   Related Works

Initially, ABSA's main tasks were addressed using knowledge-based methods based on part-of-speech tagging models and lexicons [10, 23]. Recently, machine learning including deep learning as a subset has turned out to be a more convenient solution with good rates of performance in Natural Language Processing (NLP). Whereas machine learning methods have proven to be more flexible, knowledge-based methods imply more manual labor, which makes them effective especially for in-domains sentiment classification. In [26] it was shown that these two approaches are in fact complementary. The sentiment polarities of aspects were learnt by applying an approach based on domain knowledge and a bidirectional recurrent neural network with attention mechanism. The research proves that there is not a winning option and while the neural network performs better for the laptop reviews of the SemEval 2015 dataset [17], the approach based on domain rules is more effective in the restaurant domain dataset of the same SemEval workshop.

Recently, hybrid models that take advantage of both approaches in a mixed solution have been investigated in various studies. For instance, in [20] an SVM model was trained for target sentiment classification on an input created based on the binary presence of features identified using a domain-specific ontology. Another option to enrich the input of a neural network using domain knowledge is presented in [7], where a self-defined sentiment lexicon is used to extend the word embeddings. Similar to our work, the neural network described in [8] aims to learn context-sensitive target embeddings. Next, the attention scores are computed only for relevant words of the context indicated by a dependency parser. While the previous methods focused on integrating rule-based approaches in machine learning, in [4] it is presented a different method where machine learning is used for building domain knowledge. Namely, a Long Short-Term Memory (LSTM) model with an attention mechanism is employed to create a sentiment dictionary called SenticNet 5.

Instead of integrating the two approaches in a single model, another option is to apply them sequentially [5]. This option has been demonstrated to be superior to the individual approaches in [19]. Namely, in [19] an ontology developed for restaurant domain reviews is used as the first method for sentiment classification (*positive* and *negative*). The backup model, triggered when the ontology is inconclusive, employs a bag-of-words approach trained with a multi-class SVM associated with all three sentiment polarities (*positive, neutral,* and *negative*). This work inspired [12] where the SVM model is replaced with a neural network that assigns polarities to the aspects using multiple attention layers. The first one captures the relation between aspects and their left and right contexts and generates context-dependent word embeddings. The new word vectors together with sentences and aspects embeddings created using the bag-of-words approach feed the last layer of attention.

The previous line of research is kept in [24], where the same ontology is used together with a Multi-Hop LCR-Rot model as backup. Knowing the effectiveness of the two-step approach for the SC task, and considering that the method proposed in [24] achieves the best results for the SemEval 2015 and the SemEval 2016 [16] datasets, we choose it as basis for our investigation on the benefits of contextual word embeddings. In addition, inspired by the hierarchical attention approach presented in [27] we add to the architecture of Multi-hop LCR-Rot a new attention layer for high-level representations of the input sentence.

3   Datasets Specification

The data used in this paper was introduced in the SemEval 2015 and 2016 contests to evaluate the ABSA task and is organised as a collection of reviews in

Table 1. Polarity frequencies of SemEval 2015 and SemEval 2016 datasets (ABSA).

	SemEval 2015			SemEval 2016		
	Positive	Neutral	Negative	Positive	Neutral	Negative
Train	72.4%	24.4%	3.2%	70.2%	3.8%	26.0%
Test	53.7%	41.0%	5.3%	74.3%	4.9%	20.8%

the restaurant domain. Each review has a variable number of sentences and each sentence has one or more aspect categories. Each aspect is linked to one target that has assigned a sentiment polarity (*positive, neutral,* and *negative*). Table 1 lists the distribution of sentiment classes in the SemEval 2015 and SemEval 2016 datasets.

4 Method

HAABSA is a hybrid approach for aspect-based sentiment classification with two steps. First, target polarities are predicted using a domain sentiment ontology. If this rule-based method is inconclusive, a neural network is utilised as backup. Section 4.1 introduces the ontology-based rules for sentiment classification. Section 4.2 gives an overview of HAABSA and presents our extensions based on various word embeddings and hierarchical attention. The new method is called HAABSA++, as a reminiscent of the base method name.

4.1 Ontology-Based Rules

The employed ontology is a manually designed domain specification for sentiment polarities of aspects that utilises a hierarchical structure of concepts grouped in three classes [19]. The *SentimentValue* class groups concepts in the *Positive* and *Negative* subclasses, and the *AspectMention* class identifies aspects related to sentiment expressions. The *SentimentMention* class represents sentiment expressions. To compute the sentiment of an aspect, we utilise three rules, described below.

The first rule always assigns to an aspect the generic sentiment of its connected sentiment expression. The second rule identifies the aspect-specific sentiment expression and the sentiment is assigned only if the aspect and the linked expression belong to the same aspect category. The third rule finds the expression with a varying sentiment with respect to the connected aspect and the overall sentiment is inferred based on the pair aspect-sentiment expression. All these rules are mutually exclusive.

The rule-based approach can identify only the *positive* and *negative* sentiments. By design, the neutral sentiment class is not modeled due to its ambiguous semantics. The ontology is inconclusive in two cases: (1) conflicting sentiment (predicting both *positive* and *negative* for a target) or (2) no hits (due to the limited coverage). In these cases a neural network is used as backup.

4.2 Multi-Hop LCR-Rot Neural Network Design

The LSTM-ATT [9,25] model enhances the performance of the LSTM model with attention weighting and is a standard structure integrated by numerous sentiment classifiers. The LCR-Rot model [28] utilises this structure to detect interchangeable information between opinionated expressions and their contexts. In [24], the LCR-Rot model is refined with repeated attention and the new classifier is called Multi-Hop LCR-Rot. In this paper, we explore the effect of different word embeddings on the Multi-Hop LCR-Rot model and propose a hierarchical attention structure to increase the model's flexibility.

The Multi-Hop LCR-Rot neural network splits each sentence into three parts: left context, target, and right context. Each of these three parts feeds three bi-directional LSTMs (bi-LSTMs). Then, a two-step rotatory attention mechanism is applied over the three hidden states associated with the bi-LSTMs (left context: $[h_1^l, ..., h_L^l]$, target: $[h_1^t, ..., h_T^t]$, and right context: $[h_1^r, ..., h_R^r]$, where L, T, and R represent the length of the three input parts). At the first step, the mechanism generates new context representations using target information. Initially, an attention function f is computed taking as input a parameterized product between the hidden states of the context and the target vector r^{t_p} extracted using an average pooling operation. Considering for example the left context, the function f is computed by:

$$f(\underset{1\times1}{h_i^l}, r^{t_p}) = tanh(\underset{1\times2d}{h_i^{l'}} \times \underset{2d\times2d}{W_c^l} \times \underset{2d\times1}{r^{t_p}} + \underset{1\times1}{b_c^l}), \tag{1}$$

where W_c^l is a weight matrix, b_c^l is a bias term, and d represents the dimension of the i-th hidden state h_i^l for $i = 1, ..., L$.

Then, the attention normalised scores α_i^l associated with f are defined using the softmax function as follows:

$$\alpha_i^l = \frac{exp(f(h_i^l, r^{r_p}))}{\sum_{j=1}^{L} exp(f(h_j^l, r^{r_p}))}. \tag{2}$$

In the end, context representations are computed using hidden states weighted by attention scores. For example, the left target2context vector is defined as:

$$\underset{2d\times1}{r^l} = \sum_{i=1}^{L} \underset{1\times1}{\alpha_i^l} \times \underset{2d\times1}{h_i^l}. \tag{3}$$

At the second step of the rotatory attention, target representations are computed similarly, following the previous three equations. The only difference is that instead of the r^{t_p} vector that stands for target information, the left and right contexts vectors (r^l and r^r) are employed to obtain a better target representation. Taking again the left context as example, the left context2target representation r^{t_l} is:

$$\underset{2d\times1}{r^{t_l}} = \sum_{i=1}^{T} \underset{1\times1}{\alpha_i^{t_l}} \times \underset{2d\times1}{h_i^t}, \tag{4}$$

where α^{t_l} represents the target attention scores with respect to the left context computed as above.

The right vectors, target2context and context2target (r^r and r^{t_r}) are computed in a similar way. In a multi-hop rotatory attention mechanism, the two aforementioned steps are applied sequentially for n times. In [24] the optimal n value is three (the trials were executed for four scenarios: $n = \overline{1,4}$). One should note that the r^{t_p} target vector computed using average pooling is used only for the first iteration of the rotatory attention. At the next iterations the vector r^{t_p} is replaced with one of the vectors r^{t_l} or r^{t_r}, depending on the considered context. At the end of the rotatory attention, all the four vectors are concatenated and feed an MLP layer for the final sentiment prediction.

The learning process is realised using a backpropagation algorithm by minimising the cross-entropy loss function with L2 regularization. All weight matrices and biases are initialised by a uniform distribution and are updated using stochastic gradient descent with a momentum term.

4.3   Word Embeddings

The first proposed extension examines the effect of deep context-dependent word embeddings on the overall performance of the neural network. Since the Multi-Hop LCR-Rot model already captures shallow context information for each target of a sentence, it is important to analyse how this architecture is possibly improved when we use deep context-sensitive word representations. Hereinafter, we give a short description of some of the most well-known contextual and non-contextual word embeddings.

Non-contextual Word Embeddings. Non-contextual word embeddings are unique for each word, regardless of its context. As a result, the polysemy of words and the varying local information are ignored. GloVe, word2vec, and fastText context-independent word embeddings are presented below.

GloVe. The GloVe model generates word embeddings using word occurrences instead of language models (like word2vec), which means that the new word embeddings take into account global count statistics, instead of only the local information [14]. The idea behind the GloVe model is to determine two word embeddings w_i and w_k for words i and k, respectively, whose dot product is equal with the logarithmic value of their co-occurrence X_{ik}. The relation is adjusted using two biases (b_i and b_k) for both words i and k as follows:

$$w_i^T w_k + b_i + b_k = log(X_{ik}). \tag{5}$$

The optimal word embeddings are computed using a weighted least-squares method using the cost function defined as:

$$J = \sum_{i=1}^{V} \sum_{k=1}^{V} f(X_{ik})(w_i^T w_k + b_i + b_k - log(X_{ik}))^2, \tag{6}$$

where V is the vocabulary size and $f(X_{ik})$ is a weighting function that has to be continuous, non-decreasing, and to generate relatively small values for large input values. The last two conditions for f are necessary to prevent over-weighting of either rare or frequent co-occurrences. In this paper, we choose to use 300-dimension GloVe word embeddings trained on the Common Crawl (42 billion words) [14].

Word2vec. The word2vec word embeddings were the first widely used word representations and since their introduction they have shown a significant improvement for many NLP tasks. The word2vec model works like a language model that facilitates generation of the more close word representations in the embedding space for words with similar context [13]. The word2vec model has two variations: Continuous-Bag-Of-Words (CBOW) and Skip-Gram (SG). CBOW word embeddings represent the weights of a neural network that maximize the likelihood that words are predicted from a given context of words and SG does it the other way around. Both variations exploit the bag-of-words approach and the sequencing of words in the given or predicted context of words is irrelevant. The CBOW and SG models are trained using the following loss functions:

$$CBOW : J = \frac{1}{V} \sum_{t=1}^{V} \log p(w_t|w_{t-c}, \ldots, w_{t-1}, w_{t+1}, \ldots, w_{t+c}), \qquad (7)$$

$$SG : J = \frac{1}{V} \sum_{t=1}^{V} \sum_{i=t-c, i \neq t}^{t+c} \log p(w_i|w_t). \qquad (8)$$

where $[-c, c]$ is the word context of the word w_t.

CBOW is considered to be faster to train than SG, but SG benefits of a better accuracy for non-frequent words [1]. Therefore, in the present word, both variations of word2vec are examined. The pre-trained word2vec word embeddings we use are already trained on Google News dataset (100 billion words) and their length is 300 features.

FastText. The fastText model computes non-contextual word embeddings using a word2vec SG approach where the word context is represented by its n-grams [3]. As a result, out-of-vocabulary words are better handled as they can benefit from representations closer to the ones of in-vocabulary words with similar meaning in the embedding space. Given that our employed datasets are small, we utilise already computed fastText word embeddings trained on statmt.org news, UMBC webbase corpus, and Wikipedia dumps (16 billion words). The dimensionality of word embeddings is 300.

Contextual Word Embeddings. Contextual word embeddings take into account the context of words which means that they handle better the semantics and the polysemy. Below we focus on ELMo and BERT deep contextual word embeddings.

ELMo. The ELMo word embeddings capture information about the entire input sentence using multiple bidirectional LSTM (bi-LSTM) layers [15]. The main difference between the ELMo model and other language models developed on LSTM layers is that ELMo word embeddings integrate the hidden states of all L bi-LSTMs layers in a linear combination instead of utilising only the hidden states of the last layer. The ELMo model can be considered a task-specific language model that can be adjusted to different computational linguistic tasks by learning different weights for all LSTM layers. ELMo representation of word i for a given *task* $ELMo_i^{task}$ is computed as follows:

$$ELMo_i^{task} = \gamma^{task} \sum_{j=0}^{L} s_j^{task} h_{i,j}, \tag{9}$$

where $h_{i,j}$ represents the concatenated hidden states of the j bi-LSTM layer ($h_{i,j} = [\overrightarrow{h}_{i,j}, \overleftarrow{h}_{i,j}]$), s_j^{task} is its weight, and γ^{task} scales the word embeddings accordingly to the given task.

The model we use to generate ELMo word embeddings employs two bi-LSTM layers with 512 dimension hidden state which means the size of the final word embeddings is 1024. The model is pre-trained on the 1B Word Benchmark dataset.

BERT. The BERT model unlike the ELMo language model that utilises LSTM hidden states, creates contextual word representations by averaging token vectors (unique for each vocabulary word), position embeddings (vectors for word locations in the sentence), and segment embeddings (vectors of sentence indices that contains the given word). The new sequence of word embeddings is given as input to a Transformer encoder [22] based on the (bidirectional) self-attention. The Transformer encoder has L blocks and each one contains a Multi-Head Attention layer followed by a fully connected layer. The output of each block feeds the input of the next one. Each Multi-Head Attention has A parallel attention layers that compute the attention scores for each word with respect to the rest of the words in the sentence. The word representations associated with each Transformer block are computed by concatenating all attention-based representations. Recently, Transformers have become more common than other widely applied neural networks like Convolutional Neural Networks (CNNs) and Recurrent Neural Network (RNNs) due to their capacity to apply the parallelization (as CNNs) and to control long-term dependencies (as RNNs).

The BERT model is pre-trained simultaneously on two tasks: Masked Language Model (MLM) and Next Sentence Prediction (NSP) using BookCorpus (800 million words) and Wikipedia dumps (2,500 million words). The first task employs a bidirectional Transformer to predict some masked words and the second task tries to learn sequence dependencies between sentences. The final loss function is computed as a sum of the task losses. In this paper, BERT word embeddings are generated using the pre-trained BERT Base model (L = 12, A = 12, H = 768), where H stands for hidden states and represents the size of

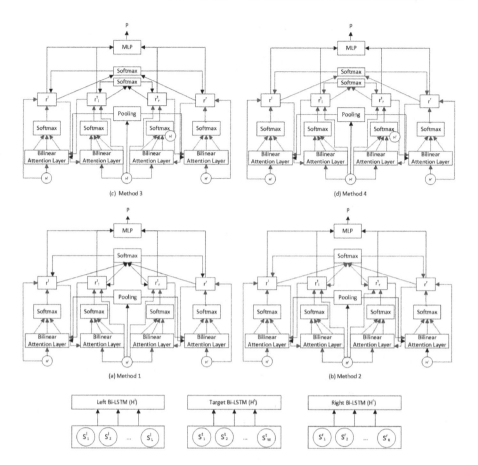

Fig. 1. Multi-Hop LCR-Rot with hierarchical attention

the word embeddings. The final representations of the word i is computed by summing the word embeddings of the last four layers (as it was suggested in [6]):

$$BERT_i = \sum_{j=9}^{12} H_{i,j}. \qquad (10)$$

4.4 Multi-Hop LCR-Rot with Hierarchical Attention

The main disadvantage of Multi-Hop LCR-Rot is that the four target2context and context2target vectors are computed using only local information. Hierarchical attention alleviates this process by providing a high-level representation of the input sentence that updates each target2context and context2target vector with a relevance score computed at the sentence level. The final sentiment prediction considers the newly obtained vectors.

First, we have to compute an attention function f defined as:

$$f(\ v^i\ ) = tanh(\ v^{i'} \times W + b\ ),$$
$$ {\scriptstyle 1\times 1} {\scriptstyle 1\times 2d} \ {\scriptstyle 2d\times 1}\ {\scriptstyle 1\times 1} \qquad (11)$$

where v^i is the representation i of the input sentence ($v^i \in \{r^r, r^l, r^{tr}, r^{t_l}\}$, $i = \overline{1,4}$), W is a weight matrix, and b is a bias. The attention function f is used to compute new attention scores α^i for each input v^i:

$$\alpha^i = \frac{exp(f(v^i)}{\sum_{j=1}^{4} exp(f(v^j))}. \qquad (12)$$

The new scaled context2target or target2context vectors are:

$$v^i = \alpha^i \times v^i , \qquad (13)$$
$${\scriptstyle 2d\times 1} \quad {\scriptstyle 1\times 1} \quad {\scriptstyle 2d\times 1}$$

We consider four methods to introduce hierarchical attention in the architecture of the Multi-Hop LCR-Rot model:

- **Method 1:** attention weighting is applied on the final four vectors of the rotatory attention (Fig. 1 (a)).
- **Method 2:** attention weighting is applied in each iteration of the rotatory attention, on the intermediate four vectors (Fig. 1 (b)).
- **Method 3:** attention weighting is separately applied on the final two context and target vectors pairs of the rotatory attention (Fig. 1 (c)).
- **Method 4:** attention weighting is separately applied in each iteration of the rotatory attention, on the intermediate context and target vectors pairs (Fig. 1 (d)).

To optimise the performance of the newly proposed methods based on hierarchical attention, we have to tune again some of the model's hyperparameters like the learning rate, the momentum term, the L2 regularization term, and the dropout rate (applied to all hidden layers). The algorithm we employ for tuning is a tree-structured Parzen estimator (TPE) [2].

5 Evaluation

We compare our extensions with the baseline Multi-Hop LCR-Rot neural network, a state-of-the-art model in the SC task for both SemEval 2015 and SemEval 2016 datasets. Like [24], our main classifier is a domain sentiment ontology. The importance of the hybrid method is pointed out in [19] where all the inconclusive cases of the domain sentiment ontology are assigned to the majority class of the dataset. The accuracy reported for the reference approach on the SemEval datasets is 63.3% and 76.1%, respectively, much lower than the accuracy of the hybrid approach.

The evaluation is done in terms of training and testing accuracy. Since our work is an extension of the baseline model, we re-run the Multi-Hop LCR-Rot to

Table 2. Comparison of word embeddings for the Multi-Hop LCR-Rot model using accuracy. The best results are given in bold font.

	SemEval 2015		SemEval 2016	
	in-sample	out-of-sample	in-sample	out-of-sample
Context-independent word embeddings				
GloVe (HAABSA)	**88.0%**	80.3%	89.6%	86.4%
CBOW	84.8%	74.6%	82.7%	83.5%
SG	84.7%	76.0%	85.4%	84.1%
FastText	87.4%	79.0%	87.3%	86.5%
Context-dependent word embeddings				
ELMo	85.1%	80.1%	**91.1%**	**86.7%**
BERT	87.9%	**81.1%**	89.2%	**86.7%**

assure a fair comparison. First, the embedding layer is optimised by trying different word embeddings; the results thereof are shown in Table 2. Given that our base model [24] utilises the GloVe embeddings, we start presenting the results for context-independent word representation models. CBOW and SG models lead to the worst predictions and, as it is already expected, the SG model performs better than CBOW by 1.4%–0.6%. The difference between the performance of the fastText and SG models is equal to three percentage points in the SemEval 2015 test dataset, which means that the fastText model is clearly an improvement of the SG model. Even if fastText outperforms the GloVe model by 0.1% for the SemEval 2016 test dataset, given the overall performance of the GloVe model, we can conclude that it is the best context-independent word representation option.

Table 3. Comparison between the four methods proposed for HAABSA++ using accuracy. The best results are given in bold font.

	SemEval 2015		SemEval 2016	
	in-sample	out-of-sample	in-sample	out-of-sample
Method 1	87.9%	81.5%	88.0%	**87.1%**
Method 2	87.9%	**81.7%**	88.7%	86.7%
Method 3	87.8%	81.3%	88.7%	86.7%
Method 4	**88.0%**	**81.7%**	**88.9%**	87.0%

As regards deep contextual word embeddings, we notice that a context-sensitive approach not always leads to better results (the ELMo model outperforms the GloVe model only for the SemEval 2016 dataset). However, the BERT model seems to have the best performance, recording the same testing accuracy as the ELMo model for the SemEval 2016 datasets and exceeding the GloVe model by more than one percentage point for SemEval 2015 datasets.

Table 4. Comparison between HAABSA++ (Method 4) with state-of-the-art models in SC task using accuracy. SW stands for the SemEval Winner (the most effective result reported in the SemEval contest). The best results are given in bold font.

SemEval 2015		SemEval 2016	
HAABSA++ (Method 4)	**81.7%**	XRCE (SW) [16]	**88.1%**
LSTM+SynATT+TarRep [8]	**81.7%**	HAABSA++ (Method 4)	87.0%
PRET+MULT [9]	81.3%	BBLSTM-SL [7]	85.8%
BBLSTM-SL [7]	81.2%	PRET+MULT [9]	85.6%
Sentiue (SW) [17]	78.7%	LSTM+SynATT+TarRep [8]	84.6%

The second extension we present is an adjustment of the rotatory attention to a hierarchical architecture using BERT word embeddings. Table 3 shows that adding new attention layers leads to a more accurate sentiment prediction than the baseline model with BERT word embeddings listed in Table 2. Overall it is fair to consider that the best approach to tackle the hierarchical attention is the Method 4, given the small difference between the first rank and the second rank on the SemEval 2016 test dataset.

Further on, we compare the fourth method with other similar neural networks, state-of-the-art models in SC task. The results are listed in Table 4. We do not replicate previous works and give the results as reported in papers. The best results reported in the SemEval contests are mentioned as well. While for the SemEval 2015 data, our method achieves the highest accuracy (together with the LSTM+ SynATT+TarRep [8] model) for the SemEval 2016 data, it is ranked on the second position.

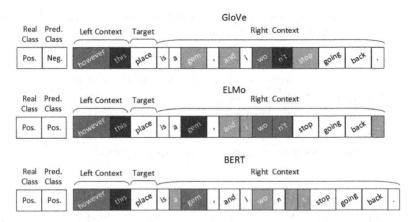

Fig. 2. Target2Context vectors of the Multi-Hop LCR-Rot model computed using GloVe, ELMo, and BERT word embeddings. (Color figure online)

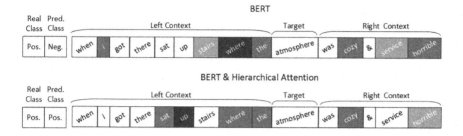

Fig. 3. Target2Context vectors of the Multi-Hop LCR-Rot model with or without hierarchical attention computed using BERT word embeddings.

As we already mentioned, the Multi-Hop LCR-Rot model turns the input sentence into four vectors. Knowing that the length of the target expression is small and usually void of sentiment, we can infer that target2context vectors determine the neural network's performance to a greater extent than context2target vectors. Taking as example two sentences from the SemEval 2016 test dataset, we explore how the embedding layer and the hierarchical attention affects the predicted sentiment polarity via target2context vectors.

Figure 2 graphically presents attention scores associated with target2context vectors for GloVe, ELMo, and BERT word embeddings. The intensity of the blue colour shows the significance of words indicated by the attention scores. The target of the first sentence is the word "place" and the opinionated expression (the word "gem") indicates a positive polarity, and is located in the right context. The left context is too short and irrelevant for the target word. Only ELMo and BERT word embeddings assign the highest attention score to the opinionated word which leads to a good sentiment prediction. On the contrary, the GloVe model finds the word "n't" to be the most relevant for the given example, leading to a negative sentiment prediction. One should note that the BERT model has a slightly different approach to extract tokens of a sentence. This is due to the internal vocabulary used by the BERT model to guarantee the high recall on out-of-sample.

The second example explores the effect of hierarchical attention (Method 4) using BERT word embeddings. The selected sentence given in Fig. 3 has two target expressions with different sentiment polarities. Considering the target "atmosphere", the left context is again irrelevant while the right context contains the sentiment expression together with the second target "service" and its opinionated expression. Even if the simple Multi-Hop LCR-Rot model without hierarchical attention assigns the highest attention scores to the words "cozy" and "horrible", it finds the word "service" as relevant. As a result the sentiment prediction of the target "atmosphere" is wrong. Differently, the neural network with hierarchical attention achieves a good prediction, considering the word "cozy" to be the most relevant to the given target.

6   Conclusion

In this work we extended the backup neural network of the state-of-the-art hybrid approach method for ABSA introduced in [24] using deep contextual word embeddings. Further on, the architecture of the model is integrated with a hierarchical structure that enforces the rotatory attention vectors to take into account high-level representations at the sentence level. Both extensions boost the testing accuracy from 80.3% to 81.7% for SemEval 2015 dataset and from 86.4% to 87.0% for SemEval 2016 dataset.

As deep learning architectures have the tendency to forget useful information from the lower layers, in future work we would like to investigate the effect of adding word embeddings to the upper layers of the architecture. Also we would like to have a better understanding of the model's inner working by applying diagnostic classification to the various layer representations.

References

1. Ay Karakuş, B., Talo, M., Hallaç, İ.R., Aydin, G.: Evaluating deep learning models for sentiment classification. Concurr. Comput.: Pract. Exp. **30**(21), e4783 (2018)
2. Bergstra, J.S., Bardenet, R., Bengio, Y., Kégl, B.: Algorithms for hyper-parameter optimization. In: 25th Annual Conference on Neural Information Processing Systems, NIPS 2011, pp. 2546–2554 (2011)
3. Bojanowski, P., Grave, E., Joulin, A., Mikolov, T.: Enriching word vectors with subword information. Trans. Assoc. Comput. Linguist. **5**, 135–146 (2017)
4. Cambria, E., Poria, S., Hazarika, D., Kwok, K.: SenticNet 5: discovering conceptual primitives for sentiment analysis by means of context embeddings. In: Thirty-Second AAAI Conference on Artificial Intelligence, AAAI 2018, pp. 1795–1802. AAAI Press (2018)
5. Chikersal, P., Poria, S., Cambria, E.: SeNTU: sentiment analysis of tweets by combining a rule-based classifier with supervised learning. In: Proceedings of the 9th International Workshop on Semantic Evaluation, SemEval 2015, pp. 647–651. ACL (2015)
6. Devlin, J., Chang, M.W., Lee, K., Toutanova, K.: BERT: pre-training of deep bidirectional transformers for language understanding. In: 2019 Annual Conference of the North American Chapter of the Association for Computational Linguistics, NAACL-HLT 2019, pp. 4171–4186. ACL (2019)
7. Do, B.T.: Aspect-based sentiment analysis using bitmask bidirectional long short term memory networks. In: 31st International Florida Artificial Intelligence Research Society Conference, FLAIRS 2018, pp. 259–264. AAAI Press (2018)
8. He, R., Lee, W.S., Ng, H.T., Dahlmeier, D.: Effective attention modeling for aspect-level sentiment classification. In: 27th International Conference on Computational Linguistics, COLING 2018, pp. 1121–1131. ACL (2018)
9. He, R., Lee, W.S., Ng, H.T., Dahlmeier, D.: Exploiting document knowledge for aspect-level sentiment classification. arXiv preprint arXiv:1806.04346 (2018)
10. Kiritchenko, S., Zhu, X., Cherry, C., Mohammad, S.: NRC-Canada-2014: detecting aspects and sentiment in customer reviews. In: 8th International Workshop on Semantic Evaluation, SemEval 2014, pp. 437–442. ACL (2014)

11. Liu, B.: Sentiment Analysis: Mining Opinions, Sentiments, and Emotions. Cambridge University Press, Cambridge (2015)
12. Meškelė, D., Frasincar, F.: ALDONA: a hybrid solution for sentence-level aspect-based sentiment analysis using a lexicalized domain ontology and a neural attention model. In: 34th ACM Symposium on Applied Computing, SAC 2019, pp. 2489–2496. ACM (2019)
13. Mikolov, T., Sutskever, I., Chen, K., Corrado, G.S., Dean, J.: Distributed representations of words and phrases and their compositionality. In: 27st Annual Conference on Neural Information Processing Systems, NIPS 2013, pp. 3111–3119 (2013)
14. Pennington, J., Socher, R., Manning, C.: Glove: global vectors for word representation. In: 2014 Conference on Empirical Methods in Natural Language Processing (EMNLP), pp. 1532–1543. ACL (2014)
15. Peters, M.E., et al.: Deep contextualized word representations. In: 2018 Conference of the North American Chapter of the Association for Computational Linguistics-Human Language Technologies, NAACL-HLT 2018, pp. 227–2237. ACL (2018)
16. Pontiki, M., et al.: SemEval-2016 task 5: aspect-based sentiment analysis. In: 10th International Workshop on Semantic Evaluation, SemEval 2016, pp. 19–30. ACL (2016)
17. Pontiki, M., Galanis, D., Papageorgiou, H., Manandhar, S., Androutsopoulos, I.: SemEval-2015 task 12: aspect-based sentiment analysis. In: 9th International Workshop on Semantic Evaluation, SemEval 2015, pp. 486–495. ACL (2015)
18. Schouten, K., Frasincar, F.: Survey on aspect-level sentiment analysis. IEEE Trans. Knowl. Data Eng. **28**(3), 813–830 (2015)
19. Schouten, K., Frasincar, F.: Ontology-driven sentiment analysis of product and service aspects. In: Gangemi, A., et al. (eds.) ESWC 2018. LNCS, vol. 10843, pp. 608–623. Springer, Cham (2018). https://doi.org/10.1007/978-3-319-93417-4_39
20. Schouten, K., Frasincar, F., de Jong, F.: Ontology-enhanced aspect-based sentiment analysis. In: Cabot, J., De Virgilio, R., Torlone, R. (eds.) ICWE 2017. LNCS, vol. 10360, pp. 302–320. Springer, Cham (2017). https://doi.org/10.1007/978-3-319-60131-1_17
21. Schwartz, B.: The Paradox of Choice: Why More is Less. HarperCollins, New York (2004)
22. Vaswani, A., et al.: Attention is all you need. In: 31st Annual Conference on Neural Information Processing Systems, NIPS 2017, pp. 5998–6008 (2017)
23. Wagner, J., et al.: DCU: aspect-based polarity classification for SemEval task 4. In: International Workshop on Semantic Evaluation, SemEval 2014. ACL (2014)
24. Wallaart, O., Frasincar, F.: A hybrid approach for aspect-based sentiment analysis using a lexicalized domain ontology and attentional neural models. In: Hitzler, P., et al. (eds.) ESWC 2019. LNCS, vol. 11503, pp. 363–378. Springer, Cham (2019). https://doi.org/10.1007/978-3-030-21348-0_24
25. Wang, Y., Huang, M., Zhu, X., Zhao, L.: Attention-based LSTM for aspect-level sentiment classification. In: Proceedings of the 2016 Conference on Empirical Methods in Natural Language Processing, EMNLP 2016. pp. 606–615. ACL (2016)
26. Yanase, T., Yanai, K., Sato, M., Miyoshi, T., Niwa, Y.: bunji at SemEval-2016 task 5: neural and syntactic models of entity-attribute relationship for aspect-based sentiment analysis. In: 10th International Workshop on Semantic Evaluation, SemEval 2016, pp. 289–295. ACL (2016)

27. Yang, Z., Yang, D., Dyer, C., He, X., Smola, A., Hovy, E.: Hierarchical attention networks for document classification. In: 2016 Conference of the North American Chapter of the Association for Computational Linguistics-Human Language Technologies, NAACL-HLT 2018, pp. 1480–1489. ACL (2016)
28. Zheng, S., Xia, R.: Left-center-right separated neural network for aspect-based sentiment analysis with rotatory attention. arXiv preprint arXiv:1802.00892 (2018)

Just the Right Mood for HIT!
Analyzing the Role of Worker Moods in Conversational Microtask Crowdsourcing

Sihang Qiu[✉], Ujwal Gadiraju, and Alessandro Bozzon

Web Information Systems Group, Delft University of Technology, Delft, Netherlands
{s.qiu-1,u.k.gadiraju-1,a.bozzon}@tudelft.nl

Abstract. Conversational agents are playing an increasingly important role in providing users with natural communication environments, improving outcomes in a variety of domains in human-computer interaction. Crowdsourcing marketplaces are simultaneously flourishing, and it has never been easier to acquire large-scale human input from online workers. Recent works have revealed the potential of conversational interfaces in improving worker engagement and satisfaction. At the same time, worker moods have been shown to have significant effects on quality related outcomes. Little is known about the role of worker moods in shaping work in conversational microtask crowdsourcing. In this paper, we conducted a crowdsourcing study addressing 600 unique online workers, to investigate the role that worker moods play in conversational microtask crowdsourcing. We also explore whether suitable conversational styles of the agent can affect the performance of workers in different moods. Our results show that workers in a pleasant mood tend to produce significantly higher quality results (over 20%), exhibit greater engagement (an increase by around 19%) and report a lower cognitive load (by over 12%), and a suitable conversational style can have a significant impact on workers in different moods. Our findings advance the current understanding of conversational microtask crowdsourcing and have important implications on designing future conversational crowdsourcing systems.

Keywords: Crowdsourcing · Conversational agent · Conversational style · Worker moods · Worker performance · Moods

1 Introduction

Microtask crowdsourcing is widely being used to gather human input in decomposed tasks called HITs (human intelligence tasks) [12]. Crowdsourcing HITs have been used for a variety of purposes – to build ground truths, understand human behavior, evaluate systems, among others [2,17,30]. Most of the popular commercial microtasking platforms (such as Amazon Mechanical Turk and FigureEight) provide workers with traditional web interfaces for task consumption

© Springer Nature Switzerland AG 2020
M. Bielikova et al. (Eds.): ICWE 2020, LNCS 12128, pp. 381–396, 2020.
https://doi.org/10.1007/978-3-030-50578-3_26

and execution. However, engaging workers in large batches of HITs is challenging. Task abandonment and drop-out effects are commonly observed in microtask marketplaces due to fatigue, boredom or other task-related factors [8].

Conversational interfaces have been argued to have advantages over traditional graphical user interfaces due to having a more human-like interaction [20]. Moreover, recent work has shown that conversational interfaces can be used to improve worker engagement and satisfaction in microtask crowdsourcing [9,18]. Worker *moods* are known to influence the quality of work in the workplace [26], including online microtasking platform where microtasks are executed using traditional web interfaces [28,31]. For example, workers in pleasant moods were found to significantly outperform those in unpleasant moods in a series of information finding HITs [6]. There is a limited understanding however, of how moods of workers interact with conversational interfaces in shaping the quality of their work. An unexplored opportunity to improve conversational microtasking further, lies in analyzing the potential impact of conversational styles [25] of agents on quality related outcomes of workers in different moods. Psychologists and linguists have found that conversational styles play an important role in communication [15,24,25]. Our recent study has investigated whether adapting and personalizing the conversational style of an agent to that of a worker can improve the quality of work [23]. We aim to fill this knowledge gap by addressing the following research questions:

> **RQ1:** *How do worker moods affect their performance, engagement and cognitive load in conversational microtask crowdsourcing?*
> **RQ2:** *How does the conversational style of a conversational agent affect the performance of workers in different moods?*

In this paper, we designed and implemented a conversational interface with different conversational styles that supports workers in the execution of HITs. We carried out a crowdsourcing study with 600 unique workers, across four types of tasks and three different interfaces ($3 \times 4 = 12$ experimental conditions in total). To answer **RQ1**, we evaluate the performance of workers, their engagement (using the User Engagement Scale-*UES*) and cognitive load (NASA-TLX) across different tasks. Results reveal that workers in a pleasant mood tend to produce significantly higher quality results (over 20% improvement), exhibit greater engagement (over 18% improvement) and report a lower cognitive load (a decrease by nearly 13%). To address **RQ2**, we considered three different interfaces (traditional web interface, and conversational interfaces with two conversational styles). Results demonstrate that a suitable conversational style can have a significant impact on workers in terms of their engagement and cognitive task load.

2   Related Work

2.1   Conversational Agents and Crowdsourcing

Conversational agents have been widely used in crowdsourcing workflows. Most studies have used conversational agents with an aim to train natural language understanding and processing models [14]. Another popular application is the usage of conversational agents to connect users with crowd-powered Q&A systems. Such conversational agents act like a representative of the crowd, working for aggregating and conveying information from the crowd to the user. Lasecki et al. designed a conversational agent named Chorus, to help users acquire general knowledge from the crowd [16]. Huang et al. designed a series of conversational systems that improve the effectiveness of collaborative work done by workers [10,11]. In contrast, Curious Cat was designed for acquiring knowledge from users [1]. In this paper, we design and implement a conversational agent that is fully functional on an HTML-based webpage, and supports the execution of HITs.

2.2 Worker Moods in Crowdsourcing

Prior studies have established that worker moods in real-life can affect their task performance; workers in a happy mood were found to exhibit a better performance than those who were less happy [27,29]. Others have shown that worker moods can also impact task execution time [19]. Recent work in the context of online crowdsourcing has revealed the relationship between worker moods and crowdsourcing task performance [31], where moods were measured using the Pick-A-Mood instrument [3]. Statistical tests indicated that worker moods had significant effects on their engagement. Based on these findings, others analyzed the impact of worker moods in struggling web search tasks [6]. Due to the evident impact of worker moods on quality related task outcomes on traditional web interfaces, in this paper we analyze how worker moods interact with conversational interfaces to shape work quality.

3 Method

3.1 Workflow and Task Design

The entire task execution process across different conditions consists of four main stages: self-reported mood (Pick-A-Mood), a short demographic survey, the crowdsourcing HITs, and a post-task survey, as illustrated in Fig. 1.

1) *Pick-A-Mood*. Workers are first asked to self-report their moods using the Pick-A-Mood instrument shown in Fig. 2. Nine moods are presented, and can be grouped into three categories, which are **pleasant** moods (A: *cheerful*, B: *excited*, H: *relaxed* and G: *calm*), **unpleasant**-moods (C: *tense*, D: *irritated*, E: *sad* and F: *bored*) and a **neutral** mood (I).
2) *Demographic Survey*. Next, workers are asked to respond to simple background questions pertaining to their gender, age, ethnicity, educational background, and sources of income.
3) *Crowdsourcing HIT Design*. The actual crowdsourcing HITs are executed on either the conversational interface or the traditional web interface as per the experimental condition. The microtasks batch has 5 mandatory HITs and

45 optional HITs. Workers must complete the 5 mandatory HITs to proceed to the next stage. On completing the mandatory HITs in the conversational interface condition(s), the agent asks the workers if they want to continue on and complete more HITs. In case of the traditional web interface condition(s), workers can click a button named 'I want to answer more questions' to complete more optional HITs.

4) *Post-task Survey.* The last stage of the workflow presents workers with a survey, to gather the worker's perception about the HITs completed. Workers are first asked to complete the User Engagement Scale Short Form [21,22] (UES-SF). Within this, 12 questions need to be answered by adjusting the slider bar ranging from "*1: Strongly Disagree*" to "*7: Strongly Agree*". O'Brien designed the UES for systematically measuring user engagement through self-assessment [21], and later developed the short form of UES (UES-SF) to be suitable for time-sensitive contexts [22]. Next, workers are asked to complete the NASA Task Load Index (NASA-TLX) questionnaire[1], which includes six questions corresponding to different kinds of cognitive task load (ranging from "*0: Very Low*" to "*100: Very High*").

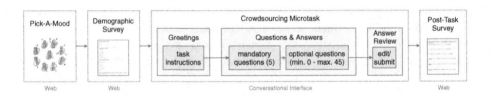

Fig. 1. Crowdsourcing microtask workflow in the conversational interface conditions.

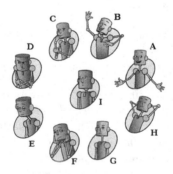

Fig. 2. Pick-A-Mood scale to measure the self-reported mood of crowd workers in different conditions.

---

[1] https://humansystems.arc.nasa.gov/groups/TLX/.

3.2   Conversational Interface

To support the execution of HITs on a conversational interface, we incorporate the following aspects.

1) *Greetings.* Drawing from the essential structure of conversation, the conversational interaction begins with greetings. The goal here is to let workers familiarize themselves with the conversational interface. Next, the conversational interface then helps workers understand how to execute HITs by introducing the task instructions using dialogues.
2) *Questions & Answers.* The conversational interface asks questions to workers, and workers can answer these questions by either typing answers or using provided UI (user interface) elements.
3) *Answer Review.* On the traditional web interface, a worker can easily go back to a question and edit its answer. To realize this affordance in the conversational interface, workers are provided with the opportunity to review and edit their answers if needed, before submitting the HITs.

The user interfaces of most common crowdsourcing platforms mainly support HTML/CSS and Javascript. To make sure the conversational interface can be directly embedded into such platforms, the conversational interface is developed based on a HTML/Javascript chatbot project `chat-bubble`[2]. This allows us to avoid redirecting workers to an external chatting or messaging application.

The conversational interface supports two modes of input– free text and multiple choices, since these two types of input can enable workers to effectively provide judgments for most popular crowdsourcing task types [5]. As shown in Fig. 3, `bubble-like buttons` and `textarea` (at the bottom of UI) are used for supporting the input modes of multiple choice selection and free text entry respectively. For HITs that need special functions (for example, drawing bounding boxes), the input mode of the conversational interface can be ported from traditional web interfaces with little effort, as the conversational agent that we developed fully supports HTML elements.

3.3   Conversational Style

We also investigate whether a suitable conversational style of the conversational agent can affect the performance of workers in different moods. According to Deborah Tannen's seminal theory, conversational styles can be classified into two broad categories, namely *High Involvement* and *High Considerateness* [24]. A conversational style is actually the superimposition of multiple linguistic features and devices [25]. To this end, we selected features and devices that can be applied in our case to create conversation agents emulating High Involvement and High Considerateness conversational styles according to the design criteria from the previous work [23]. Selected features are shown in Table 1. Table 2 shows examples of how the conversational agent opens a conversation while emulating the two different conversational styles.

---

[2] https://github.com/dmitrizzle/chat-bubble.

(a) Button-based input   (b) Text-based input

Fig. 3. Conversational interfaces for execution of HITs provide two input means: (a) buttons and (b) free text.

Table 1. Features of conversation used to design the conversational agents emulating different conversational styles [23].

Features	High-involvement	High-considerateness
Pace	Fast	Slow
Introduction of topics	Without hesitation	With hesitation
Use of syntax	Simple	Complex
Enthusiasm	Enthusiastic	Calm
Directness of content	Direct	Indirect
Use of questions	Frequent	Rare

4   Experiments and Setup

4.1   Experimental Design

In our experiments, we consider two data types (image and text) and two input types (free text and multiple choices), resulting in 4 HIT types (2 data types × 2 input types) - Information Finding (text data + free text input), Sentiment Analysis (text data + multiple choices), CAPTCHA Recognition (image data + free text input) and Image Classification (image data + multiple choices). The experiment is approved by the ethics committee of our university.

In **Information Finding (IF)** tasks, workers are asked to find and provide the rating (stars) of a given store from Google Maps. In **Sentiment Analysis (SA)** tasks, workers are asked to read given reviews of stores and determine the overall sentiment of the review. In **CAPTCHA Recognition (CR)** tasks, workers are asked to observe the image and determine which letters the image contains, and then provide the letters in the same order as they appear in the image. In **Image Classification (IC)** tasks, workers are asked to determine which animal the image contains.

We consider three distinct interfaces: 1) **Traditional web interface (web)** where all the HITs are displayed and answered using traditional HTML elements;

Table 2. Examples of greetings with High-Involvement and High-Considerateness styles.

High involvement	High considerateness
— *Hey! Can you help me with a task called Information Finding?*	— *Thank you in advance for helping me with a task called Information Finding*
— *You must complete this task within 30 min, otherwise I won't pay you*	— *I think 30 min should be more than enough for you to finish*
— *Here is the task instructions. Take a look!*	— *I kindly ask you to have a look at the task instructions*

2) Conversational interface with High-Involvement style (Con+I), where the HITs are presented through an agent with a High-Involvement style; **3) Conversational interface with High-Considerateness style (Con+C)**, which is similar to Con+I, except that the agent converses with workers using a High-Considerateness style.

Thus, the four task types and three interfaces result in a cross-section of 12 experimental conditions. These 12 experimental conditions were published on Amazon Mechanical Turk (MTurk) as HIT batches in our experiments.

4.2 Evaluation Metrics

The evaluation metrics in our experiments are *output quality, worker engagement*, and *cognitive task load*.

Output quality is measured using the accuracy of workers. A worker's accuracy is calculated as the fraction of correct responses over the total number of responses provided by a worker. Here, we consider a HIT to be accurately completed if and only if the response is identical to the ground truth (case insensitive).

Worker engagement is measured using: 1) worker retention, quantified by the number of optional HITs completed (ranging from 0 to 45); and 2) the UES-SF scores ranging from 1 to 7. A higher UES-SF score indicates that the worker is relatively more engaged.

Cognitive task load is evaluated by unweighted NASA-TLX form, consisting of six questions. Workers are asked to give scores ranging from 0 to 100 to these questions. The final TLX score is the mean value of scores given to the six questions. The higher the TLX score is, the greater is the task load perceived by a worker.

4.3 Workers and Rewards

In our setup, each experimental condition consists of 50 HITs and we recruited 50 unique workers to participate and complete the workflow in each case. As a result, we acquired judgments from $12 \times 50 = 600$ unique workers.

After a worker provided a valid `task token` and successfully submitted the HITs on MTurk, the worker was immediately paid 0.5 USD, a fixed payment for successful submission. To reach an average hourly wage of 7.5 USD, we provided bonuses to workers according to the number of optional HITs that they completed. Workers working on image-based tasks (CAPTCHA Recognition and Image Classification) received 0.01 USD for each optional HIT, while workers working on text-based tasks (Information Finding and Sentiment Analysis) received 0.02 USD for each optional HIT.

4.4 Quality Control

Although MTurk allows task requesters to set a qualification type to prevent workers from executing tasks in multiple HIT batches, workers are still able to execute multiple HITs from a single batch. To ensure each worker at most submits once, we recorded unique worker IDs on our server using Javascript, to prevent repeated participation. To ensure reliability of results, validity of responses, and control for potential malicious activity [4,7], we restricted participation by using an MTurk qualification attribute, only allowing crowd workers whose HIT approval rates were greater than 95% to access our tasks.

5 Results

5.1 Worker Demographics

Of the unique 600 workers, 36.6% were female and 63.4% were male. The majority of workers were found to be Asian (46.37%), while 39.12% of workers were Caucasian. Most workers (89.2%) were under 45 years old, and education levels of most workers (74.5%) were higher than (or equal to) Bachelor's degree. In terms of source of income, 38.0% of the workers claimed MTurk was their primary source of income, while 55.4% of the workers worked on MTurk part-time and considered it as their secondary source of income. We publicly released all data (HITs deployed and responses from workers across the different experimental conditions) to facilitate further research for the benefit of the community[3].

5.2 Distribution of Worker Moods

According to the results from the Pick-A-Mood instrument, 74.45% of workers reported to be in a pleasant mood, and 22.67% of workers reported unpleasant moods. Only 2.88% of workers reported to be in a neutral mood. As shown in Fig. 4(a), most workers reported to be in a cheerful mood. Consistent with prior findings in microtasking marketplaces [6,28,31], we found that a majority of workers were in pleasant moods.

---

[3] Companion page: https://sites.google.com/view/icwe2020mood.

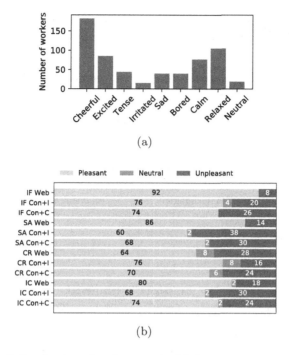

(a)

(b)

Fig. 4. (a) Overall distribution of worker moods; (b) Percentages of workers in pleasant, neutral and unpleasant moods across different experimental conditions.

Figure 4(b) shows the distribution of worker moods across all experimental conditions, where IF, SA, CR and IC represent Information Finding, Sentiment Analysis, CAPTCHA Recognition, and Image Classification respectively. Web, Con+I and Con+C refer to the web interface, conversational interface with involvement-style and conversational interface with considerateness-style in each case. The mood distribution of workers within each experimental condition is similar to the overall mood distribution. Moreover, there were no workers who reported a neutral mood in web interface conditions of Information Finding and Sentiment Analysis tasks, and the conversational interface with High-Considerateness style of Information Finding (IF Web, IF Con+C and SA Web). Since there were only a few workers with a neutral mood who executed HITs across different experimental conditions, we excluded the workers in a neutral mood in our analysis presented further.

5.3   Worker Performance

We analyzed the performance of workers across different experimental conditions. Figure 5 shows the output accuracy of workers. Due to the relative ease of tasks, in case of image-based HITs (CAPTCHA Recognition and Image Classification), the output accuracy of workers is generally higher and more stable across different interfaces and worker moods, compared to that in text-based HITs (Information Finding and Sentiment Analysis).

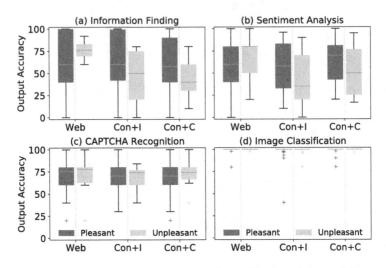

Fig. 5. Boxplots showing the output accuracy (unit: %) of workers in different moods, across different experimental conditions. Red lines in boxplots indicate the median value. (Color figure online)

To assess whether moods can affect worker performances in different interfaces, we conducted t-tests (two-tailed, $\alpha = 0.05$) to test the significance of pairwise differences between different interfaces within one conversational style. Results show that the performance of workers in unpleasant moods, using the conversational interface with High-Considerateness style (Con+C, $\mu = 43.1$, $\sigma = 23.0$) is significantly lower than those using the web interface (Web, $\mu = 76.1$, $\sigma = 11.6$) in Information Finding task (unpleasant, IF Con+C vs. IF Web, $p = 0.02$). In general, we found that the output quality corresponding to workers in unpleasant moods using conversational interfaces (both Con+I and Con+C) is generally lower than those using the traditional web interface on text-based tasks. This can intuitively be explained by the potential aversion of workers to engage with a conversation when in an unpleasant mood [13].

To investigate how workers with different moods perform under the same condition, we tested the statistical differences between the performance of workers across the two conversational styles using t-tests (two-tailed, $\alpha = 0.05$). Workers in pleasant moods performed significantly better than those in unpleasant moods, while using conversational interfaces with High-Involvement (pleasant $\mu \pm \sigma = 68.2 \pm 28.0$ vs. unpleasant $\mu \pm \sigma = 46.3 \pm 28.6$) and High-Considerateness styles (pleasant $\mu \pm \sigma = 63.3 \pm 29.8$ vs. unpleasant $\mu \pm \sigma = 43.1 \pm 23.0$) for executing Information Finding HITs (pleasant vs. unpleasant on IF Con+I and IF Con+C, $p = 0.031$ and $p = 0.033$ respectively). In general, our results suggest that workers in pleasant moods exhibited a higher quality while using conversational interfaces, in comparison to workers in unpleasant moods.

5.4   Worker Engagement

Worker Retention. Fig. 6 shows the number of optional questions that workers answered across different task types, interfaces and moods. Since the number of optional HITs completed does not follow a normal distribution, we conducted Wilcoxon rank-sum tests (two-tailed, $\alpha = 0.05$) to test for statistical significace.

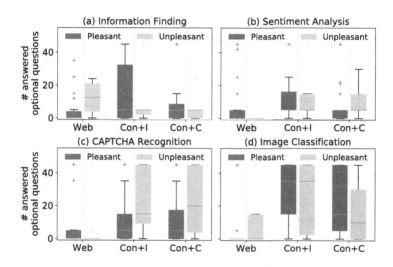

Fig. 6. Boxplots showing the number of optional HITs completed by workers in different moods across different experimental conditions. Red lines in the boxplots represent the median value. (Color figure online)

By comparing worker retention of different moods within each experimental condition, we found that the retention of workers in pleasant moods ($\mu = 7.2$, $\sigma = 10.7$) is significantly lower than that of workers in unpleasant moods ($\mu = 10.8$, $\sigma = 8.1$) using conversational interfaces with the Considerateness style for executing the Sentiment Analysis HITs (pleasant vs. unpleasant on SA Con+C, $p = 0.027$). This suggests that conversation interfaces with a particular conversational style can have the potential to improve worker retention based on the task type.

We found that workers in pleasant moods using conversational interfaces (both High Involvement and High Considerateness, Con+I and Con+C) answered significantly more optional HITs than workers in pleasant moods using traditional web interfaces across all four types of tasks (pleasant, all task types, $p < 0.05$). Workers in unpleasant moods also answered more optional HITs using conversational interfaces (both Con+I and Con+C) than those using web interfaces in Sentiment Analysis and CAPTCHA recognition with significant differences (unpleasant, SA and CR, $p < 0.05$).

User Engagement Scale (UES-SF). We aggregated and analyzed the responses of workers in the post-task survey. Figure 7 depicts the UES-SF scores of workers across all types of tasks, interfaces and two different moods (pleasant vs. unpleasant). To understand the effect of worker moods on user engagement, t-tests (two tailed, $\alpha = 0.05$) are used to test the significance of differences.

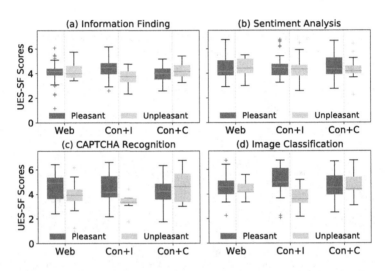

Fig. 7. UES-SF scores across different experimental conditions and worker moods. Red lines in the boxplots indicate the median value. (Color figure online)

Workers in pleasant moods reported significantly higher UES-SF scores than those in unpleasant moods on conversational interfaces with an involvement style (Con+I) for executing Information Finding (pleasant: $\mu = 4.4$, $\sigma = 0.8$ vs. unpleasant: $\mu = 3.7$, $\sigma = 0.7$), CAPTCHA Recognition (pleasant: $\mu = 4.4$, $\sigma = 1.1$ vs. unpleasant: $\mu = 3.4$, $\sigma = 0.8$), and Image Classification (pleasant: $\mu = 5.1$, $\sigma = 1.1$ vs. unpleasant: $\mu = 3.8$, $\sigma = 0.8$) HITs (pleasant vs. unpleasant on IF Con+I, CR Con+I and IC Con+I, $p = 0.02$, $p = 0.014$ and $p = 0.0001$ respectively).

UES-SF scores of workers in unpleasant moods using conversational interfaces with a considerateness style (Con+C) were significantly higher than those using conversational interfaces with an involvement style (Con+I) in CAPTCHA Recognition (Con+I $\mu \pm \sigma = 3.4 \pm 0.8$ vs. Con+C $\mu \pm \sigma = 4.6 \pm 1.3$) and Image Classification (Con+I $\mu \pm \sigma = 3.8 \pm 0.8$ vs. Con+C $\mu \pm \sigma = 4.7 \pm 1.0$) HITs (unpleasant, Con+I vs. Con+C in CR and IC, $p = 0.036$ and $p = 0.0125$ respectively). The High-Involvement conversational interface ($\mu = 4.4$, $\sigma = 0.8$) corresponds to significantly higher UES-SF scores than the High-Considerateness conversational interface ($\mu = 3.9$, $\sigma = 0.7$) for workers in pleasant moods working on Information Finding HITs (pleasant, IF Con+I vs. IF Con+C, $p = 0.013$).

5.5 Cognitive Task Load

We also calculated the un-weighted NASA-TLX scores of all the workers participating in the crowdsourcing experiment. We use t-tests (two-tailed, $\alpha = 0.05$) to test the significance of differences between experimental conditions and worker moods (Fig. 8).

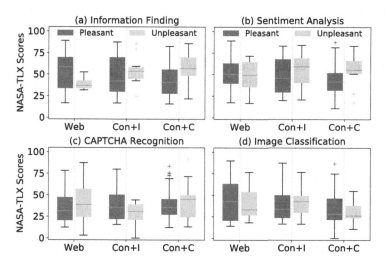

Fig. 8. NASA-TLX scores different experimental conditions and worker moods. Red lines in the boxplots indicate the median value. (Color figure online)

Workers in pleasant moods reported significantly lower NASA-TLX scores than workers in unpleasant moods in conversational interfaces with a High-Considerateness style (Con+C) for Information Finding (pleasant $\mu \pm \sigma = 42.8 \pm 19.1$ vs. unpleasant $\mu \pm \sigma = 55.4 \pm 18.1$) and Sentiment Analysis (pleasant $\mu \pm \sigma = 43.3 \pm 17.2$ vs. unpleasant: $\mu \pm \sigma = 54.9 \pm 18.1$) HITs (pleasant vs. unpleasant on IF Con+C and SA Con+C, $p = 0.046$ and $p = 0.041$ respectively). Thus, workers in pleasant moods perceived lesser cognitive task load in these conditions. Moreover, workers in pleasant moods also perceived less cognitive load while executing the Information Finding HITs on the conversational interface with a High-Considerateness style ($\mu = 42.8$, $\sigma = 19.1$), compared to the traditional web interface ($\mu = 53.5$, $\sigma = 21.1$) (pleasant, IF Con+C vs. IF Web, $p = 0.0200$).

6 Discussion

Implications. Our results clearly indicate that conversational interfaces for HIT execution can improve worker retention in general, irrespective of worker moods. Statistical tests reveal the fact that pleasant workers were more engaged than unpleasant workers in general. This calls for the development and adoption of conversational interfaces for microtask crowdsourcing, and for methods to induce pleasant moods prior to HIT execution. Our results also suggest that conversational interfaces with a High-Considerateness style exhibit the potential to improve engagement of workers in unpleasant moods, while a High-Involvement style exhibits a potential to further engage workers in pleasant moods. In terms of cognitive task load, our findings show that workers in pleasant moods can perceive less task load than those in unpleasant moods while executing text-based HITs, especially when the conversational agent uses a High-Considerateness style. These findings present opportunities for task routing based on worker moods and by leveraging different conversational styles.

Caveats and Limitations. Despite the measures we took to ensure the reliability of responses of workers, as with any research that involves human subjects using self-reporting tools, a threat to the validity of our findings is the veracity of the self-reported moods of workers. However, the overall distribution of crowd worker moods are consistent with prior works that indicate a skew towards pleasant moods [6,31]. The mood distribution of workers is naturally unbalanced. It is however, not ethically sound to elicit unpleasant moods among workers to study the interaction between their moods and conversational styles of an agent.

7   Conclusions and Future Work

Through an experimental study in this paper, we explored how worker moods can affect their output quality, engagement and cognitive task load in conversational microtask crowdsourcing (**RQ1**). We also investigated how the conversational style of the conversational agent can affect the performance of workers in different moods (**RQ2**). We addressed **RQ1** by evaluating worker performance across different tasks. We addressed **RQ2** by comparing quality related outcomes between different interfaces (and conversational styles).

We found that workers in a pleasant mood generally exhibited a higher output quality (over 20% in the best case), higher user engagement (over 18%) and around 13% lesser cognitive task load. We also found strong evidence to suggest that a suitable conversational style can have a significant impact on worker performance under some specific conditions (such as the type of HIT). In the imminent future, we will explore the relationship between worker moods and their preferred conversational style.

References

1. Bradeško, L., Witbrock, M., Starc, J., Herga, Z., Grobelnik, M., Mladenić, D.: Curious cat-mobile, context-aware conversational crowdsourcing knowledge acquisition. ACM Transactions on Information Systems (TOIS) **35**(4) (2017). Article no. 33

2. Demartini, G., Difallah, D.E., Gadiraju, U., Catasta, M., et al.: An introduction to hybrid human-machine information systems. Found. Trends® Web Sci. **7**(1), 1–87 (2017)

3. Desmet, P.M., Vastenburg, M.H., Romero, N.: Mood measurement with Pick-A-Mood: review of current methods and design of a pictorial self-report scale. J. Des. Res. **14**(3), 241–279 (2016)

4. Eickhoff, C., de Vries, A.P.: Increasing cheat robustness of crowdsourcing tasks. Inf. Retrieval **16**(2), 121–137 (2013). https://doi.org/10.1007/s10791-011-9181-9

5. Gadiraju, U., Checco, A., Gupta, N., Demartini, G.: Modus operandi of crowd workers: the invisible role of microtask work environments. Proc. ACM Interact. Mob. Wearable Ubiquit. Technol. **1**(3) (2017). Article no. 49

6. Gadiraju, U., Demartini, G.: Understanding worker moods and reactions to rejection in crowdsourcing. In: Proceedings of the 30th ACM Conference on Hypertext and Social Media, HT 2019, pp. 211–220. ACM, New York (2019)

7. Gadiraju, U., Siehndel, P., Fetahu, B., Kawase, R.: Breaking bad: understanding behavior of crowd workers in categorization microtasks. In: Proceedings of the 26th ACM Conference on Hypertext & Social Media, pp. 33–38 (2015)

8. Han, L., et al.: All those wasted hours: on task abandonment in crowdsourcing. In: Proceedings of the Twelfth ACM International Conference on Web Search and Data Mining, pp. 321–329. ACM (2019)

9. Harms, J., Kucherbaev, P., Bozzon, A., Houben, G.: Approaches for dialog management in conversational agents. IEEE Internet Comput. **23**(2), 13–22 (2019)

10. Huang, T.H.K., Chang, J.C., Bigham, J.P.: Evorus: a crowd-powered conversational assistant built to automate itself over time. In: Proceedings of the 2018 CHI Conference on Human Factors in Computing Systems, p. 295. ACM (2018)

11. Huang, T.H.K., Lasecki, W.S., Bigham, J.P.: Guardian: a crowd-powered spoken dialog system for web APIs. In: Third AAAI Conference on Human Computation and Crowdsourcing (2015)

12. Kittur, A., et al.: The future of crowd work. In: Proceedings of the 2013 Conference on Computer Supported Cooperative Work, pp. 1301–1318. ACM (2013)

13. Koch, A.S., Forgas, J.P., Matovic, D.: Can negative mood improve your conversation? Affective influences on conforming to Grice's communication norms. Eur. J. Soc. Psychol. **43**(5), 326–334 (2013)

14. Kucherbaev, P., Bozzon, A., Houben, G.J.: Human-aided bots. IEEE Internet Comput. **22**(6), 36–43 (2018)

15. Lakoff, R.T.: Stylistic strategies within a grammar of style. Ann. N. Y. Acad. Sci. **327**(1), 53–78 (1979)

16. Lasecki, W.S., Wesley, R., Nichols, J., Kulkarni, A., Allen, J.F., Bigham, J.P.: Chorus: a crowd-powered conversational assistant. In: Proceedings of the 26th Annual ACM Symposium on User Interface Software and Technology, pp. 151–162. ACM (2013)

17. Loni, B., Cheung, L.Y., Riegler, M., Bozzon, A., Gottlieb, L., Larson, M.: Fashion 10000: an enriched social image dataset for fashion and clothing. In: Proceedings of the 5th ACM Multimedia Systems Conference, pp. 41–46. ACM (2014)

18. Mavridis, P., Huang, O., Qiu, S., Gadiraju, U., Bozzon, A.: Chatterbox: conversational interfaces for microtask crowdsourcing. In: Proceedings of the 27th ACM Conference on User Modeling, Adaptation and Personalization, pp. 243–251. ACM (2019)

19. Miner, A.G., Glomb, T.M.: State mood, task performance, and behavior at work: a within-persons approach. Organ. Behav. Hum. Decis. Process. **112**(1), 43–57 (2010)

20. Moore, R.J., Arar, R., Ren, G.J., Szymanski, M.H.: Conversational UX design. In: Proceedings of the 2017 CHI Conference Extended Abstracts on Human Factors in Computing Systems, pp. 492–497. ACM (2017)
21. O'Brien, Heather: Theoretical perspectives on user engagement. In: O'Brien, Heather, Cairns, Paul (eds.) Why Engagement Matters, pp. 1–26. Springer, Cham (2016). https://doi.org/10.1007/978-3-319-27446-1_1
22. O'Brien, H.L., Cairns, P., Hall, M.: A practical approach to measuring user engagement with the refined user engagement scale (UES) and new UES short form. Int. J. Hum. Comput. Stud. **112**, 28–39 (2018)
23. Qiu, S., Gadiraju, U., Bozzon, A.: Improving worker engagement through conversational microtask crowdsourcing. In: Proceedings of the 2020 CHI Conference on Human Factors in Computing Systems, pp. 1–12. ACM (2020)
24. Tannen, D.: Conversational style. In: Psycholinguistic Models of Production, pp. 251–267 (1987)
25. Tannen, D.: Conversational Style: Analyzing Talk Among Friends. Oxford University Press, Oxford (2005)
26. Totterdell, P., Niven, K.: Workplace Moods and Emotions: A Review of Research. Createspace Independent Publishing, Charleston (2014)
27. Wright, T.A., Cropanzano, R.: The happy/productive worker thesis revisited. In: Research in Personnel and Human Resources Management, pp. 269–307. Emerald Group Publishing Limited (2007)
28. Xu, L., Zhou, X., Gadiraju, U.: Revealing the role of user moods in struggling search tasks. In: Proceedings of the 42nd International ACM SIGIR Conference on Research and Development in Information Retrieval, pp. 1249–1252. ACM (2019)
29. Zelenski, J.M., Murphy, S.A., Jenkins, D.A.: The happy-productive worker thesis revisited. J. Happiness Stud. **9**(4), 521–537 (2008). https://doi.org/10.1007/s10902-008-9087-4
30. Zhang, Z., Singh, J., Gadiraju, U., Anand, A.: Dissonance between human and machine understanding. Proc. ACM Hum.-Comput. Interact. **3**(CSCW) (2019). Article no. 56
31. Zhuang, M., Gadiraju, U.: In what mood are you today?: An analysis of crowd workers' mood, performance and engagement. In: Proceedings of the 11th ACM Conference on Web Science, WebSci 2019, Boston, MA, USA, 30 June–03 July 2019, pp. 373–382 (2019). https://doi.org/10.1145/3292522.3326010

Open Data

SolidRDP: Applying Solid Data Containers for Research Data Publishing

André Langer$^{(\boxtimes)}$ ⓘ, Dang Vu Nguyen Hai ⓘ, and Martin Gaedke ⓘ

Chemnitz University of Technology, Chemnitz, Germany
{andre.langer,dang.vu-nguyen-hai,martin.gaedke}@informatik.tu-chemnitz.de

Abstract. In the context of Open Science, researchers are encouraged to publish their research datasets in digital data repositories so that others can find and reuse it.

However, this process is commonly conducted via centralized data management platforms. Research data has to be uploaded to such a platform and this imposes the risk to become dependent from the access control and data exposure capabilities of the platform provider.

Semantic technologies are one approach to improve this situation and manage research datasets in a decentralized way with an interdisciplinary focus. We are particularly interested in Linked Data Platform - based approaches and how good Solid in particular fits for research data publishing (RDP) activities.

In this paper, we therefore present a conceptual RDP model and we assess a container-based approach to publish research data in a Solid environment in a decentralized manner, both from a researcher and developer perspective.

Keywords: Linked Data · Research data management · Data publishing · Solid · Data container · Decentralization

1 Introduction

In existing research data life-cycle models (cf. [2,20]), publishing research data following the FAIR guidelines [19] is an important step to share and reuse these datasets as encouraged by the principles of Open Science[1].

Directory projects such as OpenDOAR[2] nowadays list more than 5,200 research data repositories where research data is uploaded and provided to other interested actors worldwide. However, certain researchers hesitate to use centralized platforms and want to retain control of their research data, as shown in recent surveys from Wiley [17] or the European Union [16] on the data sharing behavior of researchers. The reasons for that are manifold [7] and especially related to data privacy, data transfer and data access concerns.

---

[1] https://www.nature.com/sdata/about/principles.
[2] https://v2.sherpa.ac.uk/view/repository_visualisations/1.html.

© Springer Nature Switzerland AG 2020
M. Bielikova et al. (Eds.): ICWE 2020, LNCS 12128, pp. 399–415, 2020.
https://doi.org/10.1007/978-3-030-50578-3_27

Decentralized approaches gain increasing attention, where research data can remain in the proximate environment and where the researcher instead of a (commercial) service provider is in control of data access regulations and other administrative settings to expose particular research data. Additionally, the demand for sharing research data for inter- and transdisciplinary purposes increases [15].

Semantic technologies already provide necessary means to annotate data with distinct meta information for cross-domain processing and reuse [18], and they allow distributed service architectures to access provided datasets in a decentralized fashion[3]. Server implementations such as in DuraSpace Fedora[4], Apache Marmotta[5] or the Social Linked Data (Solid, sometimes also SoLiD) environment[6] already exist, which implement such a Linked Data Platform behavior.

Solid in particular "proposes a set of conventions and tools for building decentralized social applications based on Linked Data principles"[7] resulting in true data ownership as well as improved data privacy. Personal Online Data Stores, so called PODs, are a key concept providing hosting and data access authorization capabilities in an application-independent proximate user environment. Solid was already applied successfully in different scenarios such as personal data, articles or images [10], but to the best of our knowledge, it has not been applied to RDM so far.

We investigated, to which extend more general research data publishing processes can also benefit from such an approach and present in the following three main contributions as part of the PIROL research project on interdisciplinary research data publishing [8]:

1. We present a reference model that can be used as an abstract framework to describe the actual activities that have to be taken into consideration for research data publishing.
2. We specify a component-based data container concept to publish research datasets and corresponding meta descriptions in a decentralized fashion.
3. We apply the Solid platform to this approach and show in a SolidRDP PoC that a technical implementation of this concept is possible together with practical extensions to use it for decentralized research data publishing.

The rest of the paper is structured in the following way: Sect. 2 describes the problem domain in detail, formalizes it in a dedicated model for research data publishing and defines requirements on a decentralized realization. Section 3 discusses a data container-based approach for that. Section 4 presents our SolidRDP implementation as a proof-of-concept, which is then evaluated in Sect. 5. Section 6 contrasts our work to other existing approaches and Sect. 7 summarizes our results and gives an outlook to future work.

---

[3] https://www.w3.org/TR/ldp/.

[4] https://duraspace.org/fedora/.

[5] https://marmotta.apache.org/.

[6] https://solidproject.org/for-developers/pod-server.

[7] https://solid.mit.edu/.

2   Conceptual Problem Analysis

Research data management (RDM) is a term that describes the way how researchers organize, publish, share, and reuse their research data during and beyond the lifetime of a research project effectively.

In the following, we do not cover the full Research Data Management life-cycle in all steps. Instead, we particularly focus on *Research Data Publishing*. In common data life-cycle models, this process is normally located after the persistent data preservation and before the discovery and reuse of datasets. Apparently, this step is crucial for efficient research according to Open Science, especially in an interdisciplinary usage context. However, it is often simplified to a single activity which is either described as *data publishing, provisioning, sharing* or *giving data access*. In contrast, we emphasize that the publication of research datasets involves multiple process steps. To the best of our knowledge, no well-accepted theoretical foundation for that was presented so far. We therefore first discuss a motivating scenario and then a reference model for research data publishing with necessary process steps, independent if they are carried out all together on a centralized platform or in a decoupled, decentralized environment.

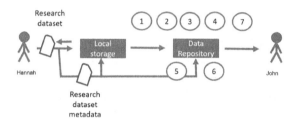

Fig. 1. Research data publishing scenario with 7 identified steps

In a practical scenario as shown in Fig. 1, a scientist with the name *Hannah* is in possession of a digital research dataset, which was created in the context of a research project activity. This dataset is saved on a local storage such as Hannah's computer or a storage device in the research institution and updated from time-to-time to a newer version. To make this data available to other researchers, it has to be transferred (i.e., uploaded) to a publicly accessible research data repository (1), where it is stored (2), (often implicitly) registered (3) in a particular persistent version (4), and described and associated with meta-information (5). Finally, the research dataset is based on additional meta-information such as access regulations and restrictions (6) exposed (7), so that other users such as *John* can find it.

2.1   Conceptual View on Research Data Publishing

The described research data publishing process can therefore be split down into seven relevant activities, as shown in Fig. 2:

Fig. 2. Basic research data publishing reference model

1. **Data Transfer**: Moving the dataset to a publicly accessible repository platform.
2. **Data Storage**: Saving the dataset in a persistent digital fashion.
3. **Data Registration**: Making the data repository aware of the transferred dataset.
4. **Data Versioning**: Handling a dataset in multiple versions.
5. **Data Annotation**: Providing meta-information to describe characteristics of the actual research dataset.
6. **Data Access Control**: Defining access rules and other constraints and restrictions.
7. **Data Exposure**: Finalizing the publishing process so that other users and services can find and access the dataset together with the provided meta-information based on the data repository configuration and access rules.

2.2 Current Situation in Practice

On common research data repository platforms such as *Zenodo, ResearchGate* or *Mendeley Data*, these publishing steps are normally carried out via a centralized infrastructure [12], where a researcher uploads a dataset which is immediately registered, provides basic meta-information online in a user input web interface and exposes the dataset by saving the entered data. Storing this data in a central fashion has the advantage that it improves the discoverability and service providers commonly offer an appealing user interface and large storage capacities for free. However, the research data itself and all related publishing activities rely on the capabilities and attitude of the trusted service provider.

Thus, certain researchers hesitate to use centralized platforms and want to retain control of their research data. Their research data is stored on centralized, institutional and sometimes even commercial server infrastructures, which means the researchers do not truly physically own and manage the data. Apart from that, we face walled gardens and obstacles between domain-specific data repositories that lead to difficulties in cross-domain data exchange and reuse.

We assessed the current situation by conducting an online user survey[8] between May and June 2019 distributed to researchers from multiple research disciplines (36% Applied Sciences, 25% Social Sciences, 21% Formal Sciences, 14% Natural Sciences, 4% Humanities) via direct message, email, and three researcher collaboration groups in social networks with a response rate of 126 full responses. Only 46% of all respondents indicated that they have shared data from their research in the past. We also asked where the participants store their research datasets currently. The results showed that 41% of all participants

---

[8] http://purl.net/net/vsr/solidrdp/presurvey.

"keep research data internally on laptop or personal computer or institutional storage", 43% share research data via Sync&Share services such as GoogleDrive, Nextcloud or Dropbox and 9% of all participants "publish research data on their private website". These are apparently places where researchers think they could have full control of data storage.

2.3 Derived Objectives

A decentralized approach on research data publishing might improve this situation. To develop a concept that enables researchers to publish and share their data in a decentralized and interdisciplinary way, the following objectives are considered:

OBJ1 **Ownership of data storage**: Research datasets shall be stored in an environment related to the owning researcher.

OBJ2 **Support for different formats, shapes and sizes of research datasets**: Publishing arbitrary kinds of research data shall be possible.

OBJ3 **Metadata integration**: Research datasets shall be published together with a corresponding metadata description that makes use of established vocabularies for interdisciplinary discoverability purposes [4].

OBJ4 **User support tools**: The setup of such a decentralized infrastructure as well as the interaction has to be user-friendly for a researcher.

OBJ5 **Data versioning control**: Different versions of research datasets can be published with persistent identifiers.

OBJ6 **Data access control**: Research dataset owners are in full control of data access regulations.

OBJ7 **Data exposure**: Research datasets are provided in a decentralized fashion, but are advertised to other services so that they can be discovered on a global level according to the FAIR principles for research data [19].

3 A Container-Based Approach for Research Data Publishing

In the following, we identify a decentralized approach enriched with semantic technologies as an appropriate way to address these objectives.

Existing solutions for decentralized research data management encompass peer-to-peer-based approaches such as the Dat Project[9] or AcademicTorrent[10], blockchain-based approaches such as datum.org[11] and git-based approaches such as DataLad[12]. We assessed all of these approaches in each of the mentioned categories and carefully compared them against our requirements[13] as shown in Table 1.

---

[9] https://dat.foundation/.
[10] http://academictorrents.com/.
[11] https://datum.org/.
[12] https://www.datalad.org/.
[13] https://vsr.informatik.tu-chemnitz.de/projects/2019/solidrdp/.

Table 1. Assessment of existing decentralized RDM solutions

	P2P-based approaches	Blockchain-based appr.	Git-based approaches
OBJ1: Ownership of data storage	o	o	+
OBJ2: Support for different formats, shapes and sizes of research datasets	+	+	+
OBJ3: Metadata integration	o	o	o
OBJ4: User support tools	+	+	+
OBJ5: Data versioning control	+	-	+
OBJ6: Data access control	-	o	o
OBJ7: Data exposure	-	o	o

+ Completely Fulfilled, o Partially Fulfilled, - Not Fulfilled

Git-based approaches already satisfy these objectives to a partial extent and a researcher can set up an own local repository for managing datasets. However, this data needs to be replicated to a searchable remote repository, e.g., *GitHub*, *GitLab* or *DataLad* so that it is discoverable and reusable by other users which raises data privacy concerns. Furthermore, there are no established Git-based solutions that focus on improving data exchange and reuse in the context of interdisciplinary research data provisioning. Hence, to overcome domain-specific boundaries, it was already suggested to not only "store and distribute (relevant data) systematically but also categorize and link (it) according to the semantic interrelations of the involved disciplinary knowledge domains" [15]. Based on this, Linked Data is considered to be a reasonable approach.

Based on that, we propose the usage of semantic data containers for research data management. Data Containers are a concept already known from the Cloud Computing community. They are practically applied e.g., in *Docker* environments. In this context, they are a bundled package which includes all dependencies to store, organize and use its contained virtual objects independent of the host infrastructure, operating system, communication protocols and storage. They are mainly used for transporting and reliably accessing data in this case. Additionally, these containers can be packed with additional information on data access regulations and privacy control.

A researcher can possess an own (online-accessible) data store in a personal environment (POD). If this personal online data store contains research datasets from multiple research projects organized in virtual research data containers, we will refer to this storage as a *ResearchPOD*. In this context, a data container will not be primarily used for transporting data to different systems to access them by multiple applications, but for giving a researcher an online location where he/she can place and control actual research datasets independently of any institution or application provider. This data can be directly accessed without the need of replications or intransparent redundant copy and check-out processes on different distributed server systems. Therefore, such a data container within a *ResearchPOD* provides different layers for the actual dataset management, semantic metadata information management, version management and access management as depicted in Fig. 3.

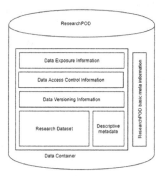

Fig. 3. Layered conceptual structure of a DataContainer within a *ResearchPOD*

In order to realize a decentralized research dataset publishing infrastructure, we identified a set of components that are needed as an extension to Linked Data Platforms such as the original Solid environment, based on our research data publishing reference model from Sect. 2. These components are depicted in Fig. 4.

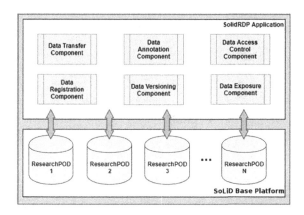

Fig. 4. Components extending the Solid base platform for RDP

In the base layer, a Solid server with its build-in tools and components "allows users to have full control of their data, including access control and storage location" [13]. A researcher can thereby own a personal storage space (*ResearchPOD*) at any location in the web. For authentication, Solid uses WebID as a globally unique decentralized identifier for the user with a mechanism to combine a traditional username-and-password authentication and WebID-TLS delegation. For authorization, Web Access Control (WAC) is used for cross-domain authorization for all particular resources.

On top of that, we identified and added six necessary components to extend a Solid base platform to make it practicably usable for research data publishing. Section 4 provides a detailed description of each component and an implementation as a proof-of-concept in our SolidRDP application. This application can connect to any *ResearchPOD* associated with a WebID of a researcher.

4   The SolidRDP Prototype

Solid Research Data Publishing (SolidRDP) is the conceptual application and extension of a Solid base platform for publishing research data. In contains six essential components in an architecture illustrated in Fig. 5. The components interact with each other to handle two primary entities: the research dataset itself and its corresponding metadata which encompasses descriptive and administrative metadata as well as technical metadata with version information and access control rules. The dotted lines in the figure represent the usage of resource references for the stored corresponding files.

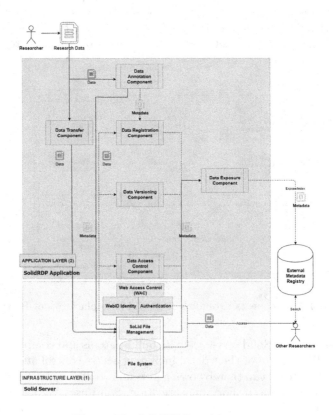

Fig. 5. The SolidRDP architecture

4.1 Components

In the following, we describe each component in detail.

Data Transfer Component. A *DataTransfer* component assists the user to place a research dataset into a data container in the online-accessible *Research-POD* on a Solid server. An upload form in a WebUI is a simple realization of such a component. Other options to pass a research dataset to the storage location use alternative protocols such as SCP or FTP, which also allow a (semi-)automated provisioning and update of research data and the transfer of multiple files at once.

Data Registration Component. As a Solid server manages files as virtual resources independently of the underlying file system, it makes sense to conceptually define a dedicated *Data Registration component*, especially when files are provided in a (semi-)automated fashion. It registers an existing physical dataset for research data publishing and associates additional information such as descriptive metadata with it.

Data Versioning Component. Research datasets are normally not static, and they constantly evolve over time. When the researchers update their datasets on the server, the system needs to preserve all versions of the data file so that other researchers can revert or retrieve a specific version at any point in time. A *Data Versioning component* ensures this persistency on a virtual and physical resource management level and provides appropriate persistent resource identifiers for the registered datasets. Additionally, it provides versioning information as additional meta-information in established vocabularies such as PROV-O and PAV.

Data Annotation Component. Annotation components assist the user in the description of the provided research dataset. This is important, as research data is commonly not self-explanatory. This can either be done by simply providing a static input form in a WebUI asking for relevant meta information such as author data, license information etc., or by using a dedicated independent metadata creation component, that exposes the meta description in an RDF serialization format by using established ontologies.

Data Access Control Component. Solid servers already provide data access definitions by using Web Access Control (WAC) and WebID. However, to manage research datasets and its metadata description, further considerations come into play. First of all, a user-friendly interface is needed, so that researchers can easily influence data privacy settings wrt. *OBJ4* of Sect. 2. Then, the access definition shall allow different levels of granularity both for the targeted audience groups as well as for the resource sets. Add it might be necessary to define individual data access rights for the datasets and for the metadata resources according to the FAIR principles to make metadata always accessible to the outside, even if the access to the actual dataset is restricted.

Data Exposure Component. With *ResearchPODs* containing scientific datasets in data containers, the research data is stored in a decentralized way. Therefore, to make data discoverable and reusable by other researchers, it needs to be exposed and indexed in external research data registries, which can be institutionally driven, domain-specific or general-purpose directories. The research data will not be disclosed to the public because of the issues of data privacy and access control. Instead, the metadata, which contains all necessary meta information and links directly to its data, will be used to expose it.

A *Data Exposure component* will provide a central user interface to present all currently published research datasets to the user and allow the exposure of recently registered datasets. For that, not only the meta-information for a particular dataset can be taken into consideration. A user can also manage additional author-related information and research project specific metadata for describing the discipline and purpose of the data containers with semantic means. The SolidRDP application can then actively report this meta-information to external services, or support harvesting protocols such as semantic versions of OAI-PMH, as shown in Fig. 6.

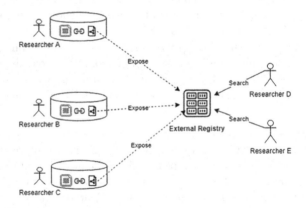

Fig. 6. Exposing metadata to external metadata registry

4.2 Prototypical Implementation

As a proof-of-concept, we implemented all components of SolidRDP in a prototypical realization based on node-solid-server[14] (5.x is the latest version), React[15]

---

[14] https://github.com/solid/node-solid-server.
[15] https://reactjs.org/.

with rdflib[16], solid-auth-client[17] and solid-file-client[18]. A demo can be found at http://purl.net/net/vsr/solidrdp. To the best of our knowledge, SolidRDP is the first Solid application particularly concentrating on research data management and publishing.

For the sake of simplicity, the *Data transfer component* is realized with a file upload control within the web-based file manager client. After uploading a new research dataset, it is currently automatically registered in the SolidRDP application and semantic metadata can be added to it as shown in Fig. 7. At the moment, we allow the explicit provision of a metadata description file by the user. Alternatively, a separate *Data annotation* component could be opened and displayed that collects relevant metadata in a semantic-aware user interface and returns it in an RDF serialization format such as Turtle, which is then added to the meta description file for the uploaded research dataset.

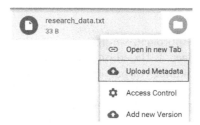

Fig. 7. SolidRDP user interface

Furthermore, the user can restrict the access to the research dataset to particular user groups or individuals by using an implemented *Data access control component*. These access control lists can be individually defined for a particular research data resource, its metadata or for an entire research data container within the *ResearchPOD* of the user. The entered information in this component is then added to the corresponding *acl* file on the Solid server. A *Data versioning component* keeps track of the current file version and adds this version information also to the corresponding metadata file. Furthermore, a user has the possibility in the web user interface to also explicitly upload a new version of a research dataset.

Finally, a *Data exposure component* handles the actual publishing step in our research data publishing scenario by providing a central access point to advertise metadata for all released research datasets in the background. Therefore, additional form input controls are provided to describe in a semantic fashion further characteristics of the author and particular research data containers, such as their knowledge domain and context, to improve interdisciplinary discoverability and reuse.

---

[16] https://github.com/linkeddata/rdflib.js/.

[17] https://github.com/solid/solid-auth-client.

[18] https://github.com/jeff-zucker/solid-file-client.

The SolidRDP application prototypically shows, that a researcher can publish a new research dataset in a decentralized fashion by simply transferring it into a pre-configured data container in an own *ResearchPOD* by using a web-based upload functionality of the SolidRDP web application together with a metadata description. Following the research data management life-cycle, this dataset can then be referenced in other research management and authoring applications by simply using the provided URI as a persistent identifier (PID) for the Linked Data resource. Also the provided SolidRDP metadata description file can be reused to publish derivations of a certain dataset while referencing provenance information of the original dataset. All other steps provided by the described RDP components are optional and give the researcher additional freedom and possibilities to integrate other existing tools or to (semi-)automate the publishing process.

5   Evaluation

To assess our SolidRDP approach, we first implemented the idea as a proof-of-concept as described in Sect. 4. Based on this demonstrator, we ran a study lab with 15 candidates. The number of participants is sufficient for usability testing in accordance to Nielsen and Landauer [11]. All participants were researchers and they were randomly invited to attend the study lab. In addition, all the participants already had experience in using a research data management systems and/or Git for data provision. The participation was voluntary without any incentives.

We conducted this study lab in a supervised fashion by sitting next to the participants, observing the way they complete a list of predefined tasks based on an instruction sheet. In order to avoid affecting their decision making, we provided an online questionnaire to them and gave time to evaluate our SolidRDP application. The standardized questions of interest were directly aligned to the criteria used for the assessment of existing solutions from Sect. 3. Finally, we used the observations and survey result[19] to assess our proposed approach.

We therefore applied the objectives-based evaluation method [14] as the most prevalent approach in program evaluation.

As the practical adoption of our approach has not yet reached a certain level so that a credible field experiment could be conducted and profoundly reviewed, an objectives-based study is a questions-oriented evaluation approach that can be performed in the meantime internally by program developers by "specifying operational objectives and collecting and analyzing pertinent information to determine how well each objective was achieved".

5.1   OBJ1: Ownership of Data Storage

To store research datasets in an environment related to the researcher, our Solid-based approach provides the researchers with the freedom to choose where their

---

[19] http://www.purl.net/net/vsr/solidrdp/postsurvey.

data resides. They have an option to set up their own Solid server (a single-user mode), which leads to the full ownership of data storage. Thus, research data is stored in only one place, in a decentralized fashion, and therefore avoid the issue of data replication or data cloning. In the survey result, 14/15 participants agreed that they had full control (add/edit/remove) of their research data via the SolidRDP application.

5.2 OBJ2: Support for Different Formats, Shapes and Sizes of Research Datasets

To publish arbitrary kinds of research data, the SolidRDP application is built on top of a Solid server, which can deal with two kinds of resources: (1) Linked Data resources (2) Everything else (binary data and non-linked-data structured text). In our usability test, all of the survey participants (15/15) confirmed that they could upload multiple files with different shapes and file types into their *ResearchPOD*.

5.3 OBJ3: Metadata Integration

To publish research datasets shall together with a corresponding metadata description that makes use of established vocabularies for interdisciplinary discoverability purposes, the SolidRDP application is designed to satisfy this requirement by integrating the metadata seamlessly into the system. The metadata we use in this application is expressed in RDF instead of plain text, HTML, or XML. It does not only contain some basic information (title, description, authors, and creation date) but also information about discipline(s), the context of research, connection to its data, and version. The metadata can also be extendable with any relevant information that can support for interdisciplinary research. In the usability test, all of the participants (15/15) confirmed that an URL of research data is saved automatically to the content of metadata after it is uploaded to the POD and the metadata can be accessed in public mode.

5.4 OBJ4: User Support Tools

To have a user-friendly setup of such a decentralized infrastructure as well as the interaction with a researcher, the SolidRDP application provides context menu and various web forms both for IT- and Non-IT-researchers, so that they can interact easily with the system. Complexity is hidden by the application and the user can accomplish all tasks via GUI. Besides, the application does not require installation of any additional tools as well as new knowledge to interact with the Solid POD. We asked the users about the ease of the User Interface and 11/15 participants agreed to the convenience when using the application.

5.5   OBJ5: Data Versioning Control

To publish different versions of research datasets with persistent identifiers, the SolidRDP application provides a Data Versioning component to control data versioning. For simplicity, this prototype supports a basic and straightforward way to backup versions. As the result of the question "Do you think the SolidRDP provides sufficient functionalities (add a new version, revert...) for Data Versioning Control?", 13/15 participants considered it as Good or Excellent. Hence, the Solid-based approach can adequately meet this requirement.

5.6   OBJ6: Data Access Control

To be in full control of data access regulations, Data access control is required to be flexible, sophisticated, as well as cross-system. Based on our analysis result, this requirement is one of the most unsatisfied requirements in other existing approaches. By using Web Access Control with access control list (.acl), data access control level downs to the granularity of files. For example, researchers can apply access control for each research data file or each container, configure private mode for sensitive data, and grant different permissions to different groups of researchers for the same research data. Moreover, the Solid-based approach uses WebID, thus, it does not restrict the researcher to have an account on a given server to have access permission. In the assessment survey, the participants were asked to run a usability test for the Data Access Control component. The test contains two tasks: (1) access a file when it is in private mode and (2) access the same file after it is set to public mode. All of the participants confirmed that the Access Control function worked adequately.

5.7   OBJ7: Data Exposure

To advertise research datasets to other services so that they can be discovered on a global level, our Solid-based approach exposes only the URL metadata instead of research data itself. By doing this way, there is no data replication, and data ownership can be guaranteed. To support interdisciplinary research projects, the metadata URL is exposed with some extra meta-information, e.g., title, authors, discipline, and relevant keywords.

6   Related Work

DataHubs are an established means to gather research datasets in a central fashion. Established solutions are commonly based on data repository systems such as CKAN, DSpace or Invenio and provide domain-specific, institutional or general-purpose platforms where research datasets can be published [9]. However, this may create user concerns wrt. data ownership, data privacy issues, and data reuse by other users as already analyzed in surveys such as [7]. This applies also to current projects such as OpenAIREs[20]] Zenodo or the EOSC (European Open Science Cloud) with a replication network of data hubs among participating countries.

A variety of alternative solutions [1] was already proposed in the past to allow actual decentralized research data management and sharing scenarios, cf. Sect. 3. Data replication among multiple instances and a lack of semantic, interdisciplinary-oriented means for metadata annotation were also here crucial issues.

The idea to use Linked Data for that purpose was already realized in LDP applications[21] such as Fedora[22], however studies such as from Khan [5] state, that "though Fedora provides the best repository framework as compared to other digital repository software systems, (but) it appeals to high technical end users and as a result there are not as many installations of the software".

Linked Open Data as a Service by Kim et al. [6] is a proposed approach, that also applied the idea to manage datasets together with metadata description files in data containers. However, its practical application DaPaas also focuses on Cloud-based publishing activities and the corresponding website was not accessible at the time of this paper submission. The Dataverse Project [3] is another alternative to build research data repositories with increasing market penetration, but focusing on the centralized concept of combining dataverses.

Instead, our suggested SolidRDP approach relies solely on standardized based technologies and proposes interchangeable, component-based extensions for the Solid environment [10,13], so that it can be directly applied for decentralized research dataset publishing scenarios.

7   Conclusion

The research contribution of this paper is a conceptual model for research dataset publishing and a container-based approach to realize this process in a decentralized environment based on Linked Data Platforms. Therefore, six exchangeable components for Research *Data Transfer*, *Data Registration*, *Data Annotation*, *Data Versioning*, *Data Annotation* and *Data Exposure* were proposed and described in an application layer on top of a Linked Data Platform and implemented as an extension to the Solid base platform for decentralized research data publishing purposes.

The SolidRDP application supports any existing Solid POD and aims to support the researcher to store their research dataset in project or knowledge discipline related data containers. Therefore, it can (1) contribute to the issue of data privacy, and (2) improve data exchange and reuse in an interdisciplinary-driven, hyper-connected world through the usage and exposure of semantic research

---

[20] https://www.openaire.eu/.

[21] https://www.w3.org/wiki/LDP_Implementations.

[22] https://duraspace.org/fedora/.

dataset meta descriptions. The assessment of a fully-functional prototype of the SolidRDP application was done by conducting a lab study with end-users, where 73,3 % of all test candidates regarded the presented user interface as usable and appropriate.

In future activities, it makes sense to investigate the presented SolidRDP components separately in more detail. The Data transfer component is so far realized in a very simple fashion as a WebUI upload control, which is not very efficient for transferring a large number of files and still involves human interaction. Similar, the integration of alternative metadata annotation components dedicated for research dataset descriptions should be considered. For the Data versioning component, currently the SolidRDP application keeps track on the version management internally itself. Last, the active and passive exposure of research data meta-information to external registries has only been briefly discussed in this paper.

Furthermore, the analysis of research dataset discovery aspects in decentralized *ResearchPOD* environments is of high interest as this paper set a primary focus on the publishing process for research datasets. Also the integration of these *ResearchPODs* in existing research environments is worth to further investigate.

Acknowledgment. This work was funded by the Deutsche Forschungsgemeinschaft (DFG, German Research Foundation) – Project-ID 416228727 – SFB 1410.

References

1. Amorim, R.C., Castro, J.A., Rocha da Silva, J., Ribeiro, C.: A comparison of research data management platforms: architecture, flexible metadata and interoperability. Univers. Access Inf. Soc. **16**(4), 851–862 (2017)
2. Charalabidis, Y., Zuiderwijk, A., Alexopoulos, C., Janssen, M., Lampoltshammer, T., Ferro, E.: The multiple life cycles of open data creation and use. In: Charalabidis, Y., Zuiderwijk, A., Alexopoulos, C., Janssen, M., Lampoltshammer, T., Ferro, E. (eds.) The World of Open Data. PAIT, vol. 28, pp. 11–31. Springer, Cham (2018). https://doi.org/10.1007/978-3-319-90850-2_2
3. Crosas, M.: The dataverse network: an open-source application for sharing, discovering and preserving data. D-Lib Mag. **17**, 2 (2011)
4. Curdt, C., Hoffmeister, D., Waldhoff, G., Jekel, C., Bareth, G.: Development of a metadata manegement system for an interdisciplinary research project. ISPRS Ann. Photogramm. Remote Sens. Spat. Inf. Sci. **I–4**, 7–12 (2012)
5. Khan, S.: Dspace or Fedora: which is a better solution? SRELS J. Inf. Manag. **56**(1), 45–50 (2019)
6. Kim, S.H., Berlocher, I., Lee, T.: RDF based linked open data management as a DaaS platform LODaaS (linked open data as a service). In: ALLDATA 2015, (2015)
7. Kim, Y., Stanton, J.M.: Institutional and individual factors affecting scientists' data-sharing behaviors: a multilevel analysis. J. Assoc. Inf. Sci. Technol. **67**(4), 776–799 (2016)

8. Langer, A.: PIROL: cross-domain research data publishing with linked data technologies. In: La Rosa, M., Plebani, P., Reichert, M. (eds.) Proceedings of the Doctoral Consortium Papers Presented at the 31st CAiSE 2019, pp. 43–51. CEUR, Rome (2019)

9. Langer, A., Bilz, E., Gaedke, M.: Analysis of current RDM applications for the interdisciplinary publication of research data. In: SEM4TRA-AMAR@SEMANTICS (2019)

10. Mansour, E., Sambra, A.V., Hawke, S., et al.: A demonstration of the solid platform for social web applications. In: Proceedings of the 25th International Conference Companion on World Wide Web, WWW 2016 Companion, pp. 223–226. International World Wide Web Conferences Steering Committee, Republic and Canton of Geneva, Switzerland (2016)

11. Nielsen, J., Landauer, T.K.: A mathematical model of the finding of usability problems. In: Proceedings of the INTERACT '93 and CHI '93 Conference on Human Factors in Computing Systems, CHI 1993, pp. 206–213. ACM, New York (1993)

12. Robinson, D.C., Hand, J.A., Madsen, M.B., McKelvey, K.R.: The Dat Project, an open and decentralized research data tool. Sci. Data **5**(1), 180221 (2018)

13. Sambra, A.V., Mansour, E., Hawke, S., et al.: Solid: a platform for decentralized social applications based on linked data (2016)

14. Stufflebeam, D.: Evaluation model. New Dir. Eval. **2001**(89), 7–98 (2001)

15. Wang, W., Göpfert, T., Stark, R.: Data management in collaborative interdisciplinary research projects—conclusions from the digitalization of research in sustainable manufacturing. ISPRS Int. J. Geo-Inf. **5**(4), 41 (2016)

16. Website of the European Commission: Open Science Monitor (2018). https://ec.europa.eu/info/research-and-innovation/strategy/goals-research-and-innovation-policy/open-science/open-science-monitor/facts-and-figures-open-research-data_en

17. Wiley: Global Data Sharing Trends (2016). https://authorservices.wiley.com/asset/photos/licensing-and-open-access-photos/Wiley%20Global%20Data%20Sharing%20Infographic%20June%202017.pdf

18. Wiljes, C., Jahn, N., Lier, F., et al.: Towards linked research data: an institutional approach. In: 3rd Workshop on Semantic Publishing (SePublica), no. 994 pp. 27–38 (2013)

19. Wilkinson, M.D., Dumontier, M., Aalbersberg, I.J., et al.: The FAIR guiding principles for scientific data management and stewardship. Sci. Data **3**(1), 160018 (2016)

20. Wissik, T., Durčo, M.: Research data workflows: from research data lifecycle models to institutional solutions. In: Selected Papers from the CLARIN Annual Conference 2015, Wroclaw, Poland, 14–16 October 2015, no. 123, pp. 94–107. Linköping University Electronic Press (2016)

Applying Natural Language Processing Techniques to Generate Open Data Web APIs Documentation

César González-Mora[✉], Cristina Barros, Irene Garrigós, Jose Zubcoff,
Elena Lloret, and Jose-Norberto Mazón

Department of Software and Computing Systems,
University of Alicante, Alicante, Spain
{cgmora,cbarros,igarrigos,jose.zubcoff,elena.lloret,jnmazon}@ua.es

Abstract. Information access globalisation has resulted in the continuous growing of online available data on the Web, especially open data portals. However, in current open data portals, data is difficult to understand and access. One of the reasons of such difficulty is the lack of suitable mechanisms to extract and learn valuable information from existing open data, such as Web Application Programming Interfaces (APIs) with proper documentation. Actually, in most cases, open data Web APIs documentation is very rudimentary, hard to follow, and sometimes incomplete or even inaccurate. To solve these data management problems, this paper proposes an approach to automatically generate Web API's documentation which is both machine and user readable. Our approach consists of applying natural language processing techniques to create OpenAPI documentations. This manner, the access to data is facilitated because of the improvement on the comprehension of the APIs, thus promoting the reusability of data. The feasibility of our approach is presented through a case study that shows and compares the benefits of using our OpenAPI documentation process within an open data web API.

Keywords: Open data Web API · Natural Language Processing · Natural Language Generation

1 Introduction

Nowadays, the Web has become an important information platform, and because of this, there is an information overload [4]. Worldwide governments and organisations are increasingly generating and publishing data online [22], producing economic and social benefits, such as innovation and transparency. While the existence of large amounts of data may be regarded as an advantage, it can actually be a pitfall because this amount of sources are difficult to be properly managed [8]. The most adopted approach to handle open data available are Web APIs [11] since they are a key feature of open data platforms, allowing developers to build their own applications and bring open data to citizens [8].

© Springer Nature Switzerland AG 2020
M. Bielikova et al. (Eds.): ICWE 2020, LNCS 12128, pp. 416–432, 2020.
https://doi.org/10.1007/978-3-030-50578-3_28

Unfortunately, the available APIs to access open data are generally incomplete because they lack adequate documentation [1]. The value of data is then limited by our ability to interpret and comprehend it [23]; therefore, having comprehensive and accurate documentation is key to reuse large amounts of data [1]. Existing works on API documentation [34] have suggested that a relevant and useful documentation, including explanations and examples of their use, is a key factor for the wide use of APIs. A proper documentation is even more important when exposing data through query-level Web APIs (i.e., Web APIs that directly access sources to retrieve required data) in order to enable the creation of third-party solutions that reuse the underlying data [12].

Furthermore, an important factor to attract users and increase the value of APIs consists of facilitating its use by an accurate, complete and interactive documentation [12]. However, this documentation is generally very rudimentary, hard to follow, and sometimes incomplete or even inaccurate [1]. Poor and incomplete documentation is one of the main obstacles faced by developers, so they need to deeply evaluate new APIs in order to understand and use them correctly [34], which entails an effort that hampers the reuse of open data. Moreover, in other cases the documentation of REST APIs is manually generated and provided as plain text, preventing users to take advantage of having a machine-readable specification automatically generated [9]. To the best of the authors' knowledge, the APIs manually documented are generally focused on descriptions understandable by humans but machine-processable descriptions are missing [24]. On the other hand, the APIs documented automatically are focus on the specification and definition of the API rather than in user-readable descriptions, such as in [15]. With the information gathered from existing research, such as [1,12,28,38], some conclusions were drawn. There are currently different types of Web APIs documentation: (i) presented as plain text without following any kind of documentation standard, which promotes the readability for users but is difficult to process by machines; (ii) documentation created manually following the OpenAPI standard, which is machine-readable but because of the human factor it is error prone and has a high cost; and finally, (iii) the documentation generated automatically in OpenAPI, which is generalisable (can be applied for any API documentation) and machine-readable, but it is difficult to read by users.

Natural Language Processing (NLP) research area could contribute to overcome the problem of lack of API documentation [15] by generating text readable by both users and machines. This would facilitate the understanding and analysis of information. Therefore, the difficulty of reading machine-readable documentation by users can be solved by applying NLP techniques, which are able to generate text readable by users. This area is a computational subfield of artificial intelligence whose main purpose relies on the analysis, processing, generation and representation of natural language [10]. Within the areas enclosed in NLP, when considering the automatic generation of documentation descriptions, the area of Natural Language Generation (NLG) is essential. The main aim of this area is to develop techniques capable of generating human utterances, whether the input to these techniques is text or non-linguistic data [6]. NLG has been used in many applications, such as text summarisation [19], dialog systems [20] or the generation of simplified texts [27]. Moreover, it has been also widely employed and integrated in different research areas, such as in computer vision, for the generation of textual descriptions for human activities in videos [2]; or in business intelligence, for the generation of reports and real time notifications about the state of a company's IT services [33]. Due to the great functionality and adaptability of NLG, the use of its techniques can be beneficial in the present research work about generation of API documentation, providing documentation with natural language descriptions.

For facilitating access to data by improving the comprehension of Web APIs, the main goal of this research is to propose the generation of suitable documentation for Web APIs in a process based on automatic, generic and standardised generation mechanisms. Our proposal is novel for the state of the art, since the main efforts of existing related work [9,12,13,18,26,29,32,36] are on the generation of documentation for many different purposes in particular scenarios, but they do not generally focus on open data Web APIs and do not take into account the positive impact that generating NL API descriptions may bring. Therefore, new approaches about the automatic generation of API documentation are needed [1] to improve the comprehension of APIs and the reusability of data. Our contributions to the field are as follows: (i) a novel freestanding approach for tackling the challenge of understanding open data available through Web APIs; (ii) a complete documentation which in addition to including easy to process specifications for machines also adds easy to read descriptions for users, facilitating the reuse of data; and (iii) the natural language descriptions included are generated automatically using a NLG template-based approach in conjunction with semantic knowledge, rather than manually for each API. It reduces the cost and effort of documenting APIs and thus enhances the data reuse process.

This article is structured as follows. In Sect. 2, the related work is described. Then, Sect. 3 presents the overview of the documentation generation approach with natural language descriptions, followed by its detailed explanation. Then, in Sect. 4, the approach is validated with different examples. Finally, the paper concludes in Sect. 5.

2   Related Work

In this section we are going to analyse and compare the existing related work about documenting APIs with NLP with our research. In this sense, the main efforts in API documentation will be discussed first and the generation of text from the NLP perspective will be further analysed.

From the point of view of the API documentation generation, the main efforts have been focused on the creation of basic documentation (i.e., a machine-readable specification), leaving in a secondary plane the natural language descriptions of the API methods. In general, the methods' descriptions are often set manually by the researchers. In other cases, these descriptions are generated as a rough draft containing a few keywords related to the overall behaviour of the method, or they are not generated at all. Some examples of this type of approaches can be found in [36], where a set of techniques for generating structured documentation of web APIs from usage examples are detailed. The authors propose a first step towards automatically learning complete service descriptions. However, the generation of methods' descriptions is not tackled. Also, the authors of this paper proposed an automatic API generation process[1] which also generates API documentation, but it includes very simple descriptions with keywords extracted from API methods, without using natural language. In [18] the authors present a new framework for generating titles for web tables. This is accomplished by extracting keywords that have potentially relevant information to the table. The proposed technique is the first to consider text-generation methods for table titles. However, NLG is not applied to generate documentation and it is based in existing table descriptions in plain text. Another paper [29] presents a technique to automatically generate human readable summaries for Java classes. The proposed tool determines the class and method stereotypes and uses them to select the information to be included in the documentation. However, this text generation approach is only valid for programming code documentation and it does not address the description of APIs in natural language. Moreover, the documentation generated is only about a general vision of the class, but the explanation of each method of the class is missing in contrast to our proposal. There are also some research works [9,12,26,32] that deal with automatically inferring API specifications from manually written documentation. In [32] it is used NLP techniques in order to infer an API specification from existing natural language documentation of the API, and in [12] they use HTTP requests to generate machine-readable documentation and combine it with existing human-readable information in order to provide complete API documentation. In [9], the authors present an approach for automatically transform HTML documentations into OpenAPI specifications. Moreover, in [26] API documents using semantics based on word embeddings for code migration purposes is analysed. However, in these investigations the problem is handled in another way contrary to ours because they assume handwritten API descriptions and then they generate machine-readable documentation based on specific keywords. But the important problem of generating complex descriptions of the API in natural language is not addressed. The importance and usefulness of API documentation, especially in OpenAPI format is emphasised in [16] and [35]. They deal with generating models from API documentations, but the problem of API documentation descriptions' quality is not addressed and they do not help in the generation of these descriptions. Moreover, the research presented in [1] is focused on improving existing data-intensive APIs and their maintenance through the analysis of their usage by users. From this analysis, the documentation of the API can then be improved. Related to the readability of Web Services, in [13] the authors propose a practical metric to quantify readability in WSDL documents, and a set of best practices to improve WSDL readability.

---

[1] https://github.com/cgmora12/AG.

From the point of view of NLP, as mentioned before, the NLG task is essential since it allows the automatic generation of text regardless of the type of input (e.g., text or non-linguistic data). This task has been commonly addressed through the use of knowledge-based approaches. This type of approaches commonly relies on the use of templates and rules for generating text [39]. For example, [14] describes an application that generates a set of sentences detailing the driving activity within a simulation environment. A set of data from the driving simulator (e.g., vehicle speed, track width, percentage of brake usage, etc.) is taken as input, and, with the use of granular linguistic model of a phenomenon techniques and templates, a summary of the driving activity is generated. PASS [25] is another example of system that describes non-linguistic data, which generates soccer reports. This system creates a summary of a specific match employing a template-based approach. The input to this system is match statistics and heterogeneous data such as the league, the date, the match events, the players, the total number of shots or the accuracy of the passes. The templates used by the system PASS were manually derived from sentences in the MeMo FC corpus [7]. Another example is the work presented in [37], where a computational system for generating linguistic descriptions from video camera images, in the context of traffic in a roundabout, is described. In this sense, the authors first analyse the image to obtain information about the vehicles in the roundabout entering lanes and then generate a description of the overall roundabout status using fuzzy logic and templates. Furthermore, within the NLG field there has been increased interest in the generation of reasoning explanations. This type of systems generates the explanation about the decisions made in order to achieve a goal, such as in the steps that a system followed in the execution of an algorithm or the decisions made in the resolution of a mathematical problem. Although this research line could not be exactly the same as our goal of generating descriptive documentation in natural language, it is closely related since this type of explanations often include the description of variables and terms, and the techniques used could be also appropriate for the purpose of our research. Some examples of reasoning explanation systems can be found in [3] where a system that generated explanation for a machine learning algorithm decision is presented; or in [5] where a semi-automatic process to analyse business models and generate a requirement documents that describes the models is proposed.

As seen in the existing related work, dealing with the automatic generation of both machine and human documentation for Web APIs is barely addressed. There are some research that deals with similar problems, but in some cases the problem arises in other scenarios such as Web services rather than APIs. Moreover, the solution proposed in this paper is novel and goes beyond the state of the art in providing the suitable documentation for web APIs.

3   NLP for Generating Open Data Documentation

In this section a further step on the documentation of open data Web APIs is proposed. In this manner, suitable descriptions in natural language are included in existing OpenAPI documentations. This process is able to document with natural language any existing open data Web API that already includes OpenAPI documentation. With this incorporation of descriptions, the Web APIs will be not only machine readable but also understandable by users. Therefore, the improvement of the comprehension of APIs will promote as a result the reuse of open data. The whole process is explained in detail in the following subsections.

3.1 Starting with an OpenAPI Documentation

The process starts with a basic machine-readable API documentation in the OpenAPI standard (Fig. 1). Then, using the proposed natural language descriptions generator approach, a set of descriptions in natural language is created and later appended to the documentation of the API, facilitating the access to the underlying data.

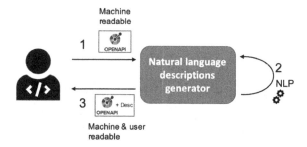

Fig. 1. Overview of the proposed approach for the automatic generation of API documentation process.

In order to apply the natural language descriptions generator, the first step of the process (Step 1 in Fig. 1) is having an Web API with an existing OpenAPI (only machine-readable) documentation. It is not easy to read by human users, so generating natural language descriptions of the API and its underlying data is essential to solve this problem.

Before being able to generate this kind of descriptions, some of the information contained in the input OpenAPI need to be extracted. In this sense, the automatic generator process first gathers the following information from the API: (i) the title given to the API, the name of each method; (ii) all the parameters from each method, with name, type and example value; (iii) and all the properties given as a result of the API, also with name, type and example data. In order to extract this information the input documentation is analysed: from the JSON object that contains all the components of the API documentation, all the information required is extracted. In order to do so, the process iterates through the JSON objects and arrays that the OpenAPI standard specifies, such as API "title", "paths", "components", "parameters" and "properties".

Once the aforementioned information is gathered, the process continues with the next step in order to automatically generate the general description of the API as well as a description for each of the API methods, its parameters and its properties. This generation process will be further explained in the next subsection.

3.2   Description Generation Employing NLP Techniques

Taking as input the information extracted in the first step of our approach's architecture, the second step (Step 2 in Fig. 1) is the generation of descriptions using NLP techniques.

From this information, the generation of natural language descriptions is performed using and integrating different NLP techniques. Specifically, tokenisation, word sense disambiguation and a NLG template-based approach are employed to generate the descriptions that will be added to the OpenAPI specification. An overview of each step of our approach is shown in Fig. 2.

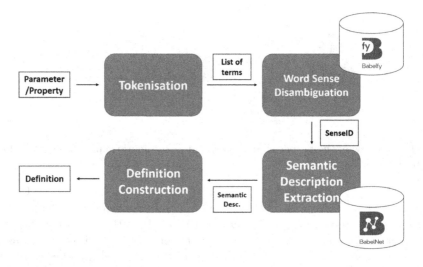

Fig. 2. Overview of our NLP approach for generating API documentation.

Template-based approaches have proven to generate relatively high quality texts and faster than other NLG approaches [25], being suitable in the case of the generation of descriptive API documentation since its integration with other systems or approaches would not affect their performance. The type of templates used in this approach is usually a text with gaps that must be filled with specific information in order to complete its semantic meaning. The information for generating the method's descriptions within the API documentation is provided by the input API specification. In this regard, the name of the methods or the parameters/properties of these methods will be used for producing semantically enriched descriptions.

The templates within the proposed approach were designed considering as reference the generic CKAN API[2] which is used by many open data platforms such as Data.gov[3] (the U.S. Government's open data platform) and Data.gov.uk[4] (the U.K. Government's open data platform), and also the descriptions shown in the *datos.gob.es*[5] API from the Government of Spain open data platform. Since the text needed in the general description of the API may not be the same than the one for a method, a variety of 3 different generic templates were hand-crafted. Therefore, depending on the case, we have separate templates for the following types of descriptions: (i) general API description; (ii) API method description; and (iii) parameter/property description.

In the first two cases (i.e., the general API and method descriptions) the information provided by the API specification is solely used, while, in the third case (i.e., the generation of parameter/property descriptions) the template is enriched with the information coming from knowledge-bases and semantic resources, also applying NLP techniques, such as word sense disambiguation. Without the use of this type of techniques is difficult to discern the meaning of a parameter/property that correctly fits the context of the API documentation. For example, in the context of an API for obtaining employment data, the word "mean" would adopt the meaning of average instead of other meanings such as a stingy person. Concerning this type of resources, Babelfy [30] and BabelNet [31] are specifically used. These resources provide semantic knowledge to the generated description, thus enriching the API documentation and providing the user with definitions and examples of the data queried by the API. The former performs word sense disambiguation, using a semantic network. The latter is a multilingual encyclopedic dictionary and a semantic network that integrates information from several sources such as WordNet [17] or Wikipedia[6]. Babelfy allows the disambiguation of a specific term (either by using only this specific term or employing it together with an example), obtaining the sense of the term in the form of an ID representing a set of synonyms. Then, searching this ID in BabelNet, the semantic description of the term is obtained. In this preliminary version of the approach, in case that a term has more than one sense, we choose the one with the highest disambiguation score[7] provided by Babelfy. Since in many cases, the parameter/property are not a single token, an intermediate processing step is needed before using BabelNet/Babelfy resources. This is due to the fact that these resources need as input a sentence or a term with the words to disambiguate correctly spelled. Therefore, in the case that a parameter/property contains more than one word in a single token (e.g., when several words are

---

[2] https://docs.ckan.org/en/latest/api/index.html.
[3] https://www.data.gov/.
[4] https://data.gov.uk/.
[5] https://datos.gob.es/es/apidata.
[6] https://en.wikipedia.org/.
[7] A value between 0 and 1 indicating the degree of confidence that the algorithm had when it performed the disambiguation of the term [21].

separated by a underscore: *Country_Code*), tokenisation[8], via regular expressions, is employed in order to separate these words. In this sense, the following cases are considered: (i) when the words are separated by non-alpha numeric characters, such as "&", "_" or "\$"; and, (ii) when the words are in camel case format, such as *"FlagsCode"* or *"CountryCode"*. Ultimately, if Babelfy is not able to disambiguate the parameter/property as a whole, or any of its components, its description will not appear in the final API documentation.

3.3 Including Natural Language Descriptions into an OpenAPI Documentation

Finally, the last step in the OpenAPI with NLG process is to create a machine and user readable documentation (Step 3 in Fig. 1).

Once the descriptions in natural language of the API, its methods and its parameters and properties are generated, they are integrated in the existing (machine-readable) documentation of the API. Hence, the documentation of the API will be now both machine and user readable, all in a single OpenAPI specification file.

In order to perform this integration, the input OpenAPI is analysed to locate where these generated descriptions in natural language have to be placed within the OpenAPI specification: the general description of the API is placed in the "info" component of the OpenAPI documentation; the description of each method of the API is placed in the corresponding OpenAPI "path"; the description of each parameter is placed in the corresponding "parameter" of each "path"; and finally, the description of each property is placed in the corresponding "property" of the "components" object.

When this process ends, the OpenAPI documentation including descriptions in natural language is returned to the user. An example of this generated documentation is shown and explained in detail in Sect. 4.1. This descriptive documentation generated by the presented process can override the initial documentation or it can be created in a separated file. At this stage, the API documentation, as aforementioned, is machine readable and also user readable, achieving a complete comprehension of the data provided by the API.

4 Validation

In this section the proposed approach is first validated with different examples and then a specific case study is introduced.

In order to ensure the correct performance of the proposed approach, a set of 5 datasets from Data.gov were randomly selected for testing the generation of their documentation. When selecting these datasets the following constraints were taken into account: (i) the format in which the dataset is available; and

---

[8] The process of splitting a stream of text into more basic units such as words, phrases or tokens (elements with an identified meaning).

(ii) the format of the column names of the dataset (i.e., words spelled correctly and, in case of having several words, these words not being in uppercase and all together in order to better generate the documentation).

Table 1. Validation results of applying our approach for OpenAPI documentation.

Title	# of instances	# of attributes	Generation time
Voter History Data	7,517,744	20	43.02 s
Biodiversity by County	20,017	13	36.54 s
Occupational Employment Statistics	6,816	10	25.88 s
Leading Causes of Death	1,380	7	24.18 s
Demographic Statistics	237	46	214.89 s

Table 1 shows a brief summary of the time spent by the proposed approach for generating the OpenAPI documentation with natural language descriptions. Before applying our approach, a basic OpenAPI documentation is generated for the datasets selected, and then, this documentation is taken as input of our approach. The time required to generate the API documentation by our proposed approach is affected by the number of attributes. In this sense, the disambiguation process would introduce a delay in generation time for each attribute. Taking into account that the datasets contain between 7 and 46 attributes, the time to generate the related API documentation including natural language descriptions is between 24 and 215 s, depending on the number of attributes of the dataset.

4.1 Case Study

A case study is introduced to illustrate the whole process and show the feasibility and usefulness of our proposal. It consists of applying the proposed approach explained in Sect. 3 to an existing open data Web API.

With this example we attempt to demonstrate that developers need to interpret and understand the available third-party open data Web APIs, but the lack of a suitable human-readable API documentation hampers the understanding and the reusability of data.

Our scenario describes a quality office in a university, aiming at developing quality assurance and enhancement strategy of different degrees. Among others, this office is in charge of monitoring employment opportunities of their students in order to support degree policy planning at the university. Therefore, this office is interested in analysing existing internal data (about enrolment, performance indicators, etc.) together with external data about employment statistics. External open data comes from a Web API providing occupational employment statistics.

Generating Documentation for Occupational Employment Data

An API providing occupational employment statistics has been chosen to illustrate this process. Data accessing this API comes from the open data website of Data.gov (the website of the U.S. Government's open data). Data.gov contains a lot of information of different topics, including statistics and employment data. As example data, the dataset *"Occupational Employment Statistics"* is used through a third-party Web API[9]. This dataset contains statistics about employment in a wide variety of professions in New York and includes information such as the occupation, the area name or the wage.

The Data.gov web offers a CKAN API to facilitate the access to the datasets' metadata. However, it is not a query-level API because it does not provide the data itself. Therefore, we used an API to access this data[9]. This API does not include natural language descriptions. Consequently, there is no means to facilitate the access and reuse of their open data, which makes the application of our approach to generate API documentation very valuable in this context.

Our process for generating open data Web API documentation where our NLP techniques are applied, includes adding natural language descriptions to an OpenAPI documentation.

The input OpenAPI specification[9] is only machine readable, so it is difficult to understand what data is offered by the API. This documentation includes a set of methods: a general method to retrieve all the data from the source; and one method to filter by the values contained in each column of the data source.

In order to include descriptive documentations to the existing specification, the natural language descriptions generator is launched. It is worth noting that this process is freestanding and it can be applied to any existing OpenAPI documentation. Taking as input the API specification in the OpenAPI standard, the generation of natural language descriptions is performed to create an API general description, an explanation of each API method and also a definition of each parameter of the API. In the example of this case study, the documentation contains now the descriptions about how to use the API and its different methods and parameters.

When the API includes the complete documentation with natural language descriptions, it is launched and exposed online so that we can just test it. This complete documentation is available online[10]. By accessing the API in a web browser, the API will return the data contained in the source dataset and the documentation with natural language descriptions, as shown in the following section. The results given by this API and the documentation of the API are both in JSON[11] format. Not only it can be easily processed by machines, but also users are able to quickly understand both the results and the documentation.

---

[9] http://wake.dlsi.ua.es/EmploymentAPI/docs/.

[10] https://wake.dlsi.ua.es/EmploymentAPI/docs/complete.html.

[11] https://www.json.org/.

API Documentation Comparison

The objective of this comparison is to visually contrast how our descriptions have benefited and increased the quality of the basic documentation we had before.

While the original documentation[9] includes a little description about the API, the documentation[10] generated using NLP includes a complete description about the data offered in the API, the different filters that can be applied, the result format and an example about how to query the API. Moreover, documentation generated about the API main method is shown in Fig. 3. The input API main method documentation (Fig. 3 above) only includes a short summary and a general description which equal to the description of other methods of the API. However, the documentation of the API main method generated by our approach (Fig. 3 below) includes an example about how to query this API method (in this case is https://wake.dlsi.ua.es/EmploymentAPI/), facilitating the use of that method directly accessing to the URL; and a complete description about the data offered by this concrete method, which can be filtered by different parameters and will bring the results with its objects and properties. The description of these parameters are empty in the original documentation, meanwhile the documentation of each parameter generated by the proposed approach includes a complete description about the type, if it is required or not, how to pass this parameter to the API, and finally, a semantic definition about the parameter itself.

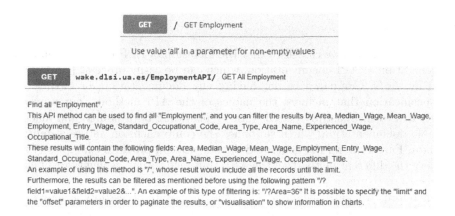

Fig. 3. Comparison of the API main method description in the OpenAPI documentation without applying our NLP-based approach (above) and integrating NLP (below).

Finally, an extract of the documentation about the API properties is shown in Fig. 4. The documentation of the API properties (Fig. 4 above) only includes the type and an example. However, the documentation of this API properties given by our proposed approach (Fig. 4 below) include information about the type of data, an example of use, and the most important part, a complete definition of the meaning of each property.

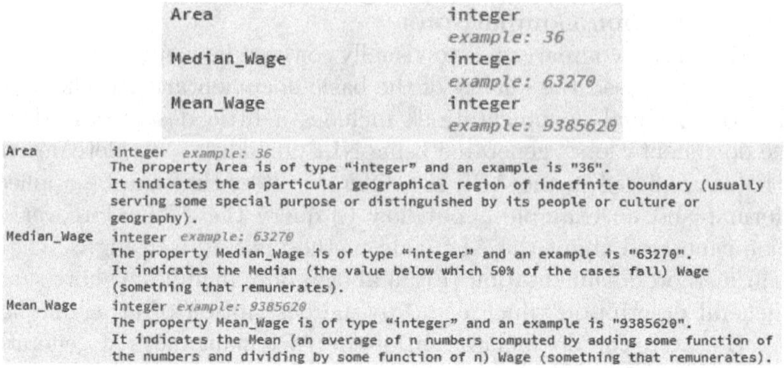

Area	integer *example: 36*
Median_Wage	integer *example: 63270*
Mean_Wage	integer *example: 9385620*

Area	integer *example: 36* The property Area is of type "integer" and an example is "36". It indicates the a particular geographical region of indefinite boundary (usually serving some special purpose or distinguished by its people or culture or geography).
Median_Wage	integer *example: 63270* The property Median_Wage is of type "integer" and an example is "63270". It indicates the Median (the value below which 50% of the cases fall) Wage (something that remunerates).
Mean_Wage	integer *example: 9385620* The property Mean_Wage is of type "integer" and an example is "9385620". It indicates the Mean (an average of n numbers computed by adding some function of the numbers and dividing by some function of n) Wage (something that remunerates).

Fig. 4. Comparison of the API properties description in the OpenAPI documentation without applying our NLP-based approach (above) and integrating NLP (below).

Therefore, from the comparison of a basic open data Web API documentation without integrating NLP approach presented previously[12], we can conclude that the documentation generated by our approach is more complete and is useful for users in order to know the data offered by web APIs. With this help, data reusers can easily promote the use of public information and contribute to the open data environment, improving the actual reuse of data.

4.2 Discussion

From this validation we can state that the inclusion of NLP techniques improve the generation of API documentation, which can be easily processed and understood by users. Compared to not having any documentation, or having only the specification that includes the names of the API methods, our approach contributes to the existing related work by providing both human and machine readable documentation, which simplifies the comprehension and reusability of the data. Furthermore, the generated documentation provides examples of how to query the different methods of the API, thus facilitating, as mentioned before, the access to the data.

Therefore, we have validated that the proposal successfully achieves the objective of generating the suitable Web API descriptive documentation in different situations. The importance of including natural language descriptions in OpenAPI documentation is that it actually helps open data reusers to reuse existing data and citizens to be able to access the data offered on the web.

5 Conclusions and Future Work

In this paper we have presented an approach that integrates NLP techniques to generate suitable documentation of open data Web APIs. Our approach starts

[12] https://github.com/cgmora12/AG.

with a basic machine-readable API documentation in the OpenAPI standard, which is easy to process by machines but difficult to understand by common users, hindering the reuse of data. From this documentation, our proposed natural language descriptions generator is used to create a set of descriptions in natural language and append them to the existing machine-readable documentation of the API. For validating the proposed approach, we tested the automatic generation of documentation process with several machine-readable documentations of datasets from the Data.gov open data portal. After that, we have presented a case study in which our approach is applied within a specific scenario. In this sense, we illustrated and described a real-based situation where a developer must obtain specific data from an open data platform.

The proposed approach (which is publicly available at GitHub[13]) is a key element for improving data management and analysis. This is because enhanced API documentation would lead to a better understanding of the API by developers, facilitating the access and handling of data available online.

As future work, the generation process will be extended by using semantic web technologies to apply data integration mechanisms. With regard to the generation of descriptions within the API documentation, the NLP area also provide of techniques that allow the adaptation or customisation of the generated descriptions depending on the user needs. In this sense, the descriptions could be simplified according to a specific linguistic level or could also include more technical terms if required. In addition to this, this approach could be easily extended to other languages (i.e., multilingual) since the semantic resources employed (i.e., BabelNet and Babelfy) are linked to many languages, which would facilitate the reuse of code.

Acknowledgments. This work has been partially funded by the following projects: TIN2016-78103-C2-2-R, PROMETEU/2018/089, RTI2018-094653-B-C22, RTI2018-094649-B-I00, TIN2017-90773-REDT and COST Action CA18231. Furthermore, the author César González-Mora has a contract for predoctoral training with the Generalitat Valenciana and the European Social Fund by the grant ACIF/2019/044.

References

1. Abelló Gamazo, A., Ayala Martínez, C.P., Farré Tost, C., Gómez Seoane, C., Oriol Hilari, M., Romero Moral, Ó.: A data-driven approach to improve the process of data-intensive API creation and evolution. In: Proceedings of the Forum and Doctoral Consortium Papers Presented at the 29th International Conference on Advanced Information Systems Engineering, CAiSE 2017, pp. 1–8 (2017)
2. Alharbi, N., Gotoh, Y.: Natural language descriptions for human activities in video streams. In: Proceedings of the 10th International Conference on Natural Language Generation, pp. 85–94 (2017)
3. Alonso, J.M., Ramos-Soto, A., Castiello, C., Mencar, C.: Explainable AI beer style classifier. In: The SICSA Reasoning, Learning and Explainability Workshop 2018 (2018)

---

[13] https://github.com/cgmora12/NL4OpenAPI.

4. Atzeni, P., Merialdo, P., Mecca, G.: Data-intensive web sites: design and maintenance. World Wide Web **4**(1), 21–47 (2001)
5. Aysolmaz, B., Leopold, H., Reijers, H.A., Demirörs, O.: A semi-automated approach for generating natural language requirements documents based on business process models. Inf. Softw. Technol. **93**, 14–29 (2018)
6. Bateman, J., Zoch, M.: Natural Language Generation. Oxford University Press, Oxford (2003)
7. Braun, N., Goudbeek, M., Krahmer, E.: The Multilingual Affective Soccer Corpus (MASC): compiling a biased parallel corpus on soccer reportage in English, German, Dutch. In: Proceedings of the 9th International Natural Language Generation conference, pp. 74–78 (2016)
8. Braunschweig, K., Eberius, J., Thiele, M., Lehner, W.: The state of open data - limits of current open data platforms. In: Proceedings of the 21st World Wide Web Conference 2012, Web Science Track at WWW 2012 (2012)
9. Cao, H., Falleri, J.-R., Blanc, X.: Automated generation of REST API specification from plain HTML documentation. In: Maximilien, M., Vallecillo, A., Wang, J., Oriol, M. (eds.) ICSOC 2017. LNCS, vol. 10601, pp. 453–461. Springer, Cham (2017). https://doi.org/10.1007/978-3-319-69035-3_32
10. Cole, R. (ed.): Survey of the State of the Art in Human Language Technology. Cambridge University Press, New York (1997)
11. Daga, E., Panziera, L., Pedrinaci, C.: A BASILar approach for building Web APIs on top of SPARQL endpoints. In: Proceedings of the 3rd Workshop on Services and Applications over Linked APIs and Data, vol. 1359, pp. 22–32 (2015)
12. Danielsen, P.J., Jeffrey, A.: Validation and interactivity of Web API documentation. In: IEEE 20th International Conference on Web Services, pp. 523–530 (2013)
13. De Renzis, A., Garriga, M., Flores, A., Cechich, A., Mateos, C., Zunino, A.: A domain independent readability metric for web service descriptions. Comput. Stan. Interfaces **50**, 124–141 (2017)
14. Eciolaza, L., Pereira-Fariña, M., Trivino, G.: Automatic linguistic reporting in driving simulation environments. Appl. Soft Comput. **13**(9), 3956–3967 (2013)
15. Ed-douibi, H., Cánovas Izquierdo, J.L., Cabot, J.: Example-driven web API specification discovery. In: Anjorin, A., Espinoza, H. (eds.) ECMFA 2017. LNCS, vol. 10376, pp. 267–284. Springer, Cham (2017). https://doi.org/10.1007/978-3-319-61482-3_16
16. Ed-douibi, H., Cánovas Izquierdo, J.L., Cabot, J.: OpenAPItoUML: a tool to generate UML models from OpenAPI definitions. In: Mikkonen, T., Klamma, R., Hernández, J. (eds.) ICWE 2018. LNCS, vol. 10845, pp. 487–491. Springer, Cham (2018). https://doi.org/10.1007/978-3-319-91662-0_41
17. Fellbaum, C.: WordNet: An Electronic Lexical Database (Language, Speech, and Communication). MIT Press, Cambridge (1998)
18. Hancock, B., Lee, H., Yu, C.: Generating titles for web tables. In: The World Wide Web Conference, pp. 638–647 (2019)
19. Hardy, H., Vlachos, A.: Guided neural language generation for abstractive summarization using abstract meaning representation. In: Proceedings of the 2018 Conference on Empirical Methods in Natural Language Processing, pp. 768–773 (2018)
20. Huang, C., Zaiane, O., Trabelsi, A., Dziri, N.: Automatic dialogue generation with expressed emotions. In: Proceedings of the 2018 Conference of the North American Chapter of the Association for Computational Linguistics: Human Language Technologies, vol. 2, pp. 49–54 (2018)

21. Iacobacci, I.: Neural-grounded semantic representations and word sense disambiguation: a mutually beneficial relationship, Ph.D. thesis (2018)
22. Janssen, M., Charalabidis, Y., Zuiderwijk, A.: Benefits, adoption barriers and myths of open data and open government. Inf. Syst. Manag. **29**(4), 258–268 (2012)
23. Keim, D.A.: Information visualization and visual data mining. IEEE Trans. Vis. Comput. Graph. **8**(1), 1–8 (2002)
24. Kopecký, J., Vitvar, T., Pedrinaci, C., Maleshkova, M.: RESTful services with lightweight machine-readable descriptions and semantic annotations. In: Wilde, E., Pautasso, C. (eds.) REST: From Research to Practice, chap. 22, pp. 473–506. Springer, New York(2011). https://doi.org/10.1007/978-1-4419-8303-9_22
25. Van der Lee, C., Krahmer, E., Wubben, S.: PASS: a Dutch data-to-text system for soccer, targeted towards specific audiences. In: Proceedings of the 10th International Conference on Natural Language Generation, pp. 95–104 (2017)
26. Lu, Y., Li, G., Zhao, Z., Wen, L., Jin, Z.: Learning to infer API mappings from API documents. In: Li, G., Ge, Y., Zhang, Z., Jin, Z., Blumenstein, M. (eds.) KSEM 2017. LNCS (LNAI), vol. 10412, pp. 237–248. Springer, Cham (2017). https://doi.org/10.1007/978-3-319-63558-3_20
27. Macdonald, I., Siddharthan, A.: Summarising news stories for children. In: Proceedings of the 9th International Natural Language Generation Conference, pp. 1–10 (2016)
28. Maleshkova, M., Pedrinaci, C., Domingue, J.: Investigating web APIs on the World Wide Web. In: 2010 8th IEEE European Conference on Web Services, pp. 107–114 (2010)
29. Moreno, L., Aponte, J., Sridhara, G., Marcus, A., Pollock, L., Vijay-Shanker, K.: Automatic generation of natural language summaries for Java classes. In: 21st International Conference on Program Comprehension, pp. 23–32 (2013)
30. Moro, A., Raganato, A., Navigli, R.: Entity linking meets word sense disambiguation: a unified approach. Trans. Assoc. Comput. Linguist. **2**, 231–244 (2014)
31. Navigli, R., Ponzetto, S.P.: BabelNet: the automatic construction, evaluation and application of a wide-coverage multilingual semantic network. Artif. Intell. **193**, 217–250 (2012)
32. Pandita, R., Xiao, X., Zhong, H., Xie, T., Oney, S., Paradkar, A.: Inferring method specifications from natural language API descriptions. In: Proceedings of the 34th International Conference on Software Engineering, pp. 815–825 (2012)
33. Ramos-Soto, A., Janeiro, J., Alonso, J.M., Bugarín, A., Berea-Cabaleiro, D.: Using fuzzy sets in a data-to-text system for business service intelligence. In: Kacprzyk, J., Szmidt, E., Zadrożny, S., Atanassov, K.T., Krawczak, M. (eds.) IWIFSGN/EUSFLAT -2017. AISC, vol. 643, pp. 220–231. Springer, Cham (2018). https://doi.org/10.1007/978-3-319-66827-7_20
34. Robillard, M.P., DeLine, R.: A field study of API learning obstacles. Empirical Softw. Eng. **16**(6), 703–732 (2011)
35. Rodríguez, R., Espinosa, R., Bianchini, D., Garrigós, I., Mazón, J.-N., Zubcoff, J.J.: Extracting models from web API documentation. In: Grossniklaus, M., Wimmer, M. (eds.) ICWE 2012. LNCS, vol. 7703, pp. 134–145. Springer, Heidelberg (2012). https://doi.org/10.1007/978-3-642-35623-0_14
36. Suter, P., Wittern, E.: Inferring web API descriptions from usage data. In: 3rd IEEE Workshop on Hot Topics in Web Systems and Technologies, pp. 7–12 (2015)
37. Trivino, G., Sanchez, A., Montemayor, A.S., Pantrigo, J.J., Cabido, R., Pardo, E.G.: Linguistic description of traffic in a roundabout. In: International Conference on Fuzzy Systems, pp. 1–8 (2010)

38. Uddin, G., Robillard, M.P.: How API documentation fails. IEEE Softw. **32**(4), 68–75 (2015)
39. Vicente, M.E., Barros, C., Agulló, F., Peregrino, F.S., Lloret, E.: La generacion de lenguaje natural: análisis del estado actual. Computación y Sistemas **19**(4), 721–756 (2015)

Liquid Web Applications

WebDelta: Lightweight Migration of Web Applications with Modified Execution State

Jin-woo Kwon$^{(\boxtimes)}$ (iD), Hyeon-Jae Lee, and Soo-Mook Moon$^{(\boxtimes)}$

Seoul National University, 1 Gwanak-ro, Gwanak-gu, Seoul, Republic of Korea
{jwkwon,hyeonjae}@altair.snu.ac.kr, smoon@snu.ac.kr

Abstract. Web applications (apps) can play an important role for the era of ubiquitous computing since they can run on any smart or IoT devices equipped with a browser. This advantage of portability and simplicity can be extended further to allow an interesting user experience called *app migration*. That is, we can save the execution state of a running web app into a file named *snapshot*, transmit it to another device, and continue the execution by loading the snapshot. One issue is that saving the whole execution state of a running app including all objects in the runtime heap will be inefficient, since most of the current states are unchanged from the initial state. To reduce this inefficiency, we propose *WebDelta* which selectively saves only those that are modified from the initial state. This selective snapshot is saved as a patch file so that after migration, once the original app is launched, the current state can be restored by applying the patch file. We model the relationship between the JavaScript objects as a directed graph to efficiently and completely save the delta of the JavaScript state. We solve the challenging issues related to modified closure variables or modified event handlers attached to the DOM objects. Our framework could successfully migrate five real web apps, and we could speed up the total migration time as much as by 2.7x.

Keywords: Internet of Things · Serialization · Migration · Productivity

1 Introduction

Nowadays, we are literally living in the world of ubiquitous computing surrounded by diverse smart devices that can run apps, including phones, TVs, tablets, or even refrigerators, thanks to the IoT technology. *Web platform* is particularly attractive for such ubiquitous computing. Once developed based on web languages (HTML/CSS/JavaScript), an app can run on any device that employs a web browser, so it can be easily distributed to diverse devices without much effort. Google Android also employs web apps through the WebView components, and many IoT platforms are under development based on web languages (*IoT.js* [9], *mongoose OS* [6], and *Cylon.js* [20]).

© Springer Nature Switzerland AG 2020
M. Bielikova et al. (Eds.): ICWE 2020, LNCS 12128, pp. 435–450, 2020.
https://doi.org/10.1007/978-3-030-50578-3_29

We can extend the portability advantage of web apps to a new user experience of ubiquitous computing called *app migration* [19], which is sending an app running on a device to a different device and continue to run it seamlessly. For example, we can migrate an execution state of a game app from a phone to a TV and continue using it on a big screen. To do this, we need to save the current execution state of an app on a source device (*serialize*) and restore the execution state on a target device (*deserialize*). Web app's portability makes the process simpler. That is, we can save the execution state of a web app in the form of another web app called the *snapshot*, transmit it to another device, and resume the execution by simply running the snapshot on the browser. This app migration approach is different from other similar approaches such as *Apple Handoff* [2] or *Liquid.js* [7], which require the developers to use specific APIs, while app migration does not.

Web app migration has been consistently studied for last few years [4,15,19]. The common idea of serialization is traversing all objects in the runtime heap and saving them in the form of JavaScript code (e.g., if there is a global object obj with two properties x and y whose current values are 1 and 2, respectively, the snapshot will include var obj={x:1, y:2};). The DOM tree, possibly attached with the event handlers, is saved as well. Elaborate technique is needed to serialize the closure objects due to shared scopes [14]. The serialization is executed only in-between event handling when no function is in execution, so saving the call stack is not needed. In this way, the snapshot file is created as a text-formatted HTML/CSS/JavaScript code, which is directly executable on any browser. Hence by running the code, we can restore all heap objects and the DOM tree that were in the original state.

There is one serious issue with this approach. Saving all objects, regardless of its relevancy to an app's state, makes the snapshot size infeasibly large, leading to a long migration time. In fact, serializing all the objects in a heap might be unnecessary. In the heap of a running app, many objects are very unlikely to be modified during the life cycle of an app's execution. A typical example is a function object. Once a function object is declared, it is simply invoked at other call sites; the function body remains unchanged until the end of the execution. The serialization technique proposed by the previous works saves every object including the ones unchanged, so the file size is remarkably large, regardless of how much modification had been done during an app's execution. Therefore, the previous approaches lose scalability for heavy apps that load a lot of initial objects and functions but create only few modifications, which is common in practice. Also, they would suffer from heavy migration time when we need to migrate frequently between the source and the target (e.g., when we exploit app migration for computation offloading between the client and the server by exchanging the app state before and after executing heavy event handlers [11]).

In this paper, we propose a novel approach to selectively serialize modified states of a running web app. The scenario of our approach is shown in Fig. 1. We extract the modified states between the current state and the initial state when the app is launched, and serialize only the differences into a snapshot. Then, this

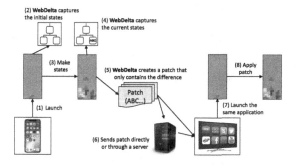

Fig. 1. Migration of modified states between two devices

selective snapshot is migrated to the target device instead of the whole snapshot. At the target device, the selected snapshot works as a patch file such that we launch the app and apply the patch file to restore the exact, current state (we assume that the same web app is pre-installed at every device where a person want to allow app migration). The scenario is straightforward, but determining which objects are changed from the initial state and creating the patch file is not a trivial problem. This paper includes detailed list of challenges and the corresponding solutions.[1]

2   Background

2.1   Execution States of a Web App

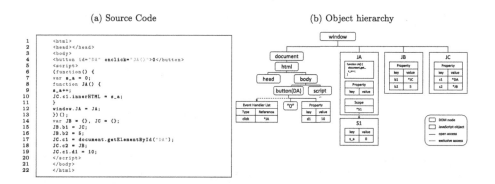

Fig. 2. Execution states of a web app (Initial state)

---

[1] The basic idea of this paper was proposed and reviewed as a 2 paged work-in-progress paper [13]. Some figures and phrases are reused, but for the most part, this paper is original.

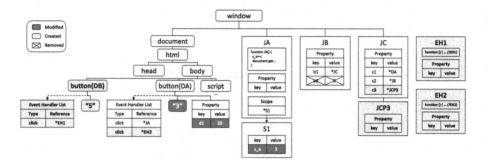

Fig. 3. Current execution state after running for some time from Fig. 2

To capture the execution states of a web app, we need to understand how web apps are executed in a common web browser. HTML and JavaScript are the two core web technologies constructing web apps. HTML constructs visual parts of a web app, while JavaScript manages interactive parts. Figure 2 shows how objects in a simple web app are created. When an app is launched, a built-in object named window is created, which acts as a root of all the heap objects throughout the execution time. HTML tags are converted to DOM (Document Object Model) nodes, and they form a tree named *DOM tree*. The DOM tree is attached under the window object. JavaScript global variables and functions are attached under the window object as well.

A JavaScript function can be lexically scoped with its environment, forming a closure. JA (lines 8–11 in Fig. 2) is a typical way of defining a closure in JavaScript. JA is defined in an anonymous function (lines 6–13), so JA becomes a closure, bounded with its surrounding scope. The scope can be accessed exclusively by the closure. We draw the relationship as a dotted arrow in Fig. 2.

DOM nodes and JavaScript objects interact with each other during app execution. A JavaScript variable can have a reference to a DOM node (JC.c1), and DOM nodes can have properties attached by JavaScript (d1 in DA node). Also DOM nodes can have JavaScript functions as handlers for certain events (JA is an event handler of DA node).

2.2 Previous Approach to Snapshot and Our Proposal

The previous approaches [4,10,14,15,19] on the web app migration simply serialize all the objects in the heap memory. They are straightforward and clear, but the performance is arguable. Even if an app is launched and only a few parts are modified from the initial state, the previous approaches have to serialize all the objects, resulting in burdensome file size. Assume Fig. 3 is the current state transited from the initial state of Fig. 2. Figures painted in dark are modified objects, and figures painted with diagonal lines are newly created objects. Even though the painted objects are the only objects that are related to an app's state, the previous approaches need to save all the objects in the graph. The snapshot code (pseudo, may not follow the actual language syntax) would be Fig. 4a. If we

(a) Snapshot   (b) Selective Snapshot (Patch Code)

```
1    /* DOM tree snapshot */                1    /* DOM tree patch */
2    buttonDB = createElement(button);      2    buttonDB = createElement(button);
3    buttonDB.addEventListener(EH1);        3    buttonDB.addEventListener(EH1);
4    buttonDB.innerHTML = 5;                4    buttonDB.innerHTML = 5;
5    buttonDA = createElement(button);      5
6    buttonDA.addEventListener(JA);         6
7    buttonDA.addEventListener(EH2);        7    buttonDA.addEventListener(EH2);
8    buttonDA.innerHTML = 3;                8    buttonDA.innerHTML = 3;
9    buttonDA.d1 = 10;                      9    buttonDA.d1 = 20;
10   script = createElement(script);       10
11   body.addChild(buttonDB);              11   body.addChild(buttonDB);
12   body.addChild(buttonDA);              12
13   body.addChild(script);                13
14                                         14
15   /* JavaScript snapshot */            15    /* JavaScript patch */
16   JA = function() {...};                16
17   JA.scope(0).s_a = 3;                  17   JA.scope(0).s_a = 3;
18   JB = new Object();                    18   delete JB.b2;
19   JB.b1 = JC;                           19
20   JC = new Object();                    20
21   JC.c1 = DA;                           21
22   JC.c2 = JB;                           22
23   JC.c3 = JD;                           23   JC.c3 = JD;
24   JD = new Object();                    24   JD = new Object();
25   EH1 = function() {...};               25   EH1 = function() {...};
26   EH2 = function() {...};               26   EH2 = function() {...};
```

Fig. 4. Previous approach compared to our approach

remove all the snapshot codes that are needed to restore the unmodified objects, the result will be Fig. 4b. Since many lines are removed, the snapshot size will be reduced. Thus, selectively serializing modified objects is a promising way to efficiently migrate app states.

3   The WebDelta Approach

(a) Source device   (b) Target device

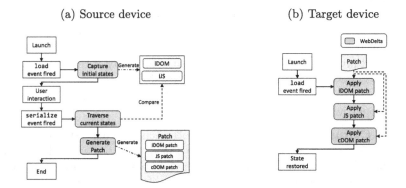

Fig. 5. Process of WebDelta

Figure 5 depicts the overall process of *WebDelta*, a serializer for modified web states. At the source device, the serialization process can be divided into two phases. The first phase is an *initial phase*, which starts right after the page is completely loaded (when `onload` event is fired). At this moment, WebDelta traverses and captures the initial DOM states (iDOM) and the initial JavaScript states (iJS). We duplicate all the initial DOM nodes and JavaScript objects so that we can preserve the initial values. Then, the app is ready for user interaction, so the user will play the app, creating some state information. The second phase is a *serializing phase*, which starts when the user wants to migrate the app's state. The user can actively fire a `serialize` event to initiate the serializing phase. WebDelta traverses the current state and compares it with the captured initial state (iDOM, iJS) to generate a patch file. The patch file is a text-formatted code that can update the initial state to the current state when it is executed on top of the initial state. The patch file can be divided into three parts: *iDOM patch*, *JS patch* and *cDOM patch*. *iDOM patch* transits the initial DOM states into the updated DOM states. *JS patch* updates all the JavaScript objects, including the event handlers. The event handlers of the current DOM states (cDOM) are restored by *cDOM patch*.

The restoration process in the target device is straightforward. Again, the app is launched, but this time WebDelta registers an event that executes the patch code when the app is completely loaded. When the app is completely loaded and the app's state becomes the initial state, WebDelta applies the patch. The patch is applied in the order of iDOM patch, JS patch and cDOM patch. When the update is done, the user can finally continue the execution of the app with updated states.

4 Challenges to WebDelta

Dynamically Changing Object Shape. In JavaScript, object shapes can be dynamically changed during runtime. Any property can be attached and removed, which complicates finding the modified states. In Fig. 3, a property `b2` is removed from the object `JB`, and a property `c3` is attached to the object `JC` during runtime. Therefore, to check modifications on an object, we must check the names of properties first and then compare the values if they have the same names, after identifying the object by comparing its path name (see Sect. 5.2). If not, we must generate a patch code that can attach or remove the created or deleted properties.

Function Closure. Function closure is another challenging issue when we serialize the differences between two states. In Fig. 3, a scoped variable `s_a` of the closure `JA` is modified, so we need to generate a patch code. However, by definition, the scoped variable can be accessed exclusively by the closure, which means that we cannot retrieve the data in the scope from the application layer. Moreover, we cannot generate a patch code that can directly update the scoped variable. In the scenario, suppose the patch is delivered to the target device, and the same app is launched to generate the closure `JA`. The scoped variable `s_a` will have the value 0, and we need to change this value to 3. However, there is no JavaScript syntax that can change a closure's scoped variable.

Re-registering Event Handlers. If a modification is done upon event handlers that are attached to a DOM node, we need to generate a patch code reflecting the change. However, finding the target DOM node to attach or remove event handlers after the migration is a challenging issue. In Fig. 3, a new event handler EH2 is registered to the button DA, so we need to serialize it. After migration, the patch code needs to re-register the event handler (EH2) to the newly initialized button DA. The challenge is how to locate the button DA after migration. The problem is even more complicated if the target DOM node is created during the execution. For example, the DOM node DB is a new DOM node that did not exist in the initial state. Since the event handler EH1 attached to the DOM node DB didn't exist in the initial state as well, we need to serialize and re-register after migration. However, since the DOM node DB is not in the initial state, there is no existing DOM node to attach the event handler. We must wait until the patch code restores the DOM node DB, then we can re-register the event handler.

5   Patch Generation

In this section, we explain details of the patch generation, focusing on how to handle the challenges raised in the previous section.

5.1   DOM Patch Generation

To detect and capture differences of two DOM states, we need to capture both the initial state and the current state of DOM tree and compare them. We imported an open-source tool named *Virtual-DOM* [16,17] to achieve the goal. *Virtual-DOM* is capable of taking a snapshot of a DOM tree at a certain moment. *Virtual-DOM* traverses the DOM tree and creates VTree, a duplicated version of a DOM tree. A limitation of VTree is that it does not copy JavaScript properties and event handlers. It only copies DOM nodes and DOM properties, so we extended VTree implementation to compare and serialize the JavaScript related elements.

Figure 6 depicts the initial and the current states of DOM trees. We compare the two VTrees and extract the difference to generate a patch code. To compare DOM sides, we used an API function diff given from the *Virtual-DOM* library. diff can traverse two VTrees and generate a patch code that can morph one VTree to another. When diff is invoked, nodes in the initial DOM (*iDOM*) are indexed in depth-first traversal way. Then, we compare the iDOM and the current DOM (cDOM) to generate the DOM patch code. The patch is generated according to the index of iDOM because when we restore the state in the target device, the DOM state will be same as the iDOM. If a node is created (button(DB)), the patch code is generated to create a new node and attach to the parent node (iDOM[3] in this case), as shown in the first row of Fig. 6c. If an existing node is modified (iDOM[5]), the patch code is generated to update the inner data, as shown in the second row of the table.

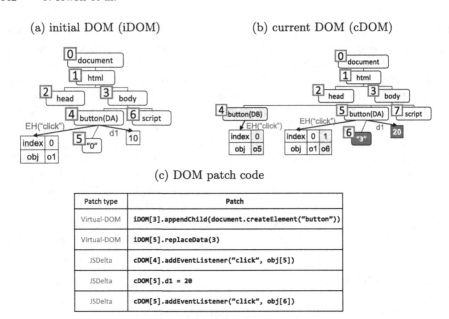

(a) initial DOM (iDOM)   (b) current DOM (cDOM)

(c) DOM patch code

Patch type	Patch
Virtual-DOM	`iDOM[3].appendChild(document.createElement("button"))`
Virtual-DOM	`iDOM[5].replaceData(3)`
JSDelta	`cDOM[4].addEventListener("click", obj[5])`
JSDelta	`cDOM[5].d1 = 20`
JSDelta	`cDOM[5].addEventListener("click", obj[6])`

Fig. 6. DOM patch generation

Since `VTree` does not copy event handlers, we need to separately serialize them. Event handlers are JavaScript functions, so we pass the handlers to *JSDelta* to generate a proper patch code. *JSDelta* is a module for serializing modified JavaScript objects, which will be explained in the following section. Once done, *JSDelta* returns index numbers that stand for location of event handlers after restoration. With the numbers, we generate patch code that can re-attach the event handlers to proper DOM nodes. The code is generated according to the `cDOM` indexes, because the nodes we are targeting might not exist in the iDOM. For example, in `cDOM[4]`, a new event handler (o5) is found. We let *JSDelta* to handle it, and in return the path `obj[5]` is obtained. Then, the patch code is generated to attach the `obj[5]` to the `cDOM[4]`, as in the third row of Fig. 6c.

5.2   JavaScript Patch Generation

We implemented *JSDelta* to compare two JavaScript states and serialize the difference. We need a solid model of the objects to clearly abstract all the states including JavaScript objects, scopes of closures, and event handlers to handle the challenges introduced in the previous section. We found that directed graph is a good solution to model the states of JavaScript objects. Figure 7a and Fig. 7b are the initial and the current states represented as directed graphs. We define an object as a node and a property as an outgoing edge that is pointing to another node. There are two types of nodes: *primitive* data type and *object* data type. Primitive data types are mere values, while object data types are JavaScript objects that are allocated in the heap. We represented primitive data types as

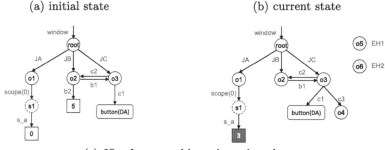

(a) initial state

(b) current state

(c) JS reference table and patch code

JS Reference	Captured Child (initial)	Path	Patch
o1	scope(0): s1	window.JA	N/A
o2	b2: 5 b1: o3	window.JB	delete window.JB.b2
o3	c2: o2 c1: DOM[4]	window.JB.b1	window.JB.b1["c3"] = obj[4];
s1	s_a: 0	window.JA.scope(0)	window.JA.scope(0)["s_a"] = 3
o4	N/A	N/A	obj[4] = {}
o5	N/A	N/A	obj[5] = function() {... //EH1}
o6	N/A	N/A	obj[6] = function() {... //EH2}

Fig. 7. JS patch generation

rectangles and object data types as circles. Notice that only circle nodes can have outgoing edges, because only the object data types can have properties.

To preserve the initial JavaScript states, we created a table named *JS reference table*. At the initial state, we traverse and search for every JavaScript object, and copy their states to the JS reference table as in Fig. 7c (o1, o2, o3, s1 entries). We also store the path that led us to reach the object.

At the current state, we traverse the directed graph to check if an object exists in the JS reference table by comparing the object's reference. If so, we compare the object's property names and values with the ones saved in the JS reference table. If a property name is new, or if the value has been changed, we generate a patch code. The patch code is generated according to the path we stored in the JS reference table. On the other hand, the object may not be in the JS reference table. This means the object did not exist in the initial state, so we need to create a new one. All the created objects are pushed to an array (obj[]) to prevent any duplicated restoration.

Figure 7 'Patch' column shows the resulting patch code. o2 does not have the property b2 anymore, so we generate a patch code that can remove the property. o3 has a new property c3 now, so we need to re-attach it. However, the object that c3 is pointing is in fact another object (o4) that was not in the initial state. So, we create the object first (obj[4]), then we create a patch code that can make c3 to point obj[4]. To update scope variables, we implemented scope(level) function that can retrieve a scope of a function at a certain level. By using the function, the scope variable s_a can be updated (i.e., `window.JA.scope(0)["s_a"]=3` can update JA's scope variable `s_a` in the near-most level). `o5` and `o6` are two objects that came from the *Virtual-DOM* in the previous section. The two objects are not in the JS reference table, so we generate a patch code that can create the objects.

6   Evaluation

In this section, we evaluate how much the size of the serialized file can be reduced. Then, we evaluate the total migration time with our approach in various network conditions. Lastly, we note the initial phase overhead, which is the weak point of our approach.

6.1   Experimental Setup

We tested our work with an open source WebKit browser [1]. We tested our work with two x86 desktops with same performance (i7-3770 CPU, 16 GB RAM), one being as a source device and the other as a target device. We selected JetStream benchmark suite [5] and five real apps listed in Table 1 to evaluate our work. During each experiment, we launch the benchmark or the app, manually execute it for some time to make some states changed, and fire the serialize event to generate the full snapshot or the selective snapshot (patch file). The file is transmitted to the target device and used to restore the states. We confirmed that all the benchmarks and apps are properly resumed.

6.2   Modified Objects Analysis

Table 1. Number of modified objects during execution

	JetStream										
	3d-cube	3d-raytrace	base64	crypto-aes	n-body	regex-dna	code-load	crypto	raytrace	richards	typescript
Initial(JS+DOM)	2,062	2,080	2,028	2,072	2,043	2,036	2,049	2,293	2,182	2,127	5,358
Modified JS	102	54	48	51	48	60	1,340	70	79	78	470
Modified DOM	N/A	N/A	N/A	N/A	N/A	N/A	N/A	N/A	N/A	N/A	N/A

	App				
	Sokoban	Snake	Tetris	Emoticolor	CentNotes
Initial(JS+DOM)	4,671	3,892	2,445	3,705	4,129
Modified JS	48	143	207	205	128
Modified DOM	12	20	8	6	49

Table 1 depicts the number of modified objects during the execution of the benchmarks and apps. *Initial(JS+DOM)* is the number of total objects (DOM nodes and JavaScript objects) at the initial state. *Modified JS* is the number of Java-Script objects that are either modified or newly created during execution. *Modified DOM* is the number of DOM nodes that are modified during execution.

For benchmark tests, the initial objects are mostly JavaScript objects since they are made for JavaScript testing. Among the initial objects, only a few objects were modified during the execution throughout the benchmarks and apps except `code-load` and `typescript` tests. These tests create a lot of new objects during execution, so the modified object counts are relatively high. We can also see that the real apps tend to have less modification than benchmarks. One reason for this is that the real apps employ JavaScript libraries. JavaScript libraries create a lot of objects while only a few of them are used. So, the unused objects will remain unchanged, lowering the number of the *Modified JS*.

6.3   Serialized File Size

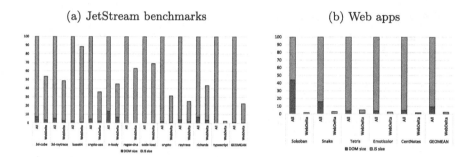

Fig. 8. Serialized file size comparison

The main purpose of our work is to reduce the serialized file size. The measurements on the file size are illustrated in Fig. 8. *All* serializes all the objects and *WebDelta* serializes the modified objects only. We depicted the relative ratio of the result of *WebDelta* when the result of *All* is set to 100. The results show that our approach can reduce 77% and 93% of the serialized file size for benchmarks and web apps, respectively. The reason why *WebDelta* is more effective on web apps is that the benchmark tests usually create few objects that are data intensive, such as very long string values. Therefore, serializing such objects enlarged the patch size. Another thing to notice in the graph is the ratio of the DOM to JS. We can see that among the modified objects, JavaScript objects are dominant, which seems to be one characteristic of modern web apps.

6.4   Total Migration Time

We measured the total time to migrate an app from one device to another, beginning from the start of the serialization at the source device to the restoration of the app's state at the target device. *Save time* stands for time to create the patch, *Transmission time* stands for time to transfer the patch file to the target device, and *Restore time* stands for time to restore the app's state at the target

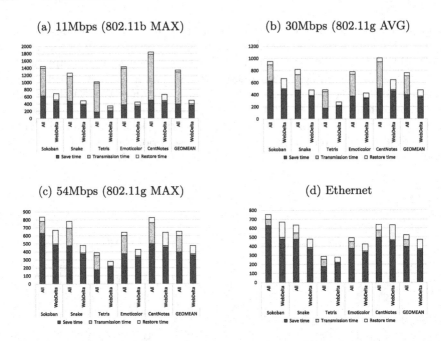

Fig. 9. Total migration time (ms)

device. We prepared four different setups for network speed, emulating three different Wi-Fi and Ethernet conditions. Figure 9 depicts the overall results. The results show that in the best case (11 Mbps), we get 63% reduced migration time (2.7x speed up), and even in the worst case (Ethernet) we get 11% reduced migration time (1.1x speed up).

Although not significant, the *Save time* was reduced in most cases except `Tetris`. We analyzed the reason and found that while in the serializing phase of *WebDelta*, the traversal could successfully find most of the current objects in the JS reference table with their states unchanged. Therefore, we could skip the entire serializing routine for those objects, which would be time-consuming. In the *All* case, all the objects except the built-in objects were serialized, so the *Save time* was higher.

6.5   Initial Phase Overhead

During the initial phase, we need to traverse and collect the initial states. We measured the time to collect the data, which is depicted in Fig. 10. *Source* refers to the time taken to load the original source code, and *DOM* and *JS* stand for time taken to create the initial states of each elements. *All* requires little overhead to traverse the initial states of the JavaScript objects, because we need to make a reference table for built-in objects initially. *WebDelta* suffered from larger initial phase overheads, taking 1.9x execution time compared to *All*. However, the initial phase overhead plus the migration overhead is still better for

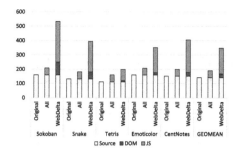

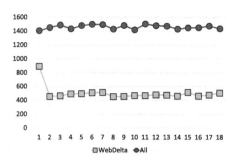

Fig. 10. Initial phase overhead (ms)

Fig. 11. Migration between two devices (Emoticolor, ms)

WebDelta. Moreover, the initial phase overhead could be amortized if there are additional migrations between the devices. Figure 11 depicts records of migration time targeting Emoticolor app consecutively held between two devices in 11Mbps network speed, including the initial phase overhead. At first migration, *WebDelta* is 1.6x faster than *All*, because *WebDelta* needs to perform the initial phase at the source device and the target device. However, at second and further migration, instead of performing the initial phase *WebDelta* updates the initial information with the patch data given, which is done instantly. Therefore, migration is done even more faster than *All* on average (3.1x).

7   Discussion

Nondeterminism. We assumed that the initial state captured from the source device is identical to the initial state at the target device when we restore the updated states. In most cases the assumption is true, but they may be different if there is a non-deterministic characteristic during initialization of an app. A random function (rand) is a typical example. If such statement exists, then the initial state changes every time we launch the app, so our work can be hardly applied. We may mitigate such limitation by analyzing non-deterministic behavior of a web app. There are studies on checking non-determinism [3,18], so we can import the studies to check if we can apply our work to an app.

Version Consistency. Our assumption is that every app installed in the devices are identical. However, the version of the apps may be different. For example, one may update an app in one device but not in another. In such case, we cannot guarantee that the patch can safely update the execution states. One solution is comparing checksums of files between two devices. If they are identical, we can proceed the migration process. If not, the source device can send the source code as well to use it as a code to create proper initial states, then apply patch to restore the updated states.

8   Related Work

Web app migration has been consistently studied through recent years. Santoro et al. [4,10] constructed the basic concept of the web app migration by serializing a web app state into a text-formatted code file. Lo et al. [15] and Oh et al. [19] advanced their work by supporting event handlers and early stage of closures. Kwon et al. [14] completed the work by supporting the advanced closure relationship. The major difference is that our work selectively serializes the modified objects while the previous approaches serialize all the objects.

There were former attempts to serializing web app states with lower file size. Voutilainen et al. [21] proposed app state synchronization through migrating DOM states. In their work, they used the *Virtual-DOM* to synchronize app states, which is the same tool we used in this paper. However, the major difference is how to treat JavaScript states. The previous approach could only serialize JavaScript event handlers, while our work can serialize every JavaScript state including event handlers. Also, to serialize the JavaScript event handler, they require the app developers to use a given API function, while our work is transparent to the app developers. Kwon et al. [12] proposed minimizing the serialized file size by excluding the JavaScript libraries. However, their work requires each implementation for each library, so their work can be hardly expanded. Our work can be applied to any web apps that employ any library (or not employing any library at all), so ours is more general and can be widely used.

Gallidabino et al. [8] proposed *Liquid Software*, which is an architectural design of web app migration. Their work is decent, but lacks details on how to implement the core migration methodology. Our work can play a role in filling that detail.

9   Conclusion

We proposed a novel approach to saving and restoring a web app's state by preserving the initial state and comparing it with the current state. We saw some promising results that can dramatically speed up the app migration process (2.7x best case). However, the results also exposed that there are large execution overheads in collecting the data at the initial state. We think improving the serialization performance is the most urgent task to work for the recent future. Rather than preserving every object in the initial state, we might need to selectively save them to reduce the comparison time. Tightly integrating *Virtual-DOM* and *JSDelta* can help as well, since there are some duplicated routines that are inevitable to run the two systems separately. These works are left for future research.

Acknowledgments. This work was supported by the National Research Foundation of Korea (NRF) grant funded by the Korea government (MSIT) (No. 2020R1A2B5B02001845).

References

1. Apple: Webkit - open source web browser engine (2017). https://webkit.org/
2. Apple: Handoff for developers (2018). https://developer.apple.com/handoff/
3. Barr, E.T., Marron, M.: Tardis: affordable time-travel debugging in managed runtimes. In: Proceedings of the 2014 ACM International Conference on Object Oriented Programming Systems Languages & Applications, OOPSLA 2014, pp. 67–82. ACM, New York (2014). https://doi.org/10.1145/2660193.2660209
4. Bellucci, F., Ghiani, G., Paternò, F., Santoro, C.: Engineering Javascript state persistence of web applications migrating across multiple devices. In: Proceedings of the 3rd ACM SIGCHI Symposium on Engineering Interactive Computing Systems, EICS 2011, pp. 105–110. ACM, New York (2011). https://doi.org/10.1145/1996461.1996502
5. browserbench: Jetstream (2017). http://browserbench.org/JetStream/
6. Cesanta: Mongoose os (2017). https://mongoose-os.com/
7. Gallidabino, A., Pautasso, C.: The liquid.js framework for migrating and cloning stateful web components across multiple devices. In: Proceedings of the 25th International Conference Companion on World Wide Web, Republic and Canton of Geneva, Switzerland, pp. 183–186 (2016). https://doi.org/10.1145/2872518.2890538
8. Gallidabino, A., Pautasso, C., Mikkonen, T., Systa, K., Voutilainen, J.P., Taivalsaari, A.: Architecting liquid software. J. Web Eng. **16**, 433–470 (2017). https://doi.org/10.26421/JWE16.5-6, http://www.rintonpress.com/journals/jweonline.html$#$v16n56
9. Gavrin, E., Lee, S.J., Ayrapetyan, R., Shitov, A.: Ultra lightweight Javascript engine for internet of things. In: Companion Proceedings of the 2015 ACM SIGPLAN International Conference on Systems, Programming, Languages and Applications: Software for Humanity, SPLASH Companion 2015, pp. 19–20. ACM, New York (2015). https://doi.org/10.1145/2814189.2816270
10. Ghiani, G., Paternò, F., Santoro, C.: Push and pull of web user interfaces in multi-device environments. In: Proceedings of the International Working Conference on Advanced Visual Interfaces, AVI 2012, pp. 10–17. ACM, New York (2012). https://doi.org/10.1145/2254556.2254563
11. Jeong, H., Moon, S.: Offloading of web application computations: a snapshot-based approach. In: 2015 IEEE 13th International Conference on Embedded and Ubiquitous Computing, pp. 90–97, October 2015. https://doi.org/10.1109/EUC.2015.10
12. Kwon, J., Oh, J., Jeong, I., Moon, S.: Framework separated migration for web applications. In: 2015 13th IEEE Symposium on Embedded Systems For Real-time Multimedia (ESTIMedia), pp. 1–10. IEEE, October 2015. https://doi.org/10.1109/ESTIMedia.2015.7351767
13. Kwon, J., Moon, S.: JSDelta: serializing modified javascript states for state sharing: work-in-progress. In: Proceedings of the Thirteenth ACM International Conference on Embedded Software 2017 Companion, EMSOFT 2017, pp. 12:1–12:2. ACM, New York (2017). https://doi.org/10.1145/3125503.3125627
14. Kwon, J., Moon, S.: Web application migration with closure reconstruction. In: Proceedings of the 26th International Conference on World Wide Web, WWW 2017, pp. 133–142. International World Wide Web Conferences Steering Committee, Republic and Canton of Geneva, Switzerland (2017). https://doi.org/10.1145/3038912.3052572

15. Lo, J.T.K., Wohlstadter, E., Mesbah, A.: Imagen: runtime migration of browser sessions for javascript web applications. In: Proceedings of the 22nd International Conference on World Wide Web, WWW 2013, pp. 815–826. ACM, New York (2013). https://doi.org/10.1145/2488388.2488459
16. marcelklehr: Github - marcelklehr/vdom-virtualize: Virtualize a DOM node (2017). https://github.com/marcelklehr/vdom-virtualize
17. Matt-Esch: Github - matt-esch/virtual-dom: A virtual DOM and diffing algorithm (2017). https://github.com/Matt-Esch/virtual-dom
18. Mickens, J., Elson, J., Howell, J.: Mugshot: deterministic capture and replay for javascript applications. In: Proceedings of the 7th USENIX Conference on Networked Systems Design and Implementation, NSDI 2010, p. 11. USENIX Association, Berkeley (2010). http://dl.acm.org/citation.cfm?id=1855711.1855722
19. Oh, J., Kwon, J., Park, H., Moon, S.: Migration of web applications with seamless execution. In: Proceedings of the 11th ACM SIGPLAN/SIGOPS International Conference on Virtual Execution Environments, VEE 2015, pp. 173–185. ACM, New York (2015). https://doi.org/10.1145/2731186.2731197
20. thehybridgroup: Cylon.js (2017). https://cylonjs.com/
21. Voutilainen, J.P., Mikkonen, T., Systä, K.: Synchronizing application state using virtual DOM trees. In: Casteleyn, S., Dolog, P., Pautasso, C. (eds.) ICWE 2016. LNCS, vol. 9881. Springer, Heidelberg (2016). https://doi.org/10.1007/978-3-319-46963-8_12

User-Side Service Synchronization in Multiple Devices Environment

Clay Palmeira da Silva$^{(\boxtimes)}$ ⓘ, Nizar Messai, Yacine Sam, and Thomas Devogele

Université de Tours, 30 Avenue du Monge, Tours, France
{clay.palmeira,nizar.messai,yacine.sam,thomas.devogele}@univ-tours.fr

Abstract. Today, a single user owning multiple devices is a reality. Moreover, with the advent of the concept of Everything-as-a-Service (XaaS), a cloud-based term that allows for a wide variety of services and applications deployed by the user, the multiple devices scenario gain more relevance, mainly due to the lack of interoperability between operating systems and services of these devices. We focus on multiple device's environments for synchronizing web services at the client-side without continuously depending on a cloud-based system. We discuss a model-based architecture that allows us to fluently migrate services/data and sessions from one device to another regardless of the operating system. The architecture, called The CUBE [12], is based on user-centric principles combined with REST and RESTful concepts. In this extension paper, we present two main contributions. First, with a description of technical and conceptual aspects of the CUBE, and its relation with the devices/applications and web services. Then, a feasibility test for a tight-coupling service such as YouTube streaming. Within a set of ten users, we presented preliminary results that had measured the wasted time to play a given video with and without the CUBE towards five different devices. The results demonstrate that when the users used the CUBE, they spend only 5.821 s to migrate the video, while without the CUBE, they spend 68.101 s to do the same procedure. That means the CUBE is up to ≈12 times faster than the traditional YouTube cloud-based synchronization procedure.

Keywords: REST · RESTful · Web Services · Multiple-devices · Cloud-based system · Client-side synchronization

1 Introduction

The concept of Everything-as-a-Service (XaaS) provides us nowadays a broad set of services that make our days more comfortable. Thus, naturally, we started to rely on cloud-based systems the task to store our data and keep tracking of all our state and behavior while using web services. In addition to the features of the cloud-based systems, we have nowadays more powerful mobile devices than ever before [14]. However, we do not explore these mobile capacities regarding

© Springer Nature Switzerland AG 2020
M. Bielikova et al. (Eds.): ICWE 2020, LNCS 12128, pp. 451–466, 2020.
https://doi.org/10.1007/978-3-030-50578-3_30

processing, storage, and security measures to using web services locally. More-over, we have mobile devices basically split into two different worlds, those with Android, and those with an iOS operating system.

With the popularity of mobile technology, we also had changed our behavior. Today it is common to find a user using two or three mobile devices concurrently, and often they have different operating systems. Thus, we are facing simultane-ously a multiple-device environment with the same or different operating sys-tems, where most of the technology and web services requiring a third-party provider to synchronizing data and keeping the state.

Furthermore, since we have adopted this behavior of storing our data some-where, we became each day more dependent on the cloud-based system. That dependency leads us to an unconscious problem, the connectivity dependency. That means, if we want to migrate a given service to a given device, the new device must ensure the same conditions required by the cloud-based system that holds the web service.

To give an example, suppose a user starts to watch a video on YouTube in a given device, then she/he wants to change device for any particular reason. The new device must ensure all required conditions: a YouTube user account, internet connection, compatible operating system, etc. Otherwise, it will not be possible to resume our YouTube video in the second device without starting from scratch, and sometime installing additional modules.

Within the popularity of the Android and iOS platforms, the problem of mov-ing applications and services between different devices without the cloud-based system to synchronize state and store data is a challenge. However, there is a technology mentioned at the end of the 90s, called Liquid Software [4], which proposes fluently moving applications and services between devices. Unfortu-nately, two decades later, all presented solutions to achieve the Liquid Software purpose involves a third-party provider such as a cloud-based system.

An alternative to server-side/cloud-based system approaches can rely on client-side management of multiple device service synchronization. In [12], the authors proposed The CUBE, a system-model architecture that addresses the challenge of web-services at user-side for a multiple-devices and operating sys-tems environment. The CUBE is fully compliant with Liquid Software principles described in 1996 by [4], and most recently described in 2016 by [1] to allow for user-side services synchronization and migration over multiple-devices.

In this paper, we provide a study of formal aspects of the CUBE, describe its technical improvements, detail additional feasibility scenario on tight-coupling (high dependency) web service interaction, and provide an evaluation based on user-experience feed-backs. We note that the previous work of the CUBE pre-sented as a feasibility test a light-coupling service (less dependency) as a client e-mail based on Gmail.

The remainder of this paper presents the following structure: Sect. 2 brings our motivating scenario and contributions. Section 3 discusses the necessary elements to build the CUBE within their descriptions and particularities. Section 4 presents our implementation insights with some challenges regarding the enhancements. Section 5 presents the feasibility test with results and evaluation. Section 6 discusses the related works from a server- and client-side perspective. Finally, Sect. 7 gives concluding remarks highlighting our future research directions

2 Motivating Scenario and Contributions

Nowadays, web services are the central use of mobile devices. As well, we are facing a real problem within a multiple-devices and operating system environment. Moreover, when we are thinking about services running over multiple devices/platforms and how this challenge had inspired researchers and industries over the years. Besides, we also have noted that all proposed solutions rely on the server or cloud-based systems to synchronize services data and state.

Today, with all available technology, and depending on the server/cloud-based system to make synchronization, we can reproduce the scenario proposed in Fig. 1, which is a migration of a YouTube video streaming across a multiple-devices environment. However, to achieve this scenario, all devices need each a YouTube account, and also they should have installed the native app from YouTube. Otherwise, it is not possible to resume the video across devices. Moreover, sometimes even with the server-cloud support, continuing a service such as YouTube streaming across devices is not assured.

Furthermore, from a resource perspective, some devices are too small or too big for a given service, e.g., a keyboard on a smartphone is too short to write an email for some users, requiring a device with an external keyboard or other with a bigger screen. In this case, a more suitable "device candidate" should be chosen by the user to reproduce such service, the CUBE deals with these challenges. Nevertheless, in this paper, we focus on a particular service (YouTube streaming), and one specific functionality, the migration of YouTube video streaming towards multiple-devices.

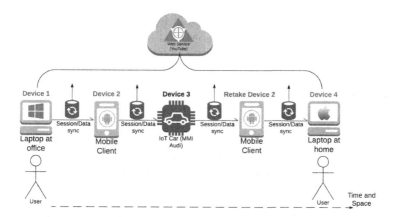

Fig. 1. Data/State synchronization managed by the server- cloud-based system.

We aim to present the migration of a tight-coupling web-service, such as YouTube, in a multiple-devices environment regardless of the operating system. In our proposition, graphically represented in Fig. 2 the user makes a connection with the web service such as the YouTube server only once. Then she/he can switch between devices while moving. It is also allowed to the user take previous equipment (Retake Device 2) until arriving at the final destination where she/he will be able to finish the video in a device of her/his choice.

We note that the user-centric principle used is applied to give the user the choice of which device to choose according to personal interest. In the CUBE environment, all control of state/data/certificate goes locally. We note this transfer is not a copy of the service or something like that. The CUBE operates within different layers and system modules to work less dependent on the server- cloud-based system. For this purpose, we enhanced our CUBE model [11–13], adding new features, described hereafter.

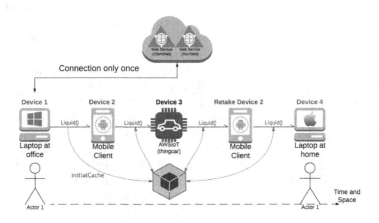

Fig. 2. A use case model describing our contribution.

– Formal description of the CUBE and demonstration of the interaction between its different elements and how they work combined;
– Enhancing our logical dock to allow migration of tight-coupling web services.

3 CUBE Model Formal Description

Our biggest challenge was to fulfill the CUBE technical principles regarding REST and RESTfull constraints. For this reason, we aimed with the formal description to make a better understanding of these constraints, and also analyze the traceability of devices and services within the only-one user scope. Furthermore, we also aim with this description to present the elements that could help developers to map their applications to work in a multiple- device/operating system environments. Figure 3 introduces our perspective of the CUBE geometrically represented.

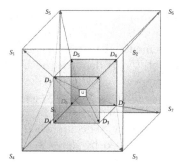

Fig. 3. In the center of the CUBE is located the user, surrounded by Devices $\mathbb{D} = \{1, 2, ..., 8\}$ and Services $\mathbb{S} = \{1, 2, ..., 8\}$

Our first steps towards the CUBE description required a review of traditional definitions since we combined multiple environments in the same scope. That means we can afford multiple devices and services running together in the same space. In this context, the macro-formalization of the CUBE relies upon three concepts that we recall here, such as Anti-Symmetric, once we have two objects that are related to each other. Reflexive because a device can relate with itself to manage a local web service. Transitive because we have a binary relation R, over a set $\mathbb{D}$ if whenever an element d_i is related to an element d_j, and d_j is related to an element d_n, where $\{d_i, d_j, d_n\}$ are devices. Therefore, we realized that the CUBE description relies indeed in an abstraction of the *Partial Orders* principle, means $d_i \preceq d_j$, where d_i and d_j are devices and $d_i \neq d_j$.

3.1 Description

Hereafter, we will present a full description of the CUBE starting from the center of the CUBE, the final-user. Thus, we need to introduce some elements that we called as essential elements. These elements are (i) the adaptation of the user-centric network for a single user, (ii) an individual user, (iii) a single device, (iv) multiple devices, (v) one service, and (vi) multiple services.

To introduce the essential element (i), we based our description from the user-centric definition proposed by Hartmann [5]. Then, we defined the user-centric network of the CUBE (UCN-CUBE) as a 4-tuple (instead of 6-tuple in [5]) by the Definition 1:

Definition 1. $\mathcal{N}_{\delta_t} := \{s, \delta_s, U_s, \mathbb{D}_{\delta_s}\}$ *where:*

1. s = *A service. Here s must not be confused with service implementation provided by the server (third-party). It preferably corresponds to local interaction initiated by the user.*
2. δ_s = *data object from service s.*
3. U_s = *The user owning service s.*
4. $\mathbb{D}_{\delta_s}$ = *set of devices forming the device pool for data object δ_s.*

Since we have defined our adaptation of the user-centric principle for a single user (i), now we can describe other essential elements. Thus, we introduce the definition of the essential elements (ii) and (iii), the individual user, and the single device, respectively. Let U (ii) denotes the User in the CUBE, and this user, in our more abstract perspective, owns one device called d_1 (iii). Then the essential elements (iv) multiple-devices, formally, let us denote by $\mathbb{D}_u$, the set of devices owned by the user U, then at this step $\mathbb{D}_u = \{d_1\}$.

The essential element (v) one service occurs when U starts to access a Service s_1 using d_1. This relation is expressed by $d_1 \leftrightarrow s_1$. Then, the essential element (vi) the multiple services, formally, let us denote by $\mathbb{S}_u$ the set of services accessed by U, then at this level $\mathbb{S}_u = \{s_1\}$.

Now, assume U has more than one mobile device at disposal d_1 and d_2. However, service migration is not already available. Let us represent the mobile devices and service for U as: $\mathbb{D}_u = \{d_1, d_2\}$, $\mathbb{S}_u = \{s_1\}$, and $d_1 \leftrightarrow s_1$, $d_2 \leftrightarrow s_1$ but, for now, there is no communication between d_1 and d_2. In this case service migration process is not possible yet. Then, U starts another Service s_2 in the same device d_1. Therefore, $\mathbb{D}_u = \{d_1, d_2\}$, $\mathbb{S}_u = \{s_1, s_2\}$ and $d_1 \leftrightarrow s_1$, $d_1 \leftrightarrow s_2$, $d_2 \leftrightarrow s_1$.

In the general case, let us assume that U is surrounded by a set of devices (multiple-devices) $\{d_1, d_2, ..., d_n\} \subseteq \mathbb{D}$. We note here that the devices in $\mathbb{D}$ are not necessarily owned by the considered user U.

Let us also assume that U is surrounded by a set of services $\{s_1, s_2, ..., s_n\} \subseteq \mathbb{S}$. Then, we denoted by $\mathbb{S}_u \subseteq \mathbb{S}$ the subset of services accessed by U.

Within the set $\mathbb{D}_u$ of devices owned by user U, we denote by d_p the main device being used by U. When switching to another device d_i in $\mathbb{D}_u$, d_i becomes the new d_p, and the old d_p remains in $\mathbb{D}_u$ as a device at user disposal.

Now, since we described the elements that surround the user, we can formally define the elements that build the CUBE, such as the INNER CUBE, the OUTER CUBE, the Pool Area. Thereby, we defined the *INNER CUBE* as a 3-tuple in Definition 2:

Definition 2. $\mathbb{I}_c := \{d_p, \mathbb{D}_u \setminus \{d_p\}, \mathcal{R}_d\}$ *where:*

- d_p *is the current device being used by user U.*
- $\mathbb{D}_u \setminus \{d_p\}$ *is the set of discovered devices owned by the user U ready to use.*
- $\mathcal{R}_d$ *is the research mechanism for devices.*

Let us denote by "$\leftrightarrow$" a connection between any device and any service: that is $d \leftrightarrow s$ means device d has established a connection to service s.

Now we define the *OUTER CUBE* (Definition 3), denoted by $\mathbb{O}_c$, as the set of Services $\mathbb{S}$ for which a connection has been established with a device in the *INNER CUBE*, $\mathbb{I}_c$.

Definition 3. $\mathbb{O}_c := \{s_i \in \mathbb{S} \text{ such that } \exists d_i \in \mathbb{D}_u \text{ and } d_i \leftrightarrow s_i\}$. *where:*

- s_i *is any current service being used by user U.*
- d_i *is any current device being used by user U.*

– $\mathbb{D}_u$ *is the set of discovered devices owned by the user U ready to use.*

Another critical element previously mentioned in [12], but not entirely described, is also defined here as *Pool Area*, Definition 4. The connection to the Pool Area is defined as $\mathbb{P}_a$, as the set of relationships established between any device d_i in $\mathbb{I}_c$ and any Service s_i in $\mathbb{O}_c$.

Definition 4. $\mathbb{P}_a = \{d_i \leftrightarrow S_i \text{ such that } d_i \in \mathbb{I}_c \text{ and } s_i \in \mathbb{O}_c\}.$

Now, based on the previous definitions, we can define the CUBE as a 4-tuple in Definition 5.

Definition 5. $\mathbb{C} = \{U, \mathbb{I}_c, \mathbb{O}_c, \mathbb{P}_a\}.$

The CUBE $\mathbb{C}$ defines a whole platform formed by a User U, surrounded by a set of communicating devices she/he owns, $\mathbb{I}_c$, a set of Services she/he accessed, $\mathbb{O}_c$, and the set of established connections, $\mathbb{P}_a$.

3.2   Model Scenario Representation

Following this formalization is given hereafter a use-case describing how the elements of the CUBE can work combined to achieve the scenario proposed in Fig. 2, introduced in our motivating scenario section.

The following use-case, shown in Fig. 4, makes use of both the Webmail client implemented for the initial feasibility (light-coupling) test of the CUBE and presented at [13] and the LiquidTUBE, our second feasibility test (tight-coupling) and the focus of this paper. We note the necessary settings of the CUBE is previously described in [11], and all devices are related to a single user, that is why we used the user-centric principle. Thus, for now, it is not possible to connect to another device outside the "user network".

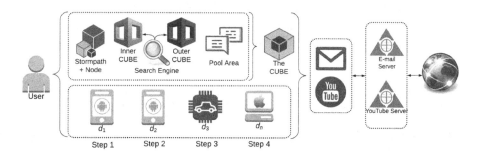

Fig. 4. Our second feasibility test scenario of the CUBE.

To start, we must assume three conditions:

1. The user chooses a connected mobile as her/his first device;

2. She/he decides to run an email service or watch a YouTube video;
3. The Car Operating System (COS) has an available compatibility interface, e.g., AUDI MMI Connection.

First, the user has at her/his disposal a set $\mathbb{D}$ of known and $\mathbb{D}_{OUT}$ of unknown devices which are found by our search engine $\mathcal{R}_d$. Then, the user manually selects those to be added to the INNER CUBE ($\mathbb{I}_c$) (Definition 2), which in turn starts the synchronization process and creates the CUBE session. Thus, using device d_p, the user requests some services $s_i \in \mathbb{S}$, e.g., start a video from YouTube.

We note that our description is linear. However, several procedures run in the second plan as callback procedures. At the moment of step 1, there already run all internal procedures required for the authentication process and connection availability. Thus, the Application and Request layers, both REST, with StormPath and Node.js respectively, make the token creation and send the HTTP responses for the required service. Also when the session starts, the Pool Area(Definition 4) deals with the first connection between d_p and s_i. Simultaneously created, the OUTER CUBE ($\mathbb{O}_c$) (Definition 3) deals with s_i as a set of services $\mathbb{S}$.

Thus, we have updated the *INNER CUBE* ($\mathbb{I}_c$), Pool Area ($\mathbb{P}_a$), and *OUTER CUBE* ($\mathbb{O}_c$) with the appropriate sets of devices, connections, and services, respectively, following the dynamic interactions within the environment. At this moment, it possible to add any new device to the CUBE (Definition 5) without compromising its structure. Also, the user does not need to be concerned regarding authorizing to the newly added device any service already discovered.

Next, in step 2, the user continues to watch the video at the exact moment previously stopped but using a different device (d_2). Still, in d_2, some callback procedures run under semantic rules to deal with hypermedia requests for the data changing status across the environment of multiple operating systems. That is why the Pool Area $\mathbb{P}_a$ is built fully RESTful because only with RESTful we can control hypermedia status. Therefore, for any request that arrives from the client or server, we assure privacy by encrypting data using the token created in step 1. Despite being shown as a linear model, the Conversation Layer is continuously available, allowing for data-change between devices and operational systems.

In step 3, our user will move by car. Hosted by a COS, the CUBE displayed as an icon, retrieves all data, session, and connections previously achieved. At this time, the available multiple devices are synchronized, allowing a resume of any task, at any time.

Finally, the user arrives at her/his destination, leaving step 3 with all synchronized data in her/his mobile. Then, on her/his laptop, based on iOS, the CUBE will retrieve all data produced so far, making it possible to resume the video at step 4.

4   Implementation Insights

With the achievement of the first feasibility test presented in [13], it was necessary to submit the CUBE to another real-world scenario in an environment that requires a third-party to work, but at this time, a tight-coupling service. Thus, we chose the streaming service from YouTube as a scenario to apply the CUBE, and aim to achieve the proposed outcome of fluently moving a YouTube video streaming towards native apps. We note that we do not consider HTML5 solutions due to its limitations regarding plugins devices.

At the same time, we added to the CUBE new functionalities, such as the enhancement of the device search engine, the authentication process with database tracked by a token, and the management of the devices that belong to the user. That means, now we can change the ID of the equipment inside the CUBE and not only rely upon the ID present on the device description. We present the CUBE architecture in Fig. 5 that shows where some functionalities work. We noted that the external element 107 in our previous version interacted with the 106 component. However, the behavior of the tight-coupling web-service required a change of the architecture. Then, in the new version, element 107 now interacts directly with the 105 component.

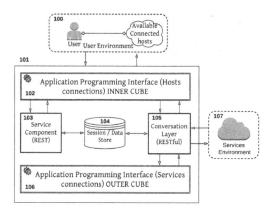

Fig. 5. The CUBE architecture and its internal modules.

In this uncontrolled scenario of YouTube streaming, the user experience is the central feature to evaluate. Thus, at this point, the behavior presented in the CUBE changed comparing with our previous test. Therefore, now, accessing the CUBE requires a more secure authentication step to get access to what we called the logical dock. This logical dock is the CUBE abstraction (a run-time file) based on the formal description previously described. It is represented in the form of a native application deployed from d_p, where a user can start the web services modeled to work from the CUBE.

It is essential to mention, at this moment, the CUBE works as a sort of a new session without making any change on the user device. That means once the user decides to leave the logical dock, all her/his previous activity is stored, e.g., the last video, viewed events, historical, etc.

Regarding the user-experience, since YouTube can work from a browser and also from native apps, we drive our efforts to make the Liquid experience as simple as possible. Thus, to work in a desktop station with a web browser, we preferred to create an extension of the CUBE for browsers. Therefore, we assumed that the Liquid feature should be more intuitive to the user. Thus, Fig. 6 shows the extension added on the browser (on the right top corner), where the user can liquid the content, that means, the control, state and data are transferred to another device, d_i in $\mathbb{D}_u$, d_i which becomes the new d_p.

On the other hand, for the native apps, we added the Liquid feature inside the button "share" that is native in all versions of the YouTube apps regardless of the operating system.

Fig. 6. The CUBE extension allows to the User liquid the content without Server synchronization.

5   Feasibility Test, Results, and Evaluation

For the test, we sent through the CUBE the elapsed time of the video, without a third-party to synchronize it. In this feasibility test, we used five different devices. Devices one (d_1) and two (d_2), a desktop HP Pentium Dual-Core 3GHz, and 8GB Ram, with a Windows 7 64 bits Professional. The device three (d_3), a Tablet Samsung A6 Chipset Exynos 7870 octa-core 1.6 GHz, Wi-Fi 802.11 a/b/g/n, and Wi-Fi Direct, Bluetooth v4.2 LE-A2DP with Android 8.0 Oreo. The device four (d_4), an iPhone 5 S 16 GB, Chipset Cyclone Apple A7 - 1.3 GHz Dual-Core, Wi-Fi 802.11 a/b/g/n, Bluetooth 4.0-A2DP with iOS 10.2. The device five (d_5), an iPad 32 GB, Chipset 1Ghz Single-Core ARM Cortex-A8, Wi-Fi 802.11 a/b/g/n (2.4 Ghz), Bluetooth 2.1-A2DP with iOS 4.0.

With a set of ten persons with no prior training with the CUBE, the test consists of starting a YouTube streaming video on the device one d_1 (Desktop Windows). Then, migrate by clicking on the extension icon in the browser on d_1, and then choose fluently move the video to d_2 (Desktop Windows) with the actual time elapsed. In the sequence d_2 sends the content to d_3 (Tablet Android).

This sequence repeats towards $d_3 \rightarrow d_4$ (Android to iOS) and $d_4 \rightarrow d_5$ (iOS to iOS) to finally going back to the first device d_1 (Desktop Windows). We note that the user must migrate the video towards the five different devices. Figure 7 shows the steps towards different devices.

Fig. 7. The YouTube content is fluently moved around different set of devices $\mathbb{D}$ owned by a User.

In the context of multiple-devices within multiple operating systems, there are different aspects to consider regarding the evaluation in the CUBE scenario, for example, privacy, throughput, user-experience, interaction time. Since there is no other proposition that synchronizes web-service at the user-side, the way we found to evaluate the CUBE was comparing its execution with YouTube itself synchronized at Server-side. For this test, we consider the wasted time to play a given video with and without the CUBE.

5.1 Results

In this second feasibility test, we achieved the expected results regarding the design of the CUBE within the modification of the user-centric perspective. Moreover, the separation of the CUBE as an extension to adding in-browser changed only a few things from the implementation perspective, without compromising the CUBE structure already defined.

We also could achieve the RESTful principles presented in the CUBE, such as high interoperability, security in all devices, system performance, etc. Regarding the constraints RESTful, we respected several, such as stateless interaction, resource linking, uniform interface, identification or addressability of resources, hypermedia for decentralized resources, etc.

Regarding the dependency and security of the third-party to retrieve data from YouTube, the CUBE worked as expected. We note the formal description of devices and services helped us from an implementation perspective to understanding and adequately mask the traceability of the devices. Therefore, the server was not aware of the migration between devices. Since the continuity of the video in the $\{d_2, d_3, \dots d_5\}$, is independent on each device, the request to the server was "resume" the task. That means, to the third-party server, the behavior was just a "pause/resume" action rather than a new connection. Therefore, the formal description helped us to assure that the CUBE works as the only responsible for maintaining a state of a given service, even if a third-party is required. Any further information regarding the functionalities or user-experience, a video with another test of the LiquidTube is available on YouTube on the following link: https://youtu.be/-TYPRXtC7Lw.

462   C. P. da Silva et al.

5.2 Evaluation

We used a video[1], with 2'31" long and followed the following protocol. We requested to 10 different users to watch the video and reproduce the same behavior with and without the CUBE. The user should fluently migrate the video at an exact point (minute, second, and milli-second) from a device to another one. We measure the interaction time wasted by each user when trying to move towards the five types of equipment.

We report the results of the CUBE in Fig. 8. In (a) the interaction time when users are trying to move from one device to another fluently. In (b), the total time wasted to fluently moving across all five types of equipment. The results show the interest of our approach as an alternative to the classical server-side approach.

The analysis reveals that the users average with the CUBE spent 5.821 s to migrate the video across five devices completely. On the other hand, without the CUBE, the same users spent 68.101 s to reproduce the same procedure. Thereby, the CUBE is up to ≈12 times faster than the traditional YouTube cloud-based synchronization procedure.

Finally, since there is no particular procedure to follow, those already familiar with browser navigation, such as buttons or extensions, or even in mobile since the CUBE deploys natively on the share button. Therefore, users considered intuitive and easy to follow and migrate the video using YouTube from the CUBE.

To the best of our knowledge, our work is the only one that synchronizes web services at the user-side.

6 Related Work

To better positioning this paper contribution regarding the existent works on the state-of-art, we recall that the CUBE relies its principles upon the user-centric approach for managing devices interaction and owning services. Our aim here is a better understanding of how authors are dealing with web-services synchronization at the user-side without continuously depending on a cloud/server-based system. Moreover, we are trying to find a solution that addressed web-service synchronization at the user-side without a server dependency and applied in a multiple- devices/operating systems environment.

6.1 Server-Side Synchronization

Companies such as Apple have their outstanding Handoff's, which keep track of state and services on their Cloud and can migrate these features and functions over multiple devices running iOS. On the other hand, the Nextbit's Baton or Google Docs is the Android solution for devices with their operating system. While Nextbit concentrates on native apps, Google Docs does web service synchronization through a web browser.

---

[1] https://www.youtube.com/watch?v=nuPZUUED5uk.

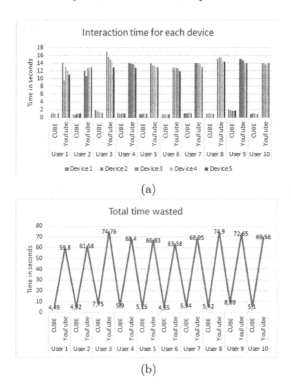

Fig. 8. The evaluation demonstrates difference regarding the user experience with and without the CUBE.

On the path of multiple device approaches, the work presented by Hamilton et al. [3] deals with the services synchronization in Android devices through a framework called Conductor that make use of WebSockets, and a color system for pairing devices.

The work of Wolters et al. [15], deals with Android cross-device synchronization. They use a collaborative service over a single external device where a different subscriber can change some data and send it back to the original user. However, they do not present any screen capture, neither achieved results.

Iyer et al. [8] present an Android cross-device platform to provide seamless integration with a simplified programming model. They work over a run-time binding of the services with the application rather than at the compile time. They also deal with the behavior of mobile devices. However, there are no further information, os feasibility tests.

In a collaborative scenarios of multiple connected devices, the platform Mobilis from [10] has a purpose of supporting developers to create collaborative apps. Mobilis works as a third-party provider with some features to deploy web services over multiple devices within same operating system.

The last contribution of Server-Side synchronization is the work of Gallid-abino et al. [2], called Liquid.js. Several papers previously mentioned Liquid Software principles, e.g., fluidity, seamless moving, etc. However, this work in specific presents Liquid Software bases over Hartman's work, as we also do.

They proposed a framework that implements multiple-device within different operating systems and services, but all rely on an API or browser to run. In this case, the sense of running on iOS or Android over a browser does not fit multi-OS since there are no native apps deployed. However, it is inspiring to see functionalities such as cloning and migration over a framework under Liquid Software concepts.

6.2   User-Side Synchronization

The paradigm User-side versus Server-Side well described by Paulheim et al. in [9]. Their work presents concepts of the real World problems regarding the available technologies. They are also concerned about web services concepts, such as modularity, seamlessly integration, and the service state. They also mentioned an implemented prototype working as a middleware running over a single device, but and there is no cross-device.

Baoping et al. present another work that proposed middleware [6]. Here authors presented a request-based mediation framework that works for dynamic invocation of web services for generating the corresponding mediator. However, there is no demonstration or feasibility test, only mention of improvement without further details.

Regarding shared data over multiple devices, the work of Nicolai et al. [7] demonstrates data transfer (copy/paste) in Android devices by proximity using a pattern. Regarding the devices and OS, no more details are given.

Regarding the User-side synchronization, there is a gap of approaches that deals web service synchronization within multiple-devices and different operating systems. Therefore, we present at Table 1 the current works regarding the main axes from the CUBE, that means, server or client-side synchronization, same or multiple-devices, and same or multiple-operating systems.

Table 1. Approaches and contributions from State-of-the-Art.

	The CUBE	Paulheim [9]	Baoping [6]	Nicolai [7]	Hamilton [3]	Wolters [15]	Iyer [8]	Mobilis [10]	Gallidabino [2]
Server-side synchronization	NO	NO	NO	NO	YES	YES	YES	YES	YES
User-side synchronization	YES	YES	YES	YES	NO	NO	NO	NO	NO
Multiple operating system	YES	NO	NO	NO	NO	NO	NO	NO	NO
Same operating system	YES	YES	YES	YES	YES	YES	YES	YES	NO
Multiple device	YES	NO	NO	YES	YES	YES	YES	YES	YES
Same device	YES	YES	YES	NO	NO	NO	NO	NO	NO

7   Conclusions

In this paper, we described in further detail the CUBE. A system-model architecture that uses concepts of REST, RESTful, and user-centric to give a solution that fluently migrates web services instances synchronized at user-side within a multiple-devices/operating system environment. The CUBE, as modeled, converges towards the ability required to dealing with the challenges of the user-side synchronization.

Across the existent works of server- user-side synchronization, we could also demonstrate the lack of approaches that deal with web services synchronization at user-side in a multiple-devices environment, and regardless of the operating system.

Thus, with a formal description of the necessary elements required to build the CUBE, we were also able to better understanding traceability measures within devices and services. Moreover, dealing with a tight-coupling service such as YouTube, has required an adaptation of our architecture to deal with the RESTful constraint of hypermedia controls to change data/status. Then, we were able to propose an enhancement in our Pool Area to deal with this challenge.

We have also presented the feasibility test, called LiquidTube, in an uncontrolled scenario with a tight-coupling service such as YouTube, to move a video through multiple-devices fluently. An individual analysis demonstrated that users are more comfortable with the CUBE to migrate the video. For each user, the wasted time to migrate the video per device was 1.1642 s with the CUBE, while users spent 13.6202 s without the CUBE, which means users are up to 11.6991 faster while using the CUBE. This individual analysis converges with the average founded and explained in the Evaluation subsection. The analysis of this information demonstrates the feasibility of the CUBE, and also reflects the interest of our approach.

Regarding our future steps, further tests will be done to take into account other parameters like network throughput for Wi-Fi, 3G, 4G and cable connections, and also privacy requirements to deploy multiple services. Moreover, regarding the user experience, we will conduct other different tests based on System Usability Scale formats (SUS) with different web services deployed from the CUBE. We also note that we drive our efforts towards a patent procedure for the CUBE.

We also intend to make the CUBE a shared resource environment. That means we may be able to create a model-system, like a cluster, to enhance processing and store capacities for a given web service without depending on a cloud-based system. These functionalities drive us to follow the principle of elastic systems but applied at the user-side. Furthermore, we intend to explore mobile sensors to fluently moving web services according to user movement and point of interest. Thus, the CUBE will also address the IoT device's perspectives.

References

1. Gallidabino, A., et al.: On the architecture of liquid software: technology alternatives and design space. In: Proceedings of 13th Working IEEE/IFIP Conference on Software Architecture (WICSA). IEEE (2016)
2. Gallidabino, A., Pautasso, C.: The liquid.js framework for migrating and cloning stateful web components across multiple devices. In: Proceedings of the 25th International Conference on World Wide Web, WWW 2016, Montreal, Canada, 11–15 April 2016, Companion Volume, pp. 183–186 (2016)
3. Hamilton, P., Wigdor, D.J.: Conductor: enabling and understanding cross-device interaction. In: Proceedings of the SIGCHI Conference on Human Factors in Computing Systems, CHI 2014, pp. 2773–2782. ACM, New York (2014)
4. Hartman, J., Manber, U., Peterson, L.L., Proebsting, T.: Liquid software: a new paradigm for networked systems. University of Arizona, Tucson, AZ, USA, Technical report (1996)
5. Hartmann, F.: User-Centric Networking: Privacy- and Resource-Awareness in User-to-User Communication. Ph.D. thesis, Karlsruhe Institute of Technology, Germany (2017)
6. Lin, B., Gu, N., Li, Q.: A requester-based mediation framework for dynamic invocation of web services. In: 2006 IEEE International Conference on Services Computing, pp. 445–454 (2006)
7. Marquardt, N., Ballendat, T., Boring, S., Greenberg, S., Hinckley, K.: Gradual engagement: facilitating information exchange between digital devices as a function of proximity. In: Proceedings of the 2012 ACM International Conference on Interactive Tabletops and Surfaces, ITS 2012, pp. 31–40. ACM (2012)
8. Narayana, I.A., Roopa, T.: Extending android application programming framework for seamless cloud integration. In: Proceedings of the 2012 IEEE First International Conference on Mobile Services, MS 2012, pp. 96–104. IEEE Computer Society, Washington (2012)
9. Paulheim, H.: Ontology-based System Integration. In: Ontology-based Application Integration, pp. 27–59. Springer, New York (2011). https://doi.org/10.1007/978-1-4614-1430-8_3
10. Schuster, D., Lübke, R., Bendel, S., Springer, T., Schill, A.: Mobilis - comprehensive developer support for building pervasive social computing applications. In: PIK - Praxis der Informationsverarbeitung und Kommunikation, vol. 36 (2013)
11. da Silva, C.P., Messai, N., Sam, Y., Devogele, T.: Diamond - a cube model proposal based on a centric architecture approach to enhance liquid software model approaches. In: Proceedings of the 13th International Conference on Web Information Systems and Technologies-WEBIST, pp. 382–387. ScitePress (2017)
12. da Silva, C.P., Messai, N., Sam, Y., Devogele, T.: CUBE system: a REST and RESTful based platform for liquid software approaches. In: Majchrzak, T.A., Traverso, P., Krempels, K.-H., Monfort, V. (eds.) WEBIST 2017. LNBIP, vol. 322, pp. 115–131. Springer, Cham (2018). https://doi.org/10.1007/978-3-319-93527-0_6
13. da Silva, C.P., Messai, N., Sam, Y., Devogele, T.: Liquid mail - a client mail based on CUBE model. In: 38th IEEE International Conference on Distributed Computing Systems, ICDCS, Vienna, Austria, 2–6 July 2018, pp. 1539–1540 (2018)
14. Suckling, J., Lee, J.: Integrating environmental and social life cycle assessment: asking the right question. J. Ind. Ecol. **21**(6), 1454–1463 (2017)
15. Wolters, D., Kirchhoff, J., Gerth, C., Engels, G.: Cross-device integration of android apps. In: Sheng, Q.Z., Stroulia, E., Tata, S., Bhiri, S. (eds.) ICSOC 2016. LNCS, vol. 9936, pp. 171–185. Springer, Cham (2016). https://doi.org/10.1007/978-3-319-46295-0_11

An Approach to Build P2P Web Extensions

Rodolfo Gonzalez[1], Sergio Firmenich[1,2(✉)], Alejandro Fernandez[1], Gustavo Rossi[1,2], and Darío Velez[1]

[1] LIFIA, CIC, Facultad de Informática, Universidad Nacional de La Plata, Buenos Aires, Argentina
`{rgonzalez,sfirmenich,casco,gustavo}@lifia.info.unlp.edu.ar`
[2] CONICET, Buenos Aires, Argentina

Abstract. Web extensions are currently the most frequently used mechanism for end-users to externally adapt and enrich the web. While most functionality offered by extensions runs on the browser, extensions that offer collaboration, complex computation, or massive storage rely on a centralized server. Relying on a server increases the cost of building, deploying, and maintaining web extensions (even small ones). This paper presents a novel P2P approach to build web extensions. It removes the need for a centralized server while hiding behind a framework the complexity of building P2P extensions. It uses a middleware to manage the resources offered by the browser so multiple P2P extensions can coexist, without degrading the browser's performance. This paper discusses the main challenges of building P2P web extensions, presents the approach, and shows its potential with a proof of concept.

Keywords: Web extensions · Peer to peer

1 Introduction

From the perspective of the average web user, the web browser has not changed much since it was first introduced. Most of the browser's evolution over the years was aimed at handling richer and more interactive content, offering better security, and dealing with aspects of the web that most users are unaware of. Browser plug-ins (currently well-known as web extensions) were introduced to enable customization of the browser by third parties. Web extensions [1] are nowadays the *de facto* standard to customize the web browser and consequently augment the user's experience with the web. Web extensions can change the browser behavior, introduce changes to visited websites and also to provide new web pages delivered with the extension once installed in the Web browser. A web extension is made of a combination of Javascript, HTML, CSS, and configurations files. A well-defined API [1] governs the interaction of extensions with the browser and with the visited web pages. Extensions can communicate with external services (via HTTP requests), for example, to augment the visited web page with content from other sources, to store information on the cloud, to perform complex computation, and to support collaboration. In most cases, regardless of the complexity of the functionality they offer, such networked extensions are designed in a client-server architecture.

© Springer Nature Switzerland AG 2020
M. Bielikova et al. (Eds.): ICWE 2020, LNCS 12128, pp. 467–474, 2020.
https://doi.org/10.1007/978-3-030-50578-3_31

This means that they depend on a server-side component/service, which increases the technical skills required to create the web extension. In addition, depending on a server component complicates maintenance and increases the costs associated with deployment for production.

We argue that building web extensions in a P2P style opens new opportunities to augment the web, especially when collaboration is involved, by removing the need for a server component. Following the P2P philosophy, web extensions are designed in order to allow users to collaborate by sharing the computation, storage and networking capabilities of their browsers, and by explicitly solving tasks for one another. In this article, we discuss the challenges that building P2P extensions present and outline our proposed approach based on a middleware that manages the resources offered by the browser so multiple P2P extensions can coexist, without degrading the browser's performance.

This article is structured as follows. Section 2 motivates the approach through an example. Section 3 outlines our approach, and Sect. 4 presents a proof of concept. Related works are discussed in Sect. 5. Finally, in Sect. 6 we conclude and reflect on future works.

2   Motivation: Augmenting News Portals with Visualizations

Consider that we want to improve navigation in news portals by augmenting them with visualizations of its latest articles and related articles from other news portals. One alternative to creating such augmentation implies:

1. Harvesting the articles in the portals, starting from those featured on the homepage and recursively following the links to other articles in the portal, until a maximum level N has been reached.
2. Extracting for each article its author, date, media type, title, text, and links to other articles in the portal.
3. Characterizing each article by topic (for instance, using TF-IDF) and by sentiment (using an opinion lexicon), and then computing article similarity.
4. Building and presenting alternative visualizations of the articles (topics cloud, timeline, sentiment, etc.) that visitors can use to navigate.

The augmentation can be realized as a web extension. With the support of the extension, visitors annotate web sites' DOM to define how to harvest articles and their properties (for example, using the approach defined in [2]). They annotate the portal's home page (to identify entry points), and one article (that serves as a prototype). Upon visiting an annotated news portal, the extension automatically and transparently crawls those news portals for which an annotation is available, harvests the content, and builds or updates the visualization.

Simple as it sounds, building such an extension presents some challenges. For any mainstream news portal, the number of articles to process can easily be in the order of hundreds. On such scale, crawling and processing are both time-consuming and computation-intensive, rendering the visualization (and possibly the news portal) unusable. Moreover, all this work would be performed by each visitor using the extension unless some collaboration mechanism to avoid unnecessary work duplication is used. To respond to these challenges, and assuming that many users will install the extension, we propose designing it in a P2P style. Doing so yields the following benefits:

- Extensions can collaborate to reduce time and workload. When an extension starts the process, it can delegate part of the crawling, harvesting and processing tasks to other available peers. In fact, performing these tasks would be unnecessary if a peer has already performed them and the results are available.
- Navigable visualizations of news articles as well as the results of harvesting (i.e., article's data), and processing (i.e., topic, sentiment, and similarity models) may be replicated and shared without the need of a central server.

3   The Approach in a Nutshell

To simplify development, and reducing development and execution errors, we separate different concerns into two supporting artifacts. First, a middleware that manages all P2P extensions installed in the browser, handling message exchange, and monitoring workload. Next, a framework that abstracts the key domain objects (such as message and peer), provides a clear interface to send messages and hides interaction with the middleware. Following this approach, developers do not require any other technical skill than those required to write any other web extension: JavaScript, HTML, and CSS and also the same kind of deployment process, i.e. just to install the extension in a Web browser.

Figure 1 shows the overall approach. A web extension implements the P2P middleware and exposes the P2P API to any other web extension installed on the same browser. Other web extensions can directly execute functions in the middleware API via the message passing mechanisms [1]. However, the recommended way to interact with the middleware is via the P2P framework. Developers include the framework as a dependency of their extensions (it is JavaScript library). As it may be appreciated, all the messages pass through the middleware and are later routed to the corresponding web extension. For the concrete web extension, a message is a JSON object with the features the developers desire. When the messages pass through the middleware (using the behavior provided by our framework), it is encapsulated with the information required in the middleware layer (the type of message, timestamp, the extension's metadata among others), as Fig. 1 shows at the right.

The P2P extension that delivers the middleware comes with a minimalist user interface, which allows the user to have control of the messages.

Communication between peers is currently based on WebRTC[1]. WebRTC brings real-time video and audio communication to the browser and can be used to transport other forms of content. It robustly solves the technical challenges in P2P communication. To establish a direct connection between peers in WebRTC, a discovery and negotiation method called *signaling* is used. It involves both parties connecting to a commonly agreed upon service to decide the mechanisms they will use to connect (as they may

---

[1] WebRTC. https://webrtc.org/ - Last accessed on January 5th, 2020.

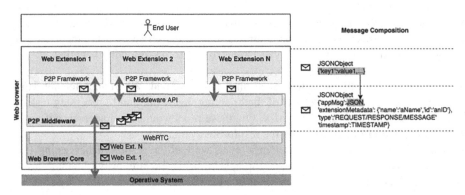

Fig. 1. The approach in a nutshell

be located behind firewalls, in NAT'd networks, etc.). The signaling process can be implemented with any technology compatible with WebSocket/XHR. WebRTC depends on a commonly known signaling server that introduces a unique point of failure and turns the architecture into a hybrid P2P. However, it must be noted that our approach still removes the need for writing and deploying a specific server for each web extension. We consider this to be a good trade-off while we explore other alternatives.

3.1 Framework

The framework is packaged as a JavaScript library. Once included in the web extension project, the user must create a class that represents the application (for instance, *P2PNewsVisualization*), and make this class inherit from the extension point offered by the Framework, which is called *AbstractP2PExtension*. This extension point lets developers specify the behavior of their web extensions considering two communication modes: (a) to send a message to another peer without expecting a response, (b) to send a request message for which a response is expected and must be managed by the peer that made the request when it arrives. The following list presents the main aspects to be considered for using the *AbstractP2PExtension* extension point:

- The developer must instantiate the concrete class and send to the new instance the *connect()* message (it is inherited from the extension point), whose purpose is:

  - to send the *initialize()* message to the new instance, which is a method for which developers must offer concrete behavior in their classes, among other things, to set instance variables related to the extension's metadata (*name* and *id*), in order to uniquely identify the extension.
  - to initialize the P2P communication mechanism for the web extension.
  - to register the extension in the middleware.

- Developers may use other inherited behaviors to look for peers, and to send messages/requests to other peers:

- *getPeers(callback)*: obtains the peers currently connected. Since this method is asynchronous, a callback function must be passed as a parameter.
- *sendMessage(msg, peer)*: sends a message (first parameter) to a specific peer (second parameter).
- *broadcasting(msg)*: send a message to all the peers.
- *sendRequest(msg, peer)*: send a request message (first parameter) to a specific peer (second parameter). It is expected to receive a response.
- *sendResponse(msg, peer)*: send a response using a message (first parameter), and to a specific peer (third parameter). In this case, the *msg* (a *JSON* object) should be populated with further information about the original request.

- To handle messages and requests according to its needs, the extension must implement some of the following methods (or all of them):

  - *receiveMessage(msg, peer)*: this method will be executed when a new message is sent to the extension. It is not expected to deliver a response. It receives the message as a first parameter and the peers who sent it as the second parameter.
  - *processRequest(msg, peer)*: this method will be executed when the extension receives a request. It is not expected to create and deliver a response during the method execution. This method is suitable for human (interactive) collaboration. Its response depends on the user's interaction which occurs asynchrously.
  - *automaticProcessing(msg, peer)*: this method will be executed when the extension receives a request and this request was marked as *automatic* (it is just a flag in the message). This method must return a JSON object intended to be used as a response, and the framework automatically delivers it when the method finishes. This method is specially designed for computing collaboration, that can be automated, i.e. without depending on user intervention.

- If the extension sends requests, it must implement the *processResponse(msg, peer)* method to manage the responses to the requests previously done.

Figure 2 shows a simplified version of our framework plus another class showing how to inherit from the extension point, named AbstractP2PExtension. The P2PConnector class is the one that uses the middleware API. Two other classes provide simple abstractions for the peer and the message. The Message class is managed by the AbstractP2PExtension and the P2PConnector objects, meanwhile, the concrete class representing the web extension (P2PNewsVisualization) always work with the JSON Object defined by the developer.

4 Proof of Concept

As proof of concept, we have developed a variation of the P2P extension discussed in Sect. 2. In this case, we have chosen to collaboratively perform the scraping and the processing of news articles. Note that in the P2P extension, the collaboration among peers could be organized with different granularity levels, which at the end depends on

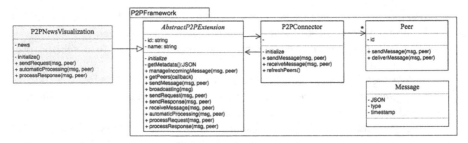

Fig. 2. The framework and its extension point, the class AbstractP2PExtension

developers' decisions. For the sake of space, in this example, we use a coarse granularity to simplify the source code shown in Fig. 3. The main idea is that the peer that starts the process (*pA*) requests another peer to handle an extraction template. The extraction template includes a news portal home's URL, the annotations to extract the news on this home page, and the annotations to extract information for a particular news article. In this way, each peer will be requested to start the scraping process from a particular news portal, applying the same extraction template to each news article crawled. As a result, each peer will follow a different crawling and scraping path. For each news article, the peer must also extract the topics (basically, calculating the most relevant words) and then compute the sentiment analysis. Then, the extracted and processed news articles are sent to *pA* together with their metadata.

```
class P2PNewsVisualization extends AbstractP2PExtension{
  startCollaborativeScraping(){
      this.getPeers(this.collaborativeScraping);}
  collaborativeScraping(peers){
      templates = this.restoreExtractionTemplates();
      for (peer in peers){
          ...
          msg = {'extractor':templates[j], 'automatic':true};
          this.sendRequest(peer, msg);
          ...
          }
  }
  processResponse(msg, peer){this.storeNews(msg.news);}
  automaticProcessing(msg, peer){
      let news = this.processWebSiteExtractor(msg.extractor);
      return {'news':news};
  }
  processWebSiteExtractor(templateExtractor){
      let news = this.extractNewsFrom(templateExtractor);
      news = this.augmentNewsWithTopics(news);
      news = this.applySentimentAnalysis(news);
      return news;}
}
```

Fig. 3. Source code excerpt for the news visualization scenario.

Figure 3 shows an excerpt from the source code (focused on those aspects related to our approach), whose main class is shown in Fig. 2, named P2PNewsVisualization.

The source code example is illustrative, so we do not take into account in this excerpt the number of peers in relation to the number of news portals.

For the proof of concept, we defined extraction templates for three news portals. We execute scraping and processing of news considering two scenarios:

- Stand-alone: *pA* processes all the available extraction templates.
- P2P: *pA* processes one extraction template and delegates the rest of the available extraction templates to other peers (one extraction template per peer).

A total of 228 web page's DOMS were processed. For the stand-alone scenario, it took 298 s. For the P2P scenario, which was based on three web browser (*pA* plus two peers), it took 120 s. Although the difference is remarkable, we did not take the best advantage of the P2P approach, given that using more peers and more fine granurality in the tasks requested, probably would improve the total time.

5 Related Works

To the best of our knowledge, there are two well-known applications of P2P in web browsers. First, there are approaches to support collaborative computing. For instance, Pando offers a platform in which a user must install a server and run it in his own machine. Then, other users may access this back-end application with their browsers to offer it for computing [5]. On the other hand, it has been proposed to use the browser as a distributed platform for content delivery [6, 9]. Over this idea, a work studies the use of a communication protocol [7] that improves how to program over WebRTC. [10] proposes a generic distributed application server which is also currently supported by existing web browsers such as Beaker Browser [11]. Other approaches use P2P communication for specific aims, such as improving virtual environments [8].

Although these works show that decentralizing the Web is a current topic, these are far to be applicable to web extensions with the final goal of improving the overall user's web experience. Server-side support for web extensions was already studied and analyzed [4], in which authors propose a Model-Driven Web Augmentation approach to model back-end requirements. Although the complexity for developing, deploying and maintaining the back-end component is clearly better than using an ad-hoc approach, we believe that a P2P approach based exactly on the same technology required for programming web extensions is a more suitable and convenient way, at the same time that it removes any need of a centralized server application.

6 Conclusions and Future Works

External Web structures (i.e. "defining hypermedia structures externally of the involved documents" [3]) are software artifacts that improve the overall Web experience. Web extensions are the most common and convenient way to develop and deploy this kind of software. Without an intermediate server, a web extension cannot communicate to the same web extension installed in another user's browser. Even more, when some communication between different web browsers is required, new technical barriers appear (for instance, dealing with back-end technologies beyond HTML, CSS, and JavaScript). Sever-side support has been very important for different reasons [4].

This paper presented an approach build P2P web extensions, which aims to eliminate the need for a centralized server to communicate web browsers and users. A signaling back-end service has been designed and implemented. It may connect peers for any web extension or for a specific one without requiring changes on it, neither on the P2P web extensions source code because it was conceived as a generic single-purpose (to connect peers) platform. Although we believe that our approach improves the potential of web extensions without requiring a centralized application, we still need to create and evaluate more scenarios. For instance, pervasive and distributed storage should be supported by the framework. However, we already could apply our approach in several scenarios. Besides future evaluations and experiments in this regard, it is also mandatory to study which is the power of a P2P web browser, as well as how to continuously measure and limit this kind of collaboration in order to not spoil the overall Web experience.

References

1. Browser Extensions. Draft Community Group Report 23 July 2017. https://browserext.git hub.io/browserext/. Accessed 20 Jan 2020
2. Bosetti, G., Firmenich, S., Rossi, G., Winckler, M., Barbieri, T.: Web objects ambient: an integrated platform supporting new kinds of personal web experiences. In: Bozzon, A., Cudre-Maroux, P., Pautasso, C. (eds.) ICWE 2016. LNCS, vol. 9671, pp. 563–566. Springer, Cham (2016). https://doi.org/10.1007/978-3-319-38791-8_49
3. Bouvin, N.O.: From notecards to notebooks: there and back again. In: Proceedings of the 30th ACM Conference on Hypertext and Social Media, pp. 19–28, September 2019
4. Urbieta, M., Firmenich, S., Bosetti, G., Maglione, P., Rossi, G., Olivero, M.: MDWA: a model-driven web augmentation approach - coping with client- and server-side support. Softw. Syst. Model. (2020, in press)
5. Lavoie, E., Hendren, L., Desprez, F., Correia, M.: Pando: personal volunteer computing in browsers. In: Proceedings of the 20th International Middleware Conference, pp. 96–109 (2019)
6. Kobusińska, A., Wolski, A., Brzeziński, J., Ge, M.: P2P web browser middleware to enhance service-oriented computing—analysis and evaluation. In: 2017 IEEE 10th Conference on Service-Oriented Computing and Applications (SOCA), pp. 58–65 (2017)
7. Tindall, N., Harwood, A.: Peer-to-peer between browsers: cyclon protocol over WebRTC. In: 2015 IEEE International Conference on Peer-to-Peer Computing (P2P), pp. 1–5. IEEE, September 2015
8. Koskela, T., Vatjus-Anttila, J., Dahl, T.: Communication architecture for a P2P-enhanced virtual environment client in a web browser. In: 2014 6th International Conference on New Technologies, Mobility and Security (NTMS), pp. 1–5, IEEE, March 2014
9. Vogt, C., Werner, M.J., Schmidt, T.C.: Leveraging WebRTC for P2P content distribution in web browsers. In: 2013 21st IEEE International Conference on Network Protocols (ICNP), pp. 1–2. IEEE, October 2013
10. Jannes, K., Lagaisse, B., Joosen, W.: The web browser as a distributed application server: towards decentralized web applications in the edge. In: Proceedings of the 2nd International Workshop on Edge Systems, Analytics, and Networking, pp. 7–11, March 2019
11. Beaker Browser. https://beakerbrowser.com. Accessed 29 Jan 2020

Web-Based Learning

Blended or Distance Learning?

Comparing Student Performance Between University and Open University

Erkki Kaila[1]($\boxtimes$) and Henri Kajasilta[2]

[1] University of Helsinki, Helsinki, Finland
erkki.kaila@helsinki.fi
[2] University of Turku, Turku, Finland

Abstract. Programming and computer science are nowadays taught in various institutions to a very heterogeneous group of people. Open universities are a typical example of non-traditional educational institutes. Online learning and blended learning models are often utilized in open universities because the students rarely study full time. In this paper, we present a study where four programming and computer science courses were taught in the Open University and in the university at the same time. A blended learning methodology was used to teach the courses in the university. The students in the open university could decide freely whether they wanted to take the courses fully online or to participate into classroom sessions as well. Moreover, no lectures were given in the open university. Instead, the students could download lecture handouts and other material online. The results from continuous assessment and the final exam of four shared IT/CS courses were analyzed. We found out that although there are some statistical differences in the results of individual sections, in general the course results are quite similar in both universities. However, the incomplete data of chosen methodologies prevents us from fully answering the research questions.

Keywords: Online learning · Open University · CS education · Learning analytics · Blended learning

1 Introduction

Computer science, and especially programming, are gaining more and more interest among all people. In addition to traditional universities and other official schools, it is nowadays quite common to learn to program by using MOOCs (see for example [1] or [2]) or in the open university courses. Because the number of students attending the classes can get high (as the largest MOOCs can host tens of thousands of students), and because the students may be located all around the world, online learning has become the only reasonable method for teaching these courses. Although the usage of modern technology opens a variety of possibilities, online education also means that some of the traditional forms of teaching, such as lectures, may not be as feasible as they were before.

© Springer Nature Switzerland AG 2020
M. Bielikova et al. (Eds.): ICWE 2020, LNCS 12128, pp. 477–484, 2020.
https://doi.org/10.1007/978-3-030-50578-3_32

In this article, we compare learning by using somewhat traditional approach in the University and more open and free approach in the Open University. The same four courses were taught side by side in University of Turku, Finland during the academic year of 2017 to 2018 in both universities. The students in the Open University had more freedom of choice in their study methodology, but the course contents and the staff responsible were the same for both universities. We are presenting the results from all shared courses in both universities, including the final scores of the exams and the points collected from assignments and exercises throughout the course. Based on the results, we try to predict the significance of the differing features in the course methodologies. Hence, this article tries to answer to the following research questions:

RQ1. Are there differences in learning results between students utilizing blended learning and distance learning methodologies?
RQ2. Is there difference in learning between different types of courses in the shared curriculum?

2 Related Work

Selecting the most efficient study methodology (or even defining what we mean by efficiency in learning) might be a cumbersome task. According to a systematic study of methods for teaching programming [3], the courses that utilize relatable content and pair programming lead to the best learning results, alongside using a CS0 course before the first programming course. The methodology used in all courses in this study is utilizing these findings as closely as possible. For example, a mechanism similar to pair programming (see [4]) is used in all courses, regardless of whether they are "pure" programming courses or not.

Blended learning models (in other words, models that combine online learning and "traditional" classroom learning) have proven to be quite beneficial in learning to program. In [5] the authors presented a blended model to teach programming, with focus on developing tools for online education. The model proved to be quite successful in relation to pass rates. Several other experiments to incorporate blended learning into computer science (and especially programming) education have been presented later, see for example [6].

In some cases, there have been difficulties in the adaptation of blended models: according to [7], the students in a blended machine learning course where students "had concerns about the coupling of online and in-class components". In [8] the authors analyzed the student outcomes in a web-enabled blended learning course, and out of 29 variables (or actions), determined the ones that correlated most with the course grade. According to the author, the actions that influenced the course success the most were "reading and posting messages", "wiki edit" and "content creation contribution". [9] goes one step deeper by presenting 21 "brain-compatible" learning principles that should be utilized in blended learning courses.

Distance learning, e-learning or online learning typically refers to education where learning scenarios take place entirely over internet. However, even the usage of terminology itself can be inconsistent. According to [10] the terms distance learning, online learning and e-learning are considered exactly the same thing by some researchers, but some think they mean different things. For example, e-learning was considered as "learning that happens with computers while distance learning is done by postal mail" by some, or as a model that was blended with face-to-face learning by others.

3   University and Open University

For the study, a four-course combination from University of Turku, Finland was selected. The same four courses were taught at the same time in the University and in the Open University, mainly by the same staff. The Open University is open for anyone interested with no prerequisite knowledge or degrees. In practice, the students in the Open University are usually either interested in applying to a university or just having a general interest towards the topic with no deeper goals. The students taking the courses in the University are typically computer science or engineering majors or other majors from the Faculty of Science and Engineering.

3.1   Shared Curriculum

The curriculum in the Open University contains four courses. The same four courses are taught in the University. The courses are listed in Table 1.

Table 1.   The courses included in the study

Course name	Period	ECTS	Abbreviation
Introduction to Computer Science 1	1st	5	CS1
Introduction to Algorithms and Programming	2nd	6	AP
Introduction to Object-Oriented Programming	3rd	7	OOP
Introduction to Computer Science 2	4th	5	CS2

The CS1 course is designed to be the first introduction to the topic in the curriculum. The topics include algorithmic thinking, binary and hexadecimal systems and Boolean algebra. *The AP course is* a typical introductory course to programming using Java as the programming language. *The OOP course* focuses on object-oriented programming. The topics covered include writing classes, inheritance, interfaces, abstract classes, polymorphism and advanced error handling. Finally, in *the CS2 course,* the functional principles of computers are covered starting from logic circuits to machine language.

All courses are taught on the same schedule. In the Open University, one course per eight-week study period is taught. In the University, additional courses are included in the curriculum. Considering content, the courses are exactly similar in both universities. Moreover, the same staff members are involved in teaching the courses in both universities.

3.2 Methodology Description and Comparison

The methodology utilized in both universities emphasizes active learning. Each course is built upon the same basic principles of the tutorial-based learning methodology [11]. Some of the key features are shortly explained below.

The courses are divided into seven weekly modules. Each week the lecture material is accompanied with automatically assessed exercises that are meant to be completed before other material. Active learning is enabled with automatic assessment and made meaningful with immediate feedback. *Continuous assessment* is emphasized by making the exercises compulsory and by giving a reward for completing them: completing more than the minimum required amount earns students bonus points for the final exam. Gamification is utilized by elements such as virtual trophies and progress bars.

In tutorial-based learning, tutorials (combination of learning material and digital exercises) are completed in collaboration with another student. The students use the same computer and the controller is frequently changed. This kind of collaboration has been proven quite beneficial for learning (see for example [12]). One tutorial was provided each week with one-week time to complete it.

The main difference between methodologies were lectures. In the University, each week consisted of a lecture (followed with weekly exercises) and a tutorial session. In the Open University, the lecture handouts were shared with students, but no lectures were organized. The only exception was a single summary lecture at the end of each course. Participation into the session was optional, and by estimation, a little less than half of the students did participate.

Another difference between universities were the required attendances: in the University, the students were required to participate in six out of all seven tutorial sessions. In the Open University, the students could attend the sessions or answer the tutorials at home, however they preferred. The attendances were not registered, but according to course staff the number of students attending the sessions was the largest in the first course and then slowly decreased towards the end of the year.

A summary of methodologies in both universities is displayed in Table 2.

Table 2. Methodologies summarized

Feature	University	Open University
Lectures	Optional, bonus awarded for attendance	Materials only, one summary lecture at the end of each course
Tutorials	Min. 50% of points and attendance required	Min. 50% of points required
Weekly exercises	Min. 50% of points required	Min. 50% of points required

4 Research Setup

The study was conducted in the academic year of 2017 to 2018. The academic year is divided into four study periods, with one course in each period. The data was collected automatically by ViLLE [13], the online tool utilized for the exercises, tutorials and as a learning management system (LMS). In the University courses, Moodle (see e.g. [14]) was used as an LMS, but all tasks involving active learning were still done in ViLLE.

4.1 Participants

The number of participants varies between courses. In the University, not all courses are mandatory for all students in the faculty. In the Open University, dropping out after the first course(s) is more common than in the University. To keep the results comparable, we counted a student as a participant in a course if he/she collected at least some points in the first week's tasks. The total number of (active) participants in all four courses are listed in Table 3.

Table 3. Number of active students in each course

Course	University N	Open University N
CS1	288	51
AP	264	54
OOP	216	39
CS2	150	25

As seen from the table, the number of students in the Open University is a lot smaller than in the University courses. The number also is much smaller in the final course, CS2. In the University, the number is likely smaller because the first three courses are mandatory for many students in the faculty, but the final course is not. In the Open University, the students can apply to University by completing the first three courses with good enough grade, so the fourth course probably attracts less students.

4.2 Method

In this study, we were interested in measuring the differences in average scores between the Open University and the University courses. Usually, measuring the value of a parameter of a population is too difficult. However, bootstrapping gives us a simple and powerful way to obtain valuable information from our sample parameters. Bootstrapping is based on random sampling with replacement and allows us to estimate for example variance, standard error or confidence intervals. In this case, we used bootstrapping to calculate confidence intervals for our observed average differences.

Majority of the students completed most of the course assignments. On the other hand, some of the students did not manage to get enough points to take part in the exam. This score distribution led to high skewness in our data and we hence decided to use a bootstrapping method called bias-corrected and acceleration bootstrapping [15]. It requires calculating bias and acceleration constants, which are adjusting non-stable variance and taking into account the skewness in the data.

Three sections were isolated from all courses: (weekly) exercises, tutorials and exam results. Only the shared assignments, i.e. assignments that were used in both universities, were included in the analysis. For the results, average differences and confidence intervals were calculated and compared. Confidence intervals were reported in the 95% confidence level.

5   Results

In this Section, we first present the results of the individual courses and then a summary of results combined. The average scores collected from tutorials and from weekly exercises, respectively, are displayed in Fig. 1.

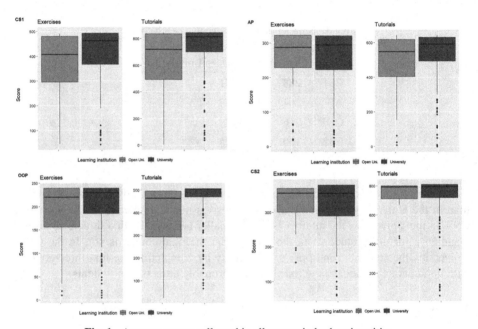

Fig. 1. Average scores collected in all course in both universities.

A summary of differences between the two universities is displayed in Table 4.

6   Discussion

The differences between the two universities are mostly quite small. However, there are some numbers worth taking a closer look. The differences in CS1 and OOP tutorials were significant (CS1: difference 111.4 points with confidence interval [78. 36, 143.29] and OOP: 73.2 points with confidence interval [55.89, 103.76]). Moreover, there was as significant difference in AP tutorials (36.1 with [8.58, 62.45]) and CS1 exam 7.6 with [−1.67, 10.2]. Curiously, the Open University students seemed to outperform the

Table 4. Differences between average scores in all courses. Positive value indicates that the University score was higher.

Course	Exercise diff.	Tutorial diff.	Exam diff.
CS1	10.5%	13.2%	7.6%
AP	0.9%	5.6%	5.2%
OOP	6.5%	14.4%	−2.7%
CS2	−1.3%	0.5%	−13.6%

University students in the two latter courses, but as the number of students in these two courses in the Open University was quite small (see Table 3), reliable conclusions could not be made.

Some likely reasons for the differences, visible in Table 4 and Fig. 1 can be presented. First, we can assume that the students in the Open University were more heterogeneous in their skills and background. Second, the dropout rate in the Open University was quite high. These two assumptions connected would somewhat explain the bigger difference in favor of the University in the first courses, which then gradually disappeared in the latter courses. Better performance of the Open University students in the final two exams could be maybe explained by students with less skills (and perhaps not as clearly defined goals in their studies) dropping out during the school year.

There were two major differences between methodologies in the two universities. First, the students in the Open University could take the courses as blended or as distance learning, since no attendances were required. Moreover, there were no lectures in the Open University; instead, the lecture materials were shared online. Unfortunately, there are no statistics about which methodology – blended or fully online – the students in the Open University selected.

7   Conclusions and Future Work

The statistical differences in the results seem to point towards positive answers to both research questions: there seems to be some differences between students following different methodologies, and the differences vary between different courses. Nevertheless, the differences are quite small and the limitations with data too big to reliably answer the questions. In the future, it would be beneficial to collect more data on the students. Background information, motivation and the attendance data from the Open University would be highly useful when analyzing the data.

References

1. Spyropoulou, N., Demopoulou, G., Pierrakeas, C., Koutsonikos, I., Kameas, A.: Developing a computer programming MOOC. Procedia Comput. Sci. **65**, 182–191 (2015)

2. Vihavainen, A., Luukkainen, M., Kurhila, J.: Multi-faceted support for MOOC in programming. In: Proceedings of the 13th Annual Conference on Information Technology Education, pp. 171–176. ACM. (2012)
3. Vihavainen, A., Airaksinen, J., Watson, C.: A systematic review of approaches for teaching introductory programming and their influence on success. In: Proceedings of the Tenth Annual Conference on International Computing Education Research, pp. 19–26. ACM (2014)
4. Salleh, N., Mendes, E., Grundy, J.: Empirical studies of pair programming for CS/SE teaching in higher education: a systematic literature review. IEEE Trans. Softw. Eng. **37**(4), 509–525 (2010)
5. Boyle, T., Bradley, C., Chalk, P., Jones, R., Pickard, P.: Using blended learning to improve student success rates in learning to program. J. Educ. Media **28**(2–3), 165–178 (2003)
6. Deperlioglu, O., Kose, U.: The effectiveness and experiences of blended learning approaches to computer programming education. Comput. Appl. Eng. Educ. **21**(2), 328–342 (2013)
7. Bruff, D.O., Fisher, D.H., McEwen, K.E., Smith, B.E.: Wrapping a MOOC: student perceptions of an experiment in blended learning. J. Online Learn. Teach. **9**(2), 187 (2013)
8. Zacharis, N.Z.: A multivariate approach to predicting student outcomes in web-enabled blended learning courses. Internet High. Educ. **27**, 44–53 (2015)
9. Van Niekerk, J., Webb, P.: The effectiveness of brain-compatible blended learning material in the teaching of programming logic. Comput. Educ. **103**, 16–27 (2016)
10. Moore, J.L., Dickson-Deane, C., Galyen, K.: e-Learning, online learning, and distance learning environments: are they the same? Internet High. Educ. **14**(2), 129–135 (2011)
11. Kaila, E.: Utilizing Educational Technology in Computer Science and Programming Courses. TUCS Dissertations 230 (2018)
12. Rajala, T., Lokkila E., Lindén R., Laakso M.-J., Salakoski T.: Students' perceptions on collaborative work in introductory programming course. In: ICEE 2015 - International Conference on Engineering Education (2015)
13. Laakso, M.-J., Kaila, E., Rajala, T.: ViLLE - collaborative education tool: designing and utilizing an exercise-based learning environment. Educ. Inf. Technol. (2018). https://doi.org/10.1007/s10639-017-9659-1
14. Cole, J., Foster, H.: Using Moodle: Teaching with the Popular Open Source Course Management System. O'Reilly Media, Inc., Newton (2007)
15. Efron, B.: Better bootstrap confidence intervals. J. Am. Stat. Assoc. **82**(397), 171–185 (1987)

On Teaching Web Stream Processing
Lessons Learned

Riccardo Tommasini[2]([✉]), Emanuele Della Valle[1], Marco Balduini[1],
and Sherif Sakr[2]

[1] DEIB, Politecnico di Milano, Milan, Italy
{emanuele.dellavalle,marco.balduini}@polimi.it
[2] DataSystem Group, University of Tartu, Tartu, Estonia
{riccardo.tommasini,sherif.sakr}@ut.ee

Abstract. Web Stream Processing (WSP) is a field that studies how
to identify, access, represent and process flows of data using Web technologies. One of the barriers that currently limits the adoption of WSP
is the paradigm shift from Web data at-rest to Web data in-motion.
This barrier is especially high when teaching undergraduate students.
To quantify the effort required to learn Web Stream Processing, we run
an Action Research audit with master students at Politecnico di Milano.
In this paper, we present the results of this inquiry, and we discuss the
lesson learned.

Keywords: Web Stream Processing · Stream Reasoning · RDF
Stream Processing · Action Research

1 Introduction

Information is no longer only stored, cleaned and queried to answer precise
questions. Instead, data is collected from all the available sources and analyzed in
real-time, as noisy as it is, exploring all the possible correlations that may occur.
This paradigm shift towards data-in-motion requires not only new approaches
but also some fundamental changes in the underlying assumptions [3].

As members of the Stream Reasoning [4] research community[1], we focus on
developing Web Stream Processing solutions that can tame data variety and
velocity simultaneously and, to this extent, we repeatedly question the existing
paradigms. We accept these changes because we observe the problems from a
research perspective. Instead, as practitioners, we notice that stakeholders are
naturally reluctant to fundamental changes since they strive to describe their
needs when they lose reference points, e.g., when we try to explain a problem
that involved both data variety and velocity. Moreover, as educators, we are
concerned about the effort that it takes to build the competencies necessary to
conceive, design, implement, test, validate and deploy continuous applications.

---

[1] http://streamreasoning.org.

© Springer Nature Switzerland AG 2020
M. Bielikova et al. (Eds.): ICWE 2020, LNCS 12128, pp. 485–493, 2020.
https://doi.org/10.1007/978-3-030-50578-3_33

To foster the adoption of innovative solutions like web stream processing, we advocate the need for educational resources that can (1) reduce the teaching effort solving technical challenges, and (2) prepare better professional figures.

In this paper, we present the results of an Action Research (AR) [8] audit that we run at Politecnico di Milano, in the context of a course on *Interoperability and Semantic Technologies*. The *contribution* of this paper is evidence from the trenches that i) formulating a continuous information need is difficult, ii) designing a Web stream processing solutions is doable, and iii) implementing it is hard due to the excessive effort required to set up an experimental environment.

Outline. Section 2 presents the course structure, briefly introducing the content of the syllabus with tools used in the project works assigned to the students. Section 3 explains the Action Research methodology. Section 4 and Sect. 5 present the result of the audit and conclude the paper.

2   The Course

This section introduces the course content, the structure of lectures and the different phases of the project work. The course involved 44 students from the first and the second year of the master degree in Computer Science and Engineering. For the project work students were divided in groups of 2 or 3. The 29% of the students were Italian, while the remaining 71% were from different nationalities. All the classes were taught in English.

The Course Content. The course of *Interoperability and Semantic Technologies* (IST) aims at teaching (i) technologies and methodologies to tame data variety, i.e., RDF, OWL, SPARQL and Ontology Based Data Access (OBDA) [6]; (ii) solutions for efficient data integration, e.g., Ontop[2] [2]; (iii) the essence of stream processing, i.e., solutions like Esper[3], Spark Streaming[4], and Flink[5] that tackle data velocity; (iv) the fundamentals of Stream Reasoning [4], i.e., RDF Stream Processing (RSP) [3] to address variety and velocity simultaneously.

Semantic Technologies are the pillars of data integration on the web. *RDF* is the core graph data model that simplifies data integration proposing triples (subject-predicate-object) as basic building blocks of any data model. *OWL 2*, i.e., the Web Ontology Language, is the W3C recommendation for knowledge representation on the Web. *SPARQL* is both the query language for RDF data on the Web and the Web-based protocol for clients to access SPARQL services. Additionally, the course dives into *Ontology-Based Data Access*(OBDA), i.e., a data integration methodology that combines semantic technologies and RDBMS. OBDA systems keep data in RDBMS and rewrite SPARQL queries in SQL by the means of mapping. Ontop is a prominent tool for OBDA that supports conjunctive queries expressed in SPARQL 1.0 and most of the RDBMSs.

---

[2] http://ontop.inf.unibz.it/.

[3] http://esper.espertech.com.

[4] https://spark.apache.org/streaming/.

[5] https://flink.apache.org/.

Stream Processing (SP) is a programming paradigm that allows to process data streams, i.e., unbounded sequence of timestamped data. Stream Processing Engines (SPEs) are systems able to satisfy continuous information needs. SPEs typically require to write continuous queries using SQL-like languages. The course covers the foundational aspects of SP and three prominent SPEs (Esper, Spark streaming, and Flink).

Web Stream Processing (WSP) is a research field that aims at taming variety and velocity at the same time. The course covers *C-SPARQL* [1] – a SPARQL 1.1 extensions with the continuous semantics –, the C-SPARQL engine – an RSP engine that can answer continuous queries written with C-SPARQL –, and *TripleWave* [7] – an engine for publishing streams on the Web.

The Course Structure. During the course, we alternate lectures and practical classes to engage the students into a collaborative working environment. The practical sessions consists of three main phases, i.e., `Concept Generation Phase`, `Design Phase`, and `Implementation Phase`. Each phase was followed by an evaluation where the educators assessed the quality of the work.

In the `Concept Generation Phase` the students had to formulate an information need on data streams and static collections from the Telecom Italia Big Data Challenge 2015[6]. The success criteria for this phase was the identification of a continuous information need that addresses data velocity and variety.

In the `Design Phase`, the students had to elaborate a solution that solves the information need they previously formulated. The solution design is a task that requires technical competencies. During the course lectures, we went through all the necessary knowledge to produce a good design. Our success criteria for this phase required that the designed solution was adequately justified and able to tackle both variety and velocity. In practice, the student had to (i) design a conceptual model for data integration, e.g., an ontology and some mappings from the data streams to the ontology; (ii) write a SPARQL query that could solve the continuous information need if submitted with a given frequency; and (iii) write a C-SPARQL query that satisfies the continuous information need. Moreover, the students were asked to provide a detailed description of the solution explaining whether a particular design decision addresses data variety, data velocity or both.

In the `Implementation Phase`, the students were asked to develop a solution based on the design they produced using two architectures: (i) an *OBDA* one based on R2RML and *Ontop* and; (ii) an *RSP* one that includes TripleWave and the C-SPARQL engine.

3   Investigation Methodology

To collect and analyze the course data we used Action Research (AR) that is a systematic inquiry method, usually conducted by educators, designed to understand how the learning environment performs [5].

---

[6] http://www.telecomitalia.com/tit/en/bigdatachallenge/contest.html.

Table 1. Action Research for Web Stream Processing.

What?	Action Research	IST Teaching
Who?	Conducted by educators on students	Authors
Where?	In schools and Classrooms	During IST Course
How?	Explore the reality and effects of interventions on it using qualitative and quantitative methods	Establishing an educators/students feedback loop by Using Web-forms.
Why?	To take action and possibly induce changes in the studied environment	To estimate the effort required to learn WSP

Since we could not control who enrolled in the course, we opted for AR as methodology to structure the audit. Indeed, in AR studies, the educators are considered the authorities. They (1) choose the area of focus; (2) they formulate the research questions; (3) they select the Key Performance Indicators (KPI); (4) they determine data collection techniques (5) they analyze data to derive data-driven conclusions, and (6) they define action plans based on them. We summarized our choices concerning AR methodologies in Table 1.

Our investigation focuses on the students who did the project of the IST course. Indeed, AR privileges a combination of theory and practice in the audit. For each phase we formulate a research questions: (Q1) *Can the participants formulate a Continuous Information Need (CIN)?* (Q2) *Can the participants design a Web stream processing solution to answer a CIN?* (Q3) *Can the participants implement a Web stream processing solution to answer a CIN?*

Moreover, we were interested in exploring the issues concerning the teaching, and we did not aim at (dis)proving any hypotheses. AR fits well this scenarios as it exploits both quantitative or qualitative methods for gathering and analyzing data. To explore the reality of how students absorb the subjects we opted for a qualitative analysis of one KPI, i.e., the relative difficulties of the task to solve.

We collected data during each phase independently, using Web-forms, interviews and written exams. As prescribed by AR methodology, the students were asked to provide feed-backs. In particular, we asked them to evaluate the difficulty of each phase using Likert Scale questions, to indicate technical difficulties with the topics, and to report technological issues with the tools using open questions.

4   Results

In this section, we present the results of the investigation. Each phases includes one or more round of feed-backs. Thus, we additionally report the results of the feedback survey we run at the end of the course. Notably, we are not trying to generalize our conclusions but we focus on presenting the lessons we learned.

Concept Generation Phase aimed at assessing the students' ability to formulate a continuous information need starting from the data of the Telecom Italia Open Big Data challenge. Notably, the students were not domain experts, thus they were also required to understand the meaning of the data consulting the available documentation.

We collected the information needs using a web-form. And, as prescribed by AR, we graded the quality of the information needs. Notably, the data velocity and variety dimensions were critical points of the evaluation. Moreover, we considered the complexity of the information needs in the grading, but we ensured that all the formulations had a comparable complexity.

We established a feedback loop with the students interviewing the groups whose information needs did not meet a satisfactory score. Since we want to ensure that all the students reached the next steps of the project, we allowed any number of resubmissions, iterating the process until we were satisfied.

Eight groups out of 21 were requested to resubmit at least once. Two of these groups had to follow up the second round of feedback. Among the remaining groups, about the half received only minor corrections.

Table 2 presents an example of information need that went through two rounds of refinement. The initial version does not consider data velocity, but it treats data as a time-series. After the first round of feedback, the students were able to reformulate the informa-

Table 2. Information needs formulated and refined.

I	How many calls were made to "Milan's Dom" from anywhere in Milan during rainy weekends?
II	Report the calls number made to "Milan's Dom" from anywhere in Milan, every weekend if it rained for 24 h.
III	Report every hour the number of calls that were made to "Milan's Dom" from in Milan, if was raining within 24 h

tion need as continuous. Finally, the last attempt improved the clarity highlighting the requirement of a sliding window.

During this phase it emerged a common difficulty in distinguishing between processing *time-series* and *data streams*, i.e., the difference between temporal information needs and continuous information needs. Our observation is that dealing with historical stream (such as those in the Telecom Italia Big Data Challenge) was a source of confusion.

We tested this critical point later on during the written exam. Indeed, we asked the students to identify between three information needs, written in natural language, whether any of them presented a problem of data velocity. We did not indicate that only one answer was correct.

With 42 respondents, 10% did not indicate the correct answer; 50% indicated the correct one and the remaining 40% indicated the correct answer but also a second one that, instead, was considering an information need over a time-series. These numbers indicate that students tended to misunderstand the two ways to interpret the temporal dimension.

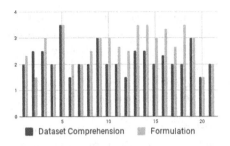 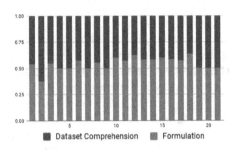

Fig. 1. Dataset Comprehension vs Information Need Formulation. On the y-axis: complexity 1 (easiest) to 5 (hardest).

Fig. 2. Dataset Comprehension vs Formulation of information needs. On the y-axis: avg complexity of the task

Figure 1 shows that the students ranked the Conceptual Phase with a medium-high level of complexity in the course survey. Moreover insights can be derived from Fig. 2. It shows how hard was to understand the datasets in contrast with the formulation of the continuous information need. It emerges that the tasks have similar complexities. On the other hand, we learned that the choice of the data is crucial and impacts the overall complexity of the phase.

The **Design Phase** aimed at assessing the students' ability to design a solution that solves the continuous information need. In particular, a stream processing solutions. As in the previous phase, we collected design proposals using a Web-forms. However, we did not allow resubmitting because our final evaluation focused on the students' explanations, i.e., we asked them to defend their design choice both in a written from and in an oral presentation.

As explained in Sect. 2, we accepted two alternative approaches: a SPARQL query to evaluate periodically, and a C-SPARQL query. Figure 3 presents a comparative view of the designs using the two query languages. Surprisingly, it emerged that the two tasks had similar complexities. Our lesson learned is that once students understand SPARQL, learning the continuous extension of C-SPARQL requires a small effort.

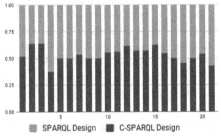

Fig. 3. Design hardness: C-SPARQL vs SPARQL.

Figures 5 and 4 show that both the ontology design and the mappings of the data streams do not require substantially more effort than understanding the data streams (i.e., in average they differ for less than 10%). This is because we asked the students to design a simple conceptual model instead of using existing vocabularies. Moreover, the students designed mostly direct mappings from the data to the ontology.

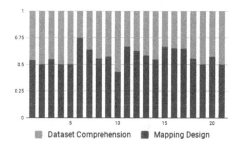

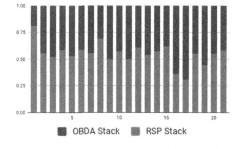

Fig. 4. Dataset comprehension vs mapping design.

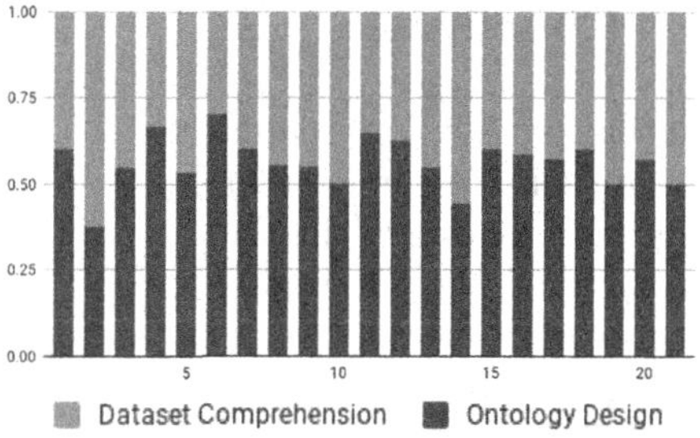

Fig. 5. Dataset comprehension vs ontology design.

The `Implementation Phase` aimed at assessing the students' ability to implement the designed solution. As explained in Sect. 2, the task required to realize two alternative architectures of increasing complexity: one based on OBDA and one based on RSP. Due to the complexity of the task, we reserved 5 h of class-work where the student worked under our supervision.

We collected the projects with web form. Moreover, we asked the student

Fig. 6. Implementation hardness: RSP vs OBDA.

to self-evaluate their project as *complete* or *incomplete*. We interviewed those who evaluated the project as complete, while we asked the other to write down a retrospective during the final exam.

Figure 6 presents how hard the OBDA solution was perceived compared to the RSP solution. What emerges is that the RSP solution causes more problem than the OBDA one. Indeed, from the retrospectives and the responses to the open questions in the final feedback survey, it emerged that most of the groups struggled with the implementation because of technical issued caused by the immaturity of the RSP prototypes.

5   Conclusion

In this paper, we presented an Action Research audit that we conducted in the context of the Interoperability and Semantic Technologies course at Politecnico di Milano.

Our investigation aimed at estimating the hardness of teaching and learning Web Stream Processing. Thus, we analyzed how the student interacted and perform during the course,

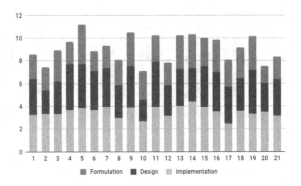

Fig. 7. Total project complexity. The x-axis: the IST project groups; the y-axis: the avg complexities of the project phases.

structuring a three-phase evaluation pipeline. From the collected material, i.e., feedback during the course, the exams, and a post-hoc survey, it emerges that the overall complexity of the project was quite high. Figure 7 shows the sum of the effort each group spent on the aforementioned phases.

This finding highlights the urgency of further investigations on the Web Stream Processing teaching methods. Moreover, from the analysis we presented in Sect. 4, we understood that: (i) Given continuous data, the task of formulating an information need is more intricate than in situations that involve only static data. (ii) Designing a simple Web Stream Processing solutions is doable and it requires an analogous effort to a data integration task. (iii) Implementing a simple Web Stream Processing solutions is strenuous because it requires to set up an entire experimental environment made with immature prototypes.

As research future work, we aim at investigating more the challenges of formulating continuous information needs. We are considering to extend the scale of the investigation and test different educational environments, e.g., tutorials, or intense courses. From the educational point of view, our action plan prioritizes the adoption of a standard experimental environment that reduces the complexity of the implementation tasks, e.g., RSPLab [9].

Acknowledgements. The work of Sherif Sakr is funded by the European Regional Development Funds via the Mobilitas Plus programme (grant MOBTT75). The work of Riccardo Tommasini is funded by the European Regional Funds through IT Academy programme.

References

1. Barbieri, D.F., Braga, D., Ceri, S., Della Valle, E., Grossniklaus, M.: C-SPARQL: a continuous query language for RDF data streams. Int. J. Semant. Comput. 4(1), 3–25 (2010)

2. Calvanese, D., et al.: Ontop: answering SPARQL queries over relational databases. Semant. Web **8**(3), 471–487 (2017)
3. Della Valle, E., Dell'Aglio, D., Margara, A.: Taming velocity and variety simultaneously in big data with stream reasoning: tutorial. In: Proceedings of the 10th ACM International Conference on Distributed and Event-Based Systems, DEBS 2016, Irvine, CA, USA, 20–24 June 2016, pp. 394–401 (2016)
4. Dell'Aglio, D., Della Valle, E., van Harmelen, F., Bernstein, A.: Stream reasoning: a survey and outlook. Data Sci. **1**(1–2), 59–83 (2017)
5. Gay, L.R., Mills, G.E., Airasian, P.W.: Educational Research: Competencies for Analysis and Applications 10th Edition. Pearson Higher Ed (2011)
6. Lenzerini, M.: Ontology-based data management. In: Proceedings of the 6th Alberto Mendelzon International Workshop on Foundations of Data Management, Ouro Preto, Brazil, 27–30 June 2012, pp. 12–15 (2012)
7. Mauri, A., et al.: TripleWave: spreading RDF streams on the web. In: Groth, P., et al. (eds.) ISWC 2016. LNCS, vol. 9982, pp. 140–149. Springer, Cham (2016). https://doi.org/10.1007/978-3-319-46547-0_15
8. Stringer, E.T.: Action Research. Sage Publications (2013)
9. Tommasini, R., Della Valle, E., Mauri, A., Brambilla, M.: RSPLab: RDF stream processing benchmarking made easy. In: d'Amato, C., et al. (eds.) ISWC 2017. LNCS, vol. 10588, pp. 202–209. Springer, Cham (2017). https://doi.org/10.1007/978-3-319-68204-4_21

Teaching Container-Based DevOps Practices

Jami Kousa[1]([⊠])(iD), Petri Ihantola[1](iD), Arto Hellas[2](iD), and Matti Luukkainen[1](iD)

[1] University of Helsinki, Helsinki, Finland
jami.kousa@helsinki.fi
[2] Aalto University, Espoo, Finland

Abstract. We present the design of a online course that focuses on container-based virtualization as part of the DevOps toolchain. In addition, we outline the professional background of participants taking the course, and describe how this affects perceived previous knowledge of DevOps. We found out that the self-evaluated conceptual understanding of DevOps topics is nearly equal regardless of the participants professional identity (e.g., student or developer). However, there are significant differences in how much participants have used tools like Docker before. We conclude that there is a clear need for lifelong learning among software engineering professionals as (future) developers often struggle in operations related skills such as command line or networking.

Keywords: DevOps · Education · Lifelong learning

1 Introduction

Traditionally the development and operation of software have been separated. However, bringing these functions together to provide an optimal flow of software from ideas to production is getting mainstream in software engineering [3]. The joint operation of developers and operations people is referred to with the term DevOps. DevOps has numerous definitions, which show different views of the term and the field. A systematic mapping study by Jabbari et al. combines them by stating [6]: *"DevOps is a development methodology aimed at bridging the gap between Development and Operations, emphasizing communication and collaboration, continuous integration, quality assurance, and delivery with automated deployment utilizing a set of development practices."*

Based on our observations, the operations (and consequently DevOps) have at most a lightweight role in many CS or even Software Engineering programs. Deployment, operation, and maintenance are part of in ACM Curricula recommendation for CS but are not apparent in the course examples [1]. DevOps-related skills were poorly trained also at our university a few years ago [9].

We argue that integrating DevOps into the university curricula can be used to introduce the operations to students as well as rehearse and strengthen existing knowledge in software development in general. However, teaching DevOps can

© Springer Nature Switzerland AG 2020
M. Bielikova et al. (Eds.): ICWE 2020, LNCS 12128, pp. 494–502, 2020.
https://doi.org/10.1007/978-3-030-50578-3_34

be challenging as it crosses boundaries of traditional computer science courses [4]. The work presented in this article emerges from our personal experiences of teaching DevOps practices at the University of Helsinki.

2 Background

A major effort for DevOps to succeed is to make the overall software delivery flow continuous and using a meaningful set of tools [11]. Containers are a concrete example of this. They are operating-system-level virtualization designed to be a standard unit of software that packages up code and all its dependencies, so the application runs reliably from one computing environment to another. Containers facilitate DevOps by allowing the use of code to perform infrastructure management tasks automatically (i.e, Infrastructure-as-Code) [13] and by removing the need to manually install software when setting up servers [12]. Moreover, containers enable fast deployment and recovery, supporting continuous deployment [7]. Docker is an open software for containerization that has been adopted as the de-facto method for virtualization in the industry [14].

One of the most comprehensive reports on teaching DevOps was published in 2016 by Christensen [4], who describes the challenges and proposes teaching methods for DevOps. Discussion in the paper is done in relation to a course in which students developed web software that scales to tens of thousands of concurrent users. In conclusion, they recommend emphasizing the programming process and realistic context for teaching DevOps skills.

In a similar vein, Pengxiang and Leong [10] published a study on teaching DevOps related hybrid-skills in the cloud computing environment. They analyzed the skill-set wanted by the industry, and identified a gap in a current polytechnic cloud computing curriculum. Their proposed an approach where students deployed web software for other students to submit their learning diaries.

A recent publication by Kuusinen and Albertsen [8] explores university-company collaboration in teaching Continuous Delivery and DevOps in a two weeks intensive course. The first week was theoretical, while the second was practical. Authors found the approach where industry partners up-to-date technical knowledge was integrated into university education successful.

Finally, Christensen et al. acknowledge the scarcity of research done on teaching DevOps, especially in teaching methodology and culture of DevOps. Some DevOps practices are introduced in other courses to provide some experience of their usage. Version control management systems, which may be classified as DevOps tools, such as git, can be introduced in many courses as Haaranen and Lehtinen describe [5]. Other tools, such as continuous integration using CircleCI[1], are integrated into software engineering projects. These kinds of integrations make it possible for students to learn DevOps tools and practices during courses that do not focus on DevOps as a methodology.

---

[1] https://circleci.com/.

3   Research Questions and Methodology

Based on the previous research, we have developed course that introduces DevOps via relevant tools. In this study, we investigate how our approach works. In addition, we are interested in what kinds of students come to the course, and how the background is linked to the participants previous knowledge. The concrete research questions we will answer are:

RQ1 What is the professional background of participants taking the course?
RQ2 How does the professional background affect participants' perceived previous understanding of DevOps?
RQ3 What are the core challenges for students when learning DevOps?

3.1   DevOps with Docker Course

Our DevOps with Docker course is based on study material first used in the internal training of an industry partner. The material was then tailored to create an introductory course to containerization for students at the university level. So far the *DevOps with Docker* course have been held three times. The latest instance of the course was held in Autumn 2019 as a MOOC for anyone. In the following, we will briefly introduce the course design. (see https://devopswithdocker.com/).

The course consists of four parts. The first part focus on setting up the environment by installing docker and testing it works. The next two parts are an introduction to containerization with Docker and container orchestration with docker-compose. More precisely, this is about containerization of an existing web application (Fig. 1, items 1 & 2) that was created for the purposes of this course. In the third part, the application is integrated with other services; cache (3), database (4) and a reverse proxy (5). In the fourth part, students still work with the same web application but the tasks are related to improving the build process and security. The course size is 1–3 ECTS points (depending on how many sections students will complete).

The main application containerized and configured throughout the course is a simple web service implementing the automated assessment and thus providing immediate feedback for students. The service returns a web page with a single button. Pressing the button returns either an ok message (if tasks are correctly solved) or an error message relates to one of the services. After students have

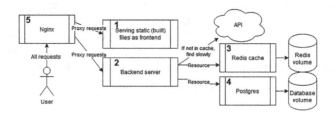

Fig. 1. Multiple services were required in the configuration to complete the exercises. The order of the exercises are numbered from 1 to 5.

completed a session, they were requested to push their progress to GitHub and submit a link to their GitHub repository.

3.2   Participants and Measures

We will answer our research questions based on the data collected from the last iteration of the course. At the beginning of the first section of the course, students were asked about their background, previous experiences in DevOps and Containers, and personal learning objectives. The detailed items related to the background were BG1: I have a general understanding of containers (1 = strongly disagree, ... 5 = strongly agree), BG2: I have understanding of problems containers solve (1 = strongly disagree, ... 5 = strongly agree), BG3: I have used Docker before (1 = none, ... 5 = daily), BG4: I'm familiar with DevOps or have general understanding what it is (1 = strongly disagree, ... 5 = strongly agree), and BG5: My background is (student, developer, data scientist, DevOps engineer, other).

At the end of the course (i.e., at the end of Sect. 2, 3, or 4), there was a feedback questionnaire where we asked, e.g., *Which exercise did you consider to be the hardest and why?*. In addition, as the pre-course survey was anonymous, the question about student professional background (BG5) was repeated at the end of the course. The initial survey was answered by 651 participants. Phases 1, 2, 3, and 4 of the course were submitted by 219, 175, 142 and 98 participants, respectively. Post-course feedback was provided by 140 participants.

Table 1. (Spearman) correlations between items related to previous knowledge, their count (N), means (M) and standard deviation (SD). $*p < .05$, $**p < .01$, and $***p < .001$

	2	3	4	N	M	SD
1. BG1	0.49***	0.13**	0.17***	632	2.67	1.24
2. BG2		0.19***	0.16***	632	2.60	1.16
3. BG3			0.03	630	1.91	1.05
4. BG4				627	2.78	1.10

Related to RQ1, participants of the pre-survey were grouped based on professional identity (BG5). Moreover, while answering RQ2, non-parametric analyses of variance (Kruskal-Wallis) were used to investigate group differences in the previous knowledge and skills (BG1–BG4). In the case of significant differences were observed, pairwise Man-Whitney tests were conducted with p-values adjusted by using the Benjamini-Hochberg method. The effect sized were estimated with Cliff's delta. Although all the items were related to the previous understanding of DevOps, they were not combined into a single factor because of relatively small correlations (Table 1). RQ3 was answered based on the open-ended answers in the post questionnaire that were coded manually by one of the authors. Coding was verified by an another person. Course staff was interviewed to triangulated the observations.

4 Results

4.1 Background and Previous Knowledge

629 participants answered something to the question about their professional status. The biggest groups were students (43%) and Developers/Software Engineers (35%). Sizes of other groups are provided in Table 2. Professions in the category other included answers such as system administrator, consultant, network engineer, manager, and software tester. Group-wise medians and median absolute deviations of previous knowledge are also provided in Table 2.

Table 2. Sized of professional identity groups together with medians and median absolute deviations of background variables per groups

	n	BG1		BG2		BG3		BG4	
		med	mad	med	mad	med	mad	med	mad
Student	270	2.00	1.48	2.00	1.48	1.00	0.00	3.00	1.48
Developer	218	2.00	0.74	2.00	0.00	2.00	1.48	2.00	0.74
DevOps engineer	34	3.00	1.48	2.00	0.00	3.00	1.48	2.50	1.48
Data scientist	24	2.00	0.00	2.00	0.00	2.00	0.00	2.00	0.0
Other	83	2.00	1.48	2.00	1.48	2.00	1.48	2.00	1.48

Table 3. Dunn's post-hoc (pairwise Mann-Whitney) analysis and possible effect sizes.

Comparison	BG1			BG2			BG3		
	Z	P.adj	d	Z	P.adj	d	Z	P.adj	d
Data scientist - DevOps eng	−2.756	.015	−0.38	−1.340	.360	−	−2.131	.041	−0.41
Data scientist - Other	−0.695	.696	−	−0.071	.943	−	1.549	.135	−
DevOps eng - Other	2.818	.024	0.31	1.673	.314	−	4.553	.000	0.52
Data scientist - Software eng	−1.026	.610	−	−0.434	.738	−	−0.288	.774	−
DevOps eng - Software eng	2.789	.018	0.28	1.431	.381	−	2.744	.010	0.29
Other - Software eng	−0.461	.716	−	−0.596	.788	−	−3.259	.003	−0.23
Data scientist - Student	−0.634	.658	−	0.549	.729	−	2.998	.005	0.38
DevOps eng - Student	3.297	.010	0.33	2.606	.092	−	6.632	.000	0.62
Other - Student	0.208	.835	−	1.063	.480	−	2.228	.037	0.16
Software eng - Student	0.941	.578	−	2.309	0.105	−	7.674	.000	0.38

Professional background affects general understand of containers - BG1 ($H(4) = 12.03$, $p = .017$), understanding of problems that containers solve - BG2 ($H(4) = 9.94$, $p = .041$), and whether authors have used the docker or not - BG3 ($H(4) = 86.78$, $p < .000$). However, a professional background does not affect how familiar participants are with DevOps or whether they have a general understanding of what DevOps is - BG4 ($H(4) = 6.00$, $p = .20$). The results of the post-hoc analysis, together with the effect sizes (d), are illustrated in Table 3.

4.2 Completers and Challenges

The most difficult topics mentioned in the feedback were networking (37 times), volumes (23), application frameworks (14), Nginx (16), Postgres (8), and CORS (8). Based on the feedback collected from the course staff, the usage of operating systems, namely Linux, was challenging at the beginning of the course as many students were not familiar with the usage of the command-line interface and, for example, creating small script files using bash. In addition, the students were requesting more realistic, production-like, environments, and tool sets to practice. There was a demand for an additional part about cloud services such as AWS or Google Cloud and advanced tools such as Kubernetes. Distribution of the professional profiles at the end of the course is similar to the beginning of the course, and illustrated in Table 4.

Table 4. Professional identity of those who started vs. those completed the course

	Data scientist	DevOps eng	Other	Software eng	Student
Pre-course	3.8%	5.4%	13.2%	34.7%	43.0%
Post-course	1.4%	5.0%	8.6%	33.6%	51.4%

5 Discussion

One of the contributions of this paper is to introduce the DevOps with Docker course design. While DevOps imposes cultural changes to software development and organizational structure, we decided to approach the topic from the tools perspective. The decision is supported by the fact that main effort for DevOps to succeed is to make the overall process continuous [11]. We recognize that containers themselves do not offer a complete picture of DevOps, lacking key subjects such as monitoring. However, containers offer the means against a subset of the presented problems, such as "works on my machine". This divide between the development and production environments is a significant hurdle as the classic "works on my machine" divide opposes DevOps principles [2]. Moreover, the teaching of methods to solve this problem offers students the possibility to design development pipelines when confronted with such a task.

There were practically no differences between professional identity groups in self evaluated conceptual understanding of DevOps (BG4) or container (BG1 and BG2). Even those who identified themselves as DevOps engineers stood out from the crowds only in one questions (BG1) where the effect sizes were small. Surprisingly, students and software developers reported similar amounts of knowledge on containers. This similarity between the two groups indicates that there is a need for life long learning courses for software industry. It is unclear if software engineers attending the course are representative sample of developers in general. It is possible to argue that only developers lacking DevOps skills would take the course in the first place. However, even those who identified themselves as DevOps engineers (and were more skilled) came in the course.

One possible explanation for only small differences is that more you know, the better you understand what you don't know. This is supported by the fact that the differences in the more concretely framed question about how often participants have used Docker were pretty clear. As assumed, DevOps engineers had most experience in using the Docker, while students were the least experienced. The effect size between DevOps engineers and both software developers and data scientists is medium, no differences were observed between developers and data scientists.

Networking was the most commonly reported challenge by the participants. In contrast to the networking course where students learn, e.g., how the internet works and the layers in the OSI model, the course we offered focused mostly on the transport layer with port configuration between applications and containers. This was challenging despite the theoretical understanding of the transport layer most university student attendees had from a mandatory networking course.

The perceived challenge in volume usage, the mapping of data in the container to the host, may also be partially explained by lack of experience with filesystems - linking it into the challenge of operating systems and CLI mentioned in other feedback. The third challenge was adapting to changing tools, services and application frameworks used as part of the exercises. To proceed in the challenging exercises attendees did not have to program in a new language but had to read the documentation, often a readme file, on what the exercise specific services required, such as open port or environmental values designating an API endpoint. For some attendees, this was a challenge as the errors encountered during these exercises were often unfamiliar at first but contained the necessary information to continue.

In the end, students requested advanced tools and more realistic context. Deployment in real cloud environments is different from simulating the same with containers in a local environment. The limited amount of realistic context in the course was identified as an area of improvement, and recommended earlier by Christensen as well [4]. Moreover, we believe that in advanced topics such as DevOps, authentic environments may be easier to master.

The threats to validity are the selection, maturation and attrition of the group. The course material was open to anyone regardless of signing up for the course and the surveys were an optional exercise during the course and as such the answers include attendees that did not sign up for the course as well as miss students that did take the course. Selecting only attendees who wanted to complete the optional survey may have an effect on the results. As attendees were able to progress the course at any pace, it was possible for them develop their skills independently of the course, for up to 9 months between the start of the course and the end. This may limit the amount of feedback on challenges of the earlier sections of the course. The attrition influences the number of answers between the beginning and ending surveys, but the distribution of professional identity remained closely the same between the surveys.

6   Conclusions

When answering our first research question (*what is the professional background of participants taking the course*), we found out that the DevOps course attracted especially those who identified themselves as Students or Software Engineers. While looking at the second question (*how does the professional background affect participants' perceived previous understanding of DevOps?*), we observer that self reported previous skills of these two groups were surprisingly similar.

Based on this, we conclude that there is a demand for lifelong learning around DevOps practices for software engineers as the relatively new methodology interests and challenges professionals working in the industry. For the last research question (*the core challenges for students when learning DevOps*) multiple topics related to administration were identified. The multidisciplinary skills emphasis of DevOps requires an introduction in a more practical approach for otherwise familiar concepts. We believe that such skills are best learned in as authentic environments as possible.

References

1. ACM Computing Curricula Task Force: Computer Science Curricula 2013: Curriculum Guidelines for Undergraduate Degree Programs in Computer Science. https://doi.org/10.1145/2534860
2. Anderson, C.: Docker [software engineering]. IEEE Softw. **32**(3), 102–c3 (2015). https://doi.org/10.1109/MS.2015.62
3. Bolscher, R., Daneva, M.: Designing software architecture to support continuous delivery and DevOps: a systematic literature review. In: 14th International Conference on Software Technologies, May 2019. https://doi.org/10.5220/0007837000270039
4. Christensen, H.B.: Teaching DevOps and cloud computing using a cognitive apprenticeship and story-telling approach. In: ACM Conference on Innovation and Technology in CS Education, pp. 17–179 (2016). https://doi.org/10.1145/2899415.2899426
5. Haaranen, L., Lehtinen, T.: Teaching git on the side: version control system as a course platform. In: Proceedings of ACM Conference on Innovation and Technology in Computer Science Education, pp. 87–92 (2015). https://doi.org/10.1145/2729094.2742608
6. Jabbari, R., Bin Ali, N., Petersen, K., Tanveer, B.: What is DevOps? a systematic mapping study on definitions and practices. In: Proceedings of Scientific Workshop Proceedings of XP2016. ACM (2016). https://doi.org/10.1145/2962695.2962707
7. Kang, H., Le, M., Tao, S.: Container and microservice driven design for cloud infrastructure DevOps. In: IEEE International Conference on Cloud Engineering (IC2E), pp. 202–211 (2016). https://doi.org/10.1109/IC2E.2016.26
8. Kuusinen, K., Albertsen, S.: Industry-academy collaboration in teaching DevOps and continuous delivery to software engineering students: towards improved industrial relevance in higher education. In: 41st International Conference on Software Engineering: Software Engineering Education and Training (2019). https://doi.org/10.1109/ICSE-SEET.2019.00011

9. Luukkainen, M., Vihavainen, A., Vikberg, T.: Three years of design-based research to reform a software engineering curriculum. In: Proceedings of 13th Conference on Information Technology Education, pp. 209–214 (2012). https://doi.org/10.1145/2380552.2380613
10. Pengxiang, J., Leong, P.: Teaching work-ready cloud computing using the DevOps approach. In: International Symposium on Advances in Technology Education (2014)
11. Rajkumar, M., Pole, A.K., Adige, V.S., Mahanta, P.: DevOps culture and its impact on cloud delivery and software development. In: International Conference on Advances in Computing, Communication, Automation, pp. 1–6 (2016). https://doi.org/10.1109/ICACCA.2016.7578902
12. Spinellis, D.: Don't install software by hand. IEEE Softw. **29**(4), 86–87 (2012). https://doi.org/10.1109/MS.2012.85
13. Syed, M.H., Fernandez, E.B.: A reference architecture for the container ecosystem. In: Proceedings of the 13th International Conference on Availability, Reliability and Security, pp. 1–6. ACM (2018). https://doi.org/10.1145/3230833.3232854
14. Zhang, Y., Vasilescu, B., Wang, H., Filkov, V.: One size does not fit all: an empirical study of containerized continuous deployment workflows. In: 26th ACM Joint Meeting on European Software Engineering Conference and Symposium on the Foundations of Software Engineering (2018). https://doi.org/10.1145/3236024.3236033

PhD Symposium

Predicting the Outbreak of Conflict in Online Discussions Using Emotion-Based Features

Maksymilian Marcinowski[1](✉) [iD] and Agnieszka Lawrynowicz[1,2] [iD]

[1] Faculty of Computing and Telecommunications, Poznan University of Technology, Poznań, Poland
{mmarcinowski,alawrynowicz}@cs.put.poznan.pl
[2] Center for Artificial Intelligence and Machine Learning (CAMIL), Poznan University of Technology, Poznań, Poland

Abstract. Anti-social online behaviour, such as harassment or vulgarity, leading to conflicts aimed at destroying any merit of the discussions, is a serious problem for the Internet community. Recognising the characteristics of conflict discussions and modelling their trajectory might help to predict and prevent derailing. My PhD thesis focuses on using emotion labels as such characteristics and building an explainable prediction model based on them. As a part of the thesis we have proposed a new dataset of discussions containing knowledge about their emotion-based features. It is a set of dialogues from Wikipedia Talk Pages annotated during a crowdsourcing experiment with labels from Plutchik's model of emotions and described with EmoWordNet lexicon scores.

With this explainable model we hope to introduce a new way of moderating Internet discussions and provide useful educational tool.

Keywords: Online discussions · Emotions · Conflict prediction

1 Problem Context and Definition

One of the most common problems faced by the Internet community is the frequent pointless, offensive disputes in Internet discussions between users taking part in the conversation. They occur in discussions in forums, in social networks as well as in comments on content posted on news portals. These conflicts consist of numerous cases of anti-social behaviour in subsequent posts. Nowadays, this problem is often solved with post-hoc moderation. An offensive message (or comment or post) is reported by users and after some time removed by the moderator. Usually removing such a message does not stop the conflict, because it has already spread - on some forums there can be seen long sequences of messages removed "due to violation of the rules".

In my PhD thesis the aim of the research is to build a mechanism that could predict the occurrence of a conflict by estimating the risk/probability of an offensive message before it appears. Such a mechanism would have a cautionary

© Springer Nature Switzerland AG 2020
M. Bielikova et al. (Eds.): ICWE 2020, LNCS 12128, pp. 505–511, 2020.
https://doi.org/10.1007/978-3-030-50578-3_35

application, analogous to a person observing a dispute between two people and trying to soften their emotions a little, as well as educational - especially for young users who may not be aware of the effects of their expressions on the Internet. The first research question that the goal requires to be addressed is:

RQ1. Are there any patterns or linguistic features of conflict discussions?

Zhang et al. assumed that there are such patterns and they are related to the rhetorical functions of comments (such as e.g. moderation, opinion, factual check) [14]. We hypothesize that the emotions occurring in discussions may be a good descriptor differentiating conflict and non-conflict conversations. Therefore, further research questions arose:

RQ2. How to effectively represent emotions for machine analysis?

RQ3. Are there any recurring sequential patterns of emotions occurring in conflict discussions?

RQ4. Is it possible to notice the escalation of conflict in dialogue by recognizing emotions?

2   Related Work

Prior works most related to the issues raised in my PhD thesis concerns: i) descriptors of derailed online conversations, and ii) other datasets containing online conversations with emotion labels.

Descriptors of Derailed Online Conversations. One of the syndromes of discussion's derailment is the occurrence of hate speech, which can be recognized automatically. The state of this field was presented by Fortuna and Nunes [6]. Recent studies [1,5] have also computationally operationalized prior formulations of politeness by extracting linguistic cues that reflect politeness strategies. There has also been research carried out to assess the relationship between politeness strategies and the trajectory of the discussions in which they are deployed [14]. Sociological and linguistic descriptors of discussions' dynamics are also considered. Wang and Cardie [12] classified disputes using lexical, topic, discussion, and sentiment features. One of their features, sentiment transition, estimates the probability of sentiment changing from one sentence to the next. Cheng et al. [4] found that an individual's mood and contextual features of a given discussion (e.g., how recently others had posted flag-worthy comments, how much time had passed since their own last comment) are related to an individual's likelihood of writing a flagged comment.

Datasets of Online Conversations Tagged with Emotion Models. A simple model of emotions was used in SemEval-2019 Task 3: EmoContext Contextual Emotion Detection in Text. Chatterjee et al. gathered a dataset of three-turn tweets, where the labels include: happy, sad, angry and "other" [3]. Li et al. developed a multi-turn dialog dataset DailyDialog [9], which includes human written daily communications. Six basic emotion labels from the Ekman's model (happiness, surprise, sadness, anger, disgust and fear) and the "neutral" label are used in this case. Another dataset that uses Ekman's and the "neutral" label is MELD by Poria et al. [11], which contains utterances from dialogues from the TV series *Friends*. Zahiri and Choi developed yet another collection [13] of scripts from *Friends*. This dataset uses different emotion labels than MELD: neutral, sad, mad, scared, powerful, peaceful, and joyful.

3 Proposed Approach

The approach we propose is a sequence of steps that aim at answering consecutive aforementioned research questions. Exploring patterns and features of discussions needs creation or adaptation of a dataset of online discussions, that would contain information about the conflict or non-conflict nature of these discussions (preferably a binary attribute).

To represent the emotions occurring in the posts an existing and acclaimed model of emotions must be used which should allow to obtain the fullest knowledge needed to analyse the posts. The dataset of conflict and non-conflict dialogues would be annotated by human annotators with emotions from this model.

Results of the annotation would thereafter be analysed (e.g. with techniques of sequential pattern mining) and on the basis of these analyses (allowing ultimately to map phrases and words into emotions used in the posts) an explainable model could be build and learned using deep neural networks. The last step is to build a black-box model, train it on raw data and finally compare predictive power of both models: black-box and the explainable one.

4 Methodology

4.1 Models of Emotions

We have selected two models for describing discussions' posts: Plutchik's model [10], which provides emotion intensity as well as similarity between them that helps to prepare guidelines for human annotators, and the model of the EmoWordNet lexicon [2], which helps us to link the emotion labels with the natural language.

Plutchik's model is a theory of emotions [10] distinguishing eight basic emotions: anger, anticipation, disgust, fear, joy, sadness, surprise and trust. Usually the model is presented on the diagram called "wheel of emotions". The adjacency of emotions on the wheel represents their similarity, and the additional dimension represents levels of *intensity*. Three levels of emotion together form a *petal*, labelled with the name of the basic emotion. Emotions in empty spaces (between petals) are called the *dyads* i.e. feelings that are compositions of two basic emotions. A *primary dyad* links common emotions that are one petal apart.

EmoWordNet [2] is a lexicon, containing 67 000 words and terms from English WordNet, expanded with 8 scores for each one, which represent 8 emotions: afraid, amused, angry, annoyed, don't care, happy, inspired and sad. The scores take values from 0 to 1 that estimate expressiveness and intensity of the emotion and they add up to 1 for each element of the lexicon.

4.2   Datasets

In order to perform experiments facilitating our research we expect to use or prepare by ourselves at least two datasets. The first one is a corpus provided by Zhang et al. [14]. We decided to extend the dataset by means of an experiment with help of students whose task was to annotate each of the comments/posts presented to them by clicking on a Plutchik's wheel of emotion in a place that represents the emotion which in their opinion dominates the post (or choose "none"). Each respondent annotated 10 posts and each post was annotated by 3 different respondents to verify compliance. Furthermore, the dataset has been expanded with values from EmoWordNet lexicon. After lemmatising all posts and removing "stop words", the scores of particular emotions in each term were summed up for each post and divided by the number of terms in the post to provide 8 mean emotion scores of each post. Therefore the new dataset contains fields with following content: (i) basic information about the posts and their belonging to the conversations, (ii) emotions from Plutchik's model the posts were annotated with and (iii) eight scores for each post based on EmoWordNet.

4.3   Analyses

Closed Sequential Patterns Mining. In order to answer research question RQ3 we performed closed sequential patterns mining. A sequence of items is an ordered list of elements (in our case - posts in a conversation and emotions they were annotated with) that can be denoted as $<s_1, s_2, ..., s_i>$. Sequential pattern mining consists of finding subsequences that occur in a given set of sequences with given frequency (support). Closed sequential patterns are patterns not included in any other patterns with the same support. The analysis was performed with the ClaSP algorithm [8], using the implementation from SPMF library [7].

Analysis of Escalation. To answer research question RQ4, we analyse the emotion intensity level and whether it grows in conflicting discussions. We understand this growth of emotions over the course of conversation as an escalation. We have verified the occurrence of this phenomenon in EmoWikipediaTalkPages dataset by using two methods of evaluating the intensity of emotions: (i) the level of intensity of emotions occurring in posts according to the annotations based on Plutchik's model of emotions and (ii) the aggregated value of scores of particular words or terms occurring in posts according to the EmoWordNet lexicon - the scores of particular emotions in each term were summed up for each post and divided by the number of terms in the post to provide 8 mean emotion scores of each post and, for the statistics, the maximum of these values (denoted by v) for each post was selected.

4.4   Future Analyses and Black-Box Model Generation

The objective of future analyses will be to potentially find alternative answers for the research questions (including RQ1 and RQ2 with the issue of linguistic feature representation for machine learning purposes) and to finally build a possibly optimal model. We will consider performing an identical experiment on another dataset to see whether a higher compliance between annotators is achievable. To link the emotions with natural language we're going to map phrases from posts with emotions the posts were annotated with, using NLP methods. The model will also be enriched with other features of the conversations, such as e.g. specific occurrence of emoticons or punctuation. On thus constructed explainable model a deep neural network would be learned and optimised. As an alternative a black-box model will be prepared, using a ready-made deep neural network learned on raw representation of dialogues, such as e.g. sequences of posts given in HTML format. We expect that the final results of the work will be a machine learning model (models). However, we will also share the results of experiments with analyses allowing for further research on these issues.

5   Results

Variety of the annotations was significant. Only approximately 6% of the posts were annotated by 3 respondents unanimously (mostly with *none* annotation) and 54% posts were annotated with three different emotions. Slightly greater amount of posts (55%) were annotated with domination of emotions from the same petal, so 45% were annotated with emotions belonging to three different petals. Among the 66 unanimous decisions, most annotations had been made with emotions from the *anger* petal.

5.1   Closed Sequential Patterns Mining

We mined patterns within four experimental settings: (i) for all of the annotations for single emotions, (ii) for all of the annotations to the level of detail of a petal with a primary dyad treated as a separate petal, (iii) for all of the annotations to the level of detail of a petal with a primary dyad treated as one of the adjacent petals and (iv) for triplets of annotations. Only one closed pattern consisting of more than one element has a support greater than 50% - it is <anger, anger> (59% support, 88 occurrences), discovered in the setting with a primary dyad treated as one of the adjacent petals. Taking all settings into account there are 21 multi-elemental closed patterns with a support greater than 20%, all of which were discovered in conflict discussions. The most common pattern for non-conflict dialogues in any setting is the same - <none, none>.

5.2   Analysis of Escalation

We measured escalation with the following values: (i) in the annotations based on Plutchik's model with mean level of intensity of emotions, (ii) in the EmoWord-Net lexicon with average v value. In both cases the value for the post at the end of conflict discussions is clearly higher than at their beginning, regardless of their length, whilst it does not occur in non-conflict discussions in any case. Moreover, all conflict conversations end with mean higher emotional intensity score than non-conflict dialogues.

6   Conclusions and Future Work

The experiment of annotating online conversations showed that it is a difficult challenge to clearly define what emotions dominate in a posts, and thus to model the trajectory of discussion using them. However, differences between conflict and non-conflict conversations are noticeable. We expect that repetition of the experiment on another dataset and enrichment of the analysis results with non-linguistic features of conversations could allow to prepare a reliable prototype model. Creating this mechanism would provide a useful tool with positive social impact for moderators of Internet discussions or an educational tool for young users to aware them of the consequences of their online behaviour.

Acknowledgements. This research has been partially supported by the statutory funds of Poznan University of Technology.

References

1. Aubakirova, M., Bansal, M.: Interpreting neural networks to improve politeness comprehension. In: Proceedings of the 2016 EMNLP, pp. 2035–2041. ACL, Austin, November 2016. https://doi.org/10.18653/v1/D16-1216
2. Badaro, G., Jundi, H., Hajj, H., El-Hajj, W.: EmoWordNet: automatic expansion of emotion lexicon using English WordNet. In: Proceedings of the Seventh Joint Conference on Lexical and Computational Semantics, pp. 86–93. ACL, June 2018. https://doi.org/10.18653/v1/S18-2009
3. Chatterjee, A., Narahari, K.N., Joshi, M., Agrawal, P.: Semeval-2019 task 3: emocontext contextual emotion detection in text. In: Proceedings of the 13th International Workshop on Semantic Evaluation, pp. 39–48. ACL, Minneapolis, June 2019. https://doi.org/10.18653/v1/S19-2005
4. Cheng, J., Bernstein, M., Danescu-Niculescu-Mizil, C., Leskovec, J.: Anyone can become a troll: causes of trolling behavior in online discussions. In: Proceedings of the Conference on Computer-Supported Cooperative Work 2017, CSCW, February 2017. https://doi.org/10.1145/2998181.2998213
5. Danescu-Niculescu-Mizil, C., Sudhof, M., Jurafsky, D., Leskovec, J., Potts, C.: A computational approach to politeness with application to social factors. In: ACL, vol. 1, pp. 250–259. ACL (2013). http://dblp.uni-trier.de/db/conf/acl/acl2013-1.html#Danescu-Niculescu-MizilSJLP13
6. Fortuna, P., Nunes, S.: A survey on automatic detection of hate speech in text. ACM Comput. Surv. **51**(4), 1–30 (2018). https://doi.org/10.1145/3232676
7. Fournier-Viger, P., Gomariz, A., Gueniche, T., Soltani, A., Wu, C., Tseng, V.S.: SPMF: a Java open-source pattern mining library. JMLR **15**, 3389–3393 (2014). http://www.philippe-fournier-viger.com/spmf/
8. Gomariz, A., Campos, M., Marin, R., Goethals, B.: ClaSP: an efficient algorithm for mining frequent closed sequences. In: Pei, J., Tseng, V.S., Cao, L., Motoda, H., Xu, G. (eds.) PAKDD 2013. LNCS (LNAI), vol. 7818, pp. 50–61. Springer, Heidelberg (2013). https://doi.org/10.1007/978-3-642-37453-1_5
9. Li, Y., Su, H., Shen, X., Li, W., Cao, Z., Niu, S.: DailyDialog: a manually labelled multi-turn dialogue dataset. In: Proceedings of the Eighth IJCNLP, IJCNLP 2017, Taipei, 27 November–1 December 2017, vol. 1, pp. 986–995 (2017), https://www.aclweb.org/anthology/I17-1099/

10. Plutchik, R.: A psychoevolutionary theory of emotions. Soc. Sci. Inf. **21**(4–5), 529–553 (1982). https://doi.org/10.1177/053901882021004003
11. Poria, S., Hazarika, D., Majumder, N., Naik, G., Cambria, E., Mihalcea, R.: MELD: a multimodal multi-party dataset for emotion recognition in conversations (2018)
12. Wang, L., Cardie, C.: A piece of my mind: a sentiment analysis approach for online dispute detection. In: Proceedings of the 52nd Annual Meeting of the ACL, vol. 2, pp. 693–699. ACL, Baltimore, June 2014. https://doi.org/10.3115/v1/P14-2113
13. Zahiri, S.M., Choi, J.D.: Emotion detection on TV show transcripts with sequence-based convolutional neural networks. In: Workshops at the Thirty-Second AAAI Conference on Artificial Intelligence (2018)
14. Zhang, J., et al.: Conversations gone awry: detecting warning signs of conversational failure. In: Proceedings of ACL (2018)

An APIfication Approach to Facilitate the Access and Reuse of Open Data

César González-Mora$^{(\boxtimes)}$, Irene Garrigós, and Jose Zubcoff

Department of Software and Computing Systems,
University of Alicante, Alicante, Spain
{cgmora,igarrigos,jose.zubcoff}@ua.es

Abstract. Nowadays, accessing open data is a difficult task since current Open Data platforms do not generally provide suitable strategies to access their data. Moreover, Linked Open Data requires knowledge in different technologies, which is a challenging task especially for novice developers. In order to manage this open data, Web APIs with accurate documentation are highly recommended features that not all platforms include. Providing these APIs would help developers to easily access data, but this access is still limited for end-users, particularly those with disabilities. Therefore, there is a gap between open data and users in which our APIfication approach can help by creating APIs for available datasets. It consists of a model-based generation of suitable APIs with natural language documentation to access open data, a universal API to access linked open data easily and a Web augmentation framework to improve data accessibility, helping users with disabilities. Accordingly, the aim of this PhD is to provide suitable mechanisms to easily access and reuse open data.

Keywords: Data access · Web accessibility · Open data · Linked data · API

1 Introduction and Motivation

Nowadays, a great effort is being made to publish open data [2]. In addition, there is a great deal of awareness on a global scale about open data, but a large gap has opened up between the data available on open data portals and the actual access to them. Some of the companies with the biggest presence on the Internet, such as Google with its dataset search [5], have made efforts to help find hundreds of millions of open datasets, yet they have only been able to index their source portal, and in some cases, include a download link. In order to take advantage of the full value of open data, as many people as possible should be able to explore and analyse this data.

Among the most adopted approaches to access open data are the Web APIs [7], as they are an important feature of open data platforms, allowing developers to make open data accessible to citizens [4]. Although organisations and other

© Springer Nature Switzerland AG 2020
M. Bielikova et al. (Eds.): ICWE 2020, LNCS 12128, pp. 512–518, 2020.
https://doi.org/10.1007/978-3-030-50578-3_36

organisms under the umbrella of smart cities started creating public data cat-
alogues recently [15], there is still a lack of suitable APIs to access online data
in open data platforms around the world. Several studies [6,15] suggest the creation of Web APIs to fill the gap between data and users. However, only about
the 6.6%, on average, of datasets from open data platforms include a query-level
API to ease the access to data, which means a Web API to consult directly
that data. In many cases, these platforms include an API following the DCAT[1]
standard, such as a CKAN API[2], which is oriented to access only metadata that
provides, at most, a download link for entire datasets.

In order to promote the use of these APIs to access open data, relevant and
useful documentation, including natural language explanations and examples of
use, is a key factor [8,16]. There are studies [10,17] about the generation of API
documentation but in particular scenarios. Therefore, the documentation available online remains generally very rudimentary, hard to follow, and sometimes
incomplete or even inaccurate [1], hampering the reuse of open data.

There also exist interfaces to query data on the Web with powerful query
capabilities such as SPARQL endpoints or direct download of data in RDF
format such as data dumps. However, exploring Linked Open Data (LOD) by
structured query languages is tedious and error-prone, because queries must
conform to the SPARQL syntax, which is a challenging task especially for novice
developers and end-users [9]. Therefore, there is a larger set of developers who
are more familiar with REST-like APIs than SPARQL [7]. Consequently, the
current best practice solution to this problem seems to be the deployment of
custom Web APIs on top of Linked Data sources [12], such as an interface to
easy access data from SPARQL endpoints. Research [13,18] that address the
exploration of Linked Open Data facilitates its access through interfaces such as
APIs, but they generally require knowledge in RDF or SPARQL technologies or
they only provide access to specific endpoints.

Although providing Web APIs with documentation will help the majority of
developers and end-users to access easily open data, this access is still limited to
certain type of users. Specifically, users with disabilities find serious barriers when
accessing data on the Web [14]. According to the World Health Organisation[3],
over 1 billion people - about 15% of the worldwide population - globally live
with disability. Providing easy and comfortable access to the Web for everyone
should therefore be a mandatory requirement for every website [11]. However,
nowadays not everyone is able to access the Web equally [14]. Thus, the concept
of Web accessibility consists of making data from the Web approachable and
available to everyone, particularly for impaired people [3].

In order to reduce the gap between open data and all kind of users, the
main contribution of our approach is to provide these users with the suitable
mechanisms to easily access, understand and reuse open data. These mechanisms
follow an APIfication approach, which means the creation of APIs for available
open data.

---

[1] https://www.w3.org/TR/vocab-dcat/.
[2] https://docs.ckan.org/en/2.6/api/.
[3] https://www.who.int/disabilities/world_report/2011/report/en/.

2   Research Proposal

The main objective addressed along the PhD is to facilitate and improve the access to open data for every user: developers and other users, considering also users with disabilities. To easily and better access data, we propose the generation of suitable mechanisms shown in Fig. 1:

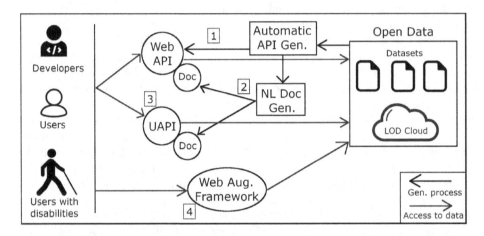

Fig. 1. Facilitating the access to open data through suitable mechanisms.

1. **Model-based generation of Web APIs to access open data.** First of all, we propose the automatic generation of Web APIs that help developers to reuse open data and thus end-users to easily access that data. This approach[4] addresses problems related to accessing and reusing open data available online, such as the shortage of query-level Web APIs to directly access data with suitable documentation. It is based on automatic, model-driven, generic and standardised mechanisms to generate APIs with machine-readable documentation following the OpenAPI 3.0 standard. Therefore, we provide an automatic generation process to better access open data through Web APIs with models and documentation to simplify the open data reuse process.
2. **Generation of natural language documentation for open data Web APIs.** Related to accessing data through Web APIs, the generation of suitable documentation through NL processing techniques is proposed. The input is a basic machine-readable API documentation following the OpenAPI standard, which is easy to process by machines but difficult to understand by common users, hindering the reuse of data. From this documentation, the generator of NL documentation is used to create a set of descriptions in

---

[4] https://github.com/cgmora12/AG.

natural language and append them to the existing machine-readable documentation of the API. Therefore, with this approach[5] we complement existing Web APIs with easy to read documentation so that the use of these existing APIs is improved.

3. **A Universal API (UAPI) to access and reuse Linked Open Data.** Furthermore, we also propose a step forward on the access and reuse of Linked Open Data by providing a mechanism which allows users to access data from the semantic web in a common way. It consists in a Universal API that includes a Web interface[6] and the suitable documentation to better access and reuse the data, even for experts in the semantic web who do not have any previous knowledge about the dataset to analyse. On the one hand, when using the UAPI by the web interface: the developer can be helped in the search of relevant information by useful OpenAPI documentation; then, the requests of the users are transformed into auto-generated SPARQL queries; and finally, the query is launched to the endpoint and the results obtained are restructured into easily reusable structures and formats. On the other hand, using the UAPI by web or mobile applications allow to directly and programmatically reuse linked data from SPARQL endpoints.

4. **Web Augmentation Framework to access open data for users with accessibility needs.** Finally, we present a *Web Augmentation Framework for Accessibility* (WAFRA[7]) in order to facilitate impaired users to access open data. The WAFRA framework provides end users with accessible websites to more easily obtain open data by voice. First of all, an intermediary user annotates the important parts of a website using the WAFRA framework, and then, end users with disabilities can perform different accessibility operations to get the desired data. This acquisition of data is made by using APIs that easily access the data directly. Among the set of operations offered are: reading aloud the data, facilitating the navigation through the Web and increasing the font size; but more operations can be easily incorporated in the framework by the users with programming knowledge. The accessibility improvement process based on Web Augmentation can be applied to any website, although the accessibility operations are tailored to open data platforms' websites. With our proposal, the accessibility of such websites can be widely improved, addressing readability problems and structural issues through voice and manual interaction.

3   Research Methodology and Planning

In order to achieve the main purpose of this research, which consists in providing users with easy access to open data, we have identified different research goals, corresponding to 1–4 from previous section.

---

[5] https://github.com/cgmora12/NL4OpenAPI.

[6] https://wake.dlsi.ua.es/UniversalAPI.

[7] https://github.com/cgmora12/Web-Augmentation-Framework-for-Accessibility.

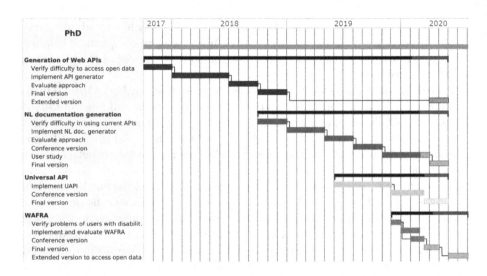

Fig. 2. Gantt chart with tasks during the whole PhD.

The main tasks performed during the PhD and also the remaining ones are detailed in Fig. 2 (including their duration and sequencing). Firstly, during the first year of the PhD, before addressing the different research goals, we analysed the availability of data in open data platforms. From this analysis, we concluded that it is generally difficult for data reusers to access these data because of the lack of suitable APIs. Therefore, developers find it difficult to create applications with interesting information for the citizenship. In order to solve these problems about accessing open data, an approach for generating Web APIs from data sources was defined during the first year of the PhD. This approach was presented in ICWE 2018 and its extension has been submitted to a journal, which is now under review. Moreover, we have also analysed the documentation of these APIs, which is mostly not easy to read by users or it is not easy to process by computers. To provide documentation which is at the same time easy to read by humans and computers, we propose an automatic NL documentation generator during the second and third year of the PhD. Furthermore, for facilitating developers to access linked data we are working on a universal API from the third year of the PhD. Finally, we also propose to help users with disabilities to access data from the Web through a Web Augmentation framework during the last year of the PhD. The proposals for generating NL documentation, facilitating the access to semantic Web and making online data accessible have been submitted to ICWE 2020. At this point of the PhD there is still work to be done: the documentation generated is going to be evaluated through user studies in order to enhance its usability and understanding, the access to open data is going to be improved using data integration techniques, and the WAFRA framework is going to be further evaluated. These improvements will be submitted to different journals.

Acknowledgments. This research work has been partially funded by the following projects: PROMETEU/2018/089 and TIN2016-78103-C2-2-R. Furthermore, the author César González-Mora has a contract for predoctoral training with the Generalitat Valenciana and the European Social Fund by the grant ACIF/2019/044.

References

1. Abelló Gamazo, A., Ayala Martínez, C.P., Farré Tost, C., Gómez Seoane, C., Oriol Hilari, M., Romero Moral, Ó.: A Data-driven approach to improve the process of data-intensive API creation and evolution. In: Proceedings of the Forum and Doctoral Consortium Papers Presented at the 29th CAiSE, pp. 1–8 (2017)
2. Attard, J., Orlandi, F., Scerri, S., Auer, S.: A systematic review of open government data initiatives. Gov. Inf. Q. **32**(4), 399–418 (2015)
3. Bradbard, D., Peters, C.: Web accessibility theory and practice: an introduction for university faculty. J. Educ. Online **7**, 1–14 (2010)
4. Braunschweig, K., Eberius, J., Thiele, M., Lehner, W.: The state of open data - limits of current open data platforms. In: Proceedings of the 21st World Wide Web Conference (2012)
5. Brickley, D., Burgess, M., Noy, N.: Google dataset search: building a search engine for datasets in an open web ecosystem. In: The World Wide Web Conference, pp. 1365–1375 (2019)
6. Cabot, J.: Open data for all: an API-based approach (2016). https://modeling-languages.com/open-data-for-all-api/. Accessed 31 July 2019
7. Daga, E., Panziera, L., Pedrinaci, C.: A BASILar approach for building web APIs on top of SPARQL endpoints. In: CEUR Workshop Proceedings, vol. 1359, pp. 22–32 (2015)
8. Danielsen, P.J., Jeffrey, A.: Validation and interactivity of web API documentation. In: IEEE 20th International Conference on Web Services, pp. 523–530 (2013)
9. Grafkin, P., Mironov, M., Fellmann, M., Lantow, B., Sandkuhl, K., Smirnov, A.V.: SPARQL query builders: overview and comparison. In: BIR Workshops (2016)
10. Hancock, B., Lee, H., Yu, C.: Generating titles for web tables. In: The World Wide Web Conference, pp. 638–647 (2019)
11. Hanson, V.L., Richards, J.T.: Progress on website accessibility? ACM Trans. Web **7**(1), 2:1–2:30 (2013)
12. Meroño-Peñuela, A., Hoekstra, R.: grlc makes GitHub taste like linked data APIs. In: Sack, H., Rizzo, G., Steinmetz, N., Mladenić, D., Auer, S., Lange, C. (eds.) ESWC 2016. LNCS, vol. 9989, pp. 342–353. Springer, Cham (2016). https://doi.org/10.1007/978-3-319-47602-5_48
13. Meroño-Peñuela, A., Hoekstra, R.: Automatic query-centric API for routine access to linked data. In: d'Amato, C., et al. (eds.) ISWC 2017. LNCS, vol. 10588, pp. 334–349. Springer, Cham (2017). https://doi.org/10.1007/978-3-319-68204-4_30
14. Power, C., Freire, A., Petrie, H., Swallow, D.: Guidelines are only half of the story: accessibility problems encountered by blind users on the web. In: Proceedings of the CHI Conference on Human Factors in Computing Systems, pp. 433–442 (2012)
15. Rittenbruch, M., Foth, M., Robinson, R., Filonik, D.: Program your city: designing an urban integrated open data API. In: Proceedings of Cumulus Helsinki 2012 Conference: Open Helsinki-Embedding Design in Life, pp. 24–28 (2012)
16. Robillard, M.P., DeLine, R.: A field study of API learning obstacles. Empir. Softw. Eng. **16**(6), 703–732 (2011). https://doi.org/10.1007/s10664-010-9150-8

17. Suter, P., Wittern, E.: Inferring web API descriptions from usage data. In: 3rd IEEE Workshop on Hot Topics in Web Systems and Technologies, pp. 7–12 (2015)
18. Verborgh, R., et al.: Triple pattern fragments: a low-cost knowledge graph interface for the Web. J. Web Semant. **37**, 184–206 (2016)

A Personal Health Trajectory API: Addressing Problems in Health Institution-Oriented Systems

Javier Rojo$^{(\boxtimes)}$ ⓘ, Juan Hernandez ⓘ, and Juan M. Murillo ⓘ

University of Extremadura, Cáceres, Spain
{javirojo,juanher,juanmamu}@unex.es

Abstract. Each person interacts with multiple health institution's systems along their life. These systems are usually developed to fulfill the specific needs of sanitary organizations or Web of Medical Things manufacturers. However, most of the times these information systems aren't interconnected, making it very difficult to put in common the information of a patient scattered in various systems. Thus, it's necessary to develop solutions that allow health information systems developers to consult all the information of an user across the multiple health's information systems it is scattered and to offer this information organized as the Personal Health Trajectory of the user (a succession of Personal Health Records ordered by time). This paper proposes a solution for the integration of heterogeneous health information systems, the processing of their data and its provisioning in a health trajectory perspective through an API. Thus, software developers of healthcare solutions can leverage this API to develop a new generation of person-oriented solutions.

Keywords: Personal Health Record · eHealth · Personal Health Trajectory · APIs

1 Introduction

Technological advances in the field of health information systems are making it possible to improve the services provided to patients. Specifically, the use of smart connected devices from the Web of Medical Things (WoMT) [10] in combination with traditional medical data is used to provide advanced solutions.

Nevertheless, most of these solutions work on data from a single information system. In a globalized society, like the present one, a person will surely interact with several health systems along their life. Not to mention the pervasive presence of WoMT devices, which generate data outside these institutions. Each of these systems keeps its data separate, which could mean that crucial information for the person's health could be not available when needed [13]. All these data are useful, but they take on added value when put together.

To better exemplify the problems this entails we present Paula's case. *Paula is a Spanish women who suffers from diabetes. On one of her trips to China,*

© Springer Nature Switzerland AG 2020
M. Bielikova et al. (Eds.): ICWE 2020, LNCS 12128, pp. 519–524, 2020.
https://doi.org/10.1007/978-3-030-50578-3_37

Paula suffers a fainting spell due to hypoglycemia. She is treated in a health center in China, where she is measured for blood glucose. However, when Paula returns to Spain, she cannot give the data of those measurements to her usual doctor, because they have been registered in the Chinese health system. Something similar happens with her smart glucometer. Only a few of the measurements she takes at home are transcribed to her health record. If Paula has another fainting spell, her doctor cannot access Paula's latest blood glucose measurements.

Providing a way to combine a person's health data and offering it in a way that can track the health of a person over time could be a solution to the previous problem and an advance in what is known as *Precision medicine*, moving from *Electronic Health Records* (EHR) to *Personal Health Records* (PHR) [11]. EHRs are computer records created and managed in healthcare systems by physicians, while PHRs are records that can be generated by physicians, patients, hospitals, pharmacies, and other sources and are managed by the patient.

The creation of health systems that are aware of a patient's health trajectory has been demanded by the fields of medicine and nursing for years [5]. Works like [7] [12] start to address this problem. However, as far as the authors know, there are no technical proposals that combines all the data from the different health related systems and processes it to provide it to software developers in an unified API.

In this paper, we propose a *Personal Health Trajectory API* (PHT API). With this API, healthcare application developers will be able to access a patient's health trajectory data and create applications with more complete and higher quality data, following the *data-driven medicine* approach. This approach argues that the use of the latest analytical techniques can lead to better health outcomes and help many more people.

To detail this proposal, the rest of the paper is structured as follows. In Sect. 2, the related works are described. In Sect. 3, the aims, objectives and research methodology of this work are detailed. Section 4 presents the current state of the work. And finally, Sect. 5 discusses the future work plan, alongside the conclusions.

2   Related Works

Looking at a patient complete health trajectory is not a new idea. For years, solutions to the above-mentioned problems have been demanded [5].

Due to this demand, some proposals have attempted to address this situation. In [7], H. La propose a framework for the collection of data from the user's own WoMT wearable devices and the use of that information to predict the probability of suffering certain diseases. A specific device is also proposed to integrate the different sensors needed to collect all the necessary data from the user. Similarly, in [8], Moguel et al. propose to collect information about the adherence to pharmacological treatments by using their own WoMT device.

However, these works are focused on the incorporation of WoMT devices in diagnostics and forget the problem of information dismissal between different health systems. For this reason, in [12] Shameer et al. study the components and information that should be included in a system that tries to offer solutions oriented to people and not solutions oriented to health institutions.

Finally, the authors of this paper have been working in making systems aware of their users needs and preferences. Starting from the People as a Service paradigm [4], different frameworks and solutions have been proposed to simplify the interoperability between smart things and humans (like Situational-Context [2]). The authors have already taken advantage of these concepts in the development of health related solutions [9], and the work presented here is the next step in developing a virtual representation of the personal health trajectory of a user.

3   Research Aims, Objetives and Methodology

To implement our proposal, a number of issues will have to be addressed. The main objective will be to develop an API that provides access to the health trajectory of users. In order to achieve this, concerns like the interoperability of WoMT devices or the integration of data from different sources should be addressed. There are works in the literature that can help us address these concerns. In the area of data integration, works like [6] propose the use of blockchain technology to integrate the electronic health records of the user among different healthcare systems and WoMT devices; and [11] implements a PHR model that integrates distributed health records using blockchain technology and the openEHR [1] interoperability standard. To integrate the data from WoMT devices, Flores et al. propose a semantic web-based solution [3].

Starting from these works, the main scientific contributions of this proposal are focused on:

- **Distributed data integration.** This problem is not new in the field of information technology and there are different approaches to solving it [1]. In recent years the use of blockchain to store EHR [6] is expanding, so our solution should allow the integration of data from different blockchains and the interaction between them, creating a "blockchain federation".
- **WoMT device data flows.** The devices provide a continuous flow of data that can sometimes be interesting, but in other cases provide too much information. Process mining techniques will be used to filter and interpret this information collected from user devices.
- **Data enrichment.** Once integrated, patient data can be used to infer additional information that separately they did not give before. Data mining processes will be used to give greater expressiveness to the integrated "raw" data from different sources.
- **Personal Health Trajectory.** Orient the approach of the medical data to follow the health of a person along their life and offer this data through an API.

---

[1] https://www.openehr.org/.

To achieve the proposed objective, we are following the Design Science methodology, where researchers see an artifact as something that should support people in practice. The development of this work passes through different stages: (1) reviewing the state of the art of proposals for health systems oriented to the trajectory of people; (2) developing an architecture that allows us to offer an API to access a person's health data along their life; and (3) developing the API, which will allow to offer the advantages of the *Personal Health Trajectory*.

4   Preliminary Key Results or Contributions

Figure 1 shows the proposed architecture that would allow software developers to consult the integrated data through a single access point.

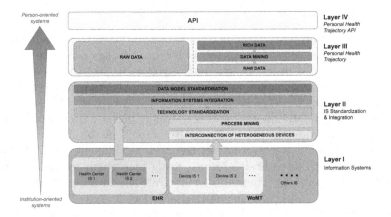

Fig. 1. Proposed architecture

This architecture is composed by software layers added over the current medical and WoMT devices information systems. An alternative solution, storing the information from the different system in a centralized repository, following a common ontology for data representation, could be explored. However, it would imply a greater compromise by healthcare institutions and manufacturers of WoMT devices, which can be difficult to achieve.

In general terms, the mission of each of the four main layers of the architecture is as follows:

– **Layer I: Information Systems.** Maintainer of patient data. It is composed by the current information systems.
– **Layer II: IS Standarization & Integration.** Responsible, firstly, for standardizing the information stored in the previous layer, including the use of different technologies and different data models; and secondly, for unifying the data of each information system. In the case of WoMT devices, it will also be responsible for their interoperability and the processing of the stored data streams.

- **Layer III: *Personal Health Trajectory*.** Responsible for providing health trajectory data for a person. This data may be provided "raw" (unprocessed) or with greater expressiveness, after applying Data Mining techniques on them.
- **Layer IV: *Personal Health Trajectory API*.** Responsible for providing a point of access to a person's health trajectory data to all those who want to develop software on *Personal Health Trajectory*.

5   Conclusions and Work Plan

Current health systems maintain patient records separately between their different information systems. The same applies to the user's WoMT devices. If a user or healthcare system wants to access all medical information along the patient's life, they do not have a way to find all this information together in a contrasted and organised manner.

To solve this problem, this paper proposes a *Personal Health Trajectory API*, which integrates the EHRs of the healthcare systems that the patient has visited and the data from their WoMT devices and offers them through a single access point.

The future work associated with this doctoral work is shown in Fig. 2 where some of the most important tasks are detailed. The initial version of the architecture has been done for the development of this paper.

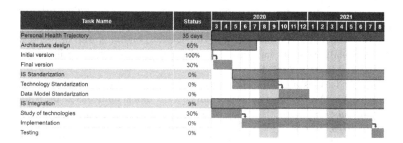

Fig. 2. Gantt chart

Acknowledgment. This work was supported by the project 0499_4IE_PLUS_4_E funded by the Interreg V-A España-Portugal 2014-2020 program, by the project RTI2018-094591-B-I00 (MCIU/AEI/FEDER, UE), by the Department of Economy and Infrastructure of the Government of Extremadura (GR18112, IB18030), and by the European Regional Development Fund.

References

1. Open data for all: an API-based approach (interested?). https://modeling-languages.com/open-data-for-all-api/

2. Berrocal, J., Garcia-Alonso, J., Canal, C., Murillo, J.M.: Situational-context: a unified view of everything involved at a particular situation. In: Bozzon, A., Cudre-Maroux, P., Pautasso, C. (eds.) ICWE 2016. LNCS, vol. 9671, pp. 476–483. Springer, Cham (2016). https://doi.org/10.1007/978-3-319-38791-8_34

3. Flores-Martin, D., Berrocal, J., Garcí-a-Alonso, J., Canal, C., Murillo, J.M.: Enabling the interconnection of smart devices through semantic web techniques. In: Bakaev, M., Frasincar, F., Ko, I.-Y. (eds.) ICWE 2019. LNCS, vol. 11496, pp. 534–537. Springer, Cham (2019). https://doi.org/10.1007/978-3-030-19274-7_41

4. Guillén, J., Miranda, J., Berrocal, J., García-Alonso, J., Murillo, J.M., Canal, C.: People as a service: A mobile-centric model for providing collective sociological profiles. IEEE Softw. **31**(2), 48–53 (2014). https://doi.org/10.1109/MS.2013.140

5. Henly, S.J., Wyman, J.F., Gaugler, J.E.: Health trajectory research: a call to action for nursing science. Nurs. Res. **60**(3 SUPPL.), S79 (2011). https://doi.org/10.1097/NNR.0b013e31821cc240

6. Kassab, M., Defranco, J., Malas, T., Graciano Neto, V.V., Destefanis, G.: Blockchain: a panacea for electronic health records? In: Proceedings - 2019 IEEE/ACM 1st International Workshop on Software Engineering for Healthcare, SEH 2019, pp. 21–24. Institute of Electrical and Electronics Engineers Inc., May 2019. https://doi.org/10.1109/SEH.2019.00011

7. La, H.J.: A conceptual framework for trajectory-based medical analytics with IoT contexts. J. Comput. Syst. Sci. **82**(4), 610–626 (2016). https://doi.org/10.1016/j.jcss.2015.10.007

8. Moguel, E., Azabal, M.J., Flores-Martin, D., Berrocal, J., Garcıa-Alonso, J., Murillo, J.M.: Asistente de voz para el recordatorio de tratamiento farmacológico. Jornadas de Ingeniería del Software y Bases de Datos (JISBD) (2019)

9. Moguel, E., Berrocal, J., García-Alonso, J.: Systematic literature review of food-intake monitoring in an aging population. Sensors **19**(15), 3265 (2019). https://doi.org/10.3390/s19153265

10. Philip, N., et al.: Design of a restful middleware to enable a web of medical things. In: 2014 MOBIHEALTH, pp. 361–364, November 2014. https://doi.org/10.1109/MOBIHEALTH.2014.7015986

11. Roehrs, A., da Costa, C.A., da Rosa Righi, R., da Silva, V.F., Goldim, J.R., Schmidt, D.C.: Analyzing the performance of a blockchain-based personal health record implementation. J. Biomed. Inform. **92**, 103140 (2019). https://doi.org/10.1016/j.jbi.2019.103140

12. Shameer, K., Badgeley, M.A., Miotto, R., Glicksberg, B.S., Morgan, J.W., Dudley, J.T.: Translational bioinformatics in the era of real-time biomedical, health care and wellness data streams. Brief. Bioinform. **18**(1), 105–124 (2017). https://doi.org/10.1093/bib/bbv118

13. Stiell, A., Forster, A., Stiell, I., Van Walraven, C.: Prevalence of information gaps in the emergency department and the effect on patient outcomes. CMAJ **169**(10), 1023–1028 (2003). https://www.scopus.com/inward/record.uri?eid=2-s2.0-0344515549&partnerID=40&md5=a93a898d90f493d07542cf5aa9dd6542. Cited By 151

Context-Aware Encoding and Delivery
in the Web

Benjamin Wollmer[1]([⊠])[iD], Wolfram Wingerath[2][iD], and Norbert Ritter[1]

[1] University of Hamburg, Hamburg, Germany
{wollmer,ritter}@informatik.uni-hamburg.de
[2] Baqend GmbH, Hamburg, Germany
wolle@baqend.com

Abstract. While standard HTTP caching has been designed for static
resources such as files, different conceptual extensions have made it applicable to frequently changing data like database query results or server-
generated HTML content. But even though caching is an indispensable
means to accelerate content delivery on the web, whether or not cached
resources can be used for acceleration has always been a binary decision:
a cached response is either valid and can be used or has been invalidated and must be avoided. In this paper, we present an early-stage
PhD project on a novel scheme for content encoding and delivery. Our
primary goal is minimizing the payload for client requests in the web by
enabling partial usage of cached resources. We discuss related work on
the topic and analyze why existing approaches have not been established
in practice so far, despite significant gains such as reduced bandwidth
usage and loading times for end users. We then present open challenges,
derive our research question, and present our research goals and agenda.

Keywords: Web caching · Efficiency · Compression algorithms · Delta
encoding · Benchmarking · Runtime optimization · User experience

1 Introduction

In the web, performance is crucial for user satisfaction and business-critical metrics such as conversion rate or revenue per session [17]. But even though new
devices and browsers are being developed year after year, the principles of data
transfer in the web seem stuck. To illustrate this phenomenon, consider how
traditional web caching is used in practice. For decades, the browser's decision
whether to use a cache or to load a resource via network has been determined by
(1) whether the resource's identifier is present in the cache, (2) whether it has
been invalidated already, and (3) whether its cache lifetime (time to live, TTL)
is still valid. However, this procedure is inefficient in certain scenarios. For example, state-of-the-art caching approaches do not make use of cache entries that are
similar (but not exact matches) to a requested resource. Invalidated resources
are discarded entirely, even if only a minor update occurred and major portions

© Springer Nature Switzerland AG 2020
M. Bielikova et al. (Eds.): ICWE 2020, LNCS 12128, pp. 525–530, 2020.
https://doi.org/10.1007/978-3-030-50578-3_38

of the invalidated resource could be reused in theory. As another example, compression algorithms are typically not chosen based on runtime parameters, even though information such as available bandwidth or processing power may well be performance-critical factors for choosing the right method in a given situation. Intuitively, though, performance and efficiency could be improved, if parameters such as image resolution or compression codec were chosen based on whether the user is on a high-bandwidth fiber cable or an unstable mobile connection with limited data allowance. We think these inefficiencies in the web content delivery chain are mere implementation artifacts that can be removed in practice. We intend to prove it.

This paper describes our research and development agenda to achieve this goal. In Sects. 2 and 3, we briefly survey the state of the art in content encoding and delivery, list the most critical open challenges, and formulate our research question. In Sect. 4, we then present the main research goals of this PhD project and a brief outline of our research agenda. Section 5 concludes the paper.

2 Content Encoding: State of the Art

Even though introduced in the early 1990s, the purely text-based Gzip is still the most widely used compression method in the web: As of 2019, it is used for more than 30% of all mobile requests and for over 40% of requests for text-based web resources overall [4]. While more efficient approaches have been developed in the last decades, none of them has become as widespread in practice as Gzip which is natively supported by all relevant browsers and web servers today.

Classic compression algorithms like Gzip remove redundancy within individual transmissions, thus increasing efficiency compared with transmitting uncompressed raw data. However, redundancy between different transmissions is not addressed, so that requesting two very similar versions of the same resource will essentially double the transmitted amount of data, compared with requesting only one. **Delta encoding** addresses this weakness by transferring only changes whenever a prior version of the requested resource is already known to the client. Since changes in websites (HTML) and web assets (e.g. stylesheets or JavaScript files) are often small, delta encoding can have a significant impact on page load times: A study from the late 1990s [11] showed potential savings of more than 80% of transferred bytes for text-based web content.

There were plans to standardize delta encoding [10] and even full-fledged user-facing implementations (e.g. [9]). All these efforts failed in practice, though, because calculating deltas fast enough to be used by requesting clients turned out prohibitive. To the best of our knowledge, the only commercial implementation of delta encoding is Cloudflare's **Railgun**^{TM} which merely optimizes data transfer between web servers and the Cloudflare CDN. Since end users still request their web content through standard HTTP requests in this scheme, however, they do not profit from delta encoding directly [5]. As another limitation, Railgun^{TM} is reportedly difficult to deploy and operate: According to architectural lead Nick Craver [6], Railgun^{TM} had been evaluated at Stack Exchange for over a year, but was eventually canceled as the deployment never became stable.

Another way to exploit similarities between data entities is **shared dictionary compression** [15]. As the basic idea, client and server share a common dictionary, so that portions of the payload can be encoded as references to dictionary entries instead of the actual content. As the only implementation we are aware of, Google's **SDCH** (pronunciation: "sandwich") [3] was supported by Chrome-based browsers and tested at LinkedIn where it outperformed Gzip compression by up to 81% [13]. Unfortunately, though, support was never added to other browsers and was eventually removed from Chrome [14], because virtually no website provider apart from LinkedIn overcame the high technical complexity of computing and maintaining shared dictionaries. To address this challenge, Google developed **Brotli** [1] compression as a derivative of SDCH where the dictionary is shipped with the library itself and does not have to be tailored to individual websites. Brotli's dictionary is still tuned for web content[1], but generic enough to be used across different websites. While this makes it more widely applicable than SDCH, it also bars Brotli from exploiting frequently occurring page-specific strings that would be efficiently encoded in SDCH.

Choosing a compression method or **compression level** always is a trade-off between minimizing computation time and minimizing transmitted bytes [8]. But even though the sweet spot depends on dynamic parameters such as the available computing power of both parties and the bandwidth between them, modern web servers typically use static heuristics like "always use default compression levels" or "use Brotli when available and Gzip otherwise" [4].

There are many **other evolutionary optimizations** to content encoding and delivery mechanisms such as HTTP/2 (incl. server push, header compression, pipelining, multiplexing) [2] or eTags [12, Sec. 14.19], and even advanced approaches for caching dynamic data [7]. However, new technologies are often adopted slowly, because they are complex (and thus expensive) to integrate with legacy architectures or because they are only supported by a relatively small share of the end users' devices and browsers.

3   Open Challenges and Research Question

Today's web infrastructure relies on technology that is several decades old. While more advanced compression algorithms than Gzip do exist, none of them has gained broad adoption. Delta encoding and other advanced approaches have failed, because they are hard to deploy or not noticeably useful for end users. Summing up, we see several critical challenges for content delivery in the web:

C_1 *Lack of Client Support.* While delta encoding with Railgun[TM] optimizes communication between backend servers and the CDN, it does not provide an actual (noticeable) benefit for users of an enhanced website. Approaches that do improve performance for users significantly, in contrast, typically also rely on browser support for broad adoption and cannot succeed without it. The history of SDCH illustrates this dilemma.

---

[1] Brotli's dictionary contains frequent terms from natural and programming languages.

C_2 Lack of Backend Support. Disregarding support for end users, just implementing the backend for advanced technologies already is a major challenge: The technical complexity alone can be prohibitive (cf. Railgun^{TM} at Stack Exchange), but even with that resolved lack of third-party support can still cause a project to fail (cf. SDCH at LinkedIn).

C_3 Inefficient Cache Usage. State-of-the-art caching discards a data item entirely as soon as it expires or is invalidated by an ever so slight change. Delta encoding exploits similarities between the current and expired/invalidated versions of the same entity, but no current approach exploits similarities between *different* entities: Requesting two similar resources (e.g. two different product pages in a web shop) always means transmitting highly redundant data.

C_4 Inflexible Protocol Negotiation. Compression protocols and their parameterization are typically selected according to static rules, although performance ultimately depends on runtime parameters. For example, CPU-intensive Brotli compression is preferable for a user while on a flaky mobile connection, but using Gzip may be faster as soon as the user comes home and connects to the local Wi-Fi. We consider neglecting the runtime context for performance optimization a major flaw in current technology.

We are convinced that the above challenges can be resolved with a careful end-to-end system design. We therefore set out to address the following **research question**: *How can partial caching and encoding methods be used to accelerate data access in a distributed architecture with heterogeneous clients and servers?*

4   Research Goals and Agenda

In order to address these challenges and our research question, we aim to devise a unified system design that enables efficient and context-aware encoding methods, exploits partial cache hits, and builds on widely supported browser and web server features to facilitate widespread adoption. Our research goals are:

R_1 Efficiency Gold Standard. To evaluate the potential gains of different encoding methods, we will collect real-world Internet traffic over a period of time and compute the optimal compression savings using hindsight knowledge: Our gold standard encoding will thus work under the unrealistic assumption of perfect knowledge of all relevant factors. We think this will help us assess the maximal possible benefit of our approach in concept and the efficiency of our implementation in practice.

R_2 Pluggable Server-to-Client Content Encoding. Two major roadblocks for earlier approaches have been poor support for end users (C_1) and high complexity of deployments (C_2). To address both these challenges, we will design an extensible architecture for content encoding that only relies on widely available browser features on the user side (cf. C_1) and that does not require tight integration with web servers in the backend (cf. C_2). We will build our prototype on the JavaScript-based technology Speed Kit [16], because it allows hooking into the client-server communication in a transparent way and because it is supported by more than 90% of all browsers.

R_3 **Cross-Entity Delta Encoding.** Current approaches for delta encoding only exploit similarities between different versions of the same entity, but disregard similarities between different entities (cf. C_3). We will develop a storage engine with the ability to exploit the similarity between stored entities: When a certain product page htmlA is queried, for example, our intended cross-entity storage engine may not respond with htmlA directly, but rather with the information required to construct htmlA from information that is already known to the client (e.g. from an old version of htmlA or from an entirely different product page htmlB).

R_4 **Context-Aware Runtime Optimization.** Our approach will let the storage engine choose a content encoding based on client-provided context information at runtime (cf. C_4). From the context information provided in Query 1.1, for example, the storage engine could derive that (1) it may encode htmlA as a diff to either htmlB or htmlC (if that is more efficient than sending the full document) and that (2) Gzip may be preferable over Brotli, because the client has broadband Internet access but only limited CPU power.

```
GET htmlA WITH CONTEXT (
    inClientCache: [htmlB, htmlC]
  , bandwidth: high
  , processingPower: low
)
```

Query 1.1. Clients will provide context information with every request, so that our storage engine can choose the most efficient encoding on a per-request basis.

As the first step in our **research agenda**, we plan to evaluate the potential gains of different encoding algorithms (R_1). We are going to start with delta and cross-entity encoding as they are pivotal in our research plan. We expect to find that both approaches yield a significant performance uplift, given the unrealistic premise of perfect knowledge. Next, we will devise a client-to-server architecture for web content delivery (R_2). One of the critical challenges in our architecture will be the context-aware storage backend (R_3). We envision an implementation in different modules for different types of content (e.g. uncompressed text-based content, compressed/bundled scripts, images). To guide and evaluate our efforts, we will benchmark our implementation (R_4) against the gold standard (R_1) for the theoretically most efficient way of cross-entity encoding.

5   Wrapup

Choosing the right encoding for content delivery has a crucial impact on performance in any globally distributed architecture. But while many attempts have been made to establish more efficient content encoding and delivery methods in the web, only few have found widespread adoption. This paper presents an ambitious research plan for addressing this issue. Our basic idea revolves around (1) the client attaching runtime context information to every server request and (2) the server dynamically optimizing every response based on the given context. To make this practically feasible, we strive for a system design that builds on widely available browser technologies and is easy to integrate for website administrators. While we plan to publish our follow-up research results in the future, we hope to spark interesting discussions on the topic right away.

References

1. Alakuijala, J., Szabadka, Z.: Brotli Compressed Data Format. RFC 7932 (2016)
2. Belshe, M., Peon, R., Thomson, M.E.: RFC 7540. Hypertext Transfer Protocol Version 2 (HTTP/2) (2015)
3. Butler, J., Lee, W.H., McQuade, B., Mixter, K.: A proposal for shared dictionary compression over http (2008). https://pdfs.semanticscholar.org/c53e/e3d44f1314c2c4d14dca7d25d1858cf55246.pdf. Accessed 20 Feb 2020
4. Calvano, P.: Web Almanac: Compression (2019). https://almanac.httparchive.org/en/2019/compression. Accessed 20 Feb 2020
5. Cloudflare: Optimierung des Ursprungsnetzwerks mit Railgun^{TM} (2018). https://www.cloudflare.com/website-optimization/railgun/. Accessed 20 Feb 2020
6. Craver, N.: HTTPS on Stack Overflow: The End of a Long Road (2017). https://nickcraver.com/blog/2017/05/22/https-on-stack-overflow. Accessed 20 Feb 2020
7. Gessert, F., Schaarschmidt, M., Wingerath, W., et al.: Quaestor: query web caching for database-as-a-service providers. PVLDB **10**, 1670–1681 (2017)
8. Jarrod: Gzip vs Bzip2 vs XZ Performance Comparison (2015). https://www.rootusers.com/gzip-vs-bzip2-vs-xz-performance-comparison/. Accessed 20 Feb 2020
9. Korn, D., MacDonald, J., Mogul, J., Vo, K.: The VCDIFF Generic Differencing and Compression Data Format. RFC 3284, June 2002
10. Mogul, J., et al.: Delta Encoding in HTTP. RFC 3229, January 2002
11. Mogul, J.C., Douglis, F., Feldmann, A., Krishnamurthy, B.: Potential benefits of delta encoding and data compression for HTTP. SIGCOMM Comput. Commun. Rev. **27**(4), 181–194 (1997). https://doi.org/10.1145/263109.263162
12. Nielsen, H.F., Mogul, J., Masinter, L.M., Fielding, R.T., et al.: Hypertext Transfer Protocol - HTTP/1.1. RFC 2616, June 1999. https://doi.org/10.17487/RFC2616
13. Shapira, O.: Shared Dictionary Compression for HTTP at LinkedIn (2015). https://engineering.linkedin.com/shared-dictionary-compression-http-linkedin. Accessed 20 Feb 2020
14. Sleevi, R.: Shared Dictionary Compression for HTTP at LinkedIn (2016). https://groups.google.com/a/chromium.org/d/msg/blink-dev/nQl0ORHy7sw/HNpR96sqAgAJ. Accessed 20 Feb 2020
15. White, H.E.: Printed English compression by dictionary encoding. Proc. IEEE **55**(3), 390–396 (1967). https://doi.org/10.1109/PROC.1967.5496
16. Wingerath, W., et al.: Speed kit: a polyglot GDPR-compliant approach for caching personalized content. In: 36th ICDE 2020, Dallas, Texas, 20–24 April 2020 (2020)
17. Young, J., Barth, T.: Akamai Online Retail Performance Report: Milliseconds Are Critical (2017). https://www.akamai.com/en/us/about/news/press/2017-press/akamai-releases-spring-2017-state-of-online-retail-performance-report.jsp. Accessed 20 Feb 2020

Demos and Posters

An OpenAPI-Based Testing Framework to Monitor Non-functional Properties of REST APIs

Steven Bucaille[1], Javier Luis Cánovas Izquierdo[2]($\boxtimes$), Hamza Ed-Douibi[2], and Jordi Cabot[2,3]

[1] Katholieke Universiteit Leuven, Leuven, Belgium
steven.bucaille@student.kuleuven.be
[2] UOC, Barcelona, Spain
{jcanovasi,hed-douibi}@uoc.edu
[3] ICREA, Barcelona, Spain
jordi.cabot@icrea.cat

Abstract. REST APIs have become key assets for any company willing to have online presence and provide access to its services. Several approaches have been proposed to describe this kind of APIs, being OpenAPI the dominant proposal in the last years. OpenAPI allows any consumer to understand the operations and data elements of a REST API. However, it does not cover any kind of non-functional properties, such as performance and availability. In this paper we present GADOLINIUM, a framework that leverages the OpenAPI specification to test non-functional properties of REST APIs. GADOLINIUM automatically tests performance and availability in different geographical locations by means of a master/slave architecture. The results of the test can eventually be injected in the original OpenAPI definition of the REST API.
Demo: http://hdl.handle.net/20.500.12004/1/C/ICWE/2020/001

1 Introduction

The Web has become the main source of information and services for both developers and big companies. Nowadays the most popular way to access this information is via REST APIs. REST APIs have been usually documented in natural language only, which hampers its understanding and use. In the last years a number of specifications have appeared to formalize the definition of APIs and solve this problem. OpenAPI is now the *de facto* standard for this.

OpenAPI provides a specification language to describe the operations and data structures of REST APIs. OpenAPI covers the functional and actionable elements of a REST API, however, it does not support Non-Functional Properties (NFPs) like performance or availability, which are crucial to help developers choose and integrate the most suitable API for their applications.

Work supported by the Spanish government (TIN2016-75944-R project).

M. Bielikova et al. (Eds.): ICWE 2020, LNCS 12128, pp. 533–537, 2020.
https://doi.org/10.1007/978-3-030-50578-3_39

In this demo paper we present GADOLINIUM, a framework that relies on OpenAPI to automatically test NFPs of REST APIs. The framework provides data schemas to describe NFPs and the required testing process, which relies on a master/slave architecture. The results of the test can eventually be stored in the OpenAPI description to enrich API information and make sure it is even more helpful for future developers evaluating its adoption. Our current implementation covers the test of performance and availability NFPs, and supports the deployment of clients in the Google Cloud platform.

To the best of our knowledge, ours is the first general approach to automatically test NFPs in OpenAPI. While some works have explored the definition of NFPs in Web development (e.g., [2–4]) and others have studied how to benchmark quality aspects in Web APIs (e.g., [1]), none of them mix the study and testing of NFPs in OpenAPI. Only some commercial tools (e.g., SOAP UI[1]) propose NFP testing for REST APIs but mostly focusing on load testing.

2   Our Proposal

We propose a framework called GADOLINIUM that relies on the OpenAPI description of REST APIs to test NFPs of their operations.

Our proposal currently supports two NFPs: performance and availability. Others can be added following a similar approach to the one explained herein. Performance is measured by calculating the latency or time interval between a request and the response. Availability is measured via the API uptime (i.e., percentage of time the API is ready to receive requests). We use random values for mandatory parameters of the requests and omits values for optional ones.

Both properties should be evaluated considering that APIs can be transparently replicated in different locations and therefore users can access them from diverse geographical places. As such, NFPs values can change on a per geographical basis. To deal with this, GADOLINUM follows a master/slave architecture where slaves are geographically distributed and deployed in different locations to ensure a good coverage of the test.

Figure 1 illustrates our proposal. As can be seen, GADOLINIUM takes as input the OpenAPI description to be tested and monitored. Once the OpenAPI description is loaded, the user configures the testing process. At that point, the testing process launches several slaves to test the NFPs and report back the results. The master element of this architecture controls the slaves, monitors the sequence of events and displays a dashboard to the user summarizing the status of the testing process and its results. The user can then review and analyze the results, which can also be exported into the OpenAPI description provided initially using the standard extension mechanism of the OpenAPI specification.

Figure 2 shows an example of using GADOLINIUM. Figure 2a shows the importation dialog, where the user provides the OpenAPI description and configure the process. The configuration involves (1) setting the number of times the API will

---

[1] https://www.soapui.org/.

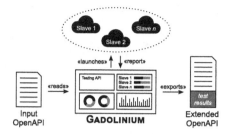

Fig. 1. General overview of GADOLINIUM.

be tested, (2) the time between tests and (3) the geographical zones to deploy the slaves for each NFP. Figure 2b shows an example of the results page. On top, it shows the importation and slaves execution data, including the progress until reaching the final stage. At the bottom, it shows the results of the uptime (on the left) as a pie chart and latency (on the right) as a bar chart that can be filtered according to either operations or geographical zones.

3   Architecture

This section provides some more details on the architecture and implementation of GADOLINIUM. As we described above, the two key components are the master and the slaves. While the master can be deployed anywhere, slaves must be physically distributed and deployed in different locations of the world to ensure a good coverage for the NFPs tested. Next we describe the implementation of both master and slaves.

Master. The Master is the central piece of GADOLINIUM and provides a dashboard to import OpenAPI files, monitor the APIs being tested and download results. The backend has been developed in NODEJS, providing an HTTP server for the frontend and a communication channel via SOCKETIO for slaves. The frontend has been developed in ANGULAR, allowing the user to provide an OpenAPI description and configure the testing process.

Slaves. A slave is created to test a specific non-functional property of a REST API from a location. The lifecycle of a slave includes its deployment, configuration, connection to the Master to get the instructions (i.e., NFP and API to test), test execution and send back the results. Slaves have been developed as independent NODEJS applications running on Google's data centers.

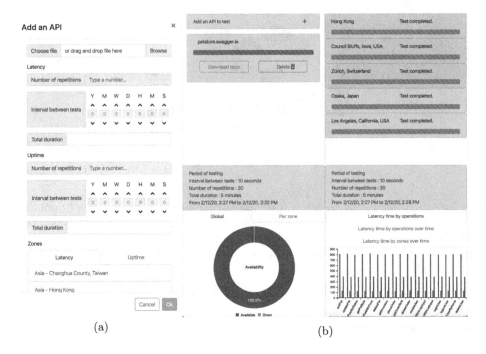

(a)   (b)

Fig. 2. Example of dashboard in GADOLINIUM. (a) Adding an API and configuring the NFP metrics. (b) Results of the testing process.

4   Conclusion

We have presented GADOLINIUM, a framework to test and monitor NFPs of REST APIs by leveraging the OpenAPI specification. The approach currently supports testing and monitoring latency and uptime NFPs and provides a dashboard view to control the complete lifecycle of the testing process. GADOLINIUM has been made available on GitHub[2], where additional information about its inner workings can be found.

As further work, we plan to support additional NFPs (e.g., throughput and reliability) as well as other cloud platforms to improve the geographical coverage. We are also interested in exploring new visualization techniques to help developers study how structural properties (e.g., the size or structure of the payload of the operations) may affect the NFPs.

References

1. Bermbach, D., Wittern, E.: Benchmarking web API quality. In: Bozzon, A., Cudre-Maroux, P., Pautasso, C. (eds.) ICWE 2016. LNCS, vol. 9671, pp. 188–206. Springer, Cham (2016). https://doi.org/10.1007/978-3-319-38791-8_11

---

[2] http://hdl.handle.net/20.500.12004/1/A/GADOLINIUM/001.

2. Galster, M., Bucherer, E.: A taxonomy for identifying and non-functional requirements in service-oriented development. In: IEEE Congress on Services, pp. 345–352 (2008)
3. Junghans, M., Agarwal, S.: Web service discovery based on unified view on functional and non-functional properties. In: International Conference on Semantic Computing, pp. 224–227 (2010)
4. Ortiz, G., Hernández, J., Clemente, P.J.: How to deal with non-functional properties in web service development. In: Lowe, D., Gaedke, M. (eds.) ICWE 2005. LNCS, vol. 3579, pp. 98–103. Springer, Heidelberg (2005). https://doi.org/10.1007/11531371_15

OpenAPI Bot: A Chatbot to Help You Understand REST APIs

Hamza Ed-Douibi[1]([✉])[iD], Gwendal Daniel[1][iD], and Jordi Cabot[1,2][iD]

[1] UOC, Barcelona, Spain
{hed-douibi,gdaniel}@uoc.edu
[2] ICREA, Barcelona, Spain
jordi.cabot@icrea.cat

Abstract. REST APIs are an essential building block in many Web applications. The lack of a standard machine-readable format to describe these REST APIs triggered the creation of several specification languages to formally define REST APIs, with the OpenAPI specification currently taking the lead. OpenAPI definitions are consumed by a growing ecosystem of tools aimed at automating tasks such as generating server/client SDKs and API documentations. However, current OpenAPI documentation tools mostly provide simple descriptive Web pages enumerating all the API operations and corresponding parameters, but do not offer interactive capabilities to help navigate the API and ask relevant information. Therefore, learning how to use an API and how its different parts are interrelated still requires a considerable time investment. To overcome this situation we present our OPENAPI BOT, a chatbot able to read an OpenAPI definition for you and answer the questions you may have about it.

1 Introduction

REST APIs are a key component of many modern Web applications. In recent years, the OpenAPI specification has positioned itself as *de facto* choice to describe these APIs. The OpenAPI specification is "a standard, programming language-agnostic interface description for REST APIs"[1].

Several tools leverage OpenAPI definitions to automate API development tasks such as generating Software Development Kits (SDKs) for a number of frameworks and languages (e.g., APIMATIC and SWAGGER CODEGEN) or generating documentation (e.g., SWAGGER UI and REDDOC). We are specially interested in this latter group as, in our opinion, understanding how to properly use a new API is a very error-prone and time-consuming task. Unfortunately, current doc tools do not help much here as they focus on generating simple descriptions of individual API components. Developers cannot ask more advanced questions or have any kind of more interactive exploration to find the info they are looking for.

---

[1] https://github.com/OAI/OpenAPI-Specification.

Work supported by the Spanish government (TIN2016-75944-R project).

M. Bielikova et al. (Eds.): ICWE 2020, LNCS 12128, pp. 538–542, 2020.
https://doi.org/10.1007/978-3-030-50578-3_40

Meanwhile, chatbots applications are increasingly adopted in various domains such as e-commerce or customer services as a direct communication channel between companies and end-users. We believe chatbots could also help in the API domain by assisting developers in their API discovery process. Initial experiments in this field have targeted so far Java APIs [4] and Stack Overflow answers [1]. [5] is more similar to our initiative as it derives a bot from an OpenAPI specification but its focus is to facilitate the execution of the API, not to help developers understand the potential of the API itself.

In this paper we present OPENAPI BOT, a chatbot that leverages the Open-API specification to help developers understand REST APIs. OPENAPI BOT provides a quick way to get information about the metadata, operations, and data structures of an API, as well as advanced insights which are not directly grasped from the API specification.

2 Overview

OPENAPI BOT is built with XATKIT [2], a flexible multi-platform (chat)bot development framework. XATKIT comprises three Domain-Specific Languages (DSLs) allowing the definition of different components of a chatbot, namely: *Intent DSL*, which defines the user inputs through training sentences, and context parameter extraction rules; *Execution DSL*, which defines how the bot should respond to the matched intents; and *Platform DSL*, that details the available operations and actions available to the bot (e.g., sending a message, querying a database, etc.) depending on the platforms the bot interacts with. Platforms are provided by XATKIT itself. These languages are complemented by an execution engine that takes care of the deployment of the bots by registering the defined intents to a given NLP engine (DIALOGFLOW in our case), and manages their execution.

Figure 1 shows a snippet of the OPENAPI BOT definition[2]. The bot defines a set of intents representing typical questions and navigation queries related to an OpenAPI definition. Figure 1.a shows the intent `GetOperationByName`, which includes training sentences to get an API operation using its name. The intent creates the `Operation` context containing the `operationName` parameter which is extracted from the user input. Our bot uses two Xatkit platforms: the `ReactPlatform`, a platform that receives user inputs and sends messages through a web-based component, and the `OpenAPIPlatform`, a custom platform we created to manipulate OpenAPI definitions. The OPENAPI BOT's execution model binds the specified intents to the platform's actions. Figure 1.b shows a snippet of the execution model containing the rule to execute when the intent `GetOperationByName` is matched. This rule first invokes the `GetOperationByName` action from the `OpenAPIPlatform`, then checks the returned value to display either the requested operation or an error message if it does not exist.

---

[2] Complete sources for the example available at https://github.com/opendata-for-all/openapi-bot/.

```
intent GetOperationByName {                  a. Intent example
  inputs {
    "Explain all what you know about the operation XXX"
    "Show me the details of the operation XXX"
    "Print the information of the operation XXX"
    "Tell me more about the operation XXX"
    "Show me the operation with the name XXX"
    "Tell me about the operation which has the ID XXX"
    "Show me the details of the operation which has the ID XXX"}
  creates context Operation {
    sets parameter operationName from fragment "XXX" (entity any)
  }
}
```

```
import platform "OpenAPIPlatform"              b. Execution example
import platform "ReactPlatform"

on intent GetOperationByName do

  val operation = OpenAPIPlatform.GetOperationByName(context.get("Operation").
  get("operationName") as String)
  if(operation != null){//Display the details of the operation
    ReactPlatform.Reply("Here is what I found about the operation "
    +context.get("Operation").get("operationName"))
    ...
  }
  else {//Display an error message
    ...
  }
```

Fig. 1. A snippet of the definition of `GetOperationByName` intent.

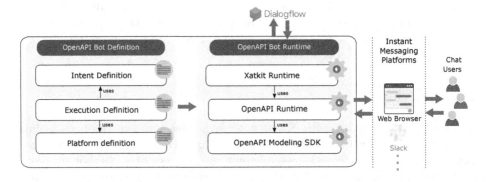

Fig. 2. OPENAPI BOT architecture overview.

Figure 2 shows an overview of the key components of the `OpenAPI Bot`. The *OpenAPI Bot Definition* presented earlier is given as input to the *OpenAPI Bot Runtime* which is composed of the core *Xatkit Runtime* (that manages the deployment and execution of the bot), as well as the *OpenAPI Runtime* that contains the concrete implementation of the `OpenAPI Platform`'s actions. To do so, it relies on the *OpenAPI Modeling SDK* [3], our model-based framework to manipulate OpenAPI definitions.

3   Example

OPENAPI BOT is up and running at https://som-research.uoc.edu/tools/openapi-bot/. The bot is initially minimized. Clicking on the button (bottom-right side) opens a chat widget. To begin with, the bot asks the user to provide the URL of the OpenAPI definition she wants to learn about. After this, the user can start asking questions about the imported API. Figure 3 shows three interaction examples related to the Petstore API[3]. The first screenshot illustrates a simple question to know the details of the operation `getPetById`. Similar questions could be asked for the other parts of the API (e.g., the schema definitions, the metadata information, etc.). The second and third screenshots illustrate two advanced questions to find which operations return instances of `Pet`, and which

---

[3] https://petstore.swagger.io/v2/swagger.json.

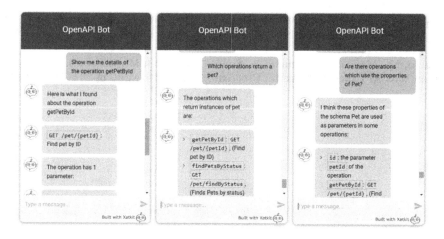

Fig. 3. Interaction examples of OPENAPI BOT using the Petstore API.

ones use the properties of the schema `Pet`, respectively. Getting this information by directly reading the OpenAPI definition is not trivial. Indeed, the OPENAPI BOT relies on a set of heuristics we implemented in the OpenAPI SDK to discover some advanced insights about OpenAPI definitions which are not obvious at first glance. See additional examples in the website.

4 Conclusion

In this paper, we presented OPENAPI BOT, a chatbot that leverages the Open-API specification (currently, the bot understands OpenAPIv2) to help developers understand REST APIs by asking questions on the API using Natural Language. Besides simple questions, OPENAPI BOT is able to provide some useful information which is not easy to infer from a more lengthy read at the specification. We are working on improving OPENAPI BOT by continuously monitoring how developers use it (e.g. to see what questions they are interested in that the bot is so far unable to answer). Also, we plan to support OpenAPI version 3 and explore how to use the bot as a new end-user interface to also execute calls on the API itself.

References

1. Cai, L., et al.: AnswerBot: an answer summary generation tool based on stack overflow. In: Proceedings of the ESEC/FSE, pp. 1134–1138 (2019)
2. Daniel, G., Cabot, J., Deruelle, L., Derras, M.: Xatkit: a multimodal low-code chatbot development framework. IEEE Access **8**, 15332–15346 (2020)
3. Ed-douibi, H., Cánovas Izquierdo, J., Bordeleau, F., Cabot, J.: WAPIml: towards a modeling infrastructure for Web APIs. In: International Conference on Model Driven Engineering Languages and Systems Companion, pp. 748–752 (2019)

4. Tian, Y., Thung, F., Sharma, A., Lo, D.: APIBot: question answering bot for API documentation. In: International Conference on Automated Software Engineering, pp. 153–158 (2017)
5. Vaziri, M., Mandel, L., Shinnar, A., Siméon, J., Hirzel, M.: Generating Chat Bots from Web API specifications. In: Proceedings of the Onward!, pp. 44–57 (2017)

A Different Web Analytics Perspective Through Copy to Clipboard Heatmaps

Ilan Kirsh[1]([✉])[ID] and Mike Joy[2][ID]

[1] The Academic College of Tel Aviv-Yaffo, Tel Aviv, Israel
kirsh@mta.ac.il
[2] University of Warwick, Coventry, UK
M.S.Joy@warwick.ac.uk

Abstract. Heatmaps are widely used in web analytics to visualize certain user activities within web pages, including mouse clicks, mouse moves and page scrolling. We propose Copy to Clipboard Heatmaps (CTCHs), to visualize what users copy from web pages. We present an implementation of CTCHs, demonstrate various types of useful information that CTCHs expose in technical-educational web pages, and discuss several possible uses.

Keywords: Web analytics · Web visualization · Clipboard · Copy · Text analysis · Heatmap · Educational technology · E-Learning

1 Introduction

Heatmaps can be very effective in visualizing accumulated data graphically. In the context of web analytics, heatmaps are widely used to visualize the frequency of visitor actions in areas of web pages. A web page can be presented to web analyzers with a varying background color. Areas of high user activity are displayed with "warm" background colors (e.g. red and orange shades), and areas with low user activity with "cold" background colors (e.g. blue and green shades). Different shades of warm and cold colors represent different levels of frequency. Website maintainers can use the visualized information to improve and optimize web page structure, navigation and content.

Špakov and Miniotas [5] proposed using heatmaps to visualize accumulated data of user eye gaze. Eye gaze data of website visitors is normally unavailable, but heatmaps can be used to visualize in-page user activity that can be tracked by modern browsers, such as mouse and scroll actions [2,3].

Three main types of heatmaps are currently available in commercial web analytics. The most common are click heatmaps, showing the distribution of mouse clicks on page elements (mainly links). The second type is cursor move heatmaps, showing frequency of mouse cursor moves in areas of the page. Cursor moves are considered to be correlated with eye gaze and user attention [1]. The third type is scroll or viewport heatmaps, visualizing the time or the number of visits in which page parts are visible to users.

© Springer Nature Switzerland AG 2020
M. Bielikova et al. (Eds.): ICWE 2020, LNCS 12128, pp. 543–546, 2020.
https://doi.org/10.1007/978-3-030-50578-3_41

Table 1. Heatmaps in 15 commercial web analytics tools

Service	Click	Move	Scroll	Service	Click	Move	Scroll
clicktale.com	✓	✓	✓	mouseflow.com	✓	✓	✓
crazyegg.com	✓		✓	plerdy.com	✓	✓	✓
cux.io	✓			sessioncam.com	✓	✓	✓
freshworks.com	✓		✓	smartlook.com	✓	✓	✓
heatmap.com	✓	✓	✓	uxcam.com	✓		
hotjar.com	✓	✓	✓	vwo.com	✓		✓
inspectlet.com	✓	✓	✓	zoho.com	✓		✓
luckyorange.com	✓	✓	✓				

Table 1 summarizes support of heatmaps in 15 popular commercial web analytics tools. We found only these three main types of heatmaps in an extensive review of commercial web analytics, with no other types of heatmaps.

Mouse clicks, mouse cursor moves and viewport scroll positions are certainly important, but modern browsers expose additional in-page user actions information [4], which may also be useful in web analytics, including copying to the clipboard. To the best of our knowledge, this paper is the first to propose and demonstrate heatmaps that visualize what users copy from web pages to their clipboards.

2   Implementation

Figure 1 shows the architecture of a CTCHs implementation. For simplicity we describe a standalone implementation, although in practice it would probably be integrated with other functions in a complete web analytics service.

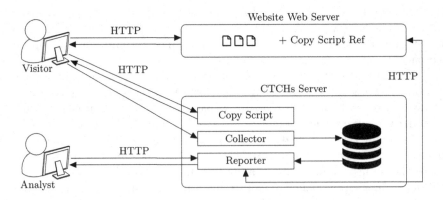

Fig. 1. High-level architecture of a CTCHs implementation

To enable CTCHs support for a website, a reference to a *Copy Script* is embedded in all the website pages. This is a common technique in web analytics and usually requires only a minor amendment to the website templates. As a result, every request for a page from the website returns a revised page that triggers an additional request to load the *Copy Script* from the *CTCHs Server*. The script tracks JavaScript Clipboard Copy events and reports back to the *Collector* component in the *CTCHs Server*, which stores the data in a dedicated database. Web analysts visit the website through the *Reporter* component of the *CTCHs Server*, which integrates aggregated copy statistical data from the database, with original web pages to form pages with heatmap background. HTTP is used for communication between the clients (the visitor and the analyst) and the servers, and between the two servers.

3   Results

We examined the CTCHs implementation on technical-educational web pages, at www.objectdb.com. The pages contain learning materials on Java Persistence API (JPA). JPA users often use the website as a reference. They copy sample code from the website and paste it later in their IDEs. Figures 2, 3, 4 and 5 demonstrate several meaningful sections of CTCHs from the website (from February 2020).

Figure 2 shows sample code from instructions on how to enable cascading detach (A JPA term). The line that starts with the *@OneToOne* annotation is the key, and in that line the core is the *cascade* parameter, and particularly the *DETACH* value. The background colors show very well the levels of importance based on user's copy frequency. This is positive visual feedback, indicating that users understand and use the sample code correctly.

Figure 3 demonstrates user preferences. The sample code lists different callback methods, and the heatmap shows which callback the users find more useful (green is considered to be warmer than blue), so we can learn about user preferences from this heatmap section.

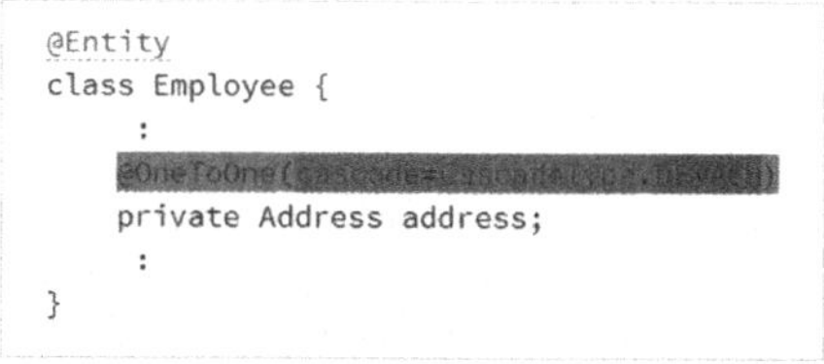

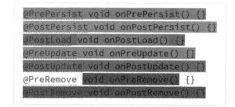

Fig. 2. Importance and centrality (Color figure online)

Fig. 3. User preferences (Color figure online)

Figure 4 shows instructions on how to create a new project in a tutorial. We can see that the suggested project name is often copied by users, probably to be pasted in the IDE. Such indications throughout a tutorial can provide valuable feedback on user progress, and may help in identifying breaking points in which users tend to abandon the tutorial (indicating that improvement of the tutorial content might be needed at these breaking points).

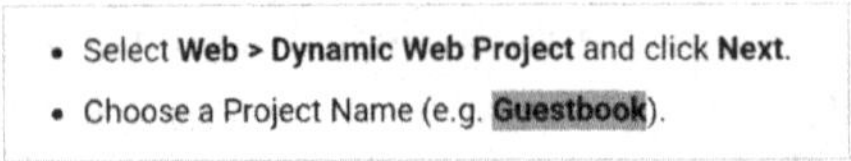

- Select **Web > Dynamic Web Project** and click **Next**.
- Choose a Project Name (e.g. **Guestbook**).

Fig. 4. Progressing in a tutorial

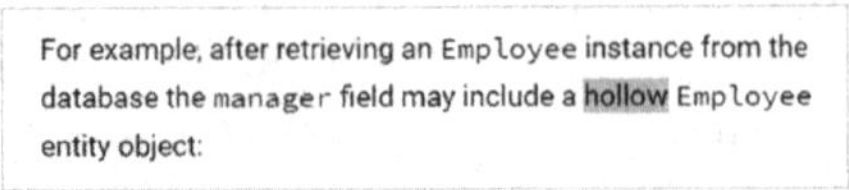

For example, after retrieving an Employee instance from the database the manager field may include a hollow Employee entity object:

Fig. 5. Unclear terminology

Figure 5 shows text with a JPA term, *Hollow*, which is painted as warm in the heatmap. It probably indicates that many readers are unfamiliar with the term (which is explained in earlier pages of the website manual), and they copy it into the clipboard in order to search for it (on the page, website, or externally in a search engine). A content editor may want to clarify the content in such cases, by adding a reminder, a link or a tooltip, to explain the term.

4   Conclusions

CTCHs can highlight various valuable information about web usage, particularly in technical-educational websites. This may include, user code preferences, how users understand and use sample code, how users follow tutorials, and which terms and concepts in the text users find unclear. We focused on visualization using heatmaps. Future work may explore quantitative methods that can utilize copy to clipboard data to improve websites and online learning materials.

References

1. Chen, M.C., Anderson, J.R., Sohn, M.H.: What can a mouse cursor tell us more? Correlation of eye/mouse movements on web browsing. In: CHI 2001 Extended Abstracts on Human Factors in Computing Systems, CHI EA 2001, pp. 281–282. Association for Computing Machinery, New York (2001)
2. Lamberti, F., Paravati, G., Gatteschi, V., Cannavó, A.: Supporting web analytics by aggregating user interaction data from heterogeneous devices using viewport-DOM-based heat maps. IEEE Trans. Ind. Inform. **13**, 1989–1999 (2017)
3. Lamberti, F., Paravati, G.: VDHM: viewport-DOM based heat maps as a tool for visually aggregating web users' interaction data from mobile and heterogeneous devices. In: Proceedings of the 2015 IEEE International Conference on Mobile Services, MS 2015, pp. 33–40. IEEE Computer Society, USA (2015)
4. Zahoor, S., Bedekar, M., Kosamkar, P.K.: User implicit interest indicators learned from the browser on the client side. In: Proceedings of the 2014 International Conference on Information and Communication Technology for Competitive Strategies, ICTCS 2014, Association for Computing Machinery, New York (2014)
5. Špakov, O., Miniotas, D.: Visualization of eye gaze data using heat maps. Elektronika ir Elektrotechnika - Med. Technol. **115**, 55–58 (2007)

A Web Augmentation Framework for Accessibility Based on Voice Interaction

César González-Mora[1]([⊠]), Irene Garrigós[1], Sven Casteleyn[2],
and Sergio Firmenich[3]

[1] Department of Software and Computing Systems, University of Alicante,
Alicante, Spain
{cgmora,igarrigos}@ua.es

[2] Geospatial Technologies Lab (GEOTEC), Institute of New Imaging Technologies
(INIT), University of Jaime I, Castellón de la Plana, Spain
sven.casteleyn@uji.es

[3] LIFIA, Facultad de Informatica, UNLP and CONICET, La Plata, Argentina
sergio.firmenich@lifia.info.unlp.edu.ar

Abstract. Even nowadays, users with disabilities still experience barriers while accessing information on the Web. In order to facilitate visually-impaired users to access this information, we propose a Web Augmentation Framework for Accessibility (WAFRA). The main focus of our framework are information-rich websites, such as Wikipedia, but it is also applicable to any website. This approach uses client-side Web augmentation techniques, extending the website with new functionality at runtime. With this Web augmentation technique, WAFRA allows users to access Web contents through a voice interface, offering a set of predefined operations to improve Web accessibility: select and read aloud fragments, increase font size, facilitate navigation and show related videos. However, new accessibility operations can be added to the framework by users, considering their own needs. Therefore, by using WAFRA the accessibility of websites is improved: users are able to interact with websites using voice commands or manually through an augmented menu to access easily specific information from the Web.

Keywords: Web accessibility · Web augmentation · Voice interaction · Client-side adaptation

1 Introduction

Today, the access to information on the Web is still impeded by serious barriers for users with disabilities [3,6]. According to the World Health Organisation[1],

---

[1] https://www.who.int/disabilities/world_report/2011/report/en/.

Electronic supplementary material The online version of this chapter (https://doi.org/10.1007/978-3-030-50578-3_42) contains supplementary material, which is available to authorized users.

© Springer Nature Switzerland AG 2020
M. Bielikova et al. (Eds.): ICWE 2020, LNCS 12128, pp. 547–550, 2020.
https://doi.org/10.1007/978-3-030-50578-3_42

more than the 15% of the worldwide population lives with disability, so that they are not generally able to access the Web [6]. In order to improve the accessibility of the Web for visually-impaired users there are several approaches. Screen readers have been proposed many years ago and they have been improved with annotation and/or transcoding of Web contents [1,5] to facilitate users with disabilities to browse the Web. However, even with these modifications, website interaction is still complex for disabled users because their needs are not (sufficiently) taken into consideration. Moreover, there are approaches that suggest voice interfaces [2,8] to improve Web accessibility. While they propose predefined operations focused on voice interaction, these are not easily applicable to every information website, and they do not offer operations to modify the presentation of contents to improve the accessibility of websites in the client. Other existing approaches [4,7] try to improve the accessibility through Web augmentation operations, but they do not offer voice interaction and do not allow the user to focus on the information they require. In summary, so far, existing approaches that deal with Web accessibility problems provide predefined voice or manual solutions, but there is still a gap between the Web and users with disabilities, especially visually-impaired users, and we believe that our approach may help to reduce this gap.

2   Web Augmentation Framework for Accessibility

In this section we present a Web Augmentation Framework for Accessibility (WAFRA) which aims to enhance accessibility specifically designed for those websites that contain a large amount of information. The main idea is to augment websites with voice-based interaction, but also with traditional manual commands, which are woven in the original website UI (Fig. 1). WAFRA operates at the client side, which allows to easily personalise its use. It is based on the existence of an intermediary user (also called volunteers in some works), such as an assistant of impaired people, who configures the augmentation for a specific website.

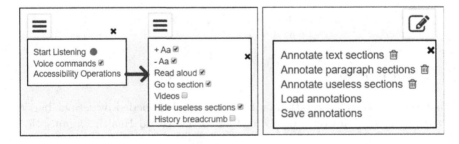

Fig. 1. Main menus of WAFRA: accessibility operations (left-hand side) and website annotations (right-hand side).

First of all, the intermediary user is required to install WAFRA by using the browser extension Tampermonkey[2], and then add our WAFRA script which is available online in Greasy Fork[3] to facilitate its installation. Once installed, the framework is ready to be used by intermediary users. They are able to identify, select and annotate particular sections or text fragments in a specific website that are important for end users. Behind the scenes, WAFRA enriches the website's DOM to include corresponding semantic information in these elements.

After the annotation of the website is done, end users are ready to use WAFRA's voice commands or main menu (see Fig. 1) to make the content more accessible. The operations, which internally manipulate the website's DOM, offered by WAFRA are: show available sections and operations; read text aloud; focus on important information hiding unnecessary data and options; increase and decrease the text size; show videos to improve the content and lower the navigation effort; and guide users with a navigation menu to jump to different sections. Since WAFRA is a framework, new operations may be developed and used in WAFRA.

Finally, end users are able to access the website augmented with these accessibility operations. When accessing a website annotated using WAFRA, it automatically reads aloud the available operations and the shortcuts to sections. At any moment, the overview of available operations can be re-heard using the voice command "welcome" or "list operations", while the available sections can be re-heard with the voice command "list sections". Then, end users are able to use voice commands in order to get specific content: "read aloud <x>" so that WAFRA will read the contents of the section specified by the user, "increase/decrease font size" to change the text size, and "go to <x>" to navigate to different sections. Other voice commands available are: "change command" to change the voice command, "stop listening" to disable the speech recognition and "cancel" to abort any operation. An example of Wikipedia after improving its accessibility is shown in Fig. 2 and in a demo video[4].

Fig. 2. Example of a Wikipedia article with improved accessibility using WAFRA.

---

[2] https://www.tampermonkey.net/.
[3] https://greasyfork.org/es/scripts/395494-wafra.
[4] https://youtu.be/LWXYeAG0lig.

3   Conclusions

In this paper, we have presented a Web Augmentation Framework for Accessibility (WAFRA) that aims to help visually-impaired users in accessing online information. Even though WAFRA is targeted to information-rich websites, it is applicable to any website. Using WAFRA, intermediary users first add annotations to a website, indicating important sections, relevant text fragments and unnecessary parts to hide. End users can subsequently rely on WAFRA's accessibility operations, using voice commands and manual interaction, to more easily get an overview of the website, adapt it to their needs or obtain specific content.

As future work, we plan to consider the reusability of annotations, so that every user can easily access websites with less intervention of intermediary users, reducing the effort to improve Web accessibility. Finally, an experiment with real users is also going to be performed in near future in order to evaluate the actual impact of our approach.

Acknowledgements. This research work has been partially funded by the following projects: PROMETEU/2018/089 and TIN2016-78103-C2-2-R. Furthermore, the author César González-Mora is funded by Generalitat Valenciana with grant ACIF/2019/044 and Sven Casteleyn is funded by the Ramón y Cajal Programme of the Spanish government with grant RYC-2014-16606.

References

1. Ashok, V., Billah, S.M., Borodin, Y., Ramakrishnan, I.: Auto-suggesting browsing actions for personalized web screen reading. In: Proceedings of the 27th ACM Conference on User Modeling, Adaptation and Personalization, pp. 252–260 (2019)
2. Baez, M., Daniel, F., Casati, F.: Conversational web interaction: proposal of a dialog-based natural language interaction paradigm for the web. In: Følstad, A., et al. (eds.) CONVERSATIONS 2019. LNCS, vol. 11970, pp. 94–110. Springer, Cham (2020). https://doi.org/10.1007/978-3-030-39540-7_7
3. Kimmons, R.: Open to all?: Nationwide evaluation of high-priority web accessibility considerations among higher education websites. J. Comput. High. Educ. **29**(3), 434–450 (2017). https://doi.org/10.1007/s12528-017-9151-3
4. Mangiatordi, A., Sareen, H.S.: Farfalla project: browser-based accessibility solutions. In: Proceedings of the International Cross-Disciplinary Conference on Web Accessibility, p. 21 (2011)
5. Plessers, P., et al.: Accessibility: a web engineering approach. In: Proceedings of the 14th international conference on World Wide Web, pp. 353–362 (2005)
6. Power, C., Freire, A., Petrie, H., Swallow, D.: Guidelines are only half of the story: accessibility problems encountered by blind users on the web. In: Proceedings of the SIGCHI Conference on Human Factors in Computing Systems, pp. 433–442 (2012)
7. Prasad, G.V.R.J.S., Soumya, M.S., Choppella, V.: Renarrating web pages for improving information accessibility. In: 2017 12th International Conference on Intelligent Systems and Knowledge Engineering (ISKE), pp. 1–8 (2017)
8. Ripa, G., Torre, M., Firmenich, S., Rossi, G.: End-user development of voice user interfaces based on web content. In: Malizia, A., Valtolina, S., Morch, A., Serrano, A., Stratton, A. (eds.) IS-EUD 2019. LNCS, vol. 11553, pp. 34–50. Springer, Cham (2019). https://doi.org/10.1007/978-3-030-24781-2_3

Annotated Knowledge Graphs for Teaching in Higher Education
Supporting Mentors and Mentees by Digital Systems

Roy Meissner$^{(\boxtimes)}$ ⓘ and Laura Köbis$^{(\boxtimes)}$ ⓘ

Faculty of Education, Leipzig University, Leipzig, Germany
{roy.meissner,laura.koebis}@uni-leipzig.de

Abstract. Digital systems that enable so-called intelligent, adaptive or personalized learning are thought to bear great potential for the future of education. Research and development towards such innovative learning systems has therefore evolved into an expanding field. Two of the key challenges are (1) to automate the extraction of expert knowledge and (2) the development of an advanced domain model, on which the system can draw. To tackle these challenges, our interdisciplinary contribution is to suggest adopting a novel approach to creating educational knowledge graphs of texts (1), which can then be further annotated and supplemented by instructors and students (2). In particular, we will outline practical use cases for blended learning scenarios in Higher Education.

Keywords: Educational software · T-Mitocar · Semantic data · Knowledge graphs

1 Introduction

University teachers spend a lot of time preparing classes, thinking about teaching methods, selecting appropriate teaching material, and much more. Reading assignments are an important part of the students' self-study, for the purposes of preparation for class and recapitulation of discussed contents. While course instructors have an interest in encouraging students to read the provided material, often they will not have time to discuss all passages in detail. Students, in turn, might shy away from asking questions about contents of the reading they failed to understand or have special interests in. These are just some of the scenarios where individual students would benefit from personal mentoring, which in this context we define as taking individual advantage of the instructor's expert knowledge. Unfortunately, in most cases proper 1:1 mentoring, which would enable effective and personal learning, is often impossible in the university context, due to the student teacher ratio necessitated by limited time and resources.

This work was supported by the German Federal Ministry of Education and Research for the tech4comp project under grant No. 16DHB2102.

To tackle these challenges, and because expert knowledge is a key component of mentoring, our contribution suggests to adopt a novel approach to create educational knowledge graphs (KG). Combining the insights of educational and computer sciences, we aim to support instructors with software, enabling them to focus on the cases in which personal contact is essential. Creating KGs, as defined by [6], fully manually is a highly time-consuming process. Therefore, in Sect. 3, we present a semi-automated, technical workflow to generate KGs by analysing available course material supplemented by the instructor's knowledge. Sections 4 and 5 describe the pedagogical implementation in an exemplary case, and discuss challenges as well as potentials for future applications.

2 Related Work

Holmes et al. demonstrated in [3] the use of digital tools to enhance education, scale mentoring processes and support students in their development of competency and self-organised learning. This is also the interdisciplinary approach of the tech4comp[1] research project, which provides the framework for our work.

Rizun [6] has provided a literature review of prior research on and application of knowledge graphs (KG) and discussed their possible use in the realm of education. Furthermore, a manually created knowledge scheme for university courses is theoretically described, whereas the input of instance data is postponed to future work. In contrast, we capture practical use cases and require data first, only then to derive a knowledge scheme from this data.

Chen et al. have discussed in [1] a novel system capable of automated KG generation for educational purposes. While they use fully automated AI based data extraction, probabilistic relation inference based on assessment data, and tutoring scenarios, their work differs from our work as we focus on mentoring scenarios, pedagogical backed modeling and separation of KGs by their domain.

3 Generating Annotated Educational Knowledge Graphs

Pirnay-Dummer et al. have created the software T-Mitocar (TM), capable of generating association nets from domain-specific texts. They elaborate their process, association nets, and their interpretation in [5]. The association nets in their work map important concepts (words) of texts to nodes and relate these nodes insofar as the concepts are related to the text itself, as shown in Fig. 2 of [5].

We use these nets as a basis for our KGs. TM allows to generate such nets in a table-based format, listing three columns: concept 1, concept 2, and association weight. We convert this data into the RDF format by using the software Tarql[2] and custom mappings[3], preserving all the information, as depicted in the left half of Fig. 1.

---

[1] https://tech4comp.de.
[2] Tarql: https://tarql.github.io/.
[3] RDF mappings: https://gitlab.com/Tech4Comp/t-mitocar-rdf-transformation.

As a second step, these basic KGs are supplemented by additional information. For this purpose, domain experts, who contributed concrete mentoring use cases, were asked which specific data is needed by a software to automate their use cases. The described information and relations were collected in an iterative, manual process, until a sufficient level of detail was reached. We refer to Sect. 5 for further automation of this process in the future. Parts of the resulting KG are inferred automatically by following OWL "same as"-statements to other data sources on the web, such as DBpedia. In addition to this process, we created a knowledge scheme that reuses as much existing vocabulary as possible, as recommended by [6], and use a domain-specific vocabulary for the TM data. The latter allows to dismantle the KG with simple SPARQL queries, enabling the operation of existing TM-based analysis on the KG. The described steps are depicted in the right half of Fig. 1.

As recommended by Hofmann in [2], we decomposed the added information into a domain graph (the educational KG), individual student graphs, and a pedagogical graph. By combining parts of these graphs for specific use cases, a software system is able to e.g. automatically and continuously recommend suitable material to students according to their personal preferences, their current progress within the curriculum and based on pedagogical predictions. See Sect. 4 for the detailed use case.

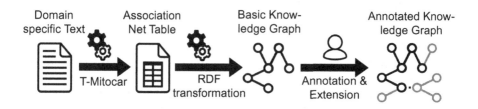

Fig. 1. Creation process of the annotated educational knowledge graph

4   Supporting Mentoring by Digital Systems

To showcase and apply our approach, we use an annotated knowledge graph (KG) constructed for a concrete reading assignment in an educational science class at the University of Leipzig. The applied text is a chapter of a text book [7, pp. 17–22] that introduces different definitions of the notion of education. TM automatically generated a KG from this text. The course instructor was then asked to develop a blended learning concept of how to best use this text for learning in the seminar context and to create an expert mind map on the basis of the TM output. Subsequently, the instructor worked together with a computer scientist to annotate and supplement TMs KG. Within the following paragraphs we describe three applications of the KG, all of which guide and support students in their reading assignment, even though many more are imaginable:

Firstly, the instructor wanted to activate the students' prior knowledge before reading, which is essential for connected learning, also in the multimedia context [4]. One example of doing so would be to ask the students: *"What are the first five words that come to your mind when you hear the word education?"* To check the students' answers against the key concepts of the text, we needed to define and highlight the key concepts in the KG. One possible output the system is now able to provide is: *"X out of the 5 words that you associated are in fact key concepts of the text you will read in a second. Please try to find more key concepts and reflect on how to combine these with the knowledge you already have of this topic."*. Naturally, adaptive responses by the system are possible.

Secondly, the instructor's aim was to test the student's reading comprehension. We therefore linked different multiple-choice questions and further explanations and definitions to specific concepts within the KG. The system is now able to present each student with personalized questions, e.g. if he or she wants to focus on a specific topic or did not understand a specific concept of the text.

Thirdly, the instructor intended to recommend further material, depending on the students' individual interests. We therefore linked videos, MOOCs, further readings, links and podcasts to key concepts within the KG.

5   Conclusion

We presented a process to support domain experts in creating knowledge graphs (KG) by automating parts of its generation. For this, we applied a text analysis tool to create basic KGs, which were supplemented with additional information to create an annotated educational KG. Our approach is also applicable to subjects other than the educational sciences, as the process itself is domain-agnostic.

In the future, we will focus on further reducing the manual workload by automating the basic KG extension processes. This includes analysing domain-specific texts for specific information, such as literature references. We also found data extraction from course planning software promising, as it provides access to fine-grained information about the course and its material. A challenge that remains is to provide user interfaces for the KGs, e.g. by integrating them into existing learning management systems.

References

1. Chen, P., Lu, Y., Zheng, V.W., Chen, X., Yang, B.: KnowEdu: a system to construct knowledge graph for education. IEEE Access **6**, 31553–31563 (2018)
2. Hofmann, S.: E-Learning und ontologisch strukturierte Planung webbasierter Lehr-Lern-Szenarien. Logos Verlag Berlin GmbH (2015)
3. Holmes, W., Bialik, M., Fadel, C.: Artificial Intelligence Education. Center for Curriculum Redesign, Boston (2019)
4. Kalyuga, S.: Prior knowledge principle in multimedia learning. In: The Cambridge Handbook of Multimedia Learning, pp. 325–337 (2005)
5. Pirnay-Dummer, P., Ifenthaler, D.: Reading guided by automated graphical representations. Instr. Sci. **39**(6), 901–919 (2011)

6. Rizun, M., et al.: Knowledge graph application in education: a literature review. Acta Universitatis Lodziensis. Folia Oeconomica **3**(342), 7–19 (2019)
7. Seel, N.M., Hanke, U.: Erziehungswissenschaft. Springer, Berlin, Heidelberg (2015). https://doi.org/10.1007/978-3-642-55206-9

A Universal Application Programming Interface to Access and Reuse Linked Open Data

César González-Mora[✉], Irene Garrigós, and Jose Zubcoff

Web and Knowledge Group, University of Alicante, Alicante 03690, Spain
{cgmora,igarrigos,jose.zubcoff}@ua.es

Abstract. In this paper we present a Universal API in order to facilitate the access and reuse of Linked Open Data (LOD). Nowadays, it is difficult to explore heterogeneous data by structured query languages, especially for end users and developers unfamiliar with SPARQL and RDF. Our solution proposes a universal access to the LOD scenario through a common interface, which automatically generates SPARQL queries to access data from any dataset available online. Moreover, the results given by this Universal API are restructured and parsed to well-known formats easily understandable by the majority of developers, such as JSON or CSV. In order to easily use the Web API proposed, there is a Web interface which guides users to get the desired data, providing appropriate documentation to facilitate the search of relevant information. The main innovation of this approach is offering programmatic access to Linked Open Data through the automatic building of SPARQL queries without requiring any prior knowledge of the data and the Semantic Web environment.

Keywords: Linked Open Data · Data reuse · Universal API · Query builder · SPARQL

1 Introduction

Nowadays, we have entered into an era of information overload: a great amount of data is being published in the Semantic Web as Linked Open Data (LOD), but only few applications really exploit its potential power [2]. For querying this data there exist interfaces with powerful query capabilities such as SPARQL endpoints. However, exploring this data by structured query languages is tedious and error-prone, because queries must conform to the SPARQL syntax, which is a challenging task especially for novice developers [4]. RDF and SPARQL

Electronic supplementary material The online version of this chapter (https://doi.org/10.1007/978-3-030-50578-3_44) contains supplementary material, which is available to authorized users.

© Springer Nature Switzerland AG 2020
M. Bielikova et al. (Eds.): ICWE 2020, LNCS 12128, pp. 556–560, 2020.
https://doi.org/10.1007/978-3-030-50578-3_44

remain relatively unknown to the wider Web community, but they are commonly required to access Linked Data [8]. Both have steep learning curves that many data consumers may refuse to face [1,8], and thus there is a larger set of developers who are more familiar with REST-like APIs than SPARQL [1]. The majority of Web developers typically need extensive training in order to use Semantic Web technologies [10].

Accordingly, the current best practice solution to reuse data from the Semantic Web for inexperienced users is the deployment of custom Web APIs on top of Linked Data sources [8,9], such as an interface to a SPARQL endpoint. Therefore, some research [9,10] address the exploration of LOD by facilitating its access through interfaces as APIs. However, they do not completely solve the problem of facilitating the access to the LOD cloud because the APIs they propose require previous knowledge in RDF and SPARQL or they only allow to access specific and predefined endpoints. Other research [3,5–7] deal with facilitating developers inexperienced in the Semantic Web environment to query SPARQL endpoints through the automatic generation of SPARQL queries. But, in most cases, they force users to access to data through an interface which requires user interaction. Programmatic access to data is not provided by these approaches, hampering the reuse of data because of the manual query building, which is time-consuming. Moreover, these existing solutions generally require previous knowledge about the information contained in the endpoints. Therefore, to the best of our knowledge, the problem of facilitating the access to LOD through easy-to-use interfaces remains unsolved. Thus, there is a gap between this data and its usage in applications.

In order to reduce this gap, we propose an approach that grants universal and simple access to semantic data via a Universal API (UAPI), especially for developers unfamiliar with RDF and SPARQL technologies but also for end users. This proposal aims to directly improve and facilitate the LOD reuse process by automatic building SPARQL queries and parsing the results to more understandable formats for users.

2   Universal API to Access and Reuse LOD

In this section the Universal API (UAPI) proposed is explained. This UAPI is universal because it can be applied to any SPARQL endpoint of the Semantic Web, by offering a common interface to manually access and programmatically reuse LOD. It consists of a REST-like API based on a NodeJS server with Express as a middleware of the Web interface, which is developed using HTML, Bootstrap, JavaScript and Ajax technologies. The implementation is publicly available online in a Github repository[1].

For using the UAPI there are two different options (Fig. 1): (1) by a Web interface[2], which facilitates users to query the underlying API with a step-by-step process, including helpful documentation[3] ; and (2) by querying the UAPI

---

[1] https://github.com/cgmora12/UniversalAPI.

[2] https://wake.dlsi.ua.es/UniversalAPI.

[3] https://wake.dlsi.ua.es/UniversalAPI/docs.

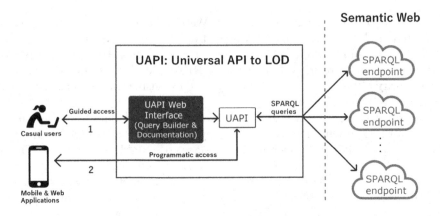

Fig. 1. Universal API to access and reuse LOD.

programmatically[4] from Web and mobile applications, allowing developers to easily reuse LOD. The step-by-step process of using the UAPI from its Web interface is:

- First, the user is required to provide the URL of one endpoint. A sample list of endpoints from the LOD cloud is offered in order to facilitate users the search of relevant data.
- In case the user wants to analyse the data presented in the endpoint, the UAPI offers the possibility of obtaining a completely detailed documentation following the OpenAPI standard. This documentation is automatically generated by the UAPI through the analysis of the endpoint with exploratory SPARQL queries. These queries obtain all the resources with their related properties and example values, helping users to learn how to programmatically query the underlying API to get the desired data from the endpoint.
- All available resources, properties and other parameters are conveniently presented to the user in the UAPI Web interface after selecting one endpoint. Users are then able to choose from these lists of resources and related properties in order that the UAPI builds the suitable SPARQL query, filling a SPARQL template depending on users specifications.
- From this query, the endpoint returns the asked data in triple format[5], which is a set of three entities (subject–predicate–object) containing information about a resource. This triple format can be a barrier not only for end users but also for some expert users [7]. Therefore, the UAPI transforms these results into easy to understand formats. This transformation of the results includes skipping irrelevant metadata such as headers of the results, merging result triples with same identifier, and finally, parsing the results into the desired format for the different users. Developers can select among JSON, JSON-LD, CSV and triple formats, which allow better processing of the data, while end

---

[4] https://wake.dlsi.ua.es/UniversalAPIQuery.
[5] https://jena.apache.org/documentation/io/rdf-json.html.

users can choose to obtain the results in table format, which is easier to read by common users.

- Finally, the generated SPARQL query is shown to users to allow them to check whether the query meets their expectations. The URL that can be used to query the underlying API directly is also shown to users, which is useful to programmatically access the data.

3   Conclusions and Future Work

In this paper we have presented a Universal API for accessing and reusing LOD. Our proposal addresses problems related to exploring LOD, searching for relevant information, reusing data and facilitating the access to that data, especially for users and developers unfamiliar with RDF and SPARQL technologies. We contribute to reduce the gap between data and its usage in applications by facilitating and unifying the access in top of the LOD scenario. A demo video is available online[6] to show an example of using the UAPI through its Web interface. As future work, the Universal API is going to be evaluated with user studies, providing the approach to end users and developers with different expertise within the Semantic Web environment. Moreover, the UAPI will also consider the data from RDF dumps in addition to endpoints.

Acknowledgments. This work has been funded by the Spanish Ministry of Economy, Industry and Competitiveness with grant TIN2016-78103-C2-2-R. Furthermore, César González-Mora has a contract for predoctoral training with the Generalitat Valenciana and the European Social Fund by the grant ACIF/2019/044.

References

1. Daga, E., Panziera, L., Pedrinaci, C.: A BASILar approach for building web APIs on top of SPARQL endpoints. CEUR Workshop Proc. **1359**, 22–32 (2015)
2. Di Noia, T., Mirizzi, R., Ostuni, V.C., Romito, D., Zanker, M.: Linked open data to support content-based recommender systems. In: Proceedings of the 8th International Conference on Semantic Systems, pp. 1–8. ACM (2012)
3. Ferré, S.: Sparklis: an expressive query builder for SPARQL endpoints with guidance in natural language. Semantic Web **8**(3), 405–418 (2017)
4. Grafkin, P., Mironov, M., Fellmann, M., Lantow, B., Sandkuhl, K., Smirnov, A.V.: SPARQL Query Builders: overview and Comparison. In: BIR Workshops (2016)
5. Heibi, I., Peroni, S., Shotton, D.: OSCAR: a customisable tool for free-text search over SPARQL endpoints. In: SAVE-SD, pp. 121–137 (2017)
6. Hoefler, P., Granitzer, M., Veas, E., Seifert, C.: Linked Data Query Wizard: A Novel Interface for Accessing SPARQL Endpoints, vol. 1184, January 2014
7. Lisena, P., Meroño-Peñuela, A., Kuhn, T., Troncy, R.: Easy web API development with SPARQL transformer. In: Ghidini, C., et al. (eds.) ISWC 2019. LNCS, vol. 11779, pp. 454–470. Springer, Cham (2019). https://doi.org/10.1007/978-3-030-30796-7_28

---

[6] https://youtu.be/cXtmas_QQ-w.

8. Merono-Penuela, A., Hoekstra, R.: grlc makes GitHub taste like linked data APIs. In: Sack, H., Rizzo, G., Steinmetz, N., Mladenic, D., Auer, S., Lange, C. (eds.) The Semantic Web, vol. 9989. Springer, Cham (2016). https://doi.org/10.1007/978-3-319-47602-5_48

9. Nolle, A., Nemirovski, G., Sicilia, A., Pleguezuelos, J.: An approach for accessing linked open data for data mining purposes. In: Proceedings of RapidMiner Community Meeting and Conference (2013)

10. Schröder, M., Hees, J., Bernardi, A., Ewert, D., Klotz, P., Stadtmüller, S.: Simplified SPARQL REST API-CRUD on JSON Object Graphs via URI Paths. arXiv preprint arXiv:1805.01825 (2018)

OntoSemStats: An Ontology to Express the Use of Semantics in RDF-Based Knowledge Graphs

Pierre-Henri Paris[✉], Fayçal Hamdi, and Samira Si-Said Cherfi

Conservatoire National des Arts et Métiers, Paris, France
pierre-henri.paris@upmc.fr, {faycal.hamdi,samira.cherfi}@cnam.fr

Abstract. For many users or automated agents, working with knowledge graphs may be a complicated task. Indeed, multiple tools using knowledge graphs rely on semantics to perform at their best. For example, in the context of data integration, some instance matching tools use semantic features such as functional and inverse functional properties or disjoint classes to discover instances that are the same (or not). Hence, in many cases, conducting an exploratory study is required to discover which semantic features are used or defined in a knowledge graph. In this paper, we propose an ontology and a large-scale ontology-based Web service that provides statistics about the use of OWL 2 and RDFS semantic features (e.g. functional properties or subclasses) in knowledge graphs. This will allow a human or automatic agent to choose the most appropriate tool or data for a given task. It also gives the data publishers a clear picture about the semantics they provide to data consumers. These statistics are represented in the form of an RDF graph (with different serialization possibilities), making them easy to use and share.

Keywords: Knowledge graph · Ontology · Semantics · Statistics · OWL · RDFS

1 Introduction

For a given task, several types of approaches can be considered when it comes to using RDF-based knowledge graphs (KGs). Some approaches rely mainly on the semantics available in the graphs, others, on the contrary, make little or no use of it. Of course, in between these two extremes, approaches can take advantage of semantics, without relying entirely on it. For example, if the task is to interconnect several KGs, approaches may use a combination of techniques such as statistics, semantics, or data partitioning algorithms. Besides, approaches relying mainly on semantics can outperform other types of approaches if semantics is very present in the KG. However, if semantics is absent, the results may not be what the user expects. Therefore, it is often necessary to conduct a first exploratory study of KG to know which tool will be best suited for a given task or to choose between topic-related graphs. Such a study helps to understand what the data may have to offer. Unfortunately, this exploratory step is time-consuming, especially if the documentation accompanying KG is missing or not

© Springer Nature Switzerland AG 2020
M. Bielikova et al. (Eds.): ICWE 2020, LNCS 12128, pp. 561–565, 2020.
https://doi.org/10.1007/978-3-030-50578-3_45

very informative. Several vocabularies or ontologies have been proposed to provide the user with an overview of the data contained in the KG. For example, Dublin Core[1] [3], Creative Commons Rights Expression Language[2], Data Catalog Vocabulary[3], or VoID[4] [1] allow KGs to be described. However, they do not give the possibility to express which elements of OWL 2 or RDFS are used.

In this paper, we propose an ontology to express which OWL 2 and RDFS features (e.g. functional properties or subclasses) a KG uses and in what proportions. This ontology allows the necessary information to be brought directly to the data consumer to select, in full knowledge of the facts, the appropriate tool for the realization of her task. Besides, we provide a Web application to instantiate the ontology for a given KG thanks to its SPARQL endpoint. The objective is to enable data consumers to know precisely how and to what extent a KG uses OWL 2 and RDFS. The aggregation of statistics on all KG vocabularies or ontologies described with OWL 2 and RDFS makes it possible to achieve this goal. We also conducted a large-scale study of the current state of the Web of data regarding the usage of OWL 2. As the paper must remain succinct, a GitHub repository[5] presents the results of the study.

2 Ontology

The ontology we propose (available online[6]) aims to explain the use of classes and properties defined with OWL 2 and RDFS features in a KG. For instance, an objective for a user could be to know the number of properties that are transitive and their number of uses in the graph.

VoID [1] is a vocabulary that can be used to describe a KG. This description facilitates KG discovery and use. Besides, VoID offers elementary statistics such as the number of classes or triples. Our ontology extends this vocabulary by providing more detailed statistics on the use of OWL 2 and RDFS features. We represent a KG as an instance of the class *void:Dataset* that can have as many *:Stat*[7] instances as it uses OWL 2 and RDFS properties or classes. Each instance of *:Stat* has one and only one *:SemanticFeature* instance. The *:hasSemanticFeature* property (see Listing 1.1) allows an instance of *:Stat* to be linked to its *:SemanticFeature*. The different types of range of *:hasSemanticFeature* are disjointed two by two, thus making it possible to detect any error in the instantiation of this ontology.

```
:hasSemanticFeature rdf:type owl:ObjectProperty ,
    owl:FunctionalProperty , owl:AsymmetricProperty ,
    owl:IrreflexiveProperty ;   rdfs:domain :Stat ;
```

---

[1] http://www.dublincore.org/specifications/dublin-core/.
[2] https://creativecommons.org/ns.
[3] https://www.w3.org/TR/vocab-dcat/.
[4] https://www.w3.org/TR/void/.
[5] https://github.com/PHParis/sem_web_stats.
[6] http://cedric.cnam.fr/isid/ontologies/OntoSemStats.owl.
[7] *Classes and properties represented without a prefix belong to our ontology.*

```
rdfs:range :SemanticFeature ;
rdfs:comment "Specify which OWL 2 or RDFS semantic
feature is the target of the given stat."@en ;
rdfs:label "has semantic feature"@en .
```

Listing 1.1. Definition of the *hasSemanticFeature* property.

For each feature of OWL 2 and RDFS, we created its own interpretation for two reasons. First, if one has an OWL 1 KG and wants to integrate the stats, then to keep the OWL profile unchanged, we must represent the semantic features with our own IRI. For example, the triple ⟨:stat :hasSemanticFeature owl:FunctionalProperty⟩ would lead to OWL 1 Full and undecidability problems[8,9] since *owl:FunctionalProperty* is a class. Therefore, for every OWL 2 and RDFS feature, we created a subclass of *:SemanticFeature*. For example, *:Owl-FunctionalProperty* represents the statistics of the functional properties. Second and more important, the different axioms of OWL 2 and RDFS can impact properties, classes, or instances. For this, we have chosen to ensure that the design of our ontology reflects these possibilities to keep a clean ontology. Depending on its purpose, an axiom will be "put" in a particular class. For example, Listing 1.2 shows the definition of *:PropertyType* (subclass of *:SemanticFeature*) used to represent the different types that a property can have (symmetrical, reflexive, etc.). Another example is the "PropertyRelation" class, which gathers, among others, statistics concerning *owl:propertyChainAxiom* or *owl:inverseOf*, which are axioms allowing the description of the nature of the relation between properties.

```
:PropertyType rdf:type owl:Class ; rdfs:subClassOf
  :PropertyAxiom ;
  owl:disjointUnionOf ( :OwlAsymmetricProperty
  :OwlFunctionalProperty :OwlInverseFunctionalProperty
  :OwlIrreflexiveProperty :OwlReflexiveProperty
  :OwlSymmetricProperty :OwlTransitiveProperty) .
```

Listing 1.2. Definition of the *Properties* class which represents the different types used to define a property.

To provide statistics for each feature of OWL 2, we have created two properties: *:definitionCount* and *:usageCount*. The first one is to state how many times the axiom is used in a definition (e.g. the number of functional properties) and the second one how many times the definitions using the axiom are used (e.g. how many triples use a functional property). Listing 1.3 shows the definition of the *:usageCount* property which allows us to declare, for example, that 3000 triples use a functional property.

```
:usageCount rdf:type owl:DatatypeProperty ,
  owl:FunctionalProperty ; rdfs:domain :Stat ;
  rdfs:range xsd:integer ;
  rdfs:comment "Number of usage of a semantic
```

---

[8] https://www.w3.org/2007/OWL/wiki/Profile_Explanations.
[9] https://www.w3.org/TR/owl2-profiles/.

feature."@en ; rdfs:label "usage count"@en .

Listing 1.3. Definition of the property allowing to specify how many times a feature is used.

3   Web Application

Our application, OntoSemStatsWeb[10], is an open-source software (under the GPL open-source license) written in C# (using dotnetRDF[11]) and JavaScript (using Comunica[12] [2]). The application has three different forms: *(i)* a Web page that is our live demonstrator[13], *(ii)* a Web API to operate seamlessly with an automated agent, and *(iii)* a command-line application. All the tools that we developed are available as Docker images (one for the command-line application and one for the Web application and the Web API), to promote ease of use and adoption.

Depending on the used tool (i.e. Web page, API, or command-line), the graph is presented in various fashions. The Web page summarizes the results through a user-friendly table and a visual representation and provides a link to download the graph. On the other side, the Web API and the command-line applications allow the graph serialization in RDF/XML, Turtle, N-Triples, Notation3, and JSON-LD.

4   Conclusion

In this paper, we proposed an ontology that described the OWL 2 and RDFS features defined and used in a given KG. Moreover, we provided tools that automatically instantiate this ontology for a given SPARQL endpoint. A human agent can use these tools through a web page and command-line or an automated agent through Web API. By offering easy access to the statistics about semantic usages, we help data consumers in choosing the right tool or KG that best suited his or her objectives. Easy access may increase KG consumption and improve user experience. Finally, to show the usefulness of our application, we conducted a large-scale study that provides an up-to-date overview of the semantic usages in the LOD. In the future, we plan to add native support for HDT files.

References

1. Alexander, K., Cyganiak, R., Hausenblas, M., Zhao, J.: Describing linked datasets. In: Linked Data on the Web. CEUR Workshop Proceedings, vol. 538. CEUR-WS.org (2009)

---

[10] https://github.com/PHParis/OntoSemStatsWeb.
[11] https://github.com/dotnetrdf/dotnetrdf.
[12] https://comunica.linkeddatafragments.org/.
[13] https://ontosemstats.herokuapp.com/.

2. Taelman, R., Van Herwegen, J., Vander Sande, M., Verborgh, R.: Comunica: a modular SPARQL query engine for the web. In: Vrandečić, D., et al. (eds.) ISWC 2018. LNCS, vol. 11137, pp. 239–255. Springer, Cham (2018). https://doi.org/10.1007/978-3-030-00668-6_15

3. Weibel, S., Kunze, J.A., Lagoze, C., Wolf, M.: Dublin core metadata for resource discovery. RFC 2413, pp. 1–8 (1998). https://doi.org/10.17487/RFC2413

Tutorial

From Linked Data to Knowledge Graphs

Storing, Querying, and Reasoning

Riccardo Tommasini[1], Raghava Mutharaju[2], and Sherif Sakr[1(✉)]

[1] Data Systems Group, University of Tartu, Tartu Estonia
{riccardo.tommasini,sherif.sakr}@ut.ee
[2] IIIT Delhi, New Delhi India
raghava.mutharaju@iiitd.ac.in

1. Extended Abstract

Knowledge Graphs (KG) are now extensively used by several enterprises across many Web domains such as e-commerce, finance, healthcare, geo-science, manufacturing, aviation, power, oil and gas. Semantic Web Technologies and Graph Management techniques play a crucial role in the construction of Knowledge Graphs. They include data models and languages for representing and processing information. Indeed, an essential characteristic of Knowledge Graphs is that resources are linked in a complex network. In the literature, the term *Linked Data* refers to Knowledge Graphs built on the Web using Semantic Technologies. However, graph databases recently gained momentum as they provide efficient data storage and rapid analytics of graph data.

In practice, KGs usually contain heterogeneous data coming from multiple sources, various contributors, produced using different methods, degrees of authoritativeness, and gathered automatically from independent sources. The size of KGs quickly reaches the Web-scale and heterogeneity. Thus, scalability issues raise storing, querying, reasoning, and data management in general. Along with these issues, benchmarking tools are essential to foster technological progress by guaranteeing a fair assessment. This tutorial aims to provide a comprehensive discussion of all these aspects and cover state-of-the-art solutions for constructing Knowledge Graphs, focusing on Linked Data. With the ever-growing relevance of Knowledge Graphs, we believe that this is a relevant and timely topic to discuss. The tutorial structure is organized as follows.

1. **Brief History of Knowledge Graphs (40m):** This part provides introduction for the basic concepts required for the tutorial such as Semantic Web, RDF, Knowledge Graphs, Property Graphs, and streaming data. Then, we will give a brief history of Linked Data and Knowledge Graphs and how multiple disciplines such as databases, machine learning, natural language processing, and information retrieval have played part in making the current Knowledge Graphs.

2. **Graph Query Processing (40m):** A number of centralized graph query processing systems have been designed to handle RDF data and generic graphs [4]. Such

© Springer Nature Switzerland AG 2020
M. Bielikova et al. (Eds.): ICWE 2020, LNCS 12128, pp. 569–571, 2020.
https://doi.org/10.1007/978-3-030-50578-3

systems do not incur any communication overhead (i.e., they process all data locally). On the other hand, they remain limited by the computational power and memory capacities of a single machine. The aim of this part of the tutorial is to provide an overview of various techniques and systems for querying graph databases and triple stores.

3. **Graph Stream Processing (30m):** Stream Graph Processing has the goal of facilitate data integration when information arrives in the forms of unbounded streams. In this part of the tutorial, we provide an overview on how such requirements are addressed in the current state of the art of RDF Stream Data processing [1, 2].

4. **Scalable Reasoning(40m):** The aim of this part of the tutorial is to provide an overview of distributed RDF reasoning systems that fall into five main categories, i.e., Peer-to-Peer, NoSQL-based, Hadoop-based, Spark-based, and shared memory RDF reasoning systems [3].

5. **Wrap-up (15m)**: In this final section, we well present open challenges and future research directions related to Knowledge Graphs.

Presenters

Riccardo Tommasini is an Assistant Professor at University of Tartu, Estonia and a member of the Data System Group. He has got his PhD Cum Laude from Politecnico di Milano, Italy. Riccardo's has experience in presenting tutorial at international venues such as ESWC, ISWC, The Web Conf, and DEBS.

Raghava Mutharaju is an Assistant Professor at the Indraprastha Institute of Information Technology, Delhi (IIIT-D), India. He got his PhD in Computer Science and Engineering from Wright State University, Dayton, OH, USA, in 2016 His research interests are in various aspects of Semantic Web such as knowledge graph construction, ontology modeling, reasoning, and querying. He co-organized workshops at WWW 2019, WebSci 2017, ISWC 2015 and tutorials at IJCAI 2016, AAAI 2015 and ISWC 2014.

Sherif Sakr is the Head of Data Systems Group at the Institute of Computer Science, University of Tartu (http://bigdata.cs.ut.ee/). He received his PhD degree in Computer and Information Science from Konstanz University, Germany in 2007. Sherif is an ACM Senior Member and an IEEE Senior Member. In 2017, he has been appointed to serve as an ACM Distinguished Speaker and as an IEEE Distinguished Speaker. He is currently serving as the Editor-in-Chief of the Springer Encyclopedia of Big Data Technologies.

References

1. Anicic, D., Fodor, P., Rudolph, S., Stojanovic, N.: EP-SPARQL: a unified language for event processing and stream reasoning. In: WWW (2011)
2. Barbieri, D.F., Braga, D., Ceri, S., Valle, E.D., Grossniklaus, M.: Querying RDF streams with C-SPARQL. SIGMOD Rec. **39**(1), 20–26 (2010)
3. Sakr, S., Wylot, M., Mutharaju, R., Le Phuoc, D., Fundulaki, I.: Querying, and Reasoning. Springer, Linked Data - Storing (2018)
4. Wylot, M., Hauswirth, M., Cudré-Mauroux, P., Sakr, S.: RDF data storage and query processing schemes: a survey. ACM Comput. Surv. **51**(4), 84:1–84:36 (2018)

Author Index

Printed in the United States
By Bookmasters